# Rhetorical Criticism

# Communication, Media, and Politics
## Series Editor: Robert E. Denton, Jr., Virginia Tech

This series features a range of work dealing with the role and function of communication in the realm of politics, broadly defined. Including general academic books and texts for use in graduate and advanced undergraduate courses, the series encompasses humanistic, critical, historical, and empirical studies in political communication in the United States. Primary subject areas include campaigns and elections, media, and political institutions. *Communication, Media, and Politics* books will be of interest to students, teachers, and scholars of political communication from the disciplines of communication, rhetorical studies, political science, journalism, and political sociology.

*The 2004 Presidential Campaign: A Communication Perspective*
　Edited by Robert E. Denton, Jr.
*Transforming Conflict: Communication and Ethnopolitical Conflict*
　Donald G. Ellis
*Bush's War: Media Bias and Justifications for War in a Terrorist Age*
　Jim A. Kuypers
*Center Stage: Media and the Performance of American Politics*
　Gary C. Woodward
*Message Control: How News Is Made on the Campaign Trail*
　Elizabeth A. Skewes
*Tag Teaming the Press: How Bill and Hillary Clinton Work Together to Handle the Media*
　James E. Mueller
*The 2008 Presidential Campaign: A Communication Perspective*
　Edited by Robert E. Denton, Jr.
*The 2012 Presidential Campaign: A Communication Perspective*
　Edited by Robert E. Denton, Jr.
*Last Man Standing: Media, Framing, and the 2012 Republican Primaries*
　Danielle Sarver Coombs
*Partisan Journalism: A History of Media Bias in the United States*
　Jim A. Kuypers
*The American Political Scandal: Free Speech, Public Discourse, and Democracy*
　David R. Dewberry
*Political Campaign Communication: Principles and Practices, Eighth Edition*
　Judith S. Trent, Robert V. Friedenberg, and Robert E. Denton, Jr.
*Rhetorical Criticism: Perspectives in Action, Second Edition*
　Edited by Jim A. Kuypers

# Rhetorical Criticism

## Perspectives in Action

*Second Edition*

Edited by
Jim A. Kuypers

ROWMAN & LITTLEFIELD
*Lanham • Boulder • New York • London*

Published by Rowman & Littlefield
A wholly owned subsidiary of The Rowman & Littlefield Publishing Group, Inc.
4501 Forbes Boulevard, Suite 200, Lanham, Maryland 20706
www.rowman.com

Unit A, Whitacre Mews, 26-34 Stannary Street, London SE11 4AB, United Kingdom

Copyright © 2016 by Rowman & Littlefield
First edition 2009

*All rights reserved.* No part of this book may be reproduced in any form or by any electronic or mechanical means, including information storage and retrieval systems, without written permission from the publisher, except by a reviewer who may quote passages in a review.

British Library Cataloguing in Publication Information Available

**Library of Congress Cataloging-in-Publication Data**
Names: Kuypers, Jim A., editor.
Title: Rhetorical criticism : perspectives in action / edited by Jim A. Kuypers.
Description: Second Edition. | Lanham : Rowman & Littlefield, 2016. | Series: Communication, media, and politics | Includes bibliographical references and index.
Identifiers: LCCN 2016006176 (print) | LCCN 2016006561 (ebook) | ISBN 9781442252714 (cloth : alk. paper) | ISBN 9781442252721 (pbk. : alk. paper) | ISBN 9781442252738 (electronic)
Subjects:  LCSH: Rhetorical criticism.
Classification: LCC PN4096 .R52 2016 (print) | LCC PN4096 (ebook) | DDC 809.5/1—dc23
LC record available at http://lccn.loc.gov/2016006176

∞™ The paper used in this publication meets the minimum requirements of American National Standard for Information Sciences—Permanence of Paper for Printed Library Materials, ANSI/NISO Z39.48-1992.

Printed in the United States of America

# Brief Contents

Detailed Contents — vii

1 Elements of Rhetorical Criticism: The Big Picture — 1
  *Jim A. Kuypers*

## Part I: Overview of Rhetorical Criticism

2 What Is Rhetoric? — 7
  *Jim A. Kuypers and Andrew King*

3 Rhetorical Criticism as Art — 21
  *Jim A. Kuypers*

4 Understanding Rhetorical Situations — 41
  *Marilyn J. Young and Kathleen Farrell*

5 Generic Elements in Rhetoric — 47
  *William Benoit*

6 On Objectivity and Politics in Criticism — 63
  *Edwin Black*

## Part II: Perspectives on Criticism

7 The Traditional Perspective — 69
  *Forbes I. Hill*

8 Close Textual Analysis: Approaches and Applications — 91
  *Stephen Howard Browne*

9 Criticism of Metaphor — 105
  *David Henry and Thomas R. Burkholder*

10 The Narrative Perspective — 125
  *Robert C. Rowland*

| 11 | Dramatism and Kenneth Burke's Pentadic Criticism<br>*Ryan Erik McGeough and Andrew King* | 147 |
| 12 | Fantasy-Theme Criticism<br>*Thomas J. St. Antoine and Matthew T. Althouse* | 167 |
| 13 | Feminist Analysis<br>*Donna Marie Nudd and Kristina Schriver Whalen* | 191 |
| 14 | Ideographic Criticism<br>*Ronald Lee and Adam Blood* | 215 |

## Part III: Expanding Our Critical Horizons

| 15 | An Eclectic Approach to Criticism<br>*Jim A. Kuypers* | 239 |
| 16 | Critical Rhetoric: An Orientation toward Criticism<br>*Raymie E. McKerrow* | 253 |
| 17 | Criticism of Popular Culture and Social Media<br>*Kristen Hoerl* | 269 |

| Appendix A: Writing Criticism: Getting Started | 289 |
| Appendix B: Additional Rhetorical Perspectives and Genres | 295 |
| Appendix C: Glossary of Terms | 301 |

# Detailed Contents

| | |
|---|---|
| Brief Contents | v |
| Preface | xiii |
| Acknowledgments | xv |

**1** Elements of Rhetorical Criticism: The Big Picture     1
   *Jim A. Kuypers*

### Part I: Overview of Rhetorical Criticism

**2** What Is Rhetoric?     7
   *Jim A. Kuypers and Andrew King*

| | |
|---|---|
| A Concise Sketch of the Rhetorical Tradition | 8 |
| The Many Meanings of Rhetoric Today | 10 |
|    The Strategic Nature of Rhetoric | 10 |
|    Rhetoric as Goal-Oriented Communication | 12 |
|    The Moral Dimensions of Rhetoric | 14 |
| A Larger Conception of Rhetoric | 15 |
| What Future for Rhetoric? | 17 |
| Suggested Readings | 18 |

**3** Rhetorical Criticism as Art     21
   *Jim A. Kuypers*

| | |
|---|---|
| Criticism as a Method | 22 |
| The Critical Act | 23 |
|    The Conceptual Stage | 23 |
|    The Communication Stage | 24 |
|    The Countercommunication Stage | 28 |
| Key Issues in Criticism | 28 |
|    What to Include | 28 |
|    Choice of Theoretical Perspective | 32 |

|  |  | Initial Approach | 33 |
|---|---|---|---|
|  |  | Objectivity or Subjectivity? | 34 |
|  | Wrapping Up |  | 35 |
|  | Suggested Readings |  | 36 |
| 4 | Understanding Rhetorical Situations |  | 41 |
|  | *Marilyn J. Young and Kathleen Farrell* |  |  |
|  | Using the Rhetorical Situation |  | 41 |
|  |  | Public Knowledge and Rhetorical Situations | 42 |
|  | Rhetoric as Situated |  | 43 |
|  | Potentials and Pitfalls |  | 44 |
|  | Situational Perspective Top Picks |  | 45 |
| 5 | Generic Elements in Rhetoric |  | 47 |
|  | *William Benoit* |  |  |
|  | The Theory and Practice of Generic Rhetorical Criticism |  | 49 |
|  |  | Situation and Genre | 49 |
|  |  | Purpose and Genre | 50 |
|  | Generic Description: An Inductive Approach |  | 52 |
|  |  | Identifying Defining Characteristic | 53 |
|  |  | Identifying Similarities | 54 |
|  |  | Explaining Observed Similarities | 55 |
|  | Generic Application: A Deductive Approach |  | 55 |
|  | Potentials and Pitfalls |  | 57 |
|  | Generic Rhetorical Criticism Top Picks |  | 58 |
| 6 | On Objectivity and Politics in Criticism |  | 63 |
|  | *Edwin Black* |  |  |

## Part II: Perspectives on Criticism

| 7 | The Traditional Perspective |  | 69 |
|---|---|---|---|
|  | *Forbes I. Hill* |  |  |
|  | Traditional Criticism |  | 69 |
|  |  | Recreating the Context of Rhetorical Events | 71 |
|  |  | Constructing Audiences for Rhetorical Events | 71 |
|  |  | Describing the Source of the Message | 73 |
|  |  | Analyzing the Message | 74 |
|  |  | Evaluating the Discourse | 79 |
|  | Critical Essay |  | 80 |
|  |  | Mr. Douglass's Fifth of July | 80 |
|  | Personal Reflections |  | 87 |
|  | Potentials and Pitfalls |  | 87 |
|  | Traditional Criticism Top Picks |  | 88 |
| 8 | Close Textual Analysis: Approaches and Applications |  | 91 |
|  | *Stephen Howard Browne* |  |  |
|  | CTA Guiding Principles |  | 92 |
|  |  | Principle 1: Rhetorical Texts Are Sites of Symbolic Action | 92 |
|  |  | Principle 2: Form and Content Cannot Be Divorced | 92 |

|  |  |  |
|---|---|---|
|  | Principle 3: Text Informs Context, and Vice Versa | 93 |
|  | Principle 4: Rhetorical Texts Exhibit Artistic Density | 94 |
|  | Critical Essay | 96 |
|  | Close Textual Analysis of Barack Obama's March 18, 2008, Speech in Philadelphia | 96 |
|  | Personal Reflections | 101 |
|  | Potentials and Pitfalls | 101 |
|  | CTA Top Picks | 103 |
| 9 | Criticism of Metaphor | 105 |
|  | *David Henry and Thomas R. Burkholder* |  |
|  | How Metaphors Work | 106 |
|  | Rhetorical Functions of Metaphor | 106 |
|  | Metaphor in Political Discourse | 108 |
|  | Critiquing Metaphor | 111 |
|  | Critical Essay | 113 |
|  | Mario Cuomo's Keynote Address to the 1984 Democratic National Convention | 113 |
|  | Personal Reflections | 118 |
|  | Potentials and Pitfalls | 119 |
|  | Metaphor Criticism Top Picks | 120 |
| 10 | The Narrative Perspective | 125 |
|  | *Robert C. Rowland* |  |
|  | Describing Narrative Form and Function | 126 |
|  | Narrative Form | 126 |
|  | Narrative Function | 128 |
|  | Approaches to Narrative Rhetorical Criticism | 130 |
|  | The Narrative Paradigm and Rhetorical Criticism | 130 |
|  | Applications of the Narrative Paradigm | 131 |
|  | Narrative Analysis: A Systematic Perspective | 133 |
|  | Summary of a Systematic Perspective on Narrative Analysis | 135 |
|  | Critical Essay | 135 |
|  | A Narrative Analysis of Stories about Children Abducted to Saudi Arabia | 136 |
|  | Personal Reflections | 141 |
|  | Potentials and Pitfalls | 141 |
|  | Narrative Analysis Top Picks | 143 |
| 11 | Dramatism and Kenneth Burke's Pentadic Criticism | 147 |
|  | *Ryan Erik McGeough and Andrew King* |  |
|  | Origins of Dramatism | 147 |
|  | Dramatism | 148 |
|  | The Pentad | 149 |
|  | Where Does It Come From? | 149 |
|  | Why Is It Important? | 151 |
|  | How Does It Work? Or, The Naming of the Parts | 152 |
|  | The Ratios | 155 |
|  | Critical Essays | 158 |
|  | Example One: Purpose and Agency in Obama's Second Inaugural Address | 158 |

x   *Detailed Contents*

|  |  |
|---|---|
| Example Two: Stressing the Agent | 159 |
| Example Three: Agrarian Concerns | 159 |
| Motives and Competing Frames | 160 |
| Finding the Dominant Term, Grappling with the Text | 161 |
| Personal Reflections | 162 |
| Potentials and Pitfalls | 162 |
| Burkean Top Picks | 163 |

**12  Fantasy-Theme Criticism** — 167
*Thomas J. St. Antoine and Matthew T. Althouse*

|  |  |
|---|---|
| Fundamental Concepts | 168 |
| Fantasy Theme | 168 |
| Chaining | 169 |
| Fantasy Type | 169 |
| Rhetorical Vision | 170 |
| How to Conduct Fantasy-Theme Criticism | 171 |
| Finding Evidence | 171 |
| Categorizing Messages | 171 |
| Constructing Rhetorical Visions | 172 |
| About Symbolic Convergence Theory | 173 |
| It Is a General Theory | 174 |
| It Is a Grounded Theory | 175 |
| It Is an Epistemic Theory | 175 |
| Critical Essay | 176 |
| Fantasy Themes for College | 177 |
| Personal Reflections | 185 |
| Potentials and Pitfalls | 185 |
| Fantasy-Theme Analysis Top Picks | 186 |

**13  Feminist Analysis** — 191
*Donna Marie Nudd and Kristina Schriver Whalen*

|  |  |
|---|---|
| Why Feminism? | 191 |
| An Introduction to Feminist Rhetorical Criticism | 193 |
| Feminist Criticism and the Challenge to Rhetoric | 195 |
| Approaches to Using Feminist Criticism | 195 |
| Redefining or Defining | 196 |
| Recovering | 197 |
| Recording | 198 |
| Revisioning | 198 |
| Critical Essay | 199 |
| A Feminist Rhetorical Analysis of *Shallow Hal* | 200 |
| Personal Reflections | 208 |
| Potentials and Pitfalls | 209 |
| Feminist Analysis Top Picks | 210 |

**14  Ideographic Criticism** — 215
*Ronald Lee and Adam Blood*

|  |  |
|---|---|
| Point of Departure | 215 |
| Ideological Turn in Criticism | 216 |
| 1. Discourse | 217 |

|  |  |  |
|---|---|---|
| 2. Power | | 217 |
| 3. Truth | | 218 |
| Rhetorical Materialism | | 219 |
| Ideographic Criticism | | 221 |
| Final Thoughts | | 224 |
| Critical Essay | | 225 |
|    The Conundrum of <Loyalty> and the <Market>: The Discourses Surrounding LeBron James's Leaving and Returning Home | | 225 |
| Personal Reflections | | 232 |
| Potentials and Pitfalls | | 232 |
| Ideographic Analysis Top Picks | | 233 |

## Part III: Expanding Our Critical Horizons

| | | |
|---|---|---|
| 15 | An Eclectic Approach to Criticism | 239 |
| | *Jim A. Kuypers* | |
| | Critical Essays | 240 |
| | Personal Reflections | 241 |
| |   Joseph M. Valenzano III on "Cowboys . . ." | 241 |
| |   Mary Evelyn Collings on "Texas . . ." | 243 |
| |   M. Lane Bruner on "Carnivalesque . . ." | 245 |
| |   Jim A. Kuypers on "From Science . . ." | 248 |
| | Potentials and Pitfalls | 249 |
| | Eclectic Criticism Top Picks | 250 |
| 16 | Critical Rhetoric: An Orientation toward Criticism | 253 |
| | *Raymie E. McKerrow* | |
| | Starting Points: Critical Rhetoric | 254 |
| | Differentiating Critiques of Domination and Freedom | 255 |
| | Enacting a Critical Stance | 257 |
| |   Critic as Inventor | 257 |
| |   Principles of Praxis | 258 |
| |   Agent as Effect | 259 |
| | The Context for Critique | 260 |
| | Critical Essay Examples | 260 |
| |   Using and/or Extending a Critical Orientation | 260 |
| | Personal Reflections | 264 |
| | Potentials and Pitfalls | 264 |
| | Critical Rhetoric Top Picks | 266 |
| 17 | Criticism of Popular Culture and Social Media | 269 |
| | *Kristen Hoerl* | |
| | Theorizing the Relationship between Culture and Power | 270 |
| | Strategies for Interpreting Popular Culture and Social Media | 273 |
| |   Selecting/Constructing the Text | 273 |
| |   Analyzing the Text | 275 |
| |   Evaluating the Text | 277 |
| | Critical Essays | 278 |
| |   Critical Essay 1: *The Hunger Games* as Allegory for Class Struggle | 278 |

        Critical Essay 2: *The Hunger Games* as the Production of Authentic Whiteness
            and Natural Femininity   280
        Critical Essay 3: The *Hunger Games* Franchise as Promotional Cynicism   281
    Personal Reflections   282
    Potentials and Pitfalls   283
    Rhetorical Criticism of Popular Culture and Social Media Top Picks   285

Appendix A: Writing Criticism: Getting Started   289

Appendix B: Additional Rhetorical Perspectives and Genres   295

Appendix C: Glossary of Terms   301

Index   307

About the Contributors   325

# Preface

*Rhetorical Criticism: Perspectives in Action*—now in its second edition—is designed to introduce students to the exciting art of rhetorical criticism.

It is no secret that rhetorical criticism can be a challenging topic to grasp. So much of criticism, although of a high quality, is difficult for "the uninitiated" to comprehend, which makes initially learning how to *produce* criticism that much more difficult. This book came about because I wanted to offer both undergraduates and beginning graduate students something they would find accessible when first encountering rhetorical criticism.

Fostering creativity was another concern. I am not the only teacher whose students desire a "template" or a "rubric" from which to work, some "formula" to use when writing criticism. Giving them just that when first teaching about rhetorical criticism is difficult to avoid. After all, we do have to begin teaching from *some* starting point, and the initial steps we take can be very much the same in most classrooms. And yet, from my conversations with others who teach criticism, it seemed I was not alone in wanting to stress the very personal nature of criticism, to expose students to both the freedoms and constraints involved. Thus, throughout this text, the chapter authors and I stress both the objective and subjective nature of rhetorical criticism.

These two concerns—accessibility and creativity—led to the creation of the book you now hold in your hands. Several additional features are designed to facilitate the effective teaching of rhetorical criticism.

First, well-known perspectives and modes of rhetorical criticism are covered, but other less known yet important perspectives are also presented. In addition to finding chapters on traditional criticism and dramatism, you will also find chapters on ideographical criticism, criticism of metaphor, and more. New to the second edition are chapters on critical approaches to rhetorical criticism and the criticism of popular culture and social media, as well as appendices covering how to begin writing a criticism paper and a listing of additional perspectives on criticism. Additionally, each chapter now includes key terms in bold that can be found in the new glossary.

Second, each chapter detailing a perspective is written by a nationally recognized scholar (or scholars) in that area. Thus, instead of one person writing a short synopsis of numerous perspectives, a noted expert with experience using a particular perspective has written about it. This approach allows students to discover quickly how personalities influence the practice of criticism and even the teaching of criticism. Because critics with well-developed voices wrote the chapters contained in this book, students will benefit from exposure to these voices, hopefully beginning the process of developing their own critical voice.

Third, each chapter in parts II and III features a "critical essay" section, showcasing the perspective in action. Often these are brief original essays written by the chapter author and composed specifically for this textbook. In other instances, the chapter authors opted instead to focus on the interpretive dynamics that their perspective encourages and so provide several short examples of criticism using their perspective. Reading through various other textbooks on criticism, I have found that they often included high-quality works of criticism for students to read—more often than not reprinted from scholarly journals. The drawback here, though, is that these articles were originally written for the readers of a particular scholarly journal; they are not easily accessible to students, many of whom will have had little previous exposure to criticism. Such scholarly essays may actually defeat their purpose of providing useful examples of criticism for new critics to emulate. On the other hand, the critical essays contained in this edition of *Rhetorical Criticism: Perspectives in Action* were originally written with *student accessibility* in mind. Each essay provides a touchstone for students to use when crafting their own essays.

The potential danger with touchstones is that they can be so good that they trample over, rather than encourage, novice critics. The chapters in this book seek to avoid this. Criticism is an artistic process, yet far too often this personal nature of criticism remains a mystery to students. There are rules, but there are also instances when if followed they would stifle the critical process and produce sterile criticism. I believe strongly, though, that students benefit from knowing a basic structure around which to organize their initial efforts at writing criticism. To this end, I asked the contributing authors, when they chose to write an original essay, to loosely follow the DAE organizational model for criticism (description, analysis/interpretation, and evaluation). Some authors did just that, and some did not follow that pattern so closely. Since not all perspectives or rhetorical artifacts lend themselves equally well to the DAE model, students are presented with instances that deviate from this model and are given reasons why this deviation is desirable—thereby empowering them to consider similar decisions for themselves.

Fourth, and stressing further the artistic and individual nature of criticism, most chapters contain the author's personal reflections on the decisions he or she made while writing the essay or short examples. Any writing project involves decisions about what to include or exclude, what to stress, and what to ignore. These personal comments allow students to see what questions and concerns guided the author as he or she wrote.

Fifth, each chapter provides a "Potentials and Pitfalls" section that calls attention to the particular strengths and weaknesses the given rhetorical perspective possesses. Authors expose those aspects of the rhetorical artifact that their particular perspective highlights, thus stressing the artistic and insight-producing aspects of the critical process. These comments shed light on how different perspectives both enable and discourage particular readings of texts.

Finally, authors provide an annotated recommended reading list for students who wish to study a particular perspective or mode of criticism in greater detail. Some authors prioritize the readings, thus helping students read, in order, those articles and books most helpful when beginning the process of writing criticism using a particular perspective.

It is my sincere hope that this book will encourage students to ask new questions about the rhetoric around them and that, in doing so, they will fulfill the critic's quest to produce both insight and understanding about the world in which we live.

Jim A. Kuypers<br>
Virginia Tech<br>
Blacksburg, VA

# Acknowledgments

The authors with whom I worked on this project were a joy; I thank them for their participation. It is with gratitude that I mention Virginia Tech, which paid my salary and also funded library services such as interlibrary loan and EBSCOhost, which were absolutely necessary to the completion of this project. The value Virginia Tech places on scholarship allows projects such as this book to be undertaken and completed. My department head, Robert E. Denton Jr., provided—as always—steadfast support, which I greatly appreciate.

I wish to give special acknowledgment for their helpful comments to Jason Edward Black, University of Alabama; John Sloop, Vanderbilt University; and Beth Waggenspack, Virginia Tech.

I would also like to thank Rowman & Littlefield's two anonymous reviewers as well as Star A. Muir, George Mason University; Leanne Stuart Pupchek, Queens University of Charlotte; and Nick Romerhausen, Eastern Michigan University, for their time and input.

# 1

# Elements of Rhetorical Criticism

## The Big Picture

*Jim A. Kuypers*

I believe in knowledge for knowledge's sake, that learning is of value in and of itself.

Certainly the exercising of our minds is as important, and often as enjoyable, as is the exercising of our bodies. That said, sometimes isn't it simply refreshing to see the immediate, practical benefits that follow the investment of your intellectual time? Think about whatever it is that you wish to do once you graduate. Then ask yourself if the ability to

- create new knowledge instead of simply echoing what others say;
- discover aspects of our world, our society, and our culture that others do not see;
- generate greater insights into human communication and civic participation;
- communicate effectively to impart greater understanding of issues, concepts, and events;
- possess a greater understanding of how and why humans communicate; and
- develop your thinking processes toward a razor-like effectiveness

will help you achieve your life goals. I suspect that in most cases the answer is yes. Importantly for us here, these are also some (yes, only some!) of the more obvious benefits derived from learning rhetorical criticism.

There is a creative, imaginative aspect to rhetorical criticism that can be exciting and enriching, having the potential to tap into the very core of our personalities. We will go into a more comprehensive definition of **rhetoric** in the next chapter, but for now, think of rhetoric as strategic, intentional communication designed to persuade or to achieve some identifiable objective. **Criticism**, whose definition we will also later expand, is a method particularly well suited to analyzing and interpreting how rhetorical communication works. Taken together, then, **rhetorical criticism** is the analysis and interpretation of the persuasive elements of communication. At least, that is the place from which we begin in this book, although later we will see just how much more expansive and rich this definition can be. Rhetorical criticism is a humanizing activity. By that I mean it produces knowledge that helps us to better understand who we are as human beings. Additionally, it is a form of activity that engages and enriches human insight, imagination, creativity, and intellect. It allows for the creation of new knowledge about who we were, who we are, and who we might become.

When first learning about rhetorical criticism, just as in any new endeavor, the essential basics can seem overwhelming: new ideas, new words, new associations, new conditions, and so on. There are new concepts; moreover, the application of those concepts will probably be unlike anything to which you will have previously been exposed. Keep pressing on; over time the new words will no longer seem so new, and eventually you will experience the opening of an entirely new intellectual world. By the end of this book you will see human communication in an entirely new light and possess understandings and insights you could not even have imagined before.

Criticism is a type of exploration. *Learning* about criticism is exploration as well. Sometimes when we explore we do not know our final destination, and that is part of the allure of our journey. This book is your guide to "the big picture" while exploring the topic of criticism. To get the most out of this experience, there are a few items to keep in mind while working your way through the ideas contained herein.

To help you with the discovery process, this book is divided into three main sections and three appendices. In the first section, "Overview of Rhetorical Criticism," you will be introduced to the concepts of rhetoric and of criticism, as well as three other important considerations. In chapter 2 you will discover rhetoric's powerful history and also be provided with a foundational definition of rhetoric. This definition, rhetoric as *the strategic use of communication, oral or written, to achieve specifiable goals*, is our starting point, and as the book progresses you will see how different critics and theorists have expanded or modified this definition. In short, this chapter will help you to develop a firm understanding of what rhetoric is, and also help you to understand the power of symbols and how they are used. As you read through this chapter, it will help to consider rhetoric as something you use every day; think of actual examples from your own life, whether personal experience or something you have seen in the news, on an entertainment show, or what have you.

Chapter 3 introduces the concept of criticism. Keep in mind when reading this chapter that criticism involves much more than offering an opinion; it is a way of generating new knowledge and insights about how communication works to persuade and how symbols interact to form meaning. Criticism is also a way to develop critical-thinking abilities, something that will only enhance your quality of life, be it in personal or professional ways. I know, it is almost certain that you have previously been promised exposure to ways of thinking critically and have walked away disappointed. Here, though, you will be introduced to **rhetorical perspectives**, which are different ways of viewing how we communicate (or theoretical orientations a critic uses to help guide the criticism of rhetoric). The idea is that by using different perspectives to view instances of communication, we can learn more about how communication works. In this chapter we will explore the nature of criticism, examine how criticism is performed, and also discover how criticism differs from other ways of producing knowledge, such as the scientific method. You will also come away from this chapter better able to think insightfully about the communication around you, and with a good understanding of how to actually begin writing criticism.

The next three chapters expose you to three key concepts in rhetorical criticism. The first is the rhetorical situation, which is a theoretical explanation for what makes certain types of communication rhetorical. Although not used as a stand-alone perspective for engaging in criticism, the concept of the rhetorical situation is very important for understanding how persuasive communication operates. The next concept is that of genre. In some senses, every example of discourse contains elements of other examples of discourse, and as situations repeat themselves, so too do the elements speakers use when addressing these situations. For example, if you have been to more than one commencement or convocation, you will have noticed that all of the main speeches sounded somewhat familiar. Sure, there were differences linked to the particular class and probably to the person giving the main speech. But there were also repeating elements that were expected in terms of what you would consider appropriate remarks for a speech concerning graduating students. This works for other types of communication as well: keynote addresses, funerals, weddings, apologies, and so on. The chapter on genre explores the importance of these repeating forms. Finally, there is a chapter on the concepts of objectivity and politics in criticism. Should a critic be objective? If so, to what degree? And what is objectivity in criticism, anyway? These questions elicit different answers from critics, and this chapter provides an excellent starting point for discussion of these issues.

The second section, "Perspectives on Criticism," contains eight chapters introducing different perspectives that you can use when performing criticism: "The Traditional Perspective," "Close Textual Analysis," "Criticism of Metaphor," "The Narrative Perspective," "Dramatism and Kenneth Burke's Pentadic Criticism," "Fantasy-Theme Criticism," "Feminist Analysis," and "Ideographic Criticism." These represent important perspectives in criticism in use now or in the past. The essential idea to keep in mind with each chapter is that you will be learning a distinct and insightful way of analyzing instances of rhetoric. Each perspective will offer new and exciting ways to view communication, thus allowing you to better unleash *your* imagination and powers of observation. As you learn about different perspectives, you will most likely discover that you like some better than others, that one or two "speak to you" in a way that the others do not. This is as it should be. Not every perspective will hold the same appeal for everyone, which is one of the reasons there are so many. Criticism is not a one-size-fits-all endeavor. Another reason that there are so many perspectives is that not all instances of communication yield insights in the same manner. Some perspectives are better suited to a particular instance of communication than are others.

The third section, "Expanding Our Critical Horizons," contains three chapters, each of which covers an orientation toward viewing rhetoric and criticism that broadens their scope beyond the more traditional or established perspectives covered in the earlier section. In a sense, they push the boundaries we have thus far created for our definitions of *rhetoric, criticism,* and *theory.* In "An Eclectic Approach to Criticism," you will discover ways to blend different perspectives in order to invent new and insightful ways to analyze instances of rhetoric. In "Critical Rhetoric," you will be exposed to what is called the *critical turn* in rhetorical studies, and also to new purposes for criticism. In "Criticism of Popular Culture and Social Media," you will be given the means to better examine contemporary and popular uses of communication, much of which you might experience every day. In each of these chapters, ask yourself how the concepts being shared modify or enlarge the definitions of rhetoric and criticism that came before. Again, you may well find that you gravitate toward some of these approaches more so than others, and that is a sign (as with the other perspectives) that you may have discovered a perspective "speaking your language."

Finally, in the appendices, you will find helpful information as you move through this book and beyond. In the "Writing Criticism: Getting Started" entry, you will discover a brief introduction to a way of initially thinking about writing criticism. It contains straightforward advice about the important elements in any piece of criticism and can act as a guide when you first begin writing your own criticism. In the "Additional Rhetorical Perspectives and Genres" entry, you will find brief overviews of other perspectives and approaches used by rhetorical critics. These are designed to give you a taste of the broader picture that is rhetorical criticism. In the "Glossary of Terms," you will find key terms used in the various chapters of this book.

Some are common throughout all the chapters, and others will be specific to a particular perspective covered in one chapter. You will know when a term is in the glossary because it will be in **bold** when you first encounter it in this book. So, for instance, you will find the terms *rhetoric* and *criticism* mentioned above in the glossary.

I (and the individuals who have contributed chapters to this book) invite you to engage with the ideas in the following pages; I hope you find them as exciting as we do, and that they will enrich your understanding of human communication.

# I
OVERVIEW OF RHETORICAL CRITICISM

# 2

# What Is Rhetoric?

*Jim A. Kuypers and Andrew King*

Rhetoric has been around for quite a while; it has many meanings, some old, some new. To get at the heart of the definition, let us first consider how the term *rhetoric* is most commonly used. When a politician calls for "action, not rhetoric," the meaning seems clear; rhetoric denotes hollow words and flashy language. It also connotes associations with deceit and tricks that mask truth and forthrightness. For example, former President Richard M. Nixon used the term *rhetoric* in this way in his 1969 inaugural address: "The simple things are the ones most needed today if we are to surmount what divides us and cement what unites us. To lower our voices would be a simple thing. In these difficult years, America has suffered from a fever of words; from inflated rhetoric that promises more than it can deliver; from angry rhetoric that fans discontents into hatreds; from bombastic rhetoric that postures instead of persuading." Although the type of rhetoric of which Nixon speaks is often worthy of study, it also leaves one thinking that it is certainly not the kind of language that an intelligent and civil person would willingly wish to use. Consider, too, this example from a recent headline: "Obama Should 'Reconcile the *Rhetoric* with *Action*' to End Religious Intolerance, Says Rev. Samuel Rodriguez."[1] Or this recent headline with a twist from a news blog: "On Energy and Climate, Obama *Action* Makes Up for Lack of *Rhetoric*."[2]

*Rhetoric* is also used to describe what some today consider embellished or overornamental language. The contemporary perception of excess has its roots in eighteenth- and nineteenth-century American oratorical practice. During these centuries before radio, television, and the Internet, public speeches were opportunities for audiences to be both informed and entertained; a certain lushness of language was both expected and desired. It was not at all uncommon for speeches to last several hours and for speakers to use no notes. This style of American speaking was most evident in patriotic orations and is well represented in George Caleb Bingham's painting, *Stump Speaking*. Albert Beveridge, in his 1898 speech "The March of the Flag," provides a common example of what we might consider embellished speech today:

> It is a noble land that God has given us; a land that can feed and clothe the world; a land whose coastlines would enclose half the countries in Europe; a land set like a sentinel between the two imperial oceans of the globe, a greater England with a nobler destiny.

> It is a mighty people that he has planted on this soil; a people sprung from the most masterful blood of history; a people perpetually revitalized by the virile, man-producing working-folk of all the earth; a people imperial by virtue of their power, by right of their institutions, by authority of their heaven-directed purposes—the propagandists and not the misers of liberty.[3]

Although the above examples are certainly forms of rhetoric, they but scratch the surface of rhetoric's deeply rich meaning. The study of rhetoric is an invention of early Western civilization, and we can trace its roots back over 2,600 years to the fledgling democracies of ancient Greece.

## A CONCISE SKETCH OF THE RHETORICAL TRADITION

The Greeks developed the original model of rhetoric, a systematic body of knowledge about the theory and practice of public speaking in the law courts, in the governing assemblies, and on ceremonial occasions. Rhetoric was codified by Aristotle in his famous treatise, *The Rhetoric*, written somewhere around 335 BC. He defined rhetoric as the "power of discovering the means of persuasion in any given situation," a much more comprehensive and intellectually respectable meaning than today's common attributions of empty words and deception. Rhetoric was viewed as a practical art and was studied, discussed, and debated by educated Greeks, who expected each other to speak well, eloquently, and persuasively. Citizens were even expected to defend themselves in court by their personal rhetorical prowess, thus making the study of rhetoric even more important. The sophists, wandering teachers in the ancient world, often taught rhetoric as popular courses designed to prepare ambitious youths for fame and success. The Greeks believed in the power of the spoken word and delighted in hotly contested debate; they even held oratorical contests as part of the Olympics. On the other hand, philosophers such as Plato condemned rhetoric, finding it a serious rival to philosophy in the ancient educational system.

Later, the Roman republican government provided many opportunities for the practice of rhetoric in their popular assemblies, in provincial governing bodies, in their law courts, and in their huge civil service and military. The best-known Roman orator was Marcus Tullius Cicero (106–43 BC), who took over the Greek ideas of rhetoric and adapted them to the needs of a far-flung world empire. From modest origins he rose to the highest office in Rome, the consulship, and was considered by many to be the greatest lawyer, speaker, and writer of his day. Fifty-eight speeches and nine hundred letters have come down to us; they still read well today and stand as models of powerfully persuasive oratory, biting wit, and incredible verbal skill. Cicero argued for an ideal **rhetorician**, an orator-statesman who would use rhetoric as a means of serving the people. A century later, Cicero's rhetorical teaching was codified by the first imperial professor of rhetoric in Rome, Quintilian (AD 35–96), who was Rome's greatest teacher and codifier of rhetorical knowledge. Thus, the Greco-Roman world established a tradition of discourse that has been taught throughout Western history and continues to grow and to develop down to our own time in the early twenty-first century.

Saint Augustine (AD 354–430) was largely responsible for early Christian uses of rhetoric, and his writings were used extensively by churchmen throughout the Middle Ages. Augustine reasoned that since the Devil had full access to all of the available resources of rhetoric, others ought to study it if only for their own protection. The Church eventually agreed, declaring that knowledge of rhetoric's great power was essential for everyone, and both "in theory and practice the Christians forever influenced the development of rhetorical thought."[4] Likewise, the influence of rhetoric on the spread of Christianity should not be underestimated. During the Middle Ages, rhetoric was at the heart of education. It was taught in the cathedral schools. It inspired the great university debates and disputations, and it set rules for the composition of sermons and royal proclamations. It even extended its domain over poetry and letter writing, and rhetorical modes of expression guided government bureaucracies.

In the Renaissance, rhetoric became even more important, recapturing the high status it had enjoyed at the time of Cicero. Renaissance leaders revered Cicero as the ideal of the practicing rhetorician, the active agent in the service of the state and the people. Jean Dietz Moss notes that "a widening wave of literacy extended beyond the church and the court to include a secular public, merchants, bankers, lawyers, artisans and others of the middle class."[5] In the fifteenth and sixteenth centuries, rhetoric dominated philosophy, literature, and politics. Early in the seventeenth century, the great Italian rhetorician Giambattista Vico took René Descartes head-on, writing that truth is discovered through the rhetorical process of invention (discussed in chapter 7), not only through scientific observation, as Descartes maintained.[6] Vico's work extended the intellectual scope of rhetoric to include the study of language and the evolution of society, and it fit in well with other works of the period that were pushing back against a growing scientism that was advancing into all aspects of life at that time.[7]

During the late eighteenth century there was a vast expansion of the middle class in Britain and North America. The tremendous growth of literacy was aligned with the growth of the press and the publishing industry. Like today's Internet, the printing press was a dynamo for the circulation and expansion of knowledge. As a result, rhetoric expanded beyond matters of political and legal conflict to areas of reading, criticism, and judgment. Vast fortunes were being made via the Industrial Revolution, and upwardly mobile and newly rich individuals were eager to assimilate the speech, ideas, and manners of their higher-status counterparts in the aristocracy. The three greatest rhetorical theorists of the period were Hugh Blair, Richard Whately, and George Campbell. Each was a Christian minister, and each emphasized matters of ethics and of individual accountability in their rhetorical theory.

The nineteenth century was a time of huge industrial, political, and educational expansion in Europe and the United States. Parliamentary democracy penetrated to many points of the globe. Nineteenth-century practitioners of rhetoric cultivated the discipline as a form of individual intellectual training. They believed that knowledge of rhetoric would prepare any speaker or writer from age fifteen to age ninety to inform, persuade, or entertain any audience at any time on any occasion. The optimistic how-to-do-it rhetorical manuals of that day were an invitation to train in the privacy of one's own home for both self-improvement and social power. One example was the young Frederick Douglass studying his rhetoric book in secret in order to prepare for a career in public life that would lift him out of both slavery and poverty. Rhetorically based eloquence was seen as a means of gaining entry to the corridors of power. Books provided strategies for persuading others and provided models of great speeches for readers to imitate. A pantheon of great orators and their greatest speeches was established through books such as Chauncey A. Goodrich's *Select British Eloquence* in 1852. The book contained the speeches of the greatest British orators together with critical guides for study and tips on rhetorical emulation. Collections of great American orators soon followed, and these became style models for ambitious youth who saw the acquisition of rhetorical skill as a path to influence and wealth.

Although rhetorical treatises had been written since before Aristotle's day, academic departments focusing on rhetoric did not come into being until the early twentieth century; beginning in America, many evolved into what we today call departments of communication.[8] In these early departments, often known as departments of speech, scholars recovered the full range of the classical tradition and greatly expanded the study of rhetoric.[9] Criticism became the major thrust of study, and theory was developed to explain the vast changes wrought by mass media, modern propaganda, and the immense social movements and revolutions of the first half of the century. In the latter half of the century and into the early twenty-first century, students of rhetoric moved far beyond the classical tradition. Traditionally scholars have focused on how exemplar speakers—gifted and influential individuals—used rhetorical arts to shape their world and affect social change. More recently scholars have inverted this relationship and have begun to study the ways in which history and culture have shaped the practice of rhetoric itself. The very conditions in which rhetoric takes place are objects of study, and they include who is allowed to speak in a public place, whose speech will be taken seriously, and the range of ideas that are considered debatable at any given time. Scholars have also emphasized the role of language and symbols in the process by which social influence occurs, and they have broken down the walls between visual, verbal, and acoustic messages. Rhetoric now includes far more than public speaking, as indispensible as that is; focusing on understanding symbolic action in many different forms and settings, it embraces discourse in print, radio, television, social media, and even our smart phones. Small wonder, then, that rhetoric is now being studied across a whole spectrum of academic subjects and is among the central disciplines of our time.[10]

## THE MANY MEANINGS OF RHETORIC TODAY

Accordingly, at the start of the twenty-first century, we find a greatly expanded study of rhetoric, along with an ever-growing litany of definitions. We begin with a pragmatic introduction to some of those meanings.

Rhetoric not only has a persuasive element; it has an informative one as well. For example, you might want to persuade someone to take a class with a certain professor, or you might want to persuade your friends to have dinner with you at your favorite restaurant. Both instances would use rhetoric. However, in order to effectively persuade, you must first provide information in the form of supporting materials such as testimony, examples, stories, definitions, and the like. In short, you must use more than mere assertions as your arguments. In this sense, rhetoric involves the proper interpretation, construction, and use of supporting materials to back up assertions and gain audience acceptance.

With this in mind, let us begin with a working definition of *rhetoric*. When we use the term **rhetoric** in this chapter we mean *the strategic use of communication, oral or written, to achieve specifiable goals*. There are two main ideas expressed by this definition. One involves the strategic, or intentional, nature of the language we use; the second involves knowing what goals we wish to reach through the language we use. This is an intentionally narrow definition of *rhetoric*, but we think using such is justified for now. After all, we need someplace to begin the inquiry, and it seems to us that a definition rooted in the most practical examples of intentional persuasion is a good place from which to launch our discussion.

### The Strategic Nature of Rhetoric

We use symbols to communicate. These symbols essentially are something we use to represent something else. Words, whether spoken or written, are such symbols. Musical notes are such symbols as well. Certain gestures are symbolic representations of meaning, too. Of importance to us here is that words, spoken or written, are symbols whose meanings are more readily agreed upon than the meanings of other symbols used in communication. That is to say, the lion's share of those hearing or reading a particular word can come to some consensus concerning its meaning, whereas this does not hold true with other types of symbols. For example, the symbols used in art, architecture, dance, and clothing are all vague in their meanings; thus a communicator would have less control over their precise interpretation by a given audience. Unfortunately, the further we travel from the *intentions* of the communicator, the closer to the *inferences* of the audience we find ourselves. Since rhetoric works using symbols, the more variation in the symbolic meaning (the meaning of a *word* versus the architectural meaning of a doorway, for example), the less precision in the communication in general.

Nonetheless, rhetoric viewed from this broader aspect should be considered. For example, Sonja K. Foss wrote that "*rhetoric* means the use of symbols to influence thought and action. Rhetoric is communication; it is simply an old term for what is now called *communication*."[11] In a later work she refines this definition of rhetoric as "the human use of symbols to communicate."[12] Rhetoric, for Foss, does involve action on the part of a communicator; it involves making conscious decisions about what to do. However, it also involves a larger conception in that it takes into consideration the impact symbols have on receivers, even if unintended. The range of potential rhetorical symbols according to Foss is vast: "Speeches, essays, conversations, poetry, novels, stories, comic books, websites, television programs, films, art, architecture, plays, music, dance, advertisements, furniture, automobiles, and dress are all forms of rhetoric."[13]

Foss presents an extremely broad definition, one that both includes and clashes with a more pragmatic conception of rhetoric. One could even argue that her definition is so broad as to claim that any form of human action or creation, when perceived by another, is a form of rhetoric. One can certainly argue what should or should not be considered as rhetoric, and Foss's conception does have merit. For the present, though, let us content ourselves with a more narrow and pragmatic definition. As Marie Hochmuth Nichols wrote, "Rhetoric is an act of adapting discourse to an end outside of itself. It serves many ends, from promoting decision to giving pleasure. It does not include ships, guns, an alluring sun, the dance, or the Cathedral of Chartres. It does not include rolling drums or the sound of marching feet; it does not include extralinguistic symbols of peace or the clenched fist of power. It does not deny that there are other symbolic forms for altering behavior, which often accompany or reinforce it."[14] Conceptions of rhetoric similar to that given by Foss minimize the important fact that as one moves further away from the use of symbols with generally agreed-upon meanings (words) to the use of symbols with imprecise meanings (furniture, dance), one finds that the *intentions* of the **rhetor**, or communicator, play less a part in the rhetorical exchange and that the *impressions* of the receiver play a greater role.[15] In this sense the meaning behind the rhetoric moves from the person crafting the message to the impressions of those receiving the message, irrespective of the intentions of the original communicator.

This distinction was not lost on Hoyt Hopewell Hudson, an early twentieth-century rhetorical theorist, critic, and poet.[16] In his landmark essay, "Rhetoric and Poetry," Hudson highlighted the differences between efforts aimed at rhetorical influence (rhetoric) and efforts aimed at symbolic expression (poetry). He began his comparison by citing numerous great poets in order to demonstrate the general focus of a poet: "The Poet . . . keeps his eye not on the audience or the occasion, but on his subject; his subject fills his mind and engrosses his imagination, so that he is compelled, by excess of admiration or other emotion, to tell of it;

compelled, though no one hear or read his utterance."[17] Hudson clearly marked where rhetoric begins and poetry ends to better discuss their differences: "For the moment, then, we shall say that poetry is for the sake of expression; the impression on others is incidental. Rhetoric is for the sake of impression; the expression is secondary—an indispensable means."[18]

This distinction is subject to exceptions, and here Hudson showed a graceful and discerning grasp of the differences between rhetoric and poetry, providing examples of how a poet might stray into the field of rhetoric. For example, a poet envisioning a speaker attempting to persuade listeners must use rhetoric—Mark Antony in Shakespeare's *Julius Caesar* and the speeches of the fallen angels in the first and second books of *Paradise Lost* are two such examples. He calls this imitative rhetoric, which may be studied for its own sake. A poet may at times consider the audience (a drama, for example), but there exist differences in the conception of the audience: "The poet thinks of a more general and more vaguely defined audience than the orator. The poet may even think of all mankind of the present and future as his audience."[19] Hudson even provided a loose scale to depict the range from the most purely poetical—personal lyrics and rhapsodic poems; then idylls and pastoral poetry; then narrative poetry, romance, and the epic—to the more purely rhetorical, such as tragedy and comedy, and finally didactic poetry, satire, odes, and epigrams. Hudson also demonstrated how an orator might cross over into the field of poetry: "Though the orator's end is persuasion, it is not hard to believe that there are moments in his discourse when this end is forgotten in his delight or wonder before some image which fills his inner eye. In such moments he has his eye on the subject, not the audience."[20]

Considering all of the above, we can clearly see the differences between the more personally *expressive* use of ambiguous symbols—poetry, painting, dance, and architecture—and the more publicly *impressive* use of symbols with generally agreed-upon meanings: words spoken and written for the sake of persuasion. It is the latter that is the focus of this chapter and many of the chapters beyond. This is not to say that other forms of more ambiguous rhetoric cannot be studied, but rather that we will take our first step on the firmer soil of rhetoric understood as strategic and intentional. Later chapters in this book will expand on this definition of rhetoric.

**Rhetoric as Goal-Oriented Communication**

Coming back to the definition of rhetoric we gave above, we find that rhetoric is strategic because it is intentional. Communicators who wish to control the manner in which their messages are understood plan ahead. They think about what they are going to say and what impact their words are likely to have on those listening to them. When they use rhetoric in this way, they provide reasons for their listeners to agree with them. Just as importantly, rhetoric is intentional in the sense that it is employed only when words can make a difference. That is to say, rhetoric is *persuasive*. It seeks to influence our personal and collective behaviors through having us voluntarily agree with the speaker that a certain action or policy is better than another action or policy. Rhetors often think about their goals so that they are better able to plan what to say for a desired effect. Since there is no scientific certainty to human affairs—that is, we do not know with complete certainty which policy will produce the absolute best results—rhetoric attempts to persuade listeners that one policy will *probably* be better than another. It is in this sense, then, that rhetoric is based on probability—communicators try to convince us not so much that their proposed course of action is the only correct one, or that it will work with guaranteed certainty, but rather that it *probably* will reap greater success than competing solutions. The trick for the person trying to persuade is to make certain that the level of probability is high enough to convince the particular audience being addressed that a certain course of action will be the best course of action for them.

Rhetoric works toward a goal, then. It may involve simply trying to have your audience believe a certain way, or it could work toward the enacting of one course of action or policy over another. In suggesting that rhetoric is policy oriented, we mean to say that it seeks to influence how those receiving the rhetoric act at either a personal or a public level. Policy at the personal level involves decisions about our beliefs or actions completely within our control: should I rent the apartment at Grosse Pointe or the one at the Aspens? Beyond this, all of us also use rhetoric to influence those around us. For example, think of the last time you were together with a group of friends and you were trying to decide where to go for dinner. You most likely had several competing options and had to advance good reasons for choosing one restaurant over another. The policy option resulting in action is simple: where to go eat. Your attempt at persuasion here involves more than just your actions; it involves deciding what to do for a group: the outcome is not solely under your control. At a more public level, consider the November 20, 2014, words of President Barack Obama concerning his executive order on immigration. He asserted that it would fix the system "while giving undocumented immigrants a pathway to citizenship if they paid a fine, started paying their taxes, and went to the back of the line."[21] The public policy here involves allowing up to five million illegal immigrants to stay in the country with federal assistance should they meet certain requirements. Senator Jeff Sessions of Alabama offered a competing policy option, one that would deny funding to the president's executive order and add "enforcement-only measures like universal E-Verify, ending catch-and-release, mandatory repatriation for unaccompanied alien minors, ending asylum loopholes, and closing off welfare for illegal immigrants."[22] The public policy here involves ending the president's plan to provide the means of citizenship for illegal immigrants and tightening border security. Which option one prefers depends on many factors, including the evidence each politician presents to show how his plan would produce the best results for the greatest number of citizens, as well as the personal values of each citizen.

A more detailed yet common example of how rhetoric works shows that the good reasons rhetoric uses to persuade us very often incorporate the human qualities we use every day when communicating with a goal in mind. A friend of ours was president of her neighborhood's homeowners association for several years. At one point during her tenure her neighborhood experienced a rash of mail thefts. The sheriff's department could do little; this was a rural setting, wooded, with little likelihood of catching whoever was stealing unless someone was willing to keep watch twenty-four hours a day. Our friend decided that the post office could be prevailed upon to install lockboxes in place of the old stand-alone mailboxes. The post office agreed but decided to place the new boxes in a wooded area alongside the road where there was no light during the evening hours. Our friend asked that they be placed in a more central, lighted area near the road, but the postal worker said no. Not to be swayed, our friend continued her use of rhetoric.

She used common examples in her efforts: Many of those who would be getting the mail would be women, driving alone or with their children. With daylight savings time soon to end, they would be driving home at night after a day at work. Where the postal service wanted to place the mailboxes would necessitate the women getting out of their cars and walking away from them in order to get the mail. Our friend pointed out that all it would take is one woman being attacked and then that particular postal worker would feel terrible. She also pointed out the very real possibility of the postal service being held responsible for any attacks that were facilitated by poorly placed boxes. The next day she had a phone conversation with the regional director of the postal service, and by the next week the new boxes were in, and in a new location so that nobody driving at night would have to get out of his or her car in order to collect the mail.

The persuasive effort used by our friend tells us a great deal about the nature of rhetoric. She used no extravagant arguments; rather, she used everyday logic and reasoning (common sense), evoked a little emotion within her listeners (feelings about someone getting hurt), and ended up getting what was best for those in her neighborhood. It was not that her arguments had no weakness or that they were scientifically reasoned out. Rather the arguments she used were constructed in order to convince the postal authorities that there was a high possibility that what she said would happen would indeed happen. And that possibility was just high enough to persuade them to agree with her. So, this example shows how rhetoric is used every day. Importantly, though, it also points out that rhetoric is concerned with contingent matters, too. Simply put, rhetoric addresses those problems that can be changed through the use of words. Put another way, the outcome of the situation is contingent upon what is said. So, for example, it was only because the possibility existed for having the location of the mailboxes moved that rhetoric was able to effect a change.

As the above example shows, rhetoric is goal directed. Our friend knew she wanted those mailboxes in a different location. She then thought of ways of constructing her arguments so that they would work with her particular audience—in this case, the postal workers who could change the location of the boxes. As you think about the goals communicators have in mind, it is important to remember another important aspect of rhetoric. When rhetoric is used, it is concerned with *informed opinions*. Most of us are not a mathematician trying to prove an equation or a chemist following a formula. Instead we deal with human beings thinking on uncertain matters; we deal with their facts and their opinions. Humans act based on what appears probable to them, not always on what they know for certain.

When we deal with questions of what we should do in a particular situation, there is no way to demonstrate using the scientific method that a certain course of action will be the best. Although *we* might know with certainty, those with whom we communicate may feel just as certain about a different course of action. What rhetors do, then, is try to persuade their listeners that their proposed course of action has the maximum probability of succeeding. Successful rhetors attempt to narrow the choices from which their audiences can choose. These audiences may have many choices for action; rhetoric helps them to decide which course is the best to take. Summing up such a position, Gerard Hauser wrote, "Rhetoric, as an area of study, is concerned with how humans use symbols, especially language, to reach agreement that permits coordinated effort of some sort. In its most basic form, rhetorical communication occurs whenever one person engages another in an exchange of symbols to accomplish some goal. It is not communication for communication's sake; rhetorical communication, at least implicitly and often explicitly, attempts to coordinate social action."[23] As Donald C. Bryant so competently put it, rhetoric is not a body of knowledge but a means of applying knowledge: "It does rather than is."[24]

## The Moral Dimensions of Rhetoric

The foregoing example has illustrated the strategic and goal-oriented nature of rhetoric. Rhetoric always presupposes the existence of an audience. A rhetorician addresses a particular audience anchored in time, space, culture, and circumstance. Intellectuals who dismiss rhetoric and wish to present unvarnished truth are often people who do not understand the power of audiences. Like Plato, they believe that what they see as clear ideas, strong evidence, and a rational plan of reform are enough. They underestimate the influence of emotion, self-interest, fear of change, and the ways in which unequal power distorts communication.

The very practice of rhetoric has an impact on the practitioners. But persuading others is always a matter of negotiating between ever-changing local conditions and the enduring principles of political judgment. Deliberation helps nurture audiences by strengthening the norms of fairness. Consider for a moment that communities do not exist prior to talk. Neither do they exist simply because someone says that this or that grouping of people is a community. They are built over time through communal understanding, argument, negotiation, and common action. Rhetorical practice is ethical in nature because it is advisory, and this advice has consequences for which the advice giver is held accountable. As Richard Weaver wrote, "it has the office of advising men with reference to an independent order of goods and with reference to their particular situation as it relates to these. The honest rhetorician therefore has two things in mind: a vision of how things should go ideally and ethically and a consideration of the special circumstances of his auditors. Toward both of these he has a responsibility."[25] Rhetoric is not an ethically neutral act such as target shooting or throwing clay pots on a wheel. Participation in rhetorical discourse involves people in building citizenship and constructing community. And the decisions they make or the ideas they embrace can ruin or enrich their lives. Thus, rhetoric is an ethically significant practice that seeks to engage audiences in sound judgment; those judgments have consequences that we can judge to be good or bad.[26]

Finally rhetoric sustains democratic culture. Rhetoric uses accepted beliefs to produce new beliefs and in so doing builds the stock of communal wisdom. It safeguards the stable beliefs that provide communal identity yet allows the community to manage change in ways that do not rend it apart and leave its people adrift.

## A LARGER CONCEPTION OF RHETORIC

We mentioned earlier that the concept of rhetoric is expansive. In our discussion above we intentionally focus on a pragmatic conception of rhetoric. As will be reflected by some of the chapters in this book, rhetoric can be conceived in slightly larger ways. For instance, Charles Bazerman wrote that

> [rhetoric is the study] of how people use language and other symbols to realize human goals and carry out human activities. Rhetoric is ultimately a practical study offering people greater control over their symbolic activity. Rhetoric has at times been associated with limited techniques appropriate to specific tasks of political and forensic persuasion. . . . Consequently, people concerned with other tasks have considered rhetoric to offer inappropriate analyses and techniques. These people have then tended to believe mistakenly that their rejection of political and forensic rhetoric has removed their own activity from the larger realm of situated, purposeful, strategic symbolic activity. I make no such narrowing and use rhetoric (for want of a more comprehensive term) to refer to the study of all areas of symbolic activity.[27]

"All areas of symbolic activity" certainly widens the scope of rhetoric's influence. Additionally, some have enlarged our understanding of rhetoric by making the argument that it can also have unintentional, even unconscious elements in its persuasive effect. As Kenneth Burke noted in the mid-twentieth century, rhetoric can work toward the promotion of "'**identification**,' which can include a partially unconscious factor in appeal."[28] Burke explained his concept of identification this way: "A is not identical with his colleague, B. But insofar as their interests are joined, A is identified with B. Or he may identify himself with B even when their interests are not joined, if he assumes that they are, or is persuaded to believe so. You persuade a man only insofar as you can talk his language by speech, gesture, tonality, order, image, attitude, idea, identifying your way with his."[29] For example, a person might use symbols associated with wealth or class when writing a news story. Upon exposure to these symbols, a reader might identify with the nuances of wealth or class without being fully aware of doing so.[30] Brooke Quigley explained that "the need to identify arises out of division; humans are born and exist as biologically separate beings and therefore seek to identify, through communication, in order to overcome separateness. We are aware of this biological separation, and we recognize additional types of separation based on social class or position. We experience the ambiguity of being separate yet being identified with others at the same time."[31] As Burke wrote, humans are "both joined and separate, at once a distinct substance and consubstantial with another."[32] Burke was interested in the "processes by which we build social cohesion through our use of language. His goal [was] that we learn to perceive at what points we are using and abusing language to cloud our vision, create confusion, or justify various and ever present inclinations toward conflict, war and destruction—or our equally-present inclinations toward cooperation, peace and survival."[33]

Other ways that critics examine this notion of the unintentional aspects of rhetoric involve the study of **ideology** in the language we use. Ideology in this context is any system of ideas that directs our collective social and political action. We can't escape some form of ideology since we are raised and educated within a society that is organized around a particular ideology. A more specific definition suggests that an "ideology is a set of opinions or beliefs of a group or an individual. Very often ideology refers to a set of political beliefs or a set of ideas that characterize a particular culture. Capitalism, communism, socialism, [fascism,] and Marxism are ideologies."[34] Thus a speaker using rhetoric would, intentionally or not, be grounding the ideas in his or her speech in a particular ideology. Critics looking at ideology generally do so from two broad perspectives. One involves looking at how ideology exists in society as systems of belief. Critics here simply want to know how ideology works in our society. In our speaker case above, how did ideology manifest itself in the speech? Most critics who study ideology go beyond this, however, and ground their understanding of ideology in the works of Marx, Engels, and Lenin. According to Jim A. Kuypers,

> One views ideology in this tradition as a false consciousness; it is a negative influence that distorts one's ability to think and perceive the world. In this perspective, ideologies contribute to the domination of the masses because they present a distorted picture of the world, thus debilitating one's ability to reason (think of an infection of the mind). For instance, consider religious and nationalist components to American ideology (America: land of the free, home of the brave; the American dream). Following the ideology as distortion metaphor, these components act to dominate members of the working class because the ideology has these workers believing that they actually are working for God and country, when in reality, according to Marxists, they are working for the dominant power elite (and the Capitalist system that steals their labor from them).[35]

In this case, then, a critic looking at our same speech mentioned above would be looking for how that speaker possessed a false consciousness imposed by a particular ideology, many times looking in particular at how it impacts race, gender, or class, and then make suggestions about how to break free from the constraints imposed by that ideology. James Jasinski offers insight into these two broad ideological trends of criticism, stating that "the difference between the traditions is primarily one of emphasis; the Marxist tradition considers ideology as an object of critique or something that needs to be overcome, whereas the belief system tradition views ideology as an object of disinterested analysis or something that needs to be studied."[36]

## WHAT FUTURE FOR RHETORIC?

But despite our friend's success in the matter of the postboxes, is there still an important future for rhetoric? Some persons worry that the places for public deliberation are becoming smaller and fewer. They remind us that beyond the scope of the town meeting and neighborhood conclave, significant issues are selected and framed by the mass media, not local citizens. These issues are debated by so-called experts while the citizenry watches, sometimes enjoying the "illusion" of participation, but often feeling like powerless spectators. Scholars such as Jürgen Habermas argue that such civic voyeurism could undermine the legitimacy of our institutions. After all, most Americans have never discussed beyond the comfort of their own homes public education, free enterprise, the income tax, or our immigration laws, yet they are imposed upon us by the dead hand of the past. These systems were largely developed before we were born and are imposed upon us without our consent. Their direction is mostly in the hands of unaccountable public officials who enjoy lifetime tenure as unelected public servants. Policy details are complex, often known only to special-interest groups.

Since many of our problems of race, ethnicity, poverty, and aging have been placed in the hands of government and state bureaucracy, they are in many ways removed from the arena of public discussion. Further, the sheer number of issues and the volume of information concerning them are mind numbing and intimidating. Matters that were once seen to be the province of ordinary citizens are now the property of specialized technical elites. We may fear that although these "intellectuals" can organize data and design complex "solutions," they may understand very little about the fears, prejudices, and aspirations of ordinary people. Denied participation in civic debate, we become less skilled in managing discourse. Increasingly, we may view ourselves as mere masses manipulated by experts, not active citizens who are in charge of their own fate.

Finally, it can be argued that the ever-increasing elite focus on diversity and multiculturalism has destroyed the basic consensus that the practice of rhetoric requires. Rhetoric was born in the Greek polis, a small face-to-face homogenous community in which civic identity was girded by the premise that everyone shared a common destiny. Our society is becoming vast congeries of warring interest groups characterized by unbridgeable controversies and sedimented suspicion. Thus some critics argue that rhetoric is a method that only worked in the past and that it no longer has a place in twenty-first-century life.

We argue that these criticisms are nothing new and actually predate the rise of a multicultural, technologically advanced megastate. In one form or another they have been made for the past century. Despite numerous pronouncements about the death of rhetoric and civil culture, persuasive discourse persists. The practice of rhetoric is alive and well. Audiences and speakers are still engaged in building practical wisdom. Common dilemmas are still being attacked and resolved. Can rhetoric still be powerful, useful, and moral? Roderick P. Hart and Courtney Dillard think so:

> Is deliberation still possible? Some say no, others find the question fatuous. In defense of deliberation they point to democracies in which women were given the vote by men and in which blacks were enfranchised by whites. They find wars being stopped by college students, environmental laws

being passed by the children of corporation executives, and Nelson Mandela's cause assisted by a distant band of college professors. They point to an American president being driven out of office by free press, a Russian president honored for dismantling a mighty Communist machine, and an Iraqi dictator stopped in his tracks.[37]

We simply cannot do without rhetoric. In fact, knowledge about the wise use of discourse has never been more necessary than it is today. Just as we begin to think that people are not communicating in the public sphere as much as they did in the past, we discover that social media such as Twitter, Pinterest, Tumblr, Instagram, VK, Vine, and Meetup are bringing them together in new and creative ways.[38] We also discover that blockbuster console video games such as *Grand Theft Auto*, *Call of Duty*, and *Halo* are dynamic productions using rhetoric to enhance game play.[39] Little wonder the study of rhetoric is enjoying a vast revival throughout our system of higher education. And after a one-hundred-year hiatus, the study of rhetoric is also seeing a resurgence in Europe.[40] The chapters that follow will give you a sense of the variety and artistry of rhetorical discourse and of the cultural and historical faces that have shaped it. As you move through each chapter, you will find that the conception of rhetoric it advances modifies or moves beyond the working definition we provided above. This is as it should be. Take note of *how* the conception changes. Rhetoric is nuanced and may be understood on many different levels. Each chapter that follows underscores this idea and will present a point of view that will add rich variety to the definition given above.

## SUGGESTED READINGS

Bryant, Donald Cross. "Rhetoric: Its Function and Its Scope." *Quarterly Journal of Speech* 39 (1953): 401–424.

Hauser, Gerard A. *Introduction to Rhetorical Theory*. 2nd ed. Prospect Heights, IL: Waveland Press, 2002.

Hudson, Hoyt Hopewell. "Rhetoric and Poetry." *Quarterly Journal of Speech Education* 10, no. 2 (1924): 143–154.

Nichols, Marie Hochmuth. "Rhetoric and the Humane Tradition." In *Rhetoric: A Tradition in Transition*, edited by Walter R. Fisher, 178–191. Lansing: Michigan State University Press, 1974.

Smith, Craig R. *Rhetoric and Human Consciousness: A History*. 4th ed. Prospect Heights, IL: Waveland Press, 2013.

## NOTES

1. Michael Gryboski, "Obama Should 'Reconcile the Rhetoric with Action' to End Religious Intolerance, Says Rev. Samuel Rodriguez," *Christian Post*, February 5, 2015, emphasis ours, http://www.christianpost.com/news/obama-should-reconcile-the-rhetoric-with-action-to-end-religious-intolerance-says-rev-samuel-rodriguez-133642.

2. Amy Harder, "On Energy and Climate, Obama Action Makes Up for Lack of Rhetoric," *Wall Street Journal: Washington Wire*, January 20, 2015, emphasis ours, http://blogs.wsj.com/washwire/2015/01/20/on-energy-and-climate-obama-action-makes-up-for-lack-of-rhetoric.

3. Speech contained in Ronald F. Reid, *American Rhetorical Discourse*, 2nd ed. (Prospect Heights, IL: Waveland Press, 1995), 657.

4. James L. Golden, Goodwin F. Berquist, and William E. Coleman, *The Rhetoric of Western Thought*, 4th ed. (Dubuque, IA: Kendall/Hunt, 1989), 128–129.

5. Jean Dietz Moss, "Renaissance Rhetoric: An Overview," in *Encyclopedia of Rhetoric* (Oxford University Press, 2001), 681.

6. Giambattista Vico, *De Italorum Sapientia*, 1710.

7. For a more detailed explanation of this growing scientism, see Craig R. Smith, *Rhetoric and Human Consciousness: A History*, 4th ed. (Prospect Heights, IL: Waveland Press, 2013), 234–257.

8. Andrew King and Jim A. Kuypers, "Our Roots Are Strong and Deep," in *Twentieth-Century Roots of Rhetorical Studies*, ed. Jim A. Kuypers and Andrew King (Westport, CT: Praeger, 2001).

9. For examples of such growth, see Theodore Otto Windt Jr., "Hoyt H. Hudson: Spokesman for the Cornell School of Rhetoric," *Quarterly Journal of Speech* 68, no. 2 (1982): 186–200; and Edward P. J. Corbett, "The Cornell School of Rhetoric," *Rhetoric Review* 4, no. 1 (September 1985): 4–14.

10. For overviews of the development of rhetorical theory, see the following: Hoyt Hopewell Hudson, "The Tradition of Our Subject," *Quarterly Journal of Speech* 17, no. 3 (1931): 320–329; Smith, *Rhetoric and Human Consciousness*.

11. Sonja K. Foss, "The Nature of Rhetorical Criticism," in *Rhetorical Criticism: Exploration and Practice* (Prospect Heights, IL: Waveland Press, 1989), 4.

12. Sonja K. Foss, "The Nature of Rhetorical Criticism," in *Rhetorical Criticism: Exploration and Practice*, 4th ed. (Prospect Heights, IL: Waveland Press, 2009), 3.

13. This and the immediately preceding quote, Foss, *Rhetorical Criticism*, 4th ed., 5.

14. Marie Hochmuth Nichols, "Rhetoric and the Humane Tradition," in *Rhetoric: A Tradition in Transition*, ed. Walter R. Fisher (Lansing: Michigan State University Press, 1974), 180.

15. As will be seen in chapter 3 on "Rhetorical Criticism as Art," one "receiver" of the rhetoric is the critic who examines the instance of rhetorical discourse. The further removed from agreed-upon meaning the symbols under consideration are, the more power the critic has over deciding what they mean (over and above what the author of the rhetorical discourse intended them to mean). This can, and sometimes does, lead to abuses by the critic. For more on this see Jim A. Kuypers, "*Doxa* and a Critical Rhetoric: Accounting for the Rhetorical Agent through Prudence," *Communication Quarterly* 44, no. 4 (1996): 452–462.

16. For the contributions of Hoyt Hopewell Hudson, see Jim A. Kuypers, "Hoyt Hopewell Hudson's Nuclear Rhetoric," in *Twentieth-Century Roots of Rhetorical Criticism*, ed. Jim A. Kuypers and Andrew King (Westport, CT: Praeger, 2001); Windt, "Hoyt H. Hudson."

17. Hoyt Hopewell Hudson, "Rhetoric and Poetry," *Quarterly Journal of Speech Education* 10, no. 2 (1924): 145.

18. Ibid., 146.

19. Ibid., 148.

20. Ibid., 153.

21. Barack H. Obama, "Remarks by the President in Address to the Nation on Immigration" (White House, Office of the Press Secretary, November 20, 2014), http://www.whitehouse.gov/the-press-office/2014/11/20/remarks-president-address-nation-immigration.

22. Jeff Sessions, "Immigration Handbook for the New Republican Majority," Office of Senator Jeff Sessions, January 20, 2015, http://www.sessions.senate.gov/public/_cache/files/67ae7163-6616-4023-a5c4-534c53e6fc26/immigration-primer-for-the-114th-congress.pdf.

23. Gerard A. Hauser, *Introduction to Rhetorical Theory*, 2nd ed. (Prospect Heights, IL: Waveland Press, 2002), 2–3.

24. Donald C. Bryant, "Rhetoric: Its Function and Its Scope," *Quarterly Journal of Speech* 39 (1953): 401–424. In honor of the fiftieth anniversary of this landmark essay, *Advances in the History of Rhetoric* published a special collection of essays from noted rhetorical critics (see vol. 7, no. 1, 2004). See, too, Bryant's "Rhetoric: Its Function and Its Scope: *Rediviva*," in *Rhetorical Dimensions in Criticism* (Baton Rouge: Louisiana State University Press, 1973), 3–23.

25. Richard M. Weaver, "Language Is Sermonic," in *Dimensions of Rhetorical Scholarship*, ed. Roger I. Nebergall (Norman: Department of Speech, University of Oklahoma, 1963), 54. This essay is conveniently

found in Richard L. Johannesen, Rennard Strickland, and Ralph T. Eubanks, eds., *Language Is Sermonic: Richard M. Weaver on the Nature of Rhetoric* (Baton Rouge: Louisiana State University Press, 1970), 201–225.

26. For more on the relationship of rhetoric, ethics, and the communication discipline, see Pat J. Gerhrke, *The Ethics and Politics of Speech: Communication and Rhetoric in the Twentieth Century* (Carbondale: Southern Illinois University Press, 2009).

27. Charles Bazerman, *Shaping Written Knowledge: The Genre and Activity of the Experimental Article in Science* (Madison: University of Wisconsin Press, 1988), 6.

28. Kenneth Burke, "Rhetoric—Old and New," *Journal of General Education* 5 (1951): 203.

29. Kenneth Burke, *A Rhetoric of Motives* (Berkeley: University of California Press, 1969), 20, 55.

30. Burke, *A Rhetoric of Motives*.

31. Brooke L. Quigley, "'Identification' as a Key Term in Kenneth Burke's Rhetorical Theory," *American Communication Journal* 1, no. 3 (1998), http://ac-journal.org/journal/vol1/iss3/burke/quigley.html.

32. Burke, *A Rhetoric of Motives*, 21.

33. Quigley, "'Identification' as a Key Term."

34. Vocabulary.com, s.v. "Ideology," http://www.vocabulary.com/dictionary/ideology. The *Oxford English Dictionary* defines ideology as "A systematic scheme of ideas, usually relating to politics, economics, or society and forming the basis of action or policy; a set of beliefs governing conduct," http://www.oed.com.ezproxy.lib.vt.edu/view/Entry/91016?redirectedFrom=ideology&.

35. Jim A. Kuypers, "The Rhetorical River," *Southern Communication Journal* 73, no. 4 (2008): 353.

36. James Jasinski, *Sourcebook on Rhetoric: Key Concepts in Contemporary Rhetorical Studies* (Thousand Oaks, CA: Sage Publications, 2001), 313.

37. Roderick P. Hart and Courtney L. Dillard, "Deliberative Genre," in *Encyclopedia of Rhetoric*, ed. Thomas O. Sloane (New York: Oxford University Press, 2001), 213.

38. Joel Penney and Caroline Dada, "(Re)Tweeting in the Service of Protest: Digital Composition and Circulation in the Occupy Wall Street Movement," *New Media & Society* 16, no. 1 (2014): 74–90; Todd Lewis, "Religious Rhetoric in Southern College Football: New Uses for Religious Metaphors," *Southern Communication Journal* 78, no. 3 (2013): 202–214; Jeffrey T. Grabill and Stacey Pigg, "Messy Rhetoric: Identity Performance as Rhetorical Agency in Online Public Forums," *RSQ: Rhetoric Society Quarterly* 42, no. 2 (2012): 99–119.

39. Rasmus Karkov, "GTA Is the Great Contemporary Novel," *Scientific Nordic*, April 1, 2012, http://sciencenordic.com/gta-great-contemporary-novel; Gerald Voorhees, "Play and Possibility in the Rhetoric of the War on Terror: The Structure of Agency in Halo 2," *Game Studies* 14, no. 1 (2014), http://gamestudies.org/1401/articles/gvoorhees; Shaun Cashman, "The Rhetoric of Immersion in Video Game Technologies" (PhD diss., North Carolina State University, 2010), http://repository.lib.ncsu.edu/ir/bitstream/1840.16/6105/1/etd.pdf.

40. For example, see the Rhetoric Society of Europe, http://eusorhet.eu.

# 3

# Rhetorical Criticism as Art

*Jim A. Kuypers*

The previous chapter provided a working definition of *rhetoric*. This chapter introduces you to another concept: *criticism*. The purpose of this chapter is to show you how you can be a critic of rhetoric, and why this is an important, enriching activity. **Criticism** is "the systematic process of illuminating and evaluating products of human activity. [C]riticism presents and supports one possible interpretation and judgment. This interpretation, in turn, may become the basis for other interpretations and judgments."[1] When we critique instances of rhetoric, we are allowing ourselves to take a closer, critical look at how rhetoric operates to persuade and influence us. Specific acts of rhetoric that critics single out to analyze are called **rhetorical artifacts**. Criticism has many broad applications, but in general it is a *humanizing* activity. That is to say, it explores and highlights qualities that make us human—the good and the bad, the sublime and the droll, the beautiful and the ugly. It is not about being negative or finding fault in everything. For Donald C. Bryant, "common notions of criticism seem to involve or to imply some analytical examination of an artifact or artifacts, of some human transaction or transactions, toward the end of comprehension and realization of the potential of the object or event. Most notions of criticism extend also to appreciation and on to appraisal or judgment."[2] For our purposes, we are interested specifically in **rhetorical criticism**: the analysis and evaluation of rhetorical acts. We are looking at the many ways that humans use rhetoric to bring about changes in the world around them.

T. S. Eliot is reputed to have said, "We do criticism to open the work to others." This is exactly what we are about when we perform rhetorical criticism. On this point Wayne Brockriede wrote, "By 'criticism' I mean the act of evaluating or analyzing experience. A person can function as critic either by passing judgment on the experience or by analyzing it for the sake of a better understanding of that experience or of some more general concept or theory about such experiences."[3] More to the point concerning rhetorical criticism, Donald Bryant wrote that it is "systematically getting inside transactions of communication to discover and describe their elements, their form, and their dynamics and to explore the situations, past or present, which generate them and in which they are essential constituents to be comprehended and judged."[4] Rhetorical critics have varied reasons and purposes for producing criticism, but for those viewing it as a form of art, we engage in criticism for two broad reasons: *appreciation* and *understanding*. Simply put, we wish to enhance both our own and others' understanding of the rhetorical act; we wish to share our insights with others and to enhance their appreciation of the rhetorical act. These are not hollow goals but quality-of-life issues. By improving understanding and appreciation, the critic offers new and potentially exciting ways for others to see the world. Through understanding we also produce knowledge about human communication; in theory this should help us to better govern our interactions with others.

## CRITICISM AS A METHOD

In its most basic form, a method is a particular manner or process for accomplishing a task. The researcher's task—humanist, social scientist, or scientist—is to generate knowledge. The methods researchers use to accomplish this task differ greatly, however. The use of rhetoric is an art; as such, it does not lend itself well to scientific methods of analysis. Criticism is an art as well; as such, it is particularly well suited for examining rhetorical creations. Numerous critics have commented upon this humanistic nature of the study of rhetoric. Marie Hochmuth Nichols, for instance, wrote that humane studies, of which the study of rhetoric is a prominent example, are "concerned with the formation of judgment and choice." Such studies teach us that "technical efficiency is not enough, that somewhere beyond that lies an area in which answers are not formulary and methods not routine." Beyond "the area of the formula lies an area where understanding, imagination, knowledge of alternatives, and a sense of purpose operate."[5] That area of which she writes is, of course, criticism.

The ways that the sciences and the humanities study the phenomena that surround us differ greatly in the amount of the researcher's personality allowed to influence the results of the study. For example, in the sciences, researchers purposefully adhere to a *strict* method (the scientific method). All scientific researchers are to use this same basic method, and successful experiments must be 100 percent replicable by others. The application of the scientific method may take numerous forms, but the overall method remains the same—and the personality of the researcher is excised from the actual study. Generally speaking, the researcher's likes and dislikes, and his or her religious and political preferences, are supposed to be as far removed as possible from the actual study. Even the language scientists use to describe the results of their studies distances them from the results of those studies. For example, in scientific essays, one normally finds a detached use of language, with researchers forcing themselves into the background by highlighting the study itself: "This study found that . . . ."

In sharp contrast, criticism (one of many humanistic methods of generating knowledge) actively involves the personality of the researcher. The very choices of what to study, and how and why to study a rhetorical artifact, are heavily influenced by the personal qualities of the researcher. In criticism this is especially important since the personality of the critic is considered an integral component of the study. Further personalizing criticism, we find that rhetorical critics use a variety of means when examining a particular rhetorical artifact, with some critics even developing their own unique perspective to better examine a rhetorical artifact.[6] Even the manner in which many critics express themselves in their writing brings the personal to the fore. Many use the first-person singular in their writing: "I found . . . " instead of "This study found . . . ." These distinctions were apparent to Edwin Black, who forcefully wrote,

> Methods, then, admit of varying degrees of personality. And criticism, on the whole, is near the indeterminate, contingent, personal end of the methodological scale. In consequence of this placement, it is neither possible nor desirable for criticism to be fixed into a system, for critical

techniques to be objectified, for critics to be interchangeable for purposes of [scientific] replication, or for rhetorical criticism to serve as the handmaiden of quasi-scientific theory. [The] idea is that critical method is too personally expressive to be systematized.[7]

In short, criticism is an art, not a science. It is not a scientific method; it uses probability-based methods of argument; it exists on its own, not in conjunction with other methods of generating knowledge (i.e., social scientific or scientific). As Marie Hochmuth Nichols articulated so well, "It is reason and judgment, not a [computer], that makes a man a critic."[8] Put another way, insight and imagination top statistical applications when studying rhetorical action.

## THE CRITICAL ACT

At this point you should have a general idea of what rhetorical criticism is. Yet a question remains: How is it performed? In short, how does one actually "do" criticism? Where does one begin? And how does one ensure that criticism is more than mere opinion? Superior criticism is not performed mechanically, similar to following a recipe or a set of instructions to build something. It is, however, quite rigorous and well thought out, with critics following certain norms when producing criticism. After all, good critics are trying to generate understanding and insight; they are not supposed to be simply flashing their opinions about. In general, there are three stages involved in the **critical act**, in producing criticism: conceptual, communication, and countercommunication.

### The Conceptual Stage

The conceptual stage takes place in the mind of the critic; it is an act of cerebration. It is a private act, and its purpose is to generate some type of insight concerning the rhetorical artifact. Since this is a very personal act—that is, not mechanistic—there is no standardized way critics go about flexing their cerebral muscles. What works for one critic might not work for another. Often, though, insight is generated in one of two very broad ways. The first is a type of spontaneous inception. Think of the *Eureka!* of Archimedes, or of the proverbial lightbulb popping on inside your head. Critics often generate involuntary, almost instinctive reactions to rhetorical artifacts. This involves more than a simple reaction to the artifact, however, because critics are trained to observe, and their training has a bearing on what they see in an artifact. In a sense, the experienced critic has assimilated particular ways of viewing rhetoric; these modes of seeing are part and parcel of the critic's personality. Some critics may even come to see rhetorical artifacts in such a way that others recognize it as characteristic of that particular critic. The more a critic learns about rhetoric, the more that critic sees the world with a rhetorical understanding, and the more likely that critic will be to generate spontaneous insights.

The other broad way a critic might generate insight is through a somewhat systematic examination of a rhetorical artifact. With this approach the critic uses some type of guide, formal or informal, that allows for an orderly progression through the rhetorical artifact. A more formal guide might take the form of a theoretical perspective on rhetoric, which we will discuss below. A more personal and informal guide could be a question the critic has about the workings of the world (often called a research question). Simply put, the critic starts with a question or two in mind and then examines various rhetorical artifacts looking for answers to that question. For example, the authors of the chapter on "Fantasy-Theme Criticism" state in their critical essay that they were guided by questions such as, "What do we expect from our universities?" and "Why do we go to college?" With those questions in mind, they decided that using a type of criticism called fantasy-theme analysis would be a fruitful perspective to use when looking at different rhetorical artifacts. In this way the authors were guided by their initial research questions in both the decision about what perspective to use and also in what to look for in the rhetorical artifacts they examined.

Whether a critic spontaneously generates an insight or searches a rhetorical artifact for information, it should be the critic, not the method or perspective, that is in control of the insights and knowledge generated. As Black wrote, "The critic's procedures are, when at their best, original; they grow ad hoc from the critic's engagement with the [rhetorical] artifact."[9] Of course, not all insights generated prove sound, and some ideas are never meant to move beyond mere personal musing. In my experience, it is only a small minority of ideas that sprout roots and actually grow. These ideas move to the next stage of the critical act: communication.

**The Communication Stage**

The second stage of the critical act is a quasi-public act of writing out the criticism in preparation for sharing it with others.[10] This stage of the critical act encompasses the private act of writing, sharing initial ideas with trusted friends and colleagues, and ultimately sharing with a wider audience. Your reasons for writing criticism will help to determine the particular audience for whom you write. For example, you could be writing a letter to the editor of your local paper concerning the rhetorical efforts of a politician running for office, you could be writing an entry for readers of your blog, you could be writing a term paper for your professor, or you could be writing with a specific scholarly journal in mind. When writing you must always keep in mind the audience with whom you intend to share your criticism. Recall that part of the purpose of criticism is to enhance the understanding and appreciation of others concerning the rhetorical artifact. On this point Black wrote, "The critic proceeds in part by translating the object of his criticism into the terms of his audience and in part by educating his audience to the terms of the object. This dual task is not an ancillary function of criticism; it is an essential part of criticism."[11]

When sharing your criticism with others, it is not simply a matter of providing a detailed picture of your opinions. You are instead sharing *propositions* with those who will be reading your work. Propositions are only naked assertions, however, until you provide a very basic step: giving supporting evidence with which to back up those assertions. Craig R. Smith wrote that critics must hold themselves to high "standards of argumentation" when writing criticism. Specifically, he suggested that, "when we write criticism . . . we ought to confine ourselves to solid argumentation inclusive of valid arguments built on sufficient and high quality evidence produced from close textual readings and masterings of context."[12] In short, critics must *invite* their audiences to agree with them. This is accomplished through stating their case and then providing evidence for their audience to accept or reject.

For example, consider the short speech given by Baltimore Ravens running back Ray Rice on May 23, 2014, following the February 19, 2014, release of a video showing him dragging his unconscious wife (then fiancée Janay Palmer) from an Atlantic City casino elevator.[13] Police said the part of the tape not released showed that Rice struck his wife "with his hand, rendering her unconscious," before dragging her out of the elevator.[14] After over a month of negative publicity for Rice, the Ravens, and the NFL in general, including charges of sexism and turning a blind eye toward domestic violence, the situation was only getting worse. On

March 27, 2014, Rice was indicted on aggravated assault charges, eventuating in a plea deal that involved counseling. The next day he and Janay Palmer were married. The NFL continued to stand up for Rice, and the negative publicity continued to grow as well. Finally, on May 23, 2014, Rice held a press conference along with his wife, during which time he addressed the situation.

After watching the video and reading the transcript of his apology, I can honestly say that it was not only a rhetorical dud but a failed speech as well.[15] Yet so far we have only my opinion, only one, undifferentiated among so many others. I might go one step further, however, and make specific assertions concerning the speech. I could say that Rice's speech did not work well in that it simply failed on several levels. For instance, it showed a lack of preparation; it lacked true elements of an apology; it demonstrated a lack of logical consistency; he potentially insulted his wife during the speech; and, ultimately, it failed as an apology.

At this point you would find yourself with additional information, but still I have only provided you with *unsupported assertions*. I have merely given you my opinions about the speech. I move into the realm of criticism when I provide support for these assertions of mine, when I provide you with evidence that asks you to agree with me or that makes you aware of some aspect of the speech that you had previously overlooked (the sharing of insights). For example, I could provide specific sentences from Rice's speech that I feel support my assertions. On the matter of lack of preparation, I could quote Rice: "I usually prepare my speeches just coming off the top [of my head], but during the time I had, I had a chance to jot a lot of things down."[16] Yet the speech was full of awkward grammatical structures and lacked any real sense of organization. For instance, Rice said although we know no "relationship is perfect, but me and Janay together, what counseling has done for us . . . ."[17] Concerning lacking true elements of an apology, I could mention that he failed to actually apologize to his wife Janay for knocking her unconscious, and she was sitting right next to him. Additionally, he never said exactly what he was apologizing for; instead, he used the vague "this situation that me and my wife were in" or "this thing [that] happened with me and my wife."[18] In a sense, he was shifting the blame onto a situation instead of onto his own shoulders.[19] In terms of logical consistency I could point out this passage: "Throughout this time, we really had the time to reflect on each other . . . but me and Janay together, what counseling has done for us—we want the world to see that it definitely did help us out."[20] He adds that he is working to change and become a better husband, father, and role model. Yet Rice then turns around and tells the listening press, "I want you to know that I'm still the Ray Rice that you know or used to know or grown to love. I'm still the same guy." And later, "We're still the same people, and I'm still the same person."[21] One does not logically say, "I have done all this self-help work that has been effective" and then go and say, but "I'm still the same old guy." In terms of insulting his wife, recall that the tape showed him dragging his unconscious wife out of the elevator, and that police said the full tape showed him striking her with his hand prior to that. Speaking of avoiding failure, of bouncing back from this legal and moral quagmire in which he found himself, Rice said, "Failure is . . . It's not getting knocked down, it's not getting back up."[22] Who knocked whom down, and who didn't get back up and was dragged unconscious from an elevator? Finally, evidence of the speech's failure comes when the criticism persists and even grows following his speech, and Rice is compelled to re-apologize months later on July 31, 2014. At this press conference, Rice actually stated, "Last time [in the May press conference], I didn't publicly apologize to my wife. I realize that hit home with a lot of people."[23]

The main point to remember from this example is that critics are trying to argue for a certain understanding of the rhetorical artifact. In this sense they are actually using rhetoric to try to gain acceptance of their ideas. The best critics simply do not make a judgment without supplying good reasons for others to agree with them. On this point, Bernard L. Brock et al. wrote, "Statements of tastes and preference do not qualify as criticism. [Criticism is] an art of evaluating with knowledge and propriety. Criticism is a reason-giving activity; it not only posits a judgment, the judgment is explained, reasons are given for the judgment, and known information is marshaled to support the reasons for the judgment."[24]

The idea of rhetorical criticism being a form of argument is not new. For example, Wayne Brockriede wrote in 1974 that useful rhetorical criticism must function as an argument to be effective criticism.[25] In his landmark essay, Brockriede advanced five interanimated characteristics of how rhetorical critics could construct a strong argument:

> (1) an inferential leap from existing beliefs to the adoption of a new belief or the reinforcement of an old one; (2) a perceived rationale to justify that leap; (3) a choice among two or more competing claims; (4) a regulation of uncertainty in relation to the selected claim—since someone has made an inferential leap, certainty can be neither zero nor total; and (5) a willingness to risk a confrontation of that claim with one's peers.[26]

More significant arguments will have a greater number and strength of the five above characteristics than less significant arguments. This is to say, the five qualities of arguments given above are on a sliding scale of sorts. The fewer of the five, or the weaker in form, the less the criticism is an effective argument. The greater the number of the five, or the stronger in form, the greater the likelihood that the criticism is an effective argument. As Brockriede wrote, "When a critic only appreciates the rhetoric or objects to it, without reporting any reason for his like or dislike, he puts his criticism near the nonargument end of the continuum. On the other hand, when an evaluating critic states clearly the criteria he has used in arriving at his judgment, together with the philosophic or theoretic foundations on which they rest, and when he has offered some data to show that the rhetorical experience meets or fails to meet those criteria, then he has argued."[27]

*Rhetorical Perspectives*

The propositions and claims used by a critic are generally contextualized through the use of different perspectives on criticism. A **rhetorical perspective** is a theoretical orientation a critic uses to help guide criticism of a rhetorical artifact. Because a rhetorical artifact is a multidimensional, complex, and nuanced event, there is not one best way of viewing it (although some ways can be better for certain artifacts than others). Moreover, no one effort to describe or evaluate the artifact will yield all the knowledge that there is to know about that artifact. Although changing, a large share of academic criticism today takes its structure from a particular perspective. Perspectives allow critics to view the rhetorical artifact from different angles. Since the 1960s there has been an incredible expansion of perspectives critics have used to better understand the rhetoric that surrounds us. By one count, over sixty formally recognized perspectives have been cataloged,[28] with many more being used and with some critics even blending perspectives. Later in this book you will be exposed to many popular perspectives designed for generating insight and understanding about rhetorical artifacts, and even more are mentioned in the appendices.

Using an established perspective to produce criticism has both strengths and weaknesses. One particular strength is that adopting a perspective allows you to see an artifact differently than if no perspective had been adopted. In a sense, using a perspective allows you to see the world in a particular way. A perspective will highlight certain features of a rhetorical artifact not featured by another perspective. Adopting a rhetorical perspective also allows you to stay focused because, when properly used, the perspective *guides* (rather than dictates) your analysis. This can be particularly useful for novice critics who often are at odds with the enormous range of options any one rhetorical artifact offers for analysis.

On the flip side of the coin, adopting a particular perspective will introduce certain biases into the criticism. A perspective is partial and encourages you to view the world in a certain manner. So, while some aspects of a rhetorical artifact are highlighted, others are screened out. The potential problem with this, as Lawrence Rosenfield wrote, is that a "critic who comes upon a critical object [rhetorical artifact] in a state of mind such that he has a 'set of values' handy (or, indeed, any other system of categories) does not engage in a critical encounter so much as he processes perceptual data."[29] Insomuch as this is true, a critic who follows too closely the dictates of a particular perspective runs the risk of producing stale and lifeless criticism. Such a critic is simply looking for what the perspective suggests should be identified. In short, improperly used, a perspective would be allowed to *dictate* rather than guide what a critic does in the analysis.

The perspectives presented in this book represent a wide array of critical possibilities. Some are well known and widely practiced; others are less known but extremely potent in their potential. As you become familiar with these perspectives, you will see how they differ in the type of material they allow a critic to focus on, as well as the type of material they exclude. A central question remains, however: *How does a critic choose which perspective to use?* The choice will be guided by several factors. First, the critic's personal interest will play a crucial role in determining which perspective to adopt. As you study the perspectives detailed in this book, you will find that some appeal to you, while others do not. This attraction or aversion is natural, so your first clue to which perspective to use should be your personal interest in that perspective. Second, and just as important, a critic must consider the unique characteristics of the rhetorical artifact being examined. As already mentioned, perspectives focus a critic's attention on certain aspects of a rhetorical artifact. A critic should take this into consideration when choosing a particular perspective to use, since any given perspective will not fit every rhetorical artifact. Some, even when there is a sound fit, might need modification. More experienced critics may choose to combine perspectives, modify perspectives, or develop a completely novel perspective, and this is something we will look at in the chapter on "An Eclectic Approach to Criticism"—the choice is the critic's to make. Of course, the greater your understanding of rhetoric and of the nuances of different perspectives, the greater your ability to discern the intricacies of individual rhetorical texts, and thus the greater the likelihood of producing vibrant criticism.

Advancing your propositions through different perspectives also makes an important contribution to the development of a critical vocabulary for both you and other critics to use. You will be contributing to both the understanding of human communication and the development of rhetorical theory. In one sense, you will be accumulating knowledge for others to draw upon. Ultimately, though, I agree with Stephen E. Lucas, who wrote, "In the last analysis, our scholarship will be judged, not by the perspectives from which it proceeds, but by the quality of the insight it produces."[30]

### The Countercommunication Stage

Once the criticism is actually performed, the final stage of the critical act, countercommunication, is entered. This is a public act, and at this stage the critic shares openly with others. For instance, your criticism could take the form of a submission to venues such as the *Huffington Post* or the *American Thinker*. If published, it will allow others (possibly tens of thousands) the opportunity to share your thoughts and possibly to respond. In more academic settings, students will submit their essays and receive feedback from their professors and possibly their classmates; or perhaps professors and some students will have written their essays for a conference presentation or for submission to a scholarly journal. The idea is to share your criticism with some segment of the public with the hope that it will provoke some type of feedback; the best criticism attempts just this.

Feedback can take many forms, as can public exchanges about the critic's ideas. Students will receive comments from their professor, and professors receive comments from their reviewers. If published, an essay then receives wider responses. The point is, once released to this public realm, a critic's work takes on a life of its own. Feedback, positive or negative, should be viewed as what it is: evidence of the critic entering into a larger conversation. A problem critics often encounter, though, is a reply of *de gustibus non est disputandum*, "there is no disputing taste." In other words, you might hear from others that your point of view is simply a subjective opinion and that their point of view is equally valid. Yet we have already seen that criticism is far more than mere opinion. So, if you made certain to provide the good reasons mentioned above, then the exchange does not boil down to "I'm right, you're wrong," but to arguing who can see the fullness of the rhetorical artifact better, or who has an actual insight. As Brockriede wrote, "Critics who argue are more *useful* than critics who do not."[31] Along these same lines, Black wrote, "The critic can only induce us, and therefore it is we, the readers of criticism, who demand the critic's compliance with certain of our expectations. We expect the critic to see things for us that we are unlikely to see for ourselves until the critic has called them to our attention."[32]

What we are about during this stage of the critical act is none other than entering into dialogue about matters of importance. The exchange and discussion of ideas is crucial to criticism; only the best criticism provokes this. Actually, the cry of many critics might well be, "Love me, hate me, but don't ignore me." Remember that good criticism *is* an act of rhetoric.

## KEY ISSUES IN CRITICISM

When you begin to write your criticism, it will be helpful to know about five key issues with which all critics wrestle at some time or another. These issues are long-standing and have various resolutions, with different critics taking different approaches to the same issue. For now it is enough to know the important questions these issues invite you to ask, not that you have the answers. By conscientiously thinking about these issues, you will be in a better position to produce deliberate, thoughtful, and well-informed criticism.

### What to Include

One important issue involves the most basic element in criticism: *what to include in your writing*. Of course, there are many ways one could write criticism, but generally speaking your essay should contain three components: a description, an analysis, and an evaluation. Every critical essay should have these components in some form, but each essay will present them in a slightly different manner (and this will be seen in examples contained in the chapters that follow).

*Description*

Description refers to both a description of the rhetorical artifact and, in more academic settings, a description of the theoretical background or perspective used in the essay. A description of the artifact is crucial if your readers are to be able to follow you. The way you describe the artifact may well be the only exposure they have to it, so you must take care in presenting as accurate a picture as possible. In more formal instances of criticism (e.g., term papers, conference presentations), a discussion of the theory being used to perform the criticism is also expected. On this point, William L. Nosthstine et al. wrote, "'Theory' has become virtually the singular objective of criticism. . . . [C]ontributing to theory *is* regarded as the fundamental goal of [rhetorical] criticism."[33] Although perhaps true then of many academic journals, there are numerous exceptions. As noted by James Jasinski, the "two most common patterns in the [communication] literature are (a) theory provides a [perspective] that is utilized in critical practice (theory serves criticism) or (b) criticism contributes to theorization through its heuristic capacity, through illustration and hypotheses testing, and through the reflexive implementation of theoretically-derived [perspectives] (criticism serves theory)."[34] Many academic readers (and most academic journal editors) want to know in which rhetorical theories your perspective is grounded, exactly how you are using the theory to guide your analysis, and how your analysis has added to the pool of theoretical knowledge. This allows them to learn from your examples and also adds to the theoretical body of knowledge, an ever-growing element of academic criticism. This drive toward generation of theory is so strong for some critics that the very quality of criticism is judged by the contributions made to the growing body of rhetorical theory. Sonja Foss represented this point of view when she wrote that the "purpose of rhetorical criticism is to explain how some aspect of rhetoric operates and thus to make a contribution to rhetorical theory. The critic who is attempting to contribute to rhetorical theory does not view an artifact for its own qualities alone but instead moves beyond the particularities . . . to discover what that artifact suggests about symbolic processes in general."[35]

For others, theory is a means to an end: the generation of insights into a rhetorical artifact with the ultimate goals of producing understanding and appreciation of that artifact and of our common humanity. From this point of view, the artifact comes first, then theory development only if convenient; critics are seen here as artists, not builders of theory. In a summary of the tension between criticism for insight and criticism for theory, Richard Gregg pointed out that "critics need not consciously set out to contribute to theory; it is often enough to gain a thorough understanding of a rhetorical event for its own sake. On the other hand . . . critical interpretations always imply theoretical positions, whether consciously articulated or not."[36] I have written elsewhere that mandating that critics produce theory forces them into a mode of production that diminishes the personal and artistic qualities of criticism. As the role of theory lessens, with theory as an "increasingly gentle influence rather than prescription, the greater role the critic's personality assumes and the humanistic aspects of rhetorical criticism come to the fore. Of course, this later form of criticism is difficult to publish today given the theory-centric nature of our discipline."[37] For now, though, at least among scholarly journals, theory building is almost mandatory; there are signs of change, however, especially with eclectic criticism and conceptually oriented criticism.[38]

When you describe the artifact and the perspective used to examine it, you will also want to relay the importance of the artifact, the study, or both. In short, at some point you will want to justify what you are doing. Given the countless appeals for our attention each day, readers may well ask, "Why is this important for me to know?" Although *you* might think what you are doing is important, not everyone else will think the same way. It is up to you to share with others the reasons why they should invest their time and energy to read what you have written.

*Analysis/Interpretation*

After you share with your readers what you will be examining (the rhetorical artifact), how you will be going about that examination (rhetorical theory), and the importance of what you are doing, you move on to the actual analysis of the rhetorical artifact. This section of your essay will generally consume the most space. When I say *analysis*, I mean both analysis *and* interpretation. They are not the same, but neither are they completely separate. In one sense, **analysis** is discovering *what is in* a rhetorical artifact, and **interpretation** is determining *what a rhetorical artifact means*. Analysis asks us to explain how the rhetorical artifact works; it provides a sketch of sorts, showing how the artifact is put together: what its parts are, how they go together, and what the whole looks like. The type of analysis depends on the temperament of the critic, but also on the theoretical perspective guiding the criticism.

*Interpretation* was once a strongly contested term in criticism. Some critics held that rhetorical criticism should involve a minimum of interpretation. For example, Barnett Baskerville, writing at a time (1953) when critics looked primarily at speeches, suggested that they were fairly straightforward in their meaning. They are "seldom abstruse or esoteric. . . . A speech, by its nature, is or should be immediately comprehensible, hence the interpretive function of the critics is seldom paramount."[39] Not all critics agreed with Baskerville on the nature of interpretation. Thomas R. Nilsen, for example, wrote a few years later that "if within the meaning of the speech are included the many attendant responses, the more subtle understanding and conceptions evoked by the speech and their possible consequences, then interpretation is a much needed function of the critic."[40] By the late 1970s some degree of interpretation had become an accepted part of criticism. Critic Michael Leff pointed out that it is with "the act of interpretation by which the critic attempts to account for and assign meaning to the rhetorical dimensions of a given phenomenon."[41] Such interpretations can focus on the external or internal dynamics of a rhetorical artifact. External interpretations focus on how the rhetorical artifact interacts with the situation that surrounds it, and internal interpretations focus on how different parts of the rhetorical artifact act together in forming a whole.

During the 2008 Democratic primary season, then-senator Barack Obama gave an important speech that may very well have saved his candidacy. It also demonstrated well the dual critical functions of analysis and interpretation. Increasingly in early 2008, Senator Obama was enduring criticism about his association with Reverend Jeremiah Wright, the leader of Trinity Unity Church of Christ. In response, Senator Obama delivered a speech, "A More Perfect Union," in which he responded to Wright's ardent anti-Americanism, including statements indicating America deserved 9/11.[42] An *analysis* could discover many things about this speech, including Senator Obama's use of analogy. Take, for example, this passage:

> I can no more disown [Reverend Wright] than I can my white grandmother—a woman who helped raise me, a woman who sacrificed again and again for me, a woman who loves me as much as she loves anything in this world, but a woman who once confessed her fear of black men who passed by her on the street, and who on more than one occasion has uttered racial or ethnic stereotypes that made me cringe. These people are a part of me. And they are a part of America, this country that I love.[43]

Analysis allows us to see this passage as analogy; beyond this, analysis ends and interpretation begins. Just what does this analogy mean? One interpretation of the meaning of this passage could be that Senator Obama was trying to show that racial tensions exist and are active in America; that whites and blacks have suspicions, anger, and even hatred inside. Along these lines, consider this statement made in response to Obama's speech:

> [He] challenged Americans to learn something about their country, to seek to understand those whose emotions seem threatening, wrong-headed, even un-American. He asked whites to understand that the anger behind Rev. Wright's comments, while paralyzing, was also valid, the result of decades and centuries of real discrimination and oppression suffered by African Americans. And he asked blacks to understand that whites who resent affirmative action and whose fears of crime lead them to stereotype blacks should not be dismissed as racists, because their concerns and fears are real and valid, too.[44]

Of course, analogies are a form of argument and thus can invite alternate interpretations. Take, for instance, another interpretation of then-senator Obama's speech, one which asserted that one plank in Senator Obama's defense was the idea of moral equivalence:

> Sure, says Obama, there's Wright, but at the other "end of the spectrum" there's Geraldine Ferraro, opponents of affirmative action and his own white grandmother, "who once confessed her fear of black men who passed by her on the street, and who on more than one occasion has uttered racial or ethnic stereotypes that made me cringe." But did she shout them in a crowded theater to incite, enrage and poison others [as did Rev. Wright]?
> 
> "I can no more disown (Wright) than I can my white grandmother." What exactly was grandma's offense? Jesse Jackson himself once admitted to the fear he feels from the footsteps of black men on the street. And Harry Truman was known to use epithets for blacks and Jews in private, yet is revered for desegregating the armed forces and recognizing the first Jewish state since Jesus' time. He never spread racial hatred. Nor did grandma.
> 
> Yet Obama compares her to Wright. Does he not see the moral difference between the occasional private expression of the prejudices of one's time and the use of a public stage to spread racial lies and race hatred?[45]

In the end, these examples might make it seem as if analysis and interpretation are two separate steps. That is not the case at all. The very first step a critic takes, deciding what the rhetorical artifact actually is, is itself an interpretive act. For instance, is Senator Obama's speech an apology, an attack, or a statement of policy? We separate out these steps for the sake of discussion. As you write criticism, become aware of how analysis and interpretation interanimate each other. On this point, Michael Leff cogently wrote,

> The act of interpretation mediates between the experiences of the critic and the forms of experience expressed in the [rhetorical artifact]. To perform this act successfully, critics must vibrate what they see in the [rhetorical artifact] against their own expectations and predilections. What critics are trained to look for and what they see interact in creative tension; the two elements blend and separate, progressively changing as altered conceptions of the one reshape the configuration of the other.[46]

Through the analysis and interpretation section of your essay, you share your insight and understanding of the artifact, and you actively make a case for your conclusions, which leads to the final component of a criticism essay: evaluation.

*Evaluation*

Evaluation of the rhetorical artifact boils down to the judgments you make about it. However, judgment is more than an expression of like or dislike. It necessitates first that you know the thing that you are studying; it also necessitates that your judgments are shared with the goal of enriching both understanding and appreciation. Judgments may certainly be made, and appreciation or disdain expressed, but they must be made after two conditions are met: one, the fair-minded description of the inner workings of the rhetorical artifact have been presented for the world to see, and two, the standards of judgment used by the critic are provided for all to see. In short, the expression of judgment is conjoined with the reasons you think the way you do. The standards of judgments used will differ depending on the type of perspective used and also on the critic's personality. As you acquire information on each perspective, notice what type of information the perspective allows you to gather about the rhetorical transactions. This is a clue about the types of value judgments that particular perspective allows. Usually these will revolve around differing combinations of the ethics, effects, truth, and aesthetics involved in the rhetorical transaction.[47] The standards of judgment you use should flow from the perspective you use to examine the rhetorical artifact; thus, how the concepts above will be understood is directly related to the perspective you use.

**Choice of Theoretical Perspective**

Another important issue facing critics is the seemingly easy decision concerning *which perspective to use in their critical endeavor*. Simply put, how will a critic go about producing criticism? As you read additional chapters in this book, you may well find that a certain perspective appeals to you. You may not know why, but you seem to gravitate toward it; you just like it for some reason. It seems natural for you to use. As you use it, you become increasingly familiar with its nuances and potentials. Some critics are well known for producing insightful and nuanced work using a particular perspective. For example, Andrew King is well known for using Burkean theory in his work; Marilyn Young's work using the situational perspective is another such example; critical rhetoric and the name Raymie McKerrow are no strangers.

Perspectives are not to be used as templates or rubrics, however. Although they do suggest a particular way of viewing the world, as the critic you must direct the criticism. When novice critics first begin to use a perspective, they often do apply it *rigidly* to the rhetorical artifact. Yet criticism, like any activity worthy of learning well, benefits from practice. As critics become more knowledgeable about the perspective they use, they often become more *flexible* in its application, allowing for personal insight and interests to guide the criticism. The personality of the critic begins to blend with the perspective used. The best criticism involves this. As Michael Leff has written, "Interpretation is not a scientific endeavor. Systematic principles are useful in attempting to validate interpretations, but the actual process of interpretation depends on conjectures and insights particular to the object [rhetorical artifact] at hand."[48]

Regardless of the perspective chosen, a critic must be cautious in its application. Perspectives are to help a critic, not control the criticism; a successful critic's ideas blend in with those of the perspective. Perspectives are not molds to be forced on a rhetorical artifact—mechanistic and rigid criticism. Black puts this idea, and the consequences, in proper perspective:

> Because only the critic is the instrument of criticism, the critic's relationship to other instruments will profoundly affect the value of critical inquiry. And in criticism, every instrument has to be assimilated to the critic, to have become an integral part of the critic's mode of perception. A critic who is influenced by, for example, [Burkean dramatism] and who, in consequence of that influence, comes to see some things in a characteristically dramatistic way—that critic is still able to function in his own person as the critical instrument, and so the possibility of significant disclosure remains open to him. But the would-be critic who has not internalized [Burkean dramatism], who undertakes to "use" it as a mathematician would use a formula—such a critic is certain (yes, *certain*!) to produce work that is sterile. An act of criticism conducted on mechanistic assumptions will, not surprisingly, yield mechanistic criticism.[49]

Some critics, myself included, take the process of assimilation one step further by blending and developing their own framework from which to proceed with criticism. This type of criticism is often called *eclectic* criticism. This type of criticism will be discussed in chapter 15; it involves "the selection of the best standards and principles from various systems of ideas."[50]

## Initial Approach

Yet another issue involves *how one should approach a rhetorical artifact* (what Ed Black below calls rhetorical "transactions"). Should one begin with a theoretical orientation or should one begin with the artifact itself?[51] Black described this distinction as *etic* and *emic* orientations. One using an etic orientation "approaches a rhetorical transaction from outside of that transaction and interprets the transaction in terms of pre-existing theory." In contrast, one using an emic orientation "approaches a rhetorical transaction in what is hoped to be its own terms, without conscious expectations drawn from any sources other than the rhetorical transaction itself."[52] These orientations are quite distinct, and although there are instances in which they might blend, such are infrequently encountered.

Both orientations have strengths and weaknesses. An etic orientation allows for a fuller development of rhetorical theory. The major end of criticism would be to develop and advance rhetorical theory, thus adding to our overall knowledge concerning human communication. An emic orientation allows for a more nuanced description of the rhetorical artifact and also provides more room for the critic's personality and intuition to play a part in the criticism. A weakness with the etic orientation is that critics may very well find exactly what they expect to find, even if it's not really there in the rhetorical artifact; in short, the rhetorical artifact is forced into a mold. A weakness with the emic orientation can arise because critics may "aspire to so sympathetic an account [during the descriptive and interpretive phases of criticism] that the critic's audience will understand that object as, in some sense, *inevitable*."[53] This is to say that the rhetorical artifact might be viewed as never having a possibility of being in any other form, that those who created it had no choice but to create it in the form they did. On this point Leff wrote, "The critic at some point . . . in the interpretive process comes to form a conception of the object as a whole. . . . This conception . . . is something other than the actual expression in the text; otherwise, there would be no interpretation. Consequently, while still engaged in the interpretive act, the critic constructs a meaning for the object, an hypothesis or model that explains what it is."[54] The difficulty in this process lies with the "good faith" of the critic. After such a sympathetic account of the rhetorical artifact, the critic will be hard pressed to return to a more objective role during the evaluative phase of criticism.[55]

### Objectivity or Subjectivity?

Yet another concern involves *the notion of criticism as an objective or a subjective (even political) endeavor*. It is clear that criticism is not a scientific act; the very best criticism involves the personality, insights, and imagination of a critic. Yet for all that, there are critics—I among them—who maintain that a certain degree of objectivity is necessary for honest, productive criticism. I do not mean that critics ought to possess or are capable of possessing a computer-like detachment from the object of criticism. This would surely produce a sterile criticism devoid of its lifeblood: the critic's intermingled intuition, insight, and personality. What I am suggesting with the term *objective criticism* is that the critic approach the artifact under consideration with a fair and open mind, with a *detached curiosity*. In this sense the critic sets aside personal politics or ideological "truths" and approaches the artifact with a sense of curiosity. The artifact under consideration should not be altered to fit the prejudgments of the critic but allowed to voice its inner workings to the world. The work of the critic is to make certain that this voice is intelligible to and approachable by the public.

This in no way detracts from the critic's bringing to bear an individual stamp upon the criticism produced; nor is it the antiseptic application of theory upon an unsuspecting rhetorical artifact. It suggests instead that the critic must learn how to appreciate the inner workings of a text, even if, personally, the critic finds that text to be repugnant or wishes it to be other than it is. In this sense, the critic is being "objective," or disinterested, when approaching and describing a text.[56] My notion of objectivity is somewhat similar to the notion of "appreciation" put forth by Lawrence W. Rosenfield. I position my notion of objective criticism between a politically partisan criticism and detached scientific objectivity; Rosenfield positions "appreciation" between ideologically driven criticism and scientific objectivity. For Rosenfield, appreciation is "founded on an inherent love of the world, while [scientific] objectivity, the effort to establish distance on the world (for whatever laudable ends) sometimes betrays an essential distrust of the world, a fear that one will be contaminated in some manner if one is open to its unconcealment."[57]

Although I agree heartily with Rosenfield that "partisan involvement may be a civic virtue, but insight derived therefrom must be continually suspect,"[58] other critics disagree with us, as you will find while reading some of the chapters that follow. For these critics, the act of criticism involves a more active attempt at persuasion of their audience in all three phases of criticism—description, analysis/interpretation, and evaluation. Very often the direction of this persuasion takes its cue from the political ideology of the critic. For example, Robert L. Ivie defined productive criticism as "a detailed and *partisan* critique."[59] According to Ivie, a critic "intentionally produces a strategic interpretation, or structure of meaning, that privileges selective interests . . . in specific circumstances."[60] The purpose of criticism is made clear: those who engage in rhetorical criticism are, or should be, advocates. Viewed in this manner, "criticism, as a specific performance of general rhetorical knowledge, yields a form of scholarship that obtains social relevance by strategically reconstructing the interpretive design of civic discourse in order to diminish, bolster, or redirect its significance. [Criticism] is a form of advocacy."[61]

Often some attempt at political fairness is made, although the result is still the politicization of the critical act. For example, Michael Calvin McGee wrote, "When interpellating 'the critic' and 'criticism,' the first thing a rhetorician should do is to identify her political orientation. Her syllabus should contain a paragraph describing the trajectory of her course. Her book should have a Chapter that aligns her politics with that politics practiced in the workaday world by political parties competing for control of the State. She must be fair, describing the politics of those who disagree with her in a light that leans more toward portraiture than caricature."[62] However, regardless of the attempt, I am inclined to agree with Rosenfield when he asserts that a difficulty with ideological criticism is that the "very notion of commitment to an ideology, no matter what its value system, implies a kind of immunity to those experiences of the world which in any way contradict the ideology."[63] Further clarifying this politicization of criticism, McGee stated, "That which [ideologically driven] critics do today is proactive, openly political in its acknowledgment of its bias and its agenda to produce practical theories of culture and of social relations (including political relations)," and thus appears to embrace the very action Rosenfield described above.[64]

Although summarizing a much larger conversation on this topic, the positions advanced are clear. On the one hand we have critics striving to keep personal politics from the initial stages of the criticism—most notably, during the description and analysis phases of the critical act. This position presupposes that part of the purpose of criticism is to produce knowledge that disputants can draw upon when making decisions about how to live—academic critics should not be partisan agents of social change. On the other hand we have academic critics allowing their personal politics to guide them during all three stages of criticism.[65] This position presupposes that critics begin by seeing the world differently than the public they seek to persuade and that the job of the critic is to produce partisan social change in the direction of that critic's choosing.[66] A good example of this contrast is found when looking at the chapters on traditional criticism and feminist criticism.

## WRAPPING UP

We have covered a great deal of ground in this chapter. Most notably we have explored the definition and nature of criticism, particularly rhetorical criticism. We specifically looked at how criticism is a method of generating new knowledge just as the scientific method is a method of generating new knowledge. The three stages of the critical act (conceptual, communication, and countercommunication) alerted us to basic elements involved in producing good criticism, and also to rhetorical perspectives. Finally, we looked at four key concerns in criticism today: what to include in our criticism (description, analysis, and interpretation), the choice of a theoretical perspective, how to initially approach a rhetorical artifact, and objectivity and subjectivity in criticism.

The chapters that follow will give you a sense of the variety and artistry of rhetorical criticism. As you move through each chapter, you will find that the way the author(s) practice criticism both modifies and moves beyond the definition I shared with you in this chapter. Take note of *how* the nature and scope of criticism changes in each chapter. Criticism is not a sterile endeavor, and you will find that some of the chapters resonate more strongly with you than do others. Just like rhetoric, criticism is nuanced and may be understood on many different levels. Each chapter that follows underscores this idea and presents a point of view that will add rich variety to your overall understanding of the critical act.

## SUGGESTED READINGS

Black, Edwin. *Rhetorical Criticism: A Study in Method* (Madison: University of Wisconsin Press, 1978), ix–xv, 1–9.

Brockriede, Wayne. "Rhetorical Criticism as Argument." *Quarterly Journal of Speech* 60 (April 1974): 165–174.

Jasinski, James. "Criticism in Contemporary Rhetorical Studies." In *Sourcebook on Rhetoric*, 125–144 (Thousand Oaks, CA: Sage Publications, 2001).

Kuypers, Jim A., ed. *Purpose, Practice, and Pedagogy in Rhetorical Criticism* (Lanham, MD: Lexington Books, 2014).

Rosenfield, Lawrence W. "The Experience of Criticism." *Quarterly Journal of Speech* 60, no. 4 (1974): 489–496.

## NOTES

1. James Andrews, Michael C. Leff, and Robert Terrill, "The Nature of Criticism: An Overview," in *Reading Rhetorical Texts: An Introduction to Criticism* (Boston: Houghton Mifflin, 1998), 6.

2. Donald C. Bryant, *Rhetorical Dimensions in Criticism* (Baton Rouge: Louisiana State University Press, 1973), 25.

3. Wayne Brockriede, "Rhetorical Criticism as Argument," *Quarterly Journal of Speech* 60 (April 1974): 165.

4. Bryant, *Rhetorical Dimensions*, 35. These characteristics might well appear in other forms of criticism, and Bryant points out that in "rhetorical criticism . . . the essential *external* reference of discourse, the context both immediate and antecedent, the suasory potential in the situation, plays an organic part different from the part it plays in other criticism" (35).

5. Marie Hochmuth Nichols, *Rhetoric and Criticism* (Baton Rouge: Louisiana State University Press, 1963), 7.

6. See "The Experiential Perspective," in *Methods of Rhetorical Criticism: A Twentieth-Century Perspective*, 3rd ed., ed. Bernard L. Brock, Robert L. Scott, and James W. Chesebro, 85–95 (Detroit, MI: Wayne State University Press, 1989).

7. Edwin Black, *Rhetorical Criticism: A Study in Method* (Madison: University of Wisconsin Press, 1978), x–xi.

8. Marie Kathryn Hochmuth, "The Criticism of Rhetoric," in *A History and Criticism of American Public Address*, vol. 3, ed. Marie Kathryn Hochmuth (New York: Russell and Russell, 1954), 13. Hochmuth later changed her name to Marie Hochmuth Nichols.

9. Edwin Black, "On Objectivity and Politics in Criticism," *American Communication Journal* 4, no. 1 (2000), http://ac-journal.org/journal/vol4/iss1/special/black.htm.

10. This is not to say that one could not orally deliver criticism. Certainly a critic could prepare a response as a speech or public presentation. One could even prepare criticism for a podcast or YouTube video. Since the majority of academic criticism is written, my primary focus is on that form in this chapter.

11. Black, *Rhetorical Criticism*, 6.

12. Craig R. Smith, "Criticism of Political Rhetoric and Disciplinary Integrity," *American Communication Journal* 4, no. 1 (2000), http://ac-journal.org/journal/vol4/iss1/special/smith.htm.

13. For a complete timeline of the situation, see Louis Bien, "A Complete Timeline of the Ray Rice Assault Case," *SB Nation*, November 28, 2014, http://www.sbnation.com/nfl/2014/5/23/5744964/ray-rice-arrest-assault-statement-apology-ravens.

14. The State of New Jersey vs. Raymell White, Complaint Number 0102-S-2014-000728, February 15, 2014, http://gamedayrcom.c.presscdn.com/wp-content/uploads/2014/02/ray-rice-police-report-arrest-hit-girlfriend.jpg.

15. Video of the speech can be viewed here: http://www.baltimoreravens.com/videos/videos/Ray-Rices-Full-Press-Conference/405fea46-d4d4-44c7-b381-33497bf6d12f?mobile-id=827459&media-type=V.

16. "Full Transcript from Ray Rice News Conference," *Baltimore Sun*, May 23, 2014, http://www.baltimoresun.com/sports/ravens/ravens-insider/bal-full-transcript-from-ray-rice-news-conference-20140523-story.html.

17. Ibid.

18. Ibid.

19. This is where using rhetorical theory and previous examples of criticism could come in. For instance, I could use Bruce E. Gronbeck, "Underestimating Generic Expectations: Clinton's Apologies of August 17, 1998," *American Communication Journal* 2, no. 2 (February 1999), http://ac-journal.org/journal/vol2/Iss2/editorials/gronbeck/index.html. Or perhaps look at the classic study by B. L. Ware and Wil A. Linkugel, "They Spoke in Defense of Themselves: On the Generic Criticism of Apologia," *Quarterly Journal of Speech* 59 (1973): 273–283. The insights these critics share concerning how apologia works could then influence how I see Rice's speech and what insights I might have.

20. "Full Transcript from Ray Rice News Conference."

21. Ibid.

22. Ibid.

23. Cindy Boren, "Ray Rice Apologizes for Domestic Violence Incident, Calls It 'Biggest Mistake of My Life,'" *Washington Post* (*The Early Lead* blog), July 31, 2014, http://www.washingtonpost.com/blogs/early-lead/wp/2014/07/31/ray-rice-apologizes-for-domestic-violence-incident-calls-it-biggest-mistake-of-my-life.

24. Brock, Scott, and Chesebro, *Methods of Rhetorical Criticism*, 13.

25. Brockriede, "Rhetorical Criticism as Argument," 165–174.

26. Ibid., 166.

27. Ibid., 167.

28. For instance, see Ronald Matlon and Sylvia Ortiz, *Index to Journals in Communication Studies through 1995* (Annandale, VA: National Communication Association, 1997).

29. Lawrence W. Rosenfield, "The Experience of Criticism," *Quarterly Journal of Speech* 60, no. 4 (1974): 491.

30. Stephen E. Lucas, "Renaissance of American Public Address: Text and Context in Rhetorical Criticism," in *Landmark Essays on American Public Address*, ed. Martin J. Medhurst (Davis, CA: Hermagoras Press, 1993), 199.

31. Brockriede, "Rhetorical Criticism as Argument," 173.

32. Black, "On Objectivity".

33. William L. Nosthstine, Carole Blair, and Gary A. Copeland, *Critical Questions: Invention, Creativity, and the Criticism of Discourse and Media* (New York: St. Martin's, 1994), 34. See also James Darsey, "Must We All Be Rhetorical Theorists? An Anti-Democratic Inquiry," *Western Journal of Communication* 58 (1994): 164–181.

34. James Jasinski, "The Status of Theory and Method in Rhetorical Criticism," *Western Journal of Communication* 65, no. 3 (2001): 252.

35. Sonja K. Foss, "Constituted by Agency: The Discourse and Practice of Rhetorical Criticism," in *Speech Communication: Essays to Commemorate the 75th Anniversary of the Speech Communication Association*, ed. Gerald M. Phillips and Julia T. Wood (Carbondale: Southern Illinois University Press, 1990), 34–35. This view is in keeping with that expressed by Roderick Hart, "Contemporary Scholarship in Public Address: A Research Editorial," *Western Journal of Speech Communication* 50 (1986): 283–295. See, too, the collection of essays in the *Western Journal of Communication* 77, no. 5 (2013), which, in summary, essentially state that, *at the very least*, "editors, reviewers, and authors should give priority to explicit contributions to theory" (558).

36. Richard B. Gregg, "The Criticism of Symbolic Inducement: A Critical-Theoretical Connection," in *Speech Communication in the Twentieth Century*, ed. Thomas W. Benson (Carbondale: Southern Illinois University Press, 1985), 60.

37. Jim A. Kuypers, "Artistry, Purpose, and Academic Constraints in Rhetorical Criticism," in *Purpose, Practice, and Pedagogy in Rhetorical Criticism*, ed. Jim A. Kuypers (Lanham, MD: Lexington Books, 2014), 87.

38. Additional signs of the potential turn toward appreciation of unique insight over theory generation or extension can be found in several of the chapters in Jim A. Kuypers, ed., *Purpose, Practice, and Pedagogy in Rhetorical Criticism* (Lanham, MD: Lexington Books, 2014).

39. Barnett Baskerville, "The Critical Method in Speech," *Central States Speech Journal* 4, no. 1 (1953): 2.

40. Thomas R. Nilsen, "Interpretive Function of the Critic," *Western Speech* 21, no. 2 (1957): 70. Essay reprinted in Thomas R. Nilsen, ed., *Essays on Rhetorical Criticism* (New York: Random House, 1968), 86–97.

41. Michael Leff, "Interpretation and the Art of the Rhetorical Critic," *Western Journal of Speech Communication* 44 (1980): 342.

42. Examples of this can be found here: Brian Ross and Rehab El Buri, "Obama's Pastor: God Damn America, U.S. to Blame for 9/11," ABC News, March 13, 2008, http://abcnews.go.com/Blotter/Story?id=4443788.

43. The speech, entitled "A More Perfect Union," may be found here, http://blogs.wsj.com/washwire/2008/03/18/text-of-obamas-speech-a-more-perfect-union/?mod=googlenews_wsj, and here, http://www.barackobama.com/2008/03/18/remarks_of_senator_barack_obam_53.php.

44. James Carney, "Obama's Bold Gamble on Race," *Time*, March 18, 2008, http://www.time.com/time/nation/article/0,8599,1723302,00.html.

45. Charles Krauthammer, "The Speech: A Brilliant Fraud," *Real Clear Politics*, March 21, 2008, http://www.realclearpolitics.com/articles/2008/03/questions_for_obama_1.html.

46. Leff, "Interpretation," 345.

47. For detailed examples of these, see Karlyn Kohrs Campbell and Thomas R. Burkholder, *Critiques of Contemporary Rhetoric*, 2nd ed. (Belmont, CA: Wadsworth, 1997), 109–127.

48. Leff, "Interpretation," 343–344.

49. Black, *Rhetorical Criticism*, xii. The pentad is explained in chapter 11.

50. Pauline Kael, *I Lost It at the Movies* (Boston, MA: Little, Brown, 1964), 309.

51. This is not a new problem in rhetorical theory. See Leff, "Interpretation."

52. Edwin Black, "A Note on Theory and Practice in Rhetorical Criticism," *Western Journal of Speech Communication* 44 (1980): 331–332.

53. Black, "A Note on Theory and Practice," 334.

54. Leff, "Interpretation," 345.

55. For a different take on the etic/emic orientation that includes a methodological suggestion for emic criticism, see W. Charles Redding, "Extrinsic and Intrinsic Criticism," in *Essays on Rhetorical Criticism*, ed. Thomas R. Nilsen (New York: Random House, 1968), 98–125.

56. The preceding two paragraphs can be found in Jim A. Kuypers, "Must We All Be Political Activists?," *American Communication Journal* 4, no. 1 (2000), http://ac-journal.org/journal/vol4/iss1/special/kuypers.htm.

57. Rosenfield, "The Experience of Criticism," 495.

58. Ibid., 492.

59. Robert L. Ivie, "A Question of Significance," *Quarterly Journal of Speech* 80, no. 4 (1994), emphasis mine.

60. Robert L. Ivie, "Productive Criticism," *Quarterly Journal of Speech* 81, no. 1 (1995).

61. Robert L. Ivie, "The Social Relevance of Rhetorical Scholarship," *Quarterly Journal of Speech* 81, no. 2 (1994).

62. Michael Calvin McGee, "On Objectivity and Politics in Rhetoric," *American Communication Journal* 4, no. 3 (2001), http://ac-journal.org/journal/vol4/iss3/special/mcgee.htm.

63. Rosenfield, "The Experience of Criticism," 494.

64. McGee, "On Objectivity."

65. For an overview of this tension between criticism geared toward an end goal of understanding and appreciation and criticism as ideologically motivated, see Jim A. Kuypers, "The Rhetorical River," *Southern Communication Journal* 73, no. 4 (2008): 350–358. For an excellent essay that explores a method of criticism that mixes elements of both types of criticism, see Jason Edward Black, "Paddling the Rhetorical River, Revisiting the Social Actor: Rhetorical Criticism as Both Appreciation and Intervention," in *Purpose, Practice, and Pedagogy in Rhetorical Criticism*, ed. Jim A. Kuypers, 7–22 (Lanham, MD: Lexington Books, 2014).

66. How and why we practice rhetorical criticism is an ongoing conversation. Those seeking to better understand the changing nature of our critical practices have a wonderful resource in the following special collections of essays published in 1957, 1980, 1990, 2000, and 2001. Taken together they present a wonderful opportunity for students of rhetoric to better understand criticism's changing nature. See "Symposium: Criticism and Public Address," ed. Ernest Wrage, in *Western Speech* 21 (1957). These essays were later reprinted along with five others in Thomas R. Nilsen, ed., *Essays on Rhetorical Criticism* (New York: Random House, 1968). See also, "Special Report: Rhetorical Criticism; The State of the Art," ed. Michael C. Leff, *Western Journal of Speech Communication* 44, no. 4 (1980); "Special Issue on Rhetorical Criticism," ed. John Angus Campbell, *Western Journal of Speech Communication* 54, no. 3 (1990); and "Special Issue: Rhetorical Criticism; The State of the Art Revisited," *Western Journal of Speech Communication* 65, no. 3 (2001).

A critical exchange focusing on the purposes of rhetorical criticism is found in "Criticism, Politics, and Objectivity," ed. Jim A. Kuypers, *American Communication Journal* 4, no. 1 (2000), http://ac-journal.org/journal/vol4/iss1/index.htm; "Rhetoric, Politics, and Critique," ed. Mark Huglen, *American Communication Journal* 4, no. 3 (2001), http://ac-journal.org/journal/vol4/iss3/index.htm; and the final essay in the exchange, Jim A. Kuypers, "Criticism, Politics, and Objectivity: *Redivivus*," *American Communication Journal* 5, no. 1 (2001), http://ac-journal.org/journal/vol5/iss1/special/kuypersresponse.htm.

Another resource on the historical changes in rhetorical criticism is the special issue of *Rhetoric Review* dedicated to Ed Black. See "Interdisciplinary Perspectives on Rhetorical Criticism," *Rhetoric Review* 25, no. 4 (2006).

# 4

# Understanding Rhetorical Situations

*Marilyn J. Young and Kathleen Farrell*

Lloyd F. Bitzer defines a **rhetorical situation** as "a complex of persons, events, objects, and relations presenting an actual or potential exigence which can be completely or partially removed if discourse introduced into the situation can so constrain human decision or action as to bring about the significant modification of the exigence."[1] Further, he writes, in "any rhetorical situation there will be at least one controlling exigence which functions as the organizing principle: it specifies the audience to be addressed and the change to be effected."[2] The rhetorical audience, then, is that which can alleviate the exigence. There are three main parts to the rhetorical situation: the **exigence** is "an imperfection marked by urgency; it is a defect, an obstacle, something waiting to be done, a thing which is other than it should be";[3] the **audience**, which is the group of persons who have the power to modify the exigence, is the second component. Bitzer also wrote of **constraints**, which are an important consideration in that they can influence both what can be said and what should not be said:

> [Constraints are] made up of persons, events, objects, and relations which are parts of the situation because they have the power to constrain decision and action needed to modify the exigence. Standard sources of constraint include beliefs, attitudes, documents, facts, traditions, images, interests, motives and the like; and when the orator enters the situation, his discourse not only harnesses constraints given by the situation but provides additional important constraints—for example his personal character, his logical proofs, and his style.[4]

## USING THE RHETORICAL SITUATION

Although the rhetorical situation's utility can be applied to contemporary events such as the use of Twitter in presidential campaigns[5] or the use of Internet-based résumés,[6] looking back at historical events can be particularly helpful in illustrating how the above concepts work. Thus, as an example, when President Franklin Roosevelt addressed Congress following the Japanese attack on Pearl Harbor, he was responding to that attack as the controlling exigence. The attack would seem to require a response in kind—a declaration of war. Yet Roosevelt was constrained by the Constitution, which grants Congress the responsibility for declarations of war. The attack, then, required Roosevelt to ask Congress to declare war on Japan; in that way, the controlling exigence (the attack) entailed the necessary audience (Congress) and the action to be taken (the declaration of war).

Yet it was not enough for Roosevelt to merely address Congress, for even with a declaration of war, Roosevelt needed the support of the American people. It is also true that the public needed to hear from the president. In light of this, his speech was designed to respond to two exigencies: the need for a declaration of war and the need of the people to hear from their leader.[7]

Compare this rhetorical situation to that which confronted President George W. Bush following the 9/11 attacks on the World Trade Center and the Pentagon. How were these situations different? In this case it was not immediately obvious who was responsible for the attacks; yet even when the instigators had been identified, Bush did not seek a declaration of war. When he spoke to the American people, Bush announced the military action he had ordered against Afghanistan; he did not ask either Congress or the people for permission. In the years since Pearl Harbor, presidents have found ways around the requirement to seek a declaration from Congress; in fact, no president has asked for a declaration of war since Roosevelt in 1941, even though the United States has been involved in hostilities in several countries. So we must ask ourselves, "What is the exigence, who is the audience, and what are the constraints?" What has changed since 1941 and the attack on Pearl Harbor?

## Public Knowledge and Rhetorical Situations

Bitzer's ideas about the rhetorical situation are best understood when considered in relation to his notions of **public knowledge**, where he articulates his understanding of the role of the public in rhetorical practice.[8] When he refers to the "public," Bitzer is not referring to the audience, although these concepts may overlap. Bitzer's construction of the public is a community of persons who share values, interests, and outlook. Publics form around specific values, ideas, policies, and proposals. Yet Bitzer recognizes that these publics are fluid, that specific publics can form, disband, and re-form in a different configuration. Further, there can be "subpublics" within a larger public, such as ethnic or some political groups within a particular community, or factions within a political party, such as the Tea Party subset of the Republican Party. These persons are interdependent and possess the power to validate community truths and values. It is this group that has the power to "authorize" decisions and actions—not in any formal way as with Congress, but in the sense that some decisions become part of the public sense of truth and value.[9]

Part of the function of the public in a situation such as December 7, 1941, is to authorize the president to seek declarations of war in times of attack. In a way this is the actualization of the notion imbedded in the US Constitution: "with the consent of the governed." That consent is offered formally through Congress, but it is also granted informally through the notion of public assent, a concept that is most successful when public knowledge is informed and has coalesced. Obviously, President Bush felt public support for the military action he took against Afghanistan, even in the absence of a declaration of war.

American democracy works because we believe it will and we therefore defer to its precepts. In that sense, democracy is a process of communication, and it is the role of the public through discourse to communicate—formally and informally—its assent to the actions of our leaders. For example, at the conclusion of World War II, in the face of strong public sentiment to "bring the troops home," Roosevelt could not guarantee our allies the presence of an American occupying force in Europe; Churchill's proposal for an alliance of the "English-speaking peoples" fell on deaf ears, and American women, who had been the backbone of the workforce during the war, were expecting to return home and make room for returning soldiers. The public authorization for the war effort and its exigences no longer existed; decisions had to reflect that new truth. Similarly, President Obama felt that public authorization for the war in Afghanistan had waned to the point where it was time to conclude American involvement and bring the troops home. How had the exigence changed between 2001 and 2011?

In the case of the Japanese attack on Pearl Harbor, the situation—and the exigence—was relatively clear, as was the fitting response. When things are not so clear, the development of public knowledge becomes critical; before assent can be communicated, the public must accumulate enough knowledge to

1. agree on the situation itself,
2. understand the options open for a fitting response, and
3. debate the costs and benefits of those options.

If these elements do not materialize, the notion of public assent cannot entail the notion of consent but rests instead on ignorance.

## RHETORIC AS SITUATED

Bitzer's ideas are grounded in the notion that all rhetoric is "situated." That is to say, rhetorical discourse derives its meaning from the situation in which it is created. Absent that situation, meaning is often lost. Think about the "great speeches" in American history; how many of them make real sense outside the time in which they were spoken? Certainly, there are speeches that may come alive while one is studying the era in which they were salient, and many "great" speeches have passages that ring through the ages. Usually, though, these are passages that can be given new life by applying them to a current situation; you see a lot of this sort of application on social media sites such as Facebook. Nevertheless, by far the majority of speeches given in this country during its existence have fallen into obscurity, not because they were not good examples of the art and craft of speech making, but because they no longer speak to us.

Even those speeches that carry powerful impact over time derive much of that strength from the situation they address. For example, Franklin Delano Roosevelt's Pearl Harbor Address to the Nation, judged the fourth most influential speech of the twentieth century, draws its power from the situation we described above.[10] Ronald Reagan's 1987 Brandenburg Gate Address is remembered today not so much for commemorating the 750th anniversary of Berlin as it is for its confrontation with then Communist Party secretary Mikhail Gorbachev over the Berlin Wall. In front of the iconic Brandenburg Gate, near the Berlin Wall, Reagan challenged the Soviet leader to advance the cause of "freedom and peace" when he uttered the now famous line, "Mr. Gorbachev, tear down this wall." The speech drew its power from the situation of continuing confrontation between the Soviet Union and the United States and Gorbachev's attempt at political reform within the Soviet Union. The Gettysburg Address, full of imagery and poetry, nonetheless is memorable at least in part because of the situation in which it was conceived: a commemoration of the deadliest battle in American history, a great civil war testing the strength of the union, and a challenge that tried the principles of equality and liberty on which that union was founded, as well as the fact that we need to continuously renew our commitment to those ideals. On the other hand, Lincoln's second inaugural, considered one of the best inaugural addresses ever given, is nonetheless remembered only in part, rather than in whole. Like most great addresses, those passages that one recalls are those the public has "authorized" by moving them into public knowledge.

In Bitzer's view, the situation in which rhetoric is called forth encompasses more than the context of the speech or the events that gave rise to the occasion for the speech. It includes all of the elements that influenced the moment: the events, the individuals involved, the circumstances, and the relationships among these factors. Thus, returning to Roosevelt's request for a Declaration of War, the situation would consist of Roosevelt himself and the attack on Pearl Harbor; but it would also include the Congress and the Constitution, the negotiations that had been going on between the United States and the Japanese, the ongoing war in Europe, the widespread isolationism of most Americans prior to the attack, and so on. We have used primarily military policy examples (Pearl Harbor in 1941 and 9/11 in 2001) to illustrate the situational method because those events present pretty clear-cut cases of exigence. But it is equally useful to use this approach to examine the rhetoric emanating from events such as the unrest in Ferguson, Missouri, or the rhetoric surrounding the Supreme Court decision on gay marriage, or even non-American examples of rhetoric.[11]

In analyzing a speech using the situational perspective, the critic must take into account the totality of the situation and must consider the role or roles played by each element. For sake of discussion, we offer these suggestions as guiding questions in a situational analysis:

- What are the elements that constitute the particular situation? Initially, this list should be inclusive, even exhaustive; elements can be omitted later if analysis demonstrates their role to be negligible.
- What role or roles did each element listed play?
- What is the dominant element, or exigence, that will govern the response?
- In terms of the response to the situation, was the exigence modified and the response "fitting"?

These questions are not exhaustive steps in a method to be applied as a sort of "cookie cutter." They do, however, provide a beginning point for analysis that focuses on the significance of the situation. As with any critical effort, it is the rhetorical artifact that will determine how the critical narrative develops. Situational analysis is seldom used as a stand-alone tool to evaluate a rhetorical artifact; more typically, it enriches other analytical methods by providing a deeper understanding of context in all its dimensions.[12] Only by understanding the full context of a rhetorical event can the critic comprehend and evaluate the artifact itself.

## POTENTIALS AND PITFALLS

The beauty of situational analysis is that it allows the critic to account for outside forces that impact a rhetorical event in ways that other methods do not. If we recognize that all rhetoric is situated—that it is dependent for meaning on the time, place, and circumstances in which it occurs—then situational analysis allows us to view rhetoric as an organic phenomenon. We are then able to view differently those rare instances of discourse that transcend the situation and live on in national memory. Situational analysis also allows us to examine the choices a rhetorician makes in constructing a particular discourse. Those choices are ultimately influenced by the situation in which the discourse arises—whether ceremonial or as a result of crisis. It also combines naturally with a number of other critical perspectives, allowing the critic to construct a richer, more robust analysis.

There are criticisms of the situational perspective; it is seen by some as mechanistic. Additionally, the idea of the exigence is viewed by some theorists as robbing the rhetor of invention,[13] because, in Bitzer's view, the exigence calls forth rhetoric to craft a fitting response, and if the response is not deemed fitting, the response is not rhetorical. While this is a pretty shallow view of situational analysis, it does cause some to reject its utility as a critical tool.

There is also the possibility that the critic might overlook elements that are not part of the situation but that would illuminate the rhetorical artifact, such as logical elements, rhetorical devices, and fallacies. Finally, the critic must not lose sight of the fact that the rhetor is responsible for what is said, regardless of the forces that impinge on his or her rhetorical choices.

## SITUATIONAL PERSPECTIVE TOP PICKS

Bitzer, Lloyd F. "Functional Communication: A Situational Perspective." In *Rhetoric in Transition: Studies in the Nature and Uses of Rhetoric*, edited by Eugene E. White, 21–38. University Park: Pennsylvania State University Press, 1980. Bitzer responds to his critics and offers some modifications of his theory.

Bitzer, Lloyd F. "Rhetoric and Public Knowledge." In *Rhetoric, Philosophy, and Literature: An Exploration*, edited by Don Burks, 67–94. West Lafayette, IN: Purdue University Press, 1978. In this essay Bitzer discusses his theory of public knowledge: how cultural truths are absorbed by groups and used to acknowledge new information and authorize action in response to rhetorical situations.

Bitzer, Lloyd F. "Rhetorical Public Communication." *Critical Studies in Mass Communication* 4, no. 4 (1987): 425–428. Bitzer discusses public communication, focusing on "journalists as a new and important class of rhetors."

Bitzer, Lloyd F. "The Rhetorical Situation." *Philosophy and Rhetoric* 1 (1968): 1–14. This is the essay where Bitzer first explains situational analysis.

Grant-Davie, Keith. "Rhetorical Situations and Their Constituents." *Rhetoric Review* 15 (1997): 264–279. Grant-Davie argues that the roles of rhetor and audience are dynamic and interdependent. Audience as a rhetorical concept has transcended the idea of a homogenous body of people who have stable characteristics and are assembled in the rhetor's presence.

Kuypers, Jim A., Marilyn J. Young, and Michael K. Launer. "Of Mighty Mice and Meek Men: Contextual Reconstruction of the Iranian Airbus Shootdown." *Southern Communication Journal* 59, no. 4 (1994): 294–306. The authors use criticism informed by a situational perspective to examine the rhetoric surrounding the incident in 1988 when US forces shot down an Iranian passenger airliner in the Persian Gulf.

Patton, John H. "Causation and Creativity in Rhetorical Situations: Distinctions and Implications." *Quarterly Journal of Speech* 65 (1979): 36–55. Patton notes that exigences, although necessary conditions for rhetorical discourse, are not, in themselves, sufficient conditions. Underlying this argument is the assumption that "rhetoric is essentially historical" and that it is through invention and creativity that the rhetorical situation is appropriately addressed, producing the "fitting response" that every rhetor seeks.

Smith, Craig R., and Scott Lybarger. "Bitzer's Model Revisited." *Communication Quarterly* 44, no. 2 (1996): 197–213. The authors discuss responses to Bitzer's theory and describe Bitzer's own attempts to refine it. What is most significant to Smith and Lybarger, however, is that Bitzer, in his refinements, opens the door to a more complex view of perception and situation.

Young, Marilyn J. "Lloyd F. Bitzer: Rhetorical Situation, Public Knowledge, and Audience Dynamics." In *Twentieth Century Roots of Rhetorical Criticism*, edited by Jim A. Kuypers and Andrew King, 275–301. Westport, CT: Praeger, 2001. Young reviews the criticism of Bitzer's work and argues that most of his critics have underestimated the power of the theory of the situation. Bitzer's theory gains power and becomes more complete when considered in conjunction with his ideas about public knowledge.

## NOTES

1. Lloyd F. Bitzer, "The Rhetorical Situation," *Philosophy and Rhetoric* 1 (1968): 6. According to the Webster Dictionary online, http://www.merriam-webster.com, *exigence* [*exigency*] is "that which is required in a particular situation."

2. Ibid., 7.

3. Ibid.

4. Ibid., 8.

5. Janet Johnson, "Twitter Bites and Romney: Examining the Rhetorical Situation of the 2012 Presidential Election in 140 Characters," *Journal of Contemporary Rhetoric* 2, nos. 3/4 (2012): 54–64.

6. John B. Killoran, "The Rhetorical Situations of Web Résumés," *Journal of Technical Writing & Communication* 39, no. 3 (2009): 263–284.

7. See, Franklin Delano Roosevelt, "A Day That Will Live in Infamy," at http://www.americanrhetoric.com.

8. Lloyd F. Bitzer, "Rhetoric and Public Knowledge," in *Rhetoric, Philosophy, and Literature: An Exploration*, ed. Don M. Burks, 67–94 (West Lafayette, IN: Purdue University Press, 1978).

9. For an example of how situation and public knowledge interact, see Marilyn J. Young and Michael K. Launer, "KAL 007 and the Superpowers: An International Argument," *Quarterly Journal of Speech* 74, no. 3 (1988): 271–295. This essay also introduces the concept of "pre-knowledge."

10. See http://americanrhetoric.com/newtop100speeches.htm.

11. As just three examples, see Cheri Hampton-Farmer, "Slippery Dilemma: Tony Blair's Rhetorical Response to Fuel Tax Protesters," *American Communication Journal* 16, no. 1 (2014): 52–61, http://ac-journal.org/journal/2014-2015/Vol16/Iss1/ACJ_2014-018_Cheri4.pdf; Bruce Dadey, "Identity, Narrative, and the Construction of the Rhetorical Situation in Euro-American and Aboriginal Cultures," *Journal of the Canadian Society for the Study of Rhetoric* 4 (2011): 1–21; and Yao Huimin and Wang Ximing, "On Bitzer's Situational View of Rhetoric," *Journal of Xi'an International Studies University* 2 (2009): 29–33.

12. As an example of just such an analysis, see Jim A. Kuypers, Marilyn J. Young, and Michael K. Launer, "Of Mighty Mice and Meek Men: Contextual Reconstruction of the Iranian Airbus Shootdown," *Southern Communication Journal* 59, no. 4 (1994): 294–306; and Jim A. Kuypers, "The Press and James Dobson: Contextual Reconstruction after the Ted Bundy Interview," *Florida Communication Journal* 18, no. 2 (1990): 1–8.

13. For instance, Richard Vatz argues that, in explicating his theory of situation, Bitzer fails to account for the creativity of the rhetor. In making his argument, Vatz provides some of the grounding for the role of perception within a rhetorical situation. See Richard E. Vatz, "The Myth of the Rhetorical Situation," *Philosophy and Rhetoric* 6 (1973): 154–161; and Richard E. Vatz, "The Mythical Status of Situational Rhetoric: Implications for Rhetorical Critics' Relevance in the Public Arena," *Review of Communication* 9, no. 1 (2009): 1–9. Interestingly, in his 2009 article, Vatz fails to mention Bitzer's 1980 "Functional Communication: A Situational Perspective," where Bitzer addresses concerns raised by his critics.

# 5

# Generic Elements in Rhetoric

*William Benoit*

To help understand a complex and variegated world, we frequently make use of generalizations that are often referred to as stereotypes. We can use a generalization such as "Ashley's a conservative" to draw reasonable, but not certain, conclusions about Ashley. If we want to know whether Ashley supports private-school tuition vouchers, the best way to find out the answer to this question is to ask Ashley, or to locate a statement by Ashley about her position on vouchers. These kinds of direct options, however, are not always available. In the absence of better ways to answer our question, we can use Ashley's political leanings to make an educated guess about her position: Because many conservatives support vouchers, Ashley, who we happen to know is a conservative, probably supports vouchers too. Knowing something (support for private-school vouchers) about most members of a group (conservatives) allows us to make educated guesses about other members of that group (Ashley). Similar generalizations about groups of discourse or "genres" can also be helpful.

**Generic rhetorical criticism** is based on the idea that observable, explicable, and predictable rhetorical commonalities occur in groups of related discourses as well as in groups of people. A critic using the generic approach would first identify a distinctive group or category of discourse, a genre: for example, presidential nominating convention keynote speeches, graduation commencement speeches, presidential inaugural speeches, speeches of apology, or eulogies. Then, the critic utilizing the generic method adopts an *inductive* approach, examining numerous past instances of this genre to develop a description or generalization of its common characteristics. It is also important for the critic to explain *why* speeches of this kind ought to have the commonalities found in the analysis. As an example of this, let us take a look at presidential nominating convention keynote speeches as an extended example.[1] These speeches are designed to sound a "key" note or set a tone for the convention. The keynote is designed to celebrate the ideals of the party and the fitness of the nominee to represent the party in the general election campaign and, ultimately, to win the office of the presidency for the nominee. All such keynote speeches are given in a similar situation: the Republican or Democratic presidential nomination convention. The result of this process, the description of the rhetorical characteristics of a genre (keynotes, for instance), can be used in at least three important ways.

First, **generic descriptions** can be used as part of a rhetorical theory that describes rhetorical practices according to genre. Rhetorical theory can describe the practice of rhetoric, as well as offering prescriptions about how it ought to be conducted. Inductive generic descriptions can provide an empirical foundation for descriptive rhetorical theory. For example, we might want to describe the practice of campaign rhetoric (keynote speeches), political rhetoric (state of the union addresses), or ceremonial rhetoric (commencement addresses, eulogies). If so, the generalizations discovered through a generic analysis could be very useful to theory building.

Second, generic descriptions can be used by practitioners, by rhetors who seek advice about how to develop a speech that falls into that genre. Those who are confronted with a need to invent a particular kind of discourse can be guided by systematic descriptions of past instances of that kind of discourse. If you need to write a eulogy, for example, it could be very useful to know what other eulogists have said in the past. A description of the practice of past eulogies could give you ideas, a starting point, and perhaps even "model eulogies" to imitate.

Third, rhetorical critics can apply what we have learned about a genre to help understand and evaluate other, as yet unexamined instances of that genre. That is, we can compare a new instance of a genre to past practices. For example, on March 20, 2003, President Bush announced the beginning of Operation Iraqi Freedom, the war in Iraq. We can learn something about this speech by comparing it with other presidential speeches announcing military action. We could compare the 2003 speech with one or more other, earlier speeches, but it would be more efficient to compare it with the results of a generic rhetorical criticism that describes a group of similar speeches.[2] As another example, although not quite a declaration of war, we could do the same with President Obama's September 10, 2014, "Statement by the President on ISIL," in which President Obama outlined America's course of military action against that terrorist group.[3] We can ask how this announcement, on the surface similar with declarations of war, matched up with actual declarations of war. Of course, nominating convention keynote speeches are almost certain to occur in 2016, and we can use our understanding of past keynotes to understand and evaluate them.

It should be obvious that the fundamental assumption of genre criticism is that rhetorical artifacts examined by a critic to establish a genre, or to develop the inductively derived generic description, will resemble in important ways other rhetorical artifacts that fall into that genre. The power of generic criticism is that, if this assumption is reasonable, critics, practitioners, and theorists can learn something about some rhetorical artifacts by examining other similar rhetorical artifacts. Rhetorical critics, schooled in the humanistic tradition, do not ordinarily make this idea explicit, but the basic argument is that the texts studied in a generic rhetorical criticism are a sample of a larger population of texts and that the results of generic rhetorical criticism can be generalized to other similar discourses. Of course, the generalizations derived from the discourses that are being studied to identify and define the genre must be applied cautiously to other discourses. Discourses that belong to the same class or genre and therefore have *some* similarities could also be different in other important ways. For instance, Ashley may be one of the few conservatives who do not favor school vouchers.

Furthermore, the generic description is inherently limited by the characteristics of the artifacts examined to develop the description. The process of genre criticism can only describe—not improve on—the actual practice of discourse. This means that if rhetors who have created discourse in a genre have not yet discovered the best or most effective approach for that kind of rhetoric, the generic description developed using existing messages cannot possibly include the optimum approach.[4] It also means that as our culture changes through time, discourses that were effective or appropriate in the past—the discourses studied to describe the genre—may be ill suited to understanding future discourses given in different times. The remainder of this chapter covers three broad areas: the theory and practice of generic rhetorical criticism, the idea of generic description, and the idea of generic application.

## THE THEORY AND PRACTICE OF GENERIC RHETORICAL CRITICISM

A common thread in this literature is that genres are a class, set, or group of related discourses. For example, Walter R. Fisher argues that "a genre is a category" and "genres are generalizations."[5] Similarly, Jackson Harrell and Wil A. Linkugel explain that, "at base, genre means class. A genus is a class or group of things. The decision to classify a particular group of things as a genus rests on recorded observations which indicate that one group of entities shares some important characteristic which differentiates it from all other entities."[6] This statement contains an important implicit claim: a genre, or each member of a genre, is distinct from other genres.[7] A keynote is one kind of campaign speech, and these speeches are different in some ways from nominating convention acceptance addresses,[8] presidential television spots,[9] or presidential debates.[10] Because these messages are all forms of presidential campaign discourse, they probably share some features in common, but if they are distinct genres they must have distinguishing differences. Political campaign messages should be different in some ways from other kinds of discourses, such as eulogies or commencement addresses.

Generic criticism generally falls into one of four broad areas. Some genre studies seem to adopt a *situational* base, identifying a genre based on the situation in which the discourses arise, such as examination of gallows speeches or inaugural addresses.[11] Other instances of generic criticism seem to focus on *purpose*, including life termination justifications, investigations of agitation and control, redemption, and polarization.[12] Still other genre studies focus on the rhetorical characteristics of groups of *rhetors*, including studies of scientists;[13] early Afro-American feminists;[14] radical-revolutionary speakers;[15] radical, liberal, and conservative rhetors;[16] the religious right;[17] or the radical right.[18] Finally, some genre studies focus on characteristics of the *medium* of discourse, such as analysis of political blogs,[19] political pamphlets,[20] or songs.[21] There can be no question that a great deal of interesting and useful scholarship of an extremely diverse nature has been conducted under the rubric of generic rhetorical criticism. It can be difficult to explore this literature, because critics do not always label their work "generic criticism" even though we might consider it as such. In reviewing this body of literature, three areas seem to me to stand out: the relationship between situation and genre, the relationship between purpose and genre, and the relationship of genre to other elements. To each of these ideas we now turn.

### Situation and Genre

Rhetorical scholars have described recurrent forms of discourse since at least as early as Aristotle's *Rhetoric*, which identified three broad genres of rhetoric: forensic (legal), deliberative (legislative), and epideictic (ceremonial).[22] Edwin Black offered one of the earliest, if not the earliest, conceptual discussions of the assumptions of the rhetorical genre:

> First, we must assume that there is a limited number of situations in which a rhetor can find himself. . . . To be sure, there may be accidental factors peculiar to a given situation; but our assumption is that there will be a limited number of ways in which rhetorical situations can be characterized, and

that the recurrent characteristics of rhetorical situations will make it possible for us—if we know enough—to construct an accurate and exhaustive typology of rhetorical situations.[23]

Black assumes that the number of rhetorical situations—and therefore, the number of potential genres—is limited. This makes the task of identifying genres and locating a sufficient number of texts to study more practical than if there were an infinite number of rhetorical situations. Black continues his description:

> Second, we must assume that there is a limited number of ways in which a rhetor can and will respond rhetorically to any given situational type. Again, there may be accidents of a given response that will prove singular, but on the whole—we assume—there will be only a finite number of rhetorical strategies available to a rhetor in any given situation, and his playing his own variations on these strategies will not prevent the critic from identifying the strategies as characteristic of the situation.[24]

This assumption, that there are a limited number of potential responses, means that the texts of a genre are likely to share common features (which the critic can identify and describe). The alternative, an unlimited number of responses, could mean that every member of a genre could be completely different. Finally, Black discusses the possible uses of generic rhetorical criticism:

> Third, we must assume that the recurrence of a given situational type through history will provide the critic with information on the rhetorical responses available in that situation, and with this information the critic can better understand and evaluate any specific rhetorical discourse in which he may be interested.[25]

So, understanding past instances of a genre may provide insight into other examples of that kind of rhetorical message. Of course, the artifacts that participate in or belong to a genre will not be identical in all regards, but for generic criticism to be a useful method of criticism, the similarities must be important.

The emphasis on understanding genre as rooted in a particular situation is popular in the literature.[26] Harrell and Linkugel assert that genres are situationally based: "We think that rhetorical genres stem from organizing principles found in recurring situations that generate discourse characterized by a family of common factors."[27] Similarly, Karlyn K. Campbell and Kathleen Hall Jamieson's oft-quoted definition stipulates a situational base for rhetorical genres:

> Genres are groups of discourses which share substantive, stylistic, and situational characteristics. Or, put differently, in the discourses that form a genre, similar substantive and stylistic strategies are used to encompass situations perceived as similar by the responding rhetors. A genre is a group of acts unified by a constellation of forms that recurs in each of its members. These forms, in isolation, appear in other discourses. What is distinctive about the acts in a genre is the recurrence of the forms together in constellation.[28]

The term *constellation* is especially well chosen, suggesting that the recurrent elements appear in a recognizable configuration or pattern. The point that rhetors work from their perception of a situation is also important.

## Purpose and Genre

A second thread in the literature grounds genres in the rhetor's purpose.[29] Carolyn Miller points out that "genres have been defined by similarities in strategies or forms in the discourse, by similarities in audience, by similarities in modes of thinking, by similarities in rhetorical situations." Her recommendation is that "a rhetorically sound definition of genre must be centered not on the substance or form of a discourse but on the action it is used to accomplish."[30] In my opinion, there is overlap between situational and purposive approaches to genre, but they are not entirely identical.

Certainly we must keep in mind that the rhetor's purpose and the rhetorical situation frequently coincide. For example, eulogists face a situation in which a person has died. When a person dies, the survivors will never again be able to see or talk with the deceased, a cause for sadness. A death also reminds everyone concerned in a very direct fashion that they are mortal. Hence it is appropriate for a eulogist to praise the departed, to ease the transition, and to try to help auditors deal with their grief and heightened sense of mortality. As Jamieson and Campbell explain it, "In Western culture, at least, a eulogy will acknowledge the death, transform the relationship between the living and the dead from present to past tense, ease the mourners' terror at confronting their own mortality, console them by arguing that the deceased lives on, and reknit the community."[31] Here, the situation and the rhetor's purpose are completely compatible, and it is difficult to see or draw a distinction between the situation and the rhetor's purpose.

However, I believe that it is not always the case that a rhetor's purpose is completely consistent with the situation. For instance, consider a eulogy for someone killed by a gunshot wound. If the eulogist felt strongly about gun control, he or she might choose to include such an appeal in the eulogy; if the eulogist did not feel strongly about gun control, he or she would likely not discuss gun control. An appeal for gun control is not a necessary part of such a eulogy. If a eulogist failed to praise the deceased, the eulogy would seem odd and incomplete if not wrong, but if a eulogist failed to include a plea for gun control, the speech would not seem incomplete. Although the particular situation may be seen to authorize such an appeal for gun control (unless the deceased were a staunch Second Amendment supporter), it does not require it; rather, the rhetor's purpose (advocating gun control) would determine whether to include this idea in the eulogy.

To extend this analogy one step further, consider Rick Kahn's plea at Minnesota Democratic senator Paul Wellstone's memorial service: "We are begging you to help us win this Senate election for Paul Wellstone." In these cases, the rhetor's personal purpose produced discourse that was in part irrelevant to if not incongruent with the immediate situation. Nothing in this eulogy's situation authorized this topic. Although a listener might happen to agree in principle with the appeal to vote for a Democrat to replace Wellstone, such an appeal has nothing to do with the deceased or the eulogy itself. It seems inappropriate; a plea to vote for a Democrat probably detracted from the ceremony for many in the audience, particularly the Republican friends and colleagues of Wellstone who attended the service.

As a final argument for the importance of distinguishing between situation and purpose, consider any rhetorical discourse that occurs in a controversy. Those rhetors who supported and opposed Prohibition spoke and wrote in essentially the same situation. Similarly, the situation confronting pro-choice and pro-life advocates is exactly the same. These groups of rhetors—and it would be easy to add additional groups to this list—produced contradictory rhetorical artifacts, and the primary reason for those differences was their purpose, not differences in the situation. Of course, one could argue that opponents' perceptions of the situation are different, but Lloyd Bitzer at least argues that the situation consists of "objective and publicly observable historic facts in the world we experience."[32] In principle, one could say that everyone lives in a unique situation, but enough shared perceptions exist to allow genre criticism to be useful.

Thus, the rhetors' purpose can be a source of generic similarities in rhetorical messages, and while purpose may overlap with situation, conceptually they are distinct concepts.

*Genre: "Act" at the Intersection of Scene, Purpose, Agent, and Agency*

The third thread in the literature highlights the relationship of situation and purpose with three other considerations. There is no question that situation and purpose do, or should, influence the production of discourse. However, in actuality, five factors jointly influence the production of rhetorical discourse. Kenneth Burke's notion of ratios[33] helps clarify the relationships between these factors,[34] and it will be discussed in greater detail in chapter 11. For now, though, it is enough to know that ratios are found within a rhetorical artifact (actual discourse) and are comprised of two terms from what Burke called a pentad—an act, scene (or situation), agent, agency, and purpose. Ratios essentially describe the influence of one of these terms on a second one. Given that in this chapter we are discussing the production of discourse (our act), "act" is the second term in each of the possible combinations of ratios, so we are actually looking at the effect that the first term in the ratio has upon the act. So, when we examine a rhetorical artifact with genre in mind, we find these ratios:

- Scene-act: the situation (scene) in which a discourse (the act) is produced exerts an influence on that discourse.
- Purpose-act: the rhetor's purpose, goal, or intent influences the discourse he or she produces.
- Agent-act: the nature of the rhetor (the agent) influences the discourse he or she produces.
- Agency-act: the means (agency) used to create the discourse, including the communicative medium, influences the discourse.

The scene-act ratio corresponds to situationally based approaches to genre (e.g., gallows speeches, inaugural addresses). The purpose-act ratio relates to genre approaches based on the rhetor's purpose (e.g., polarization, resignation[35]). The agent-act ratio pertains to genres focused on the rhetor (e.g., radical, liberal, or conservative). Finally, the agency-act ratio corresponds to studies of kinds of discourse (e.g., pamphlets, songs). All four of these combinations can influence the production of discourse and can serve as the basis for a genre.

Situations are opportunities for discourse, which rhetors may choose to exploit to further their own purposes. This can help explain why discourse that occurs in similar situations, such as the eulogies discussed above, would share important similarities. However, some rhetors have different purposes, which can also influence the discourse they produce, even when they face similar situations. Think of the gun-control example given above, for example. However, I believe that critics are certainly capable of identifying or creating groupings of discourses that share a common source (such as situation, purpose, or rhetor) but that ordinary people have not conceptualized at any level. A little imagination can devise diverse categories that could be used to divide discourses into a variety of groupings.

## GENERIC DESCRIPTION: AN INDUCTIVE APPROACH

I want to stress that there is no single way to write a genre criticism. It is important for a rhetorical critic who wants to write a generic rhetorical criticism to read a variety of genre studies before attempting the task. Still, some observations are worth making. There are two fundamental approaches to genre criticism: generic description (inductive) and generic application (deductive).[36] **Generic application** begins with a generalization and applies it to specific members of the genre. Generic application begins with a genre that has already been described; it applies the characteristics of that genre deductively to another instance of that genre in order to explain or evaluate it.

When a critic suspects the existence of a genre, he or she may use generic description to examine particular instances of a possible genre for common features. There are three fundamental steps in this process: (1) identify the defining characteristic (e.g., the situation, purpose, or kind of rhetor that constitutes the genre); (2) carefully scrutinize examples of the possible genre to identify similarities; (3) explain the observed similarities in terms of identifying characteristics (identifying the "internal dynamic" of the genre). Each of these steps is discussed below.

### Identifying Defining Characteristic

If the critic believes that he or she may have found a useful genre, he or she must identify the defining characteristic(s) of that candidate genre. For example, the defining characteristic could be the situation/scene in which the rhetorical artifacts occur (such as keynote speech or eulogy), the rhetor's purpose that prompts the rhetorical discourses (for example, celebrating the party's presidential nominee or helping the bereaved confront their own mortality), salient characteristics of the rhetor/agent (for example, Republicans or women), or the medium/agency that shapes the artifacts (for instance, a speech, television spot, or political debate). One cannot select artifacts at random to discover genres; the critic must be able to clearly define the candidate genre in order to select appropriate particular rhetorical artifacts, that is, instances of the category, for analysis.

For example, President Bush's speech of March 20, 2003, is an example of a speech announcing a war. However, it may not be clear whether speeches about al-Qaeda and ISIS/ISIL are about *war* (perhaps the struggle against terrorism is not the same as a war against a country). The genre critic needs to make a clear decision about which messages to include in a study. However, given a clear understanding of the defining characteristics of the candidate genre, the critic can select appropriate texts for scrutiny. As another example, consider presidential speeches announcing American involvement in peacekeeping missions. In a recent study, Jason A. Edwards, Joseph M. Valenzano III, and Karla Stevenson examined instances of American presidents announcing US involvement in UN peacekeeping missions.[37] They found distinct elements that differentiated those speeches from war announcements as well as crisis speeches.

Having identified the defining characteristics of the candidate genre, the critic must acquire several instances of the discourse in question for analysis. The critic must be prepared to read, watch, and/or listen to the artifacts repeatedly, closely, and carefully in order to determine whether these texts have rhetorical commonalities and what those commonalities are. Two important questions arise in this phase of generic description: what to look for and how many discourses to examine.

Unlike most other rhetorical perspectives, generic rhetorical criticism helps the critic decide *which* artifacts to examine but does not prescribe *how* to analyze those artifacts. For example, a critic employing the generic approach could look for metaphors commonly used in war speeches. A genre critic might look to see whether such speeches displayed similar rhetorical visions or fantasy themes or used narrative in similar ways. A genre critic could also look at stylistic elements (e.g., alliterations, personification) in groups of related messages. Thus, the method of generic rhetorical criticism helps the critic decide which rhetorical artifacts to examine and it tells the critic to look for commonalities, but the generic method itself does not help the critic know precisely which sorts of rhetorical similarities to look for. The whole idea of genre criticism is that rhetorical artifacts in the past can be studied and that the results of this study will tell us about future artifacts of the same kind (or other past artifacts that were not included in the initial study). Thus, it is very important for the critic to select the appropriate artifacts to study; inclusion of artifacts that do not really belong to the genre will produce a flawed study.

In my opinion, a critic using the generic approach should be familiar with numerous ways of performing rhetorical criticism and with rhetorical theory generally. It is useful to know what features might be important in a genre. When the critic utilizing the generic approach is repeatedly reading the artifacts of the candidate genre, he or she may notice that certain kinds of metaphors are used frequently. Or the critic could notice that the rhetors seem to be engaging in a certain narrative form frequently. Critics using the generic approach who are generally familiar with numerous rhetorical perspectives are probably more likely to notice important rhetorical similarities than critics who are not widely read.

Generic description, as noted above, is an inductive approach. This means that it is subject to the tests of inductive argument. The most important test is whether a sufficient number of instances—in this case, enough rhetorical artifacts—have been examined.[38] There is no simple answer to this question: The number of instances a critic should examine to establish the nature of a genre depends in part on the complexity and variety of the artifacts examined. The greater the complexity of the artifacts in the possible genre, and the more variety in the artifacts, the greater the number of instances that ought to be studied to have confidence in the study's conclusions. The number of artifacts needed also depends on how prominently the common rhetorical features appear in the artifacts. The more obvious and important the rhetorical similarities, the fewer artifacts may be needed to persuasively establish the genre. If few artifacts are available and they are difficult to acquire, readers may accept a critic's decision to examine fewer of them.

**Identifying Similarities**

Once the texts to be analyzed have been identified and located, the generic rhetorical critic must examine them carefully to identify rhetorical similarities. If the critic discovers seemingly important similarities in the texts under scrutiny, he or she should organize those commonalities and locate clear examples from the discourses that can be used to illustrate the features of the genre. For example, if I were to simply say that war speeches often include metaphors, that would not be as clear as if I gave examples of metaphors from such speeches.

It is possible that any randomly selected group of speeches will show similarities simply through the operation of coincidence. Most speeches are supposed to have introductions, main bodies, and conclusions, but that does not mean they all belong to the same genre. I suspect this may in part account for Campbell and Jamieson's statement that "a genre is composed of a constellation of recognizable forms bound together by an internal dynamic."[39] Harrell and Linkugel write about the "organizing principles found in recurring situations that generate discourse characterized by a family of common factors."[40] The point is that the common rhetorical features that are discovered through generic description must be explained by the genre's identifying feature (or internal dynamic or organizing principle). Consider again keynote speeches. These discourses are designed to encourage viewers to support the nominee; because of this, it makes perfect sense for a keynote to praise the party's nominee. Similarly, the two presidential nominees face off in the general election campaign, so it is reasonable for a keynote speaker to attack his or her nominee's opponent. Thus, the nature of the situation facing the rhetors who deliver keynote addresses can explain the presence of certain rhetorical features in those addresses.[41] This raises the question of subgenres. For example, would it be useful to distinguish between keynote speeches after a seriously contested nomination and keynote speeches to an essentially unified party?

### Explaining Observed Similarities

Because coincidental similarities are possible in rhetorical discourse, it is important to explain the similarities found in the rhetorical texts. Those who base genres on rhetors' purposes must be able to link those purposes to the common features of the rhetorical artifacts in those genres. For example, the similarities found in messages of redemption (following Kenneth Burke) should be related to that purpose.[42] We should be able to explain why common features of discourse that is designed to polarize[43] issues and ideas should be expected to occur in artifacts with that purpose. Rhetors who engage in rhetoric designed to agitate or control[44] should produce messages that can be better understood through a consideration of that purpose.

Those who base genres on the nature of groups of rhetors must be able to link the common rhetorical features to the character of those rhetors. For instance, we ought to be able to account for similarities in messages produced by rhetors with similar political beliefs (e.g., radical, liberal, conservative) by considering those beliefs.[45] If those who belong to the religious right[46] produce similar messages, the critic using the generic approach should be able to show how their political/religious beliefs explain the existence of those similarities. We might wonder again about the possibility of subgenres: Are Republican keynote speeches different from Democratic ones? Are eulogies delivered by men different from those given by women? Should the ethnicity of the rhetor be used as the basis for developing subgenres?

## GENERIC APPLICATION: A DEDUCTIVE APPROACH

The process of generic application can occur only after someone has already conceptualized a genre. Most commonly, genres would be developed through generic description: inductively describing the nature of a conceptually related group of speeches. However, it is possible that one could generate a generic description theoretically, rather than through an examination of instances of that genre. Regardless of how the genre was conceptualized, generic application includes three basic steps.

First, a genre must have already been described. The critic pursuing generic application must identify the nature of the genre ("keynote speeches") and then describe the salient features of that genre. What would discourses in the genre be likely to look like or to have in common? Second, an artifact that is a member of the genre is identified and shown to participate in, or belong to, the genre described in the first step. For example, one might choose to apply the genre of keynote speeches to Governor Chris Christie's or Mayor Julian Castro's 2012 keynote speech. In this step, the critic refers to the defining features of the genre (in this case, situational) and demonstrates that the new artifact belongs to the genre. This is an important step, because, as Robert C. Rowland correctly observes, "if a work is inappropriately placed in a given category the analysis of it inevitably will be flawed."[47]

Sometimes this step will be quite simple. If "keynote speeches" is considered to be a genre, it should be sufficient to note that the artifact under consideration is identified as one. In other cases it could require an argument. If the genre is defined by the rhetors' purposes, the critic may need to provide evidence of the rhetor's likely purpose in the new artifact. If the genre is defined by situation, it is possible that the critic may need to provide a rationale for the claim that the rhetor and/or the salient audience perceived the situation as the critic suggests. It must be clear to the reader of the rhetorical criticism that it is reasonable to view the new artifact as a member of the genre.

Finally, we are ready to begin making arguments about the "new" artifact based on the claim that it is a member of the genre. Here, evidence for these arguments can be based on the description of the genre as a standard for evaluation as well as on the message itself. It is possible to draw a variety of conclusions in a generic application. For example, the critic might measure the new artifact against the standards articulated in the genre: based on past examples, is the new artifact well or poorly conceived? Did the rhetor include the proper elements and were they developed effectively?

If the artifact shares the common features that comprise the genre, there is no problem for the critic. The "internal dynamic" explains why these features ought to occur in the kind of genre identified by the defining characteristics. Of course, if the new artifact follows the strictures of the genre but appears to have been a failure, the critic has some explaining to do. Even more complex is when the artifact violates the expectations established during the critic's initial description of the genre. What can the critic utilizing the generic approach conclude if the artifact does not conform to the characteristics of the genre? Although there can be numerous reasons that account for deviations from the genre, there are four that deserve special attention. First, it is possible that the "new" artifact does not really belong in the genre. The critic should make certain that the discourse being examined in fact fits the defining characteristics of the genre. It is conceivable that the critic may decide either that the artifact does not really belong in the genre after all or that the defining characteristics need to be revised.

Second, the artifact could be a **generic hybrid**,[48] which means it "belongs" to two genres at once. If so, it could contain some of the rhetorical features specified in each of the genres that contribute to the rhetorical hybrid. If the critic has reason to believe that this discourse is not unique, that other messages may well resemble this one, the critic may propose the existence of a hybrid.

Third, it is possible that the rhetor who created the artifact under examination made mistakes. Perhaps the rhetor did not understand the implications of the situation. Perhaps the rhetor did not examine previous artifacts or deliberately chose to ignore them. It is possible that the rhetor did not correctly analyze the audience or chose to ignore them. Perhaps the rhetor is creating discourse in order to further a purpose that is not really inherent in the situation. The critic using the generic approach, however, should make arguments about why the differences between the artifact and the common features of the genre were mistakes if that is the claim being advanced.

Fourth, it is also possible that the rhetor is experimenting and improving the genre rather than making errors. Rhetors may not yet have discovered the optimum discourse, and the rhetor being analyzed here may have developed an idea or ideas about how to invent a better discourse. Ironically, if the audience has developed expectations, it is possible that they will not like the changes even if a more objective analysis concludes that the changes made by the rhetor are improvements. Here again, if the rhetorical critic believes that the differences between the artifact and the common features of the genre are an improvement, the critic must explain why the changes should be considered improvements.

## POTENTIALS AND PITFALLS

Generic rhetorical criticism has many advantages. First, genre criticism is well designed for attempting to understand the nature of rhetorical practice. What do speeches announcing a war, or inaugural addresses, or diatribes, or resignation speeches look like? What features do they have in common and why should these commonalities exist? Generic description can help rhetorical theorists and practitioners alike. Furthermore, generic application can help rhetorical critics understand and evaluate new examples of speeches that belong to a given genre once generic description has occurred.

The rhetorical critic must keep in mind that the generic method offers advice on which speeches to study, but not on precisely how to study them. As I suggested before, another critic could look at inaugural addresses (or any other genre) looking for metaphors, narratives, or fantasy themes. Any particular method of rhetorical criticism can be used to guide the critic's analysis of the speeches in a genre.

One limitation of generic analysis is that the method lumps good messages with mediocre and bad ones.[49] The inductive method of generic description suggests that the critic locate a sufficient number of examples of the potential genre. It never suggests that the critic only examine successful messages or place the best texts in one subgrouping and the failures in another. As discussed in the preceding section, it is conceivable that a rhetor creating a keynote speech in the future could try something new, something better than any previous keynote. Unless we believe that the best possible examples of discourse in a genre have already been created, there is always room for improvement.

It can also be argued that generic rhetorical criticism ignores the nuances of individual rhetorical discourses. I feel that this criticism applies more to rhetorical criticism that focuses too heavily on description. By its very nature inductive generic description searches for commonalities among the instances of a genre, ignoring differences between individual discourses in that genre. Because the critic who is conducting generic description is attempting to discover what these texts have in common, the differences can be considered irrelevant. Of course, subsequent generic application should focus on the individual nuances of the specific instance of the genre under examination. For example, keynote speeches from 1960–1996 attacked in 48 percent of their utterances. But Barbara Jordan's Democratic keynote in 1976 contained only a single attack.[50] A critic using the deductive generic approach could argue that Jordan failed to include enough attacks on the opposing party. However, understanding the particular nuances of this speech might shed some light on her reluctance to attack. So, while generic description must by nature ignore the nuances of individual members of the genre, generic application can and should take particulars into account.

Generic rhetorical criticism takes advantage of the fact that, while no two discourses are identical, discourses do fall into groups or genres that have important similarities. Knowing the nature of these groups and their common rhetorical characteristics can be useful to rhetors, theorists, and practitioners alike. Of course, critics must never lose sight of the fact that there *are* differences even between members of the same genre, and critics must realize that genres can develop over time and potentially improve over past practice. Still, intelligent use of generic rhetorical criticism can provide powerful insights into the nature of rhetorical discourse.

## GENERIC RHETORICAL CRITICISM TOP PICKS

Benoit, William L., Joseph R. Blaney, and P. M. Pier. "Acclaiming, Attacking, and Defending: A Functional Analysis of Nominating Convention Keynote Speeches, 1960–1996." *Political Communication* 17 (2000): 61–84. This essay takes a more explicitly content analytic approach, but it is still concerned with identifying important common features of this message form.

Campbell, Karlyn K., and Kathleen H. Jamieson, eds. *Form and Genre: Shaping Rhetorical Action*. Falls Church, VA: Speech Communication Association, 1978. This volume pulls together essays from a diverse array of scholars addressing the nature of genre.

Clark, Thomas D. "An Analysis of Recurrent Features in Contemporary American Radical, Liberal, and Conservative Political Discourse." *Southern Speech Communication Journal* 44 (1979): 399–422. This essay is interesting because unlike most genre studies, Clark contrasts three different (although related) groups of discourse.

Condit, Celeste M. "The Function of Epideictic: The Boston Massacre Orations as Exemplar." *Communication Quarterly* 33, no. 4 (1985): 284–299. A classic treatment of a genre that is often overlooked.

Jamieson, Kathleen H., and Karlyn K. Campbell. "Rhetorical Hybrids: Fusions of Generic Elements," *Quarterly Journal of Speech* 68 (1982): 146–157. Genres are not always static. This essay discusses the merging of two genres into a single new genre.

Ware, B. L., and Wil A. Linkugel. "They Spoke in Defense of Themselves: On the Generic Criticism of *Apologia*." *Quarterly Journal of Speech* 59 (1973): 273–283. One of the earlier studies of genre and a classic treatment of the important genre of apologia.

## NOTES

1. William L. Benoit, Joseph R. Blaney, and P. M. Pier, "Acclaiming, Attacking, and Defending: A Functional Analysis of Nominating Convention Keynote Speeches, 1960–1996," *Political Communication* 17 (2000): 61–84. Such knowledge about keynote addresses has even made its way into assignments given in public speaking courses. See, David C. Deifel, "The Keynote Address and Its Occasion," *Communication Teacher* 21, no. 1 (2007): 1–5.

2. For rhetorical criticism of justifications of war, see Kathleen M. German, "Invoking the Glorious War: Framing the Persian Gulf Conflict through Directive Language," *Southern Communication Journal* 60 (1995): 292–302; Robert L. Ivie, "Presidential Motives for War," *Quarterly Journal of Speech* 60 (1974): 337–345; and Mary E. Stuckey, "Remembering the Future: Rhetorical Echoes of World War II and Vietnam in George Bush's Public Speech on the Gulf War," *Communication Studies* 42 (1992): 246–256.

3. Barack Obama, "Statement by the President on ISIL" (White House, September 10, 2014), http://www.whitehouse.gov/the-press-office/2014/09/10/statement-president-isil-1.

4. William L. Benoit, "In Defense of Generic Rhetorical Criticism: John H. Patton's 'Generic Criticism: Typology at an Inflated Price,'" *Rhetoric Society Quarterly* 10 (1980): 128–135.

5. Walter R. Fisher, "Genre: Concepts and Applications in Rhetorical Criticism," *Western Journal of Speech Communication* 44 (1980): 291.

6. Jackson Harrell and Wil A. Linkugel, "On Rhetorical Genre: An Organizing Perspective," *Philosophy & Rhetoric* 11 (1978): 263.

7. Thomas D. Clark, "An Analysis of Recurrent Features in Contemporary American Radical, Liberal, and Conservative Political Discourse," *Southern Speech Communication Journal* 44 (1979): 400–401.

8. William L. Benoit, William T. Wells, P. M. Pier, and Joseph R. Blaney, "Acclaiming, Attacking, and Defending in Nominating Convention Acceptance Addresses, 1960–96," *Quarterly Journal of Speech* 85 (1999): 247–267.

9. William L. Benoit, "The Functional Approach to Presidential Television Spots: Acclaiming, Attacking, Defending 1952–2000," *Communication Studies* 52 (2001): 109–126.

10. Malin Roitman, "Constructing One's Arguments Based on Refutations of the Other's Discourse. A Study of the Traditional Presidential Debate: Chirac/Jospin (1995) versus Sarkozy/Royal (2007)," *Argumentation* 29, no. 1 (2015): 19–32 (obviously a cross-cultural application); William L. Benoit and Allison Harthcock, "Functions of the Great Debates: Acclaims, Attacks, and Defense in the 1960 Presidential Debates," *Communication Monographs* 66 (1999): 341–357.

11. Bower Aly, "The Gallows Speech: A Lost Genre," *Southern Speech Journal* 34 (1969): 204–213; Karlyn K. Campbell and Kathleen H. Jamieson, "Inaugurating the Presidency," *Presidential Studies Quarterly* 15 (1985): 394–411; Halford R. Ryan, "Roosevelt's Fourth Inaugural Address: A Study of Its Composition," *Quarterly Journal of Speech* 67 (1981): 157–166. Other recent situational examples include Ryan Neville-Shepard, "Triumph in Defeat: The Genre of Third Party Presidential Concessions," *Communication Quarterly* 62, no. 2 (2014): 214–232; Mary Lay Schuster, Ann La Bree Russell, Dianne M Bartels, and Holli Kelly-Trombley, "Standing in Terri Schiavo's Shoes: The Role of Genre in End-of-Life Decision Making," *Technical Communication Quarterly* 22, no. 3 (2013): 195–218; Tess Slavíčková, "The Rhetoric of Remembrance: Presidential Memorial Day Speeches," *Discourse & Society* 24, no. 3 (2013): 361–379; and Tammy R. Vigil, "George W. Bush's First Three Inaugural Addresses: Testing the Utility of the Inaugural Genre," *Southern Communication Journal* 78, no. 5 (2013): 427–446.

12. Mike Duncan and Jillian Hill, "Termination Documentation," *Business Communication Quarterly* 77, no. 3 (2014): 297–311; John W. Bowers, Donovan J. Ochs, Richard J. Jensen, and David P. Schultz, *The Rhetoric of Agitation and Control*, 3rd ed. (Prospect Heights, IL: Waveland Press, 2009); A. Cheree Carlson and John E. Hocking, "Strategies of Redemption at the Vietnam Veterans' Memorial," *Western Journal of Speech Communication* 49 (1988): 14–26; Andrew A. King and Floyd D. Anderson, "Nixon, Agnew, and the 'Silent Majority': A Case Study in the Rhetoric of Polarization," *Western Speech* 35 (1971): 243–255; Richard D. Raum and James S. Measell, "Wallace and His Ways: A Study of the Rhetorical Genre of Polarization," *Central States Speech Journal* 25 (1971): 28–35.

13. Carolyn R. Miller and Jeanne Fahnestock, "Genres in Scientific and Technical Rhetoric," *Poroi: An Interdisciplinary Journal of Rhetorical Analysis & Invention* 9, no. 1 (2013): 2–4.

14. Karlyn K. Campbell, "Style and Content in the Rhetoric of Early Afro-American Feminists," *Quarterly Journal of Speech* 72 (1986): 434–445.

15. James Chesebro, "Rhetorical Strategies of the Radical-Revolutionary," *Today's Speech* 20 (1972): 37–48.

16. Thomas D. Clark, "An Exploration of Generic Aspects of Contemporary American Campaign Orations," *Central States Speech Journal* 30 (1979): 122–133.

17. Bernard K. Duffy, "The Anti-Humanist Rhetoric of the New Religious Right," *Southern Speech Communication Journal* 49 (1984): 339–360.

18. Dale G. Leathers, "Belief-Disbelief Systems: The Communicative Vacuum of the Radical Right," in *Explorations in Rhetorical Criticism*, ed. G. P. Mohrmann, Charles J. Stewart, and Donovan J. Ochs (University Park: Pennsylvania State University Press, 1973), 124–137.

19. Lotta Lehti, "Blogging Politics in Various Ways: A Typology of French Politicians' Blogs," *Journal of Pragmatics* 43, no. 6 (2011): 1610–1627.

20. Carl R. Burgchardt, "Two Faces of American Communism: Pamphlet Rhetoric of the Third Period and the Popular Front," *Quarterly Journal of Speech* 66 (1980): 375–391.

21. David A. Carter, "The Industrial Workers of the World and the Rhetoric of Song," *Quarterly Journal of Speech* 66 (1980): 365–374.

22. Aristotle, *The Rhetoric*, trans. W. Rhys Roberts (New York: Modern Library, 1954).

23. Edwin Black, *Rhetorical Criticism: A Study in Method* (1965; repr., University of Wisconsin Press, 1978), 133.

24. Ibid.

25. Ibid.

26. See Lloyd F. Bitzer, "The Rhetorical Situation," *Philosophy & Rhetoric* 1 (1968): 1–14; cf. William L. Benoit, "The Genesis of Rhetorical Action," *Southern Communication Journal* 59 (1994): 342–355; Lloyd F. Bitzer, "Functional Communication: A Situational Perspective," in *Rhetoric in Transition: Studies in the Nature and Uses of Rhetoric*, ed. Eugene E. White, 21–38 (University Park: Pennsylvania State University Press, 1980). For more on the rhetorical situation, see Marilyn J. Young, "Lloyd F. Bitzer: Rhetorical Situation, Public Knowledge, and Audience Dynamics," in *Twentieth-Century Roots of Rhetorical Studies*, ed. Jim A. Kuypers and Andrew King, 274–301 (Westport, CT: Praeger, 2001).

27. Harrell and Linkugel, "On Rhetorical Genre," 263–264, italics omitted.

28. Karlyn K. Campbell and Kathleen H. Jamieson, *Form and Genre: Shaping Rhetorical Action* (Falls Church, VA: Speech Communication Association, 1978), 20.

29. Situational factors and evidence from the text and rhetor can be used to make an argument about the rhetor's likely purpose.

30. Carolyn R. Miller, "Genre as Social Action," *Quarterly Journal of Speech* 70 (1984): 151.

31. Jamieson and Campbell, "Rhetorical Hybrids: Fusions of Generic Elements," *Quarterly Journal of Speech* 68 (1982): 147.

32. Bitzer, "The Rhetorical Situation."

33. Kenneth Burke, *Counter-Statement* (1931; repr., Berkeley: University of California Press, 1968); Kenneth Burke, "Dramatism," *International Encyclopedia of the Social Sciences* 7 (1968): 445–452; Kenneth Burke, *A Grammar of Motives* (1945; repr., Berkeley: University of California Press, 1969); Kenneth Burke, "Questions and Answers about the Pentad," *College Composition and Communication* 29 (1978): 330–335. See, too, vol. 1, no. 3, of the *American Communication Journal*. There you will find essays on each of the following topics: "motive," "sacrifice and moral hierarchy," "identification," "the pentad," and the cycle of "guilt, purification, and redemption." http://ac-journal.org/journal/vol1/iss3/curtain3.html.

34. William L. Benoit, "Beyond Genre Theory: The Genesis of Rhetorical Action," *Communication Monographs* 67 (2000): 178–192.

35. Howard W. Martin, "A Generic Exploration: Staged Withdrawal, the Rhetoric of Resignation," *Central States Speech Journal* 27 (1976): 247–257; Gerald L. Wilson, "A Strategy of Explanation: Richard M. Nixon's August 8, 1974, Resignation Address," *Communication Quarterly* 24 (1976): 14–20.

36. Harrell and Linkugel, "On Rhetorical Genre"; Robert C. Rowland "On Generic Categorization," *Communication Theory* 1 (1991): 143.

37. Jason Edwards, Joseph Valenzano, and Karla Stevenson, "The Peacekeeping Mission: Bringing Stability to a Chaotic Scene," *Communication Quarterly* 59, no. 3 (2011): 339–358.

38. Edward Shiappa and John P. Nordin, *Argumentation: Keeping Faith with Reason* (Boston, MA: Pearson, 2014); David L. Vancil, *Rhetoric and Argumentation* (Boston, MA: Allyn and Bacon, 1993).

39. Campbell and Jamieson, *Form and Genre*, 21.

40. Harrell and Linkugel, "On Rhetorical Genre," 263–264, italics omitted.

41. William L. Benoit and J. J. Gustainis, "An Analogic Analysis of the Keynote Addresses at the 1980 Presidential Nominating Conventions," *Speaker and Gavel* 24 (1986): 95–108.

42. Carlson and Hocking, "Strategies of Redemption."

43. King and Anderson, "Nixon, Agnew, and the 'Silent Majority'"; Raum and Measell, "Wallace and His Ways."

44. Bowers, Ochs, Jensen, and Schultz, *The Rhetoric of Agitation and Control*.

45. Chesebro, "Rhetorical Strategies"; Clark, "An Analysis of Recurrent Features"; Leathers, "Belief-Disbelief Systems."

46. Duffy, "The Anti-Humanist Rhetoric."
47. Robert C. Rowland, "On Generic Categorization," *Communication Theory* 1 (1991): 129.
48. Jamieson and Campbell, "Rhetorical Hybrids."
49. Benoit, "In Defense."
50. Benoit, Blaney, and Pier, "Acclaiming, Attacking, and Defending."

# 6

# On Objectivity and Politics in Criticism

*Edwin Black*

In his invitation to participate in this colloquium, the editor wrote, "These are opinion pieces, so it is your thoughts on these matters our readers will be interested in."

It is my thoughts that readers will be interested in? What a luxury! Does it mean that I don't have to be "objective"? That I can write whatever I please, without restraint, without discipline, without discretion? Well, not quite. I still want to avoid appearing to be an ass. And so, out of concern for my reputation (subjective), I will try to present something that will make sense to an intelligent reader (objective). Which, in turn, suggests that the polarities of subjective and objective are not always antithetical. Sometimes they may be complementary.

I can certainly understand how the issue of objectivity in criticism arises. Scientific inquiries always seek to minimize the influence of the investigator by their methods of research and their requirement of replicability. This quest for objectivity has become, along with other attributes of scientific inquiry, an intellectual standard that some people apply indiscriminately. It's a mistake. Objectivity is not universally desirable.

No one, to my knowledge, has represented criticism as scientific. At most (or least?), it has been characterized as "prescientific"—a condescending representation that assumes, quite gratuitously, that human mental activity is a pyramidal hierarchy with something called "science" hovering halo-like above its apex and a grotesquely conceived "criticism" buried somewhere in its nether region. The conception itself is prescientific in the historic sense in which anything medieval can be called prescientific.

If we want to know about criticism, we look to people who have practiced it, who have engaged its problems and have somehow resolved some of them in tangible acts of criticism. And what accomplished critic has ever claimed that criticism should only be objective? Criticism is not supposed to be always objective. It is, of course, supposed to be always intelligent. More to the point, it is supposed to be always fair. Sometimes fairness requires objectivity, and sometimes it doesn't. Therefore, the relationship between objectivity and criticism is not constant; it is variable.

---

This essay originally appeared in the *American Communication Journal* 4, no. 1 (Fall 2000). Reprinted with permission from the *American Communication Journal*.

In my use of the term *criticism*, I cannot extricate it from its origin in the Greek term *krisis*, which translates into "judgment." The critic exercises judgment. In fact, in Greek the term for "judge" and the term for "critic" were the same term. Let's play with that ambiguity a bit.

We do not demand that a judge in a courtroom be uniformly "objective." We demand that the judge be fair. If the judge's being fair requires, at some phase of the judicial process, neutrality or detachment or distance—all qualities associated with objectivity—then those are what we expect. On the other hand, if the judge's being fair requires, at some other phase, empathy or compassion or introspection—all qualities associated with subjectivity—then those are what we expect. What is important is that the judge be whatever is required for being fair. Exactly the same obtains with the critic.

Sometimes, at some stages of the critical process, it is important to be as objective as it is possible to be. There are critical problems that require for their solution a puritanical self-control—a disciplined indifference to one's own proclivities and one's own local conditions. That is especially true of rhetorical criticism, which can be at its most valuable when it focuses on odious rhetors—bigots, demagogues, habitual liars—the understanding of whom may require critics to suspend their repugnance temporarily and, for a period, try to see the world with the cold neutrality of a sociopath. But such acts of objectivity are only intermittent, and never an end in themselves.

Of course, the analogy between the critic and the courtroom judge can be taken only so far. A critic's being fair in criticism is not wholly the same as a judge's being fair in a courtroom. Conventional procedures of law prescribe to a considerable extent the claims and counterclaims to which a judge is obliged to attend in order to be fair. Such a prescriptive order is not available to the critic. The critic's procedures are, when at their best, original; they grow ad hoc from the critic's engagement with the artifact. And because the critic has to generate not only a judgment of the artifact, but also the procedure by which the judgment was reached—because, in short, the critic's responsibilities are legislative as well as judicial—the critic may have to be subjective more often than the judge in the court. That is because critics, unlike judges, cannot lay responsibility for their judgments on any code for which the critics themselves are not individually responsible.

The critic's subjectivity is also the consequence of the critic having no powers of enforcement. The critic cannot compel our compliance with the critic's judgment. The critic can only induce us, and therefore it is we, the readers of criticism, who demand the critic's compliance with certain of our expectations. We expect the critic to see things for us that we are unlikely to see for ourselves until the critic has called them to our attention. That means that we expect the critic to tell us things that we do not already know. Because the critic's perceptions are supposed to be valuable and uncommon (otherwise, why would we bother to read about them?), there is much in critical activity that ought to be subjective in the sense of being individual, novel, unconforming, sometimes even shocking.

So, far from encouraging critics to be objective all the time, I hold rather that a critic can be excessively objective. Indeed, excessive objectivity is a failure that occurs with unfortunate frequency in criticism.

Impersonal criticism is, by definition, objective. Objectivity, therefore, is manifested in more than just a passive facticity. Objectivity inheres in the substitution of any a priori method for the critic's own perceptions and judgments. It follows, then, that the application in criticism of a political or ideological program that is not the critic's own invention is an exercise in objectivity. And such exercises frequently display the deformities common to excessive objectivity in criticism, which are predictability and pedantry and wearisome uniformity. That is why excessively objective criticism—criticism that is without personality—is so repressive to write and so deadly to read.

Political judgments are certainly relevant to criticism, and political presuppositions are probably unavoidable in criticism. But politicized criticism—criticism that is in the service of an ideology—is another matter. The problem has been that so much of politicized criticism is heavy-handed and closed to discovery. The impetus of politicized criticism is to exploit its subject for the ratification of itself.

In 1844, Karl Marx said, "The essential sentiment of criticism is indignation; its essential activity is denunciation." Marx's view is reflected in much of the dyspeptic criticism written by his acolytes, even those who are many levels removed from the master: the echoes of echoes of echoes. A critical agenda that confines itself to indignant denunciation seems to me awfully constricted. Criticism has richer possibilities.

Good criticism is always a surprise. It is a surprise in the sense that you can't anticipate what a good critic will have to say about a given artifact.

I don't think that the expression of conventional opinions constitutes interesting criticism. By "conventional opinions" I mean to refer not just to the views of the Rotarian in Peoria; I mean to refer also to the pieties of any coterie whatever. The inventory of opinions that defines a political movement—no matter whether progressive or regressive, rational or psychotic, popular or insular—must become, at least to the adherents of that movement, conventional. It must in order to function as the ideological adhesion for a collective identity. Even anarchists have an orthodoxy.

Although it seems impossible for any of us to live a civic life without subscribing to some body of received doctrine, that doctrine, even if the critic conceives it vividly and believes it ardently, is not the stuff of enlightening criticism. Whatever its merits may be, it is derivative, and it intercedes between the critic and the object of criticism by effecting trite observations and stock responses in the critic.

T. S. Eliot wrote that "the readers of the *Boston Evening Transcript* sway in the wind, like a field of ripe corn." They're not the only ones. We all have episodes of marching in the parade or dancing in the chorus. It is gratifying sometimes to move in synchrony with others. But we just shouldn't try to be professional critics while we're in the ripe corn mode.

It seems to me reasonable to demand of any writer: surprise me. If the writer can't deliver, the writer can be dismissed, no matter whether what is written is critical or political or fictional or anything else. Note that the demand is not "please me"; nor is it "comfort me." It is not a demand for conformity to any sort of bias in the reader. It is simply a demand that a writer have something to say. And repeating the pieties of an ideology is not having something to say. I think it was Truman Capote who once said of a fellow novelist's work, "That isn't writing; that's typing." The same can be said of echoic ideologues.

So that these remarks are at least the semblance of an argument instead of being simple dogma, let me try to be clear about their premise. They are predicated on a proposition having to do with the relationship between criticism and its reader. The proposition is that although criticism is generically epideictic, since it engages in praise and blame, it is not functionally epideictic. That is, I am assuming that you do not read criticism solely in order to have your own opinions confirmed, but that you read criticism in order to be brought to see something that you hadn't noticed on your own. If, on the other hand, it is personal confirmation that you want—if you want to be reassured and to have your intellectual passions licensed—you don't then sit down and read criticism. You seek an epideictic occasion—some sort of rally or ceremony where co-believers can celebrate their articles of faith. Really good criticism is too singular to be confirmatory.

We don't want to read criticism that tells us nothing that we didn't already know. We don't want to read criticism that reiterates yet again what we have heard before.

Certainly there is nothing wrong with a critic's having political convictions. It is unavoidable. Only an idiot is without political convictions—in rare cases, maybe a holy idiot, but an idiot all the same. The very term *idiot* is from the Greek word for "nonpolitical person." We don't want to read rhetorical criticism written by an idiot, which really means that we don't want to read rhetorical criticism that has no political dimension to it. It may be possible to write apolitical but still luminous criticism of pure music or of nonrepresentational painting, but it is hard to imagine apolitical rhetorical criticism that isn't desiccated. So, yes, rhetorical criticism is likely to have a political dimension, and it ought to.

The inhibiting complication is that although the critic's political convictions may merit respect, they are not necessarily going to be any more interesting or intelligent or original than the general run of political convictions. Just being a critic doesn't qualify one to have anything to say about politics that has not already been said—and maybe better said—many times. So, I think that unless the critic has something fresh and knowledgeable to say, the critic should just shut up about politics. If the critic does that, then the political convictions of the critic will be presuppositional. That is, the critic will observe, judge, and argue from some political convictions rather than to them. The critic's politics will be implicit rather than explicit. Even so, the contours of the critic's political convictions will be clear enough from the criticism.

In the end, there are no formulas, no prescriptions, for criticism. The methods of rhetorical criticism need to be objective to the extent that, in any given critique, they could be explicated and warranted. But it is important that critical techniques also be subjective to the extent that they are not mechanistic, not autonomous, not disengaged from the critics who use them. The best critics have so thoroughly assimilated their methods that those methods have become their characteristic modes of perception.

The only instrument of good criticism is the critic. It is not any external perspective or procedure or ideology, but only the convictions, values, and learning of the critic, only the observational and interpretive powers of the critic. That is why criticism, notwithstanding its obligation to be objective at crucial moments, is yet deeply subjective. The method of rhetorical criticism is the critic.

# II
## PERSPECTIVES ON CRITICISM

# 7

# The Traditional Perspective

*Forbes I. Hill*

Traditional criticism, sometimes referred to as neo-Aristotelian criticism, is usually taken to mean criticism guided by the theory of rhetoric handed down from antiquity. Although this theory takes several different shapes and forms, they are mostly variations on a theme—that while rhetoric describes reality and does not create it, our perceptions of the real world can be changed by persuaders who insist that their own perceptions are more accurate or, at least, more advantageous to themselves or to the public interest. The tools for changing other peoples' understanding of reality are arguments that can be analyzed by a rhetorician; arguments are presented in language, which in most cases is believed to have more impact when it keeps perspicuity but is made attractive with artfully plotted phrasing. Normally the arguments are marshaled in a compelling order and presented to the listeners by speakers who have mastered the art of **paralinguistic features** (varying volume or rate of speaking, for example) and the art of **kinesics** (using the body to convey meanings and emotions). This is a pragmatic conception of rhetoric.

Some critics have used traditional theory to explain advertisements, propaganda, docudramas, and even novels and films, especially those with a covert propagandistic purpose. This is, of course, not a new idea. In the early 1920s, Hoyt Hopewell Hudson advocated broadening the paths of rhetorical study to include pamphleteering, newspapers, editorial writing, radio broadcasting, advertising, propaganda, and others.[1] In short, whenever there are direct attempts at persuasion, the traditional perspective may prove useful.

## TRADITIONAL CRITICISM

The **traditional perspective** assumes that criticism entails both explication of what went on when speakers engaged listeners or readers, and evaluation of how well the speakers performed the task of changing these receivers' understanding of reality. These twin tasks, explication and evaluation, together comprise the rhetorical critique. In its simplest form, it is a critique of the assumed interaction of a speaker with his audience or an author with his readers at a particular point in time. But in their more complex forms, rhetorical critiques may be used to explicate and evaluate the performance of several speakers or writers engaged in a campaign or perhaps a social movement, for example, a study of the changing rhetorical arguments in the campaign for abortion reform during the twentieth and early twenty-first centuries.

Aristotle, often considered the fount of traditional criticism, was no doubt thinking of the interaction of an individual with a particular audience when he set out the elements that we today use for analysis: "A discourse involves three factors: the speaker, the matter about which he speaks, and the persons to whom he is speaking."[2] If we add to this, as most rhetoricians do, the occasion on which the speech is given, it is still a simple plan for a critique. This plan may be made more inclusive by using slightly more complex terms that are near synonyms for the four factors. In place of the term *speaker*, for example, we often use *source*, by which is meant ghostwriter, public-relations agent, campaign committee, advertising team, and so on. In place of the matter about which one speaks, modern writers use the term *message*; that is, whatever matter is formulated for transmission to others. In place of persons who are addressed, we use *audience*. The audience is understood as the group of people who have similar reactions to the message, and in some modern cases these auditors are not even in the same space as the person presenting the message; they may be reading the message in a book or receiving it by television or podcast. For occasion the term *context* is now used. Traditional criticism is highly contextual; it looks at source, message, and audience as they interact within a given span of time.

Ultimately, the traditional perspective's "point of view," Herbert Wichelns wrote, "is patently single. It is not concerned with permanence, nor yet with beauty. It is concerned with effect. It regards a speech as a communication to a specific audience, and holds its business to be the analysis and appreciation of the orator's method of imparting his ideas to his hearers."[3] Even if we expand this notion of audience to include a number of related groups of people, targets of a persuasive campaign for example, we are still dealing with *effect*—that is, analysis and appreciation of the method used by strategists planning the campaign to impart their ideas to these people over this limited period of time.

Wichelns's concern with effect follows Aristotle's statement, "The audience is the end—the reason for making the discourse."[4] Aristotle believed that all natural activities are directed toward some end state: **telos** in his language; hence his philosophy is said to be teleological. He thought that the telos of any activity was its purpose for being and defined its essential nature. This orientation is basic to traditional criticism. Some utterances may be entirely self-expressive—crying "Ouch!" when one touches a hot stove, for example. Rhetorical utterances, however, are not primarily expressive; they are made holding in the forefront of one's mind the impact they will have on other people upon whom one seeks to impress one's ideas. They are the product of strategic choices about how the speaker wants auditors to respond.

An account of the audience logically comes first when one is composing a critique of a rhetorical event. Nevertheless, it is in practice difficult to start a highly contextualized critique such as the one a scholar writes without answering the question, When does this audience come into being and under what conditions? Reconstructing the audience is inseparable from determining the context of a rhetorical production.

What follows is an overview of how one might begin a criticism that uses the traditional perspective, although not all critical efforts of this nature follow this exact pattern. The majority of traditional critiques do, however, touch upon the following five areas: recreation of the context, recreation of the audience, description of the source of the message, analysis of the message, and evaluation of the discourse.

### Recreating the Context of Rhetorical Events

What is the context in which the speech occurred? Context is often divided into two parts: the physical setting for the event or events, the so-called mise-en-scène, and the social and political context out of which the need for using rhetoric arose. An oft-cited example in traditional criticism is Abraham Lincoln's Gettysburg Address. Why did President Lincoln go to speak at Gettysburg? One reason is that the State of Pennsylvania had planned a ceremony dedicating a cemetery right on the battlefield where many thousands had fallen. Near the field, but somewhat removed from the burial operations, a platform was erected on which sat numerous important political figures. The audience, numbering some twenty thousand, stood near rows of graves in the crisp November sun. Is this mise-en-scène important? Definitely so in this case. The fact that Lincoln was facing the field of battle and the graves is a controlling factor over the speech: "We are met on a great battlefield of that war; we have come to dedicate a portion of that field as a final resting place." Often, however, the setting is not so important. If a contemporary president makes a statement from a news studio in a large city, a description of the scenery may actually get in the way of creating an adequate critique. The studio might be anywhere; the important question, aside from whether or not he's in prime time, is what was the political situation that this administration thought required a presidential speech?

While the actual scene is often described, the social or political context must also be described. For example, Lincoln could have turned down the invitation to appear at Gettysburg. He was not the featured speaker; the ceremony was centered on a great oration to be delivered by another. Lincoln was in a busy period of his presidency, overwhelmed by the various duties of the office and by the cares of his family life. He chose to go to Gettysburg because of the importance of the occasion: it was the celebration of a battle where many lives had been lost. It was also an opportunity to make news in anticipation of the coming presidential campaign. But above all, it was time for him to put his spin on the significance of the war, to prepare for the postwar period of reconciliation. He dropped everything to take an exhausting train journey to the battlefield.[5] This is the political context of his speech.

For the critic, creating the political context is often a difficult task. Out of all the events in the life of the speaker and the history of the times, which are those that determine the rhetorical situation? Answering this question becomes even more difficult the further removed one's rhetorical artifact is from the present day. The critic simply cannot reproduce a complete account of an era as the jumping-off place for his critique. For example, it is obviously important to President Obama's "Statement by the President on ISIL"[6] that the terrorist organization ISIL had been growing in influence despite the president's policies and had recently taken control over approximately one-third of Iraq. However, is it also important that ISIL has links with al-Qaeda, and that they were not only murdering Christians but other Muslims, and that US strategic interests in the area (crude oil in particular) were in danger of being compromised? A narrative about all these factors could overwhelm a critic's account of the statement itself. The speech maker must make these decisions about inclusion; the critic then provides an evaluation. The effect various factors have on the message should usually be the principal criterion for their inclusion in the section of an essay that recreates the context.

### Constructing Audiences for Rhetorical Events

Those receiving a message are collectively known as the audience. Traditional rhetoric regards them as free agents who make largely rational choices about the matters at hand. Their choices are influenced by their emotional states but are not infinitely malleable. Traditional rhetoricians divide audiences into three kinds: either they are jurors in a court of law, who decide about a public or private action that took place in the past (**forensic discourse**), they are legislators who decide about some course of action to be taken in the future (**deliberative discourse**), or they are spectators who come to experience a celebration or commemoration of some person or event—that is, a ceremony in the present (**epideictic discourse**). Aristotle, at least, emphasized the audience's function as decision makers; even the auditors at a ceremonial speech, who primarily serve as spectators at a performance, in the final analysis are judges of the expedience and inexpedience of decisions made by those who are praised or blamed at the occasion.[7]

One must discover, then, which of these kinds of audience a speaker was asking to make a decision. Often this choice is obvious, as in the case of Roosevelt's War Message, which ends, "I ask that the Congress declare that since the unprovoked and dastardly attack by Japan on Sunday, December 7, 1941, a state of war has existed between the United States and the Empire of Japan." But what can be said of the Gettysburg Address? What decision did Lincoln expect his audience to make? To care about the honored dead? They already cared—cared enough to have come in most cases from far away. Even those who read his speech in the newspapers undoubtedly cared at a time when everyone had a relative who fought in the war.

Lincoln also recommended a course of action, that we "take increased devotion to the cause for which they gave their last full measure of devotion." Does this phrase's orientation to the future make the speech deliberative? After a careful examination of text and context, Garry Wills judged it to be a speech that changed people's attitude toward the war: no longer were they to be caught up in the blood and guts of the fray, or even the contentiousness that brought on the war. They were to transcend such matters, which go unmentioned in the address, and to see the war as a necessary phase in the nation's progress toward a more perfect union. If we accept this interpretation, then it is clearly a ceremonial speech. It does not aim at a decision about some imminent course of action. By praising the common sacrifice of all those who struggled in the Battle of Gettysburg, it aims to change people's whole belief system from one that dwells on the strife to one that is oriented to the making of peace. Use of praise and blame to forge the auditors into an audience that agrees on common values, such as peace and progress, is what ceremonial addresses are all about.[8]

The choice of the kind of audience at which the discourse is aimed is in this, as in other cases, not obvious. Making that choice requires careful examination of the text as well as the context. This examination is complicated when rhetorical productions are designed to change the perceptions and beliefs of more than one group of people, as is often the case in modern times. Take Ray Rice's May 23, 2014, speech of apology discussed in chapter 3. This speech addresses several distinct groups and is in response to numerous competing moral and social contexts. In antiquity one could conceive of the audience as those citizens in the popular assembly. With the advent of mass media and twenty-four-hour news coverage, however, the concern with audience takes on especial importance for the critic.

Back to Roosevelt's War Message. Ostensibly addressed to Congress, it was heard on the radio by over sixty million people, with even more reading it later (with a total population of 132 million at the time); its brevity and simplicity are a clue that it was intended to be a deliberative speech aimed at a decision by the larger audience of Americans. The War Message, heard in schools and churches and public buildings throughout the country, may have been one of the last speeches where members of the media audience were in contact with another. However, then as now, an address by a great public figure is heard by an audience totally fragmented—a collection of individuals. Does this make a difference? Traditional criticism seems forced to answer this question in the negative. Here is a rationalization for this position.

Any analysis of the audience is a construct. Let us say that a speaker's audience is the US House of Representatives: 435 members from fifty states. That is a diverse group, and even in the age of maximum information, one can hardly know empirically what the range of individual opinions is, especially since there are always some curmudgeons that defy classification. A rhetorical strategist needs to make a profile: most are not young, none are poor (the 2014 rank-and-file congressional salary is $174,000 per year—in the top 5 percent of the total *household* income bracket), almost all affect some kind of Judeo-Christian religious belief, almost all are committed Democrats or Republicans, most desire to be reelected, and none of them reveal the whole truth about themselves. This profile is based on a minimum of real data. It is what Aristotle would call *probability*, that is, what one would reasonably expect about people elected every two years as representatives. Since some improbable things actually happen, we also expect that several members do not fit the profile, but we ignore them. Given the right subject—for example, the war with Iraq—the Congress can be forged into something that approaches a unity; they can become a true audience. Approximately one year after 9/11, the House (296–133) and Senate (77–23) willingly voted to authorize President Bush to use US military force to make Iraq comply with UN resolutions.

Though the media audience is fragmented, can we construct it in the same way we constructed the Congress? We do have data about them: there are polls, both formal and informal, and sometimes focus groups. The polls are often broken down demographically; regions of the country are separated; the young are separated from those in their prime and the elderly, the wealthy from the middle class and the poor, women from men, whites from blacks, and blacks from Americans of Asian descent. Aristotle provides some probable statements characterizing these groups. He states that the young are sanguine and expect life to become better for them; the elderly are more skeptical, having often experienced failure. The wealthy expect to control affairs; the poor tend to expect disappointment.[9] Although Aristotle did not characterize women as distinct from men or take into consideration racial characteristics, modern pollsters do tabulate data for women and contrast it to that for men, and consider how the races differ on issues. Such hints about the ages and fortunes of people provide us with materials to refine polling questions and to better interpret polling data.

From polling data and Aristotle's character sketches, a critic can construct a profile of the fragmented media audience. The profile, if carefully made, will probably be nearly as accurate as one's profile of a divided Congress. The critic operating from a traditional perspective should search biographies and accounts of journalists to find out how the speaker conceived of the audience so that he can contrast the speaker's construction with potentially more accurate ones.

### Describing the Source of the Message

Traditional rhetoricians have historically thought about the source as a singular person—an orator skilled in the art of speaking. The roster of speakers who fulfilled that vision is almost, but not quite, congruent with the list of great statesmen. Most orators wrote their own speeches, perhaps with a little editorial help. From this point of view it makes sense to ask questions such as, What was the nature of the orator's unique personal charm? What was his education? What were the orator's peculiar qualifications as thinker and stylist? What obstacles did the orator overcome on the road to rhetorical celebrity? Such questions are the stuff of rhetorical biography. It is still a pleasure to read a short biographical essay—one that touches the peaks of a man or a woman's speaking career, say a Bernie Sanders or a Sarah Palin. When done well, it makes the reader consider himself a close watcher of a great career.

Historical figures may still be treated this way. Imagine a retrospective of Franklin D. Roosevelt: his home schooling directed by an imperious mother, his editorship of the *Harvard Crimson*, his mediocre performance in law school, his dashing entrance into politics, his marriage to the woman who became a truly remarkable public figure in her own right, his overcoming a crippling illness to reestablish an impossible political career, his use of that remarkable voice to compensate for an inability to move around the platform, his discovery of radio, his adventurous spirit, and yes, his confidence that bordered on arrogance, making him at times a divisive figure. Such an essay can never go out of date.

As exciting as a rhetorical biography can be, though, it is only a small part of a traditional critique. In recent times a speaker is likely to serve as a spokesman for an organization: he is a cabinet member or public-relations officer of an agency or corporation. The message he delivers is not his own; even if the speaker drafted it, numerous others in the organization have edited it and revised to the point where it has become a car put together by a committee. Take the March 25, 2015, comments made by incoming White House communications director Jen Psaki. She spoke on Fox News's *The Kelly File*. Host Megyn Kelly asked Psaki if trading Sgt. Bowe Bergdahl for five Taliban terrorists last year was "worth it" given the army's recently announced desertion charges against Bergdahl. Psaki replied, "Was it worth it? Absolutely. . . . We have a commitment to our men and women serving in the military, defending our national security every day, that we're going to do everything to bring them home if we can, and that's what we did in this case."[10] Psaki was speaking for President Obama and his administration, not for herself.[11]

Under these circumstances it no longer makes sense to ask about the speaker's education, or his unique language choices. The question is, what kind of a committee of writers put together the message? What interests did they represent? For a president, this often means State versus Defense, for example. How did the writers work together and interface with the spokesman? What does the text show about how they built a favorable public image for the spokesman? How did committee and spokesman construe what would build credibility? Covering factors such as these is what we now mean by describing the source. Additionally, it is still relevant to ask, did the spokesman deliver the message with conviction? With a flair? Did he show great energy? Was he serious or lighthearted? Did he dominate the audience and seem to reach into their hearts? Appropriate delivery is itself a source of credibility.

**Analyzing the Message**

The traditional perspective begins its consideration of the message by asking about the text—a written document that recreates what a speaker said to that audience on that particular occasion. If one is going to consider questions of proof or of rhetorical style, it is desirable to have an accurate account of the verbal utterance of the moment, or at least of what the author intended a reader to read.

Often a good text is available; some independent agent has made an audio or video recording. We should be alert if the recording or document is available only from the source. Texts are often edited; it is well attested that congressmen may revise the Congressional Record at any time until the printing presses start to move. Often a speaker will be asked to write out his remarks for publication after the presentation. The importance of finding a reliable text is well exemplified by this example: the text published by the *Boston Globe* of Professor George Wald's signature utterance, "A Generation in Search of a Future," furnished to the newspaper by the speaker does not contain the lines italicized here:

> Nobody is the aggressor any more except those on the other side. *And this is why that, that Neanderthal among Secretaries of State—Rusk—went to such [applause]—went to such pains, went to such pains, stuck by his guns, because in him, uhh, stubbornness and density take the place of character, [laughter] uhh, went to such pains to insist as he still insists that in Vietnam we are repelling an aggression. And if you're repelling an aggression, anything goes.*

This characterization of Dean Rusk is grotesquely unfair; he never held that if you are repelling an aggression, anything goes, and he did not resemble Neanderthal man. Professor Wald apparently had second thoughts when he edited this passage out of the version he gave the press. The independent recording put out by Caedmon Records gives what he said unedited.[12] It also shows why the unedited version is important: Wald received by far the most vociferous reaction to these statements of anything else in his speech. They resonated wildly with an audience of 1960s radicals who were united in their hatred of established authority figures such as the secretary of state. What you know from other sources about Wald's audience is amply confirmed.

The further back one goes in history the more difficult the problem. The text of the Attic orations derives from copies made by the orators as examples for use in the schools of rhetoric. Naturally the orators transmitted to the schools only the fairest texts of what they said. Speeches in the eighteenth- and early nineteenth-century House of Commons and House of Lords were mostly recreated by reporters who stood closely packed in the galleries, where they were not supposed to make transcriptions of the proceedings. The Lincoln-Douglas debates were collated from newspaper reports by Lincoln; it is small wonder that his speeches look more finished in the received text than Douglas's. The traditional critic will often need to make a caveat about most speeches: "I don't vouch for every word of the text; I worked with the best text available."

The traditional perspective considers the message itself under the headings of *invention*, *disposition*, and *style*. By **invention** is meant the finding of appropriate materials for the discourse. This is usually done by checking through an inventory of stock materials—**topics** or topoi—looking to see whether the speaker has used all available means of persuasion, as Aristotle put it. Topical thinking is a type of systematic brainstorming using predefined categories. Although developed in ancient times, more recent applications are available. For example, John Wilson and Carroll Arnold developed sixteen topics for the contemporary student. These include the "existence or nonexistence of things"; "degree or quantity of things, forces, etc."; spatial attributes"; "attributes of time"; "motion or activity"; and "form, either physical or abstract."[13] By **disposition** is meant the arranging of these materials in a structure as well plotted as the order of battle when skilled generals make a plan for victory. Structure can be influenced by many factors, although it is generally agreed upon that your audience, topic, and purpose play a deciding role. By **style** is meant the use of the right language to make the materials of exposition and argument clear and convincing. We will now consider each of these in turn.

*Invention*

When a critic seeks to investigate invention, he is dealing with both artistic and inartistic proofs. **Artistic proofs** are the invented proofs. They are created by the speaker, the arguments that he uses to try to persuade the audience. They are usually, if somewhat inaccurately, grouped under the headings of logos, ethos, and pathos. **Inartistic proofs** are not created by the speaker but instead exist on their own: contracts, wills, or other documents, for example.

In relation to *logos*, the critic should look to see whether the appropriate commonplace arguments, deduced from the list of topics, have been used. **Logos** refers in general to logic based on reason. This is not a scientific logic, but rather a rhetorical logic, one based on probability. Those creating arguments need to construct them based on common notions of what is probable. To prosecute a company for spreading toxic waste, one looks for the green water and brown air in the neighborhood; the prosecutor seeks out people who claim to be sick and compares them to those in comparable areas who are not sick. He points to the prevalence of cost cutting among companies who look at the bottom line, the absence of witnesses and regulators, and the arrogant behavior of company executives. These are the commonplaces of environmental claims, and failure to use them should be construed as not making the most effective speech possible. A critic would look for such commonplaces.

Although there are many ways to examine the logic used in a speech, one particularly important aspect to be examined is the concept of the enthymeme. The essence of the **enthymeme** is that some parts of the logical argument are omitted when the speaker or writer can predict that the auditors will supply them. Take this example from Richard Nixon: "The American people cannot and should not be asked to support a policy which involves the overriding issues of war and peace unless they know the truth about that policy. Tonight I would like to answer some of the questions that I know are on the minds of many of you listening to me."[14]

This is a typical example of an enthymeme that builds the speaker's credibility and that also requires the listener/reader's participation in supplying a crucial missing term. Presented as a traditional **syllogism**, it would look like this:

Premise 1: All policies that the American people should be asked to support are policies about which they will know the truth.
Premise 2: The policies which I reveal when I answer your questions are policies that the American people should be asked to support.
Conclusion: The policies which I reveal when I answer your questions are policies about which you will know the truth.

Nixon's actual statement is making the claim that he will tell the truth about his policies. He says that the American people should not be asked to support his policies unless they know the truth about them. Although I supplied all three parts of the syllogism, Nixon never actually explicitly claims that he is going to tell the truth. The second premise I give is actually not stated by Nixon; rather, one is tempted to supply it in one's own mind, and if the listener supplies it, the very activity of completing the logical structure starts the process of the listener assenting to the argument. As Lloyd Bitzer wrote, "Enthymemes occur only when speaker and audience jointly produce them. . . . Because they are jointly produced, enthymemes intimately unite speaker and audience and provide the strongest possible proofs."[15] This process will be completed unless the auditor checks himself and looks at it. He is more likely to yield to the process because the formal logic behind this argument is good enough, though the second premise is unsupported and probably false.

Persuasive discourse is constructed so that there are usually a large number of ethos claims. **Ethos** is basically an interpretation by the audience of qualities possessed by a speaker as the speaker delivers his message. Thus, by the way a speaker argues, an audience makes judgments about his intelligence, character, and goodwill. A speaker becomes unpersuasive if he has to claim directly, "I did not have sexual relations with that woman" (Bill Clinton) or "I'm honest in my dealings with people" (Mitt Romney). If he needs to state it in this bald way, he has already lost credibility. An exposition of how a speaker establishes ethos is a significant part of a traditional critique. Sometimes the discourse will contain a narrative of the discovery of the right course of action. Such a narrative shows the good sense of the spokesman and his advisers, who did not make decisions off the top of their heads, but only after consideration and reflection. The way in which a speaker supports his arguments and organizes his materials can impact the assessment of his intelligence. Very often his character—moral qualities—can be assessed by how qualities such as justice, courage, generosity, and so on are exhibited in his arguments.

Finally, a speaker could also show goodwill by finding common ground with the readers/listeners. The speaker who comes to campus tells us, "I remember when I was a student; like so many of you I didn't have enough time in the day to do everything. I worked part time in the dining room and stole away to the quietest corner of the library every night. But hard as that was, it was worth it." Speakers also indulge in a little subtle flattery: "You who have a university education easily recognize that group behavior differs from individual behavior." Commenting on such statements is part of a traditional critique as it relates to ethos.

The first step in dealing with **pathos** in the critique is identifying the emotional states that dominate the discourse. The speaker's words will *invite* us to feel a particular way. Sometimes this is obvious. In the case of Roosevelt's War Message, the emotional states are anger and confidence. The anger springs from our sense of betrayal by an inferior people from whom we are entitled to receive respect. The confidence comes from our feeling of unity and our sense of righteousness. Roosevelt amplified the sneakiness of the attack and the innocent lives lost to bring people into a greater state of anger, and he represented himself as speaking for all our people, who recognize the facts of Japanese aggression, which are so obvious that they speak for themselves. When auditors are angry enough, they minimize feelings of fear; they become ready to accept with confidence hardships and sacrifices: hence the above listed *pathe* are the stuff of war messages.

Another example is seen in the commercials for the Christian Children's Fund. These commercials begin with images of children in truly impoverished conditions. Many of the children are shown playing in what might be raw waste and garbage; many have flies around their eyes and walk with distended bellies. This is quickly contrasted with images of those children helped by this charity: better clothing, healthier looking, and so forth. All this in the background reinforces the same verbal message by the speaker. Your emotional register goes from pity and perhaps guilt to hope. A critic would look for these emotional appeals and determine their effectiveness in moving us along toward doing whatever it is the speaker wishes us to do: in the case of the Christian Children's Fund, sponsor a child.[16] Not all appeals to emotion will be so easy to detect; the critic must step back and carefully look for these.

*Disposition*

The critic must also ferret out disposition, or the speech's organization *as it relates to persuasion*. In almost no case is a discourse arranged randomly, though occasionally a speechwriter will try to make it appear random. Roosevelt's War Message, Stelzner points out, falls almost into two halves, separated by the sentence, "As Commander in Chief of the Army and Navy

I have directed that all measures be taken for our defense." All material prior to that sentence is in the past tense and the Japanese Empire is the actor. What follows that sentence is in the present tense; the president, Congress, and the people become the actors.[17] Such is the disposition of this celebrated speech.

Take Lincoln's address at Cooper Union for another example; it divides into three parts: first a forensic section in which the speaker refutes the belief that Congress could not constitutionally legislate as to slavery in the federal territories; then a shorter constructive section on the idea that Republicans are the ones who perpetuate the constitutional doctrines of the Founding Fathers, and it's the Southerners who have made a radical change; and then the shortest section, a little deliberative speech to Republicans exhorting them to act with restraint while refusing to compromise their basic ideals. From accusation to constructive defense to exhortation (in long, shorter, and shortest sections) is the pattern for disposition in the Cooper Union Address. There ought to be some discernible rationale, as in the cases cited, for the disposition of the materials of the discourse. It is the task of the critic to figure out that rationale.

## Style

Traditional criticism treats the style of the discourse as part of the persuasive force of the arguments. Style must be, however, both appropriate to subject and audience. In most cases clarity is assumed as the cardinal virtue of style. Clarity is achieved with factors such as using common words, avoiding jargon, creating metaphors that make matters vivid, using active verbs, and avoiding more than the minimum of adjectives. The speaker who uses such locutions as "the optimum moment of contact" is probably not persuading as well as one who says "timing's important; there's a right moment for everything." That is, of course, unless the audience is composed of those predisposed to accept a specific technical vocabulary. When Thomas Paine refutes the argument that America has flourished under her former connection with Great Britain by writing, "We may as well assert that because a child has thrived upon milk that it is never to have meat," he chooses a metaphor that is both concrete and familiar.[18] Observations of this sort are the meat of traditional criticism in relation to clarity of style.

Yet working against this preference for the unmodified common word is the notion that style should make an impression—that statements should have a certain heft to give an idea presence. That is also a precept of traditional rhetoric; the style of public address is never colloquial, though it may be deliberately kept simple. So the speechwriter is to make a certain admixture of long words and a few unusual ones; he is occasionally to look for a unique way of phrasing something even amid the clichés.

Clarity and impressiveness are also to be gained from figures of syntax: parallel structure of clauses and sentences and the devices that reinforce it. When Lincoln declaimed, "Fondly do we hope, fervently do we pray that this mighty scourge of war may speedily pass away," he created a syntactical structure that speaks seriously; it is hard, however, to sing it to a merry tune. The contrast of hope and pray (antithesis) would be entirely broken up if he had said, "Fondly do we hope and we also pray fervently." *Fondly* and *fervently*, too, must be in the same grammatical position in each clause; then the alliteration works to reinforce the structure. The rhyming of *pray* and *away* (epistrophe) is also important to the structure. Traditional rhetoric views this artistry in structuring prose as a significant part of rhetorical effectiveness. These rhetorical figures of speech are more than window dressing; they are an important part of the persuasive process.

*Summary*

When looking at the message, a critic will look to see whether the discourse is deliberative, forensic, or epideictic. Deliberative discourse is concerned with the future, and its auditors are asked to make judgments about future courses of action. Forensic discourse is concerned with past acts, and its auditors are asked to make judgments concerning what actually happened in the past. Epideictic discourse is set in the present and concerns speeches of praise or blame. Its auditors are being asked to make judgments concerning how well the speaker accomplishes his goals.

Generally a critic looks for three items in a text: invention, disposition, and style. Under invention, a critic looks to see how well the speaker created his rhetorical appeals: were all the available means of persuasion used? Both artistic—logos, ethos, and pathos—and inartistic proofs will be examined. A critic will also look hard at the disposition or organization of a speech to determine its impact upon persuasive effect. Finally, a critic will look at the style of the speech. How might the language choices made impact the persuasive effort?

## Evaluating the Discourse

Aristotle lays down the rule that a discourse should be judged by whether it uses sound method: "it is not the function of rhetoric to persuade but to observe the available means of persuasion for situations like this one, just as in all the other arts. For example, the function of medicine is not to make healthy, but to bring the patient as far toward health as the case permits. For sometimes it is impossible to bring health, but one must give sound treatment."[19]

If he follows this rule, the critic goes through a checklist of the available lines of argument to see if any are omitted that might persuade this audience on this subject; he considers the possible ways of disposing the narrative and arguments to see if the best way has been used; he looks at the stylistic devices that clothe the arguments to see if there are others more appropriate to the situation. If everything is done, he is ready to render a judgment: this must be the best discourse—or possibly it falls short in some of the ways described below. Regardless, there is a certain concern with the aesthetics involved with the speech-making process: How well were the arguments constructed? Was the message well organized? And was the style used appropriate for the specific audience?

In practice, almost no critic is wholly satisfied with this kind of purely internal critique. Almost invariably critics add some kind of external measure. The legislature did not pass the bill. The jury did not convict. The voters did not elect the candidate. The president gave a speech on the economy, and the stock market rose or fell. These *effects* are the simplest indicators of success, but we know that they are often misleading. Sometimes legislators have commitments that make it impossible for them to respond even to the most finely crafted speech. Some juries will nullify the law because of their sympathy for the defendant even though the presentation of the case has been artistically satisfactory.

We may look to somewhat more indirect measures as well. The legislature took up the bill next session or the one after and, without much additional debate, passed it. The jury did not convict, but all the editorial writers agreed that they should have. The stock market immediately reacted like a bear to the president, but two weeks later the bull market began, and it ran a long course. Take, for example, Susan B. Anthony, who was the center of controversy throughout most of her life but never lived to see woman's suffrage. When the suffrage amendment finally passed, she was honored as the ancestor of all suffragettes. These historical results are, perhaps, more just indications of the success or failure of a persuasive campaign than a decision made in the midst of the struggle. George Orwell's critique of the totalitarian tendencies of the modern state did not result in the overthrow of any totalitarians, but it has become a standard against which states are judged; the use of Orwellian language is almost universally taken as the sign of approaching danger.

Thus a critic using the traditional perspective will discuss the speech's internal dynamics, but also touch upon its impact on its audience. Rhetoric, viewed from a traditional perspective, is used for a purpose, it is intentionally created, and this is taken into consideration when a critic offers an evaluation. A thoughtful discussion of the historical context and some speculation on the influence of the discourse forms the conclusion of a traditional critique.

## CRITICAL ESSAY

Much of the writings of those who have used traditional criticism have assumed a general knowledge concerning the classical roots of the rhetorical theory that underpinned the criticism. The essay that follows proceeds along the same path. Instead of a fully developed review of the literature, this essay instead focuses on putting into practice traditional criticism as outlined above. You should be aware, however, that if you are writing for an academic audience you most likely will need to take time to define your terms and outline your theoretical perspective.

When reading this essay, look for the reconstruction of context, the construction of audience, a discussion of the source (speaker), and an analysis of the message (look in particular for a discussion of invention, disposition, and style). Finally, look for an evaluation of the rhetorical artifact.

---

### MR. DOUGLASS'S FIFTH OF JULY

Following the Compromise of 1850 the abolitionist movement, somewhat dispirited by the failure to block the Fugitive Slave Law, renewed its efforts to publicize the evils of slavery. In Rochester, New York, which was a center of anti-slavery activity, the Rochester Ladies Anti-Slavery Society decided to mark Independence Day1852 with their own celebration featuring an address by their neighbor, the famous abolitionist speaker, Frederick Douglass. The celebration was held on July 5th since the 4th fell on a Sunday, and the custom of that era prohibited secular events on the Sabbath.

The Rochester Ladies rented Corinthian Hall, where five to six hundred people assembled, having paid 12 cents each as entry fee.[20] After the opening prayer and a reading of the Declaration of Independence, Mr. Douglass made his presentation: "What, to the Slave, is the Fourth of July?" His recitation, according to Frederick Douglass's paper, was "eloquent and admirable, eliciting much applause throughout." Before the meeting was adjourned, "A Request was . . . made that the Address be published in pamphlet form, and seven hundred copies were subscribed on the spot." It was also published in Frederick Douglass's paper on July 9 and many times subsequently. Perhaps we should now consider it an American classic. It is especially appropriate to make a critique like this using the standards of traditional rhetoric because Mr. Douglass and many in his audience were familiar with these standards.

### The Audience

In constructing Douglass's audience, let us first ask, who is to make a decision about what? Those immediately before the speaker were abolitionists, their sympathizers, and their friends.

Many of them were followers of William Lloyd Garrison, with whom Douglass had recently made a rancorous break. Douglass demanded that they condemn slavery—not just in an intellectual way, but with an emotional fierceness that would keep them agitated until it was abolished. What the audience might have expected on the Fourth of July was a speech praising our ancestors, our country, and our people. In an astonishing reversal Douglass gives them a discourse of uninterrupted blame: a true epideictic speech of vituperation.

If the audience before him consisted of anti-slavery zealots, it was nevertheless not of one mind about how slavery was to be ended. A special group of auditors were strict Garrisonians, who believed that the Constitution supported slavery, and since it did, it should be wiped away, and a new Republic without the South should be established to avoid any contact with the evil of slavery. Others present took a more centrist position, and some may have been opponents of slavery only in the sense that they thought it an evil whose spread should be prevented. The auditors were united enough in their anti-slavery sentiments that Douglass could give a speech so critical of the Republic that no patriot would sit still for it. A different audience, even in the North, might have driven him from the platform.

But what of the reading public, the ones who got the speech from the papers and pamphlets? At first the address was carried only by the abolitionist papers; there Douglass could be assured of a favorable response. Soon it was published as a pamphlet, probably circulated mostly to abolitionists and those to whom they were proselytizing. The pamphlet certainly had no circulation in the South. Three years later an extract containing the most impassioned parts of the Fifth of July oration was made an appendix to Douglass's second autobiography, *My Bondage and My Freedom*. In this form it enjoyed a national circulation. A measure of acceptance by the larger audience was guaranteed by the indubitable fact: the American Revolution did not bring freedom to the slave. On the other hand, there must have been an ample number of readers irritated by the insult to our great national holiday. We can reasonably conclude that the oration aimed at energizing the friendly rather than converting the hostile.

## The Spokesman

By 1852 Frederick Douglass was well known as a speaker: he had traveled throughout the northeast and the middle states as a full-time agitator for the Massachusetts Anti Slavery Society from 1841 to 1845. Born in 1817, he spent the first twenty-one years of life as a slave. Nevertheless, he learned to read and write as a child. In his autobiographies he tells the story of getting an important book, *The Columbian Orator*, used in the schools as a source of precepts exemplified by extracts from speeches and dramas. In 1838 he escaped from the plantation, making his way north to Massachusetts. He changed his name from Frederick Augustus Washington Bailey, but after publication of the first autobiography, *Narrative of the Life of Frederick Douglass, an American Slave*, his cover was blown; he could have been arrested as an escaped slave. He fled to England, where he lectured on temperance and abolition until his freedom was bought from his old master in 1847. In England he became the most glamorous spokesman for the anti-slavery cause; the one who spoke from firsthand experience and with great fervor and eloquence. On his return, "a series of enthusiastic reception meetings was held to honor him; he completely dominated the annual meeting of the American Anti-Slavery Society, held on May 11, 1847; and two weeks later his co-workers installed him into the Garrisonian establishment by electing him president of The New England Anti-Slavery Society."[21]

The sponsors of the Fourth of July celebration in 1852 knew what they were doing when they made Frederick Douglass their main speaker. He was at the height of his oratorical powers in 1852, a physically impressive figure, obviously strong and vital with a large head of hair, not yet gray, and a resonant baritone voice. He could be counted on to give a good show, as he had many times before. It hardly needs to be said that the whole ceremony was built around that good show the orator was expected to give. In the nineteenth century, as Garry Wills has remarked, the orator at a public celebration was intended to be a virtuoso performer who presented a long speech replete with rhetorical flourishes. Anything less would disappoint the people who came to celebrate.[22] Douglass was conscious of his obligation to perform: "I have been engaged in writing a Speech," he wrote Gerrit Smith after the fact, "for the 4th. July, which has taken up much of my extra time for the last two or three weeks. You will readily think that the Speech ought to be good that has required so much time."[23]

## Disposition and Summary of the Speech

Douglass's **exordium** is given over to a conventional expression of modesty: "He who could address this audience without a quailing sensation, has stronger nerves than I have. I do not remember ever to have appeared as a speaker before any assembly more shrinkingly, nor with greater distrust of my ability, than I do this day." In this case, as in most such expressions in 18th and 19th century orations such expressions must be taken ironically. The speaker could not have failed to know that he was among the dozen most celebrated orators of his time.

Douglass organized the central section of this address on the principle of contrast between *then* and *now*. The first third of this section consists of conventional praise for what happened in the past. He does what any 4th of July orator would be expected to do: celebrate the birth of the nation. This occasion is to you "what the Passover was to the emancipated people of God." It is "easy now to flippantly descant on how America was right and England wrong, but when your fathers first talked this way, they were accounted plotters of mischief, agitators and rebels, dangerous men." They petitioned the Throne, but the British government kept its course, with "the blindness which seems to be the unvarying characteristic of tyrants since Pharaoh and his hosts were drowned in the Red Sea." One can view this section like a classicist, as an historical narration; or one may see it as the first part of the section that is usually called the proof (which follows naturally assertions). In either case, the reason for praising the courage of the Fathers is to prepare for a contrast with contemporary politicians, and the reference to the Passover and to Pharaoh is meant to cue us to the denunciation of slavery to come. Typically in conventional speeches these historical narrations are used for foreshadowing.

Suddenly Douglass switches gears: he no longer speaks about then but now and announces his subject: "AMERICAN SLAVERY." He identifies himself as a speaker for the bondman, who knows that America is false to the past, false to the present, and solemnly binds herself to be false to the future. "What have I, or those I represent, to do with your independence. . . . The sunlight that brought life and healing to you has brought stripes and death to me. This Fourth is yours not mine. You may rejoice; I must mourn. . . . I do not hesitate to declare, with all my soul, that the character and conduct of this nation never looked blacker to me than on this 4th of July!" The rest of the proof is taken up by a development of the blackness of character and conduct of the nation. The arguments used to justify slavery are mere rationalizations, not even worthy of serious refutation. He makes outstanding use of the stylistic figure *paralepsis*, claiming not to be refuting these arguments, while in fact making a summary refutation of each.

"Must I undertake to prove that the slave is a man? Of course not; it is beyond doubt: you hold him responsible for crimes like other humans. Laws in most Southern states forbid teaching him to read. No one makes such laws about the beasts of the field. When the dogs in your streets, when the fowls of the air, when the cattle on your hills, when the fish of the sea and the reptiles that crawl shall be unable to distinguish the slave from a brute, then will I argue with you that the slave is a man!" He claims not to make the arguments that he has made. Is not man entitled to liberty? That's not a matter to be debated by Republicans, to be settled by logic and argumentation. "How should I look today, in the presence of Americans, dividing and subdividing a discourse, to show that men have a natural right to freedom?" Douglass concludes that he cannot argue this (though he has) because: "There is not a man beneath the canopy of heaven who does not know that slavery is wrong for him."

Is it not wrong "to make men brutes, to rob them of their liberty, to work them without wages, to keep them ignorant of their relations to their fellow men, to beat them with sticks, to flay their flesh with the lash, to load their limbs with irons, to hunt them with dogs, to sell them at auction, to sunder their families, to knock out their teeth, to burn their flesh, to starve them into obedience and submission to their masters?" Such a system is obviously wrong; "I have better employments for my time and strength than such arguments would imply," Douglass avers, but, of course his list of these oppressions of slavery has made the strongest of arguments.

Is slavery sanctioned by God? "There is blasphemy in the thought. That which is inhuman cannot be divine! Who can reason on such a proposition? They that can, may: I cannot." But he *has* reasoned. Thus with repeated paralepsis, Douglass minimizes the justifications for slavery into insignificance. He concludes his refutation, "What to the American slave is your 4th of July?" A day which reveals to him, more than all other days, the gross injustice and cruelty to which he is the constant victim. The extent of the gross injustice and cruelty is now to be exemplified through several examples.

There is the internal slave trade, thought somehow to be more respectable than the African slave trade. Douglass uses his unique ethos; he claims to have been born amid the sights and scenes of the trade. He lived in Baltimore near the market. After the auction the flesh-mongers gathered up their victims by dozens and drove them in chains to the general depot. A ship had been chartered to convey the forlorn crew to Mobile or to New Orleans. From prison to ship they must be driven in the darkness of night due to the anti-slavery agitation, but as a child he heard the rattle of their chains and their cries.

There is the Fugitive Slave Act, through which Mason and Dixon's line has been obliterated; New York has become Virginia, and the power to hold, hunt, and sell men, women, and children remains no longer a mere state institution but is now an institution of the United States. In court two witnesses testify that this individual is the escaped slave; he may not testify on his own behalf or bring witnesses, and at the end of the proceeding he is taken in chains back to slavery. By way of amplification, this law stands alone in the annals of tyrannical legislation.

There is the attitude of the clergy who support the Fugitive Act. Using the traditional topos (topic) of inconsistency between their behavior and their pretensions, Douglass charges: "if the Fugitive Slave Law concerned the right to worship God according to the dictates of their own consciences, a general shout would go up from the church demanding repeal, repeal, instant repeal." But the church of our country does not esteem the law as a declaration of war against religious liberty. In supporting the law the church has made itself the bulwark of American slavery, and the shield of American slave hunters.

In his **peroration** Douglass does find some hope. For the first time he explicitly invokes the Declaration of Independence, "the genius of American Institutions." It is at the head of the obvious tendencies of this age. "No nation can now shut itself up from the surrounding world, and trot round in the same old path of its fathers without interference. The time was when such could be done. . . . But change has now come over the affairs of mankind. Walled cities and empires have become unfashionable. The arm of commerce has borne away the gates of the strong city. Intelligence is penetrating the darkest corners of the globe. God speed the year of jubilee the wide world over. . . ."

It is plain that from the disposition of the material in an order where one part follows another that there is a logical structure to Douglass's oration. The arguments are vividly sketched rather than developed, and the figure, paralepsis, is used to justify not giving them a full development. What is more notable is the use of the *pathe*, which are not just sketched but are amply developed.

## Douglass's Use of Pathos and Ethos

Fundamental to the effect of this speech is pity: pain at a destructive evil when it comes on those who do not deserve it. We feel this when we think that we could easily suffer in the same way as the objects of our pity. Identification with the sufferer is a necessary condition of pity. The slave in this oration does not deserve to be shut out from the independence ceremony; we are celebrating independence, but he is not independent. He "is engaged in all manner of enterprises common to other men, digging gold in California, capturing the whale in the Pacific, feeding sheep and cattle on the hillside, living, moving, acting, thinking, planning living in families as husbands, wives and children, and, above all, confessing and worshipping the Christian's God, and looking hopefully for life and immortality beyond the grave. . . ." We can see ourselves in his position: what would it be like for us to be always subject to sale, instant separation from our families, perhaps never to see them again? The slave dealer socializes with the buyers; he is "ever ready to drink, to treat, and to gamble. The fate of many a slave has depended upon the turn of a single card; and many a child has been snatched from the arms of its mother by bargains arranged in a state of brutal drunkenness."

We who are free and believe in virtue and family are those who can feel the injustice of undeserved disaster, particularly as we are not so close to the disaster ourselves as to be filled with dread (which drives out pity). The black person is the type of those pitiable; he is never at ease; if he has committed no crime, it hardly matters; whether he is honest and industrious or the opposite, it does not make him safe. He is subject to the whim of the master; what happens to him is not tied to merit; it usually comes undeserved. No good thing occurring to a slave is ever sure for more than a minute, so good fortune is hard for him to enjoy. The listeners' pity for the slave becomes a basis for anger, the pain that is felt at an unjustified debasement of ourselves or those near to us. Anger must be directed against persons; in this case, against the slave drovers, the legislators, and the clergy. Douglass visualizes anger against the practicing slave merchants: "I see clouds of dust raised on the highways of the South; I see the bleeding footsteps; I hear the doleful wail of fettered humanity on the way to the slave markets, where the victims are to be sold like horses, sheep, and swine, knocked off to the highest bidder. There I see the tenderest ties ruthlessly broken, to gratify the lust, caprice and rapacity of the buyers and sellers of men." By definition those we get angry with are those who devalue their victims, as when they treat those we identify with as horses or swine. We get especially angry when the signs of victims' suffering are brought before the eyes (and ears) as when the "fettered marchers' footsteps bleed," and we hear them wail.

Legislators became fully complicit in this debasement of the slave with the Fugitive Slave Act. They put the power of the United States behind the right to hold, hunt, and sell men, women, and children as slaves. They made the fugitive a bird for the sportsman's gun and make the "broad republican domain a hunting ground for men. Your lawmakers have commanded all good citizens to engage in this hellish sport." The law makes mercy to the fugitive a crime and pays judges to try them. Again, anger is justified because the legislators have debased those we now identify with, making them animals to be hunted by sportsmen and forbidding making them subject to acts of humanity and mercy. Yet, these legislators have no regrets; while they enforce this law, they celebrate a tyrant-killing, king-hating, people-loving, democratic, Christian America.

The clergy, too, are targets of anger. They are indifferent to what is happening to the slaves, so they also, in effect, debase them. "If the law abridged the right to sing psalms, to partake of the sacrament, or to engage in any of the ceremonies of religion, it would be smitten by the thunder of a thousand pulpits. A general shout would go up from the church demanding repeal, repeal, repeal!" The fact that the church of our country (with fractional exceptions) does not esteem "the Fugitive Slave Law as a declaration of war against religious liberty, implies that the church regards religion simply as a form of worship, an empty ceremony, and not a vital principle, requiring active benevolence, justice, love and good will towards man. It esteems sacrifice above mercy, psalm-singing above right doing. . . ." The religious leaders consider what is happening to the slaves insignificant; in their preoccupation with the forms of religion, they belittle real humans.

Lastly there is the role of shame in the address. Shame is a pain that is felt at doing bad things that bring a person into ill repute. It is obviously most felt by people who have pretensions to virtue, like you Americans, who are tyrant-killing, king-hating, people-loving Christians. You are ready to carry democracy to all the countries of the world, so long as it does not imply freedom for the slave. Even your inferiors, like the savages or the subjects of Kings and tyrants, are not guilty of practices more shocking and bloody than are the people of these United States at this very hour. Those who stand outside the system, like God and the crushed and bleeding slave, cannot help but denounce this shamefulness, "in the name of humanity which is outraged, in the name of liberty which is fettered, in the name of the constitution and the Bible, which are disregarded and trampled upon." Acts of cruelty, such as supporting the slave trade, are particularly shameful, taking advantage of weakness, playing the coward in the face of the slave merchant, enacting laws that protect his shameful dealing.

Frederick Douglass's use of pathos is supplemented by his peculiar ethos. He lived through slavery: who is to tell him that his view of suffering by the slaves is not accurate? This is especially true of the section on the slave market:

> To me the American slave trade is a terrible reality. When a child, my soul was often pierced with a sense of its horrors. I lived on Philpot Street, Fell's Point, Baltimore, and have watched from the wharves the slave ships in the Basin, anchored from shore, with their cargoes of human flesh, waiting for favorable winds to waft them down the Chesapeake.
>
> The flesh-mongers gather up their victims by dozens and drive them chained to the general depot in Baltimore. When a sufficient number have been collected here, a ship is chartered for the purpose of conveying the forlorn crew to Mobile or to New Orleans.
>
> In the deep darkness of midnight, I have been often aroused by the dead heavy footsteps and the piteous cries of the chained gangs that passed our door. The anguish of my boyhood heart was intense; and I was often consoled, when speaking to my mistress in the morning, to hear her say that the custom was very wicked; that she hated to hear the rattle of the chains and the heart rending cries. I was glad to find one who sympathized with me in my horror.

This kind of eye-witness account, buttressed by the reluctant testimony of the slave mistress herself, is hard to deny. The emotions of pity, shame, and anger are fully exploited in these ways.

Douglass does not criticize the Revolution; rather, he identifies with the ideals of the founding fathers. Washington could not die until he had broken the chains of his slaves. The fathers in their admiration of liberty lost sight of all other interests. They believed in order, but not the order of tyranny. The Constitution they framed is a "GLORIOUS LIBERTY DOCUMENT." Douglass also picks up considerable credibility from his familiarity with the Bible. Asking him to praise the Fourth of July is like the Hebrews being asked to sing a song of Zion after having been removed to a foreign land (Psalm 137:1–6). The preachers who justify the fugitive slave law are like the scribes and Pharisees "who pay tithe of mint, anise and cumin" while ignoring the weightier matters of the law, judgment, mercy, and faith (Matthew 23:23).

Douglass even identifies his position with the Constitution. It is the fundamental law. It is a slander on the memory of the Fathers to believe that it guarantees slavery. In his peroration Douglass identifies his views with progress: "intelligence is penetrating the darkest corners of the globe . . . oceans no longer divide, but link nations together." All the good things of the Bible and history and those that are coming to us, he identifies with his cause when building ethos.

## Rhetorical Style

A traditional rhetorician would describe the language of this address as grand style. The emotional tone is enhanced by a fullness in the development of relatively simple themes. Here is a series of *parallel* phrases in which Douglass develops the statement that the 4th of July is a day which reveals to the slave, more than all other days, the gross injustice and cruelty to which he is the constant victim.

> To him, your celebration is a sham; your boasted liberty an unholy license; your national greatness swelling vanity; your shouts of liberty and equality hollow mockery; your prayers and hymns, your sermons and thanksgivings, with all your religious parade and solemnity are to him mere bombast, fraud, deception, impiety and hypocrisy—a thin veil to cover up crimes which would disgrace a nation's savages. There is not a nation on the earth guilty of practices more shocking and bloody than are the people of these United States at this very hour.

One can easily point to the rhetorical hyperbole of this series—could even an intelligent slave think that all the celebration is utterly false, that there is no pious feeling to the hymns and sermons nor anything but self deception to the feeling of national pride? Could the educated black man not have known of the shocking and bloody practices of the French troops in the Napoleonic wars or the Australia of the prison ships? We understand, of course, that this flamboyance is part of the show, and while there's more than a grain of truth to it, there's also a grain of salt.

It is justified because it is told from the point of view of the slave, though certainly not in the language of the slave. There is the exploitation of **anaphora**, the repetition of the same word or phrase at the beginning of each clause, along with the hint of a rhyme in vanity, mockery, hypocrisy, and bloody—just enough there to constitute **epistrophe**, the repetition of the same phrase at the end of each clause. More than that, however, how many words does it take to say that much of the pageantry on the 4th is hypocritical, something that we all have occasionally felt at the end of an overlong ceremony? The excess of near synonymy is there to build the rhythm into a solemn march, abruptly broken by the conclusion of that last sentence with the finality of "at this very hour."

One of the characteristics of grand style is the freedom in the use of rhetorical figures of speech. These figures, such as anaphora and epistrophe, are useful in lectures and expositions, but figures of thought such as hyperbole and paralepsis are the language of feeling. Rhetorical questions are of this sort, particularly when used in a sequence that builds, like this one:

> Would you have me argue that man is entitled to liberty? That he is the rightful owner of his own body? Must I argue the wrongfulness of slavery? Is that a question for Republicans? Is it to be settled by the rules of logic and argumentation, as a matter beset with great difficulty, involving a doubtful application of the principle of justice, hard to be understood?

This sequence in particular is an example of how a series of rhetorical questions gets a listener into the mind-set of yea- or nay-saying.

Besides rhetorical questions, there is the use of paralepsis as principle for structuring the section refuting the imagined justifications of slavery. By claiming not to refute these justifications he belittles them almost out of existence. Taken all in all, the style of this speech is exciting, as befits this kind of occasion.

## Evaluation

If we take the purpose of this speech to be vituperation, bringing people into a state of wrath and fury at the institution of slavery, a greater success at using the resources of the traditional perspective could hardly be imagined. It is a real case of strategic employment of all the available means of persuasion. As an educational tool, to be sure, it falls short. The view of slavery is without depth or nuance. All that is presented are chains, beatings, and moanings. It is stereotyped; it is the propagandist's-eye view of the institution. Douglass's purpose, however, was *arousal*, not *education*. One would like to think that he could have accomplished both purposes, but that is not what he set out to do.

It seems to have been almost a total failure in convincing the Garrisonians. Though Douglass quoted Garrison favorably three times and closed with a complete rendition of one of his anti-slavery poems, they were not mollified; they continued to hold the view that the Constitution must be re-written and the union reestablished without the South.

The many reprintings of this famous address indicate the extent to which it has intrigued readers over the years. For us it is a window onto a long lost stage dominated by men whose states of feeling are far different from ours. But it fully exploits the precepts of traditional rhetoric.

## PERSONAL REFLECTIONS

This essay could have taken forms different from that written above. For example, I decided to make the essay more of a journey through the stages of traditional criticism than a regular-style academic paper. I did this because I thought it would make traditional criticism more accessible for those new to criticism. I wanted a bit more of a conversation and less of the usual academic paper. Traditional-style criticism is not lacking in sophistication, so a more accessible journey through the stages seemed better than putting up a bunch of lists for you to follow.

It is not unusual for those drawn to traditional criticism to also be drawn to history. I am very certain this shows in many of the examples I have used in this essay. This reflects my personal interests in American political history, as does my choice for a rhetorical artifact to analyze for my essay. Frederick Douglass's 5th of July oration was one of hundreds of such orations I could have chosen to study. I decided on this one since it is the most famous and is most likely to be familiar to you; moreover, I simply like this speech. My decision to use this particular speech was also influenced by my liking for Douglass's orations in general. The efforts of almost any speaker could have been analyzed, however.

## POTENTIALS AND PITFALLS

I am certain that you noticed that in the above examples for speakers I used contemporary speakers. This represents both a potential and a pitfall of traditional-style criticism. Far too often those teaching traditional-style criticism give the impression that it is only useful for explicating historical texts. Nothing could be further from the truth. Traditional criticism will serve you well even if you decide to look at a contemporary speaker such as President Obama, Hillary Clinton, James Dobson, or Dr. Phil. The choice of rhetorical artifact is up to you. What differentiates traditional-style criticism from the other critical perspectives to which you will be exposed has to do with the type of information that is generated.

Another potential pitfall involves formulaic criticism—also known as cookie-cutter criticism. This is often the result if one simply uses theory as a checklist, looking for instances of each and every concept covered and then writing it down to share. This is simply not criticism. Yes, there is some of this type of criticism written by those using a traditional perspective; it has been, after all, practiced longer than any other perspective covered in this book. Be that as it may, it is also a common pitfall associated with numerous critical perspectives. The possibility for formulaic criticism rests more with the critic than with the perspective used. To avoid formulaic criticism, you need to learn as much about the perspective you intend to use as possible. A good place to start is with the top picks I list below. There you will find excellent examples of criticism that is reflexive, not stale.

## TRADITIONAL CRITICISM TOP PICKS

Cooper, Lane. *The Rhetoric of Aristotle, an Expanded Translation with Supplementary Examples for Students of Composition and Public Speaking.* New York, London: D. Appleton and Company, 1932. The gold standard translation for this text. It went unchallenged for decades until Kennedy's book was published in 1991. Either one will work well. See George A. Kennedy, *Aristotle on Rhetoric: A Theory of Civic Discourse* (New York: Oxford University Press, 1991).

Hitchcock, Orville A. "Jonathan Edwards." In *A History and Criticism of American Public Address*, ed. William Norwood Brigance, 213–237. New York: McGraw-Hill, 1943. This essay represents a classical application of traditional criticism.

Hochmuth [Nichols], Marie Kathryn. "The Criticism of Rhetoric." In *A History and Criticism of American Public Address*, vol. 3, ed. Marie Kathryn Hochmuth. New York: Russell and Russell, 1954. A solid definition of rhetoric as conceived during the reputed heyday of traditional criticism. The essay complements well a functional approach to communication studies and rhetorical criticism.

Howell, Wilbur Samuel, and Hoyt Hopewell Hudson. "Daniel Webster." In *History and Criticism of American Public Address*, vol. 2, ed. William Norwood Brigance. New York: McGraw-Hill, 1943. An excellent essay that shows the possibilities of traditional criticism when it moves beyond analysis of a single speech and occasion. Puts the lie to the assertion that traditional criticism is only concerned with single speeches and immediate effects.

Thonssen, Lester, A. Craig Baird, and Waldo W. Braden. *Speech Criticism.* 2nd ed. New York: Ronald Press, 1970. You may well find a copy of this once common text in your school's library. In it you will find detailed explanations of the concepts outlined in this chapter.

The following is a short selection of more contemporary essays that draw on the traditional perspective in greater or lesser degrees. They show the dynamic possibilities for using the perspective today.

Gross, Alan G. "Renewing Aristotelian Theory: The Cold Fusion Controversy as a Test Case." *Quarterly Journal of Speech* 81 (1995): 48–62.

Henry, David. "The Rhetorical Dynamics of Mario Cuomo's 1984 Keynote Address: Situation, Speaker, Metaphor." *Southern Speech Communication Journal* 53 (1988): 105–120.

Hogan, J. Michael, and L. Glen Williams. "Defining 'the Enemy' in Revolutionary American: From the Rhetoric of Protest to the Rhetoric of War." *Southern Communication Journal* 61, no. 4 (Summer 1996): 277–289.

Holcomb, Chris. "'Anyone Can Be President': Figures of Speech, Cultural Forms, and Performance." *Rhetoric Society Quarterly* 37, no. 1 (2007): 71–96.

Ritter, Kurt, and David Henry. *Ronald Reagan, the Great Communicator.* Westport, CT: Greenwood Press, 1992.

Zagacki, Kenneth. "Eisenhower and the Rhetoric of Postwar Korea." *Southern Communication Journal* 60, no. 3 (Spring 1995): 233–246.

# NOTES

1. See Hoyt Hopewell Hudson, "De Quincy on Rhetoric and Public Speaking," in *Studies in Rhetoric and Public Speaking in Honor of James Albert Winans by Pupils and Colleagues*, ed. A. M. Drummond (New York: Century, 1925), 133–152; and Hoyt Hopewell Hudson, "The Field of Rhetoric," *Quarterly Journal of Speech Education* 9, no. 2 (1923): 167–180.

2. *Rhetoric*, I 3, 1358a 37–1358b 1.

3. Herbert Wichelns is routinely given credit for broadening the communication discipline's rhetorical horizons to include written as well as oral discourse in his 1925 essay, "Literary Criticism of Oratory." However, in "Hoyt Hopewell Hudson's Nuclear Rhetoric," Jim A. Kuypers convincingly argues that Hudson is deserving of this credit. Kuypers cites Hudson's 1921 essay, "Can We Modernize the Study of Invention?" where Hudson implied the use of topics for "speech or argument." The "Field of Rhetoric" contains more explicit definitions. In this essay, Hudson fully defined the term *rhetoric*, which included the study of written as well as oral discourse. Because rhetoric is the "faculty of finding, in any subject, all the available means of persuasion," the rhetorician is "a sort of diagnostician and leaves it to others to be the practitioners; the rhetorician is the strategist of persuasion, and other men execute his plans and do the fighting. In practice, however, and in any study of the subject, this distinction can hardly be maintained, since the person who determines the available means of persuasion . . . must also be, in most cases, the one to apply those means in persuasive speech and writing." See Herbert A. Wichelns, "The Literary Criticism of Oratory," in *Studies in Rhetoric and Public Speaking in Honor of James Albert Winans by Pupils and Colleagues*, ed. A. M. Drummond (New York: Century, 1925), 209; Hoyt Hopewell Hudson, "Can We Modernize the Theory of Invention?," *Quarterly Journal of Speech Education* 7, no. 4 (1921): 326; Hoyt Hopewell Hudson, "The Field of Rhetoric," *Quarterly Journal of Speech Education* 9, no. 2 (1923): 169–170; and Jim A. Kuypers, "Hoyt Hopewell Hudson's Nuclear Rhetoric," in *Twentieth-Century Roots of Rhetorical Criticism*, ed. Jim A. Kuypers and Andrew King (Westport, CT: Praeger, 2001).

4. *Rhetoric*, I iii, 1358a 3–4.

5. Garry Wills, *Lincoln at Gettysburg: The Words That Remade America* (New York: Touchstone Books, 1993).

6. Barack Obama, "Statement by the President on ISIL" (White House, September 10, 2014, http://www.whitehouse.gov/the-press-office/2014/09/10/statement-president-isil-1).

7. *Rhetoric*, II 18, 15–17.

8. H. L. Mencken disagrees with Lincoln's assessment: "The Gettysburg speech was at once the shortest and the most famous oration in American history. Put beside it, all the whoopings of the Websters, Sumners and Everetts seem gaudy and silly. It is eloquence brought to a pellucid and almost gem-like perfection, the highest emotion reduced to a few poetical phrases. Lincoln himself never even remotely approached it. It is genuinely stupendous. But let us not forget that it is poetry, not logic; beauty, not sense. Think of the argument in it. Put it into the cold words of everyday. The doctrine is simply this: that the Union soldiers who died at Gettysburg sacrificed their lives to the cause of self determination that government of the people, by the people, for the people, should not perish from the earth. It is difficult to imagine anything more untrue. The Union soldiers in the battle actually fought against self-determination; it was the Confederates who fought for the right of their people to govern themselves." H. L. Mencken, *A Mencken Chrestomathy* (New York: Vintage, 1949), 222–223.

9. *Rhetoric*, II 2–12.

10. "Obama Administration Official Defends Bergdahl Trade Despite Charges," FoxNews.com, March 26, 2015, http://www.foxnews.com/politics/2015/03/26/bergdahl-to-be-charged-with-desertion-official-says.

11. Some have called such utterances part of an "administrative text." For a fuller explanation, see Jim A. Kuypers, Marilyn J. Young, and Michael K. Launer, "Of Mighty Mice and Meek Men: Contextual Reconstruction of the Shootdown of Iran Air 655," *Southern Communication Journal* 59, no. 4 (1994):

294–306; and Jim A. Kuypers, *Presidential Crisis Rhetoric and the Press in a Post Cold War World* (Westport, CT: Praeger, 1997), 3–8.

12. Caedmon Records, TC 1264.

13. John F. Wilson and Carroll C. Arnold, *Public Speaking as a Liberal Art*, 5th ed. (Boston: Allyn and Bacon, 1983), 83–88.

14. Nixon, "The Great Silent Majority," November 3, 1969, http://www.americanrhetoric.com/speeches/richardnixongreatsilentmajority.html.

15. Lloyd L. Bitzer, "Aristotle's Enthymeme Revisited," *Quarterly Journal of Speech* 45 (1959): 408.

16. I wish in no way to minimize the work of the Christian Children's Fund. This is an outstanding charity.

17. Jane Blankenship and Hermann G. Stelzner, eds., *Rhetoric and Communication: Studies in the University of Illinois Tradition* (Urbana: University of Illinois Press, 1976).

18. Thomas Paine, *Common Sense*, 1776.

19. *Rhetoric*, I 1, 1355b 10–16.

20. In 2013 dollars, that is somewhere between $3.00 and $5.00.

21. Gerald Fulkerson, "Exile as Emergence: Frederick Douglass in Great Britain, 1845–1847," *Quarterly Journal of Speech* 60 (February 1974): 69–82.

22. Wills, *Lincoln at Gettysburg*.

23. Douglass to Gerrit Smith, July 7, 1852. Copy of original letter in possession of author. Original located in the Gerrit Smith Papers Collection at Syracuse University Libraries.

# 8

# Close Textual Analysis

## Approaches and Applications

*Stephen Howard Browne*

**Close textual analysis** (CTA) refers to an interpretive practice, the aim of which is to explain how texts operate to produce meaning, effect persuasion, and activate convictions in public contexts. To this end CTA attends in detail to the interplay of ideas, images, and arguments as they unfold within the spatial and temporal economy of the **text**. The rewards of such an approach may be glimpsed, for example, if we think of Martin Luther King's masterful "I Have a Dream" speech of 1963. Here, we would follow the address from its first words, deliberate and restrained; note the mounting intensity, the shape and direction of its metaphors; and follow the movement of the text to its thunderous conclusion. The general conviction underlying such an approach is that rhetorical texts are active, dynamic, and complex; explaining how they work therefore requires a keen sensitivity to the play of language itself.

Practitioners of CTA generally view their art less as a method per se than as a disciplined search for the linguistic particulars that eventually comprise the whole of a given rhetorical performance.[1] Students and scholars working in this vein are thus particularly attuned to the nuances, echoes, and subtle gestures that exist in the object of their study. It thus requires a sensibility cultivated by broad reading across the humanities and asks that we bring to the task a literary critic's sharp eye for textual detail. A cultivated and disciplined engagement with history, literature, and philosophy will go a long way toward preparing the rhetorical critic for such work. Above all, however, a basic love of the human language, in all its glories and all its messiness, is requisite.

Although CTA may be put to work across a broad range of genres—critics have used it to better understand orations, films, visual rhetoric, pamphlets, and poetry—one key premise drives virtually all such analysis. This premise holds that the rhetorical force of a text can never be presumed as given or fixed; rather, its rhetorical force is the result of a complex set of symbolic forces set into play at the moment of utterance. The critic working from this perspective accordingly seeks to identify and account for this process. In the following pages, we will explore the main principles guiding the practice of CTA, we will place this approach within certain historical and disciplinary contexts, we will consider a brief case study, and we will note several lines of argument raised by critics of CTA. We turn first to four principles upon which the practice of CTA rests.

# CTA GUIDING PRINCIPLES

### Principle 1: Rhetorical Texts Are Sites of Symbolic Action

What does this "mean"? By way of an answer, it will help here and throughout this chapter to have beside you a copy of Barack Obama's Philadelphia speech of March 2008.[2] As you look it over and perhaps recall reading or viewing it previously, you might ask one of two questions: either "What does this speech mean?" or "What is it doing?" The first question encourages us to think of texts as containers of ready-made semantic units that may be extracted from the text as needed. Put another way, the speech itself may be said to offer a guide for answering the question "What is this text about?" "Well," you might reply, scanning through the paragraphs, "it means just what it says; let me quote a few lines and you'll get the gist of the matter." In one sense, of course, this is a perfectly reasonable response. It does not, however, offer a very close look at how the speech functions as a text, or, more specifically, as a rhetorical text. Why? Because the response fails to take into account the **symbolic action**, or the language-in-motion that defines the dynamics of the rhetorical performance. Close textual critics thus tend to view such texts as verbs, so to speak, *and to ask not what a text means but what it does*. If you happened to see the speech on television or YouTube, or if you have now read it for the first time, pause for a moment and ask yourself, "What does this text do?"

Once this question is posed at the outset, a world of interpretive possibilities opens into view. Imagine for a moment the nearly infinite ways in which a text may be said to act. It may disclose or camouflage, seduce, exalt, debase, deface, deflect, direct, invite, distance, defer, deny, destroy, create, recreate, form, deform, reform, silence, provoke, tickle, numb, transcend, descend, portend, threaten, demur, announce, renounce, or pronounce. Texts may inaugurate, promise, plead, deny, decry, dissemble, lie, waffle, tempt, dissuade, disabuse, or deter. They may call out, call for, call on, call in, call to, or call a cab. The point is surely evident by now, but however basic the insight, such a view of textual action attunes us to the manifold ways in which we can understand what, precisely, is rhetorical about a given text: the decisive and distinctive manner in which it acts in the world.

### Principle 2: Form and Content Cannot Be Divorced

If CTA is particularly alive to the active nature of rhetorical texts, it is similarly sensitive to the interplay of form and content shaping that action. Close textual critics accordingly seek to correct a lingering tendency, dating well back into antiquity, to view properties of **form**—that is, images, tropes, the "style" of a given rhetorical production—as somehow distinct from the essential content of its message. In its most reductive expression, this tendency suggests that we invent something to say—what it is we really want to get across to our auditors or readers—and then trick out the message with appealing drapery, the better to arrest attention or gratify the aesthetic appetite of our audience. This view of style is not uncontested, however, and theorists of language since the early twentieth century have taught us that such a view is illusory and that if we are to make plausible sense of how rhetoric works, we need to reunite what has been put asunder. Form and content belong together. To invoke King's address again, consider how integral his use of figures and other imagery is to the meaning of his message. At a minimum, they may be said to arrest attention, establish pace and meter, and make concrete otherwise abstract principles of justice and redemption.

Our second principle seems to be mere common sense, but in fact it presents us with difficult issues from the outset. For example, while it is the case that form and content cannot be separated, they are not the same thing. And if form and content are not the same, then how are they different from one another? In order to answer that question, we need a working definition of each. Here, too, we need to acknowledge that both terms are notoriously slippery and the objects of considerable academic debate. For the purposes of this chapter, let us take *form* to refer to those linguistic resources that give conspicuous structure to otherwise abstract formulations. To play with this definition for a moment, note how abstract it is. It needs form! So let's put it another way, with apologies to William Butler Yeats: "form is to content as the dancer is to the dance." Here the abstract is given heightened intelligibility by embodying itself in a concrete and dynamic image. Form and content need each other. By extension, we may take **content** to refer to that dimension of a message reducible to the level of a proposition. Let us turn to the Obama text again for an example of how this principle plays out in practice:

> I can no more disown him [Wright] than I can disown the black community. I can no more disown him than I can disown my white grandmother—a woman who helped raise me, a woman who sacrificed again and again for me, a woman who loves me as much as she loves anything in this world, but a woman who once confessed her fear of black men who passed by her on the street, and who on more than one occasion has uttered racial or ethnic stereotypes that made me cringe.

Now, what can we say about the interplay of form and content in this passage? With respect to its content, we can ask, "What is the basic proposition here?" We might answer, "The fact that Reverend Wright has his faults, like all of us, is insufficient grounds for disowning him." To leave it at this, however, is to miss the rhetorical force imported to the proposition by virtue of the form in which it is expressed. We would want also to note, for example, the parallel constructions initiating the first several lines: "I can no more disown him. . . . I can no more disown him." Not only do they establish the metrical cadence of the passage, but they rather ingeniously invoke the Obama campaign's mantra of personal empowerment. We observe, too, how the proposition is inscribed into a narrative account of the candidate's grandmother, who comes to represent a kind of universal type—human, warts and all—with whom we can identify and whose image is thereby made to soften the specter of Reverend Wright. Form and content in this way are seen to sponsor each other.

### Principle 3: Text Informs Context, and Vice Versa

The emphatic emphasis CTA places on the text as such invites the suspicion that we may have here too much of a good thing. That is, does it not stand to reason that the more closely we look at an "object," the further we remove ourselves from the **context** in which that object appears? And does this not bracket out information essential for understanding such texts, especially in their rhetorical aspect? We will attend to this question in greater detail later; here it is sufficient to stress that if indeed contextual considerations are made to drop by the wayside, then of course we have a real problem. The good news is that nothing of the kind is entailed by the practice of CTA. On the contrary, it is inconceivable that a satisfactory interpretation of rhetorical texts is possible without taking all relevant features of the context into consideration.

Still, we are left with the question as to how a given text is best attuned to its context. Once again, the answer is contingent upon a matter of definition: what, after all, is a "context"? Is it the immediate exigence to which the text responds? Certainly that plays a part, but what about those rhetorical performances that seem less beholden to such pressing forces—meditations, say, in the manner of Ralph Waldo Emerson or Elizabeth Cady Stanton? And in what sense can we say that contexts are bound by fixed conceptions of space and time? The Declaration of Independence, for example, continues to be expropriated for all manner of rhetorical purposes, not only in the United States, but in revolutionary Vietnam, Poland, and the nations of South America. At a minimum, then, we need to adapt a very elastic sense of what qualifies as relevant context, make a sound case for stipulating one rather than another, and set about the task of informing our textual analysis with systematic reference to its contextual environment.

One particularly useful approach to this interpretive work is to acknowledge that while each text is distinctive on its own terms, it yet partakes in and deploys an indefinite range of other texts and discursive modalities. Another way of thinking about this phenomenon is to view contexts as themselves texts of a kind, from which a speaker or writer borrows on an as-needed basis. For a brief example of how this works rhetorically, let us turn again to the Philadelphia speech. Clearly we have an immediate exigence: popular disapproval of comments made by Obama's minister, thought to have been racially charged and in violation of basic norms of civil and political discourse. The speech is self-evidently an effort to allay such anxieties as those Reverend Wright stirred up. But there is more to the matter than that, because part of the text's rhetorical achievement is to resituate, or recreate, another and more compelling context in which the speech itself hopes to be understood. For evidence of this process, we turn, as always, to the text itself. What other texts or discursive modes does the speaker import into his own speech? A quick glance gives us the answer:

US Constitution
Declaration of Independence
Hebrew Bible/Old Testament/New Testament
Personal narrative
Sermon
Testimony
Memoir
Novel
Supreme Court decision
Anecdote

The point is clear: texts work rhetorically by responding to exigencies, yes, but they work as well by reconstituting their own interpretive contexts. On reflection, we can see how this process moves both ways: contexts inform texts, and texts inform contexts. Thus it is not unrealistic to predict that Obama's speech will itself enter into the vast storehouse of rhetorical resources and become available to ensuing speakers as they seek to effect change in the world. The speech, that is, emerges from one context, realigns itself, and eventually becomes part of an even greater context.

## Principle 4: Rhetorical Texts Exhibit Artistic Density

Our forth principle may best be considered an extension and summary of the foregoing discussion. Like the others, it seems perhaps uncontroversial, even obvious. In fact, however, the principle of artistic density cuts to the heart of CTA. How does it do this, and why does it matter? To get at these questions we need to step back for a moment and see where CTA came from, the company it keeps, and how it distinguishes itself from other reading practices.

The discipline we now associate with communication departments in the United States originated in large measure by breaking away from the academic study of English. The major argument justifying this new development was that "speech communication" attended to related but significantly different phenomena: not literature as such, but the products of human beings moved to express themselves to persuasive ends in largely oral and public contexts. This interest could of course claim a heritage dating well into Western antiquity, but it had gradually been subsumed under the auspices of literary study. Early twentieth-century champions of the revitalized discipline thus sought to distinguish their work from that of literary critics, who were concerned to explain aesthetic properties of poems, novels, plays, and the like. Rhetorical critics, on the other hand, laid claim to those speech activities that were self-evidently more instrumental, time bound, and broadly political in character: orations, parliamentary debates, and sermons, for example. As the discipline grew and flourished throughout the century, this emphasis on the pragmatics of human communication tended to bracket out, and sometimes repudiate altogether, the aesthetic dimensions of rhetorical practice.[3]

Why this apparent indifference or even hostility to the aesthetic? For many, the answer was programmatic: the very identity of our discipline required that we sustain the differences separating rhetorical studies from literary criticism. For others, it had to do with certain political investments in situating rhetorical acts within their material and ideological milieu. To preoccupy oneself with aesthetic concerns was to forget or elide the dynamics of power (the political aspects) that superintend all rhetorical productions.

Now, there are legitimate reasons for such anxieties, but students of CTA tend to reject the premises upon which they are based. Above all, such reasoning presupposes that we cannot in principle have it both ways, that a zero-sum game seems to be in play when we consider either the rhetorical or the aesthetic. That is, to engage the one is to discount the other. On reflection, however, we must ask, is this really the case? Can we not ask after the ways in which the aesthetic can be put to rhetorical purposes? Indeed we can, if only by simply reminding ourselves that rhetoric is, after all, an art and that such an art may be glimpsed by attending to techniques of production. Surely it causes no damage to King's "I Have a Dream" oration to acknowledge its artistic achievement; more positively, a full accounting of that achievement goes a long way toward explaining its enduring rhetorical legacy. And this, in the end, may be taken as the basic rationale for CTA: by submitting texts to close inspection, we are able to see better the ways in which rhetoric works at its most fundamental levels of operation. Put another way, it is difficult to see how we can understand the whole of King's speech or any other text without attending to its parts. Ultimately, we arrive at the technical process through which that whole is rendered coherent and compelling.

Taken together, our four principles should prepare us for a sensitive and instructive reading of Obama's Philadelphia speech. We will turn to the text shortly, but here might be a place to indicate what CTA is not. This will help clear further misconceptions from our path and free us from the weight of unwanted and unwarranted concerns. We have already alluded to several of these: skilled textual critics do not turn a blind eye to context, they do not reduce the "meaning" of texts to the propositions advanced by the texts' authors, and they do not entertain the aesthetics of the text in the manner of "art for art's sake." In addition, it is worth stressing that CTA, for all its attention to the "how" of textual production, does not satisfy itself with a mere naming and listing of such techniques. The aim, rather, is to provide a comprehensive account of how the parts cohere into a whole greater than the sum of those parts. Further, CTA is clearly more than an advanced version of textual appreciation; on the contrary, it arms the critic with material with which to render judgment as to efficacy, ethics, success, and failure. Important also is the position that CTA is not a "method" as such, if we mean by that term a specific how-to program for textual analysis. This is not to imply that it is simply impressionistic. It is rather to insist on a rigorous and evidence-bound explication that nevertheless leaves ample room for the play of critical insight and authorial voice. Finally, it is useful to remind ourselves again that CTA involves a great deal more than paraphrasing what is expressed in the text; it seeks rather to ask, as we did with reference to our first principle, "What is this text doing?"

## CRITICAL ESSAY

Now let us turn to our case in point. In the following, I offer one interpretation of Barack Obama's March 18, 2008, speech in Philadelphia. The analysis is designed as an exercise in CTA and aims to illustrate several—certainly not all—features of this approach. Among the questions I ask of this text is, from what family of rhetorical acts does it take inspiration? That is, can we identify one or more **generic antecedents** that seem to guide the speaker's treatment of his theme? We are then led to ask what this theme is and how it superintends the symbolic action of the text as it unfolds. We want to ask further about the internal structure of this movement and how this structure assists in the production of the speaker's message. Similarly, what kinds of images, metaphors, and other dimensions of style animate Obama's arguments and give them conspicuous form? Mindful, too, of contextual forces at play in the text, we will need to identify both the immediate exigence to which the speech responds and the ways in which it seeks to transform the contexts in which it asks to be interpreted. A number of other questions germane to the text may be asked and answered, of course, and no pretense is made here to a final or even authoritative exposition of the text. Far from it, I encourage the reader to contest, elaborate, or otherwise engage this particular rendering. The presumptive payoff is a deeper understanding of how texts work to induce conviction and impel audiences to action.

---

### CLOSE TEXTUAL ANALYSIS OF BARACK OBAMA'S MARCH 18, 2008, SPEECH IN PHILADELPHIA

The unprecedented nature of Obama's campaign for the Oval Office all but ensured the most intense kind of public and media scrutiny. The first African American making a serious bid for the office, running against the female with realistic chances for nomination, taking place in a time of war on two fronts, a faltering economy, and widespread concern over the nation's capacity to deliver health care to its own citizens. Within such a heated environment, partisan supporters can be almost as dangerous as the official opposition, as Obama, Clinton, and McCain were each to discover from their respective camps. No supporter raised as great a firestorm, however, as the Reverend Jeremiah Wright, pastor of Chicago's Trinity United Church of Christ and longtime spiritual guide to the Illinois senator. The reverend was known for addressing his congregation in language of exceptional intensity, color, and, sometimes, provocation. One such sermon, in which he expressed his disappointment with US race relations with the recurrent phrase "Goddamn America," was captured on video, was frequently replayed across a variety of media, and was very soon the object of widespread condemnation.

All campaigns run into stumbling blocks, of course, and although some are undone by such episodes, most manage to survive and push on to their fated ends. But for many this was a different matter. At stake was not just the candidate's affiliation with the intemperate pastor, but the persistent questions haunting the nation's past and present race relations. Senator Obama had offered the prospect—however idealized—of a "post-race" America, in which an African American might run for the highest office in the land and be judged, in the words of Martin Luther King, "not by the color of his skin but by the content of his character." Now this promise appeared to be on the verge of collapse. Obama and Clinton were still neck and neck in the polls, conservative talk show hosts were banging their drums of disapproval, and it soon became obvious that the candidate had to say something. On the morning of March 18, before a nationally televised audience, Senator Barack Obama stepped to the podium across the street from Philadelphia's famed Constitutional Hall and delivered, to that point, the most important speech of his life.

The situation was thus novel in many respects, but that does not mean that the speaker was bereft of resources. On close reading, we discover that, consciously or not, he drew on a rich and enduring rhetorical genre known as the "jeremiad."[4] The term takes as its referent the imposing figure of the prophet Jeremiah in the Torah and Christian New Testament. For thousands of years, the prophet has served as a model for a particular type of rhetoric, marked by lamentation over the fallen state of a chosen people, the dangers of failing the terms of a sacred covenant, and the urgent need to restore oneself and one's community into a proper relationship with God and the world. It is not a rigid model, and had been put to different uses in different ways throughout the history of the genre. But its key components—(a) covenant, (b) violation, and (c) atonement—have remained relatively stable over time. On review of Obama's text we see that there is no need to impose this model; the speech rather gives evidence of this tradition at every step. We may then allow the text to teach us, so to speak, how to understand its rhetorical task by taking up its own cues. To this end, the following analysis is organized according to each of the three functions noted above.

The very first words out of the speaker's mouth alert us to the centrality of promise to American collective identity: "We the people, in order to form a more perfect union." By thus invoking the inaugural lines of the US Constitution, Obama reminds his audience that they, like their forebears, are bound together in a civically sacred trust. That document announced to the world the arrival a unique moment in the world, when plain white men—not yet blacks, Native Americans, or women—entered into an "improbable experiment in democracy." We are hence called to be mindful that the ideal of perfection is just that—an ideal—and moreover an ideal which remains to be fully met. But the very notion that a nation could be founded under the promise to nevertheless keep striving toward such a goal remains a fact of striking historical significance, and it gives shape and direction to all that follows.

One of the hallmarks of early colonial jeremiads was their belief that the new immigrants were a select people who had endured great hardship to enter upon a "journey into the wilderness." The scriptural resonance to the Israelite exodus from slavery into freedom is unmistakable and underscores the sense that Americans were embarked upon a journey of their own. John Winthrop's sermon on board the *Arbella* perfectly captures this sense of simultaneous righteousness and anxiety that was to mark American exceptionalism for centuries to come: "For we must consider that we shall be as a city upon a hill. The eyes of all people are upon us, so that if we shall deal falsely with our God in his work we have undertaken, and so cause him to withdraw his present help from us, we shall be made a story and a by-word through the world."[5] Winthrop understood that the success of that journey was very much a matter of literally keeping the faith, of staying on the right path. In context, of course, Obama's appeal to this imagery is secular and civic, but the rhetorical work it effects is analogous. And where the Pilgrims were severely reminded of their departures from the path, their failure to keep the covenant, so America needs its own reminder. Here was a nation blessed by freedom, bounty, and democratic government, but whose promise to form a more perfect union was stained by the "original sin of slavery, a question that divided the colonies and brought the convention to a stalemate until the founders chose to allow the slave trade to continue for at least twenty more years, and to leave any final resolution to future generations."

Now we see the first instance of a structural dynamic that will direct the course of the speech generally. Put simply, it works by first introducing a positive—in this case, America's promise to work toward an ideal. Here we see the concept of *covenant* at work. Obama then asserts a negative example (slavery) of how that promise has been broken—hence the *violation* of that covenant. The former assumes expression in the celebratory or affirmative mode—hence the location of Obama's address beside Constitution Hall in Philadelphia's historic section. The latter gets articulated in the form of accusation or lament—hence the speaker's insistence on acknowledging those moments when American's have failed their own aspirations.

On the path, off the path; but now what? In keeping with the jeremiad's purposes, the speaker is obliged not to leave matters there, but to alert his audience that a choice now presents itself: either the people can opt to remain off the path, or choose to return and keep struggling toward their professed ideal. The people, in short, have the means to redeem themselves if only they would, and it is the work of the speaker to animate them toward acting on that choice alone. Here then we see the third function of the jeremiad—the means to *atonement*. The Constitution itself contained the language upon which such action could be authorized, but ultimately, he stresses, "What would be needed were Americans in successive generations who were willing to do their part—through protest and struggle, on the streets and in the courts, through a civil war and civil disobedience and always at great risk—to narrow the gap between the promise of our ideals and the reality of their time." This commitment acting upon choice is the key to redemption itself, but it presupposes yet another promise, and that is to act together as a community or a people collectively striving toward that more perfect union. In the speaker's words, "we cannot solve the challenges of our time unless we solve them together—unless we perfect our union by understanding that we may have different stories, but we hold common hopes; that we may not look the same and we may not have come from the same place, but we all want to move in the same direction—towards a better future for our children and our grandchildren."

We are now only five paragraphs into the text, but already the basic coordinates have been set. Its overarching theme—the need to act together to form a better version of America—is activated within a given genre, the jeremiad, and unfolds through successive stages of covenant, violation, and atonement. Thus form, content, and purpose collaborate to produce an artistic whole in a process that will be recapitulated throughout the performance, in a manner suggesting variations on an orchestral motif. We now consider this dynamic at work in the second and central phase of the speech.

Barack Obama was not born in Chicago, but even as a young man he made the city his political home. Shortly after earning his law degree from Harvard University, he took up residence in Hyde Park, whence he launched a systematic and very successful campaign to insinuate himself into the complex network of Chicago politics. If every step was not calculated, most were, and before long this son of a white American mother and Kenyan father had moved to the forefront of that city's center of power. Along the way, Obama encountered and fell under the spiritual tutelage of the Reverend Jeremiah Wright, a prominent leader in the black community and, by all accounts, a spellbinding speaker. As we noted above, he could on occasion cross a line thought by many to be taboo by vehemently denouncing America and its benighted record on race relations. When one such performance hit the airwaves, Obama was severely criticized for associating with the pastor and was called upon to address the issue. He did so briefly by denouncing Wright's more excessive language, but made clear that he continued to hold his mentor in high regard. This effort did little to allay the controversy, and at length Obama undertook to settle the matter once and for all—hence the Philadelphia speech.

How the speaker manages the Jeremiah Wright issue is perforce key to the address as a whole. To better understand it, let us return to our pilgrims for a moment. One of the striking characteristics of their sermons is the way in which seemingly all events of note are relegated to the status of an example or manifestation of God's disposition. Are crops bountiful and children healthy? Evidence of divine pleasure. Are famine and sickness in the village? Evidence of divine wrath. Was a two-headed calf born on the Dooley's farm? Divine warning. In short, the latter-day Jeremiahs sought to convince their flock that virtually everything could be properly understood and acted upon not with reference to the event itself, but to an overarching narrative in which any given phenomenon is but an episode. Its meaning was not inherent to the event, but in the greater story still unfolding. For Winthrop and his fellow shipmates, for example, the meaning of their journey was not limited to a group of malcontents, or land hunger; it had to be comprehended in terms appropriate to the age-old narrative of slavery, exodus, freedom, and redemption.

Now, what does all this have to do with Obama's response to the Wright matter? On closer inspection, we see that the jeremiad provides the speaker with a means to render the controversy into a minor but noteworthy episode in America's own story and its march toward a more perfect union. By transforming the "meaning" of Reverend Wright from a media-generated bogeyman into an allegory of America writ large, Obama strips him out of the hands of his critics and re-inscribes Wright into a more meaningful and instructive lesson than could otherwise have been the case. Taking up our organizing principles, we can plot the process by which this transformation is effected:

*Covenant* (affirmation of the positive)

> The man I met more than twenty years ago is a man who helped introduce me to my Christian faith, a man who spoke to me our obligation to love one another; to care for the sick and lift up the poor. He is a man who served his country as a US Marine; who has studied and lectured at some of the finest universities and seminaries in the country, and who for over thirty years led a church that serves the community by doing God's work here on Earth—by housing the homeless, ministering to the needy, providing day care services and scholarships and prison ministries, and reaching out to those suffering from HIV/AIDS.

*Violation* (exposing and condemning the negative)

> But the remarks that have caused this recent firestorm weren't simply controversial. . . . Instead, they expressed a profoundly distorted view of this country—a view that sees white racism as endemic, and elevates what is wrong with America above all that we know is right with America. . . . As such, Reverend Wright's comments were not only wrong but divisive, divisive at a time when we need unity; racially charged at a time when we need to come together to solve a set of monumental problems.

*Atonement* (restoration and redemption)

> But I have a firm conviction—a conviction rooted in my faith in God and my faith in the American people—that working together we can move beyond some of our old racial wounds, and that in fact we have no choice if we are to continue on the path of a more perfect union.

Close textual analysis takes as a given that texts have direction, that they unfold within a temporal economy established by the text itself. Obama's oration is doubly interesting because it not only has direction, but is also about direction. We have charted this fact above by observing how the speaker avails himself of certain features native to the jeremiad. It will come as no surprise, then, that this ancient rhetorical genre is activated and sustained through conspicuous word choice, which is to say its "style" collaborates in effecting the intended message. Again, this sense of style in no way views such word choice as ornamentation or afterthought. On the contrary, it is constitutive of the message itself, which may be grasped by attending to the Judeo-Christian imagery at work throughout the text and its appeal to the path as its leading trope.

We have already made reference to a number of scriptural allusions. It may be useful at this point to pause and consider them in the aggregate. A quick list of resonant terms and phrases is suggestive:

Original sin
Promise
Bondage
Faith (repeatedly)
Love one another
God's work
Foot of the cross
David and Goliath
Moses and Pharaoh
Christians in the lion's den
Ezekiel's field of dry bones
Vessel of hope
Do unto others as we would have them do unto us
Let us be our brother's/sister's keeper

Mindful that such usage is meaningful only within the contours of the text itself, we nevertheless glimpse the point. Obama's appeal to scriptural imagery functions to underscore not only his own ethos as a man of faith, but enriches the rhetorical force of the message itself. Taken together, we may observe that each allusion invokes different facets of the covenant binding the nation to its historical mission. Broken or repaired, forgotten or remembered, this covenant weaves through the speech as it presumably weaves through America's own journey toward the full realization of its promise. Hence the Hebrew Bible/Christian Old Testament imagery of original sin, bondage, and faltering faith is transformed within the text into the New Testament emphasis on love, charity, and redemption. This sense of forward movement is punctuated further by recurrent appeals to the image of the path and its clustered associations. Thus:

Travel across the ocean
The long march of those who came before us
Path to understanding
Path of a more perfect union
That path means embracing the burden of our past

However briefly, the above rendering suggests how the formal and ideational content of the text work together to create an artistically coherent message. The overall argument—that America has within itself the moral capacity to renew its commitment to form a more perfect union—is mobilized through a series of structural and stylistic resources, which together offer the speaker's audience a reason to believe and to act on such belief.

We are now in a position to revisit the four principles of CTA inaugurating this essay. Each asks a certain kind of question the critic needs to grapple with in coming to terms with his or her particular text. Let us take them up individually in the order presented.

1. **The text is a site of symbolic action**. Such a principle prompts us to then ask: "What does a text *do*?" By way of an answer, and with reference to Obama's speech, we can

now say that *texts act by summoning rhetorical resources (i.e., the jeremiad) to impose meaningful order on the world and, if successful, to make that order a compelling basis for conviction.*

2. **Form and content cannot be divorced**. Here we must ask: "How do they collaborate to create meaning and effect persuasion?" Obama's address teaches us that *form (i.e., metaphors, allegories, etc.) imparts to content conspicuous intelligibility, and content (i.e., reasons for forgiving Reverend Wright) imparts to form propositional argument.*

3. **Texts inform contexts, and vice versa**. If this is the case, then we need to ask: "How do texts recreate or restructure context?" On reflection, we are led to see that *texts borrow from other texts and discursive traditions to reorder the terms in which they hope to be interpreted.* Thus Obama, for example, invoked founding state papers, the Bible, and sermons to reorient his critics from one view toward another.

4. **Rhetorical texts exhibit artistic density**. That said, we may well ask: "How is such artistic density manifested, and to what end?" The Obama speech illustrates that *texts reveal their own techniques of production, and to the extent that these techniques yield a coherent and compelling product, they invite attention and assent.*

---

## PERSONAL REFLECTIONS

I first came to the study of close textual analysis as a graduate student at the University of Wisconsin. There I encountered a small but remarkable group of critics who combined deep historical and philosophical learning with a keen interest in discovering how texts manage to do what they do. Then as now, such close attention to texts seemed the ideal means to open windows to other vistas and distant horizons. By peering intently at Booker T. Washington's Atlanta Exposition Address, for example, I learned not only how metaphors operate to invite interpretation, but about race relations in the New South, the importance of pageantry to regional identification, and styles of African American leadership. For this reason, CTA offered a venue for bringing into focus wide-ranging interests—indeed, kept me from ranging *too* widely and without direction.

After more than two decades in the field of rhetorical criticism, one's interests are bound to grow and change. And while I now pursue other avenues of inquiry, including rhetoric and public memory, social movements, and rhetoric in the early republic, one constant has remained firmly in place: the conviction that rhetorical texts are just as worthy as any other genre of close, patient, and imaginative interpretation.

## POTENTIALS AND PITFALLS

No interpretive practice can presume to be complete or satisfactory on every count, and CTA is no exception. Through the years, it has both attracted and provoked some of the discipline's most able critics. This essay has sought to demonstrate the gains to be had from this approach, but it would be incomplete without some attention to its limits. Several of these have been mentioned, notably, the alleged tendency to bracket out contextual dynamics. Still, at least two persistent concerns remain about the assumptions upon which CTA is built and the tendencies it encourages in practice: its reliance on an ideal critic/audience construct and its privileging of canonical texts. In the following, I briefly develop each critique but leave counterarguments to the reader's discretion.

The first criticism of CTA takes us to near ground zero in the work of interpretation. In effect, it asks, what are we really saying when we claim that a unit of language means this or that? We have already discarded the notion that meaning resides objectively and inherently in the unit itself, and we have stressed that, for rhetorical criticism at least, it is best to attend to what language does in a given context. But we are not out of the woods yet and need to press further on the question. When, as the author of this essay, I claim that such and such a passage in Obama's speech means or does something, what am I really saying? Am I making a claim about what the audience supposedly thinks? Inasmuch as I have no access to its mental activity at the moment of performance, I can make no such claim. Nor am I attributing certain intentions to the speaker, as in, "This is what Obama really means here." Again, I have no grounds for arguing along these lines: who knows what his (or his speechwriters') intentions were? And even if we did know, what would it have to do with the ways in which his listeners and readers made their own sense of the oration?

In the face of such questions, CTA (but not CTA alone) finds itself exposed to the criticism that it posits an ideal reader and an ideal audience. That is, the critic implicitly operates from a privileged position, as if to say, "I offer to you the reader the preferred interpretation of this text." True, the critic is obliged to argue for his or her rendering and be otherwise held to the highest standards of scholarship. But if we cannot plausibly ascribe intention to the speaker, or reception to the audience, then is not the critic in effect saying, "This is how I think the text works"? And if that is the case, on what basis can we generalize beyond the critic's self-reporting?

The second line of criticism advanced against CTA is more politically charged but no less insistent. It holds that practitioners of the art tend almost invariably to seize upon texts of unquestioned cultural significance and artistic achievement. There are exceptions to this argument, but then there can be no mistaking the fact that CTA in general concerns itself with canonical texts. In rhetorical studies, for example, critics associated with the practice have featured the Declaration of Independence, Jefferson's first inaugural address, Lincoln's major addresses, Elizabeth Cady Stanton's "Solitude of Self," FDR's first inaugural address, and King's "I Have a Dream" speech.[6] These are, of course, perfectly understandable as fit objects of interpretation. So what is the problem? In the view of some critics, lavishing such attention on the masterpieces of American discourse unwittingly reproduces a suspect standard of what gets to count as a masterpiece, or, more pointedly, privileges the very concept of masterpiece— itself, these critics argue, a gendered and presumably outdated category. Why not use CTA to study vernacular expressions, forgotten texts, those without the cultural cachet of a Jefferson or Lincoln? One might respond that in principle nothing is stopping critics from looking at quotidian texts; but in practice, the lion's share of attention is directed at the presumptively "great" rhetorical productions of American history. In doing so, is not CTA complicit in silencing or otherwise bracketing out the many marginal voices of our cultural heritage?

Close textual analysis came of age in the field of communication studies during the 1980s and was closely associated with the work of several rhetoricians at the University of Wisconsin. The discipline, like many in the humanities, was undergoing significant transformations, especially with respect to what was called the politics of interpretation. Critics and theorists were increasingly concerned to expose the epistemological and methodological assumptions underlying their scholarly work. Operating within this climate, CTA came under considerable scrutiny for reproducing certain habits that were thought to be suspect; we have noted above two such lines of critique. A third, and for our purposes final, such argument continues to challenge its practitioners and is in fact an extension of the concern over idealizing and canonizing the text as an object of inquiry. Put simply, this critique asks us to reconsider what it is that texts—much less textual criticism—can really tell us about the power of language and the language of power.

So what is the explanatory force of a given text? One way to get at this question is to ask another: is a text a cause or an effect? For those skeptical of CTA, the answer tends to focus on the latter. That is, the text is an effect. The line of argument runs something like this: humans are decisively shaped by the material, social, and ideological forces within which they act. Consequently, what they produce—including texts—are themselves the result or effect of these forces. To claim that a text is unique, or the hallmark of individual genius, or otherwise independent of the political milieu in which it is produced is to remain trapped in an idealized and delusory model of interpretation. Here the claim is not that texts are incapable of instigating action in the world; it is rather that texts alone can never be accorded such a primary role. They can only be, again, the effects of power relations already extant and operating in a given historical moment. Close textual critics will want to ask themselves whether such reasoning makes sense, and if so, how their own practice systematically acknowledges the point. Is CTA politically naive? Does it tend to extract the text from the very interstices of power that gives rise to texts in the first place? Or can we have it both ways, that is, justify the focus on a single text even as we place it in situ and within the material conditions of its own making?

These are all legitimate questions, but again they are perhaps best addressed by those now considering the possibilities and limits of CTA for the first time. At a minimum, we may conclude that we have in CTA a robust and systematic resource for the interpretation of rhetorical texts, that it offers a means of understanding how texts work by engaging them carefully and with great detail, and that it sets on display the very human drama of language in action.

## CTA TOP PICKS

Benson, Thomas W. "The Rhetorical Structure of Frederick Wiseman's *High School*." *Communication Monographs* 47 (1980): 233–261. Benson presents a fine-grained analysis of the famed documentary filmmaker's masterpiece, with special emphasis on the play of form and content.

Black, Edwin. "Gettysburg and Silence." *Quarterly Journal of Speech* 80 (1994): 21–36. A subtle but provocative analysis of Lincoln's address, Black's essay is sharply attuned as much to what Lincoln did not say as what he did say.

Browne, Stephen H. "Encountering Angelina Grimke: Violence, Identity, and the Creation of Radical Community." *Quarterly Journal of Speech* 82 (1996): 55–73. Browne examines the first public statement by the early abolitionist and finds evidence of a radical consciousness coming into being.

Campbell, Karlyn Kohrs. "Stanton's 'Solitude of Self': A Rationale for Feminism." *Quarterly Journal of Speech* 66 (1980): 304–312. Campbell explores Stanton's speech as a statement on the human condition, which in turn operates as a summons to enlightened political action.

Fulkerson, Richard P. "The Public Letter as Rhetorical Form: Structure, Logic, and Style in King's 'Letter from Birmingham Jail.'" *Quarterly Journal of Speech* 65 (1979): 121–136. A fine-grained and systematic analysis of the interplay between textual form and rhetorical function.

Leff, Michael. "Textual Criticism: The Legacy of G. P. Mohrmann." *Quarterly Journal of Speech* 72 (1986): 377–389. Leff explains the rationale for textual analysis and provides concrete examples of how it works.

Lucas, Stephen E. "Justifying America: The Declaration of Independence as a Rhetorical Document." In *American Rhetoric: Contexts and Criticism*, ed. Thomas W. Benson, 67–131 (Carbondale: Southern Illinois University Press, 1989). A tour de force essay combining close textual analysis, deep historical learning, and sharply observed insights into the founding text.

Lyon, Janet. *Manifestoes: Provocations of the Modern* (Ithaca, NY: Cornell University Press, 1999). Lyon provides a rich and sophisticated analysis of how texts perform ideological work.

Middleton, Richard, ed. *Reading Pop: Approaches to Textual Analysis in Popular Music* (Oxford: Oxford University Press, 2003). A wide-ranging but rigorous collection of essays in the textual analysis of contemporary musical forms.

## NOTES

1. In addition to essays noted in the "CTA Tops Picks" section, the following articles are representative of some of the notable works of close textual analysis: Michael C. Leff and Gerald P. Mohrmann, "Lincoln at Cooper Union: A Rhetorical Analysis of the Text," *Quarterly Journal of Speech* 60 (1974): 346–358; Kenneth Burke, "The Rhetoric of Hitler's Battle," in *The Philosophy of Literary Form*, 191–220 (Berkeley: University of California Press, 1971); Amy R. Slagell, "Anatomy of a Masterpiece: A Close Textual Analysis of Abraham Lincoln's Second Inaugural Address" *Communication Studies* 42 (1991): 155–171; Michael C. Leff, "Things Made by Words: Reflections on Textual Criticism," *Quarterly Journal of Speech* 78 (1992): 223–231; and Martin J. Medhurst, "Reconceptualizing Rhetorical History: Eisenhower's Farewell Address," *Quarterly Journal of Speech* 80 (1994).

2. Transcripts are readily available online. One such transcript can be found at the National Public Radio website: http://www.npr.org/templates/story/story.php?storyId=88478467.

3. For summaries of the early twentieth-century growth of the communication discipline, see Thomas W. Benson, "The Cornell School of Rhetoric: Idiom and Institution," *Communication Quarterly* 51 (2003): 1–56; Jim A. Kuypers and Andrew King, eds., *Twentieth-Century Roots of Rhetorical Studies* (Westport, CT: Praeger, 2001); and Theodore Otto Windt Jr., *Rhetoric as a Human Adventure: A Short Biography of Everett Lee Hunt* (Annandale, VA: Speech Communication Association, 1990).

4. See especially Sacvan Bercovitch, *The American Jeremiad* (Madison: University of Wisconsin Press, 1978); and James R. Darsey, *The Prophetic Tradition and Radical Rhetoric in America* (New York: New York University Press, 1999).

5. For an examination of Winthrop's sermon, see Stephen Howard Browne, "Errand into Mercy: Rhetoric, Identity, and Community in John Winthrop's 'Modell of Christian Charity,'" in *Rhetoric, Religion, and the Roots of Identity in British Colonial America*, ed. James R. Andrews, 1–36 (East Lansing: Michigan State University Press, 2007).

6. Representative essays treating these texts include Stephen E. Lucas, "Justifying America: The Declaration of Independence as a Rhetorical Document," in *American Rhetoric: Contexts and Criticism*, ed. Thomas W. Benson, 67–131 (Carbondale: Southern Illinois University Press, 1989); Stephen Howard Browne, *Jefferson's Call for Nationhood: The First Inaugural Address* (College Station: Texas A&M University Press, 2003); Garry Wills, *Lincoln at Gettysburg: The Words That Remade America* (New York: Simon and Schuster, 2005); Suzanne Daughton, "Metaphorical Transcendence: Images of the Holy War in Franklin Roosevelt's First Inaugural," *Quarterly Journal of Speech* 79 (1993): 227–246; and Drew Hansen, *The Dream: Martin Luther King and the Speech that Inspired a Nation* (New York: Ecco, 2003).

# 9

# Criticism of Metaphor

*David Henry and Thomas R. Burkholder*

On August 28, 1963, Martin Luther King Jr. began his speech on the steps of the Lincoln Memorial in Washington, D.C.: "Five score years ago, a great American, in whose symbolic shadow we stand today, signed the Emancipation Proclamation. This momentous decree came as a *great beacon light of hope* to millions of Negro slaves, who had been *seared in the flames of withering injustice*. It came as a *joyous daybreak to end the long night of their captivity*."[1] Rhetorical scholars recognize immediately the "trope" or figure of speech present in this passage—and throughout King's speech—that contributed to making "I Have a Dream" both memorable and of continuing scholarly interest: **metaphor**.

Most undergraduate students probably encounter metaphor and its companion figure, **simile**, in introductory public speaking or English composition courses. Usually, those figures are discussed as means of embellishing the style of written compositions or speeches. For example, Stephen E. Lucas asserts that "speakers can use imagery . . . to make their ideas come alive." Two means of generating imagery, he explains, are metaphor and simile.[2] Likewise, David Zarefsky points out that "analogy is a powerful form of reasoning: a comparison can help people to accommodate a new idea or new information by deciding that it is similar to what they already know or believe. Comparisons can be made vivid by using similes and metaphors."[3]

Zarefsky's comment suggests how metaphor and simile are alike: both are comparisons of one thing to another. Technically, the difference between metaphor and simile is that similes always include either *like* or *as*, while metaphors do not. Thus, saying that "lowering the drinking age to eighteen is *like* giving a stick of dynamite to a baby"[4] is a simile, while saying that "teenagers drinking *is* dynamite in the hands of babies" is a metaphor. Imagine other ways of expressing the same idea. Instead of using a metaphor or simile, one might say, "Lowering the drinking age to eighteen would be dangerous." The meaning is virtually the same, but with the metaphor or simile, the statement gains its vivid, forceful quality. Thus, regardless of whether the figure is technically a metaphor or a simile, it functions to embellish the style of a written or spoken message by making ideas vivid. In that sense, distinctions between the two figures matter little.

Despite these important stylistic or ornamental functions of metaphor and simile, critics are most interested in their *rhetorical* functions, in their capacity to influence the thoughts and actions of readers and listeners. That is especially true of metaphor, which rhetorician Kenneth

Burke has called one of the four "master tropes."⁵ In this chapter, we explore the rhetorical functions of metaphor. Then we suggest how the criticism of metaphor might proceed. Finally, we illustrate criticism of metaphor through analysis of the keynote address delivered at the 1984 Democratic National Convention by the late Mario Cuomo, former governor of New York.

## HOW METAPHORS WORK

A metaphor consists of two terms that draw a comparison between two things, people, places, situations, or events that belong to "different classes of experience."⁶ One of those two terms, usually called the *tenor* or *focus*, is *relevant* to or *continuous* with the topic under discussion. The other term, usually called the *vehicle* or *frame*, is *discontinuous* with, or of a different class of experience from, that topic.⁷ When the two terms, the *tenor* (or *focus*) and the *vehicle* (or *frame*), are brought together by a speaker or writer to form a metaphor, readers or listeners are invited to see the comparison between the two.

For example, while discussing means of coping with the pressures and stresses of contemporary life, the popular TV psychologist Dr. Phil McGraw tells his audience, "Life is a full-contact sport, and there's a score up on the board."⁸ The discussion is about life's problems, so the term *life* is the tenor of the metaphor because it is continuous with the topic under discussion. The term *full-contact sport* is the vehicle of the metaphor because it is discontinuous with that topic; in other words, it is from a different class of experience.

McGraw's metaphor serves obvious stylistic functions. It is vivid and memorable because we usually do not think of life as a sport; however, it serves potentially more powerful *rhetorical* functions as well. Listeners are invited to consider the similarities between life and a full-contact sport. In doing so, their thoughts—their perceptions or understanding of life—are altered, and perhaps their everyday actions are changed. The potential for such changes in thought and action is evident when we consider an alternative metaphor. A television advertisement for a popular Italian restaurant, Macaroni Grill, says that "life is delicious." If we follow that metaphor, the way we think about life and plan our everyday actions will be very different from a full-contact sport.

### Rhetorical Functions of Metaphor

Rhetorically, metaphors ask readers or listeners to comprehend one thing, represented by the tenor, "in terms of" another, represented by the vehicle. When that happens, certain relevant and important characteristics of the vehicle are "carried over" to the tenor, thus providing a new understanding of that term.⁹ According to Malcolm O. Sillars and Bruce E. Gronbeck, "metaphor, because it draws an analogy among situations that are unrelated (e.g., 'the war on drugs,' 'a marriage of convenience,' 'loan sharks'), is a way to create new thought through language use. Thus, it is central to making sense through language."¹⁰ That sense making, however, depends on whether or not readers or listeners can make the link—that is, whether they understand what elements or characteristics of the vehicle appropriately "carry over" to the tenor. Martha Cooper provides an additional example that explains this rhetorical function of metaphor:

> Probably the classic metaphor is, "man is a wolf." This statement encourages the audience to associate the characteristic(s) of a wolf with man. Stated more directly, the pattern is simply "man is

like a wolf." The metaphor *works like* an enthymeme in that the audience is asked to participate by supplying the characteristics of a wolf and drawing the comparison between wolves and man. The metaphor, by suggesting an association, triggers a pattern of thinking in which comparisons are chained out.[11]

When readers or listeners make the association that Cooper explains, when they complete the association in their minds, their perception or understanding of humans is changed.

That intended change in perception, however, occurs only when the appropriate characteristics of the vehicle, "wolf," are carried over to the tenor, "man." After all, wolves walk on four feet. Their bodies are covered with fur. They have tails, an acute sense of smell, and long teeth, and sometimes they howl at the moon. Although possible, it is doubtful that the speaker or writer who says, "Man is a wolf," intends for man to be seen in terms of those wolflike characteristics. On the other hand, wolves are strong, powerful, cunning predators. They are fiercely territorial. They are dangerous to other animals and sometimes to each other. It is almost certainly wolflike characteristics such as these that the speaker or writer intends for listeners or readers to "carry over" to humans. Thus, listeners or readers must "get it"; they must complete the enthymeme for the metaphor to have its intended effect.

Such rhetorical functions of metaphor grow from what anthropologist J. David Sapir calls "the simultaneous likeness and unlikeness of the two terms." According to Sapir, "by replacing a term continuous to a topic with one that is discontinuous or by putting the two in juxtaposition, we are compelled . . . to consider each term in relationship to the other."[12] Thus, to complete the association presented by the metaphor, "man is a wolf," listeners or readers must be aware simultaneously of how men and wolves are both alike and different. In the process of completing the association, the differences are discarded and the likenesses emphasized. Or, in Burke's words, the metaphor "brings out the thisness of that, or the thatness of this."[13] Michael Leff explains that the thought process involved "works in two stages; the juxtaposition of the two terms first causes the vehicle to assume a pattern of foreground associations, and then this pattern serves to direct our understanding of the tenor." The "mutual attraction of terms belonging to different classes," Leff writes, "causes a response that decomposes the elements associated with these terms and then recombines them into a new structure of meaning."[14] In the case of our example, "man is a wolf," when the process is complete the metaphor has performed its *rhetorical* function and listeners or readers begin to think of man in terms of the appropriate characteristics of wolves.

Cooper's assertion that metaphors function like enthymemes, arguments in which the audience participates in forming the conclusion, is especially important for rhetorical critics. If the function of metaphor depends on cooperation between the rhetor (the writer or speaker) and the audience (the readers or listeners) to produce meaning, then both must be part of the same "speech community." That is, they must at minimum share knowledge and experiences that allow the rhetor to form, and the audience to complete, the enthymeme. Ideally, in addition to knowledge and experience, they must also share beliefs, attitudes, and values that would permit the audience to complete the argument as the rhetor intends.[15] Imagine audience members who have no knowledge whatsoever of the vehicle, wolf. For them, the metaphor, "man is a wolf," would do little to alter their understanding of the tenor, man. Or imagine an audience whose beliefs, attitudes, and values related to "man" have been previously influenced by a competing metaphor, such as the Christian teaching that "man is a temple for the Holy Spirit." Even though that audience may understand the appropriate characteristics of wolves that the rhetor wishes them to carry over to man, they may be extremely reluctant to do so.

As Leff explains, "metaphor draws its materials from communal knowledge, achieves its effects through the active cooperation of the auditor, and assumes its form in relation to a particular context."[16] Thus, if rhetor and audience are from different speech communities, the metaphor is likely to have little rhetorical, or even ornamental, effect.

## Metaphor in Political Discourse

Sometimes the associations between the metaphoric tenor and the vehicle are relatively simple and straightforward, as in the examples provided thus far. But in other cases, those associations can become extremely complex and powerful, altering our understanding of significant issues and events. According to Leff, "Since metaphoric structure limits and organizes our perception of a situation, it seems to establish the ground for viewing that situation; it creates a perspective and hence defines the space in which we encounter the situation. A metaphoric meaning localizes our attention . . . it produces a frame within which we can synthesize our reactions to the ongoing flow of events in time."[17] In other words, metaphors can determine how we think about issues and the actions we take with regard to those issues. That function of metaphor is arguably most obvious and potentially most powerful in political discourse and continues to be a source for current research dealing with topics as diverse as Ground Zero discussions, President Obama's use of movement metaphors, and the emergence of the democracy promotion industry.[18]

"Politics" and its companion subject "government" are extremely complex issues. When we think of "politics" we may think of politicians, of the citizens whose votes determine the outcomes of elections, or we may even think of the "political process" within which politicians and citizens act. Yet as complex as that process and the relationships between those individuals are, this is just the beginning.

We "do" politics at the local, state, national, and international levels. At least at the first three, politics involves executive, legislative, and judicial functions. Elected officials are joined in those functions by tens of thousands of public employees, staff members, researchers, aides, advisers, law enforcement officers, military personnel, diplomats, and the like. Those individuals, even more so than elected officials, are the "elites"[19] of politics—highly skilled or trained individuals often with considerable experience in dealing with myriad social, economic, legal, environmental, medical, and foreign policy issues, to name only a few. In the area of foreign policy, the complexity of "politics" is magnified by similar systems and processes in the nations with which the United States must deal. Obviously, the details of "politics" are far too complex for any single individual to grasp fully. That fact holds significant implications for political discourse, the persuasive efforts to influence thought and action within the political system. To cope with the almost unending complexity of government, political discourse relies heavily on metaphor.

In one important sense, metaphors are essential simply for understanding complex political issues. Psychologist Jeffrey Scott Mio asserts that "metaphors can act as both filters that screen out much of the available information, leaving only the core ideas consistent with the metaphors, and as devices to collapse disparate information into smaller, more manageable packets."[20] That is, by drawing comparisons between complicated political issues (the tenor) and more familiar, relatively simple events or ideas (the vehicle), metaphors in political discourse render those complicated issues understandable. Thompson provides a typical example:

> [T]he flow of revenue to the Federal government is determined by, among other things, macroeconomic policy, international trade and capital flows, and the perturbations of the business cycle. The

pattern of expenditures is influenced by social entitlements, continuing programs, new defense or civilian programs, and the vagaries of disaster relief. Individuals have experience with budgets, but they are typically simple enough affairs—income determined by one's salary and perhaps investments, and expenditures largely determined by the necessities of survival at the level to which one has become accustomed. In several fundamental ways the federal budget is not just a personal or household budget writ large. But for the typical citizen, and even for the relatively sophisticated policy maker, thinking about the federal budget typically begins with the metaphor of a household or business budget: *'[I]f the government were a company, it would have gone bankrupt years ago'; 'In government, just like your own home, you can't spend money you don't have.'*[21]

Thus, for both policy-making elites and for average citizens, the federal budget (tenor) becomes understandable in terms of the more familiar and considerably less complex budgets of a business or family (vehicle).

In perhaps a more important sense, metaphors in political discourse influence not only understanding but also actions—the policies enacted in response to public issues or problems. Talking about and envisioning the issue of illegal drugs as "a problem of addiction" or as a "symptom of social dysfunction" would lead to policies that focus on the role of social workers, counselors, and medical personnel, while declaring "war" on drugs would shift the focus to law enforcement and punishment or perhaps even to the military.[22]

So important is this rhetorical function of metaphor in political discourse that competing political forces—candidates for office, political parties, liberals, and conservatives—struggle for a sort of "metaphoric superiority." The metaphor that gains widest acceptance, within the government, in the public at large, or both, often determines the outcome of political contests. During the Vietnam conflict, for instance, supporters of US military action in Southeast Asia, known metaphorically as "hawks," frequently offered the domino theory to justify continued military efforts. On the other side of the issue, opponents of military action, known metaphorically as "doves," came to label the Vietnam conflict as a "quagmire" from which the United States should extricate itself. Neither the domino theory nor the quagmire, of course, explained fully the extremely complex social, economic, political, and military situation that existed in Southeast Asia. Nevertheless, both elite policy makers and ordinary US citizens came to see that geographic region as either a line of dominoes waiting to fall or as a quagmire. Eventually, the quagmire metaphor gained wider acceptance than the domino theory and the United States withdrew its military forces from South Vietnam.

Thompson points out that metaphors function in exactly the same way in domestic politics. "As much as they would like to, policy makers are unable to control the range of metaphors available or the uses to which they are put," he explains. "Opponents and interest groups in domestic politics compete vigorously to establish the winning metaphor in policy debates and, without too much exaggeration, campaigns can be seen as struggles over metaphors."[23] How one voted in the 2004 US presidential election, for example, may have been determined by whether one saw George Bush as "Baby Bush" or "The man in the arena."

Critics must also keep in mind that these potentially powerful rhetorical functions of metaphor are not without potential risks. One of those risks is that use of metaphor may so oversimplify complex issues or problems that proposed remedies are themselves oversimplified to the point of ineffectiveness. As already noted, Mio explains that metaphors "screen out much of the available information, leaving only the core ideas." Unfortunately, the key to resolving complex political issues often lies in managing details rather than in core ideas.

Metaphors may also be a double-edged sword that can work both for and against the interests of rhetors who use them. Put differently, although metaphors may produce desired rhetorical effects, they can also entrap the rhetors who use them. As we explained earlier, declaring "war" on drugs leads to policies that feature intensified law enforcement efforts and perhaps even the use of US military forces to interdict drug shipments and to arrest and punish drug dealers. The metaphor also has significant rhetorical power to rally public support for those efforts. Nevertheless, the United States simply cannot "win" a war on drugs in the sense of "winning" a war against another nation; that is, "drugs" can never be forced to sign an "unconditional surrender" and submit to an "army of occupation" to enforce the terms of that surrender. So, although officials who declare "war" on drugs may enjoy some short-term rhetorical success in the form of public support for their programs, and those programs may produce some dramatic results, the metaphor may also create expectations for the outcome of that "war" that are simply unattainable. Continuing frustration with the drug problem in the United States may be a result.[24]

Perhaps the greatest of those risks occurs when metaphors become "literalized," that is, when we stop thinking of one thing *in terms of* another and begin to think of it as literally *being* the other. As Robert L. Ivie explains, "We are in the presence of a literalized metaphor when we act upon the figurative as if it were real, not recognizing that two domains of meaning have been merged into one despite their differences."[25] Ivie's analysis of Cold War rhetoric revealed a cluster of metaphoric images that were commonly used to characterize both the United States and the Soviet Union. "Summarized briefly, these vehicles illustrate the rhetorical essentials of the logic of confrontation," he notes. "The nation's adversary is characterized as a mortal threat to freedom, a germ infecting the body politic, a plague upon the liberty of humankind, and a barbarian intent upon destroying civilization." Equally vivid were the metaphors that depicted the United States. Ivie continues, "Freedom is portrayed as weak, fragile, and feminine—as vulnerable to disease and rape. The price of freedom is necessarily high because the alternatives are reduced symbolically to enslavement and death."[26] The problem, says Ivie, was that these metaphors became literalized in a way that severely and unnecessarily limited the policies available to the United States. According to Ivie, these metaphors "evolved over four decades into powerful conventions of public discourse that diminish the political imagination, undermine the incentive to envision better alternatives, and thus reduce the scope of practical options available to leaders of both nations. . . . Yet, the stuff of which these durable motives are made is mere metaphor."[27] In other words, Cold War rhetors were also trapped by their language.

Similarly, in his analysis of Cold War rhetoric, Edwin Black suggests that the pervasiveness of the "cancer of communism" metaphor in the rhetoric of the most radical elements of the right in US politics may have brought the world to the brink of nuclear war. Noting that the "cancer of communism" metaphor is "simply not present in 'liberal' or leftist discourses," Black argues that "it seems to crop up constantly among Rightists—Rightists who sometimes have little else in common besides a political position and the metaphor itself." Further, Black suggests that the "cancer of communism" metaphor may have been "literalized," to use Ivie's term, in a way that risked nuclear annihilation. According to Black, what we little understand is that when a radical rightist

> refers to America, he refers to a polity already in the advanced stages of an inexorable disease whose suppurating sores are everywhere manifest and whose voice is a death rattle. . . . The patient is *in extremis*. It is in this light that risks must be calculated, and in this light the prospect of nuclear war becomes thinkable. Why not chance it, after all? What alternative is there? The patient is dying; is it not time for the ultimate surgery? What is there to lose? In such a context, an unalarmed attitude toward the use of atomic weapons is not just reasonable; it is obvious.[28]

Ivie and Black are not alone in warning of the perils of literalizing metaphors of disease and illness. Steven Perry's analysis of the "infestation metaphor" in the rhetoric of Adolf Hitler helps to explain how significant segments of the German population of the 1930s and 1940s were persuaded to turn violently against their own Jewish brothers and sisters. Perry explains:

> Though there was unquestionably a very real current of anti-semitism in central Europe at the time of National Socialism's rise, the Jews nonetheless were not popularly perceived as enemies of the German nation. Hitler had to shape and channel popular anti-semitism; particularly, he had to explain how it was that the heretofore *scorned* Jew was actually a dangerous and foreign threat to the very foundation of the German nation. The use of infestation metaphors provided Hitler with the answer. Such metaphors were suitably de-humanizing, and, even more important, they provided a figurative explanation of the Jewish threat: The Jew was like the disease-causing microbe, the internal parasite, or the secretly-administered poison, wreaking an invisible but ultimately fatal havoc on the national body. Hence, it was not as though the Jew had somehow suddenly metamorphosed from a worthless but harmless object of scorn into a full-blown national threat. Rather, the Jew had always posed such a threat, and the German masses had only needed a savior, a Hitler, to rise and show them the real working of the insidious, invisible Jewish plague.[29]

Thus, Perry suggests, was Hitler able to persuade Germany to follow him into the Holocaust.

In sum, metaphors work by drawing comparisons between two things, people, places, situations, or events. In doing so, they can embellish the style of written and oral messages alike. More important, they also have the capacity to perform powerful rhetorical functions, altering the thoughts and actions of readers and listeners. Additionally, although metaphors are potentially powerful figures of speech, their use also entails potential risk. We turn now to how rhetorical critics might make use of this knowledge of metaphor.

## CRITIQUING METAPHOR

We view rhetorical criticism as a primary means for creating knowledge in the humanistic study of communication. Further, we believe strongly that for criticism to fulfill that function, it must be an "organic" or inductive process. That process ends by bringing together textual, contextual, theoretical, interpretive, and evaluative elements in a finished critique. It begins, however, with a close, exhaustive reading of the rhetorical artifact under consideration, the end of which is largely descriptive at the initial stage. When that descriptive analysis is complete, the discourse is placed within its historical and cultural **context**, and the rhetorical problems or obstacles to success faced by the rhetor must be explained. Based on a thorough understanding of both text and context, critics select or invent a theoretical framework or analytical tool, such as a theory of metaphor, that both guides the completed analysis and suggests criteria or standards for interpretation and evaluation. Only when the above is complete can the textual, contextual, theoretical, interpretive, and evaluative elements be brought together.[30]

Thus, we believe that to talk about "metaphor criticism" as a distinct form or type of rhetorical criticism is both misleading and potentially counterproductive. Rather, we see metaphor as one of many analytical tools available to critics, a theoretical framework that can guide rhetorical analysis. Put differently, critics should "do" metaphor criticism only when careful descriptive analysis of the text in question reveals that metaphor is a significant—perhaps the *most* significant—rhetorical element in that text. To reverse this process, to start with a theory of metaphor and then apply it indiscriminately to whatever text happens to be in question, renders the entire critical process fraudulent.[31] The process, then, must begin with a thorough, close reading of the text under consideration; if it reveals that metaphor is a salient rhetorical element in the text, relevant theory can become a useful analytical tool.

When metaphor is a significant element of the text, critics should determine whether a single major metaphor is developed throughout the text or whether a series of metaphors are present. If a series of metaphors are present, critics should determine whether they operate independently or whether they cohere into a single vision or image. For example, a close reading of Martin Luther King Jr.'s 1963, "I Have a Dream" reveals that three major, interrelated metaphors dominate the text: (1) the "promise" set forth in the Declaration of Independence "that all men would be guaranteed the unalienable rights of life, liberty, and the pursuit of happiness" (the tenor) characterized metaphorically as a "check" or "promissory note to which every American was to fall heir" but that had yet to be paid in full (the vehicle); (2) King's goal of a free and just society if only the check were to be cashed (tenor), characterized metaphorically as his "dream" (vehicle); and (3) King's vision of the "great nation" the United States could become (tenor), characterized metaphorically as freedom "ringing" throughout the land (vehicle).[32]

Those three major metaphors in King's speech cohere into a single vision in that they "move" chronologically from the past (the promise set forth in the Declaration of Independence), to 1963 (conditions of oppression for black Americans as a result of the failure of the United States to "cash the check"), and into the future (the vision of freedom ringing throughout the land). Moreover, the metaphors cohere even further in that they also move from bad (the social and economic conditions faced by black Americans) to good (the free and just society King envisioned).

Critics should determine as well whether minor or secondary metaphors are present in the text, and if so, how they interact with the major metaphor or metaphors. Once again, secondary metaphors appear throughout King's "I Have a Dream" speech. Some stand alone to create vivid images in the minds of listeners. For instance, social conditions (tenor) are depicted metaphorically when King explains that black Americans are "still sadly crippled by the manacles of segregation and the chains of discrimination" (vehicle). Economic conditions (tenor) are depicted when he says that black Americans are living "on a lonely island of poverty in the midst of a vast ocean of material prosperity" (vehicle). However, other secondary metaphors function to reinforce the past-present-future and bad-to-good relationship between the major metaphors: "Now is the time to lift our nation from the quicksands of racial injustice to the solid rock of brotherhood," said King. "The whirlwinds of revolt will continue to shake the foundations of our nation until the bright day of justice emerges," he continued.

When major and secondary metaphors have been identified, critics might productively ask, What elements or characteristics of the vehicle does the rhetor intend for the audience to carry over to the tenor? How do those elements or characteristics function to alter audience understanding of the tenor? How is that altered understanding related to the purpose or purposes the rhetor wishes to achieve? How do the metaphors interact with other rhetorical strategies present in the text? Finally, how might the use of metaphor best be interpreted or evaluated?

We hope this brief description suggests at least a general direction for critiquing metaphor. Now we turn to an example of metaphor criticism that incorporates all of the elements of a finished critique that we mentioned earlier: contextualization, a theoretical framework or analytical tool, application of that theory to illuminate the text, and interpretation and evaluation.

# CRITICAL ESSAY

The text we have selected for analysis in our example of metaphor criticism is the keynote address delivered on July 16, 1984, to the Democratic National Convention in San Francisco by the late Mario Cuomo, then governor of New York. Although the speech was delivered over thirty years ago, it is especially well suited for this example. Even a cursory reading of Cuomo's speech reveals that metaphor is a significant—perhaps the *most* significant—rhetorical element in that text. Thus, the speech is not only a model of rhetorical excellence, but its analysis also provides beginning rhetorical critics with a clear example of a text that warrants metaphor criticism.

---

## MARIO CUOMO'S KEYNOTE ADDRESS TO THE 1984 DEMOCRATIC NATIONAL CONVENTION[33]

Immediate reactions to New York Governor Mario Cuomo's keynote address to the 1984 Democratic National Convention were extremely positive. Delegates in the convention hall lavished praise. "'He's reaching an emotional chord that hasn't been touched since John Kennedy,' said Lucille Maurer, a Maryland legislator from Silver Spring."[34] "It was a perfect speech," added Virginia state party chairman Alan A. Dimondstein. "He talked about the middle class. We're talking about a man who stood up and expressed the feelings of the majority of people in America."[35]

Media pundits were likewise kind in their assessment of the speech. Hedrick Smith of the *New York Times* observed that Cuomo "built a speech like a lawyer making a case,"[36] and then added: "Beforehand, [Cuomo's] aides had said the keynote was 'not a stemwinder, not a podium-pounder' but a carefully constructed indictment of the Reagan legacy. Yet with eyes welling with tears and a powerful rhythmic delivery, the Governor repeatedly roused the Democrats to foot-stomping applause and roaring partisan chants."[37] Howell Raines, also of the *New York Times*, noted the "persistent, preacherly rhythm" of Cuomo's speech.[38] Lou Cannon and Helen Dewar of the *Washington Post* observed that "the delegates . . . listened in rapt attention to the New York governor and interrupted him with applause 42 times."[39]

Interesting as those comments are, they do little to explain the rhetorical force of Cuomo's speech. That is, although those comments describe Cuomo's delivery of the speech and the positive reactions of both the delegates and the press, they do not reveal the elements within the text that had the capacity to produce those positive reactions. The rhetorical force of the speech, we believe, grew from the Governor's use of metaphor to refute President Ronald Reagan's own metaphoric depiction of the United States as a "Shining City on a Hill," and then to depict the people of the United States as a "family" that must reject Reagan's policies and elect a Democrat as president.

### The Context: Obstacles to Rhetorical Success

Cuomo suggested the purpose of his keynote address in the third paragraph of the speech when he said that he would "deal immediately with questions that should determine this election and that we all know are vital to the American people."[40] But a simple enumeration of campaign issues was obviously not his ultimate aim. Instead, he sought to unite Democrats and other voters to elect Walter Mondale and Geraldine Ferraro president and vice president of the United States. At the end of the address he said:

> And, ladies and gentlemen, on January 20, 1985 . . . we will have a new president of the United States, a Democrat born not to the blood of kings but to the blood of pioneers and immigrants.

> And we will have America's first woman vice president, the child of immigrants, and she . . . will open with one magnificent stroke, a whole new frontier for the United States. Now, it will happen. It will happen—if we make it happen; if you and I can make it happen.

In his effort to achieve that purpose, Cuomo faced significant rhetorical problems growing from the generic obstacles encountered by all keynote speakers as well as from obstacles unique to his specific situation.

### Generic Obstacles

The opening of a political party's national convention is an identifiable, regularly recurring ceremony that requires that a speech be given to fulfill expectations for the occasion. Thus, Wayne N. Thompson called keynote addresses "a subgenre of ceremonial speaking,"[41] making them epideictic in Aristotelian terms and suggesting that their method should be praise and blame.[42] But the purpose of keynote addresses goes beyond traditional aims of epideictic speaking. As Edwin A. Miles observed, the "keynote speech has two primary purposes: to raise the enthusiasm of the delegates to a high pitch and to rally the voters of the nation to the party's standard."[43] That is, in addition to any purely ceremonial functions, the pragmatic aim of keynote addresses is to help the party's nominee win the coming presidential election. Cuomo's purpose reveals just that aim.

The keynote address, then, is a **rhetorical hybrid**. It employs *epideictic* means—praise and blame—appropriate to the ceremonial occasion in order to achieve *deliberative* ends, election of the party's candidate. Thus, Miles explained that highly-partisan audiences in the convention hall came to expect keynote speakers' "language . . . to be bombastic, for custom demands that he 'avoid no extravagance of speech, either in praise or blame' in glorifying the brilliant accomplishments of his own party or in lamenting the dismal failures of the opposition."[44]

Unfortunately, perhaps, for contemporary speakers, widespread television coverage of keynote addresses has been problematic. Keynoters encounter not only the partisan, immediate audience, but also a large and diverse audience watching the televised speech at home. Some members of that larger audience are equally partisan, but most vary in their conviction and many support the opposition.[45] Those **dual audiences** present keynote speakers with a dilemma. According to Thompson, "whereas emotional partisans of a speaker's own party expect a vigorous attack on the opposition, neutrals and members of the other political party are likely to find strong attacks irritating and offensive."[46]

Cuomo faced those obstacles generic to the keynote situation as he addressed the 1984 Democratic National Convention. But like any other keynote speaker, he also faced obstacles growing from the specific problems that developed as Democrats prepared to meet in San Francisco in mid-July.

### Specific Obstacles

On the eve of Cuomo's address, Democrats were dispirited and divided. Political commentators Jack W. Germond and Jules Witcover noted that many convention delegates (and probably many other Democrats as well!) despaired of Mondale's chances of defeating Ronald Reagan in November.[47] But the delegates' spirits were buoyed significantly, "when the word of Gerry Ferraro's selection [as Mondale's vice-presidential running mate] filtered out on the Wednesday night before the convention was to open." The delegates' reaction to Ferraro, according to Germond and Witcover, was "akin to pulling the living room drapes back and letting the sunshine in. . . . [W]hat shook the Democrats out of their doldrums was the evidence in Mondale's decision that he was not the storefront Indian he seemed to so many of them to be—dull, unimaginative, the cardboard New Dealer who dared to be cautious," they explained.[48]

Despite the excitement over the selection of Ferraro, opinion polls indicated that the Democratic ticket was in trouble. As Robert Strauss, former head of the Democratic National Committee, explained: "If [Mondale and Ferraro] try to win a popularity contest with Ronald Reagan, they're not going to make much headway. The people of America like Ronald Reagan too well."[49] Strauss was right. The day after Cuomo's speech, the *Los Angeles Times* reported a Gallup poll indicating that "based on in-person interviews with a national sample of registered voters . . . Reagan-Bush beats Mondale-Ferraro, 53% to 39%. When Reagan and Mondale alone are pitted against each other, Reagan's margin is 55% to 36%." Among women voters, the same poll revealed, "the contest would be a virtual toss-up, with 47% choosing Reagan-Bush compared to 45% for Mondale-Ferraro. Among men, the GOP ticket leads 59% to 34%."[50]

Whether those figures signaled distrust of Mondale, approval of Reagan's political agenda and policies, or simple affection for the amiable president, they did not look good for the Democratic candidates. Moreover, coupled with the generic obstacles faced by all keynote speakers, they constituted significant rhetorical problems for Cuomo. To overcome those problems, Cuomo relied in large part on the strategic use of metaphor.

## Metaphor as Rhetorical Strategy

Cuomo's reliance on metaphor was consistent with expectations for epideictic speaking's elevated style. Nevertheless, consideration of the non-ornamental capacities of metaphor is essential for understanding its functions in Cuomo's keynote address. That metaphor serves more than embellishment has been demonstrated by scholarship in interaction theory and adapted in critical studies illustrating the significant interplay between metaphor and topical invention, wherein metaphor "frames rhetorical situations" while "topics order the elements within the frame."[51] Figures that frame situations support George Lakoff and Mark Johnson's thesis that metaphor is "primarily a matter of thought and action and only derivatively a matter of language," instrumental to our understanding of reality, and advantageous to people in power who "get to impose their metaphors."[52] The power to create a new order by imposing a metaphor that "redescribes reality," Paul Ricoeur argues, is contingent on first "creating rifts in an old order."[53] Moreover, the creation of dissonance is promoted when the similarities selected for a metaphorical frame are experiential rather than objective similarities. As Lakoff and Johnson point out, objectivists may be correct to suggest that "things in the world" constrain our conceptual systems, but that matters only if the "things" are experienced.[54] Metaphor's capacity to displace one "reality" with another by focusing on experiential themes is central to Cuomo's speech.

## Textual Analysis: Cuomo's Use of Metaphor

Cuomo's ultimate objective was to promote a vision of the American people as a "family." Movement toward that goal proceeded through three phases. First, consonant with the dictates of Ricoeur's theory of metaphor, Cuomo aimed to raise doubts about the accuracy of a favored Reagan figure, that of America as a "shining city on a hill."[55] Next, he moved to the articulation of the American family alternative. Finally, Cuomo offered his own family's experience as an embodiment of the metaphor's reflection of the American reality.

Since the creation of a new perception of reality is enhanced by an initial denigration of an old conception, Cuomo began his appeal with a revision of a favorite Reagan metaphor:

> Ten days ago, President Reagan admitted that although some people in this country seemed to be doing well nowadays, others were unhappy, even worried, about themselves, their families and their futures.
>
> The president said that he didn't understand that fear. He said, "Why, this country is a shining city on a hill."

And the president is right. In many ways we *are* "a shining city on a hill."

But the hard truth is that not everyone is sharing in this city's splendor and glory.

A shining city is perhaps all the president sees from the portico of the White House and the veranda of his ranch, where everyone seems to be doing well.

But there's another city, another part of the city, the part where some people can't pay their mortgages and most young people can't afford one, where students can't afford the education they need and middle-class parents watch the dreams they hold for their children evaporate.

In this part of the city there are more poor than ever, more families in trouble, and more and more people who need help but can't find it.

Even worse: There are elderly people who tremble in the basements of the houses there.

And there are people who sleep in the city streets, in the gutter, where the glitter doesn't show.

There are ghettos where thousands of young people, without a job or an education, give their lives away to drug dealers every day.

There is despair, Mr. President, in the faces that you don't see, in the places that you don't visit in our shining city.

In fact, you ought to know Mr. President, that this nation is more a "Tale of Two Cities" than it is just a "Shining City on a Hill."

The "Tale of Two Cities" metaphor was designed to "displace" Reagan's vision of reality, the "Shining City on a Hill," with a new vision. Significantly, Cuomo's contrasting metaphor did not force his listeners to see America from *either* the perspective of the Shining City *or* the perspective of its opposite—perhaps a "wasteland." Rather, America was *both* the Shining City that Reagan saw *and* a much more dismal place. Cuomo built the remainder of his anti-administration appeal on the foundation of the two-cities theme as he proceeded through a series of paired consequences he described as inevitable results of Reagan's programs. Republican policies, he argued, "divide the nation: into the lucky and the left-out, the royalty and the rabble. The Republicans are willing to treat that division as victory. They would cut this nation in half, into those temporarily better off and those worse off than before, and call it recovery." The Democrats' task, he continued, was to work for the election of a "new President of the United States." The challengers' success in 1984, Cuomo maintained, was contingent on supplanting one vision of the nation with another.

The objective, he intoned, was first to "make the American people hear our 'tale of two cities,'" and then to "convince them that we don't have to settle for two cities, that we can have one city, indivisible, shining for all its people." The metaphorical framing of his theme allowed Cuomo to figuratively allege objectionable consequences of the president's policies without alienating an increasingly patriotic electorate overwhelmingly enamored of the incumbent. At the same time, by raising doubts about the opposition's ideas, he fulfilled one of the functions of the keynote speech—blaming the opposition.

Praise of the Democratic Party stemmed from the subsequent introduction of the family metaphor. The family metaphor addressed the concerns of both the immediate convention observers and the "middle America" target audience. For partisans, the figure of the family served two purposes. At one level, Cuomo's enunciation of party achievements differentiated what he termed realistic, principled Democrats from their Republican counterparts. Cuomo contended, for instance, that whereas GOP policies preclude the metaphoric "wagon train" of American progress from reaching the "frontier unless some of our old, some of our young, and some of our weak are left behind," Democrats believe that "we can make it all the way with the whole family intact." This is, he continued, attested to by "wagon train after wagon train" of success, ever since Franklin Roosevelt "lifted himself from his wheelchair to lift this nation from its knees." Democrats led the way, in Cuomo's view: "To new frontiers of education, housing, peace. The whole family aboard. Constantly reaching out to extend and enlarge that family. Lifting them up into the wagon on the way. Blacks and Hispanics, and people of every ethnic group, and Native Americans—all those struggling to build their families and claim some small share of America."

The principles that underlay Cuomo's description of the party surely meshed with the personal facts influential in the target audience's thinking—family, mutual support, equality, and progress. Cuomo made explicit the link between such values and the ideals of the middle class when, late in the speech, he extended the family theme from the past and present to the future. "We can have a future that provides for all the young of the present," he asserted in a subtly worded play on the guiding family metaphor, "by marrying common sense and compassion." Success will depend, he suggested, on continued recognition of the importance of the party's "progressive principles. That they helped lift up generations to the middle class and higher: gave us a chance to work, go to college, to raise a family, to own a house, to be secure in our old age, and before that to reach heights that our own parents would not have dared dream of."

Although it is unlikely that many members of the larger public would take issue with the desirability of the middle-class family ideals he described, Cuomo clearly believed that his perspective of the American "city" and "family" differed sharply from that of citizens who consistently expressed favor with President Reagan's performance. Consequently, he sought to revise the dominant perception of the country's status. Cuomo spoke of Republican policies guided by a philosophy that dictated that government "can't do everything," so it should settle for taking care of "the strong and hope that economic ambition and charity will do the rest. Make the rich richer and what falls from the table will be enough for the middle class and those trying to make it into the middle class." Left to their own survival skills in a nation governed by such a philosophy are the "retired school teacher in Duluth," the "child in Buffalo," the "disabled man in Boston," and the hungry in Little Rock. An alternative, Cuomo maintained, was the Democratic principle of mutuality that underlay a government committed to the "good of us all, for the love of this great nation, for the American family, for the love of God."

What distinguished his pronouncement of this litany of stock political god-terms was Cuomo's personalization of them, for the ideas were not merely lines in a speech but convictions produced of a lifetime. Thus, when he moved into his peroration he reinforced the metaphorical base of his message. In so doing he offered his own experience as a warrant for a shift in the focus of public attention, away from a now tarnished "shining city on a hill" and toward recognition of a strong future via the "American family." The philosophy of mutuality that had moved Democrats to protect the retired, the young, the disabled, and the hungry, he claimed, "is the real story of the shining city. It's a story I didn't read in a book, or learn in a classroom. I saw it, and I lived it. Like many of you." Then Cuomo's own family became the symbol of the American story:

> I watched a small man with thick calluses on both hands work 15 and 16 hours a day. I saw him once literally bleed from the bottoms of his feet, a man who came here uneducated, alone, unable to speak the language, who taught me all I needed to know about faith and hard work by the simple eloquence of his example. I learned about our kind of democracy from my father. And, I learned about our obligation to each other from him and from my mother. They asked only for a chance to work and to make the world better for their children and they asked to be protected in those moments when they would not be able to protect themselves. This nation and this nation's government did that for them.
>
> And that they were able to build a family and live in dignity and see one of their children go from behind their little grocery store in South Jamaica on the other side of the tracks where he was born, to occupy the highest seat in the greatest state of the greatest nation in the only world we know, is an ineffably beautiful tribute to the democratic process.

With the choice of the family metaphor, Cuomo not only offered an alternative to the dominant Reagan trope, but also provided through his own experience a case for the efficacy of the alternative.

## Conclusion

Assessed for its effect, Gov. Mario Cuomo's keynote address to the 1984 Democratic National Convention merits a largely negative evaluation. His aim had been to rally support for the Democratic candidates, Walter Mondale and Geraldine Ferraro. But despite his best effort, Ronald Reagan and George H. W. Bush rolled to an impressive victory in November, carrying forty-nine states with 525 electoral votes to Mondale's 13—among the largest electoral-college margins in history.[56] However, given Reagan's enormous personal popularity, it is probably unfair to expect any keynote address, no matter how brilliant, to carry the election for Mondale and Ferraro.

Judged by an aesthetic standard, however, Cuomo's speech is worthy of praise as a highly-skilled effort to overcome significant rhetorical problems. Clearly, his rhetorical strategy met the situational and audience challenges posed by the keynote setting. By first raising doubts about the accuracy of Ronald Reagan's vision of America as a "shining city on a hill," Cuomo united his diverse listeners around the shared values and experiences common to both target audiences. He did so by packaging his theme of progressive pragmatism or traditional Democratic principles in the metaphorical container of the family, thereby offering an appealing alternative to the president's preferred but allegedly misleading trope.

Convention speakers faced with similar demands thus might be well advised to give due attention to the potential of figurative language as a powerful force for framing complex issues and engaging multiple audiences. The demonstrated capacity of metaphor to challenge established images and present attractive alternatives suggests the prospective value of such endeavors.

---

## PERSONAL REFLECTIONS

Cuomo's keynote address to the 1984 Democratic National Convention provides fertile ground for rhetorical analysis. Thus, although we believe our critique that focuses on Cuomo's use of metaphor yields significant insight into how the speech was intended to work, we also know that our metaphor analysis does not exhaust the text. Other critical approaches grounded in other rhetorical theories could have produced equally insightful analyses.

For example, a close reading of Cuomo's speech reveals the presence of another figure of speech that Kenneth Burke has also labeled one of the four "master tropes"—irony.[57] Interestingly, Cuomo's use of irony grows out of the metaphors he develops in the speech. More specifically, by contrasting Ronald Reagan's metaphor of the United States as a "Shining City on a Hill" with his own metaphor of the United States as a "Tale of Two Cities," Cuomo portrays Reagan as an "ironic victim" who is blind to the true condition of the country and out of touch with the needs of the people.[58] So, rather than focusing exclusively on Cuomo's use of metaphor, critics could focus on his use of irony or even on the interaction between the two.

Likewise, although we chose to examine Cuomo's speech as a single rhetorical act bounded by a relatively narrow historical context, it could also be viewed as a member of a group or class of similar rhetorical acts—the *genre* of political convention keynote addresses.[59] Taking that approach, critics might carefully describe the keynote genre, develop from that description a set of standards or criteria that might be used to evaluate individual speeches that form the genre, and then apply those criteria to Cuomo's speech.

We are not suggesting that any one of these three critical approaches—metaphor, irony, genre—is inherently superior or inferior to the others. Quite the contrary; we believe that the richness of Cuomo's speech allows for significant, insightful analysis from any of these approaches, and probably others as well. In other words, careful descriptive analysis of Cuomo's speech indicates that metaphor, irony, and genre are all three major rhetorical elements of the text. Critics might productively exploit all three, but it would be a mistake to assume that there is one—and *only* one—approach to the speech. In the case of our critique, we chose metaphor criticism because in this chapter we wanted to illustrate that approach.

## POTENTIALS AND PITFALLS

Appropriately used, metaphor criticism has the potential to reveal the rhetorical functions of language—of tropes and figures of speech—frequently imagined to be primarily ornamental. Although texts rich in metaphor may be aesthetically pleasing, metaphor analysis can reveal their capacity to alter thought and action and to influence—for good or ill—the policy decisions made by individuals and even by entire nations. Our critique of Cuomo's speech is one example of such analysis.

Earlier we suggested that critics should engage in metaphor criticism only when close analysis reveals that metaphor is a dominant element of the text in question. Thus, we believe that the major "pitfall" of metaphor analysis would be to use that theoretical perspective when it is not warranted by the text.

For example, on July 29, 1998, US Supreme Court associate justice Clarence Thomas, a politically conservative black American, addressed the National Bar Association (NBA), a largely liberal organization of black American lawyers. In that speech, Thomas sought to answer criticisms from many members of the NBA, as well as from the public, that his conservative judicial philosophy and many of his judicial rulings were somehow inappropriate for a black American jurist. Thomas's speech is rhetorically interesting and is especially important both socially and historically as a defense of black American conservatism. A close reading of Thomas's speech reveals that it contains many metaphors: "The hope that there would be expeditious resolutions to our myriad problems has . . . evaporated," "the stench of racial inferiority still confounds my olfactory nerves," "the opaque racial prism of analysis," "some who would not venture onto the more sophisticated analytical turf are quite content to play in the minor leagues of primitive harping," "the lingering stench of racism," "the battle between passion and reason," "the caldron of ridicule," and others. However, those metaphors appear in isolation and do not cohere in a rhetorically significant fashion.[60]

Likewise, George W. Bush's justifications for the US invasion of Iraq in March 2003 are extremely important historically, and they are also interesting rhetorically. However, although close textual analysis of Bush's major speeches reveals various isolated metaphors, once again they do not cohere in a rhetorically significant fashion. Rather, Bush's discourse on Iraq is dominated by mythic images of "good versus evil" that provide fertile ground for rhetorical analysis but not for metaphoric criticism.[61] Thus, despite the fact that metaphors appear in both the speech by Thomas and that by Bush, and the fact that these speeches are important both historically and rhetorically, we do not view metaphor criticism as a productive approach to these texts.

# METAPHOR CRITICISM TOP PICKS

We believe the following essays are exemplars of metaphor criticism that should be familiar to all beginning rhetorical critics:

Ausmus, William A. "Pragmatic Uses of Metaphor: Models and Metaphor in the Nuclear Winter Scenario." *Communication Monographs* 65 (1998): 67–82. The "nuclear winter" metaphor was a dominant trope in the campaign against atomic weapons in the late twentieth century. Ausmus examines the invention and evolution of the metaphor in two articles by Carl Sagan.

Black, Edwin. "The Second Persona." *Quarterly Journal of Speech* 56 (1970): 109–119. Black's essay illustrates how rhetors can invite listeners to assume roles or personas—to think of themselves in particular ways—that heighten the persuasiveness of speeches. He illustrates that strategy through analysis of the "cancer of communism" metaphor in the Cold War rhetoric of the radical right in US politics.

Cisneros, J. David. "Contaminated Communities: The Metaphor of 'Immigrant as Pollutant' in Media Representations of Immigration." *Rhetoric & Public Affairs* 11 (2008): 569–601. Popular rhetoric about immigration often aims to make concrete images of "problem-solution" relationships. Cisneros advances an alternative view, maintaining that the "immigrant as pollutant" depicted in mediated messages can have serious consequences for the public's perception and treatment of immigrants.

Condit, Celeste M., Benjamin R. Bates, Ryan Galloway, Sonja Brown Givens, Caroline K. Haynie, John W. Jordan, Gordon Stables, and Hollis Marshall West. "Recipes or Blueprints for Our Genes? How Contexts Selectively Activate the Multiple Meanings of Metaphor." *Quarterly Journal of Speech* 88 (2002): 303–325. The authors evaluate why "recipe" did not successfully replace "blueprint" as the dominant metaphor in 1990s public discourse about genetic research. Drawing from Josef Stern's *Metaphor in Context*, they assess context as a central variable in the construction of multiple meanings in rhetorical transactions.

Foley, Megan. "From Infantile Citizens to Infantile Institutions: The Metaphoric Transformation of Political Economy in the 2008 Housing Market Crisis." *Quarterly Journal of Speech* 98 (2012): 386–410. Historically state-citizen relationships feature government as parent and the people as children. Foley argues that the response to the housing crisis reversed this relationship, with citizens as parents to "infantile institutions."

Ivie, Robert L. "Metaphor and the Rhetorical Invention of Cold War 'Idealists.'" *Communication Monographs* 54 (1987): 165–182. This critique is a compelling analysis of metaphoric depictions of both the United States and the Soviet Union in the rhetoric of the Cold War.

Jensen, Robin E. "From Barren to Sterile: The Evolution of a Mixed Metaphor." *Rhetoric Society Quarterly* 45 (2015): 25–46. Examines the evolution of reproductive metaphors in seventeenth- to nineteenth-century discourses, and then analyzes those tropes as they apply to early twentieth-century texts. Findings suggest implications for positioning women as "more or less at fault for their lack of children."

Leff, Michael. "Topical Invention and Metaphoric Interaction." *Southern Speech Communication Journal* 48 (1983): 214–229. Leff takes issue with conventional treatments of rhetorical precepts, in which argument falls discretely within the province of invention and metaphor within the rubric of style. Grounding his analysis in the teachings of interaction theory, he explores metaphor's inventional potential through a close reading of Loren Eisley's essay, "The Bird and the Machine."

Osborn, Michael. "Archetypal Metaphor in Rhetoric: The Light-Dark Family." *Quarterly Journal of Speech* 53 (1967): 115–126. In this groundbreaking work, Osborn explores the universal appeal and persuasive potential of archetypal metaphor. He illustrates those characteristics of archetypal metaphor with a discussion of metaphors of light and darkness.

**Metaphor: Additional Readings**

Condit, Celeste M. "Pathos in Criticism: Edwin Black's Communism-as-Cancer Metaphor." *Quarterly Journal of Speech* 99 (2013): 1–26.

Daughton, Suzanne M. "Metaphorical Transcendence: Images of the Holy War in Franklin Roosevelt's First Inaugural." *Quarterly Journal of Speech* 79 (1993): 427–446. FDR combined religious and military "metaphoric clusters," Daughton contends, to create a controlling image of a holy war aimed concurrently to curb public anxieties and move them to action.

Henry, David. "The Rhetorical Dynamics of Mario Cuomo's 1984 Keynote Address: Situation, Speaker, Metaphor." *Southern Speech Communication Journal* 53 (1988): 105–120. This essay forms a partial basis for our critique of Cuomo's speech that appears earlier in this essay. It is an insightful treatment of the interaction between the speaker's background, the rhetorical situation, and the choice of metaphor as a key persuasive strategy.

Osborn, Michael. "Rhetorical Depiction." In *Form, Genre, and the Study of Political Discourse*, edited by Herbert W. Simons and Aram A. Aghazarian, 79–107 (Columbia: University of South Carolina Press, 1986). This essay extends Osborn's award-winning scholarship on light-dark metaphor. Rather than replicating his earlier work, Osborn advances a theory of depiction amenable to the criticism of mediated as well as verbal discourse.

Sopory, Pradeep, and James Price Dillard. "The Persuasive Effects of Metaphor: A Meta-Analysis." *Human Communication Research* 28 (2002): 382–419. Article reviews empirical research in metaphor's effects. Variables examined include source credibility, organization, and metaphor's effect on counterarguments.

# NOTES

1. The text of King's speech appears in James R Andrews and David Zarefsky, *Contemporary American Voices: Significant Speeches in American History, 1945–Present* (New York: Longman, 1992), 78–81, emphasis ours. All quotations from King's speech are from this source.

2. Stephen E. Lucas, *The Art of Public Speaking*, 11th ed. (Boston: McGraw-Hill, 2012), 228.

3. David Zarefsky, *Public Speaking: Strategies for Success*, 7th ed. (Boston: Pearson, 2014), 301. For more on metaphor as argument, see Steve Oswald and Alain Rihs, "Metaphor as Argument: Rhetorical and Epistemic Advantages of Extended Metaphors," *Argumentation* 28, no. 2 (2014): 133–159.

4. Zarefsky, *Public Speaking*, 301.

5. Kenneth Burke, *A Grammar of Motives* (Berkeley: University of California Press, 1969), 503.

6. Michael Leff, "Topical Invention and Metaphoric Interaction," *Southern Speech Communication Journal* 48 (1983): 217.

7. Leff, "Topical Invention," 216–217; J. David Sapir, "The Anatomy of Metaphor," *The Social Uses of Metaphor: Essays on the Anthropology of Rhetoric*, ed. J. David Sapir and J. Christopher Crocker (Philadelphia: University of Pennsylvania Press, 1977), 7.

8. Marc Peyser, "Paging Dr. Phil," *Newsweek*, September 2, 2002, 55.

9. Burke, *A Grammar of Motives*, 503–504.

10. Malcolm O. Sillars and Bruce E. Gronbeck, *Communication Criticism*, 2nd ed. (Prospect Heights, IL: Waveland Press, 2001), 102.

11. Martha Cooper, *Analyzing Public Discourse* (Prospect Heights, IL: Waveland Press, 1989), 111, emphasis ours. For a review of enthymeme, see chapter 7 of this text. See, too, Lloyd L. Bitzer, "Aristotle's Enthymeme Revisited," *Quarterly Journal of Speech* 45 (1959): 399–408.

12. Sapir, "The Anatomy of Metaphor," 9.

13. Burke, *A Grammar of Motives*, 503.

14. Leff, "Topical Invention," 217.

15. On this point, see Todd Vernon Lewis, "Religious Rhetoric in Southern College Football: New Uses for Religious Metaphors," *Southern Communication Journal* 78, no. 3 (2013): 202–214.

16. Leff, "Topical Invention," 219.

17. Leff, "Topical Invention," 219.

18. Theresa Ann Donofrio, "Ground Zero and Place-Making Authority: The Conservative Metaphors in 9/11 Families' 'Take Back the Memorial' Rhetoric," *Western Journal of Communication* 74, no. 2 (2010): 150–169; Jeremy L. Cox, "Politics in Motion: Barack Obama's Use of Movement Metaphors," *American Communication Journal* 14, no. 2 (2012): 1–13; Stephen J. Heidt, "Presidential Rhetoric, Metaphor, and the Emergence of the Democracy Promotion Industry," *Southern Communication Journal* 78, no. 3 (2013): 233–255.

19. Seth Thompson, "Politics without Metaphors Is Like a Fish without Water," *Metaphor: Implications and Applications*, ed. Jeffery Scott Mio and Albert N. Katz (Mahwah, NJ: Lawrence Erlbaum, 1996) 191.

20. Jeffery Scott Mio, "Metaphor, Politics, and Persuasion," *Metaphor: Implications and Applications*, ed. Jeffery Scott Mio and Albert N. Katz (Mahwah, NJ: Lawrence Erlbaum, 1996), 130.

21. Seth Thompson, "Politics without Metaphors," 187.

22. Ibid., 190.

23. Ibid., 191.

24. For a parallel study in which a president's choice of metaphors established unrealistic public expectations in policy, see David Zarefsky, *President Johnson's War on Poverty: Rhetoric and History* (Tuscaloosa and London: University of Alabama Press, 1986), especially 21–37.

25. Robert L. Ivie, "Cold War Motives and the Rhetorical Metaphor: A Framework of Criticism," in *Cold War Rhetoric: Strategy, Metaphor, and Ideology*, ed. Martin J. Medhurst, Robert L. Ivie, Philip Wander, and Robert L. Scott (East Lansing: Michigan State University Press, 1997), 72.

26. Ibid., 71–72.

27. Ibid., 71.

28. Edwin Black, "The Second Persona," *Quarterly Journal of Speech* 56 (1970): 114–117. See also Celeste M. Condit, "Pathos in Criticism: Edwin Black's Communism as Cancer Metaphor," *Quarterly Journal of Speech* 99 (2013): 1–26.

29. Steven Perry, "Rhetorical Functions of the Infestation Metaphor in Hitler's Rhetoric," *Central States Speech Journal* 34 (1983): 232.

30. For a full explanation and illustration of the critical process, see Karlyn Kohrs Campbell and Thomas R. Burkholder, *Critiques of Contemporary Rhetoric*, 2nd ed. (Belmont, CA: Wadsworth, 1997), especially chapters 1–5.

31. Ibid., 17–20.

32. King, "I Have A Dream," in Andrews and Zarefsky, *Contemporary American Voices*, 78–81. All quotations from the speech are from this source.

33. Portions of this analysis appeared in David Henry, "The Rhetorical Dynamics of Mario Cuomo's 1984 Keynote Address: Situation, Speaker, Metaphor," *Southern Speech Communication Journal* 53 (1988): 105–120, and are used by permission of the Southern States Communication Association. Other portions appeared in Thomas R. Burkholder, "Irony through Metaphor: Burkean Master Tropes in Mario Cuomo's Keynote Address to the 1984 Democratic National Convention" (paper presented to the Speech Communication Association Convention, San Diego, CA, November 1996).

34. Quoted in Lou Cannon and Helen Dewar, "Gov. Cuomo Rouses Dispirited Delegates," *Washington Post*, July 17, 1984, A1.

35. Ibid., A8.

36. Hedrick Smith, "Cuomo Would Attack Record, Not Reagan," *New York Times*, July 17, 1984, A1.

37. Ibid., A15.

38. Howell Raines, "Democrat Calls on Party to Unify and Seek Out 'Family of America,'" *New York Times*, July 17, 1984, A1.

39. Cannon and Dewar, "Gov. Cuomo," A8.

40. Mario Cuomo, "Keynote Address," delivered to the Democratic National Convention, July 16, 1984, Associated Press transcript reprinted in *Congressional Quarterly Weekly Report* 42 (July 21, 1984): 1781–1785. All quotations from Cuomo's speech are from this source.

41. Wayne N. Thompson, "Barbara Jordan's Keynote Address: Fulfilling Dual and Conflicting Purposes," *Central States Speech Journal* 30 (Fall 1979): 272.

42. Aristotle, *Rhetoric and Poetics*, trans. W. Rhys Roberts and Ingram Bywater (New York: Modern Library, 1954), 1358a33–1358b10.

43. Edwin A. Miles, "The Keynote Speech at National Nominating Conventions," *Quarterly Journal of Speech* 46 (February 1960): 26.

44. Ibid., 26. See also Craig R. Smith, "The Republican Keynote Address of 1968: Adaptive Rhetoric for Multiple Audiences," *Western Speech* 39 (1975): 32–39. Interestingly, there are also hybrid metaphors. See Robin E. Jensen, "From Barren to Sterile: The Evolution of a Mixed Metaphor," *RSQ: Rhetoric Society Quarterly* 45, no. 1 (2015): 25–46.

45. Wayne N. Thompson, "Purposes," 272.

46. Wayne N. Thompson, "Barbara Jordan's Keynote Address: The Juxtaposition of Contradictory Values," *Southern Communication Journal* 44 (Spring 1979): 224.

47. Jack W. Germond and Jules Witcover, *Wake Us When It's Over: Presidential Politics of 1984* (New York: Macmillan, 1985), 380.

48. Ibid.

49. Quoted in Hedrick Smith, "Cuomo Would Attack Record," A15.

50. *Los Angeles Times*, July 17, 1984, I7.

51. Leff, "Topical Invention," 218, 223. Also instructive are Michael Osborn, "Archetypal Metaphor in Rhetoric: The Light-Dark Family," *Quarterly Journal of Speech* 53 (1967): 115–126; Michael Osborn, "The Evolution of the Archetypal Sea in Rhetoric and Poetic," *Quarterly Journal of Speech* 63 (1977): 347–363; William Jordan, "Toward a Psychological Theory of Metaphor," *Western Speech* 35 (1971): 169–175; Pradeep Sopory and James Price Dillard, "The Persuasive Effects of Metaphor: A Meta-Analysis," *Human Communication Research* 28 (2002): 382–419; Celeste Condit et al., "Recipes or Blueprints for Our Genes? How Contexts Selectively Activate the Multiple Meanings of Metaphors," *Quarterly Journal of Speech* 88 (2002): 303–325; and Josef Stern, *Metaphor in Context* (Cambridge, MA: MIT Press, 2000).

52. George Lakoff and Mark Johnson, *Metaphors We Live By* (Chicago: University of Chicago Press, 1980), 153, 156, and 157.

53. Paul Ricoeur, *The Rule of Metaphor*, trans. Robert Czerny (1975; Toronto: University of Toronto Press, 1977), 22.

54. Lakoff and Johnson, *Metaphors*, 154.

55. William F. Lewis makes passing reference to the wisdom of Cuomo's tack in his assessment of Ronald Reagan's reliance on, and success with, the narrative form in his presidential discourse. See "Telling America's Story: Narrative Form and the Reagan Presidency," *Quarterly Journal of Speech* 73 (1987): 280–302.

56. Germond and Witcover, *Wake Us When It's Over*, 537.

57. Burke, *A Grammar of Motives*, 503.

58. See Burkholder, "Irony through Metaphor."

59. For a discussion of generic criticism and the genre of political convention keynote addresses, see John M. Murphy and Thomas R. Burkholder, "The Life of the Party: The Contemporary Keynote Address," in *New Approaches to Rhetoric*, ed. Patricia A. Sullivan and Steven R. Goldswig (Thousand Oaks, CA: Sage, 2004), 129–148.

60. Clarence Thomas, "I Am a Man, a Black Man, an American," July 29, 1998, available online at http://archive.frontpagemag.com/readArticle.aspx?ARTID=22232.

61. For an analysis of Bush's major addresses that picks up on themes such as "good versus evil," see Jim A. Kuypers, *Bush's War: Media Bias and Justifications for War in a Terrorist Age* (Lanham, MD: Rowman & Littlefield, 2006).

# 10

# The Narrative Perspective

*Robert C. Rowland*

In the spring and summer of 2015, enormous public attention focused on the transformation of former Olympic decathlon star Bruce Jenner into Caitlyn Jenner. The *New York Times* observed that the nation's "understanding of transgender people has been shaped recently by the riveting, glamorous" story of Jenner's change in identity.[1] In the same period, the public focused far less on the ongoing conflict in Ukraine, the threat of another government shutdown, and the growing number of people receiving coverage under the Affordable Care Act. Moreover, the focus on Jenner and other celebrities as representatives of the transgender community itself was misleading. After noting the enormous coverage of Jenner, the *New York Times* added that such cases "are far from representative of an economically disadvantaged community that continues to face pervasive employment discrimination."[2]

What explains public fascination with Jenner and other celebrities, or with dramatic events such as the decision of the state of South Carolina following a church shooting to take down a Confederate flag that had flown for decades at the state capitol? The answer is that events that are easily understood as stories with compelling characters and an interesting plot draw more attention than reporting on complex issues such as foreign policy and health care, or for that matter, the problems facing transgender Americans.

It is more than that people love stories. More broadly, researchers have demonstrated that narrative is a human universal found in all cultures and throughout human history.[3] There is strong evidence in cave paintings and other artifacts that humans have told stories for tens of thousands of years. While ancient humans told stories around the fire and in caves, modern humans use all forms of human communication to tell stories. The popularity of narrative easily can be demonstrated by looking at the daily television guide, a listing of movies at the local theater, or a glance at the best-seller list. Television is dominated by shows that tell stories, from *Game of Thrones* to *NCIS*. Fifty years ago the shows might have been *Gunsmoke*, *Leave It to Beaver*, and *I Love Lucy*, but narrative always has dominated the medium. And even on programs that at first glance seem to be news or issue oriented, narrative is very common. *Sixty Minutes* is a news show, but the focus of each episode is on using narratives about real people to explore an issue or other topic. Films and books are also dominated by narrative, both fictional and in the form of biography.

Narrative is not just a form of entertainment, but also a means for understanding the world. From the law to economics, and even to the hard sciences, scholars have recognized the importance of narrative.[4] In the remainder of this chapter, I lay out in more detail why we like stories and how they work to explain our world. I begin by describing **narrative form** and explaining the functions that narrative fulfills. I also describe a number of approaches that have been taken to analyzing narratives in rhetoric and describe in some detail Fisher's "narrative paradigm." After enumerating current perspectives on narrative, I present a critical essay in which I develop a system for interpreting narratives and analyze a story concerning American children abducted to Saudi Arabia to illustrate how a rhetorical critic can break down the form and function of a social narrative. I conclude this chapter by evaluating the strengths and weaknesses of the narrative approach and citing recommended essays for further reading.

## DESCRIBING NARRATIVE FORM AND FUNCTION

What is a narrative and how is it different from other rhetoric? The answer is that **narratives** are stories, and stories function differently than descriptive or argumentative rhetoric. It is one thing to make a strong argument for fighting terrorism in the Middle East, but quite another to tell a story about how terrorists are oppressing ordinary people in the region in order to support an implicit claim that the United States should attack the bases of terrorists.

### Narrative Form

What are the component parts of any story? Any story contains characters, a setting, a plot, and a theme. Stories are not about statistics. They are about the actions of **characters** (mostly people, but sometimes animals and other beings) in relation to other characters and the environment. The main action of a story centers on one or more protagonists. We sometimes call the protagonist the hero or heroine. If there is a protagonist, there must also be an antagonist (or villain), whose narrative function is to create conflict in order to carry the story forward. Oftentimes the antagonist will be a person who fights against the protagonist, although in some cases the antagonist may be the natural environment or even some weakness inside the hero. From Old Testament narratives such as the story of David and Goliath to the present day in great popular film series such as *Star Wars*, the focus is on the conflict between the protagonist and the antagonist.

The most fundamental principle concerning the relationship between the protagonist and antagonist is that they must be of approximately equal power for the story to be compelling. *Star Wars* would not have been a good film if Darth Vader had been opposed by one of the robots. The point is that if the difference in power between the protagonist and the antagonist is too great, the plot of the narrative will not be interesting because the ultimate outcome will be a foregone conclusion. *Jaws* would have been a much less successful film and novel if the killer fish had been a crazed catfish rather than a giant shark.

The point that in effective stories the relationship between the protagonist and antagonist must be based on near parity also illustrates the difference between effective and true stories. In the real world, people often fight against insurmountable odds and have essentially no chance of success. Or a person may face an antagonist so weak that there is no question about his or her ultimate success. The point is that what makes a story true and what makes it compelling are related but different concepts.

There are a number of types of protagonists. Sometimes the protagonist will be a great hero, even an angel or god. In others cases, the protagonist will be an ordinary person who does great deeds. In still other narratives, the protagonist may be one of us or even inferior to us in ability or intellect.[5] In some stories there may be multiple protagonists and antagonists. It would seem that anyone, even a college professor, can be a protagonist in a given narrative. Although there are many possible types of protagonists, from a rhetorical perspective they fall into two basic types. The protagonist can be one of us and serve the rhetorical function of creating a sense of commonality with the audience, or the protagonist can be greater than us and serve as a model for action. When the hero is one of us, his or her rhetorical function is to create what the great critic and theorist Kenneth Burke called a sense of identification or consubstantiality.[6] This type of protagonist is a regular person who shows us what it is like to live his or her life. In other stories, the protagonist is not one of us, but instead a hero who serves as a model for action. Throughout American history, the Founding Fathers have served this kind of rhetorical function. We continue to tell stories about them in a radically different time (Madison didn't have much to say about global warming), because they serve as heroic models, and we still need such models.

Stories rarely involve just a hero and a villain. Often there are a host of other characters, including friends, acquaintances, bystanders, and so forth. These supporting characters assist the protagonist or serve as obstacles to be overcome, thereby supporting the primary conflict between the protagonist and antagonist. Supporting characters also may be used to illustrate narrative themes or create sympathy in the audience. In a film about World War II, a supporting character may be killed or wounded early in the narrative to demonstrate the inhumanity of war. Finally, supporting characters may comment on the action, either to create comic relief or to critique the actions of the protagonist or the antagonist.

The second basic component that defines any story is **setting**, where and when the story takes place. Stories can take place literally anywhere and anytime. In fact, there are science fiction and fantasy stories that take place in a different universe. The important point about setting is that stories can transport us out of our here and now to places very different from our own world. For example, although it is difficult for early twenty-first-century Americans to understand the horrors of the Holocaust, through narrative Elie Wiesel and others have taken us to Auschwitz and made us see the horrors of the death camps. Through the power of setting, narrative can be used to break down barriers to human understanding.[7]

The third component of narrative form is **plot**, the action of the story. Although literary theorists have built theories about plot types, and historians have developed approaches for explaining historical narrative, from a rhetorical perspective there are two important points to be made about plot. First, the function of the plot is to keep the attention of the audience and reinforce the message in the story. Therefore, the plot generally builds to a climax that resolves the conflict between hero and villain because the story would not be very interesting if the biggest obstacle were overcome at the beginning of the story. Similarly, the plot must be varied enough and include enough action to keep the audience's interest. The second point about plot is, as Lewis O. Mink notes, what makes a good plot and what makes a true story are sometimes different things.[8] In a gripping mystery, for instance, it may be crucial that a trash truck arrived in the first scene on Wednesday morning. In real life, however, the only meaning may be that Wednesday is trash day. Nor do real-life stories always move in a gradual pattern of escalating conflict to a final climax that resolves the conflict.

The final component of narrative form is **theme**—the message of the narrative. In some narratives, the theme may be quite explicit. In other instances, the theme may be implied but not explicitly stated. On the surface, George Orwell's classic novel *Animal Farm* is a fantasy story about animals taking over an English farm. Underneath the surface, the novel is usually treated as an allegorical attack on communism and the Soviet Union. The larger point is that some narratives require more understanding of context and rhetorical type in order to identify the theme than do other narratives. The rhetorical critic also needs to keep in mind that in stories where the theme is not explicitly stated there may be considerable variation in audience interpretation. This points to an important difference between narrative in literature and narrative in rhetoric. Although much literature is rhetorical in that it supports a persuasive message and some narrative rhetoric is also literature in the sense that it possesses great aesthetic power, what makes a good theme in the two related contexts is somewhat different. In great literature, the theme may be quite complex and very subtle. In contrast, rhetorical critics are primarily interested in narratives that attempt to persuade an audience. This persuasive function of rhetorical narrative usually requires a theme that is either explicit or clearly implied. If the theme is subtle or overly complex, the audience may miss it. Consequently, great literature often fails as rhetoric because the theme is too complex for the mass audience. On the other hand, great rhetorical narratives often are inferior literature. Harriet Beecher Stowe's novel about the horrors of slavery, *Uncle Tom's Cabin*, is generally not considered to be great literature. The characters are based on simple stereotypes and show little subtlety. But there is no question that Stowe's novel had an immense rhetorical impact on popular attitudes about slavery in the North in the years leading up to the Civil War.

In summary, the four primary components of narrative form are characters, setting, plot, and theme. The first three components define what narrative form is, and together they create the theme, which is what the narrative means. To this point, I have focused on narrative rhetoric that tells a complete story in order to make a point. In some cases, however, the rhetor may not retell a complete narrative but only give the audience a scene from that narrative or tap into a narrative that is well known to the audience. In these variants of narrative form, the rhetor relies on the capacity of the audience to fill in the meaning of the narrative from the scene that is presented or to pull out of the well-known narrative the appropriate meaning.

After considering the formal components that define narrative rhetoric, it is appropriate to consider the rhetorical functions that narrative fulfills. If the components of narrative *form* describe what narrative is, the components of **narrative function** describe what rhetorical narrative does to an audience.

## Narrative Function

There are two related but somewhat different sets of functions fulfilled by narrative form: epistemic and persuasive. Epistemology is the study of how we come to know. We often use narrative, as Mink suggests, as a "primary cognitive instrument" for comprehending the world.[9] Thus, we make sense of the impact of global warming by considering stories of how it is affecting real people around the globe. Al Gore powerfully used narrative in his award-winning book, *An Inconvenient Truth*, to achieve this function, thereby providing the audience with a means of understanding the problem and what to do about it.[10]

While people use narrative to understand the world, they also sometimes create narratives to persuade others. This rhetorical function is fulfilled by stories in four ways. The first function of narrative is to keep the *attention* of the audience. I made the point earlier that popular culture is chock full of narrative, because people like stories. You would have to look long and hard in the television guide to find a show on a topic such as "Dartmouth College experts talk statistics." But virtually every channel runs fictional or nonfictional stories about people and their lives.

Popular reaction to the events of 9/11 illustrates the power of narrative to energize an audience. Previous to September 2001, experts on terrorism were well aware that there was a serious risk that terrorists might use weapons of mass destruction. Although the risk was known, there was little public attention to it because it did not fit into what the public found to be a credible narrative. Airplanes flying into tall buildings was perceived to be the stuff of summer adventure movies, not real life. After September 11, however, there was a powerful narrative to go with the warnings of the experts. That narrative energized the audience to support action dealing with terrorism.

It is important to note that the key issue in terms of persuasiveness is not the truth of the narrative, but its credibility. Prior to September 11, a narrative about terrorists using weapons of mass destruction against the United States was not perceived to be credible, no matter how many experts suggested that such an attack could occur. On the other hand, a narrative may be perceived to be credible when there is little support for it. It is widely believed, for instance, that the nuclear power accident at Three Mile Island was a major disaster. In fact, the best data suggests that there was very little radiation released and that many of the safety systems worked effectively.[11] However, the strong data I have mentioned in no way undercuts the powerful social narrative describing Three Mile Island as a nuclear disaster.

The second rhetorical function of narrative is to create a sense of *identification* between the audience and the narrator or characters in the narrative. Great novels such as Harper Lee's *To Kill a Mockingbird* played a role in the civil rights movement because they helped create a sense of identification between white and black Americans. Lee's novel and many other stories showed the audience that the black characters in the books were people just like them. The publication of Lee's new novel, *Go Set a Watchman*, with its depiction of Atticus Finch not as a saintly protector of the innocent but as a segregationist, may undercut the capacity of *Mockingbird* to produce that same sense of identification in the future.[12] Even so, one of the most powerful functions of narrative is to generate in the reader/viewer/listener the understanding that "I'm like him or her."

The third rhetorical function of narrative is to *break down barriers* to understanding by transporting us to another place or time. This function is similar to the identity-related function, but it deals with place, time, and culture rather than personal identity. People view the world based on their own experiences and culture, meaning that they often find it difficult to understand a radically different culture or time. Narrative works better than other forms of rhetoric for ripping us out of our time and culture and placing us in another place/time. For example, contemporary Americans may have great difficulty understanding the strict social regulation of women's role in the mid-nineteenth century. While works of history can describe women's roles in that period, narrative is a more powerful vehicle for bringing home the restrictions women faced.

The final persuasive function of narrative is to *tap into values and needs* in order to create a strong emotional reaction. A story about the death of an innocent child or the horrors of the Holocaust can link to emotions in a way that statistical data and other forms of argument cannot do. A study proving that several hundred children die a year because of improperly installed car seats, for example, lacks the emotional punch of a narrative about the death of a single baby. The narrative produces this emotional reaction because the story links directly to basic values and needs such as life and security.

After identifying the form and function of narrative rhetoric, it is important to consider approaches that rhetorical critics have taken to the study of narrative. In the next section, I summarize various approaches to narrative, paying special attention to Walter Fisher's seminal analysis of the "narrative paradigm."

## APPROACHES TO NARRATIVE RHETORICAL CRITICISM

With the rebirth of the study of rhetoric early in the twentieth century, rhetorical critics tended to follow the example of Aristotle in building theories of rhetoric and methods for analyzing it. As mentioned in chapter 7, critics who were influenced by Aristotle, often called neo-Aristotelian or traditional critics, usually focused on the three modes of proof identified by Aristotle (logos, ethos, and pathos), which broadly speaking defined rational argument, appeals to credibility, and rhetoric that produced an emotional reaction. In this system, there was little room for the analysis of narrative. As recently as forty years ago, there was not a sizable literature identifying narrative approaches to rhetorical analysis. Walter R. Fisher and Richard A. Filloy got at this point in a 1982 essay on "Argument in Drama and Literature: An Exploration," where they noted that "argument has been conceived traditionally in terms of clear-cut inferential structures, a judgment that limited the study of narrative forms of persuasion."[13] They went on to argue that many works of narrative, including novels such as *The Great Gatsby* and plays such as *Death of a Salesman*, make arguments. Although Fisher and Filloy cited a number of modern critics, including Kenneth Burke and Wayne Booth, who had focused on narrative forms of rhetoric, their main point was that critics had not recognized the importance of narrative. In retrospect, the failure to focus on narrative is astonishing.

In this crucial essay, Fisher and Filloy saw a need for a method to test "one's interpretation of a dramatic or literary work."[14] They outlined a four-step process in which the critic first determines "the message, the overall conclusions fostered by the work." At a second step, the critic tests the message by evaluating the "reliability" of the narrator, the words and actions of the other characters, and the descriptions of the scenes in the story. At a third step, the analyst considers the outcomes of the story as a means of asking "whether the story rings true as a story in itself." Finally, the critic should test "(a) whether the message accurately portrays the world we live in and (b) whether it provides a reliable guide to our beliefs, attitudes, values, and/or actions."[15]

### The Narrative Paradigm and Rhetorical Criticism

Although Fisher and Filloy provided a method for analyzing argument in narrative, their approach remained quite close to traditions that emphasized rational communication. The final step in their narrative methodology essentially called on the critic to do an argumentative analysis of the claim in a given story. Fisher, however, had realized that narrative was more than just a type of argument. It also was a basic form of human communication, what he would call a "paradigm" for understanding all communication.

In a series of essays and an important book, Fisher laid out the characteristics of the **narrative paradigm** and claimed that it functioned as an alternative to traditional rationality, which he believed provided little guidance for citizens concerned with issues of public moral conflict. He argued that traditional rationality privileged the perspectives of experts and created a situation in which ordinary citizens felt disempowered.[16] His solution was to claim that human beings were essentially storytellers, what he called "homo narrans."[17] He based this judgment on the fact that narrative is a human universal found in all cultures, concluding that all communication, "whether social, political, legal or otherwise, involves narrative."[18] In his book he reemphasized that all communication is narrative, stating, "All forms of human communication need to be seen fundamentally as stories."[19]

Instead of traditional rationality, Fisher argued for the value of narrative rationality. He argued that narrative rationality is a human universal since everyone knows what makes a good story and that, as a consequence, standards of narrative rationality provided a way around the elitism inherent in what he called the "rational world paradigm."[20] Fisher embraced two principles for testing narrative reason: *narrative probability* and *narrative fidelity*. He defined **narrative probability** as a standard for testing "what constitutes a coherent story."[21] He later explained that narrative probability involved three related tests of coherence: structural coherence, which involves testing the internal consistency of the narrative; material coherence, which involves "comparing and contrasting stories told in other discourses"; and characterological coherence, which tests the consistency of action by the characters.[22] In addition to narrative probability, Fisher argued that the critic should apply the standard of **narrative fidelity**, in which an audience considers "whether the stories they experience ring true with the stories they know to be true in their lives."[23] He later added that standards of formal and informal logic also could be applied at this point "*when relevant.*"[24]

According to Fisher, the narrative paradigm was superior to other approaches to understanding human communication because narrative is a universal form of communication. Second, he argued that the standards of narrative rationality provided a way around expert domination and a means of identifying stories that recognize "the truths humanity shares in regard to reason, justice, veracity, and peaceful ways to resolve social-political differences." He cited stories by Lao-tse, Buddha, Zoroaster, Jesus Christ, and Mohammed, as well as works by political leaders such as Lincoln, Gandhi, and Churchill, as meeting these standards.[25]

The narrative paradigm drew a great deal of critical attention. Many critics praised Fisher and the paradigm for illuminating the way that narrative functions in human communication. Others argued that the narrative paradigm was unclear or overly broad. Barbara Warnick and Robert Rowland both argued that the parameters of the paradigm were unclear, that the standards of narrative rationality were not adequately specified, and that there was a difference between a credible and a true story.[26] Rowland also claimed that narrative was better understood as a mode of discourse as opposed to a paradigm and that it was important to distinguish between works that actually told stories and works that described a topic or made arguments.[27] He also argued that Fisher's criticism of traditional rationality was overstated and that the standards of narrative rationality could not be applied to works of fantasy or science fiction, because those genres were judged by criteria different from realistic fiction.[28] Although there was considerable debate about the value of the narrative paradigm, there was no disagreement about the importance of studying narrative. Fisher had highlighted the importance of narrative as a form of human communication.

## APPLICATIONS OF THE NARRATIVE PARADIGM

Fisher's work awakened rhetorical critics to the importance of narrative. The result was a huge increase in narrative criticism. The narrative criticism that was produced fell into two main categories. A number of critics borrowed from Fisher's terminology, especially the standards of narrative rationality, as the primary method of their critique. Others used an inductive approach to narrative analysis to discover the specific narrative pattern at the heart of a given story.

An example of the first category of narrative criticism is Ronald H. Carpenter's analysis of "Admiral Mahan, 'Narrative Fidelity,' and the Japanese Attack on Pearl Harbor."[29] Carpenter uses Fisher's terminology to critique the narrative power of works by Alfred Thayer Mahan on naval power. Mahan was a US Navy officer who wrote extensively on naval history and strategy. According to Carpenter, the Japanese government was influenced by Mahan's work because it possessed strong narrative fidelity that made his story "'ring true' for the Japanese prior to the attack on Pearl Harbor."[30] Another example of a critique that drew heavily on Fisher's terminology was Thomas A. Hollihan and Patricia Riley's "The Rhetorical Power of a Compelling Story: A Critique of a 'Toughlove' Parental Support Group."[31] In this essay, Hollihan and Riley analyzed the narratives found in a "toughlove" support group that advocated parents taking extremely strong stands against adolescent children who behaved badly. They concluded that the "toughlove" narrative "met the needs" of group members and "fulfilled the requirements for a good story," including both narrative fidelity and probability. Hollihan and Riley went on to argue that the "toughlove" story was a dangerous one because it could encourage parents "to get a quick-fix to their problems by ejecting their children from the house when far less drastic actions would be more appropriate."[32]

Numerous works utilizing terminology drawn from Fisher's analysis of the narrative paradigm could be cited. In general, these essays used a two-step critical process, first breaking down the narrative into coherent themes and then applying the standards of narrative rationality to assess those themes. It is important to recognize that these critics tended to use Fisher's terminology for a purpose quite different than that originally proposed by Fisher. Fisher touted the narrative paradigm as an alternative to traditional rationality. In contrast, critics used the standards of narrative rationality to explain why a particular audience found a given narrative to be persuasive. It also should be apparent that the narrative paradigm did not provide critics with a complete road map for how to identify the themes and strategies in a given narrative. This led critics to develop inductive approaches to narrative analysis.

Under the inductive approach, the critic does not apply a preexisting theory of narrative but instead discovers the implicit narrative pattern in a given story. Many examples of scholars taking this approach could be cited. Thomas Rosteck analyzed narrative form in Martin Luther King Jr.'s final speech. Martha Solomon and Wayne J. McMullen argued that the film *Places in the Heart* was an "open text" that possessed a number of conflicting ideological themes. Sally J. Perkins discovered the narrative structure found in two feminist plays about the sixteenth-century feminist Queen Christina of Sweden. Robert Rowland and Robert Strain argued that Spike Lee's film *Do the Right Thing* possessed an underlying narrative form similar to Greek tragedy.[33] Stephanie Kelley-Romano uncovered the structure of conspiracy narratives, and Mike Milford and Robert Rowland identified allegorical form in the contemporary science fiction series *Battlestar Galactica*.[34] Many other examples could be cited.

William F. Lewis's essay "Telling America's Story: Narrative Form and the Reagan Presidency"[35] is a typical example of the inductive approach. Lewis argues that much of Reagan's persuasiveness can be traced to his success as a storyteller. He identifies two different kinds of stories in Reagan's rhetoric: anecdotes and myths. Anecdotes are small stories that Reagan used to keep the interest of his audience. In contrast, myth "informs all of Reagan's rhetoric."[36] Lewis shows how Reagan used both kinds of stories to generate support for his program and explains why the American people found Reagan's narratives to be so compelling, even though according to Lewis they often were inaccurate.

Lewis brilliantly illuminated much of the reason for Reagan's popularity; at the same time, Lewis's analysis also illustrated the difficulty with the inductive approach to narrative analysis. Inductive critics do a detailed analysis of the narrative and pull out of that analysis the narrative theory that applies to the particular work of rhetoric. In effect, they build a new theory of how to approach narrative in every essay. This doesn't provide much guidance for future criticism. Thus, there is need for a general approach to narrative analysis that provides the critic with tools for discovering the narrative pattern in any given story. In the following section, I develop such an approach.

## NARRATIVE ANALYSIS: A SYSTEMATIC PERSPECTIVE

The narrative critic needs a perspective that is clear and provides a means to explore the complexity present in any given narrative. The best means of achieving both of these ends is to apply a critical approach that moves in a three-step process from the *form* of the narrative to the *functions* fulfilled by the story, and finally to an *evaluation* of how effectively the narrative functions persuasively with a given audience.

The first step in this process is to identify the four formal elements that define all stories: characters, setting, plot, and theme. In relation to characters, it is important to think not only about who the characters are, but what they represent and their function in the story. It is especially important to consider whether the protagonist is an "everyman" or "everywoman" or whether he/she is a hero to be followed. After identifying the protagonist(s), it is important to identify the antagonist and supporting players and consider their role in the story. Discovering the fundamental conflict between the protagonist and the antagonist will provide the critic with a major clue concerning the plot structure and also the theme of the narrative. Similarly, it is important to consider the roles played by supporting characters and how they are depicted.

After identifying the characters, the critic should focus on the setting. In many cases the setting will be both a particular place and also by implication other places of relevance to the audience. So, a film such as *Selma* clearly is set in the American South during the civil rights movement, but more broadly it can be seen as a story about human empowerment that has relevance for anyone fighting against oppression in any culture. The next step is to identify the plot. The primary function of the plot is to keep the attention of the audience, but careful analysis may reveal the underlying message of the narrative. The plot often moves in a pattern of rising action in which more and more difficult problems occur, leading to the final crisis in which the issue is resolved. The critic should list the main events in the story and consider what those events reveal about the message of the story.

Finally, based on the analysis of characters, setting, and plot, the critic should be able to identify the theme or themes in the story. Here, it is important to recognize that narratives often work by implication and that explicit calls for specific action are rare. In fact, there are many stories in which the underlying narrative form supports a different theme than that enunciated by the narrator. Even so, careful consideration of the interaction of the characters, setting, and plot should reveal the theme or themes in the story.

In summary, the first step in narrative analysis is to identify the characters and the roles they play, the setting in which the action occurs and any more general implied setting, and the plot pattern present in the narrative and what that plot pattern implies about how the audience should react. From this information, the critic should be able to identify the themes in the story and the actions requested of the audience.

In the second step, the critic tests the degree to which the narrative fulfills the four rhetorical functions identified earlier. Initially, this means considering whether the story is compelling for the audience. The critic also should consider whether the narrative is designed to create a sense of identification between the audience and characters (or the narrator) in the story. Questions to consider include, Who does the author want us to like or admire? Does the author create a sense of identity between the reader/viewer/listener and the protagonist or other characters? Third, the critic should consider whether the story is designed to bring the message home by placing the audience in a setting very different from their own lives. If the story is set in Des Moines, the answer is probably no. But if the story is set in a sweatshop in China, the story may well be designed to show ordinary Americans what life is like in a developing nation. Finally, the critic should consider whether the narrative taps into basic values or needs in order to produce an emotional reaction in the audience. In testing this rhetorical function, it is important to remember that the story does not directly tug on the heartstrings of the audience. Instead, it uses the incidents in the story to tap into values and needs shared by audience members in order to produce the emotional response.

The last step in narrative analysis is to take the findings of the first two steps and make a coherent argument about the functioning of the particular story. Here, the critic links together the formal and the functional analysis to make an argument about how the story functions (or why it fails to function) for a given audience. Public opinion data or reports of public response to a given narrative may be cited as additional evidence to support an overall claim. At this stage, the critic should ask three final questions. First, the critic should consider whether the formal elements of the narrative are compelling. For example, Is the plot interesting? Are the characters appealing (and in the case of the antagonist revolting)? Does the author transport us to the setting of the story? Second, the critic should summarize the degree to which the story fulfills the four rhetorical functions of narrative. If the story fulfills all four, that is a sign that it is a powerful and coherent narrative. If it fails to fulfill any of the functions, that suggests strongly that it failed as a story. If, on the other hand, it fulfills some of the functions, but not all, the critic must consider the importance in the particular context of the functions that were fulfilled.

Finally, the critic should consider the credibility of the story for the audience. I mentioned earlier that the truth and credibility of a story are very different things. In the run-up to the Iraq War, the story that Iraq was quite close to developing nuclear weapons clearly resonated with the audience. While it was a powerfully resonant narrative, it also was not true. As this example illustrates, it is important to consider whether the narrative is a credible one for a given audience and to recognize the risk that some false stories may resonate strongly.

Earlier, I noted problems with the standards of narrative rationality (narrative probability and narrative fidelity) developed by Walter Fisher in his discussion of the narrative paradigm. Although those standards may have limited value for evaluating the accuracy or truth of a narrative, they are immensely useful for making judgments about the credibility or believability of a narrative. Narrative probability and fidelity get at two aspects of narrative credibility. Humans tend to believe stories that are coherent and stories that are consistent with personal experience. Thus, we expect people to behave in a consistent fashion, and we interpret events through the lens of our own experience in society. Therefore, the critic can use standards of narrative fidelity and probability to assess whether a story had credibility for a given audience.

At the end of the third step, the critic should be able to make a coherent argument about the rhetorical effectiveness of the narrative for a given audience. It is important to note that this judgment is always in relation to a particular audience. What seems coherent to an early twenty-first-century American audience might seem ludicrous to an audience in Japan or elsewhere. An example may make this point clear. It has widely been reported that many in the Arab world believe that Israel organized the 9/11 attacks and that several thousand American Jews did not show up for work at the World Trade Center on September 11. In fact, there is exactly no data supporting this story. However, a significant portion of the Arab world apparently finds it to be credible. This audience has been exposed to extremely harsh anti-Israeli rhetoric for many years in the context of the Israeli-Palestinian conflict. In this context, what would seem obviously absurd to almost any American apparently seems quite credible to Arabs.

### Summary of a Systematic Perspective on Narrative Analysis

Step 1—Form Identification
- A. Identify characters, character types, and what they represent.
- B. Identify the place in which the narrative is set and what it represents.
- C. Sketch the plot pattern and identify points of conflict.
- D. Reason from the characters, setting, and plot to the stated or implied theme.

Step 2—Functional Analysis
- A. Does the narrative energize the audience?
- B. Does the narrative create a sense of identification between characters or the narrator and the audience?
- C. Does the narrative transport the audience to a place or time different from contemporary life?
- D. Does the narrative tap into basic values or needs of the audience?

Step 3—Linking Formal and Functional Analysis: An Evaluation
- A. Are the formal elements and the plot compelling?
- B. Does the narrative effectively fulfill narrative functions?
- C. Is the narrative credible for a particular audience?

In the last few pages, I have explained an approach to narrative analysis that can be applied systematically to any narrative. It also can be used to critique speeches and essays that tap into societal narratives. However, I have not provided an approach to testing the epistemic function of narrative. How can the critic apply rhetorical standards in order to test the accuracy of a given narrative? The short answer is that rhetorical standards are of very limited value in making such a judgment. The stories told to justify going to war in Iraq illustrate this point. The American people found those stories to be quite coherent, but coherent and true are not the same thing. A story about a popular president risking his presidency and his legacy by having sex with a young White House intern would have to be viewed as incoherent. So would a story about hanging chads and butterfly ballots deciding a presidential election. But these incoherent stories did occur. The point is that rhetorical critics are in a good position to judge the persuasiveness and credibility of a narrative, but the tools of the critic are not nearly as useful for judging the accuracy of the story.

# CRITICAL ESSAY

In this section, I illustrate the systematic perspective on narrative criticism by analyzing a narrative concerning children abducted to and held in Saudi Arabia. In a number of instances,

Saudi men have married American women and, after the marriage failed, abducted their children to Saudi Arabia, where the children have been held against their will. A congressional hearing told the stories of several mothers who had their children taken from them and their efforts to get them back.

## A NARRATIVE ANALYSIS OF STORIES ABOUT CHILDREN ABDUCTED TO SAUDI ARABIA

On June 12, 2002, Representative Dan Burton, then chairman of the House Government Reform Committee, held a hearing on "U.S. Citizens Held in Saudi Arabia."[37] In the introduction of that hearing Representative Burton made the following statement:

> Today we're going to hear the stories of three mothers who had their children snatched away from them. Three things stand out in each of these stories: One, the brutal treatment of women in Saudi Arabia; the incredible courage of these women who did everything they could to rescue their children; and finally, the total lack of effort by our State Department to challenge the Saudi government.
>
> These stories are all so powerful that I'd like to talk about each one of them in detail. But I'm not going to do that, because I can't tell their stories nearly as well as they can. But I do want to mention a few key facts.
>
> Pat Roush has been living this nightmare for 16 years. In those 16 years, she has seen her two daughters one time for two hours. Her ex-husband came to the United States in 1986, kidnapped their two young daughters in violation of a court custody order, and took them to Saudi Arabia. An arrest warrant was issued here in the U.S., but the Saudi government did absolutely nothing.
>
> The year before that, when Pat went to Saudi Arabia to try to salvage their marriage, her husband beat her so badly that two of her ribs were broken and the Saudi police didn't do anything then either.
>
> Over the last 16 years, U.S. ambassadors have come and gone in Riyadh. Some have tried to help and some have not. But it's clear that the Saudis were never told by senior officials that this was a problem that was going to affect the relationship between our two countries.
>
> In 1986, the U.S. ambassador was told by his boss that he had to maintain impartiality in the Roush case. Why? Pat Roush's husband broke the law. An arrest warrant was issued. Why should we maintain impartiality? To me, that attitude goes right to the heart of this problem. Ambassador Ray Mabus deserves special credit in this case. In 1996, he started a new policy: No one from this man's family was allowed to get a visa to come to the United States, it caused a big problem for them.
>
> Unfortunately, after a year, Ambassador Mabus returned to the United States and his policy was discontinued. If this policy had been kept in place, it might very well have put the pressure on them to return these children to their mother. I'm very disappointed that that didn't happen.
>
> We were told just this week that Pat's youngest daughter, Aisha, who is now 19, was recently forced into a marriage with a Saudi man. Pat's older daughter, Alia, was forced to marry one of her cousins a year ago.
>
> Now let me say a few words about Monica Stowers. In 1985, she went to Saudi Arabia with her husband and two young children. When she arrived, she realized for the first time that her husband had a second wife and another child. She didn't know about that. Their marriage fell apart after six months. Her husband divorced her and had her deported without her children.
>
> In 1990, Monica heard that her ex-husband was abusing her children. She went back to Saudi Arabia. She took her children and went to the U.S. embassy to ask for help. Did they put her on the next plane to America? No. At the end of the day, they told Monica that she had to leave the embassy. She pleaded with them not to kick her out. She told them that she would be arrested for overstaying her visa. But the counsel general had the Marine guards carry them out. Sure enough, she was arrested. That actually happened.
>
> Can you imagine that? An American citizen is in a crisis, a mother and her young children, and the embassy staff tell the Marines to drag them out of the embassy so they could be arrested. That actually happened.

Monica is not here today. For most of the last 12 years she has stayed in Saudi Arabia to protect her children. She can leave any time she wants, but her husband refuses to allow their daughters to go. Her ex-husband tried to force her daughter into a marriage when she was only 12 years old. And Monica will not abandon her. While Monica can't be here to testify, her mother, Ethyl Stowers, is here to speak on her behalf, and we're very glad to have her here.

The third story we're going to hear about today is about Miriam Hernandez-Davis and her daughter Dria. They're both here to testify today. The reason they can both be here today is not because anybody in the United States government came to their rescue. The reason that Miriam's daughter is here today is that Miriam was able to scrape together $180,000 to pay two men to smuggle Dria out of Saudi Arabia.

Even though Miriam's husband kidnapped their daughter in 1997, and even though the FBI issued an international warrant for his arrest, she got almost no help from the State Department or our embassy.

The courage of these women, Pat Roush, Monica Stowers and Miriam Hernandez, and their kids, is just incredible to me. You've all endured terrible pain as a result of what's happened, and it's a real honor to have all of you here today.

These are not isolated incidents. These are three examples of a much bigger problem. The State Department has a list of 46 recent cases involving as many as 92 U.S. citizens who have been held against their will in Saudi Arabia.

The root cause of this problem is the Saudi government. They have refused to respect U.S. law and U.S. arrest warrants. The law in Saudi Arabia lets Saudi men keep American women and children in Saudi Arabia even when they're in violation of court orders, even when arrest warrants have been issued, and even when they've abused their wives and their children. And that's just wrong.

We can't let this go on. Our relationship with Saudi Arabia is important, but this just can't be allowed to continue. The only way we're going to resolve this problem and get these kids home again is by elevating this issue, letting the American people and the people throughout the world know about it. This has to be raised with the Saudis at the highest levels. The Saudis have to be made to understand that if they let this go on, their relationship with us is going to suffer. And I don't think that's happened yet.

## Approaching Burton's Statement from a Narrative Perspective

At first glance, Representative Burton's statement does not look much like the narratives that dominate popular culture in film, fiction, and television. He seems to be making an argument to change US policy toward Saudi Arabia. Underneath the surface, however, Burton skillfully uses narrative to support his political agenda. The stories that he tells reflect his anger at both the Saudis and US officials who fail to confront them. My starting point for approaching Burton's story is a comment by Walter Fisher: "what makes one story better than another" can be explained based on two "features" of the story—"formal and substantive."[38] Fisher is getting at two fundamental goals of narrative analysis, to identify how the story works on an audience and the characteristics of narrative form and content that allow it to produce that impact.

Before the critic can discover the functions served by Burton's narrative, he or she must first uncover the defining characteristics of the story itself. Just as a cook begins with a list of ingredients, the analyst must pull out of the story the ingredients making up the narrative. Since Fisher and Filloy focused on how drama and literature often serve an argumentative function, critics have recognized that narrative themes come out of the interaction of characters (including the narrator), the setting, and the plot.[39] Thus, the narrative analyst should begin by identifying the rhetorical forms (characters, setting, plot, and theme) that define the story and move from there to a consideration of rhetorical function.

After the linkage between narrative form and function has been identified, the rhetorical critic can assess the persuasive value of the narrative. Here, the key goal is to consider whether the narrative will be perceived as a "coherent story" that will "ring true" for the audience.[40] Three rules of thumb are particularly useful in that regard. In general, persuasive narratives will contain formal characteristics (plot, setting, characters, and theme) that the particular audience will find interesting. (This is the principle that explains why so many television shows focus on emergency room doctors, homicide cops, or high-profile prosecutors and so few on college professors). A second rule of thumb is that narratives which effectively fulfill the four functions I have described are more likely to influence an audience than narratives that do not fulfill those functions. Finally, narratives that possess "formal coherence,"[41] or credibility for a particular audience because they draw on aspects of that audience's world, are more likely to have persuasive impact than those that do not. Thus, by moving from form, to function, and then to how the form influenced the function, the critic can explain what was in the narrative, how it worked (or failed to work) on an audience, and draw an overall conclusion about the impact of the story. In the following section, I apply this approach to narrative criticism to the statement of Representative Burton.

## Narrative Form and Function in Burton's Statement

Representative Burton's statement combines narrative with appeals to basic American values and rational argument. In the conclusion, he builds the argument that "The root cause of this problem is the Saudi government." He also appeals to values of justice and concern for the innocent when he attacks the Saudi government for failing to "respect U.S. law." Burton's ultimate claim is that the President should pressure the Saudi government to release the abducted children. Implicitly, Burton assumes that a threat from the President to Saudi leaders that failure to release the children could cause "their relationship with us . . . to suffer" would be sufficient to motivate the Saudis to act.

Although Burton relies upon an appeal to basic values and rational argument in the conclusion of his statement, the dominant strategy is narrative. Burton uses the stories of three American women—Pat Roush, Monica Stowers, and Miriam Hernandez-Davis—to build the case that the US government has failed its citizens and must take remedial action. In Burton's three related mini-narratives the protagonist is the American mother. All three women are depicted as strong and loving mothers who have sacrificed mightily for their children and suffered greatly. Pat Roush tried to salvage her marriage and suffered broken ribs as a consequence. She worked for sixteen years to protect her children. Monica Stowers stayed in Saudi Arabia for "most of the last 12 years . . . to protect her children." And Miriam Hernandez-Davis "scrape[d] together" $180,000 of her own money in order to save her daughter Dria. These three women are in a sense everywoman. In a desperate situation, they refused to give in and instead fought for their children.

There are three different, but related antagonists in Burton's narrative. At one level, the role of antagonist is played by the husbands who took the children, abused them by forcing them into marriage or other acts, and prevented them from leaving Saudi Arabia. In Burton's narrative, the husbands and their abuse are not described in any detail. They figure far more prominently in the testimony of the women later in the hearing. At a second level, the antagonist is the Saudi government. In his brief retelling of Roush's story, Burton states that in response to both the kidnapping of Roush's children and physical abuse that broke "two of her ribs" "the Saudi police didn't do anything." Although Burton clearly views the Saudi government as tyrannical and Saudi society as uncivilized, the focus of his fury is on the US government, which in his telling was more concerned with trouble free relations than with the rights of American citizens. In relating Roush's story, Burton cites an American ambassador who "was told by his boss that he had to maintain impartiality in the Roush case." Burton then asks "Why? Pat Roush's husband broke the law. An arrest warrant was issued. Why should we maintain impartiality?" Later, he tells about how when Monica Stowers and her children sought help in the American embassy, "the counsel general had the Marine guards carry them out." In Burton's narrative, the government has become utterly spineless. The one government official who wasn't gutless was Ambassador Ray Mabus who tried to pressure the Saudis into releasing Pat Roush's children. In Burton's narrative, Mabus plays a heroic role, but in another sense his personal story supports the larger point that American policy has been quite weak. While Mabus's policy "might very well have put the pressure on" the Saudis, after he returned to the United States, "his policy was discontinued."

The only other characters in Burton's narrative are the children who are not discussed in any detail. Their role is that of innocent victim. These innocent children have suffered not only from being taken from their mothers, but also from being abused by their fathers. Both daughters of Pat Roush were forced into arranged marriages. The children of Monica Stowers also were abused. The only child who has been saved is Dria, the daughter of Hernandez-Davis. And Dria is safe not because of the action of the United States, which provided Ms. Hernandez-Davis with "almost no help," but because Hernandez-Davis spent her own money to get her child back.

The primary setting of Burton's narrative is in Saudi Arabia. Saudi government and society are described as uncivilized. They do not respect law. Worse, they do not protect innocent women and children from abusive husbands. It is a society in which the child of Monica Stowers can be forced into a marriage at the age of twelve. While the primary setting of the story is in Saudi Arabia, there is a sense in which the story is set in a soulless bureaucracy that no longer understands the difference between policy and principle. In Burton's narrative only the mothers and Mabus understand that the lives of innocent children must be protected at all cost.

The primary plot devices in Burton's narrative are betrayal and commitment. The women and their children are betrayed first by their husbands, but in a more fundamental sense by their own country. In Burton's narrative the husbands are almost faceless. He describes their actions as terrible, but as typical of their society. His real fury is reserved for the US government, which has failed its citizens by kowtowing to the Saudis. In sharp contrast to the government, the three mothers acted with great courage. Burton's feeling about them comes through quite clearly: "The courage of these women . . . and their kids, is just incredible to me. You've all endured terrible pain as a result of what's happened, and it's a real honor to have all of you here today." There clearly is a relationship between the two plot devices. Burton's narrative is based on the premise that if the government had not betrayed the women and their children, but had acted with the commitment shown by the mothers, the kids would have been saved.

There are two primary themes in Burton's narrative. One theme simply concerns the women and their children. In Burton's narrative these innocent people have been abused because of their betrayal by their husbands (and fathers). The other theme is implicit. While Burton explicitly attacks the State Department for failing to fight for the abducted children, by implication he argues that if we just had the courage to stick by our principles as the mothers and Ray Mabus did we would have been able to force the Saudis to release the kids.

The analysis of Burton's narrative makes it quite clear that the story fulfills all four functions of narrative. First, the narrative is well designed to grab the attention of the audience. At the end of the statement, Burton notes that the three stories "are not isolated incidents." He adds that "The State Department has a list of 46 recent cases involving as many as 92 U.S. citizens who have been held against their will in Saudi Arabia." The statistic that Burton cites is not nearly as compelling as the three narratives. Later in the hearing Deputy Assistant Secretary of State for Near Eastern Affairs Ryan C. Crocker testified that "we [the State Department] have no higher priority than the safety and security of our citizens. I believe our record shows a consistent and sustained engagement on child custody cases in line with this priority. But as noted above, we operate in accordance with the laws of our two governments, laws that do not mesh well on civil and social issues."[42] After hearing the stories of Roush, Stowers, and Hernandez-Davis, Crocker's statement comes across as mere rationalization. The stories of the three women send the message that when the welfare of small children who are American citizens is at stake the government of the United States of America, the strongest nation by far on the planet, should have acted far more strongly.

Burton's story also fulfills the second and third functions of narrative rhetoric. Burton uses the three stories to create identification between the audience and the three mothers. Implicitly, he tells us that this could happen to your sister or your daughter or granddaughter. He also draws on the power of narrative to transport us to a different place or time. This function is most clearly fulfilled in his description of how Monica Stowers fled with her children to the American embassy and then was kicked out by American marines on the order of the counsel general. Although Burton's description is brief, one image comes through quite strongly—an American bureaucrat ordering marine guards to escort a mother and small children out of the embassy to be arrested by the Saudi police. Here, Burton takes us to two uncivilized places—Saudi Arabia that does not respect the law or the rights of women and children and an American embassy that no longer fights for American citizens.

Burton's narrative also clearly taps into basic American values such as justice, freedom, and honor and also basic human needs concerning family and children. The narrative produces two strong emotional reactions, anger and guilt. It produces anger at the government for selling out our own citizens and guilt that we haven't done more to help the women and their families.

Although Burton's retelling of the three stories is brief, it is also quite powerful. His narrative brings life to what otherwise might seem a complex foreign policy dispute. The setting, characters, and plot produce a powerful theme that transforms the arcane diplomatic fight into a call for justice. Burton also effectively fulfills the functions of narrative, especially in relation to shared identity. Clearly, he creates a sense of identification between the women and their children on the one hand and other Americans on the other. He also uses the power of narrative scene to take us out of our here and now to force us to see that similar actions could happen to members of each of our families.

Burton's story also has great narrative credibility. The story possesses internal coherence and also rings true with what we know about treatment of women and children by some Islamic fundamentalists. The story is coherent in two senses. First, the Saudi husbands and their government consistently act to deny the women and their children any rights. Second, the story is coherent in its depiction of an American State department more interested in geopolitics than protecting the rights of American citizens. Finally, the story clearly rings true with what people know about Saudi society, a culture so traditionalist that women are not allowed to drive. In summary, Burton's narrative powerfully sets forth the case that the United States should use all of our power and moral authority to pressure the Saudi government to release children of American mothers and Saudi fathers to the custody of the American mothers and allow them to leave the country.

The previous analysis does not, however, tell us if such a policy in fact would be a good idea. Burton's narrative is by its very nature one-sided favoring the rights of the mothers over the fathers. We have no rhetorical means of testing whether the stories he tells are accurate. Nor do we know whether US pressure would be effective in gaining release of the children. Citizens of the United States would be outraged if a foreign government pressured this nation to act because it perceived our culture to be immoral. Surely the Saudis are no different. It is quite possible that pressuring the Saudis might be counterproductive.

There is also the possibility that larger issues involving oil supplies and stability in the Persian Gulf simply require that the United States look the other way on this issue. I find that position distasteful and immoral, but the effect of US pressure on the stability of the Saudi regime is certainly a relevant question. The key point is while the standards of narrative criticism are quite useful in revealing how Burton's narrative effectively presents a particular perspective, they do not provide much guidance in determining whether that narrative is either factual or would be the basis of good public policy. Those questions are at their base not rhetorical in nature.

## PERSONAL REFLECTIONS

The key decision that I made in approaching the Burton story was to let the rhetorical analysis emerge from the form and function of the narrative. One of the perils of rhetorical analysis is the danger that the critic will use a method as a set of blinders rather than as a powerful lens to explain how the rhetoric functions. Thus, an argumentation critic might always find rhetoric to be dominated by argument. Any rhetorical theory and the terminology associated with it can be turned into a similar set of blinders that essentially shapes the critical process.

To avoid the danger of a terminology becoming a set of blinders, while still producing theory-based criticism, my approach is always to begin by identifying the defining formal characteristics of the rhetoric in question, to move from that analysis of form to a consideration of rhetorical function, and then to consider how rhetorical theory illuminates the linkage between rhetorical form and function. The three-step approach developed in the essay is designed to achieve that aim.

In sum, rhetorical critics need a wide-ranging knowledge of rhetorical theory and methodology, but along with that knowledge, they need a healthy skepticism about those theories as well. That skepticism helps critics avoid a situation in which a theory no longer illuminates rhetorical action but becomes a set of blinders.

## POTENTIALS AND PITFALLS

The discussion of a variety of approaches to narrative analysis and the presentation of a systematic approach to narrative criticism suggests several potentials and pitfalls associated with the rhetorical analysis of narrative. The most significant potential is the importance of revealing the power of narrative in our society. There is no question that narrative is an extremely powerful rhetorical form. If the battle is between strong statistics on one side and a compelling narrative on the other, there is little doubt that at least in the short run, the narrative will be more influential. People love stories, and stories are powerful means of making connections with others and tapping into basic values and needs. The immense power of narrative makes it especially important that critics uncover how narratives function. Although a number of theorists (myself included) have critiqued the narrative paradigm, the field of rhetorical criticism owes an enormous debt to Walter Fisher for pointing out so forcefully the importance of narrative.

Although narrative criticism can be quite useful, it is not without pitfalls, three of which are particularly important. First, narrative criticism is most easily and appropriately applied to rhetoric that is clearly a story. However, much rhetoric draws on stories that are in some sense out there in the society. A speaker or writer might refer to a story about the Founding Fathers or a story about Lady Gaga or Monica Lewinsky and assume that the audience would fill in the details. The problem is that it is difficult for the critic to know how the audience fills in those details or exactly what gets filled in. There is also a fine line between an example included as support material in a speech or essay and a developed narrative. While the line between these two types of rhetoric is a fine one, the line is also important. There is a difference between a member of Congress citing the example of Pat Roush and the more developed story told by Burton. Narrative criticism is much more applicable to the developed story as opposed to the implied reference or short example. The critic can distinguish between these two rhetorical types by considering whether the story in any rhetoric is developed in such a way that it fulfills any or all of the persuasive functions of narrative that I identified earlier. If it does fulfill those functions, the story usefully can be treated as narrative. If it fails to fulfill those functions, it may be more appropriate to consider it an extended example.

A second pitfall of narrative criticism relates to the variability in how human beings interpret stories. Narrative critics need to recognize that not all people prefer the same kinds of stories. A glance at the best-seller list for fiction supports this judgment. Some of us love fantastic novels about space or romantic stories about dashing men and ravishing women; others like murder mysteries or historical novels. My point is that human beings like very different types of stories. If that is true in relation to fiction, it probably is true about other types of narratives as well. While Fisher is right that narrative is a human universal, it seems clear that the standards by which people evaluate stories are culturally based, rather than universal. I made this point earlier when I noted that many in the Arab world found the story that Israeli intelligence had orchestrated the September 11 attacks to be quite credible, when nearly all Americans found that story to be absurd. Consequently, rhetorical critics need to ground their analysis of a narrative in the attitudes of a given audience and recognize that stories that they find to be credible may not be credible to others.

The final pitfall of narrative analysis relates to variation in narrative type. Narrative criticism works best on stories that support a clear theme and that are grounded in the real world as we know it. Narrative analysis of works of fantasy, science fiction, or allegory is more difficult because the critic must not only discover the underlying narrative pattern, but also translate the message out of the category of science fiction or fantasy into the category of realistic narrative.[43] An example may make this point clear. Janice Hocker Rushing has interpreted the first two *Alien* films from a psychological perspective, concluding that in the films "the patriarchy has induced the feminine to fight itself," creating a situation in which "the feminine is actually subverted."[44] My own reading of the films would focus on how the protagonist (Ripley) is both feminine and powerful, thereby sending a message of feminist empowerment, but also on how the films strongly suggest that power and money often produce corrupt decision making.

However, I think it would be very difficult to determine one "correct" interpretation of these films because they are works of science fiction set in a time and place quite far from our reality. There inevitably will be much more variation in the interpretation of works of science fiction, fantasy, and allegory than of realistic narratives, such as that of Burton. This point is easily illustrated in relation to allegory, a type of narrative in which the author uses a story set in a place very different from the contemporary world to imply a judgment about our world. Even when a work of allegory has a very clear theme, such as Orwell's attack on communism in *Animal Farm*, interpretation is more difficult than in realistic narratives. Allegorical interpretation requires the critic to translate the allegory into a realistic narrative prior to analyzing it. This translation stage adds complexity to the interpretive process. Thus, the third pitfall of narrative criticism is that the perspective works most effectively on realistic narratives that lay out a clear conclusion.

Storytelling is one of the hallmarks of human culture. From the time that humans developed the capacity to use symbols, we have told stories. And stories are among the most powerful forms of persuasion. Yet, until relatively recently, rhetorical critics shied away from analyzing narratives and focused instead on rational argumentation and other rhetorical forms. While argument is clearly important, narrative plays a crucial role in every human culture. Rhetorical critics need a systematic way of explaining how narratives work to persuade audiences. The approach developed in this chapter is a starting point that the critic can use to break down both the forms present in a given narrative and how those forms function in relation to an audience.

## NARRATIVE ANALYSIS TOP PICKS

Fisher, Walter R. *Human Communication as Narration* (Columbia: University of South Carolina Press, 1987). In his book, Fisher fleshes out all aspects of the narrative paradigm.

Fisher, Walter R. "Narration as a Human Communication Paradigm: The Case of Public Moral Argument." *Communication Monographs* 51 (1984): 1–22. This essay is the original statement of the narrative paradigm and the most influential article about narrative published to date in a communication journal.

Hollihan, Thomas A., and Patricia Riley. "The Rhetorical Power of a Compelling Story: A Critique of a 'Toughlove' Parental Support Group." *Communication Quarterly* 35 (1987): 13–25. Hollihan and Riley provide one of the clearest applications of principles of narrative rationality to a real-world story.

Lewis, William F. "Telling America's Story: Narrative Form and the Reagan Presidency." *Quarterly Journal of Speech* 73 (1987): 280–302. Lewis's essay is among the best examples of the inductive approach to narrative analysis. It is accessible and clearly argued.

Milford, Michael, and Robert C. Rowland. "Situated Ideological Allegory and *Battlestar Galactica*." *Western Journal of Communication* 75 (2012): 536–551. Milford and Rowland show the importance of finding the particular nature of the story in rhetorical analysis, in this case identifying an ideological allegory.

Rowland, Robert C., and Robert Strain. "Social Function, Polysemy and Narrative-Dramatic Form: A Case Study of *Do the Right Thing*." *Communication Quarterly* 42 (1994): 213–228. Rowland and Strain illustrate the advantages of the inductive approach, but also the difficulty with the approach as a method of criticism.

## NOTES

1. "The Struggle of Transgender Workers," *New York Times*, July 9, 2015, A24. The *Times* also referenced the story of the actress Laverne Cox.

2. Ibid.

3. See Hayden White, "The Value of Narrativity in the Representation of Reality," *Critical Inquiry* 7 (1980): 6.

4. For example, Wallace Martin, *Recent Theories of Narrative* (Ithaca, NY: Cornell University Press, 1986), 7. The most important scholar in rhetoric to focus on its importance is Walter R. Fisher. See "Narration as a Human Communication Paradigm: The Case of Public Moral Argument," *Communication Monographs* 51 (1984): 1–22; Walter R. Fisher, *Human Communication as Narration* (Columbia: University of South Carolina Press, 1987).

5. Northrop Frye has built an entire theory of narrative around the level of heroic power present in the protagonist. See Northrop Frye, *Anatomy of Criticism: Four Essays* (Princeton, NJ: Princeton University Press, 1957).

6. See Kenneth Burke, *A Rhetoric of Motives* (Berkeley: University of California Press, 1969).

7. See Elie Wiesel, *Night*, trans. Stella Rodway (New York: Avon, 1958).

8. Lewis O. Mink, "Narrative Form as a Cognitive Instrument," in *The Writing of History: Literary Form and Historical Understanding*, ed. Robert H. Canary and Henry Kozuchi (Madison: University of Wisconsin Press, 1978), 129–130.

9. Ibid., 131.

10. Al Gore, *An Inconvenient Truth: The Planetary Emergency of Global Warming and What We Can Do about It* (Emmaus, PA: Rodale, 2006).

11. See *Report of the President's Commission on the Accident at Three Mile Island: The Need For Change; The Legacy of TMI* (Washington: Government Printing Office, 1979); Robert C. Rowland, "A Reanalysis of the Argumentation at Three Mile Island," in *Argument in Controversy: Proceedings of the 7th SCA-AFA Conference on Argumentation*, ed. Donn Parson (Annandale, VA: SCA, 1991): 277–283.

12. Michiko Kakutani, "Kind Hero of 'Mockingbird' Returns as Racist in Sequel," *New York Times*, July 11, 2015, A1, A3.

13. Walter R. Fisher and Richard A Filloy, "Argument in Drama and Literature: An Exploration," in *Advances in Argumentation Theory and Research*, ed. J. Robert Cox and Charles A. Willard (Carbondale: Southern Illinois University Press, 1982), 343.

14. Ibid., 360.

15. Ibid.

16. Fisher, "Narration as a Human Communication Paradigm," 4–9; Fisher, *Human Communication as Narration*, 67.

17. Fisher, "Narration as a Human Communication Paradigm," 6.

18. Fisher, "Narration as a Human Communication Paradigm," 7.

19. Fisher, *Human Communication as Narration*, xi.

20. Fisher, *Human Communication as Narration*, 75; Fisher, "Narrative as a Human Communication Paradigm," 8–9.

21. Fisher, "Narration as a Human Communication Paradigm," 8.

22. Fisher, *Human Communication as Narration*, 47.

23. Fisher, "Narration as a Human Communication Paradigm," 8.

24. Fisher, "The Narrative Paradigm: An Elaboration," *Communication Monographs* 52 (1985), 350.

25. Fisher, "Narration as a Human Communication Paradigm," 16.

26. See Barbara Warnick, "The Narrative Paradigm: Another Story," *Quarterly Journal of Speech* 73 (1987): 172–182; Robert C. Rowland, "Narrative: Mode of Discourse or Paradigm," *Communication Monographs* 54 (1987): 264–275.

27. In addition to "Narrative: Mode of Discourse or Paradigm?," see "On Limiting the Narrative Paradigm: Three Case Studies," *Communication Monographs* 56 (1989): 39–53.

28. See "On Limiting the Narrative Paradigm" and Robert C. Rowland, "The Value of the Rational World and Narrative Paradigms," *Central States Speech Journal* 39 (1988): 204–217.

29. Ronald H. Carpenter, "Admiral Mahan, 'Narrative Fidelity,' and the Japanese Attack on Pearl Harbor," *Quarterly Journal of Speech* 72 (1986): 290–305.

30. Carpenter, "Admiral Mahan," 291.

31. Thomas A. Hollihan and Patricia Riley, "The Rhetorical Power of a Compelling Story: A Critique of a 'Toughlove' Parental Support Group," *Communication Quarterly* 35 (1987): 13–25.

32. Hollihan and Riley, "Rhetorical Power," 23, 24.

33. See Thomas Rosteck, "Narrative in Martin Luther King's *I've Been to the Mountaintop*," *Southern Communication Journal* 58 (1992): 22–32; Martha Solomon and Wayne J. McMullen, "*Places in the Heart*: The Rhetorical Force of an Open Text," *Western Journal of Speech Communication* 55 (1991): 339–353; Sally J. Perkins, "The Dilemma of Identity: Theatrical Portrayals of a 16th Century Feminist," *Southern Communication Journal* 59 (1994): 205–214; Robert C. Rowland and Robert Strain, "Social Function, Polysemy and Narrative-Dramatic Form: A Case Study of *Do the Right Thing*," *Communication Quarterly* 42 (1994): 213–228.

34. Stephanie Kelley-Romano, "Trust No One: The Conspiracy Genre on American Television," *Southern Communication Journal* 73 (2008): 105–121; Mike Milford and Robert C. Rowland, "Situated Ideological Allegory and *Battlestar Galactica*," *Western Journal of Communication* 75 (2012): 536–551.

35. William F. Lewis, "Telling America's Story: Narrative Form and the Reagan Presidency," *Quarterly Journal of Speech* 73 (1987): 280–302.

36. Lewis, "Telling America's Story," 282.

37. *U.S. Citizens Held in Saudi Arabia* (hearing of the House Government Reform Committee, June 12, 2002), available online, Congressional Universe, LexisNexis. The passage that is included is a selection from Burton's remarks.

38. Fisher, "Narration as a Human Communication Paradigm," 16.

39. See Fisher and Filloy, "Argument in Drama and Literature," 360.

40. Fisher, "Narration as a Human Communication Paradigm," 8.

41. Ibid., 16.

42. Ryan C. Crocker, "Statement of Ryan C. Crocker Deputy Assistant Secretary for Near Eastern Affairs," *U.S. Citizens Held in Saudi Arabia* (hearing of the House Government Reform Committee, June 12, 2002), available online, Congressional Universe, LexisNexis.

43. See Rowland, "On Limiting the Narrative Paradigm."

44. Janice Hocker Rushing, "Evolution of 'The New Frontier' in *Alien* and *Aliens*: Patriarchal Co-optation of the Feminine Archetype," *Quarterly Journal of Speech* 75 (1989): 10.

# 11

# Dramatism and Kenneth Burke's Pentadic Criticism

*Ryan Erik McGeough and Andrew King*

Kenneth Burke (1897–1993) was perhaps the most influential rhetorical critic of the twentieth century. A critic, editor, poet, and traveling lecturer, Burke traversed a wide array of intellectual circles. As a result, his unorthodox ideas cut across academic disciplines (in a bookstore, Burke might be found in the communication, literary criticism, sociology, or philosophy sections) in order to explore the role of language in human action. Across his multiple books and essays, Burke developed a theory of language and human action he called **dramatism**. Dramatism contains a number of Burke's central ideas, including terministic screens, identification, and, most famously, the **pentad**.

## ORIGINS OF DRAMATISM

Kenneth Burke's unique contributions to rhetorical criticism stem from his distinctive intellectual background. Burke briefly attended the Ohio State University before dropping out and moving to New York City, where he sat in on seminars at Columbia University. During the 1920s, he integrated himself into the artistic and intellectual renaissance in Greenwich Village. During this time and into the 1930s, Burke spent time conversing, and later clashing, with Marxist intellectuals. He edited a literary magazine and engaged in long debates with other critics. All of these perspectives influenced Burke's approach to criticism. Recognizing that "every insight contains its own special kind of blindness," Burke found each perspective simultaneously valuable yet incomplete. An intellectual omnivore and pragmatist, Burke drew on insights from what he found most valuable within numerous schools of thought and combined them in novel ways.

Burke, like most major thinkers, was also profoundly influenced by the world in which he lived. He left home and started college as the First World War raged in Europe. His intellectual debates in the 1920s and 1930s focused on a wide array of topics, including art, politics, communism, fascism, democracy, and the power of language to create social change. Burke observed the power, limits, and consequences of language as the world marched toward catastrophic war for a second time. In 1938, Burke published a deeply insightful analysis of Hitler's *Mein Kampf*; he hoped that carefully analyzing Hitler's rhetoric might help prevent it from working in the United States.[1] He spent the war writing *A Grammar of Motives*, which explores the role of language in how we attribute motives and understand the actions of others. These two works not only reveal the influence of Burke's context on his writings but also demonstrate his belief in the power of language and the power of critics to intervene in the world.

## DRAMATISM

Burke labeled himself a "word man" and obsessed over words and their capacity to influence human thought and action.[2] Drawing on Aristotle, who described humans as animals who have words, Burke believed that symbol use is what separates human action from the behavior of other animals, which he called motion. Central to dramatism is Burke's contention that humans do not just use words, but that words use us. By this, Burke meant that choosing to describe the world with one set of words rather than another leads us to understand the world in a particular way, and this understanding of the world shapes how we choose to act in it. A dramatistic perspective recognizes that words are more than just the tools we use to interact with one another; they are also the fundamental building blocks by which we construct our understanding of the world. Through language, we orient ourselves in the world and call others to see the world and act as we do.

Dramatism locates this power in language because of the power of words to act as terministic screens. By **terministic screens**, Burke means the capacity of language (terminology) to encourage us to understand the world in some ways while filtering (screening) other interpretations out. Burke claims that "even if any given terminology is a *reflection* of reality, by its very nature as a terminology, it must be a *selection* of reality; and to this extent it must function also as a *deflection* of reality."[3] Thus, no matter how objective we might try to be, the specific language we use to describe an object or event will draw our attention toward some aspects of the event (selecting), and thus away from other aspects (deflecting). For example, in the rhetoric surrounding abortion, activists on both sides have sought to harness the power of language to act as a terministic screen. Activists opposed to abortion identify themselves as "pro-life," while those who support abortion being legal identify themselves as "pro-choice." The first title attempts to frame the issue as being about protecting human life, the second as being about protecting human freedom. Both labels *reflect* a position on the issue of abortion, but they *select* very different aspects of the controversy to highlight.[4] Understanding terministic screens reveals the ways in which all language can be persuasive: words shape the way we see the world by encouraging us to notice some aspects of the world over others.[5]

The capacity of language to function as a terministic screen is just one of the ways Burke argues that persuasion occurs unconsciously. Another is through what Burke labels **identification**. In fact, Burke argues that contemporary persuasion occurs less through logical weighing of arguments and more through the often unconscious processes by which we align ourselves with others. In a mass-mediated society, Burke recognized that we are awash in persuasive appeals, and we simply cannot take the time to rationally evaluate all of them. Burke felt he needed a stronger term to describe the goals of the mind-changing industries in our society (advertising, sales, politics, etc.). Persuasion in a consumer-orientated mass society involves emotion, lifestyle choices, and systematic appeals to deeply held values. Thus, Burke adopted the term *identification* as more descriptive of the goals of public rhetoric. Identification suggests more than mere like-mindedness; it connotes individuals "acting together" and sharing common feelings, "sensations, concepts, images, ideas and attitudes."[6] Dramatism is designed to give us a deep awareness of the nature and resources of identification and a discerning eye for its costs and consequences.[7]

Of course, Burke also recognized that "identification is compensatory to division."[8] By this he means that any articulation of "us" also implies (either implicitly or explicitly) "them." In recent years, activists protesting with the slogan "Black Lives Matter" have often encountered counterprotests using the slogan "Police Lives Matter." These clashes, whether in person or on social media, reveal conflicting identifications of who counts as "us" and who counts as "them." Identification occurs when you choose a path of action not simply based on weighing the pros and cons of that action, but because you perceive that action as aligning you with other people like you. Whether in aligning yourself with a political party, associating with people who share your values, or buying products designed to project a particular image of yourself, Burke recognized the power of identification in shaping our actions.

## THE PENTAD

Burke worried that because so much of persuasion is unconscious, we often embrace appeals uncritically without understanding their implications. Burke understood that our forms of language and experience are interlocked and that spokespersons in advertising, government, public relations, and media know how to use these persuasive forms. After twice watching the nations of the world follow their leaders to war, Burke hoped to provide a method that might help people become more savvy consumers of persuasive messages. He developed pentadic criticism to make visible how persuaders use language to change our beliefs and influence our actions. Burke argued that the master form was the common story, a form that was generated by the structure of our minds. Burke developed his critical method based on that form. The method he invented is simple yet complex, flexible yet straightforward, prosaic yet poetic. Its purpose is to help defend us against the tremendous flood of persuasive messages that assault us every moment of our waking lives.

Burke birthed this famous method in the last year of World War II in the pages of his 1945 book, *A Grammar of Motives*.[9] Despite its eventual celebrity, the new approach was not an immediate hit; the use of Burke's insights spread slowly at first. His work was first brought into the spotlight by rhetorical critic Marie Hochmuth Nichols,[10] who wrote two very influential articles explaining Burke's methods and theories.[11] Today dramatism is studied by a large and diverse group, including both rhetorical and literary critics, philosophers, social scientists, and even theologians. Once it was only used as a tool for textual analysis, but its uses have grown to include methods of composition and of psychological, sociological, and philosophical analysis. This chapter will confine its attention to the core mission of pentadic criticism: the development of a method that can help people resist the flood tide of persuasive messages that assault them and to develop persuasive messages of their own.[12] What follows is far from exhaustive, but it will give the reader a strong hint of the kinds of help that Burke has to offer.

### Where Does It Come From?

Burke did not so much "invent" pentadic criticism as revamp and expand schemes inherited from earlier critics. Like most perspectives, it is a combination of earlier ideas. From Aristotle's *Poetics*, Burke took the ideas of dramatic form and the power of stories in human history.[13] Aristotle affirmed the centrality of human storytelling to the formation and maintenance of community. Our stories lie at the root of our identity. It has been said that we can know a people by the kinds of stories they tell. Aristotle was also a great name giver and classifier; he believed that we need a good set of labels if we are to talk sensibly and at length about anything. Accordingly, he constructed a useful vocabulary, labeling all the parts of narrative structure. With a common set of categories, critics could better decide what made narratives strong or weak, beautiful or ugly, effective or clumsy. He left us names for the central features of the common story, names such as plot, character, spectacle, dialogue, and concept. Burke renamed these parts with the words *act, agent, scene, agency,* and *purpose*.[14]

From the great Roman poet Horace, Burke took the notion of generative categories. Generative categories are the building blocks of creativity. They not only provide the skeleton and structure of a story; they also serve as a stimulus to invent new ideas, to clothe the bones with new nerves, tendons, and sinews. Two thousand years ago in a still admired essay giving advice to would-be writers, Horace used a series of basic questions as building blocks in playwriting and storytelling. In his famous work *Ars Poetica*, Horace advised his readers on a method of composing stories, a method so universal that it did not matter whether the writers were fifteen or ninety, libertines or monks, intellectuals or merchants.[15] All they had to do was apply his categories to a subject, and they could produce a text. Horace believed that all stories were the product of the answers to a series of basic questions. Who are the main characters? What is the place in which they are set? What is the nature of their conflict or problem? What is the era in which the story is set? What is their purpose? What are the means they use to solve their problems and what obstacles do they face? And what kind of resolution can be made?

Horace argued that if you answered those questions in an imaginative way you would produce the germ of a story. Modern journalists honor Horace when they tell us that the way to write a complete news story is to answer the basic questions: What happened? Who did it? Where and under what circumstances was the action done? When did it happen? How was the thing done? Why was it done? Burke borrowed these questions and updated them. He maintained that the questions could be used to gain a complete understanding of any human action and how we explain the motives from which it arose. Burke does not use the term *motive* in the legal or formal sense. It is simply a name we give to our acts, a strategic symbolic summing-up of an action.

From the language scholar and coauthor of *The Meaning of Meaning*, Ivor Armstrong Richards, Burke took the idea of the importance of form in art.[16] Burke was interested in the aesthetic appeal of form, particularly narrative form.[17] **Form** is a pattern that invites our participation; it arouses our desires and promises to fulfill them. We see the power of form when we know a pattern and expect it to be repeated. At a wedding, we typically expect someone to officiate and for the couple to exchange vows and/or rings. At a sporting event, we know the event is beginning when we are asked to rise for the singing of the national anthem. At a religious service, we might expect each meeting to begin (or end) with a prayer or a song. Ritual forms give us a sense of order, piety, shared community, and emotional closure. Burke has made us acutely aware of the power of narrative form, a form that dominates our orientation toward the world. In tragic plays, individual conflicts are represented as clashes between good and evil; in order to restore order, evil must be vanquished. In comedies, we recognize that the characters are neither inherently good nor evil but are fools to be laughed at. Burke noted that comedians make use of our socialization to conventional forms. We expect jokes will have a punch line; we expect that football squads will punt on fourth and long, and that heroes will (usually) win out in the end. Form invites our participation; we become caught up in it. Artists and writers use form to draw us into their works; propagandists and advertisers use musical, visual, and verbal forms to gain our compliance. Burke's pentadic criticism helps us recognize the widespread use of dramatic form. Dramatic form is one of the most common ways that we interpret events. It is one of the great human lenses we employ to discover meaning in our environment. Dramatic form, Burke tells us, is much bigger than theatrical performance; it is embedded in the structure of our minds. Thus, *dramatic form exists logically prior to our experience*. It is like an actor waiting in the wings to come on stage and interpret for us what it is that we are seeing and hearing as we move through the world. In this sense, dramatic form is literal, not metaphorical. The scheme of dramatic form is not a metaphor derived from a study of lots of drama or years of going to conventional theater and watching plays. In fact, the contrary is true. The movies, plays, stories, and news events are endless imitations and reincarnations of dramatic form.

### Why Is It Important?

Frightened by the growing alliance of big commerce and big media, Burke began to worry about the future of self-government in North America. Despite his associations with leading figures of the Left, Burke was, in many ways, an old-fashioned Jeffersonian who believed that issues and ideas ought to come from the bedrock of the people, not from mandarin intellectuals and technical elites. His little farm in Andover, New Jersey, was close to his ideal, a place where groups of people met for free discussion of just about everything under the sun, but especially the local, state, and federal policies of their government. But how could this model thrive or even survive in an America now dominated by corporations, mass media, and government bureaucracies? How would American citizens maintain autonomy and agency when surrounded by agents and institutions who were trying to manipulate them? Advertising, propaganda, slanted news, and corporate public relations; political action groups, social movements, and cults; together with Hollywood and mass media have saturated the environment with persuasive images and words. During the Great Depression, Burke witnessed the rise of Hitler, Mussolini, Franco, Stalin, and later Mao, demagogues who manipulated millions of followers through messages greatly amplified by nearly absolute control of public media.

But even in the open societies of democratic Britain and the United States, he noted that large masses of Western citizenry suffered from fear, confusion, or deep cynicism as a result of being inundated by messages from every corner. After the great stock market crash of 1929 and the ruin of millions of families, our economic system seemed to have failed. Back-to-the-land agrarians, technocrats, communists, fascists, and other disaffected groups emerged from the wreckage. Spokespersons who had formerly been dismissed as cranks and utopians were getting a hearing. Burke noted that many of his fellow citizens were confused, uprooted, and fearful. He believed that without guidance they would not know how to discover the content and the consequences of these competing ides. Unlike European thinkers whose answer was guidance by a class of intellectuals, Burke thought that people ought to be able to analyze and understand public questions on their own. In particular they ought to be able to discover the personal agendas and disguised advantages that people often hide beneath idealistic rhetoric. In the old American spirit of self-help and individualism, Burke offered a perspective that would unmask personal motives and separate personal advantage from high-sounding public promises.

By the 1930s, after spending years associating with writers in Greenwich Village, translating the work of Thomas Mann, and reviewing the work of many of the leading writers of the day as editor of the *Dial* (then one of America's foremost literary magazines), Burke had become profoundly convinced of the power of artists to influence people.[18] He believed that the role of the artist was crucial in society and that the artist to a much greater extent than the psychologist and the social worker could perform a therapeutic role in society. Embracing a tradition running back to Aristotle, Burke believed that the writer could be a kind of physician of society. He was a pioneer in raising environmental awareness, an early voice warning about the polarization of class and race and about the unsustainability of our agricultural system and industrial system.[19] For the last five decades of his existence, all of his efforts were dedicated to giving people the analytic tools to resist manipulative persuaders and to seek a more poetic vision of society.

Advertisers, propagandists, and hustlers of all kinds like to have us respond rapidly and uncritically to their messages. They want us to act, without stopping to reflect deeply on the full meaning of their message. But a critical perspective means that we stop to do some analysis; and this time of reflection prevents the rapid stimulus-response kind of action so dear to mass-marketing persuasion. Charles King, a former creative director of one of the world's largest ad agencies (and brother of one of the authors), joked that he wanted people who saw the ads to respond like Pavlov's dogs. He wanted them to rush to buy the product, not to engage in an analysis of its claims and benefits. Criticism not only delays our reactions to messages; it may also *modify* our reactions. It can allow us to reframe the message in an alternative way, or adopt other attitudes toward it, or perhaps think about the intentions of the maker of the message, or about the long-term consequences of acting on such a message. In thinking deeply about one's attractions to the language and imagery of various products, one might also discover some useful things about one's mind and heart. Thus the practice of criticism not only helps us make better choices; it may also be transformational.

## How Does It Work? Or, The Naming of the Parts

Burke opens *A Grammar of Motives*—the famous book in which he first fully develops the pentad—with a question: "What is involved when we say what people are doing and why they are doing it?"[20] This question is more complex than simply "What do people do and why?" Burke's question also asks us to consider what is involved "when we *say*" what people are doing and why. Thus, Burke is interested not only in what people do, but also in how we choose to describe their actions and attribute the reasons behind those actions. Analyzing the choices a speaker makes when explaining past actions or advocating future actions can help us identify their motives. By **motive**, Burke means the underlying worldview and philosophy of the speaker and the worldview the speaker wants us to adopt (in the following sections, we identify a philosophy that corresponds with each part of the pentad).

Any given action might be explained in multiple ways (for example, a professor might condemn a student for cheating by saying he did so because he is dishonest, or excuse the action by saying he comes from a home that puts immense pressure on him to get high grades). Because of this, Burke recognizes that how a speaker chooses to explain another person's action reveals something about the speaker. Thus, the dramatistic pentad is not about finding the underlying and absolute truth of a situation. Rather it is a method of discovering multiple perspectives on why people do what they do. Which perspective a person uses to explain an action helps us to better recognize the motive of the speaker. Burke encourages us to analyze language not for its truth, but for its strategic uses. As Clarke Rountree puts it, dramatism is useful for "explaining what he, she or others, say about his, her or their own past present, and future actions or the past, present and future actions of others."[21] According to Burke, language is a mode of symbolic action, most often used as a means of presenting oneself to others. As we noted earlier Burke does not say that our daily lives resemble a drama. He says life *is* a drama. Thus we perceive the world in dramatic terms with plots, antagonists, protagonists, settings, motives, and so on. We are hardwired for drama. No wonder our news coverage, no matter how chaotic and enigmatic the events being covered, is broken into news *stories* and put into dramatic form. It is our primary way of making sense of the world. Often the dramatic frame features a battle over meanings, perspectives, and values.

The five rhetorical elements of the dramatistic pentad are act, scene, agent, agency, and purpose. Burke praises them for their universal application to discourse. He says their "participation in common ground makes for transformability."[22] The pentad is made up of five parts that are universally found in all narratives. Each of these parts is phrased as a question. What happened? Who did it? Where and when and under what constraints? With what means and modes? Alleging what purpose? The goal of pentadic analysis is not to simply name each of the five parts, but rather to identify the relationships between them. Exploring these questions allows the critic to determine which of the five parts dominates the others. This interpretation must be made by the critic. He or she will do so by answering the basic questions about an action described in the text. According to Burke, the answers to these questions will circumscribe the range and variety of reasonable interpretation.

*Act*

Act is the term for dramatic action. It answers the question, *what is* the action? What happened? What is being done? What is going on? It is associated with the philosophy of realism. Realists believe that the truthfulness of any belief rests upon the closeness of its correspondence with reality. Discourse that emphasizes the primacy of action has a deep hold on us. We admire devotees of action, and even when doing nothing would be a sensible course, or when there is little agreement about what to do, we still admire the leader who rushes headlong into an act. And we do so even when we suspect it may be a bad thing to do. We have a fear of too much reflection. We hold Hamlet in contempt because it takes him so long to act. But we love action heroes who act without hesitation or reflection. Long ago Edmund Burke noted that a big noisy destructive government policy was more admired than a wise quiet temperate policy. Too much reflection and analysis frightens people. We tend to associate thoughtful decision making with passivity, a state that fills red-blooded Americans with fear. (Burke's most succinct statement of act is found on pages 64–69 of his *Grammar of Motives*.)

*Scene*

Scene is the dramatistic term for the context of the act. Texts that emphasize the power of the surrounding environment or the coercive power of circumstances feature the philosophical doctrine of determinism. Many adventure stories that show people battling the elements or the power of nature emphasize scene. People who believe in situational ethics argue that circumstances are more important in determining our deeds than are our received moral codes. Those who argue that crime is a result of slum living and can be solved by clearing out such neighborhoods are making an argument that emphasizes scene. During the middle of the last century some literary editors came to believe that the greatest American literature could only be written in the American South. Thomas Jefferson believed that only farmers tending local, independent farms could maintain sustainable agriculture. Persons have often attributed magical properties to place. Ancient people often believed that special places such as oracles, sacred groves, or aligned hilltops possessed special power. Others attribute power to labyrinths, caves, or even buildings with special atmospherics. Many early religions adopted the idea of a sacred center. In the inner sanctum, only the gods could dwell; in the second circle, high priests; and on the profane margins, the worshippers. In romantic novels, the outer scene seems sympathetic to the inner state of the characters. Duels are fought against the background of a storm, and lovers break up in the dead of winter. (Burke's richest definitions of scene can be found on pages 127–132 of his *Grammar of Motives*.)

## Agent

Agent is the term for the person or persons who perform the actions. Not just who, but *what kind* of agent are they? Is the person performing the action a king or a servant, smart or foolish, lazy or ambitious? American folklore has honored people with strongly assertive personalities. We assume that strong leadership is vital for success in business and sports. Those who speak of the indispensable person are emphasizing the importance of the agent in human affairs. Much has been written about the charismatic leader who triumphs in spite of obstacles, setbacks, and enemies. Texts that emphasize the agent feature the philosophical viewpoint of idealism. Ronald Reagan was fond of talking about great American heroes. His celebrations of these people emphasized the power of an individual's inner resources against adverse circumstances. For Reagan the agent was always more powerful than the scene in which he or she was set. Character triumphed over circumstance. Sports analysts comparing Lebron James and Michael Jordan frequently argue for Jordan's superiority not because of his superior skills, but because Jordan is a proven winner. (Burke's clearest description of the agent can be found on pages 171–175 of his *Grammar of Motives*.)

## Agency

Agency is the dramatistic term for the means the agent uses to do the deed. It is the method, the technique, the apparatus, or the institution we use to get the thing done. Spokesmen for various technologies tend to emphasize a technological fix for all our problems. Bureaucrats tell us that the system is the solution. Arnold Schwarzenegger used to tell people that his method was the one that produced the best results. Those who emphasize agency as the dominant term in their messages tend to espouse a philosophy of pragmatism. Pragmatism is the philosophy that the most important aspect of any idea is its ability to produce good results. In other words, a good idea is one that is useful to the believer in the idea. We are bombarded with courses selling us special methods of building our bodies, transforming our personalities, or becoming immensely wealthy. Self-help books promise us seven strategies to save our marriages, three dynamic verbal techniques for successful negotiation, or a special technique to increase intelligence or expand memory. (Burke's most compelling explanation of agency can be found on pages 275–278 in his *Grammar of Motives*.)

## Purpose

Purpose answers the question, why? Moralists often emphasize this question in their messages. Purpose has to do with the justification for the action. Its driving focus is on the value of objectives, goals, and courses of action. Those who strongly emphasize purpose tend toward a philosophy of mysticism. Messages emphasizing purpose feature ends rather than means. Purposive thinkers and writers often speak of acts as small parts of a much larger system. We must protect our family as a part of helping the community. Helping the community furthers the greatness of the nation. The greatness of the nation is necessary to advance civilization. There is a natural tendency for messages centered on purpose to move toward transcendence. Cicero advised Roman youth to study rhetoric in order to enter the Senate. In entering the Senate, they preserved the republic. In preserving the republic they carried the Roman message of order and prosperity to the newly conquered peoples of the empire. In embodying the Roman message they served the gods who had clearly favored the spread of the Roman Way throughout the world. (Burke's most illuminating discussion of purpose occurs on pages 292–297 in his *Grammar of Motives*.)

**The Ratios**

Because each of these elements is interconnected in a dramatic structure of action, Burke calls them a *grammar of motives*. Thus, what is important is not simply locating and naming each of the five terms in the way a newspaper might answer, Who? What? Where? Why? and How? Rather, the pentad allows us to identify the relationships *between* each of these terms. In any one discourse, one of these elements usually dominates the others, and this ratio allows us to name or characterize the action. The predominance of one term over the others gives each drama a characteristic shape. That shape is what gives the drama its bite, its attitude, its persuasive bias. Since a text or a speech represents a persuasive act, we will pair each term with act: thus, scene-act, agent-act, agency-act, purpose-act, and even act-act. In theory one might use more than twenty ratios by simply pairing each term with every other term in sequence. This level of complexity is seldom necessary for actual critical practice, however.

*Scene-Act Ratio*

How does the place or the circumstances define the meaning of the act?

Example: Given the bad economy, I was unable to find a job.
Example: Considering the violence of urban life, we should expect city dwellers to commit more crimes.
Example: Given the distractions of Paris, it was hard to get much work done.
Example: A beautiful and revitalized downtown area will attract creative people to settle here from across the nation.

In each of the above examples, the scene dominates our understanding. The scene of an action may radically change how we understand that action. The same act (threatening someone with a weapon) might be read as unjust in one setting (at a bar) and justified in another (if your home is being broken into). The scene is also sometimes used to justify power. Leaders sometimes point to dangerous situations in order to justify expanding their powers. For example, supporters of the Patriot Act argued that surveillance of US citizens was justified in a post-9/11 world. Karl Marx believed that class conflict was a situation (scene) that would gradually ripen into revolution. During the military service of one of your authors, he was told again and again that available forces on the ground and the local terrain determine military tactics. We are often told that a failed plan might have worked in a different place. Soldiers are told that they must fight harder to defend their homeland and that fighting on native soil will bring a special zeal to their efforts.

Philosophical position: Texts that emphasize scene downplay free choice and emphasize situational determinism. They tend to emphasize the power of circumstances over individual decisions. Clarence Darrow excused the behavior of many criminals by arguing that they were victims of bad heredity and merciless environment. Supporters of social welfare programs point to bad schools and failing local economies as reasons that such programs are needed. Speakers who advise accommodating to circumstances emphasize the deterministic power of scene.

*Agent-Act Ratio*

How important is the nature of the actor in the execution of an act?

Example: Given a monster like Hitler, we should have expected that millions of people would be exterminated.
Example: Only Albert Einstein could have made this discovery.
Example: Given how corrupt our politicians are, we should expect them to pass bad laws.
Example: From a proven winner like Arnold Schwarzenegger, you can expect miracles in whatever he tries to do.

An agent-act ratio comes into play whenever we connect character and behavior. This ratio is at work when we understand an action as being a result of the person who performed it. Opponents of social welfare programs (see the scene-act example) may argue that such programs reward people who are lazy and that individuals could overcome growing up in bad schools or a failing local economy if they put their minds to it. Dynastic historians wrote histories centered on the personalities of various kings. Persons who look for charismatic leaders to solve their problems tend to speak in this mode.

Philosophical position: Texts or speeches that emphasize the agent reflect idealism. Idealism emphasizes ambitions, values, and meanings. It asserts that individuals are motivated by desires, emotion, and ambitions. Character is seen as far more important than the force of circumstances or the existence of resources or special techniques.

*Agency-Act Ratio*

What methods or tools enabled the performance of an act?

Example: Serena Williams's success is a result of her secret training methods.
Example: Only advances in technology can bring economic growth to this region.
Example: Superior training and intelligence gathering have made the CIA the greatest spy agency in the world.
Example: We failed to climb the mountain because our climbing gear was not good enough.

As Charles Kneupper observed, "Give a child a hammer and everything will be treated like a nail."[23] An agency-act ratio represents actions as a result of the available means/technologies. When an act succeeds, it is a result of having adequate means to accomplish the goal. When an act fails, it is a sign that the available means are insufficient. Or as an Indy driver once said, "Victory is 80 percent car, 15 percent team, and 5 percent driver." For those who speak from an agency perspective, the system is always the solution.

Philosophical position: Texts or speeches that emphasize agency demonstrate pragmatism. Pragmatism is the doctrine that the best idea or solution is one that produces the best outcome. Methods are judged by their consequences. The best method is the one that allows us to get things done.

*Purpose-Act Ratio*

How does a larger goal influence the act?

Example: In order to end World War II, the United States chose to drop atomic bombs.
Example: If capitalism is to function successfully, it must allow people to fail.
Example: If you want to enter the bar, you have to show your ID.
Example: I may have made several mistakes, but I had the very best intentions.

One might describe this ratio in the following manner: in order to get X you have to do Y. Another version of the purpose-act ratio is the generic, "If you want to make an omelet, you have to break a few eggs." The television program *24* depicted protagonist Agent Jack Bauer torturing captives for information. The show portrayed Bauer's action as justified because his larger goal was to prevent a terrorist attack. In a purpose-act ratio, the ends justify the means. The individual act is simply a necessary step toward the more important end. The problem is that ends often become means. Temporary methods often sabotage one's goals. Stalin promised an end to food shortages in the Soviet Union, but his method of achieving that goal brought the death of four million kulaks.

Philosophical position: Since purpose is merely another name for the goal of an act, speeches or texts that emphasize purpose suggest the concerns of mysticism. Such texts tend to move toward the transcendent. Decisions are always seen in terms of a larger program. In some examples of this kind of rhetoric, means are entirely subordinated to ends. One might be urged to break local laws for the sake of a higher or divine law. In the American civil rights movement, Martin Luther King Jr. reminded followers that they must act in accordance with God's will—even if that meant acting in ways that would lead them to be arrested. Understood from a purpose-act ratio, such actions were justified because their broader purpose warranted breaking unjust laws.

*Act-Act Ratio*

Was the action a response to a previous action?

Example: My roommate made dinner, so I washed the dishes.
Example: He made a large donation to her campaign; she will repay him once she is elected.
Example: I hit him because he hit me first.
Example: The governor passed a controversial law, so a group of citizens tried to recall him.

In an act-act ratio, an action is simply explained as a response to a preceding action. An act-act ratio might serve as justification for a series of actions: in response to the British parliament passing the Tea Act, protesters in Boston boarded a British ship and threw all of the tea into the Boston Harbor. In response to the Boston Tea Party, the British parliament passed what were known in the colonies as the Intolerable Acts; in response to the Intolerable Acts, the colonies organized the Continental Congress. Such justifications are common in political situations as well as in everyday life. Perhaps the most striking example of a policy dominated by an act-act ratio was the Cold War's doctrine of mutually assured destruction (MAD): neither the United States nor the Soviet Union wanted to use a nuclear weapon because they knew the other side would respond by using their own nuclear weapons.

Philosophical position: Texts that emphasize act suggest realism. Realism is a philosophy that says that it doesn't really matter what people *are*. What is important is what they *do*. From this position, abstractions such as "the People" or "the national character" or "the common good" are seen as silly abstractions. There is no such thing as the public; they do not believe in the "common good." People act through special interests; for them presidents or political parties are just empty agents who act on behalf of one interest group or another. Behavior is what counts, and most rhetoric is seen as a mask or a justification for self-interested action.

We could elaborate on more ratios. Any of the terms of the pentad might be seen as dominating the others. For example, how did the situation influence the means we chose (scene-agency)? How did who we are affect our goals (agent-purpose)? But the five above are enough to illustrate the twofold power of the pentad.[24] Suffice it to say that the pentad can generate discourse from a variety of perspectives and provide a lively sense of the limits of any single perspective and the necessity of viewing messages from several points of view. In looking at the feasibility and effectiveness of any public proposal, exploring the pentadic ratios allow us to critique it from a multiplicity of views. For instance, does an agent appear to understand the scene in which he or she operates? Are the agencies or methods selected by the agent appropriate to the scene? Is the agent capable of dealing with the situation? Does he or she have the character, expertise, and support? Is the purpose used in order to justify acts that seem to undermine it in an Orwellian fashion, such as militarizing the state to achieve order, or using censorship to prevent the spread of subversive ideas?

## CRITICAL ESSAYS

Thus far in this book you have read chapters that offer a single essay for you to read. Unlike these chapters, we are not offering a single example essay. To grasp the ways in which pentadic criticism can be applied, we offer instead several examples of this particular perspective, followed by a brief discussion of things to consider when grappling with motives and competing frames, as well as identifying dominant terms.

### EXAMPLE ONE: PURPOSE AND AGENCY IN OBAMA'S SECOND INAUGURAL ADDRESS

When giving his second inaugural address in 2014, President Barack Obama faced a distinct challenge since his second term began with a Republican controlled House, many of whom had run on promises to oppose or limit most government action. As such, Obama's second inaugural responded to public arguments over how much (or little) the federal government should do. Obama opens his address by quoting the Declaration of Independence:

> What makes us exceptional—what makes us American—is our allegiance to an idea articulated in a declaration made more than two centuries ago: "We hold these truths to be self-evident, that all men are created equal; that they are endowed by their Creator with certain unalienable rights; that among these are life, liberty, and the pursuit of happiness."

Today we continue a never-ending journey to bridge the meaning of those words with the realities of our time. For history tells us that while these truths may be self-evident, they've never been self-executing; that while freedom is a gift from God, it must be secured by His people here on Earth. The patriots of 1776 did not fight to replace the tyranny of a king with the privileges of a few or the rule of a mob. They gave to us a republic, a government of, and by, and for the people, entrusting each generation to keep safe our founding creed.[25]

A critic using the tools of dramatism will quickly notice a few important things about Obama's message: First, Obama seeks to create identification by articulating commonality around "what makes us American." Second, notice how Obama makes purpose the dominant pentadic term. In the first paragraph, what makes us American (Agent) is our allegiance to a common creed (Purpose). In the second paragraph, Obama states that when "entrusting each generation to keep safe our founding creed" (Purpose), the founders of the nation "gave to us a republic, a government of, and by, and for the people" (Agency). In other words, Obama portrays a world in which our common purpose is what makes us American and government is the agency by which the creed may be protected. He then claims that, "fidelity to our founding principles requires new responses to new challenges; that preserving our individual freedoms ultimately requires collective action." Again, fulfilling of purpose requires not just action, but collective action—the sort of action made possible through the agency of government. Many media pundits saw Obama's second inaugural address as a somewhat generic encomium to America. A quick application of the pentad reveals how Obama sought to undermine his political opponents by unifying Americans behind a common purpose that would justify governmental action.

## EXAMPLE TWO: STRESSING THE AGENT

Numerous students of Martin Luther King's speaking have noted that he tended to emphasize the agent. He frequently emphasized the need for soul power and the non-violent discipline over the power of the scene to provoke demonstrators to violence. He featured an agent-scene ratio, and his perspective comes down to this: Given the right kind of demonstrator, the scene can be transformed from one of hatred and exclusion to one of acceptance and forgiveness. President Jimmy Carter also emphasized agent or character. In his speeches he constantly reminded people of his background as a Christian, a nuclear physicist, an engineer, a peanut farmer, a father, a former governor, and a military officer. His personal political message was this: Given this broad range of roles, I have deep understanding and competence in a broad arena. For some listeners this litany of roles evoked identification and confidence. For others the wide list of disparate roles may have failed to produce a unifying leadership image. Carter's famous Conservation of Energy speech is a good example of bad dramatistic choices. Carter appeared in the White House in a sweater turning down the thermostat as an example of conservation of energy. He went on to blame the oil companies, several Arab nations, and the American people for bringing on the crisis. His message was that we lacked the stuff of our pioneer ancestors and that we had acted in a self indulgent and undisciplined manner. We were now suffering for our actions and must endure a lower standard of living and endure limitations imposed by the federal government on driving speeds and availability of supplies. In this way Carter used agency in a negative way. No one enjoys being blamed for a bad situation and Carter's approval ratings plummeted.

## EXAMPLE THREE: AGRARIAN CONCERNS

The Slow Food Movement, the Farmers' Market Movement, and the Neo-Agrarians are all social movements touting the need for sustainable agriculture and an organically produced food supply. Their rhetoric has a heavy scenic component. Like Thomas Jefferson and Wendell Berry, they argue that we must encourage local small individual farmers over corporate agriculture.[26] They argue that individual owners act responsibly while corporate farms overproduce, exhaust the soil, cut down tree breaks and let the precious topsoil blow away. While they destroy rural communities by displacing individual owners, they are also quick to abandon the countryside once they have exhausted the soil and the water supply. These people use many scenic words such as community, local, American earth, husbandry, organic, and home place. Like Wes Jackson they speak of the magic of "becoming native to the place" in their quest for a responsible and sustainable agriculture.[27] These repetitive patterns of good words Burke called "clusters" and therefore we should expect to find some opposite words, bad words that he called "agons." In the rhetoric of the Neo-Agrarian we find that opponents have a different group of scenic terms routinely applied to them: inorganic, rootless, unsustainable, wasteful, global, etc.

This strategic emphasis on scene has great strengths. Environmental movements have encouraged us to be more familiar and mindful of our natural surroundings. They emphasize the ways in which our environments have tremendous effects on our individual and social well-being. On the other hand, an extreme form of this emphasis might degenerate into determinism. We might be told that the scene has already determined the results and we are helpless to try to change an outcome. Opponents of scenic rhetoric might argue that in its strongest forms it reflects a philosophy of naïve materialism and determinism.

## MOTIVES AND COMPETING FRAMES

Burke taught us that motives are not fixed things but "a term of interpretation, and being such it will naturally take its place within the framework of our Weltanschauung as a whole."[28] According to Burke, "motives" are the names we give to our actions. We may use a weighted vocabulary to talk about our building of a suburban development as our contribution to the American Dream of owning one's own home, or we may call it a great opportunity for personal profit. In each case our discourse would reflect a purpose-act ratio. One can envisage a developer using both vocabularies of motive to different audiences on different occasions.

The important point here is that our orientation determines how we characterize events and therefore our motives toward events. Charles Kneupper notes how rival orientations can be at war in our discourse:

> For example, if two persons were to observe the actual event in which lumberjacks cut down trees in a forest and one describes the event as "progress" while the other describes it as "the destruction of natural resources," then significant differences of orientation and motives are implied. Both descriptions are strategic interpretations of reality. As Burke notes, "strategies size up situations, name their structure and outstanding ingredients and name them in a way that contains our attitude toward them." The "progress" observer has a favorable/supportive attitude toward the cutting witnessed. . . . [T]he "destruction of natural resources" observer has an unfavorable altitude.[29]

This example notes that people act in different ways toward the same events. And when we want to influence people's responses we will pick out certain factors that appeal to an audience and minimize or obscure factors that may not be received well. As Burke has noted, this is really a power play, a way to define or redefine a particular event. Whoever is able to define the event wins the day in most situations. Much is at stake in rival dramatic schemes. Many people routinely define the world through a tragic frame. Burke tells us tragedy usually ends in victimage, death, sacrifice, and grief. Others define events as comedy. In a comedy, there is always room for another alternative or point of view, as we recognize that each perspective is limited. It is a more open form. The late Rep. Morris Udall of Arizona used to say that the way to break through partisanship in the House of Representatives was to use humor. In this way he avoided the brutal partisan train wrecks of polarized parties. Burke was an enemy of polarization. He often noted that polarized alternatives generally ended badly, in violence, horror, and death. Pentadic criticism was his way of breaking the gridlock. The pentad suggests a variety of perspectives, standing places, and attitudes. It is generative, heuristic, creative, and frame breaking.

## FINDING THE DOMINANT TERM, GRAPPLING WITH THE TEXT

But how does one search and find the most important pentadic term? This is done during a close reading of the text. Like an accountant doing an audit, one looks for patterns. Patterns are determined by frequency of repetition. To discover the pattern is to locate the speaker's perspective. Which words are repeated more than others? How do they help explain other aspects of the text? Some texts are heavy on description or scene; others seem to focus more on the methods (agency) by which things are done, and some concentrate on the character of the person or people in the text. Yet others may deal with the justification of the actions described in the text (purpose). David Ling studied Senator Ted Kennedy's Chappaquiddick speech and discovered that most of the words used by Kennedy to characterize his actions related to the scene. Describing the car accident in which Mary Jo Kopechne died, Kennedy blamed the lack of lighting, the narrowness of the bridge, and the darkness of the road without guardrails. He noted that the car filled with water rapidly and that he was disoriented by the murky water, the cold, and the suddenness of events. In other words, the accident was produced by the scene, and Ted Kennedy and Mary Jo Kopechne were both victims of the situation; they were overpowered by circumstances.[30] And when circumstances (scene) produce an accident, it really is nobody's fault. Listeners who expect a leader to be conspicuously active might forgive one who is a victim of circumstances, but they may be disappointed with a leader who was unable to triumph over a bad situation. In Reagan's famous *Challenger* disaster speech in which he memorialized the astronauts killed when the ship exploded, he characterized them as pioneers who had sacrificed themselves so that the world might move forward to the conquest of space. All of his imagery favored the character of the agents, rather than the agency (technology) or the scene (outer space).[31] The speeches of bureaucrats typically emphasize agency (procedures) over the other pentadic terms. An audience of reformers who are enamored of purpose (moral objectives) might find this kind of speech extremely boring. An audience of bureaucrats, however, might find speeches emphasizing procedure and ritual deeply satisfying, if not inspiring.

Ultimately, texts (the speeches, the stories, the descriptions of things) represent what Burke called "multiple versions of reality." We see things in different ways, and these different ways are reflected in our choice of words. Audiences and readers respond to these different ways of seeing, these different perspectives, and they may embrace or reject them. They may find these perspectives good or bad, useful or useless, beautiful or ugly, noble or despicable. Making the perspective visible through the application of the pentad to the text allows us to see why the discourse affects us in a particular way. It also helps us to evaluate a text in terms of its power to move an audience and allows us to talk intelligently and at length about that power. By analyzing a text in terms of its images and emotions we reconnect it to the social, cultural, and political contexts that surround it.

## PERSONAL REFLECTIONS

In short, perspective matters. Burke notes that a patient might report a dream to a Freudian analyst or a Jungian or an Adlerian, or to a practitioner of some other school. In each case the "same dream will be subjected to a different color filter, with corresponding differences, in the nature of the event as perceived, recorded and interpreted."[32] Burke's point is that we can identify competing perspectives in a critical self-conscious way and come to some understanding of both their power and their limits. By imagining the same matter from perspectives other than our own, we can come to a more rounded and objective understanding of matters. In short, gaining perspective is at the heart of the pentadic critical method. Perspective shows that provisional truth lies on several sides, but that some perspectives have serious limitations.

Long ago, Marcus Aurelius, perhaps the most humane of the Roman emperors, used a similar method to make important decisions. Withdrawing temporarily from the scene of action, he would visualize the execution and outcome of several possible courses of action. Comparing these outcomes gave him a sense of distance and humility and made him consider the larger community and the long-term consequences of history. He believed that by using this method he became wiser, kinder, and more humane.

In a similar way, dramatistic analysis produces a confrontation of several perspectives, or what Burke often referred to as a perspective of perspectives.[33] While we remain living human beings, we can never transcend the limits of our bodies or our language. We can never get outside or above a message and examine its truth or falsity, its goodness or badness, in a godlike way, or after the manner of a disembodied sage. However, the pentadic method offers us the ability to at least consider a message from multiple angles. By identifying the perspective of a piece of discourse and then looking at it from several other perspectives, we can go far in discovering whether it is wise or foolish, moderate or extreme, helpful or destructive, self-interested or altruistic. In a world in which we are constantly assaulted by calls to action from media mountebanks and political demagogues, this can help us to live more sanely, humanely, and wisely.

## POTENTIALS AND PITFALLS

Clarke Rountree and others have cautioned critics against the temptation to use the pentad as a cookie cutter by unimaginatively applying the elements of the pentad to a text.[34] One of the weaknesses of Burke's method is that it could be used almost mindlessly. That is, if applied to any speech, story, or even joke, its categories will yield results. As critics we need to remind ourselves that Burke's goal was to bring deeper understanding, to shake us out of our usual ways of looking at things and to shake us up by giving us a set of fresh categories. Burke spent much of his life as an outsider, an attacker of established formulas. Thus it would be ironic to treat his pentad as a static, orthodox, tried-and-true method. Despite the formulaic nature of his five-pointed system, one needs to understand that the parts of the pentad are simply tools for analysis, aids to understanding the power and appeal of messages. For Burke, the point of the pentad was not simply to stop after identifying the parts of the pentad, or even after determining pentadic ratios. Instead, Burke hoped the tools of dramatism might help us to consider messages from multiple angles, recognize our own biases, and develop a more complete, complex, and humane perspective.

Despite its seemingly tidy structure, the pentad is a heuristic device that offers critics the ability to recognize—and analyze—change. Also, the same situation might be understood differently from different perspectives. Scenes, for example, can shrink or grow. In his famous speech on the Grenada invasion, President Reagan began talking about the difficulties on the island as an immediate threat to the safety of Americans, but he gradually expanded the scene to include meddling by Cuba and finally a larger plot by the Soviet Union. Burke himself spoke of the plasticity of terms; technology, formerly classified as agency in our culture, had (in his judgment) become an agent, a self-sustaining interest group with an agenda of accelerated technological change.[35] A leader like Castro may be presented as a forceful agent in his youth but as an icon (scene) in his dotage. Ultimately, though the assigning of ratios is an imaginative exercise, not a stodgy formula.

## BURKEAN TOP PICKS

Bello, Richard. "A Burkean Analysis of the 'Political Correctness' in Confrontation in Higher Education." *Southern Communication Journal* 61 (1996): 243–252. One of the very best studies of how political correctness went from a god term to a devil term for many embattled academics.

Blankenship, Jane, Marlene G. Fine, and Leslie K. Davis, "The Republican Primary Debates: The Transformation of Actor to Scene." *Quarterly Journal of Speech* 69 (1983): 25–36. A very imaginative treatment of the pentad and how one term can merge with another is seen in this essay.

Brummett, Barry. "A Pentadic Analysis of Ideologies in Two Gay Rights Controversies." *Central States Speech Journal* 30 (1979): 250–261. Burke treats ideology as a vocabulary that justifies the possession of power. Brummett performs a brilliant analysis of rival claims to power in this essay.

Burke, Kenneth. "Dramatism." In *Drama in Life: The Uses of Communication in Society*, edited by James E. Combs and Michael Mansfield, 7–17. New York: Hastings House, 1976. Burke himself has written a street-level, worm's-eye view of dramatism that provides a concrete set of examples. His exposition will satisfy the advanced critic as well as the neophyte.

Burke, Kenneth. "The Rhetoric of Hitler's Battle." In *The Philosophy of Literary Form*, 191–222. Baton Rouge: Louisiana State University Press, 1941. In 1938, Burke wrote a prophetic analysis of Hitler's *Mein Kampf*. This is perhaps the most lucid and penetrating article Burke ever produced.

Ling, David. "A Pentadic Analysis of Senator Edward Kennedy's Address to the People of Massachusetts." *Central States Journal* 21 (1970): 81–86. Presidential candidates are supposed to appear as active agents for us, but Ted Kennedy presented himself as a tragic victim. Ling shows that Kennedy's pentadic choice was a fateful one.

Rountree, Clarke J., III. "Charles Haddon Spurgeon's Calvinistic Rhetoric of Election: Constituting an Elect." *Journal of Communication and Religion* 17 (1994): 33–48. There is much misunderstanding of the idea of predestination in intellectual circles. Rountree uses

Burke's ideas about hierarchy and the pentad to explore the confusion over some of the most basic religious concepts in Western civilization.

One of the very best sources for practical applications of Burke's basic critical vocabulary can be found in the *Encyclopedia of Rhetoric and Composition*, edited by Theresa Enos (New York: Routledge, 1996). See Tillie Warnock, "Burke," 90–92; Bill Bridges, "Terministic Screens," 722–723, and "Pentad," 499–501; James W. Chesebro, "Dramatism," 200–201; Pat Youngdahl and Tilly Warnock, "Identification," 337–340; and H. L. Ewbank, "Symbolic Action," 710–711.

## NOTES

1. Kenneth Burke, "The Rhetoric of Hitler's Battle," in *The Philosophy of Literary Form*, 191–220 (Berkeley: University of California Press, 1971).

2. For an excellent analysis of the origins of dramatism and Burke's focus on words, see M. Elizabeth Weiser, *Burke, War, Words* (Columbia: University of South Carolina Press, 2008).

3. Kenneth Burke, *Language as Symbolic Action* (Berkeley, CA: University of California Press, 1966), 45.

4. Celeste Condit, *Decoding Abortion Rhetoric* (Champaign: University of Illinois, 1994).

5. Burke's clearest explanation of terministic screens can be found in *Language as Symbolic Action*, 44–55.

6. Kenneth Burke, *A Rhetoric of Motives* (New York: Prentice Hall, 1950).

7. Burke's best explanation of identification occurs in *A Rhetoric of Motives*, 19–46.

8. Burke, *A Rhetoric of Motives*, 22.

9. Kenneth Burke, *A Grammar of Motives* (New York: Prentice Hall, 1945).

10. For a full discussion of Nichols's contributions, see John H. Patton, "Marie Hochmuth Nichols's Voice of Rationality in the Humane Tradition of Rhetoric and Criticism," in *Twentieth Century Roots of Rhetorical Studies*, ed. Jim A. Kuypers and Andrew King, 123–142 (Westport, CT: Praeger, 2001).

11. Marie Hochmuth, "Kenneth Burke and the 'New Rhetoric,'" *Quarterly Journal of Speech* 38 (1952): 133–144. See also Marie Hochmuth, "Burkean Criticism," *Western Speech* 21 (1957): 89–95.

12. For the clearest statement of Burke's foundational theory of dramatism, see Kenneth Burke, "Dramatism," in *International Encyclopedia of the Social Sciences*, vol. 3, ed. David L. Sills, 445–452 (New York: Macmillan and the Free Press, 1968).

13. Aristotle's belief in the centrality of the polis to civilized conduct and culture is well known. For a brilliant discussion of the Aristotelian relationship between narrative culture and community, see Gabriel Lear, *Happy Lives and the Highest Good: An Essay on Aristotle's Nichomachean Ethics* (Princeton, NJ: Princeton University Press, 2004).

14. Burke, *A Grammar of Motives*, xv.

15. See Helena Detmer, *Horace: A Study in Structure* (New York: Olms-Weidmann, 1983); and also R. K. Hack, "The Doctrine of Literary Forms," *Harvard Studies in Classical Philology* 27 (1916): 1–65.

16. On this subject, I. A. Richards wrote three deeply influential books: *The Meaning of Meaning: A Study of the Influence of Language upon Thought and the Science of Symbolism*, with C. K. Ogden (1923), *Principles of Literary Criticism* (1924), and *Practical Criticism* (1929). His studies in psychology and semantics laid the foundation for the close readings of texts that dominated literary criticism for decades after.

17. Burke discusses the power of form in many places. See, for instance, the sections on "Formal Appeal" and "Rhetorical Form in the Large" in *A Rhetoric of Motives*. Also see "Literature as Equipment for Living" in *The Philosophy of Literary Form*, 2nd ed. (Baton Rouge: Louisiana State University Press), 293–313.

18. For a full discussion of Burke's association with literary figures and his editorship of *The Dial*, see Jack Selzer, *Kenneth Burke in Greenwich Village: 1915–1931* (Madison: University of Wisconsin Press, 1996); and Jack Selzer and Anne George, *Kenneth Burke in the 1930s* (Columbia: University of South Carolina Press, 2007).

19. In 1937 Burke speculated about the future importance of "one little fellow named Ecology." For a full statement of Burke's long association with the movement, see "Kenneth Burke on Ecology," in *A Synthesis: Extensions of the Burkean System*, ed. James Chesebro, 251–268 (Tuscaloosa: University of Alabama Press, 1993).

20. Burke, *Grammar of Motives*, xv.

21. Clarke J. Rountree III, "Coming to Terms with Kenneth Burke's Pentad," *American Communication Journal* 1, no. 3 (May 1998), accessed July 27, 2015, http://ac-journal.org/journal/vol1/iss3/burke/rountree.html.

22. Burke, *Grammar of Motives*, xix.

23. Charles Kneupper, "Dramatistic Invention: The Pentad as Heuristic Procedure," *Rhetoric Quarterly* (Spring 1977): 129–135.

24. Sonja Foss presents many rich examples of pentadic criticism in the chapter 11 of her *Rhetorical Criticism: Exploration and Practice* (Long Grove, IL: Waveland Press, 2004).

25. Barack Obama, "Inaugural Address by President Barack Obama," found at https://www.whitehouse.gov/the-press-office/2013/01/21/inaugural-address-president-barack-obama.

26. Berry has authored one of the most enduring books in American eco-criticism. See Wendell Berry, *The Unsettling of America* (San Francisco: Sierra Club Books, 1977). For a sense of Burke's contributions to ecology, see Tarla Rai Peterson, "The Will to Conservation: A Burkean Analysis of Dust Bowl Rhetoric and American Farming Motives," *Southern Communication Journal* 52 (1986): 1–21.

27. Wes Jackson, *Becoming Native to This Place* (Lexington: University of Kentucky Press, 1994).

28. Burke, *Grammar of Motives*, 130.

29. Kneupper, "Dramatistic Invention," 131.

30. All materials quoted from David A. Ling, "A Pentadic Analysis of Senator Edward Kennedy's Address to the People of Massachusetts, July 25, 1969," *Central States Journal* 21 (1970): 84.

31. Ronald Reagan, "Address to the American People on the Challenger Disaster," found at www.AmericanRhetoric.com.

32. Burke, *Language as Symbolic Action*, 45.

33. This is Burke's ultimate vantage point. It has roots in the ancient practice of rhetorical exercises that one reads about in Seneca, Marcus Aurelius, and in the spiritual exercises of Pierre Hadot. In preparing to argue a position or make an important decision, the ancients were wont to visualize the matter from several different points of view (from the victim's point of view, from that of the accused, from the vantage of the judge, from that of the victim's family, the accuser's family, the verdict of history, etc.).

34. Rountree, "Coming to Terms."

35. Personal conversation with Kenneth Burke at New Harmony, Indiana Convention, July 10, 1990.

# 12

# Fantasy-Theme Criticism

*Thomas J. St. Antoine and Matthew T. Althouse*

In the final game of a tied series, the Marauders and the Blue Sox struggle in an epic battle for the championship. With the score tied in the bottom of the ninth, there are two outs, and a base runner is on second. A designated hitter for the Marauders, Spikes O'Reily, steps to the plate, taps the soil from his cleats with his bat, and loosens his swing. The pitcher, ace reliever Cannonball Braden, makes eye contact with the catcher. The two Blue Sox players exchange nods, and Braden launches the ball from the mound. Before the streaking fastball can pass over the plate, O'Reily swings. Crack! The ball is struck. It races past the first baseman's glove and into right field. As the fielder stops the ball, the base runner at second, Pokey Howard, rounds third and sprints toward home. Howard slides. Simultaneously, the catcher stretches for the ball, which is rocketing from right field. From within the cloud of blinding dust plowed up by Howard's slide, the umpire makes the close call: "Safe!" Fans of the winning Marauders from the City of Champions are jubilant. They praise the speed of the base runner, the timely batting of Spikes O'Reily, and—of course—the perceptiveness of the umpire. The fans of the losing team from Baseballville, however, are livid and decry the umpire's call. Given the importance of the game, they cannot believe that an official's incompetence cost the Blue Sox their rightful claim to the title.

If you can imagine how passionate fans might tell interpretive stories about a close baseball game, you can appreciate the scope and the goals of Ernest Bormann's fantasy-theme analysis. This method is used to look at how a group dramatizes an event and at how dramatization creates a special kind of myth that influences a group's thinking and behaviors. In this context, the word *fantasy* does not refer to make-believe. Instead, it is a technical term used to understand the social reality of a group. Bormann explains that the word *fantasy* can be traced back to its Greek root, *phantastikos*, which means to be able to present or show to the mind or to make visible.[1] For instance, Blue Sox fans know that their team failed to win. However, explanations of the loss will be shaded by the way they manipulate stories about the event. Consequently, in the process of talking about the game, their discussions may lead to a number of colorful speculations. "The ump was a bum!" "The ump was biased!" Or, "The ump was paid off!" Although these reflections may not be accurate, they "make visible" a shared social reality for fans. Also, these imaginings are narrative manifestations that provide a rhetorical critic with a special perspective on the beliefs and values of a given group of people.

The purpose of this chapter is to provide a guide for using and appreciating fantasy-theme analysis, which illuminates the worldview shared by a rhetorical community. In Ball's words, fantasy-theme analysis can be used to address questions such as, "How does communication function to divide individual from individual, group from group, and community from community? How does communication function to create a sense of community, integrating individuals and groups into large, cooperative units? How does communication function to interpret reality for symbol using beings?"[2] During recent decades, scholars have used Bormann's fantasy-theme analysis to examine a myriad of topics, including group decision making, corporate communication, and political cartoons, to name a few. Regardless of the subject matter, these studies share some basic assumptions that are outlined in this chapter. The first part of this chapter surveys fundamental concepts associated with fantasy-theme analysis and with symbolic convergence theory, which provides the theoretical chassis on which Bormann's method rests. The second part of the chapter provides a case study. In this section, we examine fantasy themes that have guided perceptions of higher education in the United States during the twentieth century.

## FUNDAMENTAL CONCEPTS

To conduct a fantasy-theme analysis, a critic must understand at least four basic terms: *fantasy theme*, *chaining*, *fantasy type*, and *rhetorical vision*. Arranged here from the most basic unit to the most intricate, these concepts help us recognize how interpretations shared in small settings, like interpersonal interactions, may evolve into ways of thinking in larger, even cultural, settings.

### Fantasy Theme

The term *fantasy theme* refers to a narrative construal that reflects a group's experience and that helps a group understand that experience. Sonja K. Foss states that a fantasy theme is "a word, phrase, or statement that interprets events in the past, envisions events in the future, or depicts current events that are removed in time and/or space from the actual activities from the group."[3] Although a fantasy theme can incorporate verifiable facts, it is a dramatization, which means it is a creative and imaginative portrayal. As Bormann explains, "When people dramatize an event, they must select certain characters to be the focus of the story and present them in a favorable light while selecting others to be portrayed in a more negative fashion."[4] Through dramatization, different groups may form unique perspectives on a single event in the past and create distinctive prognostications about their respective futures.

It is not surprising that fans from the City of Champions and from Baseballville create dissimilar fantasy themes about the championship game. Fans of the Marauders praise the heavy hitter who produced the final run batted in: "Spikes O'Reily is the best player on the face of the planet! Without question, he's destined for the Hall of Fame!" To make these assessments, fans may not be objective by comparing the batter's statistics with those of other active players or with those of anyone enshrined in the Hall. However, their approximations do provide a socially constructed and accepted perspective for their community. Simultaneously, fans of the Blue Sox call O'Reily "the luckiest man alive," an estimation that may not be entirely true. He may be highly skilled. Yet the rhetorical assertion that he is "lucky" fosters a shared sense of veracity for the disappointed community of Baseballville.

## Chaining

When fantasy themes are shared and elaborated, group fantasy chains may occur. Chaining happens when dramatizations that resonate with a community "catch on." Put differently, fashionable fantasy themes created by small groups may propagate through media, including, but not limited to, public speeches, interpersonal interactions, and television. In face-to-face exchanges, evidence of chaining becomes manifest when people in a group become excited about discussing the theme and they elaborate on it. As Bormann, Knutson, and Mulsof note, "The members respond in an emotionally appropriate way. That is, they express emotions such as happiness, sadness, anger, and pleasure in a way that fits into the initial mood of the dramatization."[5] In mass-mediated communication, evidence of chaining may become manifest when creators of texts borrow, adapt, and disseminate frequently used, dramatized images and ideas.[6] Of course, not all fantasy themes find acceptance and chain out; indeed, some face disinterest and rejection. Yet, when they do stir attention, successful fantasy themes cause emotional responses reminiscent of the ones evoked by previous stories. Consequently, because of the sharing of fantasy themes, the initial dramatizations of a few people may lead to a shared symbolic reality for many.

For instance, media in Baseballville may discuss vigorously the unfairness of their team's loss. Debate is fueled by local talk radio personalities, and their shows' aggravated callers use phrases like "constant bias" and "injustice for the underdogs" to describe the game's outcome. When hearing these words, listeners familiar with the Blue Sox may become irked. Then they may contribute to further dramatizing conversations, even though they might not be avid fans who closely watched the game. With this example, we can appreciate how chaining works; people may get caught up in fantasizing about "their team" getting bested and extend relevant perceptions. What is more, common opinions that result from chaining foster a group's sense of togetherness. In a rhetorical community, shared fantasy themes make available motives that impel people to beliefs and to actions that are grounded in a "social reality filled with heroes, villains, emotions, and attitudes."[7]

## Fantasy Type

Simply put, a fantasy type is a well-known categorical example that helps identify and characterize clusters of recurring, related fantasy themes. According to Bormann, a fantasy type is a "stock scenario repeated again and again by the same characters or by similar characters."[8] This kind of scenario can include recognizable plotlines, scenes, situations, and representations of people. As William Benoit et al. put it, a fantasy type is like a noted "saga" or "myth" that "carries special meanings" for members of a group.[9] Foss offers the example of "Watergate," a landmark political controversy that provides a dramatizing label for other controversies. For instance, Watergate inspired the term "Billygate to describe Jimmy Carter's brother's Middle-Eastern affairs, Irangate to describe the Iran-contra affair during Ronald Reagan's administration, and Whitewater to describe Bill Clinton's involvement in a failed real-estate venture."[10] Once established, fantasy types enable the use of shorthand allusions to a community's shared stories. Consequently, the utilization of fantasy types provides the critic with evidence of shared fantasy themes.

Consider Baseballville, where fans expect their Blue Sox to be defeated, although they wish this situation would change. The squad has a long-standing reputation for losing in close games. So, when they were bested by the Marauders, fans from Baseballville exclaimed, "It figures! The umpire strikes again!" This may seem like a benign comment. However, if the phrase "The umpire strikes again" has recurred over the years, it may represent a fantasy type that brings to mind a number of related fantasy themes. When fans hear the phrase, they might recall stories about an umpire's peculiar expanding and contracting strike zone in the '83 series. They might also recollect tales about a fair ball called foul that resulted in a lost, pivotal game in the '94 season. Also, because fans are conditioned to see close games lost, the fantasy type provides a serviceable frame of reference for explaining the Blue Sox defeat against the Marauders.

**Rhetorical Vision**

A rhetorical vision refers to a composite drama that is made up of related fantasy themes and fantasy types. When linked together into a rhetorical vision, they reveal a coherent, unified, and holistic picture of a community's shared beliefs. Moreover, rhetorical visions feature recognizable characters and plots. When alluded to in a variety of contexts and discussions, they can trigger responses similar to those observed in the original interaction that spawned it.[11] Bormann claims that within a rhetorical vision a critic may be able to detect a "master analogy" that "pulls the various elements together into a more or less elegant and meaningful whole. Usually, a rhetorical vision is indexed by a key word or slogan [like] The New Deal, The New Frontier, Black Power, The Cold War, The New Left, The Silent Majority, and The Moral Majority."[12] Bormann states that words such as these call forth recollections of stories that resonate with specific communities.

For instance, Thomas G. Endres examines narratives of young, unmarried mothers, who must cope with the disadvantages and social stigmas of their situation. In their stories, he discerns rhetorical visions concerning being "down and out" (e.g., the mothers feel negatively about themselves and victimized by close friends, acquaintances, and family members), trying to "make the best" of their circumstances (e.g., the mothers learn to ignore social stigmas associated with having a child outside a marriage and learn to visualize a positive future), and attempting to become a "young, upwardly mobile mother" (e.g., the mothers replace feelings of victimage with feelings of empowerment).[13] Based on the results in Endres's study, one might speculate that if some details of these visions were introduced to a group of young, unmarried mothers, they would identify with and respond emotionally to the ideas presented.

In the case of the Marauders, the words "Iron Dynasty," a master analogy for a rhetorical vision, may evoke affective reactions from people in the City of Champions. They might immediately be reminded of certain fantasy types that celebrate their team's championships during the 1970s. Those fantasy types may also illuminate the team's recent, successful run for the championship against the Blue Sox. One such fantasy type might include "clutch heroes," like Pokey Howard. In fans' minds, this player's deft base running exemplifies how the Marauders always perform their best at critical moments. Another fantasy type evoked by mention of "Iron Dynasty" might be "iron toughness," a category of fantasy themes about resolve and focus in important games. In the present case, fans from the City of Champions are reminded of how the Sox gained an early lead. However, the story ended spectacularly because of Spikes O'Reily's timely run batted in. In all, remembrances of stories like these support a coherent rhetorical vision, "a unified putting-together of the various scripts that gives participants a broader view of things."[14]

# HOW TO CONDUCT FANTASY-THEME CRITICISM

Put simply, to do a fantasy-theme analysis, one needs to examine discourse for fantasy themes, chaining, rhetorical visions, and fantasy types. Yet, to accomplish these tasks, a critic should proceed with care, being aware of an important point associated with examining rhetoric for dramatizations: it matters how audiences communicate. With many frequently used methods of rhetorical criticism, the goals of analyses are to apprehend key characteristics of a *message* or to discern the appeal of a message's *source*. However, fantasy-theme analysis places emphasis on the *audience* and their reactions to and utilizations of dramatizing messages. With this in mind, a critic is ready to conduct a fantasy-theme analysis by finding evidence of dramatized messages, by categorizing those messages, and by constructing rhetorical visions.

## Finding Evidence

To find evidence of dramatized messages, a critic must first find an appropriate topic for analysis. Ball recommends considering communicative events such as "a decision-making group, a rhetorical controversy, a social group, a support group, a rhetorical community, a policy-making unit, a political campaign, a social movement, or the like that is intellectually intriguing, about which there are questions to be answered." Certainly, a critic may select virtually any topic for analysis. However, a critic must be ready to argue (1) for the topic's social significance and (2) for its role in some kind of persuasive process.

Once a topic is selected, rhetorical texts concerning the topic must be found. Therefore, a critic may gather video recordings of meetings, transcripts of speeches, interviews, and similar artifacts that may reveal dramatizations. Within these artifacts, a critic searches for "evidence of shared narratives, dramatic communication, imagery, figures of speech, and the like,"[15] while remembering the definition of a fantasy theme: it is an imaginative and dramatic message used to interpret an audience's past, present, or future, as revealed by the given texts. Bormann reminds us that for a message to be dramatic, "the action is set in a time and place other than the here-and-now of the group."[16]

For instance, in transcripts of conversations, a critic might look for words that trigger a chaining event. At a recent meeting of the Baseballville Booster Club, one person says, "I sure hope we have a better season next year." To this, another person replies, "Yes, we do not want a repeat of 'The Game.'" With mention of "The Game," other group members enthusiastically add interpretive recollections of the less-than-satisfactory results of the lost championship game: "Our lousy manager, Sparky Croft, should have brought in our all-star reliever, Cannonball Braden, sooner." "We could never win at the Marauder's Indian Rivers Stadium! We can be a horrible road team." Or, "I still can't believe that rotten call the umpire made!" Again, because of individuals' emotional responses to a remembrance of "The Game," critics might speculate that they have found evidence of fantasy themes.

## Categorizing Messages

Once critics find evidence of dramatizations in a group's discourse, they must categorize and count themes to make determinations about a group's attitudes and values. This requires a careful look at a text's characteristics. For visual media, like a film, a critic may need to examine it scene by scene. For speeches, each sentence in a transcript may need to be scrutinized.

Formulating categories requires hard work. Nevertheless, it may be helpful to start by looking for interpretations of settings, characters, and actions. For instance, Karen Foss and Stephen Littlejohn found data that fit into these three categories in the 1983, made-for-TV movie called *The Day After*. The film deals with the Cold War concern of nuclear holocaust, which prompted approximately one hundred million Americans to watch the event. In their study, Foss and Littlejohn demonstrate that themes relating to characters were few. Instead, scenic elements and plotlines dominate the film. In the shattered remains of American civilization, characters appear helpless as they labor to cope with prominent themes, including attempting to survive deadly radiation and pollution (scenic elements) and endeavoring to find limited services and resources (plotline). With this reading of the film, Foss and Littlejohn do more than the important work of finding and counting themes revealed in the discourse. The authors establish the "manner in which the film addressed various thematic components"—a critical accomplishment that illuminates America's mood in the early 1980s concerning the threat of nuclear war.[17]

In the process of categorization, a critic may also search for fantasy types. Like fantasy themes, fantasy types can be difficult to identify, especially for outsiders to a group who have not participated in a community's creation of meaning through dramatization. Nevertheless, through careful study, special "scripts" in a culture become evident, exhibiting recurrences of "particular fantasies with similar plot lines, scenes, characters, or situations."[18] For instance, a critic examining the discourse of talk radio in the City of Champions hears "Babe Ruth" and "Spikes O'Reily" uttered in the same sportscaster's breath. In this case, Ruth represents an archetypal fantasy with which O'Reily is now associated. That is, Ruth's legend is well known by many baseball fans. Because a clear comparison is being made, commentators are suggesting, for instance, that O'Reily swings a bat with the same ferocity as Ruth. Consequently, the fantasy type used provides people with a way to interpret the actions of and to set expectations for the Marauder's heavy hitter. Although not all fantasy-theme analyses search for and identify fantasy types, their discovery can substantially reinforce a critic's study.

## Constructing Rhetorical Visions

After categorizing fantasy themes and types found in discourse, a critic searches for a rhetorical vision. There is no easy, formulaic way to accomplish this task. The complexities of a vision may be many, and more than one rhetorical vision may be functioning within a given community at one time. However, Ball provides some hints a critic might consider when reaching this step of a critical study. In a rhetorical vision, there will be "heroes and villains, key personae, characterizations, attitudes about work, praising and blaming, valorization of some emotions and not others, behavior that is praised and behavior that is censured, insiders and outsiders, and a multitude of beliefs and values that, ultimately, become warrants for argument and action."[19]

Additionally, prior fantasy-theme analyses suggest that many rhetorical visions correspond to three genres—the pragmatic, the social, and the righteous. As Bormann, Knutson, and Mulsof explain, a pragmatic rhetorical vision "is shared by people who seek practical and utilitarian views." In a pragmatic rhetorical community, people extol the virtues of science, of effectiveness, and of common sense. Pragmatic people value goals and accomplishments. The social rhetorical vision "celebrates interpersonal relationships and the development of good families at the concrete level as well as in the utopian envisioning of the future achievement of the family of humankind's residing at peace on the spaceship earth." Not surprisingly, these visions feature idealistic notions of harmony and freedom, as relationships are paramount concerns. Finally, righteous rhetorical visions may be shared by those "who take part in a consciousness that is dedicated to some overarching cause or position."[20] For instance, in a certain community, soldiers killed in battle might be eulogized as brave men who wanted to "do the right thing" for their country, despite individual consequences: a "higher calling" guided the soldiers' gallantry.

In Baseballville, an examination of newspaper articles and radio talk-show transcripts reveal two complementary visions about the city's team: the Blue Sox as "hard-luck losers" and as "lovable losers." About the first vision noted here, a critic finds that the team is subject to numerous scenic impediments. Unfortunate injuries to key players, poor managerial decisions, mystical curses conjured by the trading of star players—excuses like these have kept the home team from "winning the big one," despite moderate successes. About the second vision, a critic finds evidence of character-based fantasy themes that suggest the exceptional personal attributes of players in the team's history. Generally, players are represented as altruistic, heroic, and charismatic. Because of these characteristics, Baseballville takes great pride in the team and believes they embody the persona of the city. Consequently, in their narratives about the Blue Sox, residents of Baseballville expect the team should win a championship eventually, as "good things happen to good people." Both visions appear to be social in nature, as they relate to community and to feelings of interpersonal connection. In all, by identifying rhetorical visions such as these, a critic can speculate about the values and behaviors of the rhetorical community that cheers for the Blue Sox.

## ABOUT SYMBOLIC CONVERGENCE THEORY

At this point, it is valuable to ask, why is fantasy-theme analysis an important critical tool? Simply put, it helps us see how a group's interpretations shape perceptions and, therefore, how people may act in relation to those perceptions. Yet, a more complete answer to this question rests with an understanding of symbolic convergence theory (SCT). Although fantasy-theme analysis is the tool for rhetorical criticism associated with Bormann's work, SCT is the theoretical mold in which that tool is forged. The theory underscores the human tendency to share dramatized narratives, which leads to the potential for persuasion. According to Bormann, rhetoric does not always occur through rational means. Argument, evidence, refutation—these are all parts of a traditional perspective on rhetoric. However, Bormann argues that, through the sharing of fantasies, "private symbolic worlds incline toward one another" and "come more closely together, or even overlap."[21] This overlap prompts "convergence" of ways of thinking.

To illustrate symbolic convergence, let us consider yet another hypothetical, but not unlikely, story about baseball. In the City of Champions, a decision must be made about its one-hundred-year-old sports venue, Indian Rivers Stadium. Should it be demolished and replaced by a new, state-of-the-art facility for the Marauders? Or should it be restored to its former glory? In favor of a new stadium is the owner of the Marauders, Briefcase Michaels, who is generally perceived as a well-meaning and likable fellow. Still, as an ardent capitalist, he is motivated by financial gain. Therefore, with a corporate backer, Michaels generates a profitable plan for a new facility, featuring luxury boxes and a four-star restaurant that overlooks the field. His conceptualization of "SuitCorp Park" is thoughtful and financially sound. Yet some fans view it skeptically, as they value tradition and the sense of continuity embodied by

Indian Rivers. The stadium is situated in an old, established neighborhood in the city. So the park is a landmark for the community, which is more important to many nearby residents than the conveniences of a new stadium. Therefore, as Bormann might speculate, fans are largely predisposed to consider the SuitCorp Park proposal in relation to symbolic resources created by dramatized stories of Indian Rivers. Consequently, to make a decision about the present, fans might rely more on fantasies about the past than on a business plan. In the following sections, this example concerning the future of Indian Rivers Stadium will be revisited to illustrate three characteristics of SCT.

## It Is a General Theory

Broadly speaking, a general theory deals with tendencies of humans that are readily recognized by actual participants in communicative events. Put differently, a general theory makes sense to "ordinary people." Symbolic convergence theory is general because of its emphasis on our propensities for sharing narratives. Who could deny that dramatized storytelling is an important part of phenomena such as interpersonal relationships, cultural cohesion, and public speeches? Because of its versatility and applicability, Bormann calls SCT general; it is "transhistorical and transcultural" as it is able to "account for broad classes of events."[22]

If symbolic convergence theory suggests the universality and persuasive potential of sharing dramatized stories, what might the citizens of the City of Champions say about the situation concerning Indian Rivers Stadium? To save it from the economic interests of SuitCorp, fans of the Marauders may tell dramatized stories about the stadium's past. The venue has served as the site of late-inning comebacks, of heart-pounding playoff games, and of legendary championship victories. Although the structure is a century old and in need of repair, critics of plans for SuitCorp Park argue that modern amenities cannot replace memories. In other cities, this thinking may not spare an old stadium from destruction, as newness, progress, and luxury tend to be valued. Yet, in the City of Champions, many residents say the stadium should remain to preserve the past and to provide inspiration for the team's future. An important point here is that SCT does not hold that all communities share the same fantasies. Instead, it simply posits that people do share fantasies, and they may create a common consciousness that provides the foundation upon which collective decisions are made.

Moreover, because it is a general theory, SCT is valuable because it suggests a "plausible pattern of communication."[23] That is, from a rhetorical perspective, the theory proposes a broad means by which meaningful change in a community can occur and be studied. Bormann believes that a successful persuasive campaign may hinge on dramatic stories; the use of alluring, resonating fantasy themes can entice "converts."[24] These themes encourage people to participate in a shared consciousness that fosters a sense of inclusiveness. Thus, before a referendum for renovations to Indian Rivers Stadium is due for a vote, proponents may (perhaps unknowingly) utilize principles of SCT. They may assume that the stadium embodies traditions that people in the City of Champions revere, traditions that belong to "everyone" in the metropolis. Therefore, to encourage citizens to participate in the preservation of the stadium, proponents may borrow phrases from an old, local folk song about baseball called "Swingin' Shaun Austin." Consequently, the slogan, "What would Swingin' Shaun say?" is born and becomes popular because it resonates with residents' sense of shared narratives.

### It Is a Grounded Theory

To understand symbolic convergence theory as a grounded theory, one should know that it is an empirically based undertaking that relies on both humanistic and social-scientific investigations. In a manner of speaking, all criticism is empirically based insofar as it relies on the presentation of evidence like excerpts from speeches and transcripts of meetings. However, most forms of rhetorical criticism emphasize the insights of the critic to produce the conclusions of studies. SCT, on the other hand, emphasizes audience responses to generate the results of studies. This perspective is often associated with social science. To explain the grounded nature of SCT, Bormann writes, "Thus, we begin with humanistic rhetorical qualitative analysis to analyze messages, shift to the social science methods for the study of audience response, and then return to humanistic critical analysis to explain in depth the way rhetoric functions in terms of response."[25] By saying that social-scientific methods are important to his thinking, Bormann is not claiming that every fantasy-theme analysis requires the use of surveys or experimental observations. Rather, he is claiming that social-science research enhances the critical power of SCT and, consequently, of fantasy-theme analysis.

Social science plays an important role in Bormann's thinking because he bases SCT on research conducted in the quantitative realm of small-group communication. In fact, Bormann's work is influenced significantly by the research of Robert Bales. In his book titled *Personality and Interpersonal Behavior*, Bales asserts that groups create fantasy chains for two reasons. First, communicators in small groups may harbor common psychodynamic issues. Consequently, when topics of interest are raised, the potential for sharing fantasies emerges. Second, dramatizing messages may occur when a group works on a common project that produces problems. If these problems result in tension between group members, they may employ imaginative language to soothe matters. In both cases presented here, Bales's conclusions are based on observations of participants in actual interactions.[26] What is more, because of the assumptions of social-scientific methodology, the results produced by Bales's research purport (1) to lead to some degree of predictability of human behavior and (2) to allow for replication, meaning that the conclusions of one study can be reproduced in others.

Bormann took Bales's thinking about sharing group consciousness and applied it to rhetoric. To make this leap, Bormann wanted to avoid merely relabeling the phenomenon of public discourse with terminology about small-group interaction. Therefore, over decades, he and other scholars have conducted numerous studies on symbolic convergence theory to strengthen the link between dramatizations and public discourse. Based on these efforts, he concluded that the phenomenon of group fantasizing affects and is applicable to persuasive events on a public scale.[27]

### It Is an Epistemic Theory

If a theory of communication is epistemic, simply stated, this suggests that discourse creates our sense of reality. Of course, this statement does not imply that the use of the words "pink elephant" conjures a physical one out of thin air. Instead, it implies that words can change the way people relate to the world and to one another. Words and other symbols can, according to an epistemic approach to communication, create beliefs, affect perceptions, and motivate actions, especially in the absence of certainty. As Pierre Thevenez elucidates, "Man acts and speaks before he knows. Or, better, it is by acting and in action that he is enabled to know."[28] If this statement is meritorious, then human knowledge is not final, as people continue to act and to speak. Hence, knowledge evolves over time through the processes of human interaction. In the case of symbolic convergence theory, Bormann takes the notion of rhetoric as epistemic and relates it to the public sharing of fantasies. Thus, he claims the sharing of dramatized communication can socially construct the reality of a community.

One might argue that the myth of Indian Rivers Stadium as "the greatest venue in baseball" is an epistemic construct, created by participants in a rhetorical community that chains fantasy themes. Fans of the Marauders are fond of saying, "Indian Rivers is the toughest place in which an opposing team can play. It's loud. It's crazy. It's intimidating. No one wins an important game against us at the Rivers!" Indeed, the Marauders have won pivotal games and have made spectacular plays on their home field. However, according to statistics, it is not truly the toughest place to play. The team that boasts the most wins at home is the Green Wave of Coastal City, and the team with the best winning percentage at home is the Red Streaks of Central City. In both categories, the Marauders rank second and third respectively. Nevertheless, because of fantasies perpetuated by people in the City of Champions and by sports commentators, Indian Rivers boasts a special ethos that impels fans to cheer loudly and to heckle opposing players mercilessly. That is, the myth has created the "reality" that encourages fans to be loud. What is more, because of the stadium's myth, people are mounting a very "real" campaign to curtail SuitCorp Park and to preserve Indian Rivers.

## CRITICAL ESSAY

Although we must now leave Baseballville and the City of Champions behind, we take with us our appreciation of fantasy-theme analysis to explore the legitimation of higher education in America. Many students attend college thinking that it is the "smart thing to do" or the "best preparation for the future and for a career."[29] National leaders often propose that making college more affordable will solve many social problems, including economic inequality or a lack of responsible citizenship. Moreover, higher education has been promoted as a democratic institution that provides class mobility. Even if they question the expense or practical benefits of college, Americans agree that higher learning is critically important. Yet there is ambiguity about the nature and purpose of a college education. Many Americans emphasize the professional and practical benefits of higher education. Others, however, emphasize more abstract benefits of an education, including the duty that graduates have to their communities.

In the critical essay that follows, we examine such differences and related dramatizations of higher education in public discourse. We address questions such as "What do we expect from our universities?" and "Why do we go to college?" In considering these questions, we find that two different views, or what Bormann calls rhetorical visions, of higher education emerge. One rhetorical vision, which we call the communal idealist vision, depicts a college education as an intellectual enterprise that values service to others and learning for the sake of learning. The competing vision, called the individual utilitarian vision, interprets higher education as a practical experience that prepares students for worldly success. Public discourse about higher learning is important because it shapes expectations for colleges and universities. Those expectations are important because they determine, to name just a few considerations, whether students attend college, how schools are evaluated, and what kind of public and private resources are made available to educational institutions.

## FANTASY THEMES FOR COLLEGE

Fantasy-theme analysis can help us to understand the shared realities that allow organizations, including schools, businesses, and governments to function. To create and live in a unified social reality, members of an organization participate in dramatizations that chain out in the rhetorical community. Fantasy-theme analysis is "a form of rhetorical criticism that highlights the way groups construct shared symbolic realities."[30] Essentially, this process of dramatizing motivates groups of people to work together. Moreover, group fantasizing allows layers of meaning to build, one on top of another. Imagine, for example, the deposits of calcium that form around a grain of sand as a pearl is formed in an oyster. Similarly, fantasies layer meaning around an event or a concept, which allows the perceptions of a rhetorical community to expand. If a rhetorical vision contains a group's view of symbolic reality, it will then provide members of an organization with emotions, values and attitudes, heroes and villains, and hence, guide their behavior. Bormann explains, "when a person appropriates a rhetorical vision he gains with the supporting dramas constraining forces which impel him to adopt a life style and to take certain action."[31]

The influence of the rhetorical vision on organizations is best understood from the perspective of institutional theory. According to this theory, for an organization to be legitimated, its structures and practices must be seen as consistent with the values of the society within which the organization exists.[32] Organizational structures and actions, whether rational or not, are often constructed symbolically to show that the organization meets the demands of public opinion. W. Richard Scott summarizes the environment's influence on organizations by stating, "Cultural controls can substitute for structural controls."[33] As a result, opinions about higher education establish expectations and criteria for evaluating those institutions, and fantasy-theme analysis of public discourse about higher education provides the critic with evidence that the audience has dramatized those opinions. Accordingly, if the public views a college education exclusively as career training, schools will not be seen as successful unless graduates obtain well-paying jobs. Likewise, if college is seen as training for service, schools will be judged on how well graduates exercise their citizenship.

To consider the role of public discourse in creating expectations for higher education, the critic should identify evidence of fantasy themes chaining out and clustering into fantasy types. The fantasy-theme analysis should then consider the implications of these fantasy types and their formation of a rhetorical vision of higher education. To accomplish this task, we assembled a cross section of twentieth- and early twenty-first-century discourse about higher education. The rhetorical artifacts examined here were chosen to provide a diversity of positions about the purposes of higher education and to represent the thinking of a variety of rhetors, including educators, politicians, and business leaders. We began by reviewing the indices of the periodical *Vital Speeches of the Day* and identifying speeches about higher education. We also included edited anthologies of speeches and essays on higher education and books that elaborate on the attitudes toward higher education that were seen in *Vital Speeches of the Day*. Finally, we unearthed surveys and empirical evidence that verified the fantasies found in the study were embraced by the general public. In all, the rhetoric examined provided us with evidence that the individual utilitarian and communal idealist visions of higher education had, indeed, chained out.

### The Individual Utilitarians in Higher Education

Public discourse on higher education contains evidence of two different fantasy types chaining out to create opposing visions. We first explore the individual utilitarian vision, which favors an experiential education encouraging immersion in society. This vision emphasizes the discovery of useful knowledge, practical education, and the economic benefits of learning. Unlike the idealist vision, utilitarians see education as a means of achieving ends outside the academic realm. The individual utilitarians speak positively about the development of public institutions and the access to higher education provided by programs like the GI Bill. These developments are celebrated for making college a possibility for most citizens, regardless of economic class. On the other hand, they eschew the elitism that often surrounds academic culture. Not surprisingly, their heroes are the "self-made individuals" who, despite disadvantages in life, used a college education to achieve wealth and success. The villains of this fantasy are elitist, esoteric thinkers who seem to "waste" resources pursuing impractical academic ends. The following subsections present fantasy types that construct an individual utilitarian perspective of college learning.

## The Self-Reliant Fantasy Type

The notion that a student goes to college to become self-reliant was the most common fantasy type supporting the individual utilitarian vision. Throughout the last century, proponents of this vision claimed that college graduates should gain financial self-sufficiency and have a successful career. A number of political leaders articulated the relationship between a college degree and the ability to make a living, to avoid dependence on others. President Clinton, for example, remarked, "to make the American dream achievable for all, we must make college affordable to all."[34] President George W. Bush also perpetuated this fantasy in his 2002 State of the Union when he said, "Good jobs begin with good schools."[35] The fantasy that an education makes one self-reliant began chaining out long before these recent presidents. In 1944, Allen Crow, of the Detroit Economic Club, argued, "Higher education . . . must include among its primary functions, the instruction of folks in how to acquire what they need and what they want, by taking care of themselves."[36]

Contemporary educators also recognized that students primarily go to college to improve their professional opportunities. Institutions often indulge this individualism by promising students that a degree will lead to high-paying jobs and desirable careers. Professors Robert Solomon and Jon Solomon, authors of a book on contemporary education, contended "social mobility in the United States is very largely determined by education. Education is the gateway to the professions and, these days, to managerial jobs in business and other organizations."[37] This fantasy has persisted, even as Americans have debated whether a college education is a sound financial investment. In 2013 Rickard Ekman, President of the Council of Independent Colleges, acknowledges that "While colleges did not create the economic recession, they have been hard-pressed to cope with it. Many people think that colleges cost too much."[38] He went on to say that "our colleges are repeatedly criticized for being too expensive; for not preparing students for productive lives; and for not being accessible to low-income students," and Ekman replied, in part, to these criticisms citing data showing that college graduates earn $700,000 to $1 million more over a lifetime and that high-paying jobs in today's new economy are only available to those with a degree.[39]

## The Equal-Opportunity Fantasy Type

In the twentieth century, the prospect of attending college represented a democratic equalizer meant to erase lines of social class and privilege. In 2000, Secretary of Education Richard Riley celebrated the fact that "American education has become more open, more diverse, and more inclusive."[40] Politicians such as President Clinton also used the equal opportunity fantasy type to appeal to voters, speaking of college as a privilege to which all citizens are entitled. In a speech given in 1998, Clinton said,

I have something to say to every family listening to us tonight: Your children can go on to college. If you know a child from a poor family, tell her not to give up—she can go on to college. If you know a young couple struggling with bills, worried they won't be able to send their children to college, tell them not to give up—their children can go on to college . . . we can make college as universal in the 21st century as high school is today.[41]

In the 2015 State of the Union, President Obama revealed an initiative to make community college free for all who qualify, providing evidence that the equal opportunity fantasy continues to chain out. He said, "We still live in a country where too many bright, striving Americans are priced out of the education they need. It's not fair to them, and it's not smart for our future."[42]

Along with politicians, business leaders and educators identified with America's universal access to higher education. In 1953, the chair of Standard Oil, Robert Wilson, explained, "One of the noteworthy things about higher education in America is that there is so much of it. . . . Nowhere else has it been possible to offer the advantages of higher education to so many."[43] From this perspective, the American Dream is the right of all individuals to make a living and thereby transcend class distinctions. In 1916, philosopher John Dewey elaborated, "A society which is mobile . . . must see to it that its members are educated."[44] More recently, rhetors have celebrated online learning and MOOCs as democratizing education by giving free or convenient access to an education which was once reserved for the elite.[45] Indeed, this fantasy type demonstrated that the cherished ideal of all Americans having the opportunity to prosper was linked to the notion of universal access to higher education. Along with equality of opportunity, the individualistic vision includes the theme that college develops in students a work ethic and a character suited for personal success.

### The Practical Mind Fantasy Type

From an individualistic perspective, a college education was expected to motivate a student to succeed in life, to encourage ambition, and to help a student become the type of person who can fulfill that ambition. In a 1987 commencement address, Robert Spaeth stated, "Students . . . determine for themselves what they 'want to get out of' their college experience."[46] In short, along with the acquisition of specific professional skills, the most successful students were expected to be diligent and practical. Along similar lines, Du Pont executive Chaplin Tyler, in a 1938 speech at Virginia Military Institute, observed that an overall "working philosophy" is far more important than any specific course of study. Such a philosophy includes things like logic and "unswerving faith in cold facts."[47]

### Assembling the Individual Utilitarian Rhetorical Vision

A coherent rhetorical vision of higher education emerges when one assembles the fantasy types we have discussed. This rhetorical vision, called individual utilitarianism, emphasizes the practical benefits a degree gives to individual students. Fantasy types emphasizing self-reliance, equal opportunities, and practical mindedness have chained through rhetorical communities and shaped what we expect from our colleges and universities. A variety of empirical studies from a variety of time periods verify that this fantasy has chained out in the American public. For example, survey data showed strong support for expanded access to higher education and documented the belief that college should be attainable for all economic classes.[48] Researchers at the Ford Foundation and at UCLA's Higher Education Research Institute (HERI) provided evidence that most students expected that their education would provide them with basic skills, career preparation, and better earning power.[49] Annual studies by HERI also showed that faculty embraced such a pragmatic view.[50]

As we have seen, the heroes of this vision are the graduates who use their degree to become independent and successful. These people are revered for their determination, and an education empowers them to survive in a competitive world. In the 1930s Robert Jackson honored such rugged individualists: "The world has an overabundance of those who paddle pretty well in still water. The world cries for men who can navigate 'white water.' I see plenty of it ahead."[51] Additionally, educators are honored for attempting to provide expanded access to higher learning, and elitists are the villains of the individualist vision. University president James Rosser criticized colleges for "educating the sons and daughters of the already elite, or the already able to aspire."[52] Although educators who provide practical training are granted heroic status, the vision condemns professors who are disconnected from the real world or who pursue studies that do not have tangible, material benefits. Robert Lutz of the Chrysler Corporation complained that students often get a "dumb" education "from silly classes based on trendy theory and from curricula that look like they were designed by a TV game-show programmer."[53]

Public narrative construals provide additional evidence of the utilitarian vision. This vision regards the establishment of the private colleges of the colonial era as an attempt to provide an education only to the most elite students and to offer an impractical classical curriculum. Therefore, one of the most significant narratives in the history of higher education has been the establishment of large public universities. The establishment of these land grant universities was celebrated by utilitarians because they provided expanded access to higher education and provided research and instruction in practical subjects such as business, industry, and agriculture. University of Texas President Homer Rainey celebrated this story: "In the thirty years between 1830 and 1860 there was waged in this country the battle for free public schools." According to Rainey the result was "the finest system of public education that any society has ever known."[54] Likewise, the founding of Cornell University, which pioneered the elective system, was a story often heralded as a victory for practical education. Cornell claimed to offer instruction to any student in any subject and was seen as a landmark in the struggle to develop curriculum based less on the classical liberal arts and more on the basic needs of contemporary society. Finally, the GI Bill was a popular narrative for individual utilitarians. This federal program was credited with making higher education available to the masses. When President Clinton proposed increasing educational funding for working families, he called it the "G.I. Bill for American workers."[55]

The core values of this vision embrace learning as the acquisition of skills for survival; they criticize intellectual experiences that cannot be shown to make students more employable or independent. For example, graduates are expected to find employment related to their degrees, and research is expected to discover useful information. Accordingly, a college's primary focus must be on credentialing undergraduates and advancing the economy. The vision would also privilege academic disciplines and curricula that can be clearly linked to practical benefits. One would obviously expect students who hold the individualist view to prefer classes or majors that are linked to their careers and dismiss work that does not seem to provide such skills. Additionally, schools would be expected to offer a large variety of majors to accommodate students who choose diverse professions. A final core value of the vision mandates that a college's constituency be composed of students from all socio-economic backgrounds who are pursuing the opportunities offered by the institution.

## The Communal Idealists in Higher Education

Having examined the individual utilitarian vision, we now turn to the opposing rhetorical vision of higher education. Many twentieth-century rhetors emphasized the community in legitimating higher education. They assumed that the good of an entire society is promoted by an educated citizenry. From this perspective, speakers depicted higher education as a means of encouraging students to appreciate their communities and to place service to others before self-gain, recognizing that they are attending college for the good of those around them. Put differently, communal idealism portrays college as a place to retreat from society and to exercise the intellect. This vision expects colleges to prepare graduates for leadership roles in the community. In this vision, heroes are those contemplative students and professors who seek to develop the intellect for the purpose of creating a more perfect and democratic society. Its villains include those people who selfishly use higher education for material gain.

## The Servant-Leader Fantasy Type

The communal idealistic vision of higher education is based on a clearly articulated model of leadership. Rather than encouraging selfish ends, college teaches students to lead by sharing their talents with others. In this servant-leader fantasy type, graduates are seen as a select group of people who must fill leadership roles for the community, and ideal leadership comes in the form of service. In other words, college is thought to take the finest young people and inculcate in them a sense of responsibility.

Contemporary statements by leading educators articulated the value of the leader who is committed to service. John Howard of the Rockford Institute suggested that, "although you make a living by what you get, you make a life by what you give."[56] Others claimed the desire and ability to serve others should be nurtured in college. In an essay published in 1992, history professor Ralph Ketcham defended civic education as a way of training students to participate in democracy: "Human beings do have the capacity to rise above the narrow and self-serving states of mind, and this capacity can be nourished."[57] To encourage service to others, Harvard president Derek Bok argued in 1992 that educators must teach students to "deepen their concern for those who need help, to build within them a strong sense of ethical responsibility, to help them acknowledge that exceptional talent carries with it exceptional responsibility for the welfare of others."[58]

The servant-leader fantasy type can be found throughout the twentieth century. Princeton President Harold Dodds told his graduates in 1949 that they belonged to an elite group of educated leaders. He said, "you are under, and will be under all the days of your life, the heavy responsibility of being qualified for membership in that creative minority which . . . decides the great issues of life."[59] Dodds also argued that college graduates cannot honorably escape the role as leaders and that it would be disgraceful for an educated person to shirk his or her responsibility to lead. He was concerned that educated citizens were often "guilty of the sins of civic indolence, private self-interest and slavery to party spirit. These concerns added up to gross neglect of civic duty."[60]

In sum, colleges have long been expected to teach students a sense of social and civic responsibility, and those who serve the community are those who are most suited to lead. Next, we explore higher education's role as critic.

## The Watchdog Fantasy Type

An additional communal function of higher education is the role of the independent watchdog. As this fantasy type chained out, colleges were expected to be critics in the community by checking the power of government and challenging the conventional truths of culture. The watchdog fantasy type called on schools to act as an authority that monitors the government, industry, and other powerful institutions.

Fantasy themes envisioning the academy as a watchdog were elaborated throughout the twentieth century. President of the University of Wisconsin, Glenn Frank, argued that education provides a democracy with corrective criticism: "To Jefferson the freedom of scholars to examine and the freedom of journalists to express were liberties without which neither the political nor the economic liberty of the people could conceivably be secure."[61] That is, this fantasy type used by Frank suggested that academics should use their insight and influence to keep other powerful groups in check.

Part of higher education's watchdog role also allowed independent thinkers time to contemplate freely. In a 1935 speech, Robert M. Hutchins advocated theoretical training and a separation of the academy from everyday affairs. For Hutchins, the key to fighting controversial ideas was to debate rather than ignore them: "the American people must decide whether they will . . . tolerate the search for truth. If they will, the universities will endure and give light and leading to the nation."[62] In response to the depression and the rise of fascism in Europe, Glenn Frank also emphasized the value of a system of higher education that was allowed free inquiry and used the results of that inquiry to inform other institutions. With the watchdog role comes the expectation that university research provides the world with knowledge and wisdom. The discovery and preservation of information has long been recognized as a benefit to the community. "Great universities," Frank claimed, "can prosecute and publish fearlessly objective researches into the living issues of state and nation."[63]

Educators observed that college teaches students to think insightfully and to avoid seeing the world uncritically. In 2002, author and professor John Rodden argued that "such concerns are especially compelling today in light of 9/11" because education allows students to "assess the value of data we consume every day."[64] Bloom further cautioned that people not properly educated lack critical abilities: "Lack of education simply results in students seeking for enlightenment wherever it is readily available, without being able to distinguish between the sublime and trash, insight and propaganda."[65]

## The University as Microcosm Fantasy Type

A final communal view of higher education embraced the value of schools as small communities, within which students learn to function in larger communities. When he was president of Princeton, Woodrow Wilson emphasized the need for a campus to be a community of scholars who motivate one another. As an administrator on campus, Wilson worked to shape the environment within his school, and he tried to convince students to embrace the academic community. Wilson said, "A college body represents a passion . . . a passion not so much individual as social, a passion for the things which live, for the things which enlighten, for the things which bind men together in unselfish companies."[66] Living in this community provided the student with practical lessons in how to serve his fellow citizens and, more importantly, how to selflessly serve an institution larger than oneself. Wilson elaborated: "A college is a brotherhood in which every man is expected to do for the sake of the college the thing which alone can make the college a distinguished and abiding force in the history of men . . . men shall be ashamed to look their fellows in the face if it is known that they have great faculties and do not use them for the glory of their alma mater."[67]

The notion of a miniature community was more recently articulated by Solomon and Solomon: "The university should be a model for democracy as well as a training ground for democracy."[68] Through activities such as student government and campus media, including student-run newspapers, television, and radio stations, students learned to assess, shape, and interact with public opinion. Learning to respond to the public discussion and attitudes that invariably exist on a campus will prepare students to function in the public sphere after graduation. This persisted as a key role for colleges and universities.

## Assembling the Communal Idealist Rhetorical Vision

The communal idealist vision of higher education emphasizes the servant-leader, the watchdog, and the miniature community. The fantasy themes honor those who approach higher education as a community of scholars left to contemplate freely and to teach students to lead. The vision despises the selfish individuals who are interested only in self-gain. Harold Dodds remarked, "All history teaches that struggle for power and influence divorced from unselfish ends is self-destructive and in the end unsatisfying."[69] More recently, Willard Butcher of the Chase Manhattan Corporation contended that "a total commitment to personal gain—'meism'—at the expense of society's overall well-being, even if it gets you to the top, will ensure you are *not* a leader."[70]

While the communal idealist fantasy can be seen chaining out in public discourse, empirical data provides further evidence of its popularity. Annual HERI surveys and Gallup poll data indicated support for increased interaction between students and faculty to establish a more robust academic community.[71] Studies by HERI have also shown that faculty believed a college education ought to help a student develop moral character and commitment to community service.[72] Likewise, students hoped their schooling would help to develop leadership skills.[73] In sum, communal visions have chained through the public, and, although they are not as popular as individualistic visions, research documents their persistence at the grassroots level.

Central to the communal vision are many of the same narratives that the utilitarians dramatized, but they take on a decidedly different form. The communal idealists edified the founding of the colonial colleges. This was seen as a story in which the success of the American revolution and the establishment of a democratic government was due to the availability of leaders who were trained in American colleges.[74] In 1938 Harvard President James Conant recognized the ongoing role of those early colleges in preparing the elite to be leaders: "Thomas Jefferson in the early days of the last century spoke of the necessity of 'culling the natural aristocracy of talent and virtue from every condition of the people, and educating it at the public expense for the care of the public concern.' In the great wave of enthusiasm for universal schooling, this principal of Jefferson's has tended to become submerged."[75] Speakers have regretted that universities have become so large that they do not provide an effective learning community. In a 1984 commencement address Harold Logan of W. R. Grace and Company questioned the contribution made by large state universities: "I submit that one of the things we have gotten is a weakening of the private-education system in this country by the rapid growth of our State-subsidized university which has grown to such a size as to lose all personal touch."[76]

The vision's core values emphasize the intellectual and moral benefits of learning. The ideal college prepares its students for responsible participation in the community. Its mission includes forming an educated citizenry, inculcating a sense of citizenship, and nurturing the moral character of students. The curriculum of this college is not based on practical value but on intellectual merit, and the student body is composed of students who will provide leadership after graduation. Unlike the individual vision, which could accommodate nontraditional learning, MOOCs, and online learning, the communal idealist vision would prefer the traditional experience of a residential college. Finally, faculty research would include not just the discovery of practical data but also the contemplation of values that shape community. Having described opposing visions of higher education, the next section examines their consequences.

## Implications for Education: Striking a Balance

The goal of this study is to use fantasy-theme analysis to identify the purposes of higher education as they are expressed in twentieth- and early twenty-first-century American rhetoric. Fantasy theme analyses "illuminate how individuals talk with one another about their here-and-now concerns until they come to share a common consciousness and create a sense of identity and community."[77] The public discourse we examined suggests that this symbolic convergence process has occurred among audiences. Americans have assembled fantasies into two competing rhetorical visions, and, as a result, there is not clear consensus on the purpose of college. Derek Bok explained, "the bonds of understanding between our universities and the nation have not grown stronger . . . neither educators nor community leaders share a clear, compelling view of what universities can do for the society."[78]

As demonstrated in this study, rhetorical visions shape public expectations for and sentiments about organizations. To maintain legitimacy, then, higher education must acknowledge both the individual utilitarian and communal idealist visions. Perhaps this is more challenging now than ever. American higher education has relied on a tremendous reserve of legitimacy, but it does not want to risk eroding that. Challenges to that legitimacy have become increasingly common and are reflected in books and essays with apocalyptic titles like *The End of College* and "The Death of American Universities."[79]

The ability to participate in a genuine community diminished in the twentieth century, and this breakdown has led to challenges and opportunities for higher education. Many educators lament the belief that the individualistic model dominates contemporary higher education. Robert Spaeth of St. John's remarked:

> Individualism is so rampant in American higher education today that it goes unnamed and often unnoticed. It is, I believe, our way of life . . . it has produced the very failures that critics are constantly bringing to our attention. Individualism has infected both student bodies and faculties, and the two groups encourage it in one another. Students by and large come to college today to major in a field that will lead to a career—their own career—by means of which they hope to become successful and at least materially comfortable.[80]

Examples from other spheres of public discourse also interrogate the imbalance between individualism and community. Robert A. Nisbet, in his book *The Quest for Community*, observed that "despite the influence and power of the contemporary State there is a true sense in which the present age is more individualistic than any other."[81] Nisbet argued that the release from the contexts of community have not led to freedom and rights but "intolerable aloneness and subjection."[82] Robert Putnam's best seller *Bowling Alone* links the loss of social capital with decline in education, civic engagement, economic prosperity, and public health.[83]

To truly serve contemporary culture, higher education would provide communal experiences that help students to overcome the individualism of the current age. A balanced rhetorical vision presents higher education as an enterprise for equipping students for individual success, but it also demonstrates that higher education is an enterprise for equipping students to serve others. Too often, educators fail to make this case to the public. Harvard President Derek Bok argued, "Today, universities need new ways to serve the public . . . we must associate ourselves prominently once again with efforts to solve problems that really concern the people of this country."[84] Put simply, if the communal idealistic vision is to continue to resonate with the public, advocates must make it appealing.

To conclude, fantasy-theme analysis has helped us to recognize the meaning that rhetorical communities have given to a college education. Schools have specific expectations that must be met to survive and maintain legitimacy. Over the years, fantasies have chained out in the public and have crystallized into vivid rhetorical visions. Understanding those visions will help explain why so many people feel obligated to attend college, why colleges behave as strangely as they do, what a student can expect from his or her degree, and why colleges should be preserved, revolutionized, or both. In short, we improve our understanding of institutions and what it will take to succeed within them.

## PERSONAL REFLECTIONS

We chose to write our critical essay on higher education because of the natural link between fantasy themes and institutional theory, which suggests that public opinion influences life inside organizations. As we tried to show in our theoretical considerations section, fantasy-theme analysis helps us better appreciate organizations.

Furthermore, the purpose of a college degree is an especially relevant topic. We hope that the questions raised in this essay are questions that you have already thought about. At some point, you might have talked with parents, classmates, or professional colleagues about what you expect to get from your college years. Perhaps this essay will help you to deal with these questions in a new way. Effective rhetorical criticism often raises questions and suggests solutions to problems in our everyday lives. Criticism should provide useful insights that help us to better understand and interact with our world.

The next step in this line of study might be to compare and contrast different approaches associated with different types of rhetors. For example, we might have looked at the difference between educators and those outside education. It would also be useful to conduct studies on various campuses to determine the extent to which these fantasies have chained out. A close examination of conditions on our campuses might help to determine the ways that students, faculty, and administrators apply the two rhetorical visions.

## POTENTIALS AND PITFALLS

Although fantasy-theme analysis is a serviceable, as well as fashionable, critical tool, it is not without its detractors. Prominent protests, for instance, may be found in essays written by G. P. Mohrmann. In these works, he strikes two significant blows against Bormann's method. First, Mohrmann claims that fantasy-theme analysis is not an appropriate extension of Bales's work on small-group interaction. In this context, fantasies can be used as mere jokes or as manifestations of individuals' needs to enhance their "self-picture, to feel more attractive and powerful, to discharge aggression, or dispel anxiety."[85] Put simply, fantasies may be used as a buffer against reality, not as a creation of it. If this is the case, one possible pitfall of fantasy-theme analysis may include a critic's inability to discern "meaningful" fantasies that do, in fact, chain out in the public realm. Second, because Bormann allegedly misconstrues Bales's work, Mohrmann claims fantasy-theme analysis does not show us much about human interaction. That is, he asserts Bormann's technique is simply a process of naming, with terms such as *fantasy themes* and *fantasy types*, revealing "the presence of agile minds" of critics, but telling "us little about communication, little about the human condition."[86] In short, in some cases, fantasy-theme analysis might be little more than a labeling device.

Nevertheless, used adeptly, fantasy-theme analysis boasts noteworthy potentials. For instance, Bormann claims that discursive logic and fantasy themes are interrelated, despite Mohrmann's protestations to the contrary. That is, people in public settings do, indeed, make choices based on attitudes formed by the sharing of dramatizations. Bormann writes that "discursive argument requires a common set of assumptions about the nature of reality and proof."[87] Without rhetorical visions that are produced by the sharing of fantasy themes, a community would have no common set of assumptions upon which to base the premises of their arguments. Put differently, some rationalists may posit that fantasies are not verifiable and, therefore, not remarkably influential. However, for those who subscribe to a narrative perspective, fantasies may be central to understanding human communication.

Another potential of fantasy-theme analysis it that it assumes a multistep flow of information, rather than a conventional two-step flow. Benoit et al. explain the difference between the two: "Instead of moving simply from the media to opinion leaders and to the public, information flows in all directions between all agents creating a web of interaction and making possible a unified rhetorical vision."[88] Therefore, students who hope to attend college may not get all of their information about higher education solely from newspapers or from literature produced by colleges. Rather, students may also construct their impressions of college from a variety of informal sources, including friends and coworkers. If this instance is representative of the way people formulate beliefs, then fantasy-theme analysis accounts well for the means by which messages spread from small groups to larger publics and back.

## FANTASY-THEME ANALYSIS TOP PICKS[89]

Ball, Moya A. *Vietnam-on-the-Potomac*. New York: Praeger, 1992. To examine the escalation of the Vietnam War, Ball investigates the role of small-group communication in President Kennedy's and President Johnson's administrations. Ball uses Bormann's critical method to scrutinize declassified documents and interviews with presidential advisers.

Bormann, Ernest G. "Fantasy and Rhetorical Vision: Ten Years Later." *Quarterly Journal of Speech* 68 (1982): 288–305. Here, Bormann responds to his critics, including G. P. Mohrmann and Rod Hart, who question the theoretical foundation of fantasy-theme analysis. In his response, Bormann refines the method's technical terms and discusses its growing body of literature.

Bormann, Ernest G. *The Force of Fantasy: Restoring the American Dream*. Carbondale: Southern Illinois Press, 1985. This is the acme of Bormann's work. Using fantasy-theme analysis, he traces changes in American political discourse from colonial Puritanism to Abraham Lincoln's "romantic pragmatism." More than that, Bormann spells out the basics of his method and provides rich examples.

Bormann, Ernest G. "The Symbolic Convergence Theory of Communication and the Creation, Raising, and Sustaining of Public Consciousness." In *The Jensen Lectures: Contemporary Communication Studies*, ed. John I. Sisco, 71–90. Tampa: University of South Florida Press, 1983. As the title of this essay indicates, Bormann focuses on how usage of fantasy themes develops public consciousness. Moreover, Bormann provides a remarkably lucid and concise account of the principles that underpin fantasy-theme analysis.

Bormann, Ernest G., John F. Cragan, and Donald C. Shields. "An Expansion of the Rhetorical Vision Component of the Symbolic Convergence Theory: The Cold War Paradigm Case." *Communication Monographs* 63 (1996): 1–28. The authors explain the "life" of a rhetorical vision. More specifically, they claim that the life cycle of a rhetorical vision is shaped by three kinds of communication, including consciousness creation, raising, and sustaining, and by three rhetorical principles, including novelty, explanatory power, and imitation.

Bormann, Ernest G., John F. Cragan, and Donald C. Shields. "In Defense of Symbolic Convergence Theory: A Look at the Theory and Its Criticisms after Two Decades." *Communication Theory* 4 (1994): 259–294. "Two Decades" provides readers with elaborate response to critics of symbolic convergence theory. Also, the essay provides an extensive literature review of studies utilizing symbolic convergence theory and fantasy-theme analysis.

Bormann, Ernest G., Roxann L. Knutson, and Karen Mulsof, "Why Do People Share Fantasies? An Empirical Investigation of the Symbolic Communication Theory." *Communication Studies* 48 (1997): 254–276. To address the question posed in the essay's title, the authors explore characteristics of dramatized narratives. Along the way, they provide clear explanations of kinds of rhetorical visions (i.e., pragmatic, social, and righteous) and of dimensions of dramatized messages (i.e., reality, time, moral, and emotional).

Cragan, John F., and Donald C. Shields. "The Use of Symbolic Convergence Theory in Corporate Strategic Planning: A Case Study." *Journal of Applied Communication Research* 20 (1992): 199–218. This essay boasts two enticing features. First, it provides clear explanations for terms associated with fantasy-theme analysis. Second, it provides a case study that demonstrates how Bormann's theory guided the reconstruction of a company's shattered identity.

Rarick, David L., Mary B. Duncan, and Laurinda W. Porter. "The Carter Persona: An Empirical Analysis of the Rhetorical Visions of Campaign '76." *Quarterly Journal of Speech* 63 (1977): 258–273. The authors of this essay explore audience perceptions of Jimmy Carter's personality during his campaign for the White House. In their investigation, they reinforce the notion that fantasy-theme analysis is an audience-centered method.

Zagacki, Kenneth S., and Dan Grano. "Radio Sports Talk Shows and the Fantasies of Sport." *Critical Studies in Media Communication* 22 (2005): 45–63. This study demonstrates the utility of using fantasy-theme analysis for studying mediated interactions. More important, it demonstrates how FTA may be adapted to examine ideological concerns, like hegemonic masculinity and the blurred distinction between college sports and education.

## NOTES

1. Ernest G. Bormann, "The Symbolic Convergence Theory of Communication and the Creation, Raising, and Sustaining of Public Consciousness," in *The Jensen Lectures: Contemporary Communication Studies*, ed. John I. Sisco (Tampa: University of South Florida Press, 1983), 74.

2. Moya A. Ball, "Ernest G. Bormann: Roots, Revelations, and Results of Symbolic Convergence Theory," in *Twentieth-Century Roots of Rhetorical Studies*, ed. Jim A. Kuypers and Andrew King (Westport, CT: Praeger, 2001), 221.

3. Sonja K. Foss, *Rhetorical Criticism: Exploration and Practice* (Prospect Heights, IL: Waveland Press, 1996), 123.

4. Ernest G. Bormann, *The Force of Fantasy: Restoring the American Dream* (Carbondale, IL: Southern Illinois University Press, 1985), 9.

5. Ernest G. Bormann, Roxann L. Knutson, and Karen Mulsof, "Why Do People Share Fantasies? An Empirical Investigation of the Symbolic Communication Theory," *Communication Studies* 48 (1997): 255.

6. See, for example, William L. Benoit, Andrew A. Kluykovski, John P. McHale, and David Airne, "A Fantasy-Theme Analysis of Political Cartoons on the Clinton-Lewinsky-Starr Affair," *Critical Studies in Media Communication* 18 (2001): 377–394.

7. Ernest G. Bormann, "Fantasy and Rhetorical Vision: The Rhetorical Criticism of Social Reality, *Quarterly Journal of Speech* 58 (1972): 398.

8. Bormann, *The Force of Fantasy*, 7.

9. Benoit et al., "A Fantasy-Theme Analysis," 380.

10. Foss, *Rhetorical Criticism*, 125.

11. Bormann, "Fantasy and Rhetorical Vision," 398.

12. Bormann, *The Force of Fantasy*, 8.

13. Thomas G. Endres, "Rhetorical Visions or Unmarried Mothers," *Quarterly Journal of Speech* 37 (1989): 139–141.

14. Ernest G. Bormann, "Symbolic Convergence Theory: A Communication Formulation," *Journal of Communication* 35 (1985): 133.

15. Ball, "Ernest G. Bormann," 222.

16. Bormann, "The Symbolic Convergence Theory of Communication," 72.

17. Karen A. Foss and Stephen W. Littlejohn, "The Day After: Rhetorical Vision in an Ironic Frame," *Critical Studies in Mass Communication* 3 (1986): 320.

18. Bormann, "Symbolic Convergence Theory: A Communication Formulation," 132.

19. Ball, "Ernest G. Bormann," 222.

20. Bormann, Knutson, and Mulsof, "Why Do People Share Fantasies?," 257.

21. Ernest G. Bormann, "Fantasy and Rhetorical Vision: Ten Years Later," *Quarterly Journal of Speech* 68 (1982): 134.

22. Bormann, "Symbolic Convergence Theory: A Communication Formulation," 132.

23. Ball, "Ernest G. Bormann," 221.

24. Bormann, "The Symbolic Convergence Theory of Communication," 129.

25. Bormann, "Fantasy and Rhetorical Vision," 305.

26. Robert F. Bales, *Personality and Interpersonal Behavior* (New York: Holt, Rinehart, and Winston, 1970).

27. Bormann, "Fantasy and Rhetorical Vision," 292.

28. Quoted in Robert L. Scott, "On Viewing Rhetoric as Epistemic," *Central States Speech Journal* 18 (1967): 15.

29. A *Chronicle of Higher Education* survey showed that Americans had extremely high confidence in higher education, ranking it with institutions such as the military and local police forces. However, this high ranking comes with criticism of tenure, affirmative action, big-time athletics, and ambiguity on the purpose of education. Americans seem to agree on the importance of general education and leadership training in colleges, while they place less value on the research role of higher education. Findings are presented in Jeffrey Selingo, "What Americans Think about Higher Education," *Chronicle of Higher Education* 49, no. 34 (2003): A10.

30. Linda L. Putnam and George Cheney, "Organizational Communication: Historical Development and Future Directions," in *Speech Communication in the 20th Century*, ed. T. W. Benson (Carbondale: Southern Illinois University Press, 1985), 146.

31. Ernest G. Bormann, "Fantasy and Rhetorical Vision," 406.

32. W. Richard Scott, *Institutions and Organizations* (Thousand Oaks, CA: Sage, 1995), 41.

33. W. Richard Scott, "Unpacking Institutional Arguments," in *The New Institutionalism in Organizational Analysis*, ed. Walter W. Powell and Paul J. DiMaggio (Chicago: University of Chicago Press, 1991), 181.

34. Bill Clinton, "2000 State of the Union," *Vital Speeches of the Day* 66 (2000): 260.

35. George W. Bush "2002 State of the Union" *Vital Speeches of the Day* 68 (2002): 260.

36. Allen B. Crow, "Higher and H-I-R-E Education," *Vital Speeches of the Day* 11 (1944): 379.

37. Robert Solomon and Jon Solomon, *Up the University* (Reading, MA: Addison and Wesley, 1993), 61.

38. Richard Ekman, "Myths and Reality about U.S. Higher Education" *Vital Speeches of the Day* 79 (2013): 392.

39. Ibid., 393.

40. Richard Riley, "The State of American Education," *Vital Speeches of the Day* 66 (2000): 323.

41. Bill Clinton, "1998 State of the Union," *Vital Speeches of the Day* 64 (1998): 259.

42. Barack Obama, "2015 State of the Union," https://www.whitehouse.gov/the-press-office/2015/01/20/remarks-president-state-union-address-january-20-2015.

43. Robert E. Wilson, "A Businessman Looks at Higher Education," *Vital Speeches of the Day* 20 (1954): 213.

44. John Dewey, *Democracy and Education* (New York: Macmillan, 1916), 103.

45. See, for example, Kevin Carey, *The End of College: Creating the Future of Learning and the University of Everywhere* (New York: Riverhead Books, 2015).

46. Robert L. Spaeth, "Individualism vs. Liberal Arts Education," *Vital Speeches of the Day* 54 (1987): 24.

47. Chaplin Tyler, "Industry and You: The Field for College Graduates," in *Modern Speeches on Basic Issues*, ed. Lew Sarrett and William Trufant Foster (Boston: Riverside Houghton Mifflin, 1939), 401.

48. A study conducted by the Lumina Foundation for Education ranked schools by how selective and affordable they are for average students from low-income families. The study concluded that nearly all private and most four-year public institutions are "too selective" or "too costly." Such a conclusion reveals a general belief that college ought to be widely accessible and affordable. For a discussion of the study, see Stephen Burd, "Report on College Access Angers Private Institutions," *Chronicle of Higher Education* 48, no. 19 (2002): A27. See also Sara Hebel, "Poll Shows Value Americans Place on a College Education," *Chronicle of Higher Education* 46, no. 36 (2000): A38. This article presents a public opinion survey prepared by Public Agenda which finds that "Most Americans now believe that there cannot be too many people going to college" (A38).

49. The Higher Education Research Institute at UCLA conducts annual nationwide surveys of the attitudes and aspirations of incoming freshmen. In the fall of 2014, for example, this well-known study found that 72.8 percent of freshmen identified the ability to make more money as a reason for going to college, and 77.1 percent identified training for a specific career as a reason for attending college. Results were published in Kevin Eagan, Ellen Bara Stolzenberg, Joseph J. Ramirez, Melissa C. Aragon, Maria Ramirez Suchard, and Sylvia Hurtado, *The American Freshman: National Norms Fall 2014* (Los Angeles: Higher Education Research Institute, UCLA, 2014). In a national poll on diversity in higher education by the Ford Foundation, 85 percent of voters felt that it was very important for education to provide basic skills, and 72 percent felt that career training was very important. Results are available at www.pbs.org/als/race/media/poll.

50. The Higher Education Research Institute at UCLA also conducts a national survey of faculty attitudes. In their 2013–2014 findings, 81.9 percent of faculty saw the purpose of higher education as preparation for employment, and 99.1 percent thought it was important for students to learn to think critically. Results are published in Kevin Eagan, Ellen Bara Stolzenberg, Joseph J. Ramirez, Melissa C. Aragon, Maria Ramirez Suchard, and Sylvia Hurtado, *Undergraduate Teaching Faculty: The 2013–2014 HERI Faculty Survey* (Los Angeles: Higher Education Research Institute, UCLA, 2014).

51. Robert H. Jackson, "Why a College Education?," in *Modern Speeches on Basic Issues*, ed. Lew Sarrett and William Trufant Foster (Boston: Riverside Houghton Mifflin, 1939), 59.

52. James M. Rosser, "Universal Access and Entrance and Exit Requirements," *Vital Speeches of the Day* 47 (1981): 368.

53. Robert A. Lutz, "The Higher Education System," *Vital Speeches of the Day* 62 (1996): 651.

54. Homer Rainey, "Are Too Many Youth Going to High School and College?," *Vital Speeches of the Day* 5 (1939): 461.

55. Bill Clinton, "A Bridge to the Future," *Vital Speeches of the Day* 62 (1996): 707.

56. John A. Howard, "Ennobling Obligations," *Vital Speeches of the Day* 54 (1987): 317.

57. Ralph Ketcham, "A Rationale for Civic Education," *Current* (November 1992): 12.

58. Derek Bok, "The Social Responsibilities of American Universities," *Representative American Speeches* 64, no. 6 (1992): 114.

59. Harold Willis Dodds, "The Cultivation of Individual Excellence," *Vital Speeches of the Day* 15 (1949): 555.

60. Ibid.

61. Glenn Frank, "The Critical Function in Democracy," in *Modern Eloquence*, vol. 7, ed. Ashley H. Thorndike (New York: P. F. Collier and Son, 1936), 199.

62. Robert M. Hutchins, "What Is a University," in *Modern Speeches on Basic Issues*, ed. Lew Sarrett and William Trufant Foster (Boston: Riverside Houghton Mifflin, 1939), 56.

63. Frank, "The Critical Function," 202.

64. John Rodden, "But Professor, What Are the Humanities For?," *Vital Speeches of the Day* 68 (2002): 346.

65. Allan Bloom, *The Closing of the American Mind* (New York: Simon and Schuster, 1987), 64.

66. Woodrow Wilson, "The American College," in *Modern Short Speeches*, ed. James Milton O'Neill (New York: Century, 1923), 203.

67. Ibid., 204.

68. Solomon and Solomon, *Up the University*, 89.

69. Harold Willis Dodds, "The Art of Living," in *Modern Eloquence*, vol. 7, ed. Ashley H. Thorndike (New York: P. F. Collier and Son, 1936), 137.

70. Willard C. Butcher, "Applied Humanities," *Vital Speeches of the Day* 56 (1990): 623.

71. Annual surveys of faculty by the Higher Education Research Institute at UCLA indicate that more interaction between students and faculty outside the classroom is a rising priority. The HERI has observed a steady increase in this desire for community since its inception. Changes over time are discussed in Robin Wilson, "A Kinder, Less Ambitious Professoriate," *Chronicle of Higher Education* 49, no. 11 (2002): A10–A11. See also Julie Ray and Stephanie Kafka, *Life in College Matters for Life after College*, May 6, 2014, which presents Gallup Poll data that shows students benefit from good relationships with their professors: "if graduates recalled having a professor who cared about them as a person, made them excited about learning, and encouraged them to pursue their dreams, their odds of being engaged at work more than doubled, as did their odds of thriving in all aspects of their well-being."

72. Although a much higher number of faculty in the Higher Education Research Institute's annual surveys link higher education with career preparation, a significant number in 2014 recognized that higher education could be important for character development (66.7 percent) and building commitment to community service (48 percent). Results for 2013–2014 are presented in Eagan et al., *Undergraduate Teaching Faculty*.

73. Freshmen in the Higher Education Research Institute's studies have also indicated recognition of communal idealism. In the fall of 2000, for example, 36.4 percent identified becoming a community leader as a reason for attending college, 43.1 percent wanted to influence social values, and 72.2 percent wanted to help others who were in difficulty. Results are presented in Eagan et al., *The American Freshman*.

74. See John F. Roche, *The Colonial Colleges in the War for American Independence* (New York: Associated Faculty Press, 1986), 73.

75. James B. Conant, "Education for American Democracy," *Vital Speeches of the Day* 4 (1938): 420.

76. Harold R. Logan "A Case for Preserving Higher Education," *Vital Speeches of the Day* 50 (1984): 287.

77. Bormann, *The Force of Fantasy*, 3.

78. Bok, "The Social Responsibilities of American Universities," 109–110.

79. See, for example, Kevin Carey, *The End of College* (New York: Riverhead Books, 2015); Terry Eagleton, "The Slow Death of the University," *Chronicle of Higher Education*, April 16, 2015; or Roger Scruton, "The End of the University," *First Things* 252 (April, 2015), 25–30.

80. Spaeth, "Individualism," 24.

81. Robert A. Nisbet, *The Quest for Community* (New York: Oxford University Press, 1971), 9.

82. Ibid., 25.

83. Robert D. Putnam, *Bowling Alone: The Collapse and Revival of American Community* (New York: Simon and Schuster, 2000).

84. Derek Bok, "Reclaiming the Public Trust," *Current* (November 1992): 7.

85. G. P. Mohrmann, "An Essay on Fantasy Theme Criticism," *Quarterly Journal of Speech* 68 (1982): 111.

86. Ibid., 131.

87. Ernest G. Bormann, "Fantasy and Rhetorical Vision: Ten Years Later," 292.

88. Benoit et al., "A Fantasy-Theme Analysis," 379.

89. The authors of this chapter are ultimately responsible for compiling this list. However, we are grateful to Dr. Bormann himself for providing his suggestions.

# 13

# Feminist Analysis

*Donna Marie Nudd and Kristina Schriver Whalen*

## WHY FEMINISM?

Susan Faludi once said, "All women are born feminists, but most get it knocked out of them."[1] However, the once common phenomenon of women, especially young women, declaring a belief in equality but voicing little connection with the term *feminism* shows signs of change. An in-depth poll commissioned by Lake Research Center for *Ms.* magazine, the Communications Consortium Media Center, and the Feminist Majority Foundation after the 2012 presidential election found that 55 percent of women voters consider themselves feminist—a nine-point increase from the last poll conducted in 2008. "And if those polled were given a follow-up question that included a *definition* of feminism [defined as 'someone who supports political, economic and social equality for women'], the percentage of those declaring themselves feminists or strong feminists rose to a total of 68 percent!"[2]

It's not surprising that providing a clear definition altered responses. The definition of feminism is mired in confusion, and describing feminism remains a daunting and complex task. With so many veins of thought and varying perspectives, communication scholars Cheris Kramarae and Paula Treichler tried to simply note that at its core feminism is "the radical notion that women are people."[3] Although Kramarae and Treichler's definition does not capture the theoretical disagreements that exist in feminism, it does express the common spirit of most strands of feminism. **Feminism** *is a pluralistic movement interested in altering the political and social landscape so that all people, regardless of their identity categories, can experience freedom and safety, complexity and subjectivity, and economic and political parity—experiences associated with being fully human.* It is this definition (or a close approximation) that a growing segment of the population is embracing.

Feminist advocates argue for the necessity and profitability of their activism and critical inquiry by evidencing the *patriarchal* systems that most civilizations have been operating under for several thousand years and the way it limits human potential. Allan G. Johnson writes that three principles encompass the still present patriarchal system: male domination, male identification, and male centeredness. According to Johnson, *male domination* refers to the simple fact that men have populated most positions of authority in major societies. Men head large corporations, nation-states, churches, colleges and universities, and most other positions of social and economic importance. Male domination means our social world and the way we experience it are shaped predominately by men. The things we know (only 8 percent of Wikipedia editors are women), the way we work (women hold less than 25 percent of science, technology, engineering, and math jobs), and the way we play (only 11 percent of game developers are women even though they comprise 45 percent of gamers) are under male control.[4] A few women have temporarily taken seats of prestige, such as Yahoo CEO Marissa Mayer, and other female leaders encourage women to "*lean in*" or "crack the glass ceiling," but it is clear, given how infrequently women succeed, that a patriarchal system prevents movement.[5] Once dominance is established, it's seemingly intractable. As Johnson explains, "Men can shape culture in ways that reflect and serve men's collective interest."

Johnson believes that a critique of patriarchy is incomplete if it simply notes degrees of male domination. He argues that we must also note instances of *male identification*. Male identification locates our cultural values in maleness and masculinity. According to Johnson, in a male-identified society, the activities of men underscore what is preferred, normal, and desirable. The qualities commonly associated with masculinity, such as competition, individualism, invulnerability, rationality, and physical strength, are honored. The qualities commonly associated with femininity, such as cooperation, nurturing, emotionality, and care, are undervalued or trivialized.[6]

Finally, Johnson advocates a focus on our society's *male centeredness*, meaning that our cultural attention is mainly focused on males. "Pick up any newspaper or go to any movie theater and you'll find stories primarily about men and what they've done or haven't done or what they have to say about either."[7] Sporting activities represent one of many culturally significant areas where men seek and receive acclaim. Large populations of men and women watch men's sporting events. Millions watch the Super Bowl, Monday Night Football, the World Series, and the NBA Championship series.[8] Advertisers spend copious amounts of money to market products during these events, knowing the viewing audience is large for most sports in which men take center stage.

However important it is to point out the features of patriarchy, sexist oppression is not the only oppression of interest to feminism. Late twentieth-century feminism concerned itself with interlocking systems of oppression, noting that most systems of discrimination share common characteristics and must be seen together if liberation struggles are to gain ground. For these reasons, feminist scholars such as bell hooks (who chooses not to capitalize her name) reference the dominant framework as a *white supremacist capitalist patriarchy*.[9] This term underscores that we not only live in a sexist society but a society that discriminates based on economic circumstances and race. In the last decade, a profitable discussion on "privilege" has taken root, sown by many feminist and race scholars and further fostered by the deeply personal interrogation of "white privilege" by scholar Tim Wise, whose tome *White Like Me: Reflections on Race from a Privileged Son* is taught in hundreds of colleges and even some high schools.[10] A thorough feminist critique will not fail to interrogate how all these systems of privilege work together to marginalize discrete groups of people and curry favor for others.

So, we will summarize by answering the question that heads this section: Why feminism? Most feminists believe that we live in a complex social structure guided by patriarchy. They believe this patriarchal system must change, and that criticism may be used as a tool to help foster change, thus moving beyond criticism for purposes of increasing understanding and appreciation mentioned in earlier chapters. Moreover, the understanding of patriarchy cannot be a simple calculation. Engaged human beings are likely to identify egregious cases of sexism;

however, most feminists believe that much of the sexism of the patriarchal framework remains unchallenged. Feminists therefore are motivated to expose the fundamental ways, the often subtle, taken-for-granted ways, in which societal members undervalue and diminish women. That done, feminists propose new ideas, assumptions, and viewpoints allowing for humans to realize a wide range of possibilities and promise. In the next section, we will explore these differences and their relationship to rhetorical criticism.

## AN INTRODUCTION TO FEMINIST RHETORICAL CRITICISM

Feminist thought has always been quite diverse in its theories and practices. One main theoretical difference among various feminists surrounds disagreements over gender differences. This disagreement is referred to in feminist writings as the "minimalist/maximalist debate." A feminist *minimalist* believes that men and women are more alike than different; therefore, the policies and social organizations privileging men can easily adapt to women if they are just granted access. *Maximalists* believe that women and men are more different than alike. With that premise in mind, feminist maximalists argue that women will never achieve success and comfort in social institutions created by men for men, and thus our social and political landscape must be altered or transformed to accommodate the distinctions between men and women.

From this theoretical debate, many categories of feminism have emerged. Jill Dolan notes that we can generally see American feminism separated into liberal, cultural, and materialist segments.[11] *Liberal feminist* approaches locate the oppression of women in the systematic failure to include women in dominant structures and cultural production. A liberal feminist rhetorical critique would be interested in the exclusion of women from systems of representation. Are women given a voice in the political system? Can you find women in recent films you've seen, stories you've read? Did the stories showcase the women as competent and able to solve problems, lead others, and champion a cause? Liberal rhetorical feminist critics are diligently employing language strategies within the current structures to increase the stature and number of women in places of political and social power. Sheryl Sandberg's popular book *Lean In* is a feminist voice from the liberal feminist perspective. As one scholar noted, "Sandberg's definition of feminism begins and ends with the notion that it's all about gender equality within the existing social system."[12] She advocates for personal strategies (such as carefully choosing a partner that co-parents equally) for more women to participate in corporate power positions, but she does not argue for changes to those structures. Liberal feminists are typically minimalists.

*Cultural feminists*, on the other hand, are maximalists. They argue that women's nature, primarily shaped by the ability to give birth, is decidedly different from men's. "Because they can give birth, women are viewed as instinctually more natural, more closely related to life cycles mirrored in nature."[13] Cultural feminists argue that women have a unique and valuable perspective that is not adequately reflected in today's society. This deficit of perspective creates a world of domination and violence. Moreover, some cultural feminists have situated themselves within another subcategory of feminist thought, eco-feminism. Eco-feminists believe that if society adopted the nondominating feminine perspective, the likelihood of continuing ecological devastation would diminish. But this is just one of many cultural feminist perspectives. A rhetorical critic adopting a cultural feminist perspective is likely to critique current rhetorical practices for their sexist domination as well as to suggest ways in which a feminine perspective could rehabilitate the rhetorical situation. Does a given communication artifact convey the largely feminine characteristics of caring, nurturing, cooperation, and intuition? Does it glorify aggression, competition, and individualism to the exclusion of other perspectives? How do the messages around us "normalize" a distinctly masculine perspective? How could we infuse and balance our public discourse by including a feminine perspective? These are some of the many questions guiding the explorations of a rhetorical critic that is also a cultural feminist.

Finally, *materialist feminists* believe that symbol-using humans are historical subjects that are largely socially constructed, not biologically driven. A materialist feminist is interested in analyzing social conditions, such as the influence of ethnicity, sexual orientation, and class, that work together to define women and men as categories and seemingly erase the possibility of other categories being established, such as intersexed and transgendered. As such, this strand of feminism is also interested in unearthing the symbolic systems of gender that oppress all people, not just women. Materialist feminists may study the way masculinity has been constructed in such a way that men, too, have little freedom and dimension in society. So, while liberal feminists are primarily interested in social representation, materialist feminists reveal how people "have been oppressed by gender categories."[14] A materialist feminist might approach a rhetorical artifact by noting the ways in which it situates masculinity and femininity as stale categories instead of giving the concept room for growth and movement. Do movies, or other culturally significant discourse, outfit men and women with retrograde notions of masculinity and femininity? How so? Can we point to messages around us that transform the somewhat rigid categories of gender in positive ways? These and similar questions would be of interest to the rhetorical critic with a materialist feminist perspective.

Positioning materialist feminism along the minimalist–maximalist continuum demands some attention. Since materialists stress the social construction of gender, they very rarely look for "real" differences and similarities. Instead, materialists question the constructed categories of gender and offer the concepts dimension and redefinition if it aids the attainment of freedom, safety, complexity, subjectivity, and equality—the goals of feminism.

Although these categories represent large sects of feminist thought, other feminist strands not covered in this chapter apply a feminist lens to a Marxist perspective, psychoanalytical thought, and global issues; there are even feminists operating from libertarian and conservative political perspectives.[15] Feminists in different academic fields have established a literature base specific to their field of inquiry; therefore, one is likely to see feminist legal studies, feminist international relations, and feminist medicine as well as feminist literary criticism. Women of color, who have traditionally had a complicated relationship with feminism, are interested in the way their ethnic and racial identities intersect with feminism. So, if one delves into the literature about feminism, one is likely to see discussions about Chicana feminism, black feminism, Asian feminism, and Native American feminism, to name a few.[16] When engaging in feminist rhetorical criticism, consideration should be given to how the critic positions an argument on the map of feminism so that those reading the criticism know the assumptions about gender infused in the analysis.

In this next section we will first briefly outline the history of feminist criticism within the rhetorical tradition. Next will follow an explanation of the approaches feminist rhetorical critics utilize to analyze our symbolic systems. Alongside these general explanations, numerous specific examples from feminist rhetorical critics will be provided.

# FEMINIST CRITICISM AND THE CHALLENGE TO RHETORIC

The rhetorical tradition tethers itself to a long history of oral argument and public oratory. This tradition also has an equally long history of excluding female rhetors or feminine ways of speaking.[17] Sometimes this was done either by making public address unavailable to women through systematic discrimination or by refusing to recognize the many women who did take the podium. Today, finding women at the podium is certainly more frequent but still meets disparity. For example, the wildly popular speaking venue, TED Talks, features women only 27 percent of the time.[18] Organizers are unpacking the systematic ways men are privileged by the practices surrounding TED Talks as well as barriers to women accepting an invitation to the stage.[19] An interrogation of silenced or absent voices is one challenge feminist criticism has brought to the rhetorical tradition. Another challenge is an attempt to foreground how gender is operating or being sculpted in particular ways by language choices or the positioning of rhetorical artifacts in our social and political world. By highlighting the intended and unintended meanings created about gender, feminist rhetorical scholars invite critical thinking about our gendered assumptions. So, when Jean Kilbourne, in her acclaimed series *Killing Us Softly*, looks at advertisements for the way women's bodies are positioned visually (passively), the way objects for sale are positioned in relation to the women's body (sexually), and the way claims about "liberation" are used alongside these images (consumedly), she is using this approach. Moreover, feminists are also interested in discovering new symbolic strategies, or making visible little-known language systems, in an effort to dismantle current gender hierarchies. So, another important part of feminist rhetorical criticism is suggesting that alternative, yet equally valid forms of producing symbolic meaning exist—historically this has taken form in letter writing or newspapers, or more recently zines.[20] Although we do know that many women enlisted public address as a vehicle for their ideas, we also know that women's position in society relegated message making to other terrain. Feminist rhetorical criticism reclaims this forgotten rhetorical past. All of these concerns have meant that feminist rhetorical scholars have developed somewhat unique approaches to analyzing rhetorical artifacts.

Having been introduced broadly to some examples of ways feminist rhetorical criticism is attempting to alter the patriarchal past of the rhetorical tradition, the section that follows concretely outlines some of the more common methods of feminist criticism used by rhetorical scholars. It is not meant to be an exhaustive list, but you should be able to see that many of the approaches discussed in the following section were used in the examples of feminist rhetorical criticism described above.

# APPROACHES TO USING FEMINIST CRITICISM

Feminist rhetorical scholars are important to feminism because they see patriarchy as being maintained by a symbolic system and language that defines gender in narrow and specific ways. Through our communication practices and language choices we have both a poverty and power when it comes to gender. The poverty comes when our language use sculpts masculinity and femininity in ways that are not complex, resulting in disparity and domination. Another poverty of thinking occurs when language and communication practices are used so that masculinity and femininity are seen as the only two gendered choices. Many feminists are interested in opening up our symbolic system so that many genders flourish and those wanting to express themselves outside our current gender codes feel the freedom to do so. Herein lies the power of language. By systematically analyzing our language choices and communication practices, one can in part effectively undermine the patriarchal logic of gender. This is the work of feminist rhetorical critics.

There are perhaps countless ways one could go about analyzing rhetorical artifacts for the meaning produced about gender. However, if one looks over the history of feminist rhetorical criticism, four prominent critical techniques emerge.[21]

1. Feminists are interested in *redefining* or *defining* gendered ideals and gendered behavior.
2. Feminist rhetorical scholars are *recovering* communication practices that have been forgotten or considered unimportant.
3. Feminist rhetorical criticism is interested in *recording* the cultural production of the rhetorical artifacts we consume so as to uncover the ways in which gender is created (as well as arguing that gender is created, not natural).
4. Feminist rhetorical theorists engage in a *revisioning* of rhetorical theory; they create new theories of rhetoric that champion feminist ideals.

As mentioned earlier, depending on the type of feminism to which one subscribes, some of the choices will be more or less appealing. For example, liberal feminists are interested in women's representation in the current social world. Therefore, a liberal feminist might be more interested in the second and third critical approach. Liberal feminists' particular theoretical interests make showcasing forgotten female rhetors and demonstrating how women are excluded from the communication process a priority. Materialist and cultural feminists, interested in reordering our values and institutions, might favor techniques 1 and 4, since both suggest new ways of thinking. That being said, it is possible that all feminist theoretical perspectives could use any number of these approaches, in any combination, to further knowledge about their feminist argument.

**Redefining or Defining**

While attempting to redefine what it means to be a gendered human being, feminist rhetorical critics generally undertake one of several tasks. First, feminist rhetorical critics note the way language and other meaning-making activities contribute to stereotypical gendered ideals. Second, feminist critics reclaim words or communication practices used to straitjacket masculinity and femininity and infuse them with new meaning. Third, they try to create new communication strategies that will give nonpatriarchal dimension to people's lives or a language to effectively demystify patriarchy.

Feminist scholars have long held the premise that patriarchy is largely maintained by language—both symbolic and visual. Put differently, male domination, male identification, and male centeredness are stable ideas because the meanings created by our everyday speech acts, as well as in films, media, social media, advertisements, and other artifacts of popular culture, act to keep them anchored. Thus, it is important to note the way in which all the things that convey meaning around us are often used to paint a biased picture of gender. The words we choose, the visuals we find appealing, and monuments we create often unknowingly privilege a patriarchal perspective. As such, feminists are interested in making visible the current, and inadequate, rhetorical practices in our culture. For example, the existence of only two widely used pronouns (*he* or *she*) is argued to be a language system creating a reality in which only two genders are recognized, referred to as the gender binary. In response, some feminist and gender scholars have advocated for a third pronoun, *ze*, or the avoidance of gender pronouns by circumventing grammar rules and allowing *their* to stand in for singular *he* or *she* in our language. Recently the term *cisgender* has come into use. The term is used to describe someone whose outside appearance conforms to societal expectations about their sexed body. The proliferation of its use steers thinking away from the naturalization of gender choices. In other words, before the word was adopted, people who conformed to societal expectations did not have to comment on their gender performance. It was deemed "natural." When everyone is compelled to comment on and mark one's gender performance in some way, it is argued to create a "commonality among transgender and nontransgender people." Further, "it tells us that we all experience some kind of relationship between our bodies and our selves, whatever that relationship may be," and some people should not have to spotlight that relationship while others do not.[22] So, the term *cisgender* provides a vehicle for marking different places on the gender continuum, without labeling one place as "natural" and another "deviant."

The second definitional technique used by feminists involves taking words that were once used to diminish femininity and reclaiming them for feminist purposes. Recently Slut Walks and the term "slut shaming" are potent rhetorical tools used by women (and male allies) to critique cultural narratives that suggest female sexuality is deviant. Ringrose and Renold note that one goal of Slut Walks, which started in Toronto, "is to push the gaze off the dress and behavior of the victim of sexual violence back upon the perpetrator, questioning the normalization and legitimization of male sexual aggression."[23]

Many feminist critics have taken to writing their own dictionary definitions or altogether rewriting the dictionary.[24] While inventing new language is often considered "against the rules," many feminists argue the language rules are rigged and need to be reorganized and reinvigorated. Feminist rhetorical criticism utilizing redefinition (1) explains and names how language functions to regulate femininity and masculinity and/or (2) creates or reinvents language that expands the possibilities of gender or turns on its head language used to subdue liberation.

**Recovering**

Throughout this chapter, you will hear that women and feminine ways of speaking have been systematically excluded from the public realm for much of the rhetorical tradition. However, this exclusion was not complete. For periods of time, generally around social reform platforms such as suffrage and abolition, women produced rhetorical texts. However, in most compilations of public speeches, women account for a small percentage of speakers. Although the historical exclusion of female rhetors is partly responsible for the disparity, it does not always explain their absence. Regardless of the dearth, the notable absence of women "confirms that men continue to serve as standard for communication performance and that women are peripheral in terms of significant discourse."[25]

Karlyn Kohrs Campbell's anthology *Man Cannot Speak for Her* uses the approach of recovering rhetors lost in a male-centered society. Also, Kohrs Campbell's work recovers the rhetorical options surreptitiously proposed by women facing enormous prohibitions. Despite being discouraged from taking the podium, women such as Christine de Pizan, a fourteenth-century French feminist, wrote books for women that clearly serve as rhetorical theory. Christine de Pizan's books *The Book of the City of Ladies* and *The Treasure of the City of Ladies* provide discursive theory that differs from the dominant traditions of time, but is no less valuable.

Not all feminist recovering involves archival investigations of classical texts. In contemporary artifacts, our patriarchal society often pushes women to the margins, but feminist rhetors foreground their worth. Popular actress Amy Poehler's Smart Girls social media campaign, in which girls are invited to "change the world by being yourself," could be understood as a critical act of recovery. While Smart Girls began as a web series in 2007, Poehler now reaches her 1.6 million followers, called "smarties," using a range of social media. On Twitter Poehler retweets acts of bravery and accomplishment from women and girls. On Facebook, she often features female artists or shares posts from the Women's History Museum or other sites that highlight forgotten female accomplishments. Using a webcast she interviews preteen girls that have a special talent or skill—a demographic not often valorized in society.[26] Feminist rhetorical critics approaching a rhetorical artifact by recovering are (1) acknowledging rhetors that patriarchy has erased and/or (2) recovering the lost or never seen significance of a visible female rhetor.

### Recording

Another analytical approach used by feminists is to record cultural production. This means that the techniques used to create an artifact are scrutinized. An important part of this approach is the understanding that an artifact does not stand apart from the processes that made it. By analyzing these *systems of production*, one can understand quite thoroughly how messages about gender are created and sometimes understand why a message is packaged a particular way. As Douglas Kellner notes, such an approach "can help elucidate features and effects of texts that textual analysis alone might miss or downplay."[27] In sum, this approach analyzes how the rhetorical artifact was put together, not just the end result.

If you've been following Anita Sarkeesian's work on women's representations in video-game development on Feminist Frequency, you should understand her work both as an example of feminist rhetorical criticism and the kind of criticism that delves into the historical production of representations in the lucrative video-game industry. Sarkeesian's "Damsel in Distress" web video series charts the use of the distressed damsel trope from Greek mythology, through early films like *King Kong*, to its firm entrenchment in early video games such as *Donkey Kong*. Her criticism records and categorizes the placement of Princess Peach throughout the various incarnations of the popular Mario Brothers games and how game developer icon Shiguro Miyamoto was pressured by industry moguls to turn strong playable females into passive damsels in need of rescue.[28]

A feminist approach to analyzing cultural production (1) uncovers who is behind the rhetorical artifact and (2) closely analyzes how the rhetorical artifact is put together.

### Revisioning

Finally, an important part of feminist criticism is creating new theories about rhetoric. This approach analyzes a specific rhetorical artifact or artifacts as part of a larger project that revisions what it means to engage in rhetoric. As mentioned before, the definition of *rhetoric* was once solely used to describe the written and spoken word used to persuade. Feminist theoretical thought worked hard to expand that definition. This was important feminist work since women, as historical subjects, would be significantly excluded from the rhetorical history if defined so narrowly. The work of Karen Foss and Sonja Foss in this area extrapolates new theories about what constitutes *significant* rhetoric. In their book *Women Speak*, significant rhetoric emanates from ordinary individuals not noted for their historical accomplishments. Females or even groups of females in private as well as public domains create significant rhetoric; significant rhetorical works include ongoing rhetorical dialogues that are dramatically different from speech making. This is an important theoretical departure, because as Deirdre Johnson notes, much of the work women do is ritualistic and impermanent[29]; hence, feminist rhetoric should include symbolic activities that are less concrete and finished. Revisioning these theoretical ideas, then, it is possible to see much of what women do as historically significant rhetoric. These activities include baking, children's parties, gardening, letter writing, herbology, and needlework, among others. These activities produce meaning but have had their significance diminished in the patriarchal world.

Likewise, rhetorical theorists such a Sally Miller Gearhart theoretically question some of the fundamental ideas about the way we disseminate ideas. As a society, we have for years believed that trying to persuade somebody through discourse was a rational alternative to violence. However, Gearhart notes that common rhetorical techniques have an ability to produce a personal violation as "real" as violence. Instead of trying to change someone through rhetorical message making, a feminist rhetorician opposing domination would create a rhetorical situation that makes change possible but doesn't insist on change. Using both the feminist rhetorical approach of revisioning and redefining, Gearhart brings new language into the realm of rhetoric. For example, she uses the word *enfoldment* to describe a rhetorical process whereby you offer, make yourself available, surround, listen, and create an opening with your rhetoric, rather than "penetrating the mind" of those you engage.[30] Influenced by Gearhart, other theorists have built on this premise. Foss and Griffin, for example, have outlined a theory of *invitational rhetoric*. This theory suggests a rubric for actualizing a rhetoric of nondomination that invites participants to a point of view but does not create a rhetorical imposition.[31]

The above examples are rhetorical work in which theoretical concepts revision practice and scholars closely analyze texts and "reread" them for their feminist possibilities. For example, Suzan Brydon looks at yet another Disney film in which the mother is killed off in the beginning, *Finding Nemo*, and analyzes the rhetorical choices made by the filmmakers about the parenting of Marlin, Nemo's father. She concludes that Marlin's character should be understood as performing "mothering" and that "Marlin's performance of 'mothering' in *Finding Nemo* (2003) has the potential to make a positive impact on parenting parity and freedom to pursue mothering in new ways."[32]

A feminist rhetorical criticism using the approach of revisioning (1) questions the assumptions underlying desirable rhetoric and (2) offers new rhetorical insights and possibilities as well as liberating frameworks to analyze such rhetoric.

## CRITICAL ESSAY

Feminist rhetorical critics use varied approaches and analyze a full range of communication artifacts. In this essay, you will see how feminist critics analyze approaches to criticism, arrive at the most profitable approach, review literature to inform the *kind* of artifact chosen, and apply the chosen approach to the artifact. It is important to underscore that academic articles often look at a full range of rhetorical artifacts. In the following essay, a romantic comedy, or romcom, is analyzed for its ability to make meaning. Even though the artifact is comedic and lighthearted, its implication to society's large romcom audience is anything but trivial. Humor has an immense power to move people to ideas and ideas to people. For that reason, this feminist rhetorical criticism made a conscious decision to analyze comedy and showcase how approaches to feminist criticism may be broadly applied.

## A FEMINIST RHETORICAL ANALYSIS OF *SHALLOW HAL*

In the last two decades, Bobby and Peter Farrelly have directed a dozen films. Among their most popular are *Dumb and Dumber*; *Something about Mary*; *Me, Myself and Irene*; *Shallow Hal*; and *Dumb and Dumber To*.[33] Their fourth major film, *Shallow Hal*, which they co-wrote with Sean Moynihan, was lauded by a prominent American critic as one of the ten best of 2001.[34] *Shallow Hal*'s major moral, one we would expect many feminists to embrace wholeheartedly, is that for women, *interior* beauty, not exterior beauty, is what truly counts. A feminist rhetorical analysis of the DVD of *Shallow Hal* allows us to investigate more deeply in what ways the film's proposed moral is both underscored and undermined.

We proceed with two main sections. First, we provide a brief discussion of feminist criticism as related to film and television. Feminist scholars are interested in the representations of gender in these two mediums because the messages are distributed quickly and widely. As bell hooks notes, "Television and film are critical texts . . . because they are the primary tools used to socialize oppressed peoples to internalize the thoughts and values of white supremacist capitalist patriarchy."[35] Thus, it is important to understand the ways that feminist critics unpack films for their content—how they strive to be critical cultural consumers. Second, we analyze more specifically how this particular film, *Shallow Hal*, was put together and the rhetorical choices made in its production. Doing so allows us to better discern the inherently contradictory messages in this popular Farrelly brothers film about what constitutes "a beautiful woman" in our society.

### Feminist Approaches to Film and Television Artifacts

There are numerous ways one could go about analyzing rhetorical artifacts for the meaning produced about gender. However, if one looks over the history of feminist criticism as it particularly relates to television and film, three prominent critical techniques emerge: recording, recovering, and revisioning. To each of these we now turn.

#### *Recovering*

Many feminist scholars are committed to recovering and documenting the contributions women have made in various fields. For instance, the Women Film Pioneers Project, spearheaded by Jane Gaines at Columbia University, epitomizes this type of archival work. Focusing on the period of 1894 to 1929, the Women Film Pioneers Project (WFPP) . . . showcases the hundreds of women who worked behind-the-scenes in the silent film industry as directors, producers, editors, and more. Always expanding, the database features career profiles on each pioneer . . . these profiles are written by film scholars, curators, archivists, and historians.[36] Rediscovering the work of women in the very early years of the film industry is not the only type of "recovery" work that interests feminist scholars, however. Feminist scholars also at times take a second look at women's genres within the film and television industry that the dominant culture has dismissed as trivial. A prime example here is Tania Modleski's book *Loving with a Vengeance: Mass-Produced Fantasies for Women*.[37] Modleski's sophisticated analysis of women and their complicated relationship to soap operas pioneered the way for feminists to ask questions about other genres such as women's films, which our culture has often dismissed as "chick flicks" or "weepies."[38]

## Recording

Feminists interested in studying film and television texts also are interested in recording the cultural production of the rhetorical artifacts we consume and, in doing so, shedding light on the complex ways in which gender is created. In this analytical approach, techniques used to create the artifact are intensely analyzed. Most importantly, the artifact does not stand apart from the processes that made it. By analyzing these systems of production, we can better understand how messages about gender are created and packaged. In sum, this approach analyzes how the rhetorical artifact was put together, not just the end result.

Communication scholar Sut Jhally's criticism of MTV music videos is a form of feminist criticism utilizing this approach. Jhally's highly regarded video *Dreamworlds* (I, II, III) records the processes comprising sexist music videos. He notes that music videos function as advertisements for the industry. Additionally, he documents the roles, clothing, and behavior of the men and women performing in the videos to demonstrate that music videos overwhelmingly tell a story about male sexual fantasy. Jhally's analysis also notes the camera angles that place men at the center and women at the periphery. When the camera does focus on women it usually only focuses on one part of her, generally the buttocks, legs, or breasts. These production techniques serve, argues Jhally, to visually dismember women—making women objects, and even more disturbingly, only one part of an object. He then draws connections between the composition of the videos themselves to the affiliations of the people making the videos. Music videos are overwhelmingly directed by men with strong ties to the pornography industry.[39] These are just a few examples of the way that the production of the rhetorical artifact is analyzed.

## Revisioning

Perhaps the most important contribution feminists have made to the study of film and television is in their revisioning of cinematic theory. The most referenced work in the history of feminist film theory is undeniably Laura Mulvey's "Visual Pleasure and Narrative Cinema."[40] In her essay, Mulvey reasons that because most filmmakers in Hollywood are male, the voyeuristic gaze of the camera is male; moreover, the male characters on the screen make women characters the object of their gaze. In essence, Mulvey theorizes that the dominant *male gaze* in mainstream American films reflects and satisfies the male unconscious.

Mulvey's revisioning of psychoanalytical film theory in terms of gender construction profoundly influenced the way feminist scholars and others thought about film and television texts. For many feminist media scholars, Mulvey's main thesis rang true, for it appeared that in classic films, such as Hitchcock's, women were consistently made into passive objects of male voyeurism who primarily existed to fulfill the desires and express the anxieties of male spectators.

Mulvey's pivotal 1975 concept of the "male gaze" has been revisited these last forty years by many other feminist communication scholars who have amended or revised or critiqued it in significant ways. For example, some scholars have argued that women spectators may reject the male gaze and instead identify or construct a "female gaze" in reading popular television shows, such as *Orange Is the New Black*, or mainstream movies, such as *Thelma and Louise*.[41] Scholars in queer studies have noted that Mulvey's articulation is problematic because the "male gaze" is premised on heterosexuality. These scholars have reconceptualized the way the gaze works in order to shed light on the ways homosexual as well as heterosexual audiences might be processing various mainstream films, such as *Fight Club* or *Boys Don't Cry*.[42]

## A Feminist Rhetorical Reading of *Shallow Hal*

*Shallow Hal*, released in 2001, is a film that reached a large viewing audience. As of July 2015, the film had, adjusted for inflation, grossed 101 million dollars.[43] In this essay, we scrutinize the rhetorical choices made by the directors of the film and the producers of the DVD regarding *Shallow Hal*'s representations of women, beauty, and sexuality. As feminist rhetorical critics, we approach this task in the spirit of "recording," as we are most interested in analyzing how the film was put together and the rhetorical choices made in its DVD production. We also approach the film and its DVD, however, in the spirit of "recovery" as we seek to recover one of the lost rhetors of the film.

Specifically, this essay proceeds by summarizing the plot of the film, and then analyzing the film's sight gags (overt visual comedy), its portrayal of "inner beauty," and its marketing strategies. We argue that the film *Shallow Hal* ultimately reinforces the discrimination women feel under current definitions of beauty in our society. Second, we examine the extratext in the *Shallow Hal* DVD. After analyzing the brothers' offhand remarks about women in the film as compared to their male counterparts, we conclude that many women's contributions in this film are marginalized. Finally, after analyzing the director's, special effects creator's, and Gwyneth Paltrow's take on the "fat suit," we make connections between Hollywood's fascination with the fat suit and other forms of discrimination now deemed unacceptable.

## The Plot and Proposed Moral of *Shallow Hal*

The plot of *Shallow Hal* is rather simple.[44] Before the opening credits, the audience sees a nine-year-old Hal at the bedside of his dying father, a reverend. High on morphine, his father advises the nine-year-old Hal that he should find himself "a classic beauty, with a perfect can and great toddies" because "hot young tail's what it's all about."[45] The film then opens with images of the adult Hal (Jack Black) and his closest male buddy, Mauricio (Jason Alexander), at a dance bar. Here, these two rather dumpy-looking men try pathetically and unsuccessfully to pick up only the most gorgeous, sexy women. Similar scenes follow that continue to underscore Hal's shallowness until his chance encounter with Tony Robbins in a stuck elevator. The television guru hypnotizes Hal so that, from then on, he will only see the "inner beauty" of people he encounters. Soon following the hypnosis, Hal and Mauricio return to the dance club. Hal, from his point of view, is seen dancing with three model-perfect women, while from Mauricio's point of view, Hal is seen dancing with a trio of women whom Mauricio describes as a "pack of stampeding buffalo."[46] The next day, Hal meets the woman of his dreams, Rosemary (played by Gwyneth Paltrow and, alternately, by Ivy Snitzer). Even though there are a few moments in which the audience is privy to the "real" 300-pound Rosemary, for the most part throughout the courtship, the audience vicariously sees Rosemary through Hal's eyes, which means seeing Rosemary as the movie-star-thin Gwyneth Paltrow.[47] Rosemary is a volunteer at both the hospital burn unit and a member of the Peace Corps; she also, fortuitously, happens to be the daughter of Hal's boss. Hal's dating of Rosemary and Hal's novel insights for Rosemary's father's corporation lead to an inevitable and immediate rise in Hal's career. Meanwhile, Hal's friend Mauricio mourns the loss of his immature friend and consequently secures the magic words, from Tony Robbins, to dehypnotize Hal to his old shallow ways of seeing. The ending of this romantic comedy is rather predictable in that Hal's original, real-world vision is restored; yet Hal *chooses* to see beyond Rosemary's physical characteristics to love Rosemary for who she truly is. He appreciates her humor, her altruistic worldview, and her inner beauty.

*Shallow Hal*'s repeatedly underscored moral—*that one should not judge people, in particular women, by their physical appearances*—appears to be a rather revolutionary one for Hollywood and one we would expect feminists to truly embrace. For the Farrelly brothers' film strives to argue, as Tony Robbins in the film itself testifies, that everything we "know about beauty is programmed: television, magazines, movies"; media images are all falsely telling us what is beautiful and what is not.[48] And indeed, evidence for this thesis occurs early in the film when the unenlightened Hal explains that he is seeking a woman with the "face" of Paulina in a *Sports Illustrated* layout, the "beams" and "teeth" of Heidi Klum, the "knockers" and "ass" of Britney Spears, the "grille" of Michelle Pfeiffer, and the "smile" of Rebecca Romijn-Stamos.[49] So from one angle, it would appear that feminists would rejoice in Hal's transformation in this film from an unenlightened, immature, and shallow man to a more complicated man who is genuinely in love with Rosemary, a good-natured, funny, altruistic, plus-size woman. But what's fascinating to us, as materialist feminists, is the way the Farrelly brothers' movie and the supplementary material on the DVD continuously undermine its intended revolutionary message.

## *Shallow Hal*'s Sight Gags and Construction of "Inner Beauty"

The film's title, *Shallow Hal*, rather overtly alludes to the film's intended thesis. Clearly, the film's overall message is to prove how shallow and wrong Hal's perspective is. Yet virtually all of the sight gags in the film are clichéd jokes that primarily work by reinforcing society's stereotypical, often mean-spirited assumptions about overweight people. The film's visual jokes encourage audiences to judge overweight people by the effects of their weight. Hence, the audience is prompted to laugh when they see Rosemary inhale a huge milkshake she was supposed to be sharing with Hal. Or when we see Rosemary do a cannonball that displaces such a large volume of water in the neighborhood pool that it quenches a barbeque and literally propels a child to the top of a tree.

One could counterargue that the humor lies in the audience *not* seeing the obese Rosemary in each of these instances, but rather seeing, as Hal does, the svelte Gwyneth Paltrow. For example, audience members who empathize with Hal can vicariously smile at the incongruity of seeing a model-thin woman having the freedom to consume a double burger rather than peck at a salad. Or slurp down that jumbo shake for two rather than sip a Perrier.

We do not deny that humor is undeniably complex, but we believe it is important to acknowledge that, in general, the sight gags only work because as audience members, we see the *reality* that Hal is not privy to. Sometimes, we are given glimpses of the very large Rosemary by the filmmakers. For example, we see glimpses in the film of stand-in Ivy Snitzer or see the slim Paltrow casting a huge reflection in a store window. Thus, the filmmakers continually prompt viewers to see the 300-pound Rosemary, so that we imagine her even when she is not literally in the scene. Hence when a scene features only Gwyneth Paltrow, the viewer projects the large Rosemary into the scene, and, thus, the visual gag becomes no fundamentally different than the tried-and-true "fat jokes" so pervasive in American culture. In general the humor is sophomoric in both its sexism and weightism.

If the humor in the film is problematic, so are its point of view and its construction of "inner beauty." Like most films, the point of view in *Shallow Hal* allows the audience to have full knowledge. As audience members we see many scenes that Hal is not privy to (e.g., the meeting between Tony Robbins and Hal's friend, Mauricio). But a film can privilege a particular character's perspective, and *Shallow Hal* privileges Hal's gaze. Thus, for the vast majority of the film, the audience sees what Hal sees; i.e., Gwyneth Paltrow in all her physical, film star perfection. Indeed, from the time Rosemary is introduced, we visually see Paltrow for most of the film; and we very rarely see the 300-pound Rosemary.

*Shallow Hal* fits neatly into Laura Mulvey's theory that most films are primarily designed to provide pleasure to the male spectator. There are numerous scenes in this film in which women are seen as the objects, not the subjects, of the gaze, a gaze in which women's bodies are inevitably eroticized. Hal eroticizes only sexy women before his Robbins-induced hypnosis, and, after his Robbins-induced hypnosis, he eroticizes all inherently "good" women, even unattractive ones. Perhaps if our hero discovered the erotic in a relationship with the 300-pound Rosemary, the film might have broken new ground. But Hal's bedroom scene is not shared with Gwyneth Paltrow in her fat suit; it is a conventional bedroom scene with a not-so-attractive male hero and a stunningly attractive Gwyneth Paltrow. Thus, Hal is typical of the film hero whom theorist Laura Mulvey discusses in her book *Visual and Other Pleasures*. Hal is the active hero who advances the narrative, controlling the events, the women, and the erotic gaze.[50] Gwyneth Paltrow functions primarily as erotic spectacle. In spite of their noble intentions, the Farrelly brothers offer no new language of desire.

## *Shallow Hal*—the DVD

DVDs are enormously beneficial to rhetorical scholars. Not only do they allow critics to replay scenes easily with close-captioned dialogue, but DVDs also provide supplementary materials regarding various systems of production, such as marketing, advertising, costuming, filming, or editing. Hence, a DVD is, as Brookey and Westerfelhaus note, "a synergistic package comprised of product and promotion."[51] As such, it deserves a close, critical reading. In this section, we will again consider the film's intended moral—*to not judge people by their appearances*—as we review the rhetorical packaging of images on the cover jacket of the DVD, the Farrelly brothers' own rhetoric in the DVD commentary, as well as the technical wizardry and the rhetorical implications of the fat suit.

### *Visual Images from the DVD*

Marketing of DVDs relies in part on the selection of key images that try to capture the essence of the film and strike a chord with the audience (in the case of DVDs, the renter or buyer). Similarly, prior to releasing a film, producers choose a very select amount of photos or jpegs from the actual film to send out in their press packets, photos that ideally capture the essence of the film.

The front cover of the *Shallow Hal* DVD features a curvaceous Gwyneth Paltrow, wearing a very tightly fitted, bright pink T-shirt and small-checkered, pink and white skirt. Her body is positioned mostly in profile, so that her what-can-only-be-digitally-manipulated breasts perk out quite nicely. She is holding both hands, in a rather schoolgirl way, with Jack Black. Jack Black is wearing a loosely fitting spotted yellow shirt with oversize brown trousers. The calves of Paltrow's naked legs in her slim, heeled sandals contrast with Black's workmanlike boots. Paltrow's two-inch heels also make her appear slightly taller than Black. The couple is not looking at each other; rather both appear to be looking directly at the potential purchasers of the DVD—Paltrow with a teasing, lovely smile and the wide-eyed Jack with a smirk that suggests he can't believe he's lucky enough to be holding hands with this leggy blond. Behind the couple is a blue brick wall with the couple's shadows: a slight, realistic shadow of Black and a more-defined shadow behind Paltrow which is not realistically hers, but rather that of a 300-or-more pound woman. Above the title, "*Shallow Hal*," is the film's slogan in smaller print, "True Love Is Worth the Weight!"

The DVD's cover jacket epitomizes the same paradox we have been discussing in this essay. The slogan's pun, "True Love Is Worth the Weight," alludes to this being both a story of a hero's lengthy quest for romance, while also underscoring his true love of a large or weighty woman. But the main "feel" of the front cover belies the latter reading of the slogan, for the images of the two stars is nothing more than yet another photographic reiteration of a male's pleasure and a female positioned-as-erotic-spectacle. The oversize shadow of Paltrow, like the large Rosemary in the film, is seen in only a negligible way and only to the most conscientious viewer.

The Farrelly brothers' intention on selling the film as both a stereotypical romance and as an original comedy is also shown in the selection of photos that their marketing department distributed to the press. Consider the three most reoccurring photos accompanying the reviews: the slim Paltrow as Rosemary, sweetly and jointly sipping the jumbo shake with Hal

(Jack Black); the slim Rosemary and Hal paddling a canoe, with Rosemary "anchoring" one end and Hal up in the air on the other; or Hal, looking perplexed as he stretches out sexy, lavender-laced, bikini underpants that are literally a yard wide. Similarly, in the two-minute theatrical trailer for *Shallow Hal* which establishes the slim Rosemary and Hal's courtship, no fewer than nine sight gags are featured. In essence, most of the press photos and the theatrical trailer function in much the same vein as the sight gags analyzed earlier in this essay. These images are thinly disguised fat jokes embedded in a stereotypical romance, images which are consistently at odds with the film's intended thesis.

## Farrelly Brothers' Commentary from the DVD

Robert Alan Brookey and Robert Westerfelhaus have examined how the "extra text" in DVDs functions rhetorically. They note that, "extra text offers consumers access to commentary by those involved with making the film, and it positions this commentary as authoritative."[52] In doing so, the extra texts in DVDs *direct* viewers' experience of the film. In this section, we'll look closely at the "authoritative" words of the directors of *Shallow Hal* in the DVD's extra text called "Commentary by the Farrelly Brothers" and, in the next section, we'll look closely at the "authoritative" words of the creator of the fat suit, Tony Gardner. In both cases, we'll place the "authoritative" voices of the directors and visual effects creator in a larger cultural context.

Upon listening to "Commentary by the Farrelly Brothers," we were so struck by the major differences between the way the actors playing the male minor characters were introduced as compared to the actresses who were playing the female minor characters that we did a content analysis.[53] The length of the Farrelly brothers' improvised commentary is, of course, restrained by the length of time each of the minor characters appear in the film (since the brothers are just conversing as the film runs with no sound). The 109 minor characters that were introduced range from those with a few speaking lines, such as Hal's coworkers, to local extras in the background.[54] Our analysis revealed that in the Farrelly brothers' commentary, *male* actors playing minor roles are significantly more likely, as compared to their female counterparts, to be referred to by their full names, to be identified by their professional credits, and to be re-employed by the brothers.[55] The commentary reveals the Farrelly brothers' immense loyalty to male actors and their appreciation of their career successes. On the rare occasion that the brothers mention an actress's previous professional credits, most often it is invariably about her appearing in a "*Playboy*" or "*Baywatch*" or having a career as "a model."[56]

But it was not just beautiful women who had to be cast according to the demands of the screenplay; unattractive actresses had to be cast (or supplemented by the makeup and special effects department). So let us now examine the Farrelly brothers' commentary on the performer who played perhaps the most key "unattractive" female character in the film—Ivy Snitzer, a very large actress who on some occasions serves as a stand-in for the 300-pound Rosemary in *Shallow Hal*. The audience never sees Snitzer's face in the film, though we see her back, her calves, and so on. On the occasions that she does appear in the film and in "The Farrelly Brothers' Commentary," the directors either do not comment on her or they offer unintentionally, yet somewhat problematic, comments. Without a doubt, Ivy's longest scene in the film occurs when Hal is avoiding her, after having learned from Mauricio that the hypnosis that made him believe "really ugly girls" were "supermodels" was broken. In Snitzer's longest scene in the film, the audience sees her from the back, seated at the hospital, talking to Hal on the telephone. The voice-over in "The Farrelly Brothers' Commentary" in this scene is not about Snitzer; rather it centers on the brothers' admiration of the male writer of the detective novel that Hal was reading in the last scene in the film.[57] But in all fairness to the directors, they do discuss Snitzer's contribution earlier, and their comments are revealing. Snitzer is commended for her "abundance of inner beauty" and for being the "heart and soul of the crew."[58] Ivy Snitzer is characterized, in general, as a good egg, a gal who helped Paltrow understand her part, a trouper who endorsed the film and its message, a woman whom everyone liked. And we do not mean to imply here that the Farrelly brothers and others were wrong in these assertions. What we are arguing is that regardless of her own and the directors' noble intentions, she was still somewhat exploited in the making of this film. In an interview, Ivy Snitzer noted how proud her family is about her appearance in *Shallow Hal*: "I think my mother's whole Girl Scout troop is going to opening night!"[59] Yet, sadly, in *Shallow Hal*'s listed credits, Ivy Snitzer is not credited at all, not as part of the cast, not as part of the crew, not as a stand-in or body double, not even as a consultant.[60]

To best describe the way that we believe Ivy Snitzer was used in the process of making this film, we might turn momentarily to feminist bell hooks. In *Teaching to Transgress*, hooks notes that in those of our classrooms which are still predominantly white, a "spirit of tokenism" may prevail. Often if there is one lone person of color in the classroom he or she is objectified by others and forced to assume the role of *native informant*.[61] As an example, hooks provides a classroom setting in which the students have been assigned a novel by an American author of Korean ancestry. White students turn to the sole Korean student in the classroom to explain what they do not understand. According to hooks, this practice places an unfair responsibility on the Korean student and assumes that "experience" makes him or her an expert. In the making of *Shallow Hal*, the filmmakers often put Ivy Snitzer in the position of the "native informant" as they conveniently assume that Snitzer represents all plus-size people. This is not only evident in "The Farrelly Brothers' Commentary," but it is also evident in interviews with Gwyneth Paltrow: "[M]y double, IVY SNITZER, was really supportive. I was nervous and she was so supportive of it, she said, 'I think it's so great.' She loves it when I'm in the fat suit, and that made me feel good. The only concern I had with wearing the suit was about offending people who are overweight. I was concerned about that, but actually it has been fine."[62] Thus, the Farrelly brothers and Gwyneth Paltrow rely on Snitzer to be their "native informant." The implication is that if Ivy Snitzer embraces the film, its jokes, and Paltrow's impersonation of a large person, then all overweight American audience members will embrace *Shallow Hal*.

In general, "The Farrelly Brothers' Commentary" in the DVD is most fascinating to us for what the Farrelly brothers' improvised language unintentionally reveals. Male actors playing minor characters, no matter what they physically look like, are more likely to benefit from the good old Farrelly boy network. In contrast, women, particularly attractive ones, are less likely to be cited by their complete names and, on the rare occasion that an actress's professional credits are referenced, it's typically in reference to an industry tied to the beauty culture.

## The Fat Suit

Another noteworthy section of the DVD is a mini-documentary, called "Seeing through the Layers," which shows viewers the wizardry behind the creation of very unattractive characters for *Shallow Hal*. "Seeing through the Layers" features a series of brief interviews with the makeup effects designers, the Farrelly brothers, and actresses and an actor who were made unattractive for their particular parts in *Shallow Hal*. The thirteen-minute documentary primarily focuses on the makeup artist's skill in transforming very *attractive* actresses into unattractive ones.[63] The documentary is fascinating in that the person mainly responsible, Tony Gardner, is both articulate and thoughtful as he describes the various technical challenges this particular film set forth and how he tried to meet them.

The viewer learns that there was quite a "learning curve" for the makeup artists in designing the fat suit for Gwyneth Paltrow. The major challenge being that they had to design a fat suit that was "comfortable"; a fat suit that appeared "realistic" and "not too cartoonish" and was "lighthearted" enough to work in a romantic comedy.[64] Moreover, the makeup artists had to create a prosthetically enhanced "fat" face that would allow enough of Paltrow's facial attributes to be clearly "recognizable" to an audience, while simultaneously being "elastic" enough for her acting to come through.[65] In the documentary, Tony Gardner traces the evolution of the fat suit and Paltrow describes the demands on the performer *prior* to its construction (full body cast so that the makeup artists could construct a fat suit to perfectly fit her frame) as well as *after* its construction (the time-consuming demands to literally put on the fat suit costume and the extensive prosthetics and makeup to create the fat Rosemary's face.) The documentary testifies that makeup artists, such as Gardner, can effectively create realistic fat suits that actors enjoy wearing and performing in, fat suits that meet the directors' and producers' expectations, fat suits that audience members find relatively convincing.

Gardner's fat suits for Gwyneth Paltrow and the actress that played Rosemary's mother is of course one of many recently created in Hollywood. Mojo Box Office lists the revenue generated by twenty-six films that feature actors in fat suits in the last few decades,[66] while blogger Saul Hutson ranks these and others in *"Best Movie Fat Suits: Martin Lawrence and 25 Other Actors Who Wear It Well."*[67] The mini-documentary, "Seeing through the Layers," in the *Shallow Hal* DVD and the proliferation of fat suits in Hollywood prompts us to pose an ethical question: Does the fact that makeup artists have the talent and technical know-how to create fat suits ultimately justify their use in film and television?

A number of reviewers and activists have responded to the use of fat suits in *Shallow Hal* and other films with a resounding "no." In an excellent essay on this subject, Marisa Meltzer discusses how humor aimed at minority groups has changed through the years.

> Over the past several decades, comedy has gradually become less broad and more sensitive to overt racism. . . . We've come a long way since Peter Sellers was cast as bucktoothed Chinese sleuth Sidney Wang in *Murder by Death*. By now, the cardinal rule of humor—you can only make fun of a group if you're part of it—is familiar enough to be a punch line itself. (Remember Jerry Seinfield's outrage over his Catholic dentist's Jewish jokes?) But fat people are the last remaining exception.[68]

To Meltzer's dismay, "Fat people are now America's favorite punch lines." Meltzer, like many others, contends that fat suits are the moral equivalent of blackface.

In calling for a boycott of *Shallow Hal*, the National Association to Advance Fat Acceptance (NAAFA) makes the same claim in 2001. The executive administrator, Maryanne Bodolay, explains:

> Putting thin performers in fat suits is no different than putting white performers in blackface. . . . To have these actors become "fat" and then film them gorging on food and breaking chairs is an insult to the 55% of Americans who are deemed "overweight." . . . These movies are giving people permission to make fun of fat people. . . . Hollywood is intent upon perpetuating the myth that fat people are miserable and unattractive, and that the path to happiness is through losing weight. In reality, beauty comes in all sizes, and people can find happiness at whatever size they are.[69]

Diane Bliss, the founder and chair of the Screen Actors Guild's Plus-Size Task Force (PSTF) cites an academic study that documents NAAFA's claim about the media's stereotypical representations.

> Michigan State University did a study of the representations of plus-size people in TV and film and statistically proved what our common sense tells us: people of size are more likely to be portrayed as stupid, lazy, unemployed, a member of an ethnic group, and the target of the joke. Older plus-size women are fairly frequently portrayed in a positive, non-stereotypical light as nurturing mothers, but we're seldom portrayed as desirable love interests or leading ladies.[70]

Some of the members of the Plus-Size Task Force have expressed in various interviews why they are fighting Hollywood's current depictions of large people. What emerges from these sources first is that the plus-size actresses resent the limited roles available to them. The plus-size activists also resent the industry's double standard for male and female actors of size: "Why is the chunky and average-looking Jim Belushi considered 'leading man material' a star of his own sitcom," Diane Bliss asks, "while his wife is played by the gorgeous Courtney Thorne-Smith, size 2?"[71]

With its double standard regarding acceptable size for actors and actresses, Hollywood is an industry that clearly discriminates against plus-size actresses. One can easily understand why plus-size actresses, with limited opportunities available, would be taken aback when two roles for large women in *Shallow Hal*—Rosemary and her mother—are earmarked for thin actresses. A number of reviewers concur with the plus-size actresses' observations. For example, a reviewer for the *New Daily News* writes, "Casting a heavy actress in a lead romantic role is still as impossible to imagine as it once was to think of women having the vote or serving in the military. . . . It's good that U.S. movies are giving lip service to the idea that big is beautiful, but it's time they cast those movies from real life and not from the bins of the special effects department."[72]

## Conclusion

All in all, there can be no denying that the moral of *Shallow Hal*—that one should not judge people, in particular women, by their physical appearances—is constantly undermined in both the film and in the DVD supplements. With the film's sight gags, its clichéd idea of "inner beauty," and its predominantly adolescent male point of view, when considered in conjunction with *Shallow Hal*'s iconic marketing images, the rather sexist "Farrelly Brothers' Commentary," and the political perception that Hollywood's fascination with "fat suits" echoes their previous fascination with "blackface," we are hoping that readers of this essay will agree that *Shallow Hal* undermines its intended revolutionary message. Or, as Peter Travers, a reviewer for *Rolling Stone*, articulated his experience with *Shallow Hal*: "There is something condescending, not to mention hypocritical, about asking an audience to laugh uproariously at the spectacle of a fat person being sneered at and dissed as 'rhino,' or 'hippo' or 'holy cow,' and then to justify those laughs by saying it's society's fault and tacking on a happy ending that allegedly teaches us a moral lesson. It won't wash."[73]

---

# PERSONAL REFLECTIONS

Writing the essay on *Shallow Hal* was for us as researchers an exercise in finding the limits or boundaries of feminist criticism. Although the feminist critique has opened up dramatically over the last couple of decades, a researcher employing feminist criticism still has to ask: Are the issues relevant to gender?

Initially, we wanted to write a feminist rhetorical analysis of "fat suit" films. We were excited when in our initial research we discovered a few conspicuous trends. First, male performers donning fat suits far outnumbered female performers in this genre. Second, many male performers have successfully built franchises out of the fat-suit film phenomenon; consider Mike Myers, Tim Allen, Eddie Murphy, Martin Lawrence, and Tyler Perry. Third, mainstream comedies often feature male actors donning fat suits to play female roles, but not the reverse. Consider Robin Williams in *Mrs. Doubtfire*, Martin Lawrence in *Big Momma's House*, John Travolta in *Hairspray*, and Tyler Perry in his *Madea* films. Finally, a large number of these franchise films are played by black actors; hence, *race* and *gender* are shaping these portrayals.

We quickly surmised that the construction of gender in fat-suit films is interesting and would likely produce an important piece of critical work in the area of feminist rhetoric, but that work would—minimally—need to be a *book*, not an essay. To write critically about the genre of the fat-suit film, a rhetorician would need to do more scholarly reading in other areas. For example, performance studies scholars could inform us about the history of male actors performing female roles on stage; disability studies scholars about society's treatment of fat/disabled people as social pariahs; African American studies scholars about the history of minstrel shows and films' portrayals of female stereotypes (Mammy, Jezebel, and Sapphire); political economists about the making of film franchises; and queer studies scholars about the history of drag performances. Given the collection of social, political, historical, and economic issues that inform "fat suit" films, and given that our editor asked us to write an *essay* and not a book, we understandably decided to limit our analysis.

We eventually settled on an investigation of one film in the fat-suit genre: *Shallow Hal*. *Shallow Hal* initially appealed to us because it is atypical in having a female actress donning a fat suit for a lead comic role. And we were curious as to how a film starring Gwyneth Paltrow would work given the film's intended feminist moral—*that one should not judge people, particularly women, by their physical appearance*. Sensing that the film would undermine its own revolutionary moral, we began to explore how the movie was put together, how the directors and actors theorized about the film, and how the marketers promoted *Shallow Hal*. Predictably, our opinions of the film were shaped, reshaped, and reordered as this material was viewed.

For us, an essay is successful if readers are prompted to employ similar methods to analyze other cultural texts. So, ideally, we hope readers of our essay, when viewing other films and their supplementary materials, will analyze how fatness has been represented, how femininity has been constructed, how directors' commentary can reveal implicit biases, how public-relations departments can justify ethically problematic choices by dazzling us with mini-documentaries about the technical process, and how celebrities are equally culpable when relying on the testimonies of "native informants" to justify their choice of roles. In short, we need more scholarly studies on fat-suit films.

## POTENTIALS AND PITFALLS

Feminist rhetorical analysis is well-suited for many communication artifacts that exist in our cultural world. Given that gender is one of the primary ways we determine social behavior, very few artifacts are devoid of gendered implications. It must be stressed again, though, that gender is only one of the many identities that complex humans use to interact with the world. While looking for the gendered implications of a rhetorical artifact, one must be vigilant not to undermine or dismiss the other identities at work in the communication processes and fail to understand their impact as well.

Additionally, we believe that critical work requires equal part critique and equal part solution. It is often easy to point out what is oppressive about a communication artifact and then fail to offer any solutions. Many critics of feminist theory suggest that by pointing out all the ways communication oppresses women, one runs the risk of largely positioning women as victims. A potential pitfall of feminist analysis is failing to offer concrete alternatives to the patriarchal order. For example, while the above essay primarily combined the feminist approach of recovering and recording to critically analyze the film, other approaches could be utilized as well. While one part of the feminist project is to critique existing rhetorical practices for their patriarchal logic, the other two approaches offered in this chapter center on feminist solutions. In sum, feminist rhetorical critics should offer new solutions, new ways of thinking. Therefore, as an alternative or supplement, the essay above could have focused more on creating new definitions for beauty and attractiveness, instead of critiquing the rhetorical contradictions of the directors.

In addition, the essay alludes to the need for new language and new theories of cinematic representation that transcend existing formulas and standards. This too could have been the focus of the paper or should be the focus of other researchers that build on the analysis. With that in mind, a feminist rhetorical critic might take a film such as *Shallow Hal* and compare it to *My Big Fat Greek Wedding*, another romantic comedy featuring a larger lead actress. By comparing the two films, one could argue that *My Big Fat Greek Wedding* achieves where *Shallow Hal* fails. The paper could detail the specific ways in which *My Big Fat Greek Wedding* provided a positive, transformative character, a character decidedly more interesting than Paltrow's.

In sum, a feminist critic puts together the analytical rubric that works best to elucidate all the strategies of domination made rigid by language and may also suggest new rhetorical paths to take—paths that achieve freedom, safety, complexity, subjectivity, and equality.

## FEMINIST ANALYSIS TOP PICKS

Campbell, Karlyn Kohrs. *Man Cannot Speak for Her: A Critical Study of Early Feminist Rhetoric*. Vol. 1. New York: Greenwood Press, 1989. This book simultaneously investigates feminist rhetoric and offers new ways of thinking about the rhetorical process. It is considered among the most important works in feminist rhetorical scholarship.

Campbell, Karlyn Kohrs. "Rhetorical Feminism." *Rhetoric Review* 20 (2001): 9–12. A concise essay that provides a survey of the work done by feminist scholars in the field of communication. Beginning critics will find this history very helpful.

Condit, Celeste M. "In Praise of Eloquent Diversity: Gender and Rhetoric as Public Persuasion." *Women's Studies in Communication* 20, no. 2 (1997): 91–116. Condit's article is an excellent example of feminist revisioning. She provides a thorough rationale for new ways of communicating gender. The article also will further a student's understanding of the different positions on gender that rhetorical scholars take.

Hamlet, Janice D. "Assessing Womanist Thought: The Rhetoric of Susan L. Taylor." *Communication Quarterly* 48, no. 4 (2000): 420–437. This essay provides an interesting rhetorical analysis of the former editor of *Essence* magazine. The study is an excellent example of feminist scholarship and furthers understanding of womanist scholarship.

Hanke, Robert. "The 'Mock-Macho' Situation Comedy: Hegemonic Masculinity and Its Reiteration." *Western Journal of Communication* 62, no. 1 (Winter 1998): 74–93. Well-done and easy-to-understand analysis of the television shows *Home Improvement* and *Coach*. This essay allows the student to see the ways in which portrayals of masculinity are critiqued in feminist analysis.

Lotz, Amanda D. "Communicating Third Wave Feminism and New Social Movements: Challenges for the Next Century of Feminist Endeavor." *Women and Language* 26 (2003): 1–9. This essay provides students with an overview of feminist thought from the perspective of the communication field. This article is helpful for students seeking to understand the complex and contradictory messages about feminism in the media and elsewhere.

Shugart, Helene. "She Shoots, She Scores: Mediated Constructions of Contemporary Female Athletes in Coverage of the 1999 US Women's Soccer Team." *Western Journal of Communi-*

*cation* 67, no. 1 (Winter 2003): 1–31. Shugart's analysis of famous female athletes unearths the patriarchal strategies used to subordinate these successful and empowered women. Shugart provides theoretical language for understanding these strategies.

## NOTES

1. Susan Faludi, "Whose Backlash Is It Anyway? The Women's Movement and Angry White Men," FSU Student Government Summer Lecture Series, Florida State University, Tallahassee, June 25, 1997.

2. "The Feminist Factor: More than Half of 2012 Women Voters Identify as Feminists," *Ms. Magazine*, March 18, 2013.

3. This definition appears in Kramarae and Treichler's *A Feminist Dictionary* (Urbana: University of Illinois Press, 1996).

4. Megan Rose Dickey, "23 Statistics That Prove Men Dominate the Tech World," *Business Insider*, July 15, 2013.

5. "Lean in" is a reference to the best-selling book *Lean In: Women, Work and the Will to Lead*, written by Facebook chief operating officer Sheryl Sandberg.

6. Johnson, 6.

7. Ibid., 8.

8. For example, it is estimated that on average 114 million viewers watched Super Bowl XLIX in 2015, and marketing departments spent 4.5 million for each thirty-second advertising spot. See Frank Palotta, "Super Bowl XLIX Posts the Largest Audience in TV History," CNN Money, February 2, 2015.

9. For a more thorough explanation of the use of this term, view *bell hooks: Cultural Criticism and Transformation*, directed by Sut Jhally (Media Education Foundation, 1997), DVD.

10. Tim Wise. *White Like Me: Reflections on Race from a Privileged Son*, remixed and revised ed. (Berkeley, CA: Soft Skull Press, 2011).

11. Jill Dolan, *Feminist Spectator as Critic* (Ann Arbor: University of Michigan Press, 1988), 3–16.

12. bell hooks, "Dig Deep: Beyond Lean In," *Feminist Wire*, October 28, 2013.

13. Dolan, *Feminist Spectator*, 7.

14. Ibid., 10.

15. For an example of a group that falls into this last category, see http://www.iwf.org.

16. For a more thorough listing of the categories of feminism, see Julia T. Wood's chapter 3 of *Gendered Lives* (Stamford, CT: Cengage, 2015), 62–79.

17. Karlyn Kohrs Campbell, *Man Cannot Speak for Her*, vol. 1 (New York,: Greenwood Press, 1989).

18. Pamela Fayerman, "TED Talks Presenters: Will Male Domination Continue in Vancouver Videos and Conference?," *Vancouver Sun*, August 1, 2013.

19. Allison Taylor, "TED Talks Rising to the Challenge of Gender Imbalance," *Pique News*, August 8, 2013.

20. For example, see Karlyn Kohrs Campbell, *Three Tall Women: Radical Challenges to Criticism, Pedagogy, and Theory*, Carroll C. Arnold Distinguished Lecture (Boston, MA: Allyn and Bacon, 2003), 4.

21. See Krista Ratcliffe, *Anglo-American Challenges to the Rhetorical Tradition* (Carbondale: Southern Illinois University Press, 1995). Ratcliffe's work on feminist rhetorical strategies has been adopted for this section. We have expanded her analysis beyond the Anglo-American tradition and added the examination of cultural production as an option in lieu of rereading traditional rhetorical texts.

22. Paula Blank, "Will Cisgender Survive?," *The Atlantic*, September 24, 2014.

23. Jessica Ringose and Emma Renold, "Slut-Shaming, Girl Power and 'Sexualisation': Thinking through the Politics of the International SlutWalks with Teen Girls," *Gender and Education* 24, no. 3 (2012): 334.

24. Kramarae and Treichler, *Feminist Dictionary*. See also Mary Daly, *Websters' First New Intergalactic Wickedary of the English Language* (Boston, MA: Beacon, 1987).

25. Karen A. Foss and Sonja K. Foss, *Women Speak: The Eloquence of Women's Lives* (Prospect Heights, IL: Waveland Press, 1991), 10.

26. Marianne Schnall, "SNL Star Amy Poehler on Her New Online Show 'Smart Girls,'" *Huffington Post*, January 2, 2009.

27. Douglas Kellner, "Cultural Studies, Multiculturalism, and Media Culture," in *Gender, Race, and Class in Media: A Critical Reader*, ed. Gail Dines and Jean M. Humez (Los Angeles, CA: Sage, 2015), 10.

28. Anita Sarkeesian, "Damsel in Distress (Part 1) Tropes vs Women," YouTube, Feminist Frequency, March 17, 2013, https://www.youtube.com/watch?v=X6p5AZp7r_Q.

29. *Monuments Are for Men; Waffles Are for Women: Exploring Gender Permanence & Impermanence* (University of California Extension Center for Media and Independent Learning, 2000), video recording.

30. Sally Miller Gearhart, "Womanpower: Energy Re-Sourcement," in *The Politics of Women's Spirituality: Essays on the Rise of Spiritual Power within the Feminist Movement*, ed. Charlene Spretnak (Garden City, NY: Doubleday, 1982), 143.

31. Sonja K. Foss and Cindy Griffin, "Exploring Rhetoric beyond Persuasion: A Proposal for an Invitational Rhetoric," *Communication Monographs* 62 (1995): 6.

32. Suzan G. Brydon, "Men at the Heart of Mothering: Finding Mother in *Finding Nemo*," *Journal of Gender Studies* 18, no. 2 (2009): 142.

33. "The Farrelly Brothers," Box Office Mojo, n.d., accessed June 17, 2015, http://www.boxofficemojo.com/people/chart/?id=farrellybros.htm.

34. Evan deCatanzaro, "Ebert and Roeper—Best of 2001 (Part 1/2)," *YouTube*, January 5, 2014, https://www.youtube.com/watch?v=oE0jyFRz09o.

35. Foss, Foss, and Griffin, *Women Speak*, 89.

36. Women Film Pioneers Project, Columbia University, September 2013, https://wfpp.cdrs.columbia.edu/about.

37. Tania Modleski, *Loving with a Vengeance: Mass-Produced Fantasies for Women*, 2nd ed. (1982; New York: Taylor & Francis, 2008).

38. Flo Leibowitz, "Apt Feelings, or Why 'Women's Films' Aren't Trivial," in *Post-Theory: Reconstructing Film Studies*, ed. David Bordwell and Noël Carroll, 219–229 (Madison: University of Wisconsin Press, 1996).

39. Sut Jhally, *Dreamworlds 3: Desire, Sex, & Power in the Music Industry* (Media Education Foundation, 2007), video recording.

40. Laura Mulvey, "Visual Pleasure and Narrative Cinema," *Screen* 16, no. 3 (Autumn 1975): 6–18.

41. For examples see Adrienne Trier-Bieniek's numerous books and articles, found at www.themarysue.com as well as Brenda Cooper, "'Chick Flicks' as Feminist Texts: The Appropriation of the Male Gaze in *Thelma and Louise*," *Women's Studies in Communication* 23 (2000): 277–306.

42. See Robert Alan Brookey and Robert Westerfelhaus, "Hiding Homoeroticism in Plain View: The *Fight Club* DVD as Digital Closet," *Critical Studies in Mass Communication* 19 (2002): 21–43.

43. "The Farrelly Brothers," Box Office Mojo.

44. *Shallow Hal*, directed by Bobby Farrelly and Peter Farrelly, performed by Gwyneth Paltrow and Jack Black (2001) (Twentieth Century Fox, 2002), DVD. Throughout this section of the essay, we will be citing from the Twentieth Century Fox DVD version of *Shallow Hal*. When citing from the actual film on the DVD, we will note the specific chapter number, for example: *Shallow*, chapter 3.

45. *Shallow*, chapter l.

46. Ibid., chapter 8.

47. In this description and subsequent analysis of the film, we need to distinguish between Gwyneth Paltrow, in her own body, playing the Rosemary character, and the 300-pound Rosemary (played by Paltrow in a fat suit or by Ivy Snitzer). The language available to us to describe these two different bodies of Rosemary is charged. Our cultural construction of beauty in twenty-first-century America gives us a multitude of ways to describe Paltrow's body (model-thin, perfect, svelte, normal, beautiful), all of which have positive connotations. Although we try to avoid pejorative adjectives (obese, overweight, fat) to describe the second body type of Rosemary, the adjectives available to us (very large, plus-size, 300-pound) all seem woefully insufficient in that they do not allow us to provide a bias-free or inherently positive description.

48. *Shallow*, chapter 20.
49. Ibid., chapter 6.
50. Laura Mulvey, *Visual and Other Pleasures* (Basingstoke: Macmillan, 1989).
51. Brookey and Westerfelhaus, "Hiding Homoeroticism," 25.
52. Ibid., 24.
53. For a more detailed discussion of our methodology and results, please see an earlier version of this essay in the first edition of this textbook.
54. Comments about the actors who played major characters were not included in the analysis; these include Rosemary; Hal and his friends, Mauricio and Walt; Hal's neighbor, Jill; and the TV guru, Robbins.
55. Again, these claims are made only based on the brothers' improvised comments; they do not account for the actors and actresses as cited in the actual film credits for *Shallow Hal*, nor do they represent the Farrelly brothers' actual hiring practices.
56. "Commentary," chapters 18, 7, and 8.
57. Ibid., chapter 23.
58. Ibid., chapter 9.
59. "Gwyneth's Double Breaks Her Silence," interview with Ivy Snitzer, *Entertainment Tonight Online*, November 9, 2001, http://www.etonline.com/celebrity/a7536.htm. Note: This interview was subsequently accessed on web.archive.org on June 19, 2015, using the original URL.
60. *Shallow*, chapter 28.
61. bell hooks, *Teaching to Transgress* (New York: Routledge, 1994), 43.
62. "Gwyneth Gets Heavy!," interview with Gwyneth Paltrow, *Entertainment Tonight Online*, November 9, 2001, http://www.etonline.com/celebrity/a3291.htm. This interview was subsequently accessed on June 19, 2015, on web.archive.org using the original URL.
63. Although there is a brief section on Ivy Snitzer, the three, we presume, conventionally unattractive actresses who were made even more unattractive for their scenes in the dance bar—Bonnie Aarons, Lisa Brounstein, and Fawn Irish—are *not* interviewed in this thirteen-minute documentary. Nor is Nan Martin, who played Nurse Tanya Peeler.
64. "Seeing through the Layers," *Shallow Hal*.
65. Ibid.
66. "Comedy—Fat Suits: 1980–Present," Box Office Mojo, n.d., http://www.boxofficemojo.com/genres/chart/?id=fatsuit.htm.
67. Saul Hutson, "Best Movie Fat Suits: Martin Lawrence and 25 Other Actors Who Wear It Well," IMDb, February 28, 2011, http://www.imdb.com/news/ni8156878.
68. Marissa Meltzer, "Are Fat Suits the New Blackface?," *BITCHfest: Ten Years of Cultural Criticism from the Pages of Bitch Magazine*, ed. Lisa Jervis and Andi Ziesler, 267–269 (New York: Farrar, Straus and Giroux, 2006).
69. "Fat Rights Organization Boycotts 'Shallow Hal,'" press release, NAAFA, November 7, 2001. As of 2010 this figure may be as high as 69 percent. See http://www.niddk.nih.gov/health-information/health-statistics/Pages/overweight-obesity-statistics.aspx.
70. Interview with Diane Bliss, *Big Fat Blog*, October 8, 2002, http://bigfatblog.com/interviews/bliss.php. This interview was accessed on web.archive.org on June 17, 2015, using the original URL.
71. For a review in the *Philadelphia Inquirer* that echoes these women's concerns, see Carrie Richey, "'Shallow Hal' Tries to Have It Both Ways," review of *Shallow Hal*, *Philadelphia Inquirer*, November 9, 2001, http://ae.philly.com/entertainment/ui/philly/movie.html?id=49495&reviewId=5945. This review was accessed on web.archive.org on June 19, 2015, using the original URL.
72. Jami Bernard, "Thin on Respect," review of *Shallow Hal*, *New York Daily News*, November 11, 2001, http://nydailynews.com. This review was accessed on web.archive.org on June 19, 2015, using the original URL.
73. Peter Travers, Rev. of *Shallow Hal*. *Rolling Stone*, December 6, 2001, http://www.rollingstone.com/reviews/movie/5947659/review/5947660/shallow_hal. This review was accessed on web.archive.org on June 19, 2015, using the original URL.

# 14

# Ideographic Criticism

*Ronald Lee and Adam Blood*

For most students, communication is a pragmatic discipline. It provides methods of analysis, a storehouse of strategies, and tried-and-true techniques for aiding an advocate in advancing a cause. Whether in public speaking, argumentation, or persuasion, the paradigm of an advocate moving a specific audience toward a predetermined end dominates undergraduate communication pedagogy. When students approach rhetorical criticism, they typically bring this orientation with them. Understanding the commitments of the pragmatic model, along with its limitations, provides concepts that other approaches radically recharacterize. Of particular note is the so-called **ideological turn**. Although the phrase captures a particular attitude toward criticism, it includes under its umbrella a constellation of different perspectives and methods.

This chapter focuses on Michael McGee's *rhetorical materialism* (theoretical perspective) and *ideographic criticism* (how that perspective is used in criticism). Beginning in the 1970s, McGee wrote a series of essays that changed the way a generation of critics think about, talk about, and do criticism. Even those who reject his program have been obliged to enter an ongoing conversation with his vision of rhetoric and the critical perspective he promulgated. McGee taught at the University of Memphis, at the University of Wisconsin–Madison, and for the twenty years before his death at the University of Iowa. Beyond his own writing, he influenced a generation of Iowa graduate students, a number of whom now rank among the most influential rhetorical theorists and critics in the field. In what follows, we outline a pragmatic approach to criticism. Second, we explain the ideological turn in criticism by contrasting it with the pragmatic approach. Third, we detail the particular commitments of McGee's rhetorical materialism. Fourth, we explain how rhetorical materialism is expressed in the doing of ideographic criticism. Finally, we illustrate the use of ideographic criticism in an analysis of the discourses of loyalty swirling around basketball star LeBron James's decision to leave the Cleveland Cavaliers to play for the Miami Heat and then return four years later.

## POINT OF DEPARTURE

In 1968, Lloyd Bitzer wrote a widely read essay titled "The Rhetorical Situation." It is the classic presentation of an approach that focuses on understanding the strategic way an advocate may overcome obstacles to success and points the critic toward an understanding of the persuasive influence that messages, deliberately employed, have on a targeted audience. Bitzer views a rhetorical work as "pragmatic" because it "functions ultimately to produce action or change in the world." "The rhetor," he writes, "alters reality by bringing into existence a discourse of such a character that the audience, in thought and action, is so engaged that it becomes a mediator of change."[1]

Bitzer's view presupposes that objective conditions in the external world call forth discourses. There is a brute presence to situations; these situations present exigencies (problematic circumstances); and these exigencies can be "completely or partially removed if discourse, introduced into the situation, can so constrain human decision or action as to bring about the significant modification of the exigence."[2]

Assume for a moment that you are taking a class in corporate advocacy. The instructor presents you with a series of case studies along with materials that describe the public-relations response to corporate difficulties. You follow Bitzer's approach to criticism. First, you identify the exigencies (loss of business and profit, civil and criminal prosecution, etc.). Second, you locate the audiences that can be mediators of change and thus ameliorate the exigencies (customers, investors, regulators, etc.). Third, you examine the constraints that limit the range of possible rhetorical responses (economic, legal, ethical, etc.). Finally, you evaluate the rhetorical strategies that these corporations enacted and make judgments about their effectiveness.

## IDEOLOGICAL TURN IN CRITICISM

Notice how narrow the range of judgment is in this pragmatic model of criticism. The critic is limited to assessing the skill of advocates in meeting their predetermined ends.[3] Other questions, especially those concerning competing values or the veracity of the discourse, are set aside. The danger is that conventional wisdom and tradition, typically determined in concert with entrenched interests and institutions, become equated with truth. Our student critics may feel restricted to looking at the world through the eyes of corporate officials. "We can clarify this issue," Philip Wander, himself an important figure in the ideological turn, has remarked, "by asking ourselves what in everyday language we would call the person . . . who examines or rewrites drafts of . . . statements so that their impact on specific audiences can be ascertained or improved; for whom policy, audience, and situation are a given and the overriding question is how to assess the effectiveness of the speech?" His answer is "not . . . a critic." "We would," he concludes, "be more inclined to call him or her a 'public relations consultant.'"[4] Once critics begin to ask, "Whose interests are served by these messages that construct this particular version of the truth?" they are dealing with ideology.

**Ideology** in the most general sense is "any system of ideas . . . directing political and social action."[5] The questions swirling around ideology ask, To what extent are these ideas true or false? What forces perpetuate these particular ideas? What groups benefit from and what groups are disadvantaged by these ideas?

The underlying assumption is that ideology "usually does not mirror the social world . . . but exhibits some transformation of it."[6] We generate concepts, images, and stories about the nature of our world, and these ideas are used to interpret social reality. These interpretations may create falsehood and distortion. Importantly, these distortions are not neutral in their effect, for they work to the advantage of some groups and to the disadvantage of others.

At root, ideology concerns the relationship among discourse, power, and truth. If we spend a few moments with each term, we should arrive at a workable understanding of ideology.

## 1. Discourse

The term *__discourse__* refers to "language in use, or more broadly, the interactive production of meaning."[7] This definition highlights a distinction between contextual and abstract uses of language. For the sake of illustration, consider the phrases "moral language" and "moral discourse." As we look at our bookshelves, we see several works of moral philosophy. These authors focus on "language" because they are interested in the linguistic properties of ethical propositions. These scholars provide an account of the meaning of the word *good* in the statement "X is good." Their treatment of this statement is apart from consideration of actual utterances of the word *good*. They do not examine any particular speakers, audiences, or contexts. They are not interested in whether any specific object, person, or state of affairs is in fact good. Instead, their interest is wholly theoretical.

We also have books and journals that contain treatments of "moral discourse." The authors of these works explore the moral utterances of actual speakers—Milton Friedman, Barack Obama, Pope Francis, and many others—in order to understand the meaning of their moral talk in historical context. These scholars do examine particular speakers, audiences, and contexts. Although their interest is in part theoretical, it is a theoretical interest grounded in a concern for the influence of specific moral messages in the world of practical affairs.

## 2. Power

Once the term *discourse* is substituted for *language*, the relevance of **power** becomes more obvious. Actual advocates are trying to influence the course of events in a manner that promotes their interests. Some advocates have more resources (money, access, technology, networks of influential friends) than others. Some advocates are pressing a case on behalf of established institutions and traditional ways of doing things, while others are working for groups with little social or economic standing and who find their interests at odds with the status quo. These disparities in position and resources make a huge difference in the ability to influence audiences.

Let's work from the most everyday of examples to grander illustrations of national political life. There is an old saying, "It is a poor scorekeeper who cannot win for his or her team." This aphorism captures one face of power—the illicit power exercised by those in positions of authority. So, in place of the game scorekeeper, we might just as well speak about Jeffrey Skilling, the former president of Enron, and David Duncan, the Arthur Andersen partner who oversaw the auditing of the Enron Corporation books. They are accused of profiting mightily from the creation of false reports documenting Enron's profitability. They had the power to manufacture a misleading discourse that persuaded thousands of investors to put money into their enterprise.[8]

Power is often exercised without any tinge of corruption. The president describes the crisis of terrorism, uses his authority as commander-in-chief to mobilize the armed forces, and urges the nation's citizens to sacrifice for the common good. Like the previous cases, this is an example of a powerful individual making an explicit decision that alters some state of affairs. And also like the other cases, it is done largely through the use of discourse. The president characterizes a situation as a "crisis," calls forth the historic precedents for the use of military force, and exhorts the citizenry to unite behind the cause.

In the examples we have used thus far, a person or group with power makes an explicit decision to exercise that power to bring about a particular result. Yet many of the most interesting discursive expressions of power are far more subtle and commonplace. Such cases are not the result of a single decision, but rather the product of power that is exercised by a way of talking that constitutes social and political culture. These forms of power go under a number of different names depending on the particular theorist and circumstance, including socialization, legitimation, domination, and hegemony. Each term suggests that powerful political, social, and economic interests perpetuate belief systems. Yet, it would be impossible to locate a set of decision makers that consciously decide on such matters. In advanced industrial societies, the apparatus of indoctrination is hidden and often denies its own existence.

Americans do not think of their children's education as an exercise in political propaganda. The schools are viewed as democratic institutions governed by local communities. Education is seen as the objective study of the world. Yet, it is obvious that stable societies must have an efficient way to pass on values and customs to each new generation. There are some obvious patriotic lessons taught in the early years of elementary schooling, such as reciting the Pledge of Allegiance and singing "My County 'Tis of Thee," but there are also subtle, supposedly nonpolitical, and yet important beliefs inculcated in children during these formative years. Children learn that they are required to go to school and that school officials have power over them. This power appears sweetly benign as personified by kindergarten teachers. This benevolent image of power is reinforced in the stories of the Founding Fathers, children's paternal conception of the president, and classroom visits by Officer Friendly. Students also learn the importance of order, the value placed on finishing work in a timely matter, and the rewards that come to the best and most obedient students. These are beginning lessons about the merit system in a capitalist economy.[9] As these pupils continue on in their education, they come to understand the country through the positive meanings associated with liberty, freedom, equality, tolerance, and democracy. These concepts are then organized into larger stories such as the American Dream.

The school is not the only institution socializing the citizenry. Advertising, for example, bombards viewers with the values of consumerism. Industrialization and urbanization weakened the traditional sources of socialization—church, family, and ethnic community. Commercial messages filled this void by selling consumers lifestyles, which they may purchase by selecting particular products.[10] Advertising, rather than religion and tradition, has become the dominant source of individual identity. Commercial messages construct for us a particular view of the country, where men and women are beautiful, everyone is affluent, and consumption makes people happy.

To put this point about power in yet another way, those who have the power to define the terms of the controversy have a tremendous rhetorical advantage. This is what examining the relationship between discourse and power makes evident. Powerful interests, through the communication apparatuses of an advanced society, define the very terms of discussion. The United States is a democratic republic; it has an advanced capitalist economy; and it is a predominantly Judeo-Christian nation. These traditions and institutions together create a set of belief systems that shape our view of the world. Their domination of our thinking is virtually invisible because they merely appear as the American way of life.

## 3. Truth

From what we have already said about power, we suspect that it is obvious that "truth" is dependent upon standpoint or perspective. There are often various versions of the truth, with each sponsored by a different set of interests. This subjective or contextual conception of truth (small *t*) stands in contrast with notions of universal Truth (big *T*).

If you decide to attend law school, you will be introduced to this sense of the truth. The lawyer's job is to *characterize* the facts and the law in ways that are to the advantage of the client. The law is a rhetorical enterprise, which pits opposing interpretations of the facts and the law against one another. The more persuasive version of the "truth" wins the verdict. Neither the law nor the facts are settled matters, but rather objects that may be differently constructed in discourse.

What we have said about the law is equally true of nearly any enterprise concerned with the construction of social reality. For example, many histories are written of the same event. Even when the relevant facts are generally agreed upon, the placement and characterization of those facts within a larger narrative may radically change the meaning of events.[11] So, taken together, discourse and power may create persuasive versions of the truth. These versions may be widely accepted and serve as the basis for decisions in the world of practical affairs.

We fear that the work we have done so far creates too inclusive a domain for ideology. If we define ideology as "any discourse bound up with specific social interests," then it becomes hard to think of any discourse, at least in some remote sense, which does not fall under its umbrella.[12] There is no simple way out of this problem. All we might say is that as social interests are better organized, more powerful, and their relationship to dominant cultural discourses more obvious, we can be more confident in calling such affected discourses ideological. Conversely, as social interests appear disorganized, lacking in influence, and their relationship to dominant cultural discourses are unclear or weak, we may view these discourses as relatively nonideological.

Remember that discourses that meet these criteria may resist the label "ideology." Americans do not typically refer to school curricula, advertising, or the law as examples of ideological discourse. Yet these discourses are paradigm cases of ideology. This quality of ideology denying itself is a central characteristic of the concept. In summary, ideological discourse is a "discourse bound up with specific social interests." It produces a version of the truth and perpetuates belief systems on behalf of powerful interests. This account has set aside many thorny theoretical issues, but for our purposes it is enough to recognize that discourse, power, and truth are bound up in the concept of ideology.

## RHETORICAL MATERIALISM

Michael McGee's participation in the ideological turn is based on a particular theoretical perspective on rhetoric, which underwrites a method of critical analysis. We begin with an explanation of McGee's theory, rhetorical materialism, and then proceed to his method, ideographic criticism.

McGee identified himself as a "rhetorical materialist" to distinguish his program from traditional critical-theoretical approaches that had largely dominated the field into the 1970s. This is an important point to grasp. McGee was not theorizing in a vacuum; he was instead providing a perspective that stood in opposition to what was then the prevailing disciplinary paradigm. He was reacting against a regime of rhetorical theory built on the authority of revered figures and texts. At that time, communication scholars largely thought about rhetoric through the ideas and theoretical prescriptions of such great thinkers as Aristotle, Isocrates, Cicero, Quintilian, St. Augustine, Francis Bacon, George Campbell, and Richard Whately. The result of this approach was "a 'rhetoric' which is on its face uninformed by historical or immediate contact with actual practice." "The theory and technique of rhetoric," McGee writes, "come less from human experience than from the metaphysical creativity and inspiration of particular writers." "What has been called 'rhetorical theory,'" McGee contends, "through much of our tradition is not theory at all, but a set of technical, prescriptive principles which inform the practitioner while, paradoxically, remaining largely innocent of practice."[13]

Under this old regime, a speech was determined as eloquent and effective based on the application of classical theories. So, if the speaker was found to follow the advice of Aristotle, then the speech must have been both worthy and successful. Not surprisingly, the discourse surrounding twentieth-century social upheavals, especially the antiwar, civil rights, and women's movements, did not resemble the speeches given by the ancients. The mediated age of celebrity and fifteen-second ads operates on different principles than addresses to the Athenian Assembly, the Roman Senate, or the British Parliament.

By contrast, McGee explored actual rhetorical encounters. His sense of materialism is captured in his definition of *rhetoric*: "Rhetoric is a natural social phenomenon in the context of which symbolic claims are made on the behavior and/or belief of one or more persons, allegedly in the interest of such individuals, and with the strong presumption that such claims will cause meaningful change."[14] Note how this definition expands upon that given in chapter 2; from this definition, we may proceed to unpack the dimensions of rhetorical materialism.

First, the "natural social phenomenon" is the recurring human experience of the relationships among "speaker/speech/audience/occasion/change." You cannot live in the social world without being impacted by these relationships. Each time you are addressed as an audience—for instance, as the reader of this chapter, as a student in a class, or as a citizen of the republic—you enter into this confluence of relationships. This is not simply an idea but an unavoidable part of living in the social world.

Second, the phrase "in the context of which" features for McGee the problematic relationship between "discourse" and "rhetoric." Rhetoric represents the entire experience of the complex social relationships among speaker/speech/audience/occasion/change. Discourse is residue that is left behind. It is the copy of the "speech" that has been saved. McGee uses an analogy to explain the rhetoric-discourse distinction. "We can construct," he writes, "the nature, scope, and consequence of a nuclear explosion by analyzing its residue when the raw matter and even the energy inherent in its occurrence have dissipated. Thus it is possible to reconstruct the nature, scope, and consequence of rhetoric by analyzing 'speech' even when 'speaker,' 'audience,' 'occasion,' and 'change' dissipate into half-remembered history." So, from a particular discourse we have the tracings that will permit a "reconstruction *of the whole phenomenon* . . . for it is the *whole* of 'speaker/speech/audience/occasion/change' which impinges on us."[15]

Third, the phrase "symbolic claims" suggests that "*every* interactivity of society contains or comprises a claim on some human being's belief and/or behavior."[16] Unlike conventional accounts of rhetoric, McGee does not distinguish rhetoric from coercion. He understands rhetoric as a species of coercion. It is, he writes, a "coercive agency," but certainly one that is preferable to other physical forms of coercion. It is preferable in two different senses. First, when an audience acquiesces to rhetoric, it does so feeling that some more personal account was given for imposing the speaker's will. Second, the symbolic is preferable because it sublimates the "pain" of more violent forms of coercion. So, rhetoric may be thought of as a more ethical form of coercion, but a form of coercion nonetheless.

Fourth, the phrase "behavior and/or belief" draws the reader's attention to the complexities of moving from a change in belief to altering behavior. Scholars have filled the persuasion and social psychology literature with explanations of the difficulties inherent in the process of changing beliefs to influence attitudes in order to ultimately create new behaviors. This process is complex even in the simplest of direct transactions (speaker–message–target audience), but considerably more difficult to account for in the intricate communication environment of contemporary society. Beliefs and attitudes are shaped by ideology and other diffuse discourses that influence the tenor of an entire society.

Fifth, the phrase "allegedly in the interest of the audience," McGee explains, "calls to attention the relationship between 'speaker' and 'audience' as 'leader' to 'follower.'"[17] The relationship between leader/follower and speaker/audience is a continuing theme in McGee's work. "Every 'audience,'" he writes, "comes together with an interest and the expectation that the 'speaker' will aid in procuring that interest. And every 'speaker' comes to 'audience' with the desire to accomplish an otherwise impossible task by mobilizing a collective force."[18] The tension between the interests of leader and follower, speaker and audience, is at the center of any ideological criticism. The rhetorical creation of a sense of collectivity among audience members requires the invention of messages that harmonize often divergent interests.

Finally, the phrase "the strong presumption that such claims will result in meaningful change" draws our attention to the issue of rhetorical effects. Few social science models of any stripe have much success at predicting cause-and-effect relationships. Certainly, any retrospective claim of a direct effect between a particular feature of a message and a specific historical outcome is foolhardy. The message variable is at best one among a bundle of other forces (economic, demographic, political, cultural, and so forth), and to try to draw specific causal connections is nearly impossible. Yet, in the everyday world, we "conduct a continual deliberation based on our ability to model the environment and to predict the consequences of changing it."[19] Even though we can neither explain nor control all the factors that influence change, we talk as if speech is a powerful agency that can control the environment. This talk creates a sense of the collective and then speaks as if the collective will can shape meaningful social change. In these rhetorical transactions, we construct a discourse that reveals the world in which we live. It is powerfully shaped by the ideological commitments that we share. As these commitments are modified, the messages reflect these changes. We can map the ideological shifts in society by paying attention to these messages.

Given the commitments of rhetorical materialism, how does McGee proceed as a rhetorical critic? What critical apparatus does he mobilize to glean the ideological commitments that are present in a text? The answers to these questions revolve around the concept of the "ideograph."

## IDEOGRAPHIC CRITICISM

Critics need a way to move between discourse and ideology; they need a rhetorical window on the exercise of power and the accompanying promulgation of truth. In Dana Cloud's words, they require "an analytical link between rhetoric—understood as situated, pragmatic, instrumental, and strategic discourse—on one hand, and ideology—the structures or systems of ideas within which individual pragmatic speech acts take place and by which they are constrained—on the other."[20]

McGee's concept of the **ideograph** provides just this link between rhetoric and ideology. The definition of *ideograph* is surprisingly complex, given its very ordinary and everyday nature. So, let us begin with a list of ideographs and then move to their formal characteristics. In the American context, the following words and slogans are examples of ideographs: <equality>, <freedom>, <freedom of speech>, <law and order>, <liberty>, <national security>, <privacy>, <property>, <rule of law>, and <separation of church and state>.[21]

McGee lists the "characteristics" that would constitute a "formal definition of 'ideograph.'"[22] We have commented on each of these seven characteristics:

1. *"An ideograph is an ordinary language term found in political discourse."*[23] Ideographs are not technical terms, words used by experts or privileged insiders; rather they are terms that appear regularly in ordinary public talk. These are words that you will encounter on the news, on talk radio programs, in the texts of political speeches, in grade-school classrooms, and in everyday conversation.
2. *"It is a high-order abstraction representing collective commitment to a particular but equivocal and ill-defined normative goal."*[24] On the highest level of abstraction, ideographs are ambiguous, although they have a high emotional affect. For instance, the words <liberty>, <freedom>, and <equality> are emotionally evocative, but they have little cognitive meaning unless tied to specific situations. Either side in the abortion debate might employ the ideograph <liberty>, or either side in the controversy over the meaning of <separation of church and state> may invoke it. Ideographs are "normative" because they are value terms that are used to make judgments. Ideographs are "goals" because they represent something to be obtained or a path to follow. So, political candidates might urge their audiences to pursue the path of <freedom>.
3. *"It warrants the use of power, excuses behavior and belief which might otherwise be perceived as eccentric or antisocial, and guides behavior and belief into channels easily recognized as acceptable and laudable. Ideographs such as 'slavery' and 'tyranny,' however, may guide behavior and belief negatively by branding unacceptable behavior."*[25] The essential function of an ideograph is to warrant the exercise of power. Taking or not taking action is justified in the name of ideographs. Some ideographs are positive (<liberty>, <freedom>, <equality>), and behaviors that can be justified by positive ideographs are regarded as socially acceptable. Some ideographs are negative (<tyranny>, <socialism>, <censorship>), and behaviors that further these values are branded as unacceptable.
4. *"And many ideographs ('liberty,' for example) have a non-ideographic usage, as in the sentence, 'Since I resigned my position, I am at liberty to accept your offer.'"*[26] Ideographs "signify and 'contain' a unique ideological commitment."[27] They are the public vocabulary of ideology. So, when terms such as "liberty" and "freedom" are used in nonideological contexts, they do not function as ideographs.
5. *"Ideographs are culture-bound, though some terms are used in different signification across cultures."*[28] Ideographs are universal because they exist in all societies. Specific ideographs are culture bound. The Anglo-American liberal tradition[29] features a defining set of ideographs—the focus on <liberty>, for instance—that would not appear, or at least not appear with the same significance, in other cultures.
6. *"Each member of the community is socialized, conditioned, to the vocabulary of ideographs as a prerequisite for 'belonging' to the society."*[30] Becoming a member of a culture requires understanding the society's ideographs. As part of being socialized as an American, every schoolchild learns to respect <property>, to love <liberty>, and to guard <freedom>.
7. *"A degree of tolerance is usual, but people are expected to understand ideographs within a range of usage thought to be acceptable: The society will inflict penalties on those who use*

*ideographs in heretical ways and on those who refuse to respond appropriately to claims on their behavior warranted through the agency of ideographs."*[31] These penalties may range in severity. Speaking in ways that use ideographs inappropriately may result in political marginalization. Absent the appropriate language, advocates will simply fail to find an audience. Rhetorical sanctions may be imposed as deviant rhetors are labeled "traitors," "demagogues," or "extremists." This may result in public scorn and rhetorical exile. Finally, legal and economic sanctions may be inflicted on those who are determined to be guilty of "subversion" or "treason."

Ideographs are especially important for understanding the relationship between leaders and citizens. They are the storehouse of words and phrases from which leaders select appeals to warrant exercises of power. These are the terms that are used when leaders claim to be acting in the name of <the people>.[32] "Ideographs represent in condensed form," Condit and Lucaites explain, "the normative, collective commitments of the members of a public, and they typically appear in public argumentation as the necessary motivations or justifications for action performed in the name of the public."[33]

Like other terms of value, ideographs are often in tension with one another. As McGee writes, "An ideograph is always understood in its relation to another."[34] So <freedom> is understood in relationship to <order>, <responsibility>, and the <rule of law>. In any given circumstance, advocates may argue that one ideological commitment is more important than another. For instance, in the civil rights struggles of the 1950s and 1960s, segregationists and integrationists battled over the preeminence of particular sets of ideographs. Segregationists held that <property> rights permitted proprietors of restaurants, motels, retail stores, and other <private> businesses to decide who they would serve. If owners of apartment buildings did not want to rent to black families, they should have that prerogative as controllers of private property. Integrationists held that the ideological commitment to <equality> demanded that businesses that served the <public> had an obligation to treat each customer alike. The resulting public accommodation and open housing legislation put into law regulations that elevated, in this context, <equality> over <property>.

In brief, this example depicts the synchronic and diachronic dimensions of ideographic analysis. The **synchronic** dimension explores the tension among ideographs at a particular time. In the civil rights illustration, there were advocates posing differing ideological constructions of segregation in an effort to influence passage of specific legislation. The **diachronic** dimension explores a society's changing ideological commitments through time. In America, <equality> has become an ever more important ideological commitment, and its prominence has come at the expense of other ideographs, including <property>,[35] and is even now clashing with <freedom of religion>.

We want to return for a few moments to the "point of departure" at the beginning of the chapter. Recall that we contrasted a pragmatic model of criticism (Bitzer's rhetorical situation) with ideological criticism. With the introduction to McGee's ideographic criticism, we want to spend a little time contrasting the two approaches. We draw your attention to three specific differences: the nature of effects, the concept of audience, and assumptions about reality.

*Effects.* In the pragmatic model, which few working scholars actually employ but is the focus of a great deal of undergraduate pedagogy, the critic is interested in evaluating the impact of a speaker's message on a target audience. The effects are quite narrow in conception. Did the message have the particular effect that the speaker desired? For instance, did the corporations' public-relations campaigns retain customers and investors? In ideographic analysis, the critic is interested in examining the discourse as a symptom of changes in ideology and, thus, public consciousness. Put differently, the discourse itself is understood as the effect rather than the cause. When ideographs change—for instance, when <equality> displaces <property>—this reflects a change in ideology. The society has begun to justify political actions in new ways and warrant the exercise of power in different terms.

What caused these changes in ideology? This is a very difficult question and is beyond the scope of rhetorical analysis. Typically, such changes are the result of economics, demographics, conflict, or some other social malady. The result of such forces is a change in social reality—the way Americans think about race has changed dramatically over the last century—and these changes are then reflected in the society's rhetoric. These rhetorical changes are marked by new relationships among the culture's ideographs.

*Audience.* In the pragmatic model, the audience is often assumed to be a fixed target. The audience preexists the message. Thus, the advocate adapts the message to a set of audience predispositions and behaviors. The critic's work is to assess the choices that the rhetor made. In ideographic analysis, the audience itself is taken to be rhetorically constructed. Power is exercised and political actions are justified in the name of <the people>.[36] The audience does not preexist the message but is actually constituted by it. Adolf Hitler constructed the German people as a superior Aryan race. Martin Luther King Jr. constructed a people who were judged by the "content of their character" rather than the "color of their skin." In each case, these definitions of <the people> become ideological premises upon which to justify taking particular forms of political action. Understanding the changing ideological construction of <the people> is at the center of doing ideographic criticism.

*Reality.* In the pragmatic model of criticism, there is an implicit assumption that an objective situation (circumstances, audiences, constraints) is present that may be altered by the strategic use of discourse. The situation preexists the discourse. In ideological criticism, there is an explicit assumption that rhetoric constitutes reality. As we mentioned earlier, ideological criticism concerns the relationship among discourse, power, and truth. The constellation and relationship among ideographs maps the shape of this rhetorically constituted reality.

## FINAL THOUGHTS

All criticism involves making arguments on behalf of judgments. For example, Wayne Brockriede writes that when a critic "states clearly the criteria he has used in arriving at his judgment, together with the philosophic or theoretic foundations on which they rest, and when he has offered some data to show that the rhetorical experience meets or fails to meet these criteria, then he has argued." Confronted with this form of critical argument "a reader has several kinds of choices: he can accept or reject the data, accept or reject the criteria, accept or reject the philosophic or theoretic basis for the criteria, and accept or reject the inferential leap that joins data and criteria."[37]

Using Brockriede's notion of criticism as a template, let us think through how a critic may use ideographic criticism to form an argument on behalf of a judgment. First, ideographs are a kind of *data*. They direct the critic to look for the presence of ideographs in a text. The critic looks both for the tension among ideographs at a single point in time and for the changing patterns of ideographic tensions over time. These patterns are the critic's data.

Second, the *theoretical foundation* of ideographic analysis is rhetorical materialism. It is the commitments of rhetorical materialism that underwrite the relationship among rhetoric, discourse, and ideology. It is only when rhetoric and ideology are understood in particular ways that ideographic criticism becomes compelling. The data provided by ideographs represent patterns of public consciousness. These patterns are maps of changing ideological commitments. As a result, the critic reveals the changing patterns by which power is justified.

Third, ideographic criticism does not present any single set of *criteria for evaluation*. The results of ideographic criticism provide data that underwrite several different forms of evaluation.

(A) An ideographic criticism documents progressive or regressive ideological-rhetorical trends. Celeste Condit and John Lucaites, in their book *Crafting Equality*, have documented the increasingly important role <equality> has played in American public consciousness. By and large, they tell an affirming story of an improving and more just America. The ascendancy of <equality>, they argue, has had positive consequences on the moral quality of our national discourse. Used in this way, the reader is asked to judge the positive and negative quality of the ideographic trend.

(B) Ideographic criticism believes ideology is false consciousness. For these critics, public rhetoric often rationalizes political acts that help the powerful and disadvantage the powerless. Dana Cloud, in her ideographic analysis of family-values discourse, draws precisely this type of conclusion. "<Family values> talk," she writes, "functioned during the [1992 presidential election campaign] to scapegoat Black men and poor Americans for social problems." She continues, "Ultimately, in constructing the family as the site of all responsibility and change, the rhetoric of <family values> privatizes social responsibility for ending poverty and racism."[38] Employed in this matter, readers are asked to accept or reject the discourse as a distortion promulgated for the purpose of established interests.

(C) Ideographic criticism reveals political irony. Irony lies in the incongruity between the actual result and the normal or expected result. By exposing inconsistencies among ideological warrants, it opens up semantic space for resistance. These terms begin to lose some of their positive emotive force, and ultimately these justifications for the exercise of power become less compelling. For example, Celeste Condit and Ann Selzer explored the newspaper coverage of a Kansas murder trial. They found, ironically, that the journalistic standards of <objectivity> led "to a prosecution bias in the reporting of criminal trials."[39] Ironically, objectivity led to bias. This form of ideographic criticism suggests lines of counterargument and alternative political narratives. The reader is left to judge the merits of these new ways of looking at the world.

## CRITICAL ESSAY

We have written an analysis of the discourses accompanying the departure of LeBron James from Cleveland in 2010 to play for the Miami Heat and his subsequent return to the Cavaliers in 2014. This sports transaction illustrates the ideographic tension between the <market> and <loyalty>.

---

### THE CONUNDRUM OF <LOYALTY> AND THE <MARKET>: THE DISCOURSES SURROUNDING LEBRON JAMES'S LEAVING AND RETURNING HOME

Living in the shadow of the marketplace, we plant roots in shallow ground. Market theory "teaches that leaving is a virtue" because it fosters "competition."[40] In our work lives, we can expect resources to flow across borders, and capital, labor, and materials to seek the most efficient and profitable location for production. The deindustrialized upper Midwest, now sadly called the rust belt, is a testament to this new condition. Only downsized remnants remain of the steel industry in Youngstown, Gary, and Pittsburgh, tire production in Akron, glass manufacturing in Toledo, or automobile assembly in the Michigan cities of Flint, Hamtramck, and River Rouge. Consequently, US workers can expect to move more often, change jobs more frequently, and make a living under conditions of increasing economic uncertainty.

Likewise, the marketplace weakens our attachment to goods and services. With new search engines, we shop across the range of providers to find what is cheapest and most convenient. According to philosopher George Fletcher, "The values of the marketplace apply today not only in the choice of material products like toothpaste and automobiles but in our relationships with people." "Shifting loyalties," he continues, "is an increasingly common way of coping with a weak friendship, a shaky marriage, a religious community that takes the wrong stand on an important issue, or a nation that has come into the hands of the wrong political party." "Those who exit," he observes, "cannot be faulted for assuming that newly planted roots will yield greener grass."[41]

Despite the dominance of the market, appeals to loyalty are no less prominent. Sellers invest vast sums to create bonds between the public and their wares. What changed during the last century are the rhetorical materials with which these bonds are manufactured. Commercial advertising has turned away from product-based marketing; religious evangelizing has turned away from arguments about theology; and political campaigning has increasingly turned away from issue appeals.[42] Contemporary constructions of loyalty are cobbled together from disconnected images, decontextualized historical references, and mythic fragments. They are, to borrow the language of Alasdair MacIntyre, largely incoherent as a reasoned justification for belief and action.[43]

We may not notice this incoherence because discussions of loyalty are now so frequently comingled with the vocabulary of branding. Yet, this marketing terminology is a species of loyalty with newer, less auspicious, objects of attachment. The appeals by which we claim people have obligations, duties, or owe their faithful allegiance are no small matter. When these appeals rest on shifting sands, commitment becomes hard to secure and misplaced loyalties become difficult to refute.

In this essay, we turn our attention to a case study of disputed loyalty, which garnered a great deal of national attention because it set in sharp relief the tension between the logic of the market and the loyal obligation to community. In the resulting rhetorical fireworks, the act was characterized as "desert[ion]" and "betrayal" and the actor as "narcissistic," "cowardly," "heartless," "callous," and "selfish." Fortunately, in the larger scheme of things, a basketball player exercising his prerogative to change teams in the free-agent market is hardly all that important, though the national clamor around LeBron James's decision to leave Cleveland for Miami rivaled the handwringing over Edward Snowden's supposed traitorous NSA revelations.[44]

We do believe, however, that the discourses surrounding professional sports are a useful entry point into the study of loyalty and the marketplace. Sports fandom is built on bonds of attachment among teams, communities, and athletes.[45] These bonds are stressed by the economics of free agency, which encourages players to make decisions that weigh their individual interests against considerations of loyalty.

In what follows, we describe the circumstances and characterize the discourses that swirled around James's decision to leave the Cleveland in 2010 and return in 2014. Second, we unpack the rhetorical complications in the ideographic tension between the <market> and <loyalty>. Finally, we draw conclusions about the rhetorical nature of <loyalty> in the postmodern world.

## Leave and Return

Despite being raised by a single mother in the housing projects of Akron, Ohio, LeBron James's athletic talent made him a national celebrity by his late teens. When he bypassed college, a bounce of the NBA lottery ball permitted his hometown team to select him with the first pick in the draft.[46] Cleveland had not enjoyed a championship of any kind for nearly fifty years, but now a native son of Ohio seemed destined to alter its fate.

During his first seven seasons, the league twice named James MVP and he led the Cavaliers to the 2007 NBA Finals. He was regarded as the "best player on the planet," and, befitting his iconic status, was known simply as "King James."[47] But beyond delivering on his athletic promise, James cemented his regional identity. His partner, the mother of his children (and now his wife, Savannah Brinson), had been his girlfriend since the time they were high-school classmates. He built a large home in Akron. He was a generous benefactor to his alma mater, St. Vincent–St. Mary School, and his foundation provided support to schoolchildren in Northeast Ohio. He often spoke about where he came from and how it contributed to who he was. He constructed a persona not of a person changed by good fortune, but rather as an authentic man who reflected the character of home.

Since the time of Curt Flood and the challenge to baseball's reserve clause, the free-agent market has permitted professional athletes to choose the places they work.[48] So, on July 8, 2010, on the nationally televised special, "Decision," LeBron James announced that he was going to exercise his collectively bargained right to change teams and take his "talents to South Beach." During the next four years in Miami, he played in four NBA Finals and brought two championships to the Heat. Four years later, on June 25, 2014, James decided to return to Cleveland, where he signed a two-year $42.1 million contract and transformed the Cavaliers from one of the worst teams in the league to a favorite to win the 2015 championship.[49]

We focus on two texts produced by the chief protagonists in the drama: Dan Gilbert's public letter to the Cleveland fan base released on the eve of the "Decision," and LeBron James's first-person essay announcing his return to Cleveland. In exploring these discourses, we find a window through which to examine the ideographic tension between the <market> and <loyalty>.

### Gilbert's Public Letter

Dan Gilbert was born, raised, and centers his core businesses in Detroit. His company, Quicken Loans, is the second largest retail lender in the United States with 10,000 employees who issued $70 billion in home loans in 2012. He has amassed an estimated $4.8 billion fortune transferring money across the local boundaries that used to define old time banking.[50] He bought the Cavaliers in 2005 for $375 million. Upon James's return in 2015, *Bloomberg News* estimates that the franchise was worth a billion dollars.[51] In the 2013–2014 season, Cleveland ranked 16th in NBA attendance, but after James's announced return, the team sold out every regular season game.[52] James's move to Miami cost, by some estimates, the Cleveland market $2.5 billion in economic activity.[53]

Gilbert, the man of the <market>, penned a public letter, addressed to "all of Northeast Ohio and Cleveland Cavaliers supporters," excoriating LeBron James for exercising his free-agent option.[54] The letter has three parts: the portrayal of James as traitor, the promise of the continued commitment of the Cavaliers' franchise to its supporters, and the observation that "bad karma" would "curse" James and Miami. Each part is built on a persuasive characterization of <loyalty>.

Loyalty is a virtue that characterizes a disposition of persons and their motivation toward action, and is invoked toward particular objects of attachment. So, one might be a loyal spouse, employee, or friend. In a political context, <loyalty> is understood as attachment to community, nation, or political ideals. Because dispositions are mental states, they are inferred indirectly through the interpretation of acts. For Gilbert, leaving Cleveland is an act of "desert[ion]" and "betrayal," and such "disloyalty" is associated with a person of "narcissistic," "cowardly," "heartless," "callous," and "selfish" character.

In the letter's second section, Gilbert contrasts the Cavaliers' organization with its departing player. "The good news," Gilbert writes, "is that the ownership team and the rest of the hard-working, loyal, and driven staff over here at your hometown Cavaliers have not betrayed you nor NEVER [all cap in original] will betray you." The organization's commitment will bring the Cleveland "an NBA Championship before the self-titled former 'king' wins one."

Finally, Gilbert's "[personal] guarantee" of an NBA championship is built on an understanding of vice as a harbinger of "bad karma." "This heartless and callous action," Gilbert writes, "can only serve as the antidote to the so-called 'curse' on Cleveland, Ohio. . . . James (and the town where he plays) will unfortunately own this dreaded spell and bad karma."

If the <market> is a rational arbiter of self-interest, what are the grounds for making <loyalty> claims? James neither abandoned his family, the league, nor the game; he merely changed employers in order to improve his prospects. Not surprisingly, Gilbert's scathing criticism of James does not appeal to any utilitarian calculation of interest. James is guilty of severing a mystic bond. Consider these phrases from the letter:

1. "Unlike anything ever 'witnessed' in the history of sports."
2. "This shocking act of disloyalty from our home grown 'chosen one' sends the exact opposite lesson of what we would want our children to learn. And 'who' we want them to grow-up to become."
3. "The self-declared former 'King' will be taking the 'curse' [refers to the Cleveland sports curse] with him down south."
4. "DELIVERING YOU [all caps in original] the championship you have long deserved and is long overdue."
5. "Tomorrow is a new and much brighter day."

The Chosen Nation narrative tells the story of God's covenant with the people of Israel. When this story is transferred to American shores, the Puritans adapted the myth to justify their own "errand in the wilderness."[55] The phrases "delivering you" and "new and much brighter day" evoke the Exodus narrative.[56] In the tradition of the Old Testament prophets, Gilbert warns of God's "curse" upon the unfaithful.

The term "witnessed" is a reference to the Nike advertising campaign, launched in 2005, to pay "tribute to James and acknowledges the legions of fans worldwide who are 'witnessing' his greatness, power, athleticism and beautiful style of play."[57] In the accompanying imagery, fans resemble a Black Church congregation and LeBron's pose, with arms splayed, symbolizes the cross. The "witness" language is drawn from the Book of Acts, where St. Luke speaks of those chosen to testify to the resurrection.[58] Gilbert reinforces the Christian motif with the phrases "chosen one" and "self-declared king."

In his condemnatory discourse, Gilbert allegorically compares James to Moses abandoning his quest for the Promised Land and Jesus forsaking the sacrifice of the cross. This hyperbolic criticism, invented from fragments of the most sacred stories in the Judaic-Christian tradition, ought to shock the public's rhetorical sensibility. Yet, as the *Cleveland Plain Dealer* documented in its media roundup article, "In everywhere but Miami, reaction to LeBron James' decision is overwhelmingly negative."[59] Interestingly, the authors of these negative commentaries often acknowledged the good reasons for changing franchises, but yet found in James's move evidence of his weak character.

## James's "Coming Home" Essay

On July 11, 2014, LeBron James announced in a first-person essay, published in *Sports Illustrated*, his intention to return home to play basketball in Cleveland.[60] The text mediates <loyalty> with the ideograph <opportunity>. James explains his journey in three parts. First, he was given an opportunity that required leaving home. Second, the time away was an enriching experience. Finally, upon his return, he is better prepared to help those he left.

This is a familiar genre. It resembles the story of anyone who has gone away to school and returned home. This narrative form is a staple of candidate biographies. Jimmy Carter and Bill Clinton, for instance, grew up in the South; both left home to pursue elite educational and professional opportunities (for Carter, Georgia Tech, Annapolis, and the nuclear Navy; for Clinton, Georgetown, Oxford, Yale, and the legal profession); and both returned to engage in public service so they might improve the places they left.[61]

In James's parallel account, "Miami, for me, has been almost like college for other kids. These past four years, helped raise me into who I am. I became a better player and a better man." "I learned," he continues, "from a franchise that had been where I wanted to go." As a consequence, "I see myself as a mentor now and I'm excited to lead some of these talented young guys." Like Carter and Clinton, who had opportunities to pursue a naval career or a legal career in a large urban law firm, James wanted to bring what he had learned to bear on the problems at home:

> Before anyone ever cared where I would play basketball, I was a kid from Northeast Ohio. It's where I walked. It's where I ran. It's where I cried. It's where I bled. It holds a special place in my heart. People there have seen me grow up. I sometimes feel like I'm their son. Their passion can be overwhelming. But it drives me. I want to give them hope when I can. I want to inspire when I can. My relationship with Northeast Ohio is bigger than basketball.

The reasons for returning were largely unrelated to basketball; they were ties to the mythic chords of place. "But I have two boys and my wife, Savannah, is pregnant with a girl," and "I started thinking about what it would be like to raise my family in my hometown." He elaborates, "The more time passed, the more it felt right. This is what makes me happy." In the closing sentences of the essay, James draws explicitly the parallel between his journey and the life cycle of so many others that leave so they may return better able to help improve the quality of the community:

> I want kids in Northeast Ohio, like the hundreds of Akron third-graders I sponsor through my foundation, to realize that there's no better place to grow up. Maybe some of them will come home after college and start a family or open a business. That would make me smile. Our community, which has struggled so much, needs all the talent it can get.

The appeal to <loyalty> is reconfigured, building a sense of connectedness and obligation that is differentiated from those expressed in Gilbert's message. James speaks of a familial bond, not with the Cavaliers' fan base, but the one between himself and his childhood home. This move separates James-as-person from James-as-athlete. This appeal connects <loyalty> to place rather than to an organization and its mission. Put another way, James's account moves out of the shadow of the market.

## Ideographic Tensions

An ideograph is "an ordinary language term" representing a "collective commitment to particular but equivocal and ill-defined normative goal." Yet, it has serious justificatory consequences since it "warrants the use of power" and "guides behavior and belief into channels easily recognized as acceptable and laudable." As members of a political community, we are all "socialized, conditioned to the vocabulary of ideographs as a prerequisite for 'belonging' to the society."[62] Ideographs are highly evocative but cognitively ambiguous. As ideographic terms move across contexts, they warrant social action on different grounds. As various ideographs arise in any given circumstance, the dialectical tensions among them stress their equivocal status and generate controversy.

In our discussion, we have largely focused on the tension between the <market> and <loyalty>. We have suggested that various other ideographs swirl around these key terms. Although free agency is a market term par excellence, James speaks and writes in the language of <opportunity>. He views free agency as creating a situation in which he may make a rational decision about taking advantage of <opportunity>.

In the US tradition, the <market> is but one term revolving around the ideological cornerstone of liberal-democratic thought, <property>. Broadly understood, <property> ensures a wide sphere of private action and thoughts, conscience, speech, religion, and association remain the <property> of individuals and, therefore, outside public regulation.[63] In this sense of <property>, James had a right to his own labor and could freely pursue <opportunity>. Yet, in US history <property> has had other meanings and been used as a justification for the denial of <freedom>. Property rights were the rationale for segregation, because owners of restaurants, motels, theaters, and apartment buildings had the right to determine which customers they would serve. Before the Civil War, human bondage defined slaves as <property> and denied them the right to sell their labor.

Gilbert used language that evokes, at least for some listeners, this older, discredited sense of <property>. He "speaks as an owner of LeBron and not the owner of the Cleveland Cavaliers," Rev. Jesse Jackson said in a press release, "His feelings of betrayal personify a slave master mentality. He sees LeBron as a runaway slave. This is an owner employee relationship—between business partners—and LeBron honored his contract."[64] In the context of an African American–dominated NBA, this characterization forced Commissioner David Stern to fine Gilbert $100,000 for "inappropriate" remarks and to rather gently rebuke Jackson. "However well-meaning Jesse may be in the premise of this one, he is, as he rarely is, mistaken," Stern said. "But he is a good friend of the NBA and our players. Has worked arduously on many good causes and we work together in many matters."[65] In our interpretation, we take Stern to be rejecting any characterization of athletes as the owners' property, while simultaneously acknowledging that Gilbert's language inappropriately echoed this older sense of <property>.[66]

We live in a liberal-democratic culture dominated by appeals to rights. These rights limit the range of public obligation and create a correspondingly large domain of privacy in which citizens can pursue their self-interest. In the present case, James secured his rights through a collectively bargained labor agreement, provisions in a binding contract with the Cavaliers, and the general right of citizens to freely offer their labor.

The concept of loyalty, by contrast, is traditionally conceived as a public obligation, a civic virtue with a dispositional attachment to some end apart from self. Definitions of loyalty employ synonyms such as "devotion," "attitude," "sentiment," "emotional attachment," and "identification."[67] In political terms, loyal Americans possess the requisite sentiment toward their country. The presence of this sentiment is important because it motivates acts in support of the government and leads citizens to willingly sacrifice for the common good.

In the present context, Gilbert's discourse is ambiguous about the objects of James's betrayal. Apparently, it is some combination of team, organization, mission, fan base, and home. When citizens are asked to sacrifice for country, we may ask about their reasons for national attachment. They might list a host of ideographs—<freedom>, <equality>, <opportunity>, <rights>, and so forth. In one important sense, Gilbert is asking James to forfeit the exercise of his <rights> in the name of <loyalty>. This is precisely the logic of the Red Scare, when Joseph McCarthy argued that citizens ought to be willing to sacrifice First Amendment protections of freedom of speech and association to ferret out disloyal subversives. Not surprisingly, because scholarly attention to loyalty has so frequently focused on McCarthyism, the resulting analyses have commonly joined appeals to loyalty with demagoguery.[68] Although the squabble over a basketball player's free agency is hardly momentous in comparison, it is worth examining the parallels to understand the rhetorical logic integral to liberal appeals to <loyalty>.

In the Greek, a demagogue is literally a "leader of the people."[69] Thus, with its modern pejorative connotations, the demagogue is a leader of the people who appeals to the basest instincts of the public. Thus, appeals to class, race, anti-intellectualism, and so forth are often labeled demagogic. Most instances of demagoguery have about them some tension between civic obligation and individual rights. When pressed too far, advocates of civic virtue will inevitably begin to look for "traitors." Hitler found the men who stabbed Germany in the back during World War I. The members of ISIS use a logic of loyalty in their adoption of a philosophy that allows them to deem other Muslims outside genuine Islamic faith, and thus worthy of condemnation, torture, or even execution.[70] White supremacists find the turncoats who are "traitors to their race." In one way or another, the demagogue plays on the tension between obligation to a community and individual rights.

We can ask meaningfully if Dan Gilbert's letter is demagogic. Our answer is necessarily equivocal. Certainly, in one sense, Gilbert employs all the incendiary language of treason in response to James's exercise of his rights to operate in a free <market>. Using our formula that an appeal to civic virtue is used to undermine <rights>, the Gilbert discourse has about it a necessary condition of demagoguery. On the other hand, because the legal framework of contract protected James, because fans, despite their often-indecorous displays of emotion, understand the limited nature of the stakes, and because Gilbert's outrage did not lead to a campaign of persecution, the incendiary discourse had few notable demagogic effects. We suspect, too, because this tension was between <loyalty> and <market> as opposed to <loyalty> and <national security> or <loyalty> and <our way of life>, the rhetorical consequences are muted.

Yet, the Gilbert-James exchange remains an interesting case to think with. First, as we have already said, the demagogic potential of the rhetorical logic of loyalty is clearly present in this case. Second, James's 2014 essay announcing his return home offers a productive way to think and talk about loyalty. The use of mediating ideographs, especially <opportunity>, makes clear the contingent claims of <loyalty>. In LeBron's prose, the journey home is a draw, a responsibility, but one that should not become narrow provincialism. In order to grow and mature, the loyalty to community must find new grounds of attachment.

## Postmodernity and the Coherence of Loyalty

The mix of the market and, as noted above, the sacred lend credence to our judgment that contemporary loyalty discourses are often incoherent. Was Gilbert's letter an artless aberration composed in a fit of anger and, therefore, meaningless as a cultural maker of loyalty? It may well have been artless and it was most assuredly an angry rant, but words and images expressed so spontaneously reflect patterns of socialization. Because loyalty runs counter to material self-interest, we readily turn to the realm of the sacred.

Scholars have argued that religion is the quintessential domain of loyalty. "In general," Fletcher writes, "it makes good sense to think of one's relationship to God as a commitment to loyalty." After all, "the faith of the believer is constantly subject to temptation by a false power."[71] Adam and Eve's original sin is an act of disloyalty; the Book of Job is a drama of fidelity; and Peter's denying Christ three times is fear overwhelming devotion. "In its biblical foundations," Fletcher observes, "God is king, father, and protector of his people, who in turn owe him a duty of loyalty."[72] The sacred language of faith and covenant, sin and idolatry provide terms for expressing loyalty and betrayal. Marketing specialists have long understood the usefulness of sacred appeals in establishing brand loyalty.[73] As one group of researchers put it, "Consumption has become a vehicle for experiencing the sacred."[74] Remember the original Nike "Witness" campaign connected buying shoes to the Apostles.

The Gilbert letter's intense emphasis on the most vicious kinds of disloyalty—treason, betrayal, and desertion—in the context of a contractually constructed market makes the mythic fragments of the sacred so obviously incongruent. Ads are not written in the argumentative form of premise and conclusion; they are instead composed of emotionally charged words and images, which short-circuit the consumer's critical faculties. Gilbert's use of this postmodern montage as argument rendered his discourse incoherent.

## PERSONAL REFLECTIONS

We came to this essay out of a series of conversations about the strong public reaction to LeBron James's "Decision." We discovered shared, though usually unspoken, standpoints. First, we both sympathized with LeBron James and found Gilbert's public letter an unwarranted diatribe. Second, we both remembered the bitter battle that Curt Flood had waged to overturn baseball's reserve clause. We knew that the Flood struggle had been filled with the evocative language of slavery and freedom, and we could hear echoes of this racial rhetoric in the present case. Third, we are both distrustful of the ethos of the <market>. Consumerism is a persuasive ideology that dramatically influences nearly all spheres of American life, and many of its appeals hardly deserve the description "rational."

Yet, we also brought different perspectives to the discourse. Adam was fascinated by the intensity of fan identification with the team and the resulting strong emotional response to the "Decision." Ron was struck by the parallels between Joseph McCarthy's use of loyalty during the Red Scare and the evocative phrases in Dan Gilbert's public letter. Ideographic criticism gave us the vehicle with which to meld these two perspectives. Putting to work the ambiguity and intensity of a term to further group interests is the essence of an ideograph.

Like other critics working in the tradition of the "ideological turn," we readily acknowledge that our construction of the truth is a product of our standpoint. We trust we have offered reasonable arguments for the soundness of our conclusions, but we admit that it rests on suspicions about the misuses of <loyalty> to serve establishment interests.

## POTENTIALS AND PITFALLS

Ideographic criticism is especially powerful when applied to discourses that celebrate particular values. This is so for three reasons: (1) Ideographic criticism links the celebration of particular values to the justification of power. (2) Ideographic criticism demonstrates the ways in which a particular celebrated value subordinates and organizes competing values. (3) Ideographic analysis can map alterations in value orientation over time and thus show the changes in a society's public discourse, which reflect changes in the citizenry's public consciousness.

The critic must be careful in generalizing from ideographic analysis. A single speech or a small set of messages may not represent anything particularly important about the public. In fact, the citizenry may resist government leaders' official pronouncements. One lesson we should learn from the fall of the Soviet Union and the communist regimes of Eastern Europe is that the populace often does not accept a regime's justifications for power. Kept in line by the brute force of the state, the citizens apparently never bought into the government's propaganda. When given an opportunity, they quickly seized the chance to topple their countries' leaders.

In our short essay, we tried to illustrate the increasingly problematic grounds for justifying <loyalty>. The James-Gilbert discourses are a symptom of the problems of commitment in a postmodern world.

## IDEOGRAPHIC ANALYSIS TOP PICKS

Cloud, Dana. "The Rhetoric of <Family Values>: Scapegoating, Utopia, and the Privatization of Social Responsibility." *Western Journal of Communication* 62 (1998): 387–419. This essay explores the phrase <family values> as an ideograph. It examines the ideological force of this ideograph and concludes that it works to victimize the poor. It has the force of blaming the poor for their own circumstances and absolving the fortunate of any responsibility for society's disadvantaged.

Condit, Celeste, and John Lucaites. *Crafting Equality: America's Anglo-African Word*. Chicago: University of Chicago Press, 1993. This prize-winning book is an excellent example of a diachronic analysis of ideographs. The authors trace the development of <equality> through American history.

Condit, Celeste, and J. Ann Selzer. "The Rhetoric of Objectivity in the Newspaper Coverage of a Murder Trial." *Critical Studies in Mass Communication* 2 (1985): 197–216. This essay explores the ideological commitment of journalism to the ideograph <objectivity>. In exploring the coverage of a Kansas murder trial, they demonstrate the ironic effect of <objectivity>. The commitment to <objectivity> leads, these authors contend, to reporting that is biased toward the prosecution.

Ewalt, Joshua. "A Colonialist Celebration of National <Heritage>: Verbal, Visual, and Landscape Ideographs at Homestead National Monument of America." *Western Journal of Communication* 75 (2011): 367–385. This essay is one of a growing number of critical analyses that examines the ideograph as a visual image and not just a term in a verbal text.

McGee, Michael Calvin. "An Essay on the Flip Side of Privacy." In *Argument in Transition: Proceedings of the Third Summer Conference on Argumentation*, edited by David Zarefsky, 105–115 (Annandale, VA: Speech Communication Association, 1983). This essay illustrates the ideological complexity of the abortion debate. The abortion debate implicates a series of underlying ideographic tensions among <public>, <private property>, <liberty>, and <equality>.

## NOTES

1. Lloyd F. Bitzer, "The Rhetorical Situation," *Philosophy and Rhetoric* 1 (1968): 3–4.
2. Ibid., 6.
3. Philip Wander makes this same point in commenting on the alleged sterility of neo-Aristotelian (traditional) criticism, which shares many of the same commitments as Bitzer's situational approach. See Philip P. Wander, "The Ideological Turn in Modern Criticism," *Central States Speech Journal* 34 (1983): 1–18.
4. Ibid., 9.
5. Antony Flew, "Ideology," in *A Dictionary of Philosophy* (New York: St. Martin's, 1979), 150.
6. Edward B. Reeves, "Ideology," in *Encyclopedia of Religion and Society* (Walnut Creek, CA: Altamira Press, 1998), 234.
7. Robert T. Craig, "Communication," in *Encyclopedia of Rhetoric* (New York: Oxford University Press, 2001), 135.

8. "Enron Fast Facts," CNN, April 26, 2015, http://www.cnn.com/2013/07/02/us/enron-fast-facts.

9. See David Easton and Jack Dennis, *Children in the Political System: Origins of Political Legitimacy* (New York: McGraw-Hill, 1969).

10. See Stuart Ewen, *Captains of Consciousness: Advertising and the Social Roots of Consumer Culture*, 25th anniversary ed. (New York: Basic Books, 2001).

11. See Hayden White, *Metahistory: The Historical Imagination in Nineteenth-Century Europe* (Baltimore, MD: Johns Hopkins University Press, 1973), 1–42.

12. Terry Eagleton, *Ideology: An Introduction* (London: Verso, 1991), 9.

13. Michael Calvin McGee, "A Materialist's Conception of Rhetoric," in *Explorations in Rhetoric: Studies in Honor of Douglas Ehninger*, edited by Ray E. McKerrow (Glenview, IL: Scott, Foresman, 1982), 24.

14. Ibid., 38.

15. Ibid., 39.

16. Ibid.

17. Ibid., 41.

18. Ibid.

19. Ibid., 43.

20. Dana L. Cloud, "The Rhetoric of <Family Values>: Scapegoating, Utopia, and the Privatization of Social Responsibility," *Western Journal of Communication* 62 (1998): 389.

21. Placing a term or slogan inside angle brackets, <liberty>, has become the conventional way of identifying an ideograph.

22. Michael Calvin McGee, "The 'Ideograph': A Link between Rhetoric and Ideology," *Quarterly Journal of Speech* 66 (1980): 15.

23. Ibid.

24. Ibid.

25. Ibid.

26. Ibid.

27. Ibid., 7.

28. Ibid, 15.

29. For a definition of the Anglo-American liberal tradition, see Claus Mueller, *The Politics of Communication: A Study in the Political Sociology of Language, Socialization and Legitimation* (New York: Oxford University Press, 1973).

30. McGee, "The 'Ideograph,'" 15.

31. Ibid., 15–16.

32. See Michael Calvin McGee, "In Search of the 'People': A Rhetorical Alternative," *Quarterly Journal of Speech* 61 (1975): 235–249.

33. Celeste M. Condit and John L. Lucaites, *Crafting Equality: America's Anglo-African Word* (Chicago: University of Chicago Press, 1993), xii–xiii.

34. McGee, "The 'Ideograph,'" 14.

35. See Condit and Lucaites, *Crafting Equality*.

36. See Maurice Charland, "Constitutive Rhetoric: The Case of the *Peuple Québécois*," *Quarterly Journal of Speech* 73 (1987): 133–150; and McGee, "In Search of the 'People.'"

37. Wayne Brockriede, "Rhetorical Criticism as Argument," *Quarterly Journal of Speech* 60 (1974): 167.

38. Cloud, "The Rhetoric of <Family Values>," 387.

39. Celeste Condit and J. Ann Selzer, "The Rhetoric of Objectivity in the Newspaper Coverage of a Murder Trial," *Critical Studies in Mass Communication* 2 (1985): 197.

40. George P. Fletcher, *Loyalty: An Essay on the Morality of Relationships* (New York: Oxford University Press, 1993), 3.

41. Ibid., 4, 5.

42. See William Leiss, Stephen Kline, Sut Jhally, and Jacqueline Botterill, *Social Communication in Advertising: Consumption in the Marketplace*, 3rd ed. (New York: Routledge, 2005); Neil Postman, *Amusing Ourselves to Death: Public Discourse in the Age of Show Business* (New York: Penguin, 2985), 114–141; and Kenneth L. Hacker, ed., *Presidential Candidate Images* (Lanham, MD: Rowman & Littlefield, 2004).

43. Alasdair MacIntyre, *After Virtue: A Study in Moral Theory*, 2nd ed. (Notre Dame, IN: University of Notre Dame Press, 1984).

44. "Edward Snowden: Computer Programmer (1983–)," *Bio Newsletter*, http://www.biography.com/people/edward-snowden-21262897.

45. Hans H. Bauer, Nicole E. Stokbuerger-Sauer, and Stefanie Exler, "Brand Image and Fan Loyalty in Professional Team Sport: A Refined Model and Empirical Assessment," *Journal of Sport Management* 22 (2008): 206.

46. Ryan Jones, *King James: Believe the Hype—The LeBron James Story* (New York: St. Martin's Griffin, 2005).

47. Benjamin Hochman, "Five-Man Race for MVP a Tossup," *Denver Post*, March 19, 2008.

48. Free agency came about through the collective bargaining efforts of the Major League Baseball Players Association following the loss of the Curt Flood case before the US Supreme Court in *Flood v. Kuhn* (1972).

49. Brian Windhorst, "LeBron Deal has Eye on Future Cap," ESPN, July 14, 2014, http://espn.go.com/nba/story/_/id/11207703/lebron-james-deal-cleveland-cavaliers-2-years-421-million.

50. "#341: Daniel Gilbert," *Forbes: The World's Billionaires*, June 3, 2015, http://www.forbes.com/profile/daniel-gilbert.

51. Scott Soshnick, "James Pushes Cavs Valuation Past Billion-Dollar Mark," *Bloomberg Business*, July 11, 2014, http://www.bloomberg.com/news/articles/2014-07-11/james-pushes-cavs-valuation-past-billion-dollar-mark.

52. "NBA Attendance Report—2015," ESPN, http://espn.go.com/nba/attendance; and "With LeBron James Returning to Cleveland, Cavaliers Tickets Could Be Most Expensive in NBA," *Forbes*, July 11, 2014, http://www.forbes.com/sites/jesselawrence/2014/07/11/if-lebron-james-returns-cavaliers-tickets-could-be-most-expesnive-in-nba.

53. Chris Good, "What Cleveland Lost When It Lost LeBron," *Atlantic*, July 9, 2010, http://www.theatlantic.com/national/archive/2010/07/what-cleveland-lost-when-it-lost-lebron/59480.

54. "Dan Gilbert's Open Letter to Fans: James' Decision a 'Cowardly Betrayal' and Owner Promises a Title before Heat," Cleveland.com, July 8, 2010, http://www.cleveland.com/cavs/index.ssf/2010/07/gilberts_letter_to_fans_james.html.

55. Richard T. Hughes, *Myths Americans Live By* (Urbana: University of Illinois Press, 2003).

56. Gary S. Selby, *Martin Luther King and the Rhetoric of Freedom: The Exodus Narrative in America's Struggle for Civil Rights* (Waco, TX: Baylor University Press, 2008).

57. "Nike Reminds Fans 'We Are All Witnesses,'" NBA.com, June 5, 2007, http://www.nba.com/cavaliers/news/witnesses_070606.html.

58. See Acts 1:8, 1:22, 1:26, 2:32, 3:15, 4:33, 5:32, 10:39, 10:41, 14:17, 15:8, 20:24, 22:15, 22:20, 23:11, 26:16, 28:23.

59. "In Everywhere but Miami, Reaction to LeBron James' Decision Overwhelmingly Negative: National Media Links," Cleveland.com, July 9, 2010, http://www.cleveland.com/cavs/index.ssf/2010/07/as_lebron_james_leaves_clevela.html.

60. LeBron James and Lee Jenkins, "LeBron: I'm Coming Back to Cleveland," *Sports Illustrated*, July 11, 2014, http://www.si.com/nba/2014/07/11/lebron-james-cleveland-cavaliers. Unless otherwise noted, all James's quotations in this chapter come from this letter.

61. Ronald Lee, "Electoral Politics and Visions of Community: Jimmy Carter, Virtue, and the Small Town Myth," *Western Journal of Communication* 59 (1995): 39–60.

62. McGee, "The 'Ideograph,'" 15.

63. John Durham Peters, "John Locke, the Individual, and the Origin of Communication," *Quarterly Journal of Speech* 75 (1989): 387–399; Michael Calvin McGee, "The Flip Side of Privacy," in *Argument in Transition*, ed. David Zarefsky, Malcolm O. Sillars, and Jack Rhodes, 105–115 (Annandale, VA: Speech Communication Association, 1983).

64. Brian Windhorst, "NBA's David Stern Fines Dan Gilbert $100,000 for Outburst, Criticizes LeBron James' TV 'Decision,'" *Plain Dealer*, July 12, 2010, http://www.cleveland.com/cavs/index.ssf/2010/07/nba_commissioner_david_stern_f_1.html. The imagery of slavery swirled around the original Curt Flood legal battle against professional baseball's reserve clause. The paternalistic terminology Donald Sterling used in characterizing his management prerogatives was part of the racial scandal that lead to the NBA's termination of his ownership rights to the Los Angeles Clippers. See Ian O'Conner, "Shame on Stern for Sterling Silence," ESPN, April 30, 2014, http://espn.go.com/losangeles/nba/story/_/id/10857899/shame-david-stern-nba-letting-donald-sterling-stick-around.

65. Windhorst, "NBA's David Stern."

66. Ibid.

67. Clarke E. Cochran, *Character, Community, and Politics* (University: University of Alabama Press, 1982), 25–28; Leonard William Doob, *Patriotism and Nationalism: Their Psychological Foundations* (New Haven, CT: Yale University Press, 1964), 4–9; Morton Grodzins, *The Loyal and the Disloyal: Social Boundaries of Patriotism and Treason* (Chicago: University of Chicago Press, 1956), 21; John H. Schaar, "Loyalty," in *International Encyclopedia of the Social Sciences*, vol. 9, 484–487 (New York: Macmillan, 1968).

68. J. Justin Gustainis, "Demagoguery and Political Rhetoric: A Review of the Literature," *Rhetoric Society Quarterly* 20 (1990): 155–161.

69. Mogens Herman Hanson, *The Athenian Assembly: In the Age of Demosthenes* (New York: Blackwell, 1987), 51.

70. Kurt Eichenwald "ISIS's Enemy List: 10 Reasons the Islamic State Is Doomed," *Newsweek*, September 8, 2014.

71. Fletcher, *Loyalty*, 36.

72. Ibid., 37.

73. See, for example, Russell W. Belk and Melanie Wallendorf, "The Sacred Meanings of Money," *Journal of Economic Psychology* 11 (1990): 35–67; and Priscilla A. La Barbera and Zeynep Gürhan, "The Role of Materialism, Religiosity, and Demographics in Subjective Well-Being," *Psychology and Marketing* 14 (1998): 71–97.

74. Russell W. Belk, Melanie Wallendorf, and John F. Sherry Jr., "The Sacred and the Profane in Consumer Behavior: Theodicy on the Odyssey," *Journal of Consumer Research* 16 (1989): 1.

# III

# EXPANDING OUR CRITICAL HORIZONS

# 15

# An Eclectic Approach to Criticism

*Jim A. Kuypers*

> I have tried to be as eclectic as I possibly can with my professional life, and so far it's been pretty fun.
>
> —Roland Barthes

*Eclectic* and *eclecticism* are frequently misused terms. They have been used to call attention to differences not easily categorized, and also by persons unable to find a common thread among ideas. For instance, consider this use of *eclectic*: "Typically off-year elections are used for two things: one is a sort of testing ground, as a dry run for the next year. And two: you get a real eclectic mix of issues that don't have an over-arching theme but that's a little different this year."[1] What the author actually describes is not an eclectic mixture, but a *hodgepodge*, which is a confusing or heterogeneous mixture. A more accurate use of *eclectic* would be to label as eclectics those who derive their sense of style or taste from a wide variety of sources. Although seemingly diverse, the common link among the sources is the person who puts them all together. For an eclectic, there is a theme. The task for the eclectic critic is to make that theme apparent to others.

When I speak of eclectic criticism, I am not speaking of a jumbled mess of viewpoints presented in an unwieldy manner. The best eclectic criticism takes components of various rhetorical theories and blends them together into a comprehensive whole, all to better explain the workings of an intriguing rhetorical artifact. Pauline Kael wrote that "eclecticism is the selection of the best standards and principles from various systems of ideas. It requires more orderliness to be a pluralist than to apply a single theory. . . . Criticism is exciting because you must use everything you are and everything you know that is relevant."[2] Although some, particularly those who use single perspectives to guide their criticism, might take issue with Kael's assertion about "orderliness," eclectic critics would certainly agree with Kael's depiction of excitement, not to mention Barthes's use of the term *fun*.

Beyond excitement, though, there often lies a broad sense of exploration. Eclectic critics are frequently drawn to extremely diverse rhetorical artifacts, and analysis of these diverse forms of rhetoric necessitates the development of nuanced, flexible, and diverse perspectives of analysis. On this note, theatrical director and producer David Esbjornson wrote,

> I have an eclectic past . . . but I intentionally have pursued that because there are so many interesting points of view that I want to explore. I think I'm not quite as all over the map as maybe people think. There's a certain reason that I have done all those plays. I tend to gravitate to the writers that I think are trying to say something, or who are outside of the center a bit and who are trying to break in and get their point of view expressed.[3]

Eclecticism has a long history. The term is often used to describe ancient philosophers who followed no particular philosophical school, but instead sought to take what was to them the best of established doctrines in order to construct a new system. The original Greek term, *eklektikos*, simply means choosing the best. Diogenes of Appolonia (fifth century BC) was one of the earliest eclectics. By the first century BC, the term *eclectic* was in common use. One of the better-known examples of eclectic philosophers was Cicero, who blended the Stoic, Peripatetic, and New Academic doctrines. As an approach to philosophy and to rhetoric, eclecticism eschews single perspectives and draws its power instead from insights gained from combining multiple theories or perspectives into a blend used for a specific purpose.

Writing of the eclectic critic in particular, Bernard L. Brock, Robert L. Scott, and James W. Chesebro remarked that

> the conscientious eclectic is apt to be more interested in the immediacy of experience than the abstract integrity of a system or method. Such a person will argue that [perspectives] are but more-or-less-complete sets of tools with instructions by which to build scaffoldings and frameworks. They will argue that when what is made is made, the tools are laid aside, the scaffolding torn down, and the framework absorbed. When the eclectic critic does use a [perspective], it is an "open-ended" one that does not force or prescribe a specific [plan] and provides the critic with a great deal of creative decision making. The eclectic approach stresses the critic's ability to assemble and absorb ways of working, subordinating these to the task at hand.[4]

The last sentence is especially noteworthy in that it reinforces the critic's dominant role in producing good criticism. Good critics "absorb" or assimilate theory into their personal perceptions and then bring to bear their eclectically enhanced point of view on the rhetorical artifact. Eclecticism stresses the personality and critical capacities of the critic. On this point Ed Black wrote that it

> is inevitable that any expositor will approach a work from a certain point of view. His frame of reference may be subconscious and unsystematized, but it will assuredly be present, shaping the bias of his interpretation by influencing the direction of his attention, selectively sharpening some and dulling others of his sensibilities, and molding the nuances of his judgment in a thousand imperceptible ways.[5]

In some ways, eclecticism turns the tables, allowing first the critic to influence the perspective and then the perspective to influence the critic.

## CRITICAL ESSAYS

Eclecticism is not for everyone, and despite its strengths, only a minority of critics blend and develop their own framework from which to proceed with criticism. The rest of this chapter explores the inner workings of four eclectically oriented essays. The first is "Cowboys, Angels and Demons: American Exceptionalism and the Frontier Myth in the CW's *Supernatural*," by Joseph M. Valenzano III and Erika Engstrom, published in *Communication Quarterly* 62, no. 5 (2014): 552–568. Valenzano and Engstrom blend television criticism with mythic criticism, religious communication with political communication, and incorporate elements of American exceptionalism in order to produce an eclectic and insightful piece of criticism. The combined approach allows the authors to explain how the television show *Supernatural* enacts a particularly potent message that actually serves a larger American political narrative.

The second is "Texas Vernacular Rock House Structure: Defining 'Home' through Rhetorical Depiction," by Mary Evelyn Collins, published in the *American Communication Journal* 9 (2007): n.p. Collins incorporates elements of rhetorical depiction, theoretical elements of the Arts and Crafts movement, architectural theory, and cluster criticism in order to better understand and appreciate how Texas rock house architecture rhetorically acted to create a spirit of family and home, and also a sense of place.

The third is "Carnivalesque Protest and the Humorless State," by M. Lane Bruner, published in *Text and Performance Quarterly* 25, no. 2 (2005): 136–155. Bruner looks at public protests in two different cultures using elements gleaned from several different theoretical areas that include viewing the "carnivalesque" as a form of public protest and political performance; he also employs theories of democratic citizenship. Through this analysis he provides insight into how Eastern European protests against communist dictatorships prevailed whereas protests against the communist dictatorship in China failed.

The fourth is "From Science, Moral Poetics: Dr. James Dobson's Response to the Fetal Tissue Research Initiative," by Jim A. Kuypers, published in the *Quarterly Journal of Speech* 86, no. 2 (2000): 146–167. Kuypers employs a judgmental analysis combined with Kenneth Burke's distinction between semantic and poetic meaning in order to analyze James Dobson's response to the legalization of fetal tissue research. Ultimately, using dramatistic theory, Kuypers analyzes the motive underpinning Dobson's discourse to understand how Dobson provided a way out of the moral quagmire science has placed humans in by highlighting mankind's ability to morally act.

Since there is no "one way" of performing eclectic criticism, what follows below are the personal comments of the authors of the above-mentioned essays. The authors explain how they feel their work is eclectic and highlight the truly creative aspects of an eclectic style of criticism by focusing on describing the action of creating an eclectic approach to the artifact.

## PERSONAL REFLECTIONS

### Joseph M. Valenzano III on "Cowboys . . ."[6]

Ever since 1995, eyewitnesses around the globe, but particularly in the Americas, reported seeing a small bearlike creature attacking local livestock. In Latin America the creature was dubbed the *chupacabra*, but to date it has not been found, and no sightings have been independently verified. This contemporary legend has, over the course of the last twenty years, been the subject of books, movies, and television shows. In fact, a popular way of saying you have attained the unattainable or found the unfindable is to say you have "found the Chupacabra." I like to think that in my own work, which explores the intersection of religion, politics, and popular culture, I have found the chupacabra—because I get to watch a lot of television and movies to complete my research!

I have always been interested in politics, and when I was younger one of my favorite television shows was *The West Wing*. I loved how the show seemed to mirror and discuss current issues and events. I also grew up Catholic, exposed to all the ceremonial trappings and extensive theological readings that come with that particular faith. Additionally, I have always had a very wild imagination, with a keen interest in science fiction and the supernatural. When I first began my career studying communication, I focused on politics, but soon my interests became more varied. For instance, I started to notice the same ceremonial dimensions in politics that occurred in my church. I began to see plenty of overlap between religious faith and the modern popular culture I consumed. Thus, my chupacabra emerged—I knew I wanted to explore how the modern penny dreadful[7] popular culture influenced the understanding of religion and politics for its consumers, and so I undertook the arduous mission of watching a lot of television and reading a wide array of communication research.

There are those who study media effects, those who explore popular culture, others who examine rhetorical theory, and a bevy of scholars who focus their attention on political and religious communication; however, very few bring the literature from all of these areas to bear on a text. In my work I begin with a text that "tells me something," and in my case it's usually a television show or movie. That "something" is a subtextual message that connects the imagination of the producers of the media artifact with a commentary on social, political, religious, and economic issues faced in the real world. I am fascinated with how these connections are made in the artifact and how they produce commentaries on contemporary events and issues that viewers often don't overtly recognize. To explain how the text accomplishes the "something," I noticed I needed to draw on literature from a wide range of fields, thus creating an eclectic criticism of the text. Let me share with you an example of this type of work.

A colleague of mine and I had a chance conversation one day regarding a common interest in a show called *Supernatural*, which airs on the CW network. We both were really interested in the story, but also noticed that it brought elements of multiple faiths together in a single show in a way no other program to our knowledge ever did. The result of this conversation was a set of studies regarding the intersection of politics and religion on television. The first study, published in the *Journal of Media and Religion*, used content analysis to find that *Supernatural* actually privileges the Catholic faith over other religious traditions—something that typically fails on television. The second study, which appeared in the *Journal of Communication and Religion*, analyzed the apocalyptic plotline of the show's first five seasons, illustrating how it functioned as a form of homily to a secular audience. The third article, though, serves as a terrific example of the eclectic nature of the criticism I like to conduct.

In "Cowboys, Angels and Demons: American exceptionalism and the frontier myth in the CW's *Supernatural*," we dove even deeper into our analysis of the show. Not only did it have a distinct religious message, but that religious content also served a larger political narrative as well. American exceptionalism is the idea that the United States is qualitatively better than Europe, and in some versions of the myth the United States is ordained by God to serve as the beacon of freedom for the rest of the globe.[8] This is a largely political message, but the "chosen by God" portion brings in a uniquely religious perspective that cannot be ignored.

We blended the religious notion of American exceptionalism with elements of the frontier myth. Specifically, the frontier myth has at its core certain elements of the American Wild West and expansion westward. In a wildly interesting essay on the Donner Party, Mary Stuckey identified four elements of the frontier myth that helped explain the plotlines of *Supernatural*. They were (1) an erasure of indigenous people and others who do not fit mainstream notions of the acceptable; (2) the triumph of American civilization over the wilderness;

(3) the allowance for individual aggression when it benefits the larger community's survival; and (4) the idea of movement, key to the notion of Manifest Destiny.[9] Additionally, scholars have noted other key elements of the frontier myth, such as the heroic cowboy character.[10] We then used this frame to explore the episodes of the show in the contemporary context in which they appeared in an effort to learn how they reflected and deflected perspectives about current events. What made the case for this type of analysis even clearer were certain statements made by the show's creative team that made it sound as if they wanted to push an image of a rugged American family fighting in a supernatural wilderness.[11]

So the recipe for our approach in this essay began with the premise that media, especially television, function as today's "cultural storyteller,"[12] advancing ideas, values, and beliefs through the depiction of myths central to a community.[13] We then conducted our analysis by taking the core elements of the myth of American exceptionalism, especially the part about the United States being chosen by God, and the central characteristics of the frontier myth and applied them to the episodes of *Supernatural*. The critical frame was one part media, one part political myth, with a dash of religion. We were not really concerned with demonstrating that the show contained these myths (after all, that would simply be a cookie-cutter analysis). Instead our research questions were focused on asking, What was the payoff of that approach? How did it contribute to theory? and What did it do to the messages being sent to the primarily teenage audience?

The fact is, what we did was not simply scholarship about television or religion or politics, but rather all three. We borrowed from media studies, religion, and political rhetoric to help understand the central messages of the show and the influence they have on how viewers might understand the United States and/or religion. Eclectic criticism such as ours requires researchers to fully immerse themselves in the text, current events, and a multitude of different theoretical perspectives. The more perspectives from which you can draw analytical tools, the more enriching the analysis will be.

### Mary Evelyn Collins on "Texas . . ."

I have always been intrigued with a particular style of house that is very common in the Southwestern United States, from Missouri to New Mexico, but most especially in Texas. This interest was prompted by the fact that the only house that my parents actually built was a bungalow in the "rock house" style. It was a transitional time in their lives, and this was perceived to be the house that would become their retirement home. I was not quite three when we moved in, but my older brothers were teenagers, the eldest in college. Less than two years later, with a better retirement plan promised, there was a job change and a move to another town. That house still stands, with the pecan trees my parents planted looming high above its roof, a survivor of Texas storms, a flood, and assorted families with active children.

What began to interest me in recent years was that, with the return of the bungalow in popular new home building, there was a return to Arts and Crafts movement elements used in the new "retro"-look homes. So much reminded me of the charming front porches and roof lines of the Texas rock houses.[14] The version of the Arts and Crafts, or Craftsman, bungalow in America emerged in the eastern United States with stucco walls and river stone columns or brick walls with river stone or stacked stone trim elements. In the far west, California particularly, the bungalow had stucco walls and some flat stone trim. Many "California bungalows" had a Spanish look, with tile roofs and side or rear patios rather than front porches. All over America whole neighborhoods of bungalows were built from 1900 to the early 1940s.[15] Their popularity disappeared after World War II when the new ranch-style home came into vogue.

The bungalow style in Texas used local stone, usually gathered from fields, pastures, and riverbanks. The stones are set vertically rather than horizontally, making the outside wall look like freckles, with the various colors shown on the wide, flat side of the rocks in irregular arrangement. This arrangement was economical, since fewer stones were needed for the outside wall construction than would be needed for a wall with stone set horizontally. The style was used in small, humble dwellings and in large, expensive homes, both in the countryside and in the city.

As I continued to explore the history, I was stunned by the loyalty to these rock bungalows and began to notice that elements from the original designs were appearing in new buildings. There had been many examples of this style elongated to look similar to the ranch-style house, but in recent years porches, arches, and side patios or terraces appeared in new homes. Even some exterior sections are found in the multicolored flat rock arrangement, although the majority of the exterior might be brick, white limestone, or stucco.

Certainly one can see that this form of architecture has become quite influential and has been receiving preservation interest. Here the key word is *influential*. For if influential, then rhetorical (or, paraphrasing Kenneth Burke, any good communication is rhetorical). Any influential architecture is rhetorical in its visual form. From this beginning premise, I began to look for some rhetorical means—a perspective—to help in the analysis process in order to better understand how this type of home is influential and why.

My first thought was of Burke's cluster criticism, because this type of criticism has been used very successfully in analyzing visual elements in art, architecture, and photography.[16] Looking at the history of the Texas rock house led me to believe that the house itself was highly identified with the values and concerns of those trans-South emigrants who made their way to Texas in order to start a new life in a new place. Burke's idea of identification as consubstantiality,[17] when some individual and some property share a substance, seemed very applicable to emigrants' intention to build a home in the new place that was "solid," "permanent," and connected with the very soil that would bring them their livelihood: the rock being the substance and the values the personal intention. However, this identification was only one part of the problem to be addressed in the rhetorical analysis. The question of regionality or the influence of locale and culture on the nature of the house style and the choice of building materials made it necessary for me to look for additional tools with which to analyze the influence of this particular style.

This brought to mind the rhetorical depiction method developed by Michael Osborn in a seminal essay in the collection *Form, Genre, and the Study of Political Discourse*.[18] Rhetorical depiction as explained by Osborn has five functions: presentation, intensification, identification, implementation, and reaffirmation. Each one of these functions must be addressed in the analysis in order to have a successful discussion of rhetorical depiction and the ultimate outcome of the rhetoric. In the case of the Texas rock house there seemed to be some very appropriate questions to pose from each of the five functions.

First, presentation can be repetitive, that is, showing us what we already know, or innovative, which shows us a new way of knowing when the past no longer works for us.[19] Innovative presentation depends on the use of metaphor to connect to the new way of knowing. Intensification is the expression of heightened feeling, that is, how we see the rhetoric as instigating reaction.[20] Identification, as in Burke, is a sharing of characteristics, but with a narrative quality, identification with the community story.[21] Implementation is the "What do we do?" question. How is the message of the rhetoric put into action? Osborn adds, "Implementation includes the classical idea of deliberative rhetoric for it has to do with the designs of the future."[22] Osborn also asserts that "implementation can be defined as applied identification."[23] The last function of rhetorical depiction is reaffirmation, which means that the rhetoric brings the community back to its identity with its values in a common "appreciation." "Reaffirmative depiction guards the sacred fire around which a nation or a subculture gathers periodically to warm itself in recognition of its being."[24]

The Texas rock house is evidence that families, most new to the state and region, had deliberately decided to establish homes in order to make a new start in new communities. Herein began a new subculture with its shared values. By incorporating insights gained from both Burke and Osborn, I was better able to share with others the fascinating rhetorical strength of the Texas rock houses. My approach was eclectic in that I had to blend rhetorical perspectives in order to better appreciate the underlying rhetorical dynamics that were hidden in the architecture of these houses. In the visual form, such as architecture, there are various elements that connect with values and purpose for those who live within the dwelling. This form of eclecticism is not a jumble or hodgepodge, but an evolved process that began with the classical scholars who highly influenced Kenneth Burke and then Burke influenced Michael Osborn. A close reading of either Burke or Osborn will reveal a developmental path of true eclecticism: the ability to see the influential elements in all of communication, no matter the form or genre.

### M. Lane Bruner on "Carnivalesque . . ."

Revolutionary discourses are interesting things to study. Thomas Jefferson once famously remarked that "a little rebellion" now and then was a good thing, "as necessary in the political world as storms in the physical."[25] Only the people's stormy uprisings, he believed, ensured a continued focus on republican virtue. But what are these storms? Are they all alike? What is their relationship to the virtuous state? How do we know, for example, when rebellions produce more or less freedom? How can we recognize the best kind of rebellions?

An excellent opportunity to study rebellion was provided in the late 1980s as peoples rose up in communist regimes from China to East Germany to demand more political and economic freedoms. As a rhetoric scholar interested in the relationship between discourse and politics, and how different patterns of communication create different types of political communities, I was eager to study how these rebellions worked (or not). I was especially curious to learn why the rebellions against the Soviet Union were generally nonviolent, productive of more freedom, and helped to develop the rule of law, while those against communism in China were violent, did not produce more political freedom, and made no impact on authoritarian rule.

The methods and theories most appropriate for scholars are driven by the questions they pursue, and those who want to study the world-historical relationship between the rhetorical and the political can hardly rely on one theory or method, or even a small combination of theories and methods. Instead, the *eclectic* critic is also required to be well versed in political, economic, cultural, and philosophical matters as well. This is where eclectic critics' strengths come into play: their relatively broad theoretical and historical background enables them to study the broader relationships between the ways people talk and behave and the kinds of communities they create as a result of that talk and behavior.

To be an eclectic critic, in the sense expressed here, one must follow the sage advice of Cicero and Quintilian, two famous rhetoricians concerned with the development of the virtuous orator: they must be *highly eclectic* in their learning.[26] The virtuous rhetor persuades to improve the community, but a person cannot improve the community unless he or she is exceptionally wise. To be truly eloquent, according to Cicero, the virtuous rhetor must be able to distinguish good from evil, the desirable from the undesirable, the profitable from the unprofitable, all the virtues and vices and how they arise and are transformed, the difference between just and unjust states, as well as to understand the common sense of mankind, the laws of nature, moral duties, and more. One can hardly expect to be a good *critic* of persuasive acts if unfamiliar with the learning required of virtuous persuaders themselves. Nor can the eclectic critic risk being a dilettante, knowing just a little bit about everything. As Quintilian noted, "a little learning is a dangerous thing."[27] Instead, the responsible eclectic critic must seriously study the history of ideas, comparative law, aesthetics, and any other number of similarly important subjects. The guiding principle behind all of the work of the eclectic rhetorical critic is this: what theoretical, historical, and methodological tools must be brought to bear to investigate the world-historical question at hand.

To prepare for my study of rebellion, for example, I first had to decide what my objects of study and guiding research question would be. I then had to decide what I needed to know in order to engage in such a study. I decided that, building upon my prior research on Russia (i.e., on public memory and national identity in Russia during the collapse of communism, and on the rhetorical and political dimensions of the subsequent transition to capitalism), I would limit my study to the rebellions against the Soviet Union.[28] My larger research question, however, led me to expand this initial plan: I wanted to know *why* those rebellions were so successful, so I decided to compare them to a failure. Thus, I also studied the tragic 1989 rebellion against communism in China.

I started exploring this question about productive rebellions by obtaining numerous accounts and histories of the political, economic, and cultural histories of the Soviet Union and China, and then of the rebellions in the old Soviet states and the massacre at Tiananmen Square in Beijing in 1989. One thing became immediately clear, other than the obvious fact that the political, economic, and cultural conditions in both countries were quite different: the protests against the Soviets were generally comic, while those against Chinese communists were anything but. I learned that in Poland, East Germany, Ukraine, the former Czechoslovakia, and elsewhere, resistance against the state, when most successful, was "carnivalesque," that the carnivalesque was a public and comic way of reversing "normal" social roles, and that the carnivalesque had a long and interesting history in Europe.

Not yet deeply understanding the carnivalesque, I next had to obtain the very best studies related to that concept. Here I learned that, from at least Ancient Rome up until the nineteenth century, it was a European custom to have official days set aside when community norms would be comically turned upside down. The master would be the servant and the servant the master. Some scholars saw this strange discursive practice as a means for the powerful to strengthen their grip on society by providing well-managed opportunities to release social tensions; others, however, argued that moments of carnival were excellent opportunities for disempowered people to send serious political messages under the protective cover of "just joking!"

As an eclectic critic, I first enjoyed studying the political, economic, and cultural histories of Russia and China, then studying accounts of the protests themselves, then studying the carnivalesque, and then studying performance theory and social movement theory. If I wanted to study these comic and serious public performances and understand how and why they worked (or did not), these were simply parts of the puzzle I sought to solve.

Here is what the picture looked like once the pieces were in place. In the states attempting to separate themselves from a crumbling Soviet Empire, the initially funny thing was the overly serious communist state officials themselves. Here is an illustrative example. In Poland, during the crackdown on the Solidarity movement, which paradoxically was a workers' movement against a communist state that purportedly represented the interests of the working classes, state employees went around the major cities painting big circles over pro-Solidarity graffiti, a practice that seemed especially ridiculous to some Polish dissidents. The dissidents decided, therefore, to go out at night and repaint the circles as elves, with little feet, hands, and a hat. Over the next couple of years, little elves began to appear everywhere, but the significance of the elf was unclear to state officials. Dissidents would do other silly things such as go in groups to the local zoos and demand "freedom for the bears" while singing communist songs and giving out candy to children. When arrested—though the police had no idea what these crazy people were doing—the news images of happy young people ironically singing communist songs and demanding freedom for the bears were clear enough to everyday citizens: the Soviet Union has always been symbolized by the bear.

Months later, on Children's Day, thousands of children came out of their houses dressed like elves! What was the state to do? The people identified themselves as comic characters, like Smurfs, defending the ethical state and protesting for everything from clean air to inexpensive toilet paper. Eventually, and without directly confronting the state, but instead using abstract symbols to communicate comically, the revolutions against the Soviet Union were, for the most part, peaceful and successful. This is not to say that they were successful *only* because of this widespread comic tactic. Still, the tactic worked in large part because of the cultural, economic, and political contexts in which it was used.

There was nothing "funny," however, in China, when dissidents gathered on the central public square in Beijing to demand more political liberty. The Chinese situation was quite different from the situation in the former Soviet territories. The Chinese state was economically and politically stronger. The communist leadership was already preparing to turn the country toward capitalism, but certainly not toward greater political liberties. Ultimately the protest was crushed. Tanks and gunmen opened fire on the protesters, killing thousands. Today, the vast majority of people in China have no memory of the massacre, since it has been erased from their public memory (e.g., the event is not taught in schools, memorial images or tapes are not shown on television, and references to the massacre are consistently filtered out of Chinese Internet search systems).

My initial investigation concluded, therefore, that carnivalesque tactics were best employed under specific political, economic and cultural conditions, which I outlined in my study. When deployed in most of the former Soviet territories, they helped to transform them into more economically and politically liberal states. Conversely, I concluded that comic tactics were not used in China, and serious strategies did not work at all.

When this study was concluded, I attempted to describe the specific tactics that were most successfully used, and in what specific contexts, in order to apply them to present-day protests against present-day injustices in other political contexts. Today, for example, groups are using carnivalesque tactics against large corporations, against transnational organizations such as the World Bank, and in support of environmental protection and nuclear disarmament. On the whole, however, they have not often been successful. Why? How can we apply the lessons learned by the anticommunist protests to fight for greater social justice today so that these "storms" can indeed lead to more just states?

In sum, to answer my initial research question (i.e., what constitutes a successful rebellion?), as we have seen, I first had to rely on my prior work on political transformation and public memory in the former Soviet Union, as well as histories and personal accounts of the rebellions of the late 1980s, and they, in turn, led me to study the carnivalesque. Then, however, I actually had to closely study the protest tactics themselves, for these were my "texts." Yes, I was also interested in what the protesters would say and what others would say about them, but I was also interested in the way the protesters communicated their messages through embodied performances. This required studying performance theory and social movement theory to better understand how the comic wave gained momentum. This, as if to complete the research circle, required knowing a lot about economic and political policies in the former Soviet Union and China, and how shifting economic and political policies contributed to varied social and political conditions. Only within this larger context was the function of the rhetorical artifact, the variously situated protest tactics, clear.

Of course, not all rhetorical criticism explores world-historical questions, nor does it try to improve the human condition. For scholars seeking to understand, for example, the dominant tropes and figures in a speech, or the principal metaphors in an advertisement, or the generic expectations in an inaugural address, one primary method and a handful of theoretical concepts may suffice. To critique the discursive construction of national, racial, gendered, or class identities, however, the critic must begin to move into a wider range of methods and theories, as well as broader cultural, political, and economic matters. In the same manner, to critique the larger world-historical relationship between identity and statecraft, and to determine the most virtuous forms of rhetoric, requires even more, just as it would were one to wish to become a virtuous orator. One can never feel completely successful in such an endeavor, given the limits of human understanding, but the potential payoff for the attempt can be great.

### Jim A. Kuypers on "From Science . . ."

Years ago I came across a letter written by James Dobson, then president of Focus on the Family. The letter was distributed to over two million constituents of Focus on the Family and concerned the 1993 Fetal Tissue Research Initiative, which legalized scientific experimentation on aborted fetuses. Dobson spoke out against this initiative, in particular calling attention to the immoral nature of the practice, making biblical analogies, and making predictions of eventual cloning of humans for spare body parts.[29]

The letter intrigued me on several levels, and I wanted to study it further. First, Dobson had an enormous potential impact. The audience for his monthly letters was then over two million, but his potential radio audience, to which he read the entire letter, approached 200 million in North America and 550 million worldwide. What were these audience members being asked to believe? Dobson's detractors had called him a televangelist and doctrinal speaker in the past, but this seemed simplistic criticism of someone with such a large multinational and diverse audience. I was interested in discovering whether his letters contained elements of indoctrination, or whether he was communicating truly to a worldwide audience, attempting persuasion rather than indoctrination. Dobson's letter was also noteworthy because it successfully brought together the resources of scientific and moral language. The letter seemed to be using science to argue against a scientific practice; moreover, it appeared to be asking for individual moral action in the face of an impersonal science. I was curious to discover how all of this was being accomplished. Just why did this letter have so much power as I read it? Finally, it simply interested me, having elements of science, Jewish history, God's wrath, individual morality, futuristic predictions, and charismatic appeal.

As I pondered how to go about exploring my questions, I soon realized that no single perspective would do the job I wanted it to do. So, to understand the rich moral culture Dobson's letter represents and reaches out to, I examined it in three stages: first, I performed a judgmental analysis of the letter in order to determine what Dobson's potential reading audience was being asked to believe. I sought also to understand how Dobson met the needs of his regular readers and was able to appeal to other than his usual audience, even while eschewing the type of discursive strategies often employed by doctrinal speakers. Second, using Kenneth Burke's distinction between semantic and poetic meaning as a starting point, I examined Dobson's discourse as a moral-poetic response to the amoral stance of scientific discourse. Finally, I undertook an inquiry of the motive underpinning Dobson's discourse that allowed me to better understand the actions of Dobson's envisioned moral agent.

The end result was a *method* of analysis (criticism) that blended *perspectives* (judgmental analysis and Burkean dramatism—namely, moral-poetic language and motivational analysis) into a critical point of view. This flexible combination allowed me to study the letter on three different levels, thereby more fully explaining the inner and outer workings of the letter better than if I had used any one perspective alone.

What I found amazed me. Judgmental analysis allowed me to discover that Dobson based his initial argumentative appeals upon the language of science (factual, secularly authoritative); however, halfway through his letter he resorted to a different strategy and shifted to adjudicative appeals (judgments relying upon some type of code) based upon the factual evidence he had already submitted as true. This new strategy took on a moral-poetic dimension that acted in opposition to the scientific discourse: scientific discourse (that allows for fetal tissue research) gave way to a moral-poetic discourse designed to allow for individual moral action. The moral-poetic and motivational portions allowed me to discover how Dobson pitted medical research (science) against moral action; used what Kenneth Burke called "poor semantics" (scientism: what society believes to be science; science given the status of a public philosophy) as support for his moral interpretation; and then provided a way out of the moral quagmire science has placed humans in by highlighting our ability to morally act, thereby initiating the possibility for an individual to act morally to achieve societal redemption.

## POTENTIALS AND PITFALLS

As with the other perspectives covered in this book, an eclectic approach to criticism has both potentials and pitfalls. When it works well, it certainly offers the critic a great deal of flexibility, and its potential to allow for nuanced insights and new theoretical understandings is quite high. The critic has great freedom to explore, and the potential for allowing greater personality into the criticism certainly exists. However, if a critic does not fully develop the new point of view before undertaking the criticism, the results could be scattered and meaningless observations in place of genuine criticism. In short, the effort to produce criticism might devolve into a hodgepodge of poorly related theoretical tidbits and unrelated insights. Another concern is that it is particularly easy for a critic to construct a point of view that will find exactly what that critic wants to find. Then there is the burden of acquiring enough knowledge in order to practice eclectic criticism. By this I mean that if a critic wishes to use parts of several different perspectives, theories, and ideas in order to derive a new point of view, that critic must first obtain a healthy working knowledge of all the perspectives, theories, and ideas that will be used.

Eclectic criticism offers an amazing amount of freedom in crafting an approach to examine a rhetorical artifact. We must remember, though, that imagination and knowledge go hand in hand. In order for you to create imaginative criticism you must have a great deal of knowledge on different subjects, and so eclectic criticism very often necessitates that you spend considerable time exploring new subjects. Although this can be quite exciting (and the rewards of increased knowledge, the exposure to new ideas, only serves to enrich one's criticism and enhance one's quality of life), it is a step that must be taken with deliberateness and care.

So, it is not without caution that one should approach eclectic criticism. Freedom without responsible constraints is quite often harmful. In addition to the demands upon one's time, there does exist a danger in that it can be easy to play fast and loose with the theories one uses. It can be all too easy for a critic to put together a patchwork of theoretical bits without explaining well their interconnected qualities—the unifying element. And that is a key to good eclectic criticism; the critic must present the unifying idea behind using the different theories to explain the rhetorical artifact.

## ECLECTIC CRITICISM TOP PICKS

In some ways you have already been exposed to a portion of my top picks in eclectic criticism when you read the commentary about the four essays above. There are certainly more fine examples of eclectic criticism from which to choose. Below I list two articles and a book chapter that I feel provide additional grounding in eclectic criticism should you choose to pursue this type of criticism.

Brock, Bernard L., Robert L. Scott, and James W. Chesebro, eds. *Methods of Rhetorical Criticism: A Twentieth-Century Perspective*, 3rd ed., 88–95. Detroit: Wayne State University Press, 1989. The authors provide commentary on eclectic criticism and link it with what they call the experiential perspective. Thoughtful and insightful, this is highly recommended reading if eclectic criticism is of interest to you.

Gunn, Joshua. "The Rhetoric of Exorcism: George W. Bush and the Return of Political Demonology." *Western Journal of Communication* 68, no. 1 (Winter 2004): 1–23. A beautifully written example of eclectic criticism that examines President George W. Bush's speeches following 9/11. Gunn combines a close textual analysis with elements of biblical metaphor, mythic, genre, and psychoanalytic criticism.

Rosenfield, Lawrence W. "The Anatomy of Critical Discourse." *Speech Monographs* 25, no. 1 (1968): 50–69. Rosenfield provides valuable insight into the nature and varieties of critical discourse, as well as the nature of reason giving and logic in criticism. He explains critical discourse in a manner that opens possibilities for textual analysis that benefits an eclectic approach.

## NOTES

1. "Kristina Wilfore Quotes," ThinkExist.com, http://en.thinkexist.com/quotation/typically-off-year-elections-are-used-for-two/984893.html.

2. Pauline Kael, *I Lost It at the Movies* (Boston: Little, Brown, 1964), 309. I first came across this quotation in Bernard L. Brock, Robert L. Scott, and James W. Chesebro, eds., *Methods of Rhetorical Criticism: A Twentieth-Century Perspective*, 3rd ed. (Detroit: Wayne State University Press, 1989), 89.

3. "David Esbjornson Quotes," ThinkExist.com, http://en.thinkexist.com/quotation/i-have-an-eclectic-past-but-i-intentionally-have/737562.html.

4. Brock, Scott, and Chesebro, *Methods of Rhetorical Criticism*, 89.

5. Edwin Black, "Plato's View of Rhetoric," in *Readings in Rhetoric*, ed. Lionel Crocker and Paul A. Carmack (Springfield, IL: Charles C. Thomas, 1965), 68.

6. Excerpt written by Joseph M. Valenzano III.

7. A penny dreadful was a form of serial literature in the nineteenth century that sold for one penny. They were released each week and focused on sensational stories about detectives, monsters, and the supernatural. They were printed on cheap pulp paper (and as a result were sometimes called pulp fiction) and targeted a younger working male demographic. For links to several examples, see http://vichist.blogspot.com/2008/11/penny-dreadfuls.html.

8. Trevor B. McCrisken, *American Exceptionalism and the Legacy of Vietnam: U.S. Foreign Policy since 1974* (New York: Palgrave Macmillan, 2003).

9. Mary E. Stuckey, "The Donner Party and the Rhetoric of Westward Expansion," *Rhetoric and Public Affairs* 14, no. 2 (2011): 229–260.

10. Ray Allen Billington, *Land of Savagery, Land of Promise: The European Image of the American Frontier in the Nineteenth Century* (Norman: University of Oklahoma Press, 1981); Richard W. Slatta, "Making and Unmaking Myths of the American Frontier," *European Journal of American Culture* 29, no. 2 (2010): 81–92.

11. "Ask Eric," *Supernatural Magazine* 1, no. 3 (April/May 2009): 95.

12. Stewart M. Hoover, *Mass Media Religion: The Social Sources of the Electronic Church* (Newbury Park, CA: Sage, 1988), 241.

13. David Thorburn, "Television as an Aesthetic Medium," *Critical Studies in Mass Communication* 4 (1987): 161–173.

14. This particular movement of revived interest is well documented in several publications. The most comprehensive is *American Bungalow Magazine*, published by the John Brinkmann Design Office, Santa Monica, CA.

15. Chicago is known for its bungalow neighborhoods, featuring houses that are narrow to facilitate more house on a narrow lot, with the front door on the side of the house, with the front room window wall nearest the street. Denver features bungalow neighborhoods with brick bungalows, both single story and story and a half, with front porches and garages.

16. See the discussion in Sonja K. Foss, *Rhetorical Criticism: Exploration and Practice*, 4th ed. (Carbondale, IL: Waveland Press, 2009), 63–96.

17. Kenneth Burke, *A Rhetoric of Motives* (1950; Berkeley: University of California Press, 1969), 41.

18. Michael Osborn, "Rhetorical Depiction," in *Form, Genre, and the Study of Political Discourse*, ed. Herbert W. Simons and Aram A. Aghazarian (Columbia: University of South Carolina Press, 1986), 79–107.

19. Ibid., 82–86.

20. Ibid., 86.

21. Ibid., 89–92.

22. Ibid., 93.

23. Ibid., 92.

24. Ibid., 95.

25. Jefferson's opinions, expressed in a letter to Colonel Edward Carrington on January 16, 1787, proved to be controversial in the wake of the French Revolutions and Shays Rebellion, two rebellions against the upper classes. Cited in Gerald Stourz, *Alexander Hamilton and the Idea of Republican Government* (Stanford, CA: Stanford University Press, 1970), 34.

26. See, for example, Cicero's daunting list in *De Oratore*, in *Cicero: On Oratory and Orators*, trans. J. S. Watson (Carbondale: Southern Illinois University Press, 1986), 100. Quintilian wrote that the ideal orator

must be a good person whose character is shaped by philosophy, for rhetoric is a *virtue*. See the *Institutio Oratoria*, vol. 1, ed. Charles E. Little (Nashville, TN: George Peabody College for Teachers, 1951).

27. *Institutio Oratoria*, 23.

28. See M. Lane Bruner, *Strategies of Remembrance: The Rhetorical Dimensions of National Identity Construction* (Columbia, SC: South Carolina University Press, 2002); and M. Lane Bruner and Viatcheslav Morozov, eds., *Market Democracy in Post Communist Russia* (Leeds, England: Wisdom House, 2005).

29. A mere five years later, all that Dobson suggested materialized in science circles. For example, see the December 8, 1998, BBC News article, "Human Spare-Part Cloning Set for Approval," http://news.bbc.co.uk/1/hi/sci/tech/230002.stm. By 2004, British scientists were given formal approval to clone human embryos for "therapeutic purposes." Antony Barnett and Robin McKie, "UK to Clone Human Cells," *The Observer*, June 13, 2004, http://www.guardian.co.uk/society/2004/jun/13/health.research.

# 16

# Critical Rhetoric

## An Orientation toward Criticism

*Raymie E. McKerrow*

Rhetorical criticism has had a long and distinguished history within the communication discipline. Although my purpose here is not to chronicle that history, it is important to recognize that our current endeavors have been made possible by working from our extension or alteration of earlier approaches. Critical approaches outlined in detail in other chapters of this text were based on earlier work, just as future approaches will be built upon, or emerge as counters to, current scholarly perspectives on what constitutes a useful approach.[1] The perspective labeled **critical rhetoric** emerged similarly—it was an outgrowth of key developments in critical inquiry in the 1970s–1980s as critics sought new ways to answer questions about specific discursive events. We had moved through a period in which a "public address" approach dominated scholarly inquiry in focusing on "great speakers" and their speeches.

As protests abounded during the tumultuous years of the civil rights movement and the Vietnam War, in particular, scholars began to critique older approaches as insufficient in analyzing protest discourse. As one example, Herb Simons's now classic essay on social movement rhetoric offered new tools for the critic; his work stimulated others to provide additional critical tools.[2] As early as 1972, Philip Wander and Steven Jenkins challenged the then-conventional approach to criticism in an essay titled "Rhetoric, Society, and the Critical Response."[3] At the time they were writing, the critic stood apart from the discourse and analyzed it in a purported objective fashion—his or her own political stance, and what was thought about the values of the discourse being examined were considered off limits. Their conclusion with respect to making clear one's own political stance and addressing values implicit or explicit in a discursive act is worth repeating here: "The purpose of writing criticism is to share a world of meaning with other human beings. . . . The critic offers, along with a particular judgment, and way of judging, a definition of being. . . . [T]he critic is but one human being trying to communicate with other human beings. Criticism, at its best, is informed talk about matters of importance."[4]

A decade later, Wander followed up with an essay, "The Ideological Turn in Modern Criticism,"[5] that captured the conversation that was occurring at that time. This essay went beyond the "critical response" to articulate what the aim of such criticism might be: to engage readers with judgments about what thought and/or action might follow from the critical appraisal of a given event. In essence, the critic goes beyond a description of "what happened" to "what should have happened" and/or "what should happen now." This was a dramatic "turn" toward a new engagement with events in the world and the critic's role as an "ideological critic." In its broadest sense (and there are many definitions of the term), **ideology** captures the worldview of a person, group, community, and/or society at a given moment in time. As I write, a particular event is consuming our attention—the killing of an iconic lion, Cecil, by a big-game hunter. The rationale for trophy hunting may escape those whose worldview includes preservation of endangered species, but for those inside this enterprise, it seems the most natural act to undertake. Worldviews thus differ, as positions taken may result in contrary beliefs and actions (think of the divergence in views between Tea Party members and other Republicans over matters of importance to both). As another example, the oft-used phrase "political correctness," more than likely expressed in a disparaging tone, gives a name to a difference in ideological **frames**[6] between those who see language as potentially demeaning or denigrating of the dignity of others, and those who see such concerns as trivial nonsense. An important point for us to remember is that the critic gives voice to his or her own ideological commitments in the act of evaluating the discourse of others. A "conservative leaning" critic may well come to different conclusions than another like-minded critic, and could agree on occasion with a "liberal leaning" critic. Thus, ideological stances are not tidy, discreet positions that preclude differences in judgment or the possibility of agreement across differences; nonetheless, the move in this direction among critics was a precursor to the articulation of what has become known as the "critical rhetoric project." That project takes its cue from Wander's conclusion: "Criticism takes an ideological stance when it recognizes the existence of powerful vested interests benefiting from and consistently urging politics and technology that threaten life on this planet . . . and commends rhetorical analyses not only of the actions implied but also of the interests represented."[7]

## STARTING POINTS: CRITICAL RHETORIC

What is meant by "critical rhetoric," and what does it mean to use it as a way to understand or analyze rhetorical practice? What's the point of criticism if judgment is not reached in some sense—so that we know what we think about an event? How should one frame critical rhetorical practice? Is it best conceived as a formalized *method* of rhetorical analysis? Is it the only way, or just another way, to critically appraise discursive events?

In what follows, I respond to the questions introduced above in underscoring the thesis that critical rhetoric is best viewed as a fluid and flexible **orientation**, not a formal, rule-governed method. It has never been intended to serve—either primarily or secondarily—as a conventional rhetorical perspective. I have yet to explain what it means to suggest that orientation is the preferred frame within which critical rhetoric operates. I take my cue from Kenneth Burke: "Orientation is thus a bundle of judgments as to how things were, how they are, and how they may be." He goes on to note that "orientation is a reading from 'what is' to 'what may be.'"[8] How you see the world conditions how you respond to events within it.

Thus, the adoption of an orientation—in all that the term embodies—is the best way to ensure that critical rhetoric is applied to the fullest of its emancipatory potential (meaning its ability to create possibilities for altering relations of power that currently constrain action). Conceived in this way, a critical orientation may employ other approaches or "methods" of analysis, but these are always in the service of the orientation toward how discourse operates in a fragmented and destabilized social world. Adopting a critical stance toward the world is precisely the orientation that animates the critical rhetoric project. As Kent Ono suggests, "taking a critical stance means addressing issues of power; taking such a perspective helps broaden the focus of critical scholarship and brings together varying critical traditions."[9]

Before taking up these matters in greater detail, it is important to revisit the putative "starting point" for the critical rhetoric project. From a traditional perspective, the starting point for criticism focuses on an active *agent* who seeks to effect change in his or her environment through suasive speech, symbolic expression, or other stylized means of broadcasting an idea, creating an event, or taking a public stand. Examples abound: annual "Take Back the Night" marches, environmental protests against "fracking," and the various "Occupy" protests against the "1 percent" are contemporary illustrations of citizens taking action. Each of the persons involved in these kinds of protests is, of course, identifiable as a sentient actor and may certainly be evaluated rhetorically for the words or deeds he or she has said or done at a particular time and place. Criticism that begins with the focus on the agent is a worthwhile endeavor, but it is not the only approach that might be useful in answering specific questions. Thus, while acknowledging the value of an agent-centered approach, I wish to stress that there exist other means of achieving answers to questions one might have about events and that such means are sometimes grounded upon conceptions of public space, power relations, and the nature of public speech and action that are not as accessible to analysis from an agent-centered approach. Contrary to John M. Murphy's claim that this orientation deprivileges other approaches, the intent of the original critical rhetoric article in 1989 (perhaps not as clearly achieved as I might wish) was to suggest that some questions may be better answered via approaches that work from a different position or utilize different approaches.[10] Not all criticism is created equal; some critical attempts will work better than others. Those engaged in a critical rhetoric perspective are not immune to this assessment. Nevertheless, as I've argued before,

> There is no single approach or perspective that stands above all others as the preferred means of enacting a critical perspective on any artifact. That said, it is equally the case that some approaches are better suited to analyze specific artifacts or events. The critical principle that underlies a value judgment on which approach is most likely to be helpful is first, what is the question being asked, and second, what is the best approach to use in answering that question. Some questions demand quantitative answers, while others are better suited to qualitative approaches.[11]

The starting point for the critical rhetoric project is not the active agent seeking change, though as noted above, I do not deny the efficacy or reality of **agency** as an ever-present persuasive force in human affairs. But I do, however, choose to begin elsewhere. In what may be the most oft-cited phrase in the original essay, "a critical rhetoric seeks to unmask or demystify the discourse of power. The aim is to understand the integration of power/knowledge in society—what possibilities for change the integration invites or inhibits and what intervention strategies might be considered appropriate to effect social change."[12] What this expression means in the act of critiquing discourse is the focus of the remainder of this chapter.

## DIFFERENTIATING CRITIQUES OF DOMINATION AND FREEDOM

Consistent with Wander's injunction, there are two forms of critical analysis that form the basis for a critical practice. As suggested above, both interrogate the existence of power relations between individuals, between individuals and agencies that have some influence or control over their lives, between groups (including those that are seen as belonging together and those that may be marginalized or excluded from participation), or even between nation-states. The first has been earmarked as a **critique of domination**. This critique has an emancipatory aim, what I've elsewhere noted as a "freedom from"[13] that which controls the beliefs or actions of others. In this context, power is seen as oppressive—as an example, consider the reason for the existence of "Hollaback" organizations within social communities. Women, tired of hearing leering, sexually suggestive comments from thoughtless males have taken to sharing their experiences online—"hollering back," as it were, in rejecting the, in their terms, sophomoric immaturity of grown men. In so doing, they assist in creating a sense of solidarity among those who no longer wish to be treated as an object. A critic examining the "Hollaback" movement would focus on the language and actions of both perpetrators and those who are on the receiving end of such unwanted attention. The power difference between those harassing women and the women themselves is a focus of the critique—how might one respond in a way that challenges the perceived right to annoy another?

The key problem with a sole focus on liberation or emancipation from oppression is "what happens next." The focus can be so tightly drawn that all one sees in front of them is the oppression and the possible means to remove its influence. Once "free," where does one go next? What change in life is presented in the absence of what has thus far been a controlling factor in choices made or not made? The second critical practice can be seen as the "flip side" of the domination critique, as the **critique of freedom** focuses attention on "freedom to" be other than what one is at the present moment. In this context, the focus also shifts from a view of power as solely oppressive (putting someone under one's control) to a sense of power that is potentially productive. It is "a positive force which creates social relations and sustains them through the appropriation of a discourse that 'models' the relations through its expression."[14] A cautionary note is needed here: I am not suggesting that one critical practice follows the other in every case. Rather, what I want to suggest is that these two practices have a logic that can tie them together, but they also may operate independently of each other. As an example of a sole focus on "freedom" in practice, what are the possibilities in your own life for becoming other than you are at this moment in time? What are the openings for change that a productive use of present power relations between siblings, friends, or partners (one or all) might create? Then, assume change does occur—what then? Are you satisfied, are you comfortable with your new self? Are you finished? The key assumption that I am making here is this: one is never "perfected." One may always be on the move toward perfection but never quite reach it. Something is always open to criticism and the possibility of change. This is the essence of what has been termed **continual critique**. In this instance, "new social relations which emerge from a reaction to critique are themselves simply new forms of power and hence subject to renewed skepticism."[15] You may not make a change as a result of the critique, but your changes are always open to future reconsideration. Assume for the moment that a new world order has arrived, and the feminists are in charge (review chapter 13 and pick your type of feminism here—there is more than one). Is the world a perfect place as a result of the new relations of power that exist—the new values that determine what actions are now appropriate? It may be better for some, worse for others. The point of circling back and reexamining the new social relations is precisely to determine what the possible new future might be beyond what is now present.

In promoting an analytic perspective that underscores this commitment to continual critique, it might be useful to take up Kenneth Burke's injunction that "the symbolic act is the *dancing of an attitude*";[16] conceiving of discourse in this sense is another way to understand how one operates from within a critical perspective. Following Burke, a critic understands that words matter. It is not true that "sticks and stones may break my bones, but words will never harm me." Attitudes toward the world, and the acceptance or rejection of the power relations that exist within it at a given moment in time, are either explicit or implicit in the language used to reflect the world. With this much in mind, we would stress that what the individual agent can or cannot do assumes a much different flavor when the question of how power relations intersect with the possibilities for "who can talk to whom with what impact" is raised. In particular, within the critical rhetoric project, the rhetorical emphasis does not hinge on an agent's ability to perform certain rhetorical acts. Rather, the emphasis is on those seen or unseen relational properties within which the agent—as agent—is contained and with which he or she must contend in the social world.

To use Jim A. Kuypers's language, we might say that the critical rhetoric project frames the rhetorical analysis from a different starting point than traditional approaches to criticism.[17] This is not at all to dismiss other modes of analysis or other starting points. To argue, for example, that an agent-centered point of departure is *the* premier analytic frame for all analyses of public action is as wrongheaded as arguing that the same distinction in fact belongs to critical rhetoric. Both assertions are or would be fatuous, nondemonstrable, and unhelpful. As I've noted elsewhere, what prompts the adoption of a particular perspective is not the critical frame itself but *the questions one seeks to answer* (and this is just as true under more traditional formulations as it is for the critical orientation advanced here).[18] The chosen rhetorical mode is informed by the phenomenon, not the reverse. For this reason, critical rhetoric is (or should be) as open to embrace or dismissal as any other frame of inquiry.

## ENACTING A CRITICAL STANCE

The foregoing sets the scene as a prelude to actually employing a critical stance. How one enacts critical rhetoric has been a major question. Three considerations are critical here: (1) What is the "object" of study? (2) What should one look for/at in executing a critique? and (3) What role do persons, as communicators, play with respect to enacting this critical stance?

### Critic as Inventor

With respect to the "object" of study, critical rhetoric reverses the phrase "public address" and instead focuses attention on *"that symbolism which addresses publics."*[19] If conducted as designed, the reversal assumes the critic is not looking solely at a speaker-speech scenario but is rather seeking to "invent" the object of critique out of the varying ways in which symbols influence people. This may be a speaker/speech situation, but it is not predicated on that context alone. Moreover, going beyond that "public address" to consider how the discourse operates within a broader context is also an option for the critic. The **critic as inventor** does not conceive of invention as making things up out of nothing, but rather as discerning, within the vast and complex world of signs and symbols, what influences might be present in determining how one's own orientation is formed or altered. As an example, think back to when you were entering your teen years—what were the symbols that informed your sense of who you were and how you were supposed to look and act at that time? What would you examine now if you were looking to answer this question? Would teen magazines be one resource? Would television shows from that era be another resource? How do these resources influence the actions you took at the time to improve or change yourself? The choices you make in answering the question will differ from those others will make in answering the same question for themselves—that is not a problem, as the key is not to arrive at a single uniform answer but to construct one that makes sense not only to you but to others whom you inform regarding your findings.

**Principles of Praxis**

With respect to what the critic looks for, if this were a "method," it would be fairly easy to establish guidelines for its correct use. In conducting Burkean criticism, for example, one will normally consider the pentad (see the chapter on Burke in this volume by Ryan Eric McGeough and Andrew King). If one is critiquing inaugural addresses, the methods outlined by William Benoit in this volume would be useful. An orientation lacks this precision with respect to identifying specific "tools" to utilize in engaging in criticism. However, all is not lost, as the **principles of praxis** introduced in the original critical rhetoric essay provide a direction—they serve not as guidelines for criticism, but as ways of conceiving of the rhetorical act and as potential indices to consider when beginning to critique. These are presented below with a very brief explanation of the intent behind the principle:[20]

1. "*Ideologiekritic* [ideological criticism] is in fact not a method, but a practice."[21] The intent here is not to suggest that method is unimportant, but rather to remind the critic that a slavish devotion to method may constrain the imagination. For instance, Burke never referenced the pentad explicitly in his classic essay on Hitler, nor do journalists outline their articles with subheadings indicating "who, what, when, and where." Instead, these function as possibilities to consider in examining any situation. In the same way, ideological criticism is an open-ended approach to understanding how people's worldviews condition their beliefs and actions.
2. The discourse of power is material. Quoting Göran Therborn is instructive here (though I would read "men" as an artifact of the times): "ideology operates as discourse. . . . [It] is the medium through which men make their history as conscious actors."[22] In making history, we (all of us) recognize that words matter—they reflect who's in power and what that power might do for us or against us.
3. Rhetoric constitutes *doxastic* rather than *epistemic* knowledge. In this context, **doxastic** refers to the role of opinion in forming what we know about the world. **Epistemic** refers to that knowledge which is certain—which does not change as time changes. For the most part, we argue about those things that are not self-evident, that are not certain or epistemically grounded. Rhetoric operates in the realm of contingent knowledge—that which could easily be otherwise than what it is currently perceived to be.
4. *Naming* is the central symbolic act of a *nominalist* rhetoric. This principle draws on the assumption that language assists in constituting who we are—how we see ourselves. To give someone a name is to say something specific about how you see them—as "arrogant," "foolish," "studly," or . . . the list goes on in conveying an attitude that may be appropriately or inappropriately applied. **Nominalism** (the philosophical position a nominalist takes) in this sense suggests that when you hear a general term such as "dog," you automatically relate it to a specific dog you are familiar with—the general term has no explicit existence. "Criminal," as a designation of a person, has existence only in application to specific individuals who may or may not deserve that label.

5. *Influence* is not *causality*. Why did you do that? If you've ever been asked this question, you know the person is looking for the cause of your action. Influences on your behavior are not as precise—they may or may not lead to specific actions, as they may be ignored. The presence of a particular symbol may or may not influence you to see the world in a certain way or be important in considering how you should act.
6. *Absence* is as important as *presence* in understanding and evaluating symbolic action. This principle suggests that we need to examine the "not said" or the "not present" as well as what is said and seen in evaluating a situation. It is said that history is written by the victors—which likely explains why, for years, "Custer's Last Stand" was represented only as a "white man's" memorial. Only recently has a memorial to the Native Americans that died there been constructed. Unfortunately, their presence is still "absent" in the artifacts available to purchase.
7. Fragments contain the potential for *polysemic* rather than *monosemic* interpretation. If *mono-* represents singularity, it is pretty clear that *polysemic* suggests that there is more than one reading possible in critiquing any event. Your goal as a critic is not to "get it right" in terms of the one and only meaning an event might have. Rather, it is to provide a defensible interpretation—one that seems reasonable on its face, even while others may see something else in the event.
8. Criticism is a *performance*. You are performing your sense of who you are as a critic; you are implicated in the choices made in the act of criticizing and accept an obligation to argue on behalf of the claims you advance (a position already made by Kuypers in chapter 3 on what criticism entails). The latter commitment is what Wander means in suggesting that critique has taken an "ideological turn."

### Agent as Effect

The third question, the role of the person in enacting change, is more complex. On the one hand, critical rhetoric does not deny the possibility of a person taking action to change a situation. The sense in which a person's saying or doing something is perceived as a cause is not precluded from critical rhetoric's scope. Far from it, for change would be almost impossible to consider if one were blinded to either person or agency—seen as the person's ability to act or influence an event. As I've noted, "the subject, as citizen and social actor, is capable of acting. . . . While not wholly formed through discourse, it is through that discourse that the subject gives expression"[23] to its being-in-the-world. As a speaking subject, a person expresses judgment in the form of critique—sharing or formulating a position on the world as it exists, leading to a world that it might yet become. What is implicit is that in and through its expression, the becoming world is once again subject to reflexive judgment as to its well-suitedness in the lives of those it engages. Hence, the work in this formulation is to seek to remain within a more traditional focus on the speaking subject as the source that effects all change.

On the other hand, critical rhetoric *does* pursue a reframing of the basis for that action, and it understands action's meaning(s)—in a sphere of social action—very differently. Instead of focusing on the person as the cause of an action, the emphasis shifts to their role as "an effect" of the event and/or language that has preceded their action. In other words, the critic focuses on what conditions produced the action taken—what were the constraints that limited the range of responses that were possible in this setting? The purpose is to consider the broader *rhetorical* possibilities for freedom (or limitation) of action that might exist in a given discursive context—either through its denial or resistance, or through its refashioning into an unfamiliar form—*prior* to essaying a formal evaluation of that action itself. Thus, the focus of a critical rhetoric is on unpacking and outlining the conditions that have created the present situation and from that analysis determining what the potential avenues for change are that might be further explored.

## THE CONTEXT FOR CRITIQUE

Within the context of both a critique of domination and a critique of freedom, in considering the need for continual critique, the critic must insistently acknowledge that rhetorical power lies in whatever social activities ground the discursive act under investigation.[24] The power to do and say things in or for a community, for example, presumes that power is both a discrete possession that speakers control and one that they distribute as they choose. Once again, this does not suggest that the power to act is an illusion; but once again, the starting point for critical rhetoric is not with the agent as *rhetor*. It lies with a careful study of the social or communal situation out of which the rhetor acts.

The question here is not one of protecting a preferred version of the needs (or the good) of the community but rather one of being open to the possibility of any and all avenues toward *freedom*, for two reasons. First, a "critical rhetoric" is by definition one that seeks to liberate—whether from oppression (domination) or from a complacent acceptance of life as it is currently lived (freedom). In this latter sense, "a [critical rhetor's] critique of freedom . . . has as its aim a reflexivity that grounds its actions in a constant reflection on the contingency of human relations and can best be styled as a 'freedom to' move toward new relations with others."[25] Second, to begin with the presumption that the rhetor knows best, particularly in the absence of even partial knowledge of those formation(s) which may inform, restrain, or enable other options, is shortsighted. What are needed are opportunities for a critical rhetor's engagement with the community that permit the broadest array of choices for action—but with the clear and minimal understanding that whatever action is proposed or undertaken may well make for social or communal relations that are not as good or efficient or desirable as one might have hoped, or which are simply wrong for that society at that time. Commitment to change, even when selfless and well intended, cannot be enacted in a single-minded way.

## CRITICAL ESSAY EXAMPLES

As already suggested, there are a variety of approaches one might take in exercising a critical orientation in the sense outlined in this chapter. A focus on power can take multiple forms. For that reason, I wish to illustrate by examples how several scholars have utilized this orientation, as well as ways in which some have extended it in new directions, as a way to suggest possible avenues for critical inquiry.

---

## USING AND/OR EXTENDING A CRITICAL ORIENTATION
### Using CR

Jessica Benham's analysis of gender issues in television focuses on the *Doctor Who* show.[26] She works from both critiques of domination and freedom in illustrating the portrayal of the

Doctor's female companions. This is an excellent method-driven study as it examines specific shows where a new female companion is introduced. Her study discusses five themes that implicate the role of power in both oppressive and productive senses: "violation of expected roles, lack of sexualization, destruction of the masculine power equation, development of romantic tensions, and lack of relationships between female companions."[27] A key attribute of a critical orientation is the way in which a researcher's background may influence the analysis. As noted earlier, the critic's role as a performer is an acknowledged facet of the critical act. Benham notes her fan status with respect to the show, as well as her roles as both a woman and a feminist, as her personal history impacts her interpretation of the way women are represented. In framing her study, she provides a brief account of the primary features of a critical orientation and notes specific accounts that critiqued the 1989 essay on critical rhetoric. Her conclusion provides her own recommendations for extending and improving the critical process. This essay serves as a "primer" with respect to how to integrate a systematic approach with a critical orientation toward the object of study.

Thomas Discenna's analysis of the graduate student unionization movement focuses on a "grade strike" in the 1970s at Yale University.[28] This study centers attention on power differentials, as graduate students were considered by Yale's administration to be "interns," not "employees." This distinction addresses the importance of how something is named and the reactions that follow from such decisions. In particular, graduate students were threatened with potential dismissal by their graduate programs if they participated in a "grade strike." Unlike employees, they had no recourse with respect to formal appeals if that action were taken. Discenna's analysis of the "rhetoric of academic professionalism" begins with a summary of unionization efforts by both faculty and graduate students. Are faculty "laborers" in the traditional sense of that term, or are they "professionals" and hence engaged in individual pursuits of the life of the mind, not that of workers seeking to better their working condition through collective action? Yale administrators at the time took advantage of this tension in claiming that graduate students were "apprentices" whose role was that of becoming professionals through their education and roles as "teaching assistants." Given this label, the prospect of a union was not an acceptable means for students to engage in as they sought to have a voice in improving their working conditions. The analysis is an adept illustration of how domination works to keep a group of people in a subordinate position. Discenna's conclusion recognizes that unionization remains "mired in a view of academic work as a life of the mind separate from the more prosaic field of labor."[29] This, plus the growing use of "contingent faculty" (part-time adjuncts), makes it more difficult for graduate students in particular to locate points of entry that would imply a freedom to influence their own future. The future for unionization is not bright, but Discenna notes that we must seek to alter the forced dichotomy between academic and work life in order to protect the rights we have to pursue our interests and be treated well at the same time.[30]

Jonathan Rossing merges critical, rhetorical scholarship with critical race theory (CRT) in an analysis of comedic discourse.[31] He argues that "the origins, aims and strategies of critical rhetoric and CRT present opportunities for reciprocal engagement."[32] After supporting this with a cogent examination of the similarities and the advantages that can be gained in merging these orientations, Rossing focuses attention on Stephen Colbert's use of a "satiric mock-editorial" in addressing the debate over Sonia Sotomayor's Supreme Court nomination. The analysis shows how both function "to address racial oppression and simultaneously work toward positive social transformation."[33] Comedic discourse provides an opportunity to take positions on sensitive topics while submitting values to critique. Rossing provides a detailed account of how Colbert's discourse interrogates white privilege in relation to choosing a Supreme Court justice. As an example, Colbert's satirical statement is worth noting: "Take the *Dred Scott* case. Those justices' life experiences—being white men in pre–Civil War America, some of whom owned slaves—in *no way* influenced their decision that black people were property."[34] Rossing concludes by returning to his initial premise: comedic discourse is a rich vein to be mined by rhetorical scholars to "advance critiques of racialized culture and generate opportunities to promote social transformation."[35]

As a final illustration, Kristen Hoerl's analysis of news coverage of Obama's inauguration focuses on the media's positive attention given to Martin Luther King's legacy in noting that we had just elected the first African American president. The media also crafted a "postracial version" that implied an end to a racialized America.[36] In extending "critical rhetoric's engagement with the concepts of remembrance and forgetfulness in public discourse," Hoerl argues that "this myth precludes public memory of radical black dissent that has condemned institutional racism in the United States."[37] We thus forget our history in constructing a mythic portrayal of a race-free society, what Hoerl references as "selective amnesia." She concludes that "a critical rhetoric attendant to the discursive processes by which public amnesia is constructed may help to enrich our resources for envisioning social change and the means of attaining social justice."[38] Her study advances the case for a critical orientation to discourse that creates, through amnesia, an "absence" that must be noted.

## Extending CR

Several scholars have worked from the original formulation in creating innovative extensions. For example, Perlita R. Dicochea, a professor of ethnic studies, proposes a "Chicana Critical Rhetoric to refer to a unique body of knowledge that represents a merging of Chicana feminist studies and critical rhetoric developed in both vernacular and academic forums."[39] In addition to this merger, Dicochea adapts Dana Cloud's[40] view that discourse analysis alone may not be as transformative as one may hope, and hence it is necessary to incorporate activism "as a counterpart to rhetoric in affecting material change."[41] She examines two Chicana publications that emerged in the 1970s that advocated for a critical space for "Chicana feminist consciousness" in the context of an already male-dominated La Causa movement. Her analysis reflects well on a critique of Chicana culture and the power relations that maintain a marginalization of Chicanas within not only their own culture, but societally as well.

Brian Ott and Carl Burgchardt employ a critical rhetoric orientation as a starting point in engaging ideas that culminate in a divergence from that orientation, arguing that it does not possess "the dialogic dimension essential to critical pedagogy."[42] What they are saying, in effect, is that the critical rhetoric orientation does not demand attention to talking together (dialogue) in a way that acknowledges the power differences between teachers and students (critical pedagogy is implied here). At the same time, they note the positive values of a critique of freedom and go on to suggest that "at a minimum, this means acknowledging one's own ideological commitments and positionality as they are mediated by socially contingent networks of power" in order to "foster agentive citizenship and promote political alternatives."[43] This is an excellent way of expressing what is intended in terms of a critique of freedom—permanent criticism is not a recipe for inaction, but rather a recognition that power relations are open to change across time. That action requires due diligence with respect to how current power relations either foster or inhibit the possibilities inherent in improving our lives. They illustrate what they mean by a "critical-rhetorical pedagogy" and the importance of dialogic criticism through an analysis of the film *Schindler's List*. Their analysis underscores the value of using film as a teaching tool, especially in engendering dialogue that is instructive. In the process, they evince a very positive view of student accountability in engaging a productive (in the sense of power relations) conversation that enables them to develop critical awareness of themselves and their world. They conclude in noting that "CRP conceives of criticism as a dialogic encounter with(in) a much wider (and always unfolding) constellation of discourses involving the text, critical commentary on the text, and classroom conversation surrounding the text."[44]

Art Herbig and Aaron Hess articulate a promising new direction in addressing what they term "convergent critical rhetoric"—an analysis that integrates rhetoric, ethnography, and documentary film production elements into a cohesive framework.[45] The analysis builds off prior work that brings rhetorical analysis and ethnographic methods into conversation. In the past, these have seemed to be separate approaches, but "blending the tools of the rhetorician with the skills of an ethnographer can lead to insights that neither can produce alone."[46] Adding media production tools expands the potential for the critic, especially in directing attention to the way documentary film uses language. In preparation for the analysis, they attended the Rally to Restore Sanity and taped interviews with other attendees—they reference the YouTube video they created in supporting the claims advanced. A key advance in this study is the fact that the authors "productively participate in the discourses we also seek to critique."[47] This takes a critical orientation at face value in blurring the lines between critic as observer and critic as participant.

In *Participatory Critical Rhetoric: Theoretical and Methodological Foundations for Studying Rhetoric in Situ*, Michael Middleton, Aaron Hess, Danielle E. Endres, and Samantha Senda-Cook extend prior work that links rhetorical and ethnographic approaches to criticism. They define this approach in the following terms:

> Participatory critical rhetoric describes a set of research practices that bring qualitative methods of data collection such as participant observation, interviewing, and oral history into the process of doing rhetorical criticism. . . . As a participatory research praxis, . . . [this approach] reconsiders the relationship between critic, rhetor, text/context, and audience by placing the critic in direct contact with audiences and rhetoric, inviting new perspectives on these complex rhetorical processes.[48]

Their approach is consistent with the "convergent" approach articulated above as it creates an orientation that melds together multiple approaches in a coherent whole. While each facet may not be present in every critical encounter, the approach offers an opportunity to erase artificial barriers between ways of critiquing events.

## Conclusion

This essay has sought to underscore critical rhetoric's practice as an *orientation* and to further the explanatory power of an inventional, critical modality in its engagement of discursive and artifactual fragments in the social world. How one carries the impetus to utilize its perspective forward remains open. As the above exemplars have done, you may also do: consider placing yourself inside an orientation that asks questions about the nature of language as it reveals particular formations between and among people, and interrogates the productive capability of power in inhibiting or fostering social action. Opening one's attitude toward events by considering the context whereby the event has come into being will go a long way toward realizing the potential of this critical perspective. Just as Burke eschewed using critical markers (e.g., elements of the pentad) in advancing critical judgment, we would remind readers that critical rhetoric functions as an intellectual backdrop to the critical act—it enjoins asking questions related to how the context forms discourse rather than how discourse effects publics. While recognizing the power accorded the speaker in traditional analyses of public oratory, it yet suggests that there is more to the story. By asking questions of speakers, seen as products of the discourse that produced them, we hope to understand how the discourse came to be in this rather than another time and what possibilities for freedom it hinders or makes available. Intervention as a means of remedying social ills demands no less from us than understanding how we come to be in this time and place, with these sets of attitudes toward events, ourselves, and others. Critical rhetoric is but one starting point in the path toward social action.

## PERSONAL REFLECTIONS

Exercising one's voice is about choices, whether responding to another person who has asked a question or writing a scholarly essay. There are, of course, differences in the nature of each response, but the fact remains that one could choose several different ways to "style" one's commentary. My choice in this situation was to highlight the facets of the original critical rhetoric article—the twin "critiques" of domination and freedom and the principles grounding a revised approach toward rhetorical events. Instead of providing a "critical essay" that emulates a method, I elected to illustrate the varying ways in which a critical orientation might be employed, both in terms of remaining largely within the scope of the original critical rhetoric essay's suggestions for criticism as well as exploring ways in which the orientation has been extended in new directions. These exemplars illustrate how critical reflection might work in actual practice. In making this choice, the primary difficulty is in accurately reflecting how each example works from a critical orientation. Whether I have been successful in this goal is left to the reader's judgment.

## POTENTIALS AND PITFALLS

In writing theoretical essays, one hopes to have an influence on the work of other scholars. With respect to what has become known as the "critical rhetoric project," it appears that the initial ideas have had a heuristic impact. As the preceding examples illustrate, and the following "critical bibliography" confirms, the "project" remains a viable approach to critical inquiry. These have taken form in ways that adhere fairly closely to the original theory, as extensions and improvements in responding to shortcomings or critical weaknesses, and as oppositional views in order to illustrate the fundamental flaws in the approach.

If you begin with the recognition that traditional rhetoric has a history of emphasizing the "great man speaking well," then **decentering** the role of the speaker as the origin of thought, words, and action raises significant questions. What becomes of the object of criticism if the focus is not on the person speaking?

Especially in this latter context, the following issues become relevant: (1) When you add to this purported "removal" of the active speaker/rhetor a commitment to a recursive or continual critique, a question about the possibility of criticism itself competes for attention. If critique is never ending, what can we say about any specific instance of communication as to its value in achieving specific goals? (2) If you then suggest that the nature of critique does not rest in "method" but rather exists as an "orientation" toward an object, the negative reaction becomes even more strident. How can you possibly know what it is you have, or can argue, if you cannot rest your argument on the mantle of objective, methodical assessment of an object or event?

What follows is an attempt to address two of the primary "pitfalls" that have concerned critics of the "project." First, consider the existence of a *subject*. I attempted to deal with this "flaw" in assessing the possibility of a subject (or speaker) within a critical rhetoric perspective:

> If the subject is decentered... can there be a role for the speaker as agent of social change? I answer this question in the affirmative. Resituating the subject does not necessitate the destruction of the speaker.... By giving voice to critique, the subject renews self.[49]

What is implied in this response to the issue is that the speaker, though decentered, is not "dead" to the issues involved. At the same time, it also means that we are already immersed in a set of social practices and rituals that are not of our own making—and that we speak from within a conversation that has already prefigured for us the possibilities of expression as well as the range of interpretations that might be most likely. This does not mean everything is "fixed" and determined ahead of time—but it does mean that the discursive formation is not open ended and infinite with respect to who can say what to whom with what effect. You can yell "Fire!" in a crowded room, but in so doing, you already know the possible impact of giving voice to that expression—if there were no fire, nor a possibility of one, what would happen to you as a consequence of people's believing you and acting on that belief? Jim A. Kuypers does an eloquent job of considering this issue, arguing in part that the role of critical rhetoric "diminishes" the speaker's contribution.[50] While I would not use that label, it is the case that critical rhetoric changes the landscape within which speakers act and react. In aiming for the retention of what is termed "prudence" or "practical wisdom," which in turn actively engages ethical conduct or action, Kuypers argues that a critical rhetoric perspective may fail to contain prudence or "prudent action." Ethics is not automatically removed when adopting a critical rhetoric perspective. Rather, the "scene" (to use a term from Burke's pentadic orientation toward criticism) shifts from the speaker to the context in which the speaker acts. Prudence, as reflective of moral conduct or right action, is still possible within the rhetorical moment. The critical concern is not in "not accounting for the agent as the causative force" but rather lies in "accounting for ethical action or its absence in the rhetorical context." Reminding us of the importance of ethical considerations is a valuable contribution to the project; hence, Kuypers's points are well taken—and accommodated within a slight shift from a focus on the speaker as active agent to the speaker as part of a larger context in which rhetorical action is taken.

My second pitfall involves *the possibility of criticism*. We might start with the observation that criticism and critique are different objects. Criticism is the shallower, narrower term, with a focus on "making things better." Critique, on the other hand, goes deeper and broader—its focus, while on "making things better," is also on the assumptions that ground the very object of critique. As I noted at an earlier time, the propaganda critics of the early twentieth century certainly were focused on improving democracy.[51] But they did not go beyond that to actively suggest that the very assumptions on which democracy was premised were themselves subject to revision. When invoking "critique" as the operative term, we are suggesting that not only do we want to improve our lot, but we want to subject the foundations underlying our social relations to scrutiny. Critique does not mean "everything we find is wrong"—that is, it is not inherently fault-finding. We may decide, after examination, that for now at least, specific social practices are fine the way they are. That isn't always likely, but it is at least a logical possibility—and one we need to retain in order not to fall into an irreversible litany of "this is wrong. . . . this is wrong," ad infinitum. Cloud argues, among other things, that the critical rhetoric project may well rob us of the possibility of critique.[52] If we can never finish, how do we say anything is ever "wrong" or in need of correction? Consider the possibility that rhetoric is a moral and material force: it acts on us at every moment of our lives. If that were not the case, we would not be able to affirm such phrases as "a child who lives with criticism learns to criticize." Living in a social relationship bounded by the continual expression of one's flaws may well have an impact on how one sees oneself. Kent Ono and John Sloop's articulation of a "telos" (purpose/goal) for a "sustained critical rhetoric" adds immeasurably to the power of the theoretical stance to make a difference.[53] What is suggested is simply this: we do act with purpose within discrete historical moments, and we do judge the social worth of our actions at that moment as hopefully positive. What the critical rhetoric orientation suggests is not that we can't decide anything in the moment, but that once decided, once acted on, as we move on we can't just rest on our laurels. We can't just brush the dust off our hands, say the job is done, and assume all is now right with the world. It may be for then, and for always, but we owe it to ourselves to ask: what changes in power relations does this action portend, and how do those changes affect others? Does the correction of one inequity produce another down the road—one that also should be remedied? What the orientation commits us to is not indecision in the moment, but the realization that action is never final. There is no *fini* to the play of human life.

## CRITICAL RHETORIC TOP PICKS

The following lists are not exhaustive but reflect work done in advancing the "critical rhetoric project" in both theoretical and critical terms.

### Works on Critical Rhetoric by Raymie E. McKerrow

"Critical Rhetoric: Theory and Praxis." *Communication Monographs* 56 (1989): 91–111.
"Critical Rhetoric in a Postmodern World." *Quarterly Journal of Speech* 77 (1991): 75–78.
"Critical Rhetoric and Propaganda Studies." In *Communication Yearbook*, vol. 14, edited by J. Anderson, 249–255. Newbury Park, CA: Sage, 1991.
"Critical Rhetoric and the Possibility of the Subject." In *The Critical Turn: Rhetoric and Philosophy in Postmodern Discourse*, edited by I. Angus and L. Langsdorf, 51–67. Carbondale, IL: Southern Illinois Univ. Press, 1993.
"Corporeality and Cultural Rhetoric: A Site for Rhetoric's Future." *Southern Communication Journal* 63 (1998): 315–328.
"Space and Time in a Postmodern Polity." *Western Journal of Communication* 63 (1999): 271–290.
"Critical Rhetoric." In *Encyclopedia of Rhetoric*, edited by T. Sloane, 619–622. New York: Oxford University Press, 2001.
"Critical Rhetoric." In *Encyclopedia of Communication Theory*, vol. 1, edited by S. Littlejohn and K. Foss, 234–237. Thousand Oaks, CA: Sage, 2009.

### Primarily Theoretical Works Related to Critical Rhetoric

Charland, Maurice. "Finding a Horizon and Telos: The Challenge to Critical Rhetoric." *Quarterly Journal of Speech* 77 (1991): 71–74. While finding much to commend in the perspective, it raises concerns about the potential for "continual critique" to turn into an infinite process, with no end in sight. McKerrow's response to these two pieces is "Critical Rhetoric in a Postmodern World" cited above.
Cloud, Dana L. "The Materiality of Discourse as Oxymoron: A Challenge to Critical Rhetoric." *Western Journal of Communication* 58 (1994): 141–163. This essay chronicles the shift toward a discussion of discourse as material. In particular, McGee and McKerrow's work is critiqued for its alleged shortcomings in advancing ideological criticism. Cloud proposes an alternative perspective in remedying the problems inherent within McGee's and McKerrow's formulations.
Gaonkar, Dilip P. "Performing with Fragments: Reflections on Critical Rhetoric." In *Argument and the Postmodern Challenge*, edited by R. E. McKerrow, 149–155. Annandale, VA: Speech Communication Association, 1993. This essay critiques the alleged absence of reason that follows from assuming a critical rhetoric stance.
Hariman, Robert. "Critical Rhetoric and Postmodern Theory." *Quarterly Journal of Speech* 77 (1991): 67–70. This essay, along with Charland's (see above), is an invited response to the critical rhetoric essay. The essay notes the problematic status of the rhetor as active agent affecting a specific audience if one adopts the orientation provided by a critical rhetoric perspective.

Kuypers, Jim A. "Doxa and a Critical Rhetoric: Accounting for the Rhetorical Agent through Prudence." *Communication Quarterly* 44 (1996): 452–462. As the title suggests, this analysis provides a "correction" to the absence of a central agent enacting change by recasting the sense of doxa and its corollary, "prudence" or "practical wisdom" (e.g., doing the right thing). The changes place responsibility for ethical action within an understanding of the community's will to action.

Murphy, John M. "Critical Rhetoric as Political Discourse." *Argumentation and Advocacy* 32 (1995): 1–15. This essay interrogates McKerrow's penchant for creating dichotomies (in this case—disassociations between opposites, as in permanence/change or domination/freedom) and critiques the absence of an active subject seeking change through the power of the word.

Ono, Kent A., and John M. Sloop. "Commitment to 'Telos'—A Sustained Critical Rhetoric." *Communication Monographs* 59 (1992): 48–60. This essay is sympathetic to the project, and responds directly to the criticism that continual critique makes it impossible to ever "take a stand" for some specific change, as one is always in the mode of critic rather than acting to create change.

## NOTES

1. The development of this essay is no different, as it is based on prior versions coauthored with Jeffrey St. John, published in 2005 and 2009 under the title "Critical Rhetoric: The Context for Continual Critique."
2. Herbert Simons, "Requirements, Problems, and Strategies: A Theory of Persuasion for Social Movements," *Quarterly Journal of Speech* 56 (1970): 1–11.
3. Philip Wander and Steven Jenkins, "Rhetoric, Society, and the Critical Response," *Quarterly Journal of Speech* 58 (1972): 441–450.
4. Wander and Jenkins, "Rhetoric, Society, and the Critical Response," 450.
5. Philip Wander, "The Ideological Turn in Modern Criticism," *Central States Speech Journal* 34 (1983): 1–18.
6. See Jim A. Kuypers, "Framing Analysis," in *Rhetorical Criticism: Perspectives in Action*, ed. Jim A. Kuypers, 181–204 (Lanham, MD: Lexington Books, 2009).
7. Wander, "The Ideological Turn," 18.
8. Kenneth Burke, *Permanence and Change*, 3rd ed. (Berkeley: University of California Press, 1984), 14–15.
9. Kent A. Ono, "Critical: A Finer Edge," *Communication and Critical/Cultural Studies* 8 (2011): 93.
10. John M. Murphy, "Critical Rhetoric as Political Discourse," *Argumentation and Advocacy* 32 (1995): 1–15.
11. Raymie E. McKerrow, "Criticism Is as Criticism Does," *Western Journal of Communication* 77 (2013): 547.
12. Raymie E. McKerrow, "Critical Rhetoric: Theory and Praxis," *Communication Monographs* 56 (1989): 91.
13. Raymie E. McKerrow, "Critical Rhetoric and Propaganda Studies," in *Communication Yearbook*, vol. 14, ed. J. Anderson, 249–255 (Newbury Park, CA: Sage, 1991).
14. McKerrow, "Critical Rhetoric: Theory and Practice," 99.
15. Ibid., 96.
16. Kenneth Burke, *The Philosophy of Literary Form* (Berkeley: University of California Press, 1941/1973), 9, emphasis his.
17. Kuypers, "Framing Analysis."
18. McKerrow, "Criticism Is as Criticism Does."
19. McKerrow, "Critical Rhetoric: Theory and Practice," 101.

20. The principles are derived from McKerrow, "Critical Rhetoric: Theory and Practice," 102–108.

21. Michael Calvin McGee, "Another Philippic: Notes on the Ideological Turn in Criticism," *Central States Speech Journal* 35 (1984): 49.

22. Göran Therborn, *The Ideology of Power and the Power of Ideology* (London: NLB, 1980), 15, 3.

23. Raymie E. McKerrow, "Critical Rhetoric and the Possibility of the Subject," in *The Critical Turn: Rhetoric and Philosophy in Postmodern Discourse*, ed. I. Angus and L. Langsdorf, 51–67 (Carbondale: Southern Illinois University Press, 1993), 64.

24. McKerrow, "Critical Rhetoric: Theory and Practice," 98.

25. Raymie E. McKerrow, "Critical Rhetoric," in *Encyclopedia of Rhetoric*, ed. T. Sloane, 619–622 (New York: Oxford University Press, 2001), 619.

26. Jessica L. Benham, "Saving the Mad Man in a Box: A Critical Analysis of the Role of Female Companions in *Doctor Who*" (paper presented at the National Communication Association convention, Las Vegas, November 2015).

27. Ibid., 2.

28. Thomas A. Discenna, "The Rhetoric of Graduate Employee Unionization: Critical Rhetoric and the Yale Grade Strike," *Communication Quarterly* 58 (2010): 19–35.

29. Ibid., 32.

30. Ibid.

31. Jonathan P. Rossing, "Critical Intersections and Comic Possibilities: Extending Racialized Critical Rhetorical Scholarship," *Communication Law Review* 10, no. 1 (2010): 10–27.

32. Ibid., 11.

33. Ibid.

34. Ibid., 18.

35. Ibid., 22.

36. Kristen Hoerl, "Selective Amnesia and Racial Transcendence in News Coverage of President Obama's Inauguration," *Quarterly Journal of Speech* 98 (2012): 178–202.

37. Ibid., 179.

38. Ibid., 197.

39. Perlita R. Dicochea, "Chicana Critical Rhetoric: Recrafting La Causa in Chicana Movement Discourse, 1970–1979," *Frontiers: A Journal of Women Studies* 25 (2004): 78.

40. Dana L. Cloud, "The Materiality of Discourse as Oxymoron: A Challenge to Critical Rhetoric," *Western Journal of Communication* 58 (1994): 141–163.

41. Dicochea, "Chicana Critical Rhetoric," 78.

42. Brian L. Ott and Carl R. Burgchardt, "On Critical-Rhetorical Pedagogy: Dialoging with *Schindler's List*," *Western Journal of Communication* 77 (2013): 16.

43. Ibid.

44. Ibid., 28.

45. Art Herbig and Aaron Hess, "Convergent Critical Rhetoric at the 'Rally to Restore Sanity': Exploring the Intersection of Rhetoric, Ethnography, and Documentary Production," *Communication Studies* 63 (2012): 269–289.

46. Ibid., 270.

47. Ibid., 284.

48. Michael Middleton, Aaron Hess, Danielle Endres, and Samantha Senda-Cook, *Participatory Critical Rhetoric: Theoretical and Methodological Foundations for Studying Rhetoric in Situ* (Lanham, MD: Lexington Books, 2015), xiv.

49. McKerrow, "Critical Rhetoric and the Possibility of the Subject," 64.

50. Jim A. Kuypers, "Doxa and a Critical Rhetoric: Accounting for the Rhetorical Agent through Prudence," *Communication Quarterly* 44 (1994): 452–462.

51. McKerrow, "Critical Rhetoric and Propaganda Studies."

52. Cloud, "The Materiality of Discourse."

53. Kent A. Ono and John M. Sloop, "Commitment to Telos—A Sustained Critical Rhetoric," *Communication Monographs* 59 (1992): 48–60.

# 17

# Criticism of Popular Culture and Social Media

*Kristen Hoerl*

From 2006 to 2012, more votes were cast for the winner of *American Idol*, a televised singing competition, than for the 2012 presidential election in the United States.[1] This is a troubling statistic for those of us interested in civic engagement and democracy, even though the ability for *American Idol* viewers to vote multiple times makes this statistic somewhat less frightening. Nonetheless, the voting totals for *American Idol* highlight the importance of popular media as a space for collective engagement. Indeed, it is often easier for me to strike up a conversation with someone I do not know very well by asking them what television program or movie they watched recently than by asking them their thoughts about political events.

Rhetorical criticism of popular culture begins with the premise that the study of discourses of everyday life and entertainment can offer insights about social beliefs, attitudes, and power relations. A rhetorical approach to the study of popular culture embraces a broad conception of rhetoric as "the social function that manages meanings."[2] Rather than locating rhetoric within only those texts intentionally created to achieve a specific goal, this expansive view enables critics to explain how symbolic action comprised of a combination of words, images, moving pictures, and sounds across a myriad of cultural artifacts shape our identities and communities. Raymond Williams, a foundational theorist in the field of cultural studies, famously defined culture as "a whole way of life."[3] This definition is purposefully vague, as it enables critics to explore a wide variety of cultural forms that some might consider lowbrow or trivial, including Hollywood films, television programs, popular music, and social media such as Twitter, Facebook, and Pinterest. Although my focus in this chapter is on commercial media, popular culture is broader in scope. Rhetorical critics of popular culture may be interested in other cultural practices including sporting events, tattoo art, and food culture. Why study such practices? Because the most seemingly mundane practices and discourses can shape our assumptions and worldviews. When we engage with popular culture, we inevitably participate in the political and social struggles of our time. Rhetorical criticism starts from the premise that symbolic action invites shared understanding that provides a basis for collective decision making. The study of how meaning is constructed in popular culture explains the processes by which communities share experiences, maintain social stability, and recognize the need for social change.

Although many disciplines within the humanities study films and television programs, rhetorical criticism of popular culture is distinguished by an investment in civic life. Such criticism seeks to explain how popular texts contribute to broader cultural conversations about social life and politics. An implication of this approach is that the messages of popular culture carry meanings that extend beyond the narrative or aesthetic dimensions of the text by referencing and giving meaning to sociopolitical circumstances. Conscientious rhetoric scholars attend to popular texts as products of their time and read them in the historical and political contexts in which they were created and consumed. By interpreting popular-culture texts in these contexts, critics have a basis for explaining how popular culture functions to "make some ideas, positions, and alternatives more attractive, accessible, and powerful to audiences than others."[4] Popular media offer discursive resources and interpretive frameworks for audiences to consider and discuss the social and political issues embedded in the texts of popular culture.

This chapter is different from other chapters in this book. Unlike approaches such as close textual analysis, narrative, and metaphoric criticism, the concept of popular culture is not a method per se. Instead, popular culture is an object of analysis for criticism. A variety of approaches already discussed in this book including narrative, generic criticism, feminist criticism, and conceptual criticism have been applied to the texts of popular culture. For example, Donna Nudd and Kristina Whalen's analysis of the movie *Shallow Hal* appears in this book as an example of feminist rhetorical criticism that illustrates how popular film reinforces normative ideals about feminine beauty. Hence, there is no one standard approach toward analyzing popular culture from a rhetorical perspective. In the following section, I discuss a variety of theoretical frameworks and practices that critics have applied to analyze the texts of popular culture. First I provide a brief overview of some of the most frequently referenced theoretical frameworks for interpreting the meaning of popular culture. Then I describe how scholars have made decisions about text selection and analytical approaches. Not all of these theories and strategies will be useful for one project. Critics' uses of concepts and texts depend on what they find to be most important and the central arguments they wish to make.

## THEORIZING THE RELATIONSHIP BETWEEN CULTURE AND POWER

Although rhetorical critics have analyzed popular-culture texts using a variety of approaches, their scholarship often intersects with and draws upon the work of cultural studies. **Cultural studies** is an interdisciplinary field concerned with the relationship between culture and power. It focuses on the ways that symbolic action reproduces, resists, and transforms existing power relations and conditions of inequality. This approach to criticism explains how mass media construct, affirm, and sometimes challenge social hierarchies based on categories of identity such as race, gender, class, sexual orientation, and nationality. One core tenet of cultural studies is that scholarship should be explicitly interventionist. Because all discourse is positioned within and responds to power relations, critics should be self-reflexive about the ways in which their own social locations shape their criticism. For instance, I need to be aware of how the examples I have chosen for this chapter might reflect my own perspective as a white woman who teaches students at a small university in the Midwest. This awareness should remind me to look for examples that are recognizable to a broader group of students beyond those I work with daily. With this interventionist goal in mind, rhetorical criticism of popular culture not only explains how meaning is constructed within a particular text, but also evaluates the implications of the text. For many critics, the point of criticism is to promote social change. Of course, many critics prefer to describe and explain popular culture, stopping short of active intervention.

Rhetorical scholars have drawn from a variety of theories to explain the relationship between culture and power. In this chapter I focus on four of them: ideology, interpellation, hegemony, and power/knowledge. Although this is not a comprehensive list, many rhetorical critics continue to draw upon them to interpret contemporary examples of popular culture. If you have read Ronald Lee and Adam Blood's chapter about the ideograph in this book, you should already be familiar with the concept of ideology. **Ideologies** are systems of ideas that provide the frameworks through which we understand and interpret social experience. Although language and symbolic action are the means by which ideologies are shared, ideologies are not the product of individual intention. Rather, we unconsciously adopt ideological beliefs as part of the environments into which we are born. Popular culture is a central feature of this environment.

Ideologies for humans are akin to water for fish. We take ideologies for granted because it is an intrinsic part of our everyday lives. A fish realizes the importance of water when it finds itself on the other side of the fishbowl. Likewise, it is only when we have a radically different experience such as visiting a new country that we realize how much we depended on our ideological beliefs to make sense of the world. Without that new experience, the ideologies we grow up with seem to be common sense. One important implication of ideological discourse is that it provides a partial view of reality that privileges some perspectives over others. Ideologies that hold sway in current culture are referred to as dominant ideologies.

Critics of ideology typically draw attention to the ways in which particular instances of ideological discourse make the uneven distribution of resources and other conditions of inequality seem natural. These critics explain how the mundane features of everyday life affirm the interests of powerful classes. Although this approach suggests that some ideologies are better than others, it should not imply that one can gain understanding of reality that is complete or "outside" ideology. Indeed, finding a basis for evaluating ideology is a complex issue. The concept of interpellation explains why seeking to identify discourse that is not ideological is a thorny problem.

**Interpellation** refers to the process by which ideological discourse constructs subject positions for individuals and groups from which they can make sense of their experience. That is, our own identities are the products of ideology.[5] We internalize ideological discourses that offer us a certain image of our place in the world and then use that image to guide our beliefs and behaviors. Renowned cultural studies critic Stuart Hall explains that ideologies construct for their subjects "positions of identification and knowledge which allow them to 'utter' ideological truths as if they were their authentic authors. . . . [W]e find ourselves mirrored in the positions at the centre of the discourses from which the statements we formulate 'make sense.'"[6] The theory of interpellation explains why it is impossible for us to experience the world outside ideology, but it has also been criticized for offering a static worldview. If our internalized worldview is constructed by dominant ideologies, then how does social change happen?

The concept of **hegemony** explains the role of discourse in the process of social change. Attributed to the work of Antonio Gramsci, hegemony refers to the process by which the social order remains stable by generating the voluntary consent of its members.[7] The **social order** refers to a system of social hierarchies, structures, institutions, relations, customs, values, and practices that correspond to specific ideological assumptions. Thus, consent to the social order is achieved through the construction and circulation of ideological texts. For example, capitalism is widely perceived as the only legitimate economic system in the United States because our news coverage, films, and television programs frequently extol the virtues of free enterprise and hard work as values that enable people to achieve their goals. A key to maintaining this consent to capitalism is to understand people's economic distresses as personal failures that could have been avoided if they had worked harder or smarter. If the majority of US citizens believed that economic distress itself was a result of capitalism, the social order would be in jeopardy. You may note that the concept of hegemony is very similar to that of dominant ideology. One way to distinguish between the two is that dominant ideology is a set of beliefs that suggest that the current distribution of power is common sense, and hegemony is the process by which cultural texts convince us to accept these beliefs.

The concept of hegemony recognizes that ideological discourse must convince marginalized groups that the social order exists in their best interests if that order is to remain dominant. When members of these groups conclude that the dominant ideology does not adequately reflect their experiences and values, they may build alternative ideologies that offer contrasting propositions about the nature of reality and one's place within it. Thus, interpellation is never complete. The struggle between dominant and alternative ideologies is often referred to as a struggle for hegemony. Hegemonic systems are an unavoidable aspect of social life, but they do change form through a process of negotiation between social groups.

Popular culture is an interesting site of struggle because media texts must adapt and respond to changing social conventions. Thus, hegemony is always in a process of negotiation. Counterhegemonic messages may express support for an alternative ideology and question the social order. Because ideologies are always contested, dominant ideologies must be able to absorb and reframe challenges. Such ideological adaption should not be conflated with fundamental social change or the redistribution of power. After all, slight changes in ideological discourse might discourage audiences from thinking about the system as a whole. For example, Dana Cloud explains that mediated discourses about Oprah Winfrey have challenged hegemonic whiteness in American culture by celebrating the success of an African American woman, but they also obscured the reality that black Americans are still more likely to live in poverty than white Americans. Consequently, attention to Oprah's success encourages audiences to support the current system despite ongoing racial disparities in employment, health care, and law enforcement.[8] One insight that emerges from this approach to criticism is that texts that appear to promote alternative ideologies at first glance may have hegemonic implications nonetheless. Conversely, other critics have noted that popular culture has incorporated progressive and countercultural values into its content.[9]

Another perspective on power draws from the work of Michel Foucault, who emphasizes that knowledge and power mutually inform one another.[10] Rather than think of power as a repressive force used against others, Foucault regards power as a productive force that circulates through all levels of society. **Power/knowledge** creates and sustains social relations in every instance. Critics of rhetoric find Foucault's discussion of power useful because is foregrounds how meaning is achieved through operations of power. Discourse constructs, defines, and produces objects of knowledge in an intelligible way while excluding other forms of reasoning as unintelligible.[11] Our physical bodies are subject to the regulatory power of discourse because it is through discourse that we become subjects for ourselves and others. Thus, the subject, or a sense of one's individual identity, is constituted in discourse through the specific vocabularies of knowledges that circulate in society. So, by studying those discourses, critics explain how power makes particular social identities intelligible. From this view, discourses of popular culture operate as a disciplinary technology that regulates and organizes bodies. Those who resist such regulation do not make sense within the available vocabularies of knowledge; hence, they are positioned as abnormal, or Other. For instance, relative absence of positive depictions of gays and lesbians in US films and television, particularly before the sexual revolution of the late 1960s, illustrates how Hollywood has positioned the gay community as unintelligible. Of course, that does not mean that the gay and lesbian community does not exist. That people do resist lines of intelligibility reminds us that subjectivity is never stable and is open to change.

## STRATEGIES FOR INTERPRETING POPULAR CULTURE AND SOCIAL MEDIA

### Selecting/Constructing the Text

Many critics find the aforementioned theoretical frameworks useful to explain why a particular text in popular culture is rhetorically meaningful; however, insightful criticism does not simply apply a particular theoretical framework to a text. For instance, explaining that a specific movie expresses a dominant ideology is not all that interesting because all products of commercial media reflect dominant ideological views in some way. Rather than seeking to apply a particular theory to a popular-culture text, I recommend that critics begin by identifying a text that they are curious about because it offers unique, important, or troubling commentary about public life. Critics often pursue their analysis with a hunch that a particular text gives meaning to an ongoing social conflict or political controversy. Other critics are simply interested in a particular text and want to understand its rhetorical significance more fully.

Critics should think carefully about the texts they select for analysis. They cannot assume that the existence of a text alone legitimizes it as an object of study. Since criticism itself is an act of communicating rhetorically to others, the first step is to explain why a particular text merits scholarly attention. Rhetorical critics part ways with some of their counterparts in film studies whose criticism primarily appreciates the aesthetic merits of a film. Remember that rhetorical critics of popular culture are primarily concerned with how a text contributes to shared understanding about a social or political issue, collective decision making, and/or social justice. If few people are familiar with a text, readers may be hard pressed to care about the analysis. Critics might provide a variety of reasons that explain why a text is worthy of rhetorical analysis based on its popularity, critical acclaim, or resonance with other trends in popular culture.

Some texts become interesting candidates for analysis after a public figure has referenced them to discuss a broader issue. For instance, Bonnie Dow notes that the television situation comedy *Murphy Brown* had rhetorical implications during the 1990s because then-vice-president Dan Quayle mentioned the program. In a 1992 speech about the decline of family values, Quayle famously condemned fictional character Murphy Brown for having a child out of wedlock.[12] A more recent example is public intellectual Neil deGrasse Tyson's criticism of the Academy Award–winning film *Gravity*. After the film's release in 2013, Tyson issued a series of Tweets about the film's failures to accurately depict astrophysics. These Tweets garnered additional news media attention and online debate about the status of science and science literacy. Thus, *Gravity* and social media discussions about the film may tell us something unique about how cinema participates in public controversies about the merits of scientific discovery and space exploration.

The example of *Gravity* and social media attention to the film illustrates the critic's role in defining the scope of the text. A text typically refers to a self-contained media product such as a particular film, television program, or music recording. But it may also include a variety of products that give meaning to an issue when considered collectively.[13] Barry Brummett defines a text as "a set of signs related to each other insofar as their meanings all contribute to the same set of effects or functions."[14] This definition suggests that the scope of the text may be determined according to the patterns across different products in media culture that share similar messages and themes. These patterns may be more interesting than any one individual text because they construct a structured symbolic environment that encourages audiences to share similar interpretations of the world.

For example, consider the emerging practice of Twitter trolling. One particularly pernicious form of trolling involves responding to feminists' Tweets with messages that threaten violence or rape. Although individual Tweets that threaten violence are troubling, the pattern of threatening responses that feminist advocates have received reveals a culture of misogyny that exists beyond the attitudes of a few individuals.[15] In deciding the scope of the text, critics should consider whether a particular cultural product is interesting on its own and/or to what extent it is intriguing when considered in relationship to other cultural products.

Even if critics choose to focus an analysis on one particular text, they should consider the rhetorical role of paratexts in giving meaning to the text and its surrounding issues. **Paratexts** are the variety of materials that comment on or refer to a text such as a movie or television program. Advertisements, movie trailers, DVD special features, website reviews, interviews with actors and creators, Internet discussions, and fan creations inform audiences about movies, films, and celebrities; consequently, they also guide audiences' interpretations. As Herman Gray notes, these paratexts establish frames through which audiences interpret and discuss popular media.[16] Dan Quayle's remark about Murphy Brown is an example of a paratext that gave explicit political and social meaning to the television program.

Celebrity news coverage and fandom offer another form of paratext. For instance, Beyoncé performed at the 2014 Video Music Awards in front of a giant neon sign displaying the word *feminist*. A critical analysis of her performance might analyze how Beyoncé gave meaning to the idea of feminism. In her performance, she references her husband and hip-hop artist Jay Z. Since most of her fans are likely to follow news coverage of her personal life, the critic would need to discuss how Beyoncé's highly publicized relationship with Jay Z contributed to the meaning of her performance. Alternatively, critics might interpret the controversy surrounding her performance in the Twitter posts responding to her act. Many Tweets weighed in on a debate about whether Beyoncé fit the definition of a feminist. An analysis of these Tweets would illuminate how social media gave meaning to Beyoncé's performance and to contemporary feminism.

The emergence of digital media has shifted how some critics think about the significance and scope of the text. Whereas commercial media including major television networks, Hollywood blockbuster films, and national newspapers were once thought to provide the only significant resources for shared meaning in popular culture, the proliferation of smart phones and the Internet has enabled groups and individuals to gain a public presence outside mainstream media. Kevin DeLuca, Sean Lawson, and Ye Sun observe that our social world is constructed by a complex media matrix that is an "ever-changing combination of myriad media, from writing and print and photography to television and radio and cinema to the Internet and laptops and smartphones."[17] DeLuca et al. refer to the interaction of the plurality of media that shape social life as "**panmediation**." These critics compared and contrasted national news media reports about the Occupy Wall Street movement with online political blogs to the right and left of the mainstream political spectrum. Noticing the differences between mainstream news coverage and these blogs, they conclude that panmediation enables activist groups who are routinely ignored or derided by traditional US mass-media organizations to build alternative social and political realities.

Another example of mediated communication that occurs outside traditional media is the Internet meme, which is an image, hyperlink, video, or hashtag that circulates from person to person through social networks, blogs, or direct e-mail. Rhetorical critics have just begun to explore the ideological dimensions of memes.[18] A rhetorical analysis of an Internet meme requires a broad construction of a text because a meme takes form not with an individual instance but through the repetition and adaptation of a symbol through digital space. With the proliferation of digital media, the rhetorical criticism of popular culture has focused increased attention on the confluences and contradictions across different texts responding to a particular issue, controversy, or event.

Although the critic plays a role in text construction within the analysis, the critic's scope of the text should share some semblance to audiences' consumption practices. Since most audiences view films and television programs in their entirety, an interpretive essay about a film or television program should not focus exclusively on one scene to form its conclusions. A critic's analysis would be unconvincing if the messages of one part of the film being analyzed were contradicted by another part of the film. After all, it would make no sense to solely analyze a scene of a lovers' spat if the two reconcile during the film's conclusion.

### Analyzing the Text

After you have established the scope of your text, you may begin to analyze its meaning. Rhetorical critics of popular culture explain the symbolic construction of meaning through an analysis of signifying practices within a text. **Signification** explains the process in which meaning is constructed through the relationship among signs within a text. This is something most of us understand implicitly. A sign is something that prompts the reader, viewer, or listener to think of something other than itself. For instance, the image of a stick figure on a door tells us that the room is a bathroom. Bathroom door signs are examples of iconic signs that structurally represent the objects they stand for. A map is another kind of iconic sign. Indexical signs are necessarily related to the objects that they represent. A flashing light on the dashboard of a car is a sign of a mechanical problem, and the sign of smoke at a campground indicates the presence of fire. Likewise, a train's whistle signals that a train is approaching. Alternatively, a symbol, a third kind of sign, refers to other things on the basis of shared agreement or convention. Words are symbols because their meanings are shared culturally. Thus, the English word *dog* and the Spanish word *perro* are symbols for the same thing. That English readers recognize the meaning of the word *dog* is the result of collective agreement that the furry animal and the word are related. Images and sounds such as the US flag and the tune of the national anthem are also symbols. Importantly, symbolic meaning changes over time.

The distinction between denotation and connotation elaborates on the processes of signification. Denotative meaning refers to the literal and descriptive meaning of words and other symbols shared by all members of a culture. For instance, the word *dog* evokes the image of a furry domesticated mammal with a wet nose, long tail, and propensity to bark. Connotative meaning involves the broader and more fluid associations and values attributed to particular signs. In the history of Western civilization, dogs have been symbols of loyalty and fidelity. But they are also symbols of protection and danger. Hence, a "BEWARE OF DOG" sign warns people to stay away from someone's personal property. The point of this example is to illustrate how meaning is contextual. Connotative meanings are dependent on the historical and cultural contexts in which particular signs are used. Likewise, they are shaped by their relationship with other signs within a particular context. The US flag has traditionally been associated with values such as freedom and patriotism, but when a protester holds a flag upside down at an antiwar rally, the flag symbolizes protest and criticism of US foreign policy. Roland Barthes, who introduced the concepts of denotation and connotation to cultural studies, highlighted the ideological dimensions of signification. Barthes observed that connotations attain mythic status when they are accepted as common sense.[19] To use the flag example again, every time people in the United States are asked to salute the flag, they are encouraged to express support for US institutions and government policies. In this way, the US flag promotes the myth of American exceptionalism. Protesters who refuse to salute the flag reject this myth. In 2011, Occupy Wall Street protesters replaced the stars on the flag with corporate logos including McDonald's golden arches and Nike's swoosh. By playing with the different signs on the flag, the protesters expressed an alternative ideology that is critical of the corporate influence on public policy.

A rhetorical critic looks at how different signs within a text (and possibly its paratexts) relate to one another to contribute meaning to a social or political issue. Critics have used a variety of approaches to explain the relationship among texts, both broadly and narrowly defined. An analysis of a narrowly defined text involves looking at how symbolic elements with a particular cultural product interact to create meaning. For example, to analyze a particular movie, the critic might focus on how the dialogue explains characters' motivations and facilitates narrative development. To analyze a particular magazine advertisement or web page, a critic could explain how the arrangements of words and images work together to give meaning to the featured product, issue, or topic. In any case, the critic should consider how the different formal elements that structure the text contribute to the text's meaning. An analysis of a film's dialogue might not be adequate because movies tell stories through the combination of moving images, sound, and dialogue. Thus, the connotations of a particular scene may be communicated not only through what characters say to one another but through other signs including camera angles, lighting, props, and actors' movements in front of the camera.[20] Likewise, to study popular music, a critic should pay attention not only to lyrics, but to sounds communicated through chords, rhythms, keys, and instrumentation.[21]

An analysis of a more broadly defined text involves looking at how symbolic elements interact across cultural products. In this case, the critic is analyzing the **intertextual** construction of meaning. An analysis of an Internet meme would necessarily be intertextual because the critic would need to explain how the meme's connotations shifted as it circulated and evolved with each use. An essay I wrote about press coverage of President Obama's 2008 inauguration is an example of an intertextual analysis. The mainstream press frequently described Obama's election as the fulfillment of Martin Luther King's "dream." Rather than analyze one individual news report, I examined dozens of news fragments, or the specific instances in which reporters and news pundits mentioned Martin Luther King to describe Obama's inauguration. I demonstrated how different media outlets worked in concert to give meaning to Obama's inauguration by repeating the idea that Obama's election was the conclusion to the civil rights saga. I argue that this narrative only made sense if audiences were unfamiliar with ongoing racial justice struggles that were active during the years after King's assassination.[22]

One approach to interpreting a text's meaning in relationship to other cultural discourses is through the concept of allegory. An **allegory** is a narrative that implicitly relates to historical or political issues that are not explicitly mentioned in the next. Traditional critics of allegory identify how characters and events within a narrative correspond with persons, events, and issues outside the narrative. Through this correspondence, the narrative conveys a more subtle secondary meaning beyond its surface meaning. Allegories reinforce broader myths or ideologies. One familiar example is George Orwell's novel *Animal Farm*, a story about barn animals that comments allegorically about the Bolshevik revolution and the development of the Soviet state. Recently, rhetorical critics Mike Milford and Robert Rowland interpreted the remake of the science fiction television program *Battlestar Galactica* as an allegory for criticisms of the Bush administration's War on Terror after 9/11.[23] To demonstrate that the program functioned as allegory, the authors drew comparisons between events depicted in the program and controversies debated in response to the War on Terror.

Another approach to interpreting the relationship between texts is through the concept of **homology**. Barry Brummett defines a rhetorical homology as a situation in which two or more kinds of experience appear to be structured according to the same patterns.[24] A homology is different from allegory in that it looks more at the formal patterns across discursive elements than at the content of ideas. To analyze a rhetorical homology, the critic would compare seemingly disparate sets of discourses to identify a similar underlying structure and explain how that structure is a template that orders human experience.[25] For instance, Brummett argues that the tension between something that is unique and that which is a copy is a homology that is expressed in horror films such as *Invasion of the Body Snatchers* and *The Ring* and in an academic essay by Walter Benjamin about reproductions of famous works of art. Both the fictionalized films and the serious academic essay express anxiety over the difficulties in distinguishing between the real object and the reproduction. Brummett concludes that by identifying this homology, critics can better understand why particular texts are meaningful to audiences and what motivates people to respond to them.[26]

Critics of popular culture should also be attuned to the placement of a particular text within its particular genre. William Benoit's chapter on generic elements in rhetoric explains how critics might study a particular text as representative of a larger population of texts that share specific commonalities. This approach could easily apply to the study of popular film, television, and music. If you watch many films, you are probably already familiar with genres of comedy, drama, action/adventure, documentary, and horror. Generally, rhetorical criticism of popular culture does not revolve around how a particular text fits within a particular genre. However, it is important to recognize how a text's membership within a particular genre conditions audiences' expectations and understandings. For instance, consider the television crime drama, a genre that is popularized by programs including *Law and Order*, *CSI-Miami*, *Bones*, and *Criminal Minds*. One convention of this genre is that law enforcement agents are always the protagonists. Another is that the guilty person is almost always brought to justice. These conventions implicitly teach audiences to trust in the justness and morality of police detectives and prosecuting attorneys and to be suspicious of defense attorneys and critics of the criminal justice system.[27] Critics may interpret a genre itself to explain how that genre functions ideologically, or they might simply need to note that a text fits within a particular genre to contextualize their analysis.

### Evaluating the Text

A rhetorical analysis of a particular popular-culture text typically concludes with an assessment and evaluation of the text's contribution to public life. Critics often identity the beliefs and value systems that are elicited within the text and explain how these value systems might shape audiences' responses to related social conflicts or controversies. They also often describe how the text's messages provide implicit lessons that could inform how audience members understand and act as citizens, workers, and/or family members. A key point of this evaluation should be to address the implications of the analysis for communities who have a stake in issues addressed by the text. My strategy for writing the conclusion is to identify a current event that is related to but different from the text I have analyzed. Based on my analysis, I explain how my text might encourage audiences to understand that issue. Then, I conclude with a statement about whether or not I believe such understanding promotes social justice for the people involved. For instance, one episode of the television crime drama *Blue Bloods* recently depicted the exoneration of a police officer who was accused of beating a suspect without just cause. In the context of the recent news media coverage of police brutality and killings of black suspects, this episode primes audiences to presume that police officers are innocent. This is disconcerting given the evidence that many law enforcement officers have seriously injured unarmed black people. The three critical essays in the following section of this chapter provide additional examples of how to evaluate a popular-culture text.

## CRITICAL ESSAYS

In this section, I provide three short critical essays that analyze aspects of the *Hunger Games* film franchise. Released in 2012, *The Hunger Games* is a fictional action film that revolves around Katniss Everdeen, a sixteen-year-old girl who inspires political resistance by challenging her repressive government. In the fictional country of Panem, the majority of citizens work within one of twelve districts that are each devoted to providing material resources to furnish the Capitol, a city that houses the nation's wealthy elites. To discourage the districts from rebelling against the Capitol, the government forces its citizens to participate in the Hunger Games, a televised competition in which children from each district battle to the death until one child remains. To prevent her younger sister from being forced into the game, Katniss volunteers herself. The ensuing narrative depicts Katniss's struggles as she prepares for the games, participates in them, and convinces the government to allow her and the other remaining survivor Peeta Mellark to live.

This movie is the first of four films adapted from the best-selling young adult novels by Suzanne Collins. It had the third-highest-grossing opening weekend in US history.[28] The sequel, *The Hunger Games: Catching Fire*, was the highest-grossing film released in the United States in 2013.[29] Both movies' box-office successes attest to the films' popularity. Clearly, the movies' narratives resonated with young filmgoing audiences. The first analysis is my allegorical reading of the first movie released in 2012. The second essay summarizes Rachel Dubrofsky and Emily Ryall's argument about the same movie's implications for gender and race relations.[30] The third analysis summarizes Joe Tompkins's critique of the paratexts surrounding the third movie in the series: *The Hunger Games: Mockingjay Part 1*.[31] The similarities across these three readings highlight our mutual interest in evaluating the implications of popular culture for ongoing power relations and social hierarchies. The differences between these readings reflect the diversity of ideological investments and interpretative practices within popular-culture criticism.

### CRITICAL ESSAY 1: *THE HUNGER GAMES* AS ALLEGORY FOR CLASS STRUGGLE

One explanation for *The Hunger Games*' success is that it resonated with ongoing public controversies that generated extensive media attention when Collins's novels and the movies were released. The movie revolved around the injustices of class inequality and political tyranny. This film shares similarities to alternative ideological discourses that proliferated after the economic turmoil and election of Barack Obama in 2008. I argue that themes within *The Hunger Games* have allegorical resonance to public controversies about capitalism and the role of the federal government. I also suggest that the film's emphasis on media spectacle offers implicit lessons about how advocates for change might use mainstream media to their advantage.

Stark class difference is one of the movie's central themes. The image of Katniss's District 12 contrasts sharply from images of the Capitol. The majority of District 12's workers labor in mines and live in modestly furnished homes. Many of them struggle to feed their children. By contrast, the Capitol is a technically advanced city comprised of tall, gleaming buildings and luxurious accommodations for its residents. When Katniss visits the Capitol, she is shocked by the residents' opulent displays of wealth and obsession with fashion. The theme of class difference is also presented by the strategies necessary to win the Hunger Games. Children from Districts 1 and 2, the wealthiest districts, are born and bred to compete in the games. Competitors from these districts have a clear advantage because they have developed skills and strategies through years of training that were not available to the other districts' children. In order to survive, contestants must appeal to donors to fund their resources, including food, water, and medicine. Contestants from poorer districts are at a disadvantage here as well; obviously, viewers from poorer districts have less to give their own children in the games.

The theme of wealth inequality in *The Hunger Games* resonates with issues addressed by Occupy Wall Street protesters a year before the film's release. The Occupy Wall Street movement garnered media attention when protesters occupied Zucotti Park, located in New York City's Wall Street financial district. Activists condemned economic inequality, greed, and corporate influence on government policy. Their political slogan, "We are the 99%," highlighted the statistic that the top 1 percent of the population earns 24 percent of the nation's income and holds 40 percent of its wealth.[32] A Tumblr page that helped to inspire the slogan, "wearethe99percent.tumblr.com," provides numerous examples of individuals who struggle with debt and poverty despite their college degrees and full-time employment. Like the central theme of *The Hunger Games*, the key theme of Occupy Wall Street is that income inequality unfairly advantages a small minority of wealthy citizens.

Government tyranny is another central theme in *The Hunger Games*. The Panem government enforces districts' participation in the Hunger Games through the deployment of heavily armed soldiers. Mediated messages from the Capitol "welcoming" audiences to the Hunger Games are clearly propaganda. The film's portrayal of government tyranny bears traces of the Tea Party's rhetoric that called for a reduction in the size of the federal government. During President Obama's first term in office, the Tea Party movement characterized the President's tax policies and domestic agenda as an attack on personal and economic freedom.[33] In recent years, Tea Party advocates have sponsored billboards above well-trafficked roads that compare Obama to the world's most brutal dictators. One billboard off highway I-70 in Kansas features a picture of Obama's face partially obscured by shadows next to a large caption that reads, "Wannabe Marxist Dictator." Audiences concerned about the federal government's threat to individual rights and freedom might find some similarities between the billboards' depiction of Obama and *The Hunger Games'* menacing portrayal of President Snow.

By giving cinematic form to the issues of class inequality and government tyranny, *The Hunger Games* promotes alternative ideologies that question the legitimacy of contemporary capitalism and politics. As audiences are encouraged to identify with Katniss Everdeen's struggles, they are invited to question the morality of income inequality and centralized government. Katniss Everdeen dares to challenge the tyranny of President Snow and refuses to embrace the greed inside the Capitol. Thus, she helps to legitimize Occupy Wall Street and Tea Party protesters' concerns and makes them relatable. Katniss's method of resistance might also provide lessons for resistance to real-world political problems. In this sense, *The Hunger Games* has counterhegemonic potential.

The theme of media spectacle in the movie helps to explain its counterhegemonic implications. President Snow controls the media and uses the spectacle of the Hunger Games in order to win the consent of the Capitol and the districts. The Panem government provides universal access to its state-controlled television so that everyone can watch the games. From the moment their names are announced as the participants in the upcoming game, contestants become objects of surveillance. Cameras follow them throughout their preparations and participation in the games. Although the Hunger Games are coercive, the publicity surrounding them dazzles viewers. Contestants parade around in stunning costumes in the days leading up to the games. During the games, each contestant's every movement is displayed on camera. The movie's focus on spectacle resonates with the enjoyment viewers take in watching reality television game shows in which contestants' dramatic wins and losses are sold to audiences as a form of weekly entertainment. Just as the drama of reality programming sells contestants' struggles to entertain audiences, the Hunger Games are offered to Panem citizens as compensation for and distraction from the Capitol's exploitation of them. President Snow's use of media to spread propaganda about the virtues of the Hunger Games resonates with both Tea Party and Occupy Wall Street activists' criticisms of the mainstream press. As media scholars have noted, the mainstream media promotes the hegemonic order by excluding or downplaying perspectives critical of mainstream politics and capitalism.[34]

The movie offers solutions to the problems of exploitative media, political tyranny, and economic inequality by depicting Katniss's survival strategies. Katniss uses the spectacle of the Hunger Games against the government's intended purposes. She appeals to viewers' sentiments by cultivating the impression that she and Peeta are romantically involved. When she and Peeta attempt to commit suicide together rather than be forced to kill one another, the Capitol is forced to allow them both to live. Ostensibly, to do otherwise could turn the majority of Panem's populace against the government. By performing romantic desire and threatening to kill herself for the sake of love, Katniss manipulates the government's efforts to control Panem's populace. By addressing viewers watching the games, she inspires resistance. The implicit lesson of the film is that the spectacle of popular culture may be a resource for challenging dominant hegemony. By working within its forms and manipulating its pleasures, media producers and those represented by the media may integrate new and revolutionary ideas into public life.[35] This lesson attests to the rhetorical potential of popular culture to promote radical social change in the face of a powerful hegemonic order.

## CRITICAL ESSAY 2: *THE HUNGER GAMES* AS THE PRODUCTION OF AUTHENTIC WHITENESS AND NATURAL FEMININITY

In contrast to my reading of *The Hunger Games* as a counterhegemonic allegory for class struggle and political critique, Dubrofsky and Ryalls argue that the movie conveys problematic messages about authentic whiteness and natural femininity. These critics explain how Katniss Everdeen is portrayed as more authentic than the other contestants and residents of the Capitol through her ability to "perform not performing."[36] Katniss's image of authenticity is based on her constant surveillance by the producers of the Hunger Games. Katniss appears uncomfortable and unrehearsed when she is asked to perform on camera even though she must make people like her to win the games. Her expressions of discomfort are a sign of her authenticity and trustworthiness. She is the movie's hero because she clearly does not want to play the game. As Dubrofsky and Ryalls point out, authenticity is a kind of performance; we all perform certain behaviors when we interact with others regardless of our intentions to do so. This particular depiction of authenticity is troubling to Dubrofsky and Ryalls because it draws upon the film's portrayal of Katniss as white and stereotypically feminine.

These critics analyze character development and film techniques to make their case. They observe how black characters are relegated to the background in the film. These characters are developed to the extent that they shed light on the motivations and heroic virtues of Katniss. The character of twelve-year-old Rue is important to the narrative because, as the youngest contestant, she is the most vulnerable. After Rue helps Katniss recover from an injury, Katniss is committed to helping Rue survive. On her deathbed, Rue makes Katniss promise that she will win the game. Rue's death helps to frame Katniss's efforts to win as noble. In addition to character construction, the movie's use of lighting presents Katniss as the "embodiment of natural feminine white beauty."[37] In several scenes, Katniss appears bathed in sunlight and her skin glows. By contrast, less noble characters' faces often appear in shadows. These scenes draw upon conventions in film that have associated whiteness with virtue and innocence. Ostensibly, a white character's heroism can be "read off her body."[38] By subordinating black characters and focusing on Katniss's white skin, the movie naturalizes whiteness. By privileging Katniss's whiteness as a sign of her authenticity, the film implicitly privileges white bodies over racialized bodies. In this way, the film subtly reinforces racist assumptions that black bodies are deviant and Other.

Dubrofsky and Ryalls argue that the film's message about "natural femininity" is also problematic.[39] They note that Katniss appears "naturally feminine" because she does not appear interested in performing particular gender rituals such as wearing makeup and dresses. Katniss's disinterest in performing these rituals "naturalizes her femininity."[40] Her femininity is also authenticated because she does not recognize how beautiful she is. Furthermore, many of her character traits are not explicitly feminine. Katniss does not actually seek romantic relationships, rarely expresses emotion, and does not want children. Yet she exhibits several feminine character traits nonetheless. During the games, she tends to contestants who are injured. Dubrofsky and Ryalls conclude that the movie's focus on her maternal traits suggests that "good women are always already mothers, and their value, strength, and heroism stem from their natural instincts and conventional heterosexual femininity."[41] Hence, the film promotes narrowly defined gender identities that position women who do not exhibit these character traits as outside what may be considered normal and desirable.

## CRITICAL ESSAY 3: THE *HUNGER GAMES* FRANCHISE AS PROMOTIONAL CYNICISM

While focusing on a single film within the political and historical context of its construction may help the critic explain how a popular-culture text contributes to the process of social change, attention to the paratexts surrounding that film may lead to a different set of observations that challenge the conclusions of scholars who have defined the scope of the text more narrowly. A look at the paratexts surrounding the *Hunger Games* franchise illustrates this point. Lionsgate Films, the movie's production company, marketed the third movie in the series, *The Hunger Games: Mockingjay Part 1*, through an interactive transmedia campaign that included billboard advertisements, websites, Tumblr pages, and YouTube videos. The variety of media platforms illustrates how marketers marshaled panmediation to shape the meaning and popularity of the franchise. The campaign included fake advertisements for "Hunger Games" fashion on billboards and a cross-promotional campaign with CoverGirl makeup. The cosmetics brand advertised its makeup collection "Capitol Beauty" by featuring models dressed in the flamboyant costumes of the Panem Capitol residents. The models' large wigs, dark red lips, and sequined eyebrows appear alongside images of cosmetic products and gold emblems that read, "Capitol Collection." The relationship between the bright colors on the models' faces and the text rearticulates the meaning of the film. In the ads, the citizens of the Capitol signify beauty rather than greed. They are objects of desire rather than objects of scorn.

The marketing campaign also included a website featuring news reports, propaganda, and weather forecasts for fictional Panem and a series of YouTube videos called "District Voices."[42] Both the website and the videos mimic the style of nonfiction media. The Capitol website adapts several conventions of websites designed for governments and cities, including the address, "www.thecapitol.pn," that might plausibly exist for a country. "District Voices" appears to have been produced by a television network owned by the fictional government of Panem. The YouTube series mimics the aesthetics of a video news release promoting the services of a political or commercial organization. In the episode titled "A District 9 Paean to Peeta's Bakery," two young adults, Jimmy Wong and Ashley Adams, speak directly to the camera and perform a cooking demonstration similar to those that frequently appear on morning television news programs to promote a celebrity chef or food product. The video elaborates on the character construction of Peeta Mellark as Adams explains that Peeta's family owned a renowned bakery in his home district. Wong and Adams then make an apple and goat cheese tart in his honor. The program is tongue in cheek as it combines elements of the films' narrative with the genre of a cooking demonstration. Props and dialogue reference the film's theme of class inequality. The kitchen is shabby, the oven is wood burning, and the sleeves of Adams's sweater are full of holes. Wong notes that, "depending on the district you're in, it may be difficult to find some of these ingredients, but the good citizens of Panem are endlessly resourceful, so we're sure you'll find a way." Although the video is ostensibly about cooking, it is clearly not designed to teach the audience to prepare a tart. By blurring the conventions of promotional news media with the narrative elements of *The Hunger Games*, "District Voices" simultaneously mocks the public-relations industry and promotes the *Hunger Games* franchise.

Comparing the narrative themes of the movie with its paratexts, Tompkins observes that the *Hunger Games* franchise constructs contradictory messages. On one hand, the film offers a narrative of mass revolt inspired by class injustice; on the other hand, the viral marketing campaign invites audiences to identify with the Capitol.[43] Tompkins asks, "How are we to make sense of this 'revolutionary' franchise, which essentially embodies what it claims to oppose?" Tompkins concludes that the franchise fosters an attitude of "promotional cynicism" that reflects contemporary audiences' ambivalent relationship to contemporary brand culture.[44] The marketing campaign provides multiple cues that ironically position the campaign as transparently fake. Thus, these cues enable fans of the film to recognize the campaign as a commercial ploy and consume it anyway. These cues also help to frame the meaning of the film in a way that undermines the film's counterhegemonic potential (my phrasing). Tompkins concludes that the *Hunger Games* franchise invites audiences to "entertain the *fantasy* of class revolution, while deriving pleasure from our *not* taking that fantasy seriously."[45] The panmediated marketing campaign has rhetorical implications when considered in the context of the film, recent populist movements in the United States, and prodemocracy movements in Hong Kong and Thailand. Tompkins concludes that the campaign ultimately discourages audiences from seeking social change.[46] Even though US publics are aware of economic inequality, and even though our popular entertainment addresses these conditions in fictional form, brand culture encourages us to maintain the status quo.

## PERSONAL REFLECTIONS

While my analysis shares Dubrofsky and Ryall's focus on the film itself as the scope of the analysis, we analyze the film through different frames of reference. I think the film primarily resonates with problems associated with class difference and economic exploitation, whereas Dubrofsky and Ryalls are primarily concerned with the film's implications for race and gender. Tompkins shares my interest in the film's portrayal of class struggle but defines the scope of the text differently. Consequently, he believes that the film has less potential to challenge dominant ideologies about class inequality than I do. The differences between our ideological frameworks and interpretive practices have led each of us to draw different conclusions about the film's social and political implications. Is one of these interpretations better than another? Perhaps. It is possible that each analysis offers valuable insights. But it could be equally possible that one interpretation is more meaningful than another. It depends on how well the analysis is supported by textual evidence from the film and its paratexts. It also depends on the reader's own subjectivity and ideological commitments.

## POTENTIALS AND PITFALLS

Although many academics believe that popular culture is an important site of politics and a potential resource for social change, some scholars do not believe that the texts of popular culture are worthy objects of rhetorical criticism. Given the rhetoric discipline's early investments in promoting civic engagement, some scholars are concerned that the focus on popular culture shifts attention away from public speeches, writings, and videos that directly shape democratic political decision making. For these scholars, the texts of popular culture are secondary to the texts that explicitly address audiences as citizens. Controversies regarding rhetorical criticism of popular culture highlight how critics' decisions about the texts they select for analysis are rhetorical acts. Which texts the critic chooses to study will shape how others understand his or her political and intellectual investments.

Rhetoric scholars who agree that popular culture merits serious analysis do not always share the same methodological approach or interpretive practices. Edward Schiappa contends that many academic critics of popular culture engage in what he refers to as "representational correctness," which he describes as an approach that evaluates particular texts on the basis of criteria that are impossible to meet.[47] The first criterion of *accuracy* requires that a representation of a social group should be authentic to the group's experience to avoid stereotyping; the second criterion of *purity* requires that a representation of social struggle must unequivocally advance social change and justice on behalf of marginalized groups and avoid presenting contradictory perspectives; and the third criterion of *innocence* requires that media texts avoid insulting the groups depicted.[48]

Schiappa laments that rhetorical criticism puts popular culture in a no-win situation. Critics tend to point out how popular culture reinforces stereotypes. For instance, one might critique *The Hunger Games* by pointing out that Katniss required the help of men around her to succeed at the game, reinforcing stereotypes that men are more skilled than women. When popular-culture texts do challenge stereotypes, critics often focus on how these texts reinforce normative beliefs. This kind of criticism might reason that Katniss's success at winning the Hunger Games is largely achieved through her skills as an archer, a skill that may be coded as a masculine strength. Schiappa argues that rhetorical interpretations based on criteria of accuracy, purity, and innocence have limited usefulness because all popular media texts are open to multiple interpretations, and some audiences' interpretations contradict the meanings that creators intended.[49] Further, Schiappa observes that such criticism is usually grounded in the questionable assumption that popular culture influences audiences' attitudes and beliefs.[50] Instead, he suggests that scholars need to explore how audiences respond to particular media representations.[51] To gain this information, Schiappa recommends using quantitative survey methods, which takes us far afield from rhetorical criticism.

Schiappa is not alone in faulting popular-culture critics for ignoring the ways in which different audiences may glean different meanings from the same text. Outside the rhetoric discipline, an approach to studying mass media known as reception studies has shifted away from the text and toward the reader as a site of meaning. Some of this scholarship has used ethnographic methods in which researchers observe how people use and talk about media in their everyday lives.[52] A premise of this work is that the needs and subject positions of audiences shape the reading strategies they use to make sense of a text. A prominent proponent of this position, John Fiske, advances the concept of polysemy, or the idea that different audiences may draw different meanings from the same cultural product.[53] Fiske admits that this does not mean that the text has no influence on audience interpretation. We can reasonably assume that most audiences will draw similar meanings from the combinations of signifiers in a text. However, members of different social groups may draw different associational meanings from the text based on their subject positions and experiences. For example, most viewers probably understand that *The Hunger Games* is a narrative about rebellion against an autocratic and unjust political system, but supporters of the Tea Party may read it as an affirmation that the federal government of the United States has overreached its authority, and supporters of Occupy Wall Street may believe that the movie reflects the exploitation of workers by the 1 percent. Further, people concerned by racial injustice may be more likely to critique the film's lack of empowered black characters. Each of these responses does not account for or explain the diversity of interpretations that are available to analyze the film.

One challenge for critics seeking to study the myriad ways in which audiences use popular culture is that audiences' own interpretations become texts for criticism. Schiappa might prefer to read a critical analysis of how online media blogs described and evaluated the character of Katniss Everdeen to determine whether the film promoted positive attitudes toward assertive and athletic young women. But analyzing paratexts does not avoid the critique that texts are open to multiple meanings. If different audiences can glean different meanings from a film or television program, then different scholars may also interpret a review of a film or television program from different or competing perspectives. Another problem with preferring viewers' interpretations is that it ignores how some interpretations may be better than others. For instance, a critic who tries to argue that *The Hunger Games* is a homology for fears about global warming will be unconvincing unless he or she can explain how signifiers throughout the film map onto discourses about climate change. I see few textual cues across the film's text and paratexts that support this thesis.

Rather than abandon rhetorical criticism for quantitative or ethnographic research, I am committed to rhetorical criticism because I believe that important insights about civic life can be made through thoughtful interpretations of popular culture. The approach I have recommended here is to build an analysis by drawing connections across the variety of signifiers that comprise the text. By thinking carefully about the scope of the text, the critic is in a stronger position to explain how meanings that emerge from the confluences across signifiers enable and constrain interpretation. This approach enables the critic to share important insights about a popular-culture text while acknowledging that his or her choices influence interpretation. By analyzing popular culture through this approach, the critic can explain how audiences might share understandings about social life and how those understandings evolve over time as different texts respond to one another and to their historical, social, and political contexts.

# RHETORICAL CRITICISM OF POPULAR CULTURE AND SOCIAL MEDIA TOP PICKS

This list provides just a snapshot of the myriad approaches to rhetorical criticism of popular culture and social media. My synopses of the analytical frameworks and thesis statements of each article demonstrate the variety of perspectives and types of mediated texts that are available to critics. Of course, as media culture changes, these perspectives and textual approaches will expand.

Brouwer, Daniel C., and Aaron Hess. "Making Sense of 'God Hates Fags' and 'Thank God for 9/11': A Thematic Analysis of Milbloggers' Responses to Reverend Fred Phelps and the Westboro Baptist Church," *Western Journal of Communication* 71 (2007): 69–90. This essay describes how military website blogs responded to the Westboro Baptist Church's protests of military funerals. The authors identify themes across these blogs to demonstrate how they functioned ideologically by excluding gay rights issues and queer identity from discussions about nationality and citizenship.

Buescher, Derek T., and Kent Ono. "Civilized Colonialism: *Pocahontas* as Neocolonial Rhetoric." *Women's Studies in Communication* 19 (1996): 127–153. This essay provides a narrative analysis of the Disney children's film. By substituting the history of Native American genocide with a romantic tale, the film provides ideological support for contemporary practices of colonialism.

Cloud, Dana L. "Hegemony or Concordance? The Rhetoric of Tokenism in 'Oprah' Winfrey's Rags-to-Riches Biography." *Critical Studies in Mass Communication* 13 (1996): 115–137. This is an influential essay that considers how the television and print biographies of television talk show host Oprah Winfrey functioned hegemonically to affirm the myth of the American Dream. This dream distracts attention from factors including race, gender, and class that pose limits to upward mobility for many people.

Dow, Bonnie J. *Prime-Time Feminism: Television, Media Culture, and the Women's Movement since 1970* (Philadelphia: University of Pennsylvania Press, 1996). This award-winning book analyzes how a variety of fictional television programs between 1970 and 1995 responded and contributed to cultural meanings about feminism. Dow uses hegemony theory to explain how television entertainment has represented feminism through the portrayals of white, middle-class heterosexual women. This book explains how commercial television extols the virtues of lifestyle feminism that foreground women's personal choices over political activism for women's rights.

Hoerl, Kristen, and Casey R. Kelly. "The Post-Nuclear Family and the Depoliticization of Unplanned Pregnancy in *Knocked-Up*, *Juno*, and *Waitress*," *Communication and Critical/Cultural Studies* 7 (2010): 360–380. In this essay, a coauthor and I analyze the narrative patterns across three separate fictional Hollywood films in which main characters have unplanned pregnancies and decide to give birth. We use a feminist perspective to argue that the films' portrayals of women's reproductive agency are problematic because it ignores the financial struggles that single mothers face.

King, Claire. "Rogue Waves, Remakes, and Resurrections: Allegorical Displacement and Screen Memory in Poseidon." *Quarterly Journal of Speech* 94 (2008): 430–454. This essay uses the concept of allegory to argue that the 2006 remake of the disaster film *The Poseidon Adventure* implicitly responds to the events of 9/11 and rhetorically manages their traumatizing effects.

McCann, Bryan J. "Contesting the Mark of Criminality: Race, Place, and the Prerogative of Violence in N.W.A.'s *Straight Outta Compton*." *Critical Studies in Media Communication* 29 (2012): 367–389. This essay analyzes a gangsta rap album and music video as resistant texts that challenged mainstream political discourses about race and criminality during the 1980s. McCann explains that NWA's depictions of violence should be understood as humorous parodies that draw attention to the racism of law enforcement practices and the prison system.

Stahl, Roger. *Militainment, Inc.: War, Media, and Popular Culture* (New York: Routledge, 2010). This book explains how the US war in Iraq was depicted by entertainment genres. Stahl contends that people were invited as citizens to become virtual participants in war via the rhetoric of sports, reality television, video games, and toys.

Vats, Anjali. "Racechange Is the New Black: Racial Accessorizing and Racial Tourism in High Fashion as Constraints on Rhetorical Agency." *Communication, Culture, & Critique* 7 (2014): 112–135. This essay analyzes the visual rhetorical processes that give meaning to racial and ethnic costuming of models in the fashion industry. Vats argues that these costumes discipline bodies and perpetuate the ideology of postracism that denies that categories of race function to oppress people of color.

## NOTES

1. Hunter Schwarz, "RIP 'American Idol': The Show that Proved How Bad Americans Are at Voting," *Washington Post*, May 11, 2015, accessed June 5, 2015, http://www.washingtonpost.com/blogs/the-fix/wp/2015/05/11/rip-american-idol-the-show-that-gave-us-an-easy-shorthand-for-americans-not-voting.

2. Barry Brummett, *Rhetorical Dimensions of Popular Culture* (Tuscaloosa: University of Alabama Press, 1990), xii.

3. Raymond Williams, *Culture and Society, 1780–1950* (1958; repr., New York: Columbia University Press, 1983), 325.

4. Bonnie J. Dow, *Prime-Time Feminism: Television, Media Culture, and the Women's Movement since 1970* (Philadelphia: University of Pennsylvania Press, 1996), 7.

5. Louis Althusser, *For Marx*, trans. Ben Brewer (1965; repr., London: Penguin, 1969); Louis Althusser, *Lenin and Philosophy and Other Essays*, trans. Ben Brewer (1970; repr., London: New Left Books, 1971).

6. Stuart Hall, "The Whites of Their Eyes: Racist Ideologies and the Media," in *Gender, Race, and Class in Media: A Text-Reader*, ed. Gail Dines and Jean M. Humez, 2nd ed. (Thousand Oaks, CA: Sage, 2003), 90.

7. Antonio Gramsci, *Selections from the Prison Notebooks*, trans. Quintin Hoare and Geoffrey N. Smith (1971; repr., New York: International Publishers, 2012).

8. Dana L. Cloud, "Hegemony or Concordance? The Rhetoric of Tokenism in 'Oprah' Winfrey's Rags-to-Riches Biography," *Critical Studies in Mass Communication* 13 (1996): 115–137.

9. Aniko Bodroghkozy, *Groove Tube: Sixties Television and the Youth Rebellion* (Durham, NC: Duke University Press, 2001); John Fiske, *Television Culture* (1987; repr., London and New York: Routledge, 2011).

10. Michel Foucault, *Power/Knowledge: Selected Interviews and Other Writings, 1972–1977*, ed. Colin Gordon, trans. Colin Gordon, Leo Marshall, John Mepham, and Kate Soper (1971; repr., New York: Pantheon Books, 1977).

11. Raymie McKerrow, "Critical Rhetoric: Theory and Praxis," *Communication Monographs* 56 (1989): 91–111.

12. Dow, *Prime-Time Feminism*, 5.

13. McGee argued that the proliferation of a variety of cultural products has created a fractured media environment. What we understand to be a finished discourse, such as a speech or film, is a reconstruction of fragments of other discourses from which it was made. Thus, the critic's role is to "invent a text suitable for criticism." Michael Calvin McGee, "Text, Context and the Fragmentation of Contemporary Culture," *Western Journal of Speech Communication* 54 (1990): 288.

14. Barry Brummett, *Rhetoric in Popular Culture*, 2nd ed. (Thousand Oaks, CA: Sage, 2006), 34.

15. See Kristi K. Cole, "'It's Like She's Eager to be Verbally Abused': Twitter, Trolls, and (En)Gendering Disciplinary Rhetoric," *Feminist Media Studies* 15 (2015): 356–358.

16. Jonathan Gray, *Show Sold Separately: Promos, Spoilers, and Other Media Paratexts* (New York: NYU Press, 2010), 6.

17. Kevin DeLuca, Sean Lawson, and Ye Sun, "Occupy Wall Street on the Public Screens of Social Media: The Many Framings of the Birth of a Protest Movement," *Communication, Culture, & Critique* 5 (2012): 487.

18. See for example Kathryn A. Cady, Robert Alan Brookey, and Renee M. Powers, "Seeing Dixie: Exposing Patriarchy in an Internet Meme," *Women and Language, Alternative Scholarship* (2011), accessed July 5, 2015, https://seeingdixie.wordpress.com/memes.

19. Roland Barthes, *Mythologies* (London: Cape, 1972).

20. For a detailed introduction to the aesthetics and grammars of film, see David Bordwell and Kristin Thompson, *Film Art: An Introduction*, 9th ed. (New York: McGraw-Hill, 2009). For a quick reference guide to film vocabulary, see Timothy Corrigan, *A Short Guide to Writing about Film*, 9th ed. (London: Longman, 2014).

21. For an example of rhetorical criticism of popular music that integrates the analysis of lyrics and sound, see Lisa Foster, "Populist Argumentation in Bruce Springsteen's *The Rising*," *Argumentation and Advocacy* 48 (2011): 61–80.

22. Kristen Hoerl, "Selective Amnesia and Racial Transcendence in News Coverage of President Obama's Inauguration," *Quarterly Journal of Speech* 98 (2012): 178–202.

23. Mike Milford and Robert Rowland, "Situated Ideological Allegory and *Battlestar Galactica*," *Western Journal of Communication* 76 (2012): 536–551.

24. Barry Brummett, "Social Issues in Disguise: An Introduction to Sneaky Rhetoric," in *Uncovering Hidden Rhetorics: Social Issues in Disguise*, ed. Barry Brummett (Thousand Oaks, CA: Sage, 2004), 9–10.

25. Barry Brummett, *Rhetorical Homologies: Form, Culture, Experience* (Tuscaloosa: University of Alabama Press, 2004).

26. Barry Brummett, "Rhetorical Homologies in Walter Benjamin, *The Ring*, and Capital," *Rhetoric Society Quarterly* 36 (2006): 449–469.

27. For a nuanced analysis of the rhetoric and history of the crime drama genre, see chapter 1 in Elayne Rapping, *Law and Justice as Seen on TV* (New York and London: New York University Press, 2003), 21–47.

28. Pamela McClintock, "Box Office Shocker: 'Hunger Games' Third-Best Opening Weekend of All Time," *Hollywood Reporter*, March 25, 2012, accessed July 16, 2015, LexisNexis Academic.

29. "'The Hunger Games . . .' Highest Grosser of 2013 in US," *Bollywood Country*, February 25, 2014, accessed July 16, 2015, LexisNexis Academic.

30. Rachel E. Dubrofsky and Emily D. Ryalls, "*The Hunger Games*: Performing Not-performing to Authenticate Femininity and Whiteness," *Critical Studies in Media Communication* 31 (2014): 395–409.

31. Joe Tompkins, "The Makings of a 'Revolutionary' Franchise: Promotional Cynicism and *The Hunger Games*" (paper presented for the annual meeting for the Union for Democratic Communications, Toronto, BC, May 3, 2015).

32. Ezra Klein. "Who Are the 99 Percent?," *Washington Post*, October 4, 2011, accessed July 19, 2015, http://www.washingtonpost.com/blogs/ezra-klein/post/who-are-the-99-percent/2011/08/25/gIQAt87jKL_blog.html.

33. Thomas Basile, "Once Effective, the Tea Party Has Become Toxic," *Forbes*, April 4, 2013, accessed July 19, 2015, http://www.forbes.com/sites/thomasbasile/2013/04/04/once-very-effective-the-tea-party-has-become-toxic.

34. DeLuca et al., "Occupy Wall Street"; Todd Gitlin, *The Whole World Is Watching: Mass Media in the Making and Unmaking of the New Left* (1980; repr., Berkeley: University of California Press, 2003); Kristen Hoerl, "Mario Van Peebles's 'Panther' and Popular Memories of the Black Panther Party," *Critical Studies in Media Communication* 24 (2007): 206–227; Kristen Hoerl, "Commemorating the Kent State Tragedy through Victims' Trauma in Television News Coverage, 1990–2000," *Communication Review* 12 (2009): 107–131.

35. The potential for commercial media to provide counterhegemonic messages is limited by the ownership and advertising structure of commercial media. Because commercial products must earn products for media owners, they are ultimately oriented around capitalist goals. Further, most commercial media earn profits through corporate sponsorship and cross-promotion with other commercial products. See Edward S. Herman and Noam Chomsky, *Manufacturing Consent: The Political Economy of the Mass Media* (New York: Pantheon Books, 1988).

36. Dubrofsky and Ryalls, "*The Hunger Games*," 396.

37. Ibid., 401.

38. Ibid., 401.

39. Ibid., 404.

40. Ibid., 405.

41. Ibid., 407.

42. The Capitol, accessed July 18, 2015, www.thecapitol.pn; Brooks Barnes. "With 'Hunger Games' Campaigns, Lionsgate Punches above Its Weight," *New York Times*, November 23, 2014, accessed July 10, 2015, http://www.nytimes.com/2014/11/24/business/media/hunger-games-studio-lionsgate-punches-above-its-hollywood-weight.html.

43. Tompkins, "The Makings of a 'Revolutionary' Franchise."

44. Ibid.

45. Ibid., emphasis in original.

46. Ibid.

47. Edward Schiappa, *Beyond Representational Correctness: Rethinking Criticism of Popular Media* (Albany: State University of New York Press, 2008), 9.

48. Ibid., 9.

49. Ibid., 10.

50. Ibid., 12.

51. Ibid., 23.

52. Two notable examples are David Morley, *The "Nationwide" Audience: Structure and Decoding* (London: BFI, 1980); Janice Radway, *Reading the Romance: Women, Patriarchy, and Popular Literature* (Chapel Hill: University of North Carolina Press, 1984).

53. Fiske, *Television Culture*, 15–16.

# Appendix A
# Writing Criticism: Getting Started

Writing your first piece of rhetorical criticism—not a summary of something, but rather the creation of new knowledge and the sharing of new ideas—can be a daunting task. There is no template or rubric for this type of paper, which makes answering the question, "How do I begin?" all the more important. Although there is no standard formula, there are some key elements to keep in mind as you write: theory and rhetorical artifacts, the actual analysis, writing the paper, and judging your product.

## STEP 1: RHETORICAL ARTIFACT OR RHETORICAL THEORY?

Unless you are blessed with a Eureka! moment as discussed in chapter 3, your first step in writing a piece of rhetorical criticism is determining whether you should begin with a rhetorical perspective or a rhetorical artifact. At first this decision will be challenging, but the more time you spend learning about rhetoric and criticism, the easier this step becomes. Your professor might assign one or the other starting point, or leave it up to you. If the latter, this choice should be made based on your personal interests. There are several points to keep in mind depending on whether you begin with theory or artifact.

For example, let us say that as you progressed through this book, two rhetorical theories really stood out: metaphor and Burke's notion of identification. As you think on this, you decide that you are particularly interested in how metaphor works in society and in our persuasive communication, so you decide metaphor is the theory you are going to use to write your critical paper. So far, so good. Now comes the decision about artifact. Unfortunately, you can't pick just anything, plug it into metaphor theory, and end up with a good piece of criticism. To ensure a good match with the theory, the artifact you decide on will need to have major elements of metaphor working in it. The range of potential artifacts can be broad depending on your professor's assignment—so, a speech, a debate, advertisements, a social media campaign such as NASA's #GlobalSelfie in honor of Earth Day, a popular cartoon show such as *Bob's Burgers* or *BoJack Horseman*, and many others. To keep from feeling overwhelmed by the choices available, ask your professor for examples of acceptable artifacts. Also keep in mind that whatever artifact you decide on must contain elements of the theoretical perspective you are going to use. For example, if metaphor is your theory, make certain whatever artifact you decide on has significant elements of metaphor.

There are many ways you can move from a theory that you like to finding an appropriate rhetorical artifact. For example, in terms of metaphor, say you have an interest in America's relationship with its Central and South American neighbors. You also happen to watch *House of Cards* regularly and noticed one episode that included references to South America, but you decided they were too fleeting to be meaningful. Then, in the course of reading some news articles about this area, you run across President Obama's 2015 "Remarks by the President at Opening of the CEO Summit of the Americas"[1] speech. You are excited about this speech as a possible candidate for your criticism paper. As you read through it, though, you discover that there is no significant use of metaphor. Although there are certainly other ways of analyzing the speech, using metaphor theory is just not a good fit. Later that evening, while checking out YouTube videos, you come across Denzel Washington's 2011 University of Pennsylvania commencement speech.[2] You listen to it and love it. Something he says catches your ear, and as you review the speech with metaphor in mind, you discover that you think there is a significant use of metaphor: Washington's use of "fall forward." You now have an artifact that matches up with the rhetorical perspective you are using.

However, suppose that you are able to first choose an artifact and then decide how to analyze it. If this is the case, when you initially came across President Obama's speech mentioned above, you would simply say, "I like this speech; it's interesting. *This* is the speech I'm going to analyze." As you read the speech, you are looking for elements that suggest a particular theory that will be helpful in analyzing how it works. Because the speech doesn't really make use of metaphor, you need to identify another theory that relates more directly to the content of the speech. While reading, you notice the sections about integration and technology. You feel drawn to how Obama described those ideas and believe he was making an attempt to craft a new policy by "identifying" with young voters. So you decide that if examined through the Burkean lens of identification, an analysis of the speech could bear fruit. You have now matched up a perspective to the rhetorical artifact that initially caught your eye.

## STEP 2: ANALYSIS

Before you actually begin to write your paper you will want to conduct the analysis of your rhetorical artifact. Time is necessary; lots of time. You simply cannot zoom through your artifact once and expect to produce insightful criticism, much less engage in any interpretation as discussed in chapter 3. So be certain to review your artifact extensively. I suggest reading (or watching) through several times just to become thoroughly familiar with it. Don't immediately take notes or make an outline. Simply allow yourself to walk through and engage with it—you are taking a "first look." After this, then go through and begin the process of highlighting, taking notes, and otherwise analyzing the text numerous times. Remember, you will need to be able to describe this artifact in your paper and do so in a way that allows it to speak for itself. That initial reading without preconceptions is important. As an example, let's say you were going to analyze an episode of *South Park*. You find an appropriate episode on YouTube and watch it. Then you watch it again, taking notes. (If you really want to be able to deeply analyze the text, you might obtain or make a transcript of the episode as well.)

Next, review the key concepts of the theory you are using and read through (or watch) your artifact with those in mind. How did they play out in the artifact? Were some stronger than others, or were some missing? How is the artifact better explained when viewed through the lens of the theory? What insights are gained? Some critics bring these key concepts to the artifact when first reviewing it. This certainly works well for many critics. I prefer to engage the artifact first, to try to get a feel for it on its own terms, and then bring theory to bear.

At some point you ought to develop a research question or questions. Although these can be informal—that is, kept to yourself—many critics prefer formal questions that can be shared in the essay. Research questions help guide you as you conduct your analysis. Depending on your purpose, you could have a narrowly tailored research question that seeks its answer from your particular artifact (e.g., What are the dominant metaphors in Washington's speech?), or it could be broader in that numerous artifacts or studies would be necessary for a complete answer, although your own study would certainly contribute to the answer. This latter focus is the more popular. For example, one could ask, "How does metaphor work to create audience unity in commencement speeches?" You would need more than just the one study of Washington's speech, but it would certainly produce information that would help answer this question.

I have always appreciated research questions: we critics are explorers, and research questions help guide us and keep us on track without being too controlling of our imaginations. There are no formal hypotheses in criticism as in the sciences. Remember, insight and appreciation are the twin goals of the art of criticism, although in more formal academic criticism, theory building is considered quite important by many scholars. With that in mind, consider asking yourself how your study sheds light on how the theory you used works; does it extend the theory or modify it in some way? Ask your professor about this issue and whether or not he or she wishes this in your paper. If theory building is an important part of what you are doing, then that ought to be reflected in your research question(s).

Remember, you are not concerned with finding one true interpretation of your artifact—the ultimate reality of your artifact. That is impossible. You are instead offering an interpretation to enrich us, to provide insight and foster appreciation, and perhaps to contribute to rhetorical theory. Your work, then, is a type of argument, asking others to agree with your way of viewing, your way of understanding the artifact. This necessitates that your essay be well reasoned. That is, your claims must be supported by actual evidence from the artifact, other sources, and your own reasoning about how the evidence supports your claims.

## STEP 3: WRITING THE PAPER

Although there is not a standard organizational formula for writing a rhetorical criticism paper, there are certain elements that ought to be included, and these are found within the common organizational pattern of introduction, body, and conclusion.

An introduction provides an overview of the subject on which you are writing, providing brief exposure to the main elements that will be in the body of your paper. Be certain to get straight to the point in your introduction. Although you may start by broadly contextualizing what you are doing, you want to quickly zero in on the specific analysis you are going to conduct. Do not forget to make a statement about the importance of what you are studying—not just why *you* find it important, but why *others* reading what you have written will find it important as well. Not all such statements begin with, "This study is important because . . ."; however, they do imply why the study is worthy to read. Here are two examples:

1. We believe that our study of the Netflix original series *Orange is the New Black* contributes to our understanding of the nuances of postfeminist narratives embedded in the show and their relationship to contemporary feminist themes operating in American society.

    This could also be reworded to read,

    This study is important because it contributes to our understanding of the nuances of postfeminist narratives embedded in the show and their relationship to contemporary feminist themes operating in American society.

2. "I argue actor-networks are not only rhetorical, as many ANT scholars claim, but that the entire network can and is often invoked in rhetorical practice as an inventional resource, an important insight that will help scholars further understand how scientific controversies are engaged in contemporary contexts."[3]

It is important that you include some variation of a topic statement (some say thesis statement), which is really a sentence or two about the general subject of your rhetorical criticism paper. Usually it shares the general *argument* you are advancing or the *understanding* you are sharing. Importantly for a criticism paper, you are making some type of assertion with it, not simply relaying the general area you are writing on. It has the crucial function of focusing your readers' attention on the specific area where you will be taking them, letting them know what it is that you seek to prove. The topic statement is usually followed by a listing of the main ideas or main points you will share in your paper: "The pages that follow are divided into four sections: first, I will . . . ; second, I . . ."; and so on.

Here is an example of a topic statement (albeit extended) and listing of the forthcoming main points from a published essay of criticism:

Specifically, we aim to demonstrate that *Supernatural*'s New Testament–based stories centering on the Four Horsemen of the Apocalypse . . . gave its audience messages about life grounded in Biblical lessons, essentially serving the purpose of a homily that one might hear in a church on a Sunday morning. While the Four Horsemen serve as antagonists to the series' two protagonists, we argue that their symbolism became a way to convey lessons about contemporary everyday life regarding the destructiveness of war, the fear created by pestilence, famine of spirituality, and the inevitability of death. To illustrate how these secular homilies function, we first briefly discuss research on television and religion. We then describe hermeneutics and homiletics, concepts central to understanding how a nonreligious fictional mainstream program can "preach" the Bible to an audience. Following this, we explain the nature and success of the show *Supernatural* and the group of episodes that serves as the case study for our analysis. Finally, we investigate those episodes we see as clearly offering homilies and the messages beyond the obvious Biblical interpretation inherent in them.[4]

After reading this, one knows what the main arguments are going to be and how the essay will be organized. It serves as an orienting gateway into the body of the essay.

The body of your essay will include both a description of the artifact and the theory you use, followed by your analysis/interpretation. The description of your rhetorical artifact is crucial to allowing your audience to follow you as you conduct your analysis, since not everyone will be familiar with your artifact. When describing the artifact, you should maintain a detached sense of curiosity about it. As you point out the artifact's important elements, keep in mind that your task at this point is not to judge it, or to express like or dislike, but to be fair minded. Try to describe it in such a way that the major elements you are going to analyze are shared and so that the artifact's voice is heard, not your own.[5]

The description section also involves a review of relevant literature. Generally you will need to review literature that covers both the artifact you are examining and also the theory you are using to guide your analysis. Are there previous studies on your artifact? If not, don't worry; you are going to be creating new knowledge about something—how exciting! If so, what did they say, and how does that relate to what you are going to do in your essay? What, in particular, are the key elements of the theory you are using, and how do they relate to how you are using the theory in your analysis? What have others written about this theory that is relevant to what you are doing? You do not have to summarize every idea and every study, but you do need to define key terms and explain key ideas enough so that someone unfamiliar with the theory can follow along and know how they relate to what you are doing. In a sense, you are *positioning* your study in relation to what has previously been written about your artifact and the theory you are using.

There is a tendency among beginning critics to overquote other critics. Unless a particular critic makes an especially cogent point or contributes in a significant way to your understanding of a concept or the artifact you are analyzing, don't feel you have to quote every person who has written on your subject. It could be, though, that a particular critic raised an issue to which you are responding, or perhaps the critic leaves off where you are beginning and you wish to establish that you are extending this critic's work, or even that you are quoting a particular critic who agrees with you on a particular point. What you want to avoid is a patchwork of quotes from other critics about your artifact or the theory you are using instead of presenting your ideas about how your analysis is going to work.

The conclusion to your rhetorical criticism paper should be brief and to the point. You will need a short summary of your major findings and then extend from there. Make certain that you relate how you made the case put forth in your topic statement. If you actually wrote out your research questions, make certain you answer them in your conclusion. Be certain to discuss how what you found relates to what others have said. This is where you highlight your essay's contributions to our insight and appreciation, and also perhaps how it contributes to rhetorical theory. You want others reading the conclusion to have a sense of what it was that you did that adds to the conversation about your topic.

## STEP 4: JUDGING YOUR PRODUCT

There is no such thing as good writing, only good rewriting.[6] Good criticism is like that. After following the steps above, you will have a draft, not a completed product of criticism ready to share with the world (or even with your professor). Set it aside for a while (good criticism takes time) and then come back to it with fresh eyes that will allow you to rework your essay in various ways. The more times you can repeat this, the better—until ultimately you feel it is complete. To successfully arrive at that point, keep in mind several questions as you move through the draft process:

- Do I have a strong topic statement?
- Have I provided a rationale for doing this study? Have I relayed the importance of what I have found?

- Have I provided clear statements of my claims that are then followed by actual examples?
- Is my essay well organized? If uncertain, let someone else read it with organization in mind.
- In my conclusion have I actually moved beyond summary and provided clearly the insights generated in my analysis?
- Have I reviewed the instructions provided by my professor?

What I have written here is only one way of writing a rhetorical criticism essay, although it is in keeping with what would be considered normal inclusions and concerns. Ultimately the best way to learn how to write good criticism is to read examples of published criticism, write your own criticism, and allow others to provide you with feedback.

## NOTES

1. Barack Obama, "Remarks by the President at Opening of the CEO Summit of the Americas" (White House, Office of the Press Secretary, April 10, 2015), https://www.whitehouse.gov/the-press-office/2015/04/10/remarks-president-opening-ceo-summit-americas.

2. https://www.youtube.com/watch?v=QyDo5vFD2R8.

3. Richard D. Besel, "Opening the 'Black Box' of Climate Change Science: Actor-Network Theory and Rhetorical Practice in Scientific Controversies," *Southern Communication Journal* 76, no. 2 (2011): 122.

4. Joseph M. Valenzano III and Erika Engstrom, "Homilies and Horsemen: Revelation in the CW's Supernatural," *Journal of Communication and Religion* 36, no. 1 (2013): 52.

5. See note 9 in Jim A. Kuypers, "Must We All Be Political Activists?," *American Communication Journal* 4, no. 1 (2000), http://ac-journal.org/journal/vol4/iss1/special/kuypers.htm; and also Jim A. Kuypers, "Criticism, Politics, and Objectivity: Redivivus," *American Communication Journal* 5, no. 1 (2001).

6. I have seen this quote attributed to novelist Robert Graves, Samuel Clemens, Supreme Court Justices Oliver Wendell Holmes and Louis Brandeis, and my high school American literature teacher.

# Appendix B

## Additional Rhetorical Perspectives and Genres

Critics have a rich variety of perspectives and genres of criticism at their disposal, including but by no means limited to those discussed in more detail in the preceding chapters. Likewise, the following is not meant to be a comprehensive list of *every* perspective and genre available. Rather, it represents a sampling of areas not already covered in this text, as well as areas that represent my (the editor's) own interests and the interests of numerous critics with whom I regularly converse. Arranged alphabetically, each entry provides a brief overview and highlights one exemplary essay.

**Apologia:** This is a genre of discourse explored by critics rather than a perspective for engaging in criticism. *Apologia* is the term used to describe a variety of apology strategies. For example, B. L. Ware and Wil A. Linkugal list four basic apology strategies: denial, bolstering, differentiation, and transcendence.[1] One type of apologia is "image restoration." Bill Benoit suggests five strategies rhetors may employ when repairing their public images: denial, evading responsibility, reducing the event's offensiveness, taking corrective action, and mortification.[2] Given the prevalence of apologies in public life, there is a rich and long history of apologia examples and literature.

See: Noreen Wales Kruse, "Apologia in Team Sport," *Quarterly Journal of Speech* 67, no. 3 (1981): 270–283.

**Cluster Analysis:** Initially developed by Kenneth Burke, it is one way of determining the worldview of rhetors through the analysis of key terms within their discourse. Using this approach a critic identifies key terms in a rhetorical artifact. Key terms are determined by either their intensity (how strongly they are used) or their frequency (how often they appear) or a combination of both. Once these key terms are discovered, the critic then charts "clusters" or groupings of other terms surrounding the key terms; these subordinate terms help to provide the meaning for the key terms. Finally, the critic analyzes how the cluster of terms coordinate, or produce patterns, in order to discover what messages are being presented to those exposed to the rhetorical artifact.

See: Adriana Angel and Benjamin Bates, "Terministic Screens of Corruption: A Cluster Analysis of Colombian Radio Conversations," *KB Journal* 10, no. 1 (2014), http://kbjournal.org/angel_bates_terministic_screens_of_corruption.

**Conceptually Oriented Criticism:** A flexible orientation (as opposed to perspective) on criticism. The starting premise is that a text in which a critic is interested will itself suggest a "concept" or a "conceptual" question the critic can explore. A critic with this orientation is particularly interested in how the text interacts with its historical context and the central concept(s) within the text itself. There can emerge an evolving interaction between the critic, the text, the historical context, and the concept as the critique unfolds; this process can lead to insightful discoveries about the text's impact on human consciousness. The key idea here is that the "conceptual orientation examines the way that particular concepts that shape or inform symbolic activity are expressed in significant texts and using this exchange to explore shifts in human consciousness and standards of judgment."[3]

See: Stephanie Houston Grey, "Conceptually-Oriented Criticism," *Rhetorical Criticism: Perspectives in Action*, ed. Jim A. Kuypers, 341–362 (Lanham, MD: Lexington Books, 2009).

**Framing Analysis:** Critics using framing analysis examine the process whereby communicators act—consciously or not—to construct a particular point of view that encourages the facts of a given situation to be viewed in a particular manner, with some facts made more or less noticeable (even ignored) than others.[4] Framing analysis can be used to better understand any rhetorical artifact, with critics examining a text to discover how some aspects of reality are highlighted over others, and also how frames act to define problems, diagnose causes, make moral judgments, and suggest remedies. Frames are central organizing ideas within a narrative account of an issue or event; they provide the interpretive cues for otherwise neutral facts.[5]

See: Michael C. Sounders and Kara N. Dillard, "Framing Connections: An Essay on Improving the Relationship between Rhetorical and Social Scientific Frame Studies, Including a Study of G. W. Bush's Framing of Immigration," *International Journal of Communication* 8 (2014): 1008–1028.

**Judgmental Analysis:** Seeks to examine the ideas expressed in discourse by asking what judgments a text is asking its audience (readers, viewers, listeners) to make. These are called judgmental appeals. Judgmental analysis is useful in exposing "the judgments audiences are asked to make by a speaker."[6] It allows critics to determine the standards of reason that a rhetor asks his or her audiences to use when judging the situation under discussion. In some senses this type of analysis allows critics to "chart" the rhetorical patterns of persuasive appeals made in a text.

See: Jim A. Kuypers, "From Science, Moral Poetics: Dr. James Dobson's Response to the Fetal Tissue Research Initiative," *Quarterly Journal of Speech* 86, no. 2 (2000): esp. 148–150, 163.

**Movements (social, rhetorical):** Critics in this area examine the discourse of rhetors who are part of a large, noninstitutionalized group or collective seeking to change, remove, or protect some aspect of the current economic, political, or social order. Such efforts at public advocacy, when popularly (grassroots) generated and of a sustained nature, are generally called social or rhetorical movements. Examples include the civil rights movement, the pro-life movement, the slow foods movement, the men's rights movement, and the animal rights movement.

Critics may be interested in individual speakers (movement leaders) or specific manifestos or single-event messages, although it is more typical to look at broad rhetorical strategies used in making a particular movement successful (or not), as well as in identifying the core, common rhetorical features of movements.

See: Eric C. Miller, "Phyllis Schlafly's 'Positive' Freedom: Liberty, Liberation, and the Equal Rights Amendment," *Rhetoric & Public Affairs* 18, no. 2 (2015): 277–300.

**Mythic Criticism:** Richard Slotkin defined myths as "stories drawn from a society's history that have acquired through persistent usage the power of symbolizing that society's ideology and of dramatizing its moral consciousness. . . . Myths are formulated as ways of explaining problems that arise in the course of historical experience."[7] Critics exploring myth often use rhetorical theory mixed with psychological and anthropological theory. Archetypal myths can provide patterns from which similar stories are made, and critics operating from a mythic perspective attempt to discover how myths operate rhetorically in everyday discourse.

See: Janice Hocker Rushing and Thomas S. Frentz, "The Mythic Perspective," *Rhetorical Criticism: Perspectives in Action*, ed. Jim A. Kuypers, 231–256 (Lanham, MD: Lexington Books, 2009).

**Postcolonial Criticism:** A critical perspective starting from the premise that third world and non-Western countries are influenced by Eurocentrism and Western cultural imperialism inherent in Western discourses. "Articulated mainly within the intersectional critical space of cultural studies, postcolonialism primarily challenges the colonizing and imperialistic tendencies manifest in discursive practices of 'first world' countries in their constructions and representations of the subjects of 'third world' countries and/or racially oppressed peoples of the world."[8] Critics using this perspective often ask questions such as, How do global media practices, especially those of the United States, act as a forceful cultural insertion into other cultures, fomenting a type of cultural imperialism, perpetuating racism and a type of neocolonialism? and How do the discursive practices of Western nations, "in their representations of the world and of themselves, legitimize the contemporary global power structures?"[9] Some current efforts in this area focus on "decolonization," or a kind of responsible corrective to the difficulties caused by colonization; this "reconstruction" seeks to find respectful and responsible solutions to problems perceived by the critic.

See: Jason Edward Black, "Rhetorical Circulation, Native Authenticity, and Neocolonial Decay: The Case of Chief Seattle's Controversial Elegy," *Rhetoric & Public Affairs* 15, no. 4 (2012): 635–646.

**Public Memory:** "A shared sense of the past, fashioned from the symbolic resources of community and subject to its particular history, hierarchies, and aspirations."[10] For critics it is in part the analysis of public sites created for remembrance. Critics working with public memory are concerned with the rhetorical process of how public memory is created, stored, and retrieved. They ask questions such as, How does public memory become "embedded in the available structures of lived experience"?[11] and How is public memory discursively constructed? They often begin with the assumption that "public memory lives as it is given expressive form; its analysis must therefore presume a theory of textuality and entail an appropriate mode of interpretation." Thus not only museums and memorials, but also reenactments, ceremonies, and rituals can be analyzed for their role in public memory.

See: Nicole Maurantonio, "Material Rhetoric, Public Memory, and the Post-It Note," *Southern Communication Journal* 80, no. 2 (2015): 83–101.

**Queer Rhetoric:** A critical perspective tracing its main academic roots to the mid-1990s gay, lesbian, bisexual, and transgendered rights movement. Critics in this area look at how GLBT groups' activism shapes and interacts with public discourse, specifically asking what constitutes the various rhetorical modes of GLBT expression. Distinct from gay cultural studies, a queer rhetoric suggests that the GLBT rights movement "as it enters a new phase of consciousness [in the mid-1990s] could be accountable for having developed a specific rhetorical practice in the public sphere."[12] Contemporary practices have expanded on the earlier examples of queer rhetoric to embrace a larger concern of critiquing discourses of sexuality that establish norms (what is considered normal) for sexuality in the public sphere. Such critiques often offer counterdiscourses that actively seek to offer alternate views on sexuality. In short, "queer rhetorical practice focuses in particular on *sexual* normalization and the regimes of discursive control through which [human] bodies" are categorized as sexually normal or as Other.[13]

See: Charles E. Morris and John M. Sloop, "'What Lips These Have Kissed': Refiguring the Politics of Queer Public Kissing," *Communication and Critical/Cultural Studies* 3, no. 1 (2006): 1–26.

**Rhetoric of Argument:** Critics examining arguments certainly look at types of arguments and how they function in certain contexts: inductive or deductive, enthymemes, signs, parallel cases, analogies, and many others. These critics are interested in how people "justify their beliefs and values and [how they] influence the thought and action of others."[14] Beyond analysis of particular argument types, critics are also interested in "the rationality or reasonableness of claims put forward in discourse."[15] A wide range of artifacts can be analyzed, from specific instances of argument in a text to broad national or international issues discussed over a period of time, such as the degree to which human activity is responsible for climate change.

See: Eric C. Miller, "Fighting for Freedom: Liberal Argumentation in Culture War Rhetoric," *Journal of Communication & Religion* 37, no. 1 (2014): 102–125.

**Rhetoric of Music:** There are two broad aspects examined by critics in this area: the analysis of song lyrics and the analysis of music (without words) for its persuasive effects. Critics are interested in music and song because they "can create socially shared meanings in both the artistic and rhetorical sense."[16] In terms of song lyrics, "music functions both as an expression of the artist and as an invitation to the audience to identify with the themes, ideas, and emotions expressed. If rhetoric is conceptualized either as constructing or interpreting reality, music is a powerful part of that process."[17] Song lyrics may be analyzed from any number of rhetorical perspectives. Of particular interest to critics are songs designed to inspire attitude change. Yet one can analyze the music that carries the song lyrics, or even nonvocal music composition, for rhetorical dynamics as well. Music is, after all, a symbolic language, with a particular vocabulary and grammar. Musical notes, keys, harmony, and other elements have parallel structures to written and oral language and may be analyzed to determine the rhetorical aspects of a musical composition. The idea is that music can represent emotions and ideas and thus have effects similar to that of written and spoken language.

See: Caroline C. Koons, "The Rhetorical Legacy of 'The Battle Hymn of the Republic,'" *Southern Communication Journal* 80, no. 3 (2015): 211–229.

**Rhetoric of Science** (also known as rhetoric of inquiry): Critics in this area explore the interrelationships among reality, language, and the nature of knowledge, in particular questioning the idea of an absolute grounding for knowledge. There is a particular focus on analyzing the discourse of scholars and scientists when transmitting their "knowledge" to others. The idea is that both scholars and scientists write rhetorically (whether to a greater or lesser degree).[18] Thus critics in this area are critiquing both the reading and writing practices of scholars and scientists.

See: Celeste Condit, "Insufficient Fear of the 'Super-flu'? The World Health Organization's Global Decision-Making for Health," *Poroi: An Interdisciplinary Journal of Rhetorical Analysis & Invention* 10, no. 1 (2014): 1–31.

## NOTES

1. B. L. Ware and Wil A. Linkugel, "They Spoke in Defense of Themselves: On the Generic Criticism of Apologia," *Quarterly Journal of Speech* 59, no. 3 (1973): 273–283.
2. William Benoit, *Accounts, Excuses, and Apologies: A Theory of Image Restoration Strategies* (New York: State University of New York Press, 1995).
3. Stephanie Houston Grey, "Conceptually-Oriented Criticism," in *Rhetorical Criticism: Perspectives in Action*, ed. Jim A. Kuypers, 341–362 (Lanham, MD: Lexington Books, 2009), 342–343.
4. Jim A. Kuypers, "Framing Analysis as a Rhetorical Process," *Doing News Framing Analysis*, ed. Paul D'Angelo and Jim A. Kuypers, 286–311 (New York: Routledge, 2010).
5. For an example of this, see Joseph M. Valenzano, "Framing the War on Terror in Canadian Newspapers: Cascading Activation, Canadian Leaders, and Newspapers," *Southern Communication Journal* 74, no. 2 (2009): 174–190.
6. Roderick P. Hart, *Modern Rhetorical Criticism* (New York: HarperCollins, 1990), 102.
7. Robert Slotkin, *Gunfighter Nation: The Myth of the Frontier in Twentieth-Century America* (New York: Atheneum Books, 1992), 5–6.
8. Raka Shome, "Postcolonial Interventions in the Rhetorical Canon: An 'Other' View," *Communication Theory* 6, no. 1 (1996): 41.
9. Ibid., 42.
10. Stephen H. Browne, "Reading, Rhetoric, and the Texture of Public Memory," *Quarterly Journal of Speech* 81 (1995): 248.
11. Ibid., 248.
12. Philippe-Joseph Salazar, "Queer Rhetoric," in *Encyclopedia of Rhetoric*, ed. Thomas O. Sloane (New York: Oxford University Press, 2001), 649.
13. Jonathan Alexander and Jacqueline Rhodes, "Queer Rhetoric and the Pleasures of the Archive: Introduction," *Enculturation: A Journal of Rhetoric, Writing and Culture* (January 16, 2012), http://enculturation.net/files/QueerRhetoric/queerarchive/intro.html.
14. David Zarefsky, "Argumentation," in *Encyclopedia of Rhetoric*, ed. Thomas O. Sloane (New York: Oxford University Press, 2001), 33.
15. Zarefsky, "Argumentation."
16. Karyn Rybacki and Donald Rybacki, "The Rhetoric of Song," *Communication Criticism: Approaches and Genres* (Belmont, CA: Wadsworth, 1991), 275.
17. Michael McGuire, "'Darkness on the Edge of Town': Bruce Springsteen's Rhetoric of Optimism and Despair," in *Rhetorical Dimensions in Media: A Critical Casebook*, ed. Martin J. Medhurst and Thomas W. Benson, 2nd ed. (Dubuque, IA: Kendall-Hunt, 1991), 305.
18. Alan G. Gross, *Starring the Text: The Place of Rhetoric in Science Studies* (Carbondale: Southern Illinois University Press, 2006); Nathan Crick, "When We Can't Wait on Truth: The Nature of Rhetoric in the Rhetoric of Science," *Poroi: An Interdisciplinary Journal of Rhetorical Analysis & Invention* 10, no. 2 (2014): 1–27.

# Appendix C

## Glossary of Terms

**agency:** refers to a person's ability to enact change in a specific situation.

**allegory:** a narrative in which characters and events correspond with persons, events, and issues outside the text to convey a secondary meaning beyond its surface meaning.

**analysis:** discovering what is in a rhetorical artifact and explaining how the rhetorical artifact works. Analysis provides a sketch of sorts, showing how the artifact is put together: what its parts are, how they go together, and what the whole looks like.

**anaphora:** a rhetorical figure of speech that involves the repetition of the same word or phrase at the beginning of each clause.

**artistic proofs:** arguments invented by the speaker as evidence or "proof" to believe him or her. (See *logos*, *pathos*, and *ethos*.)

**audience**, rhetorical: within a rhetorical situation perspective, this is the collection of persons who are capable of modifying the situation's exigency.

**characters:** stories are driven by the conflict between the protagonist or hero and the antagonist or villain, who may be a person or some other obstacle that must be overcome.

**close textual analysis:** an approach to rhetorical criticism seeking to account for the ways in which texts produce meaning and activate convictions in public contexts.

**constraints:** within a rhetorical situation perspective, these are elements that can influence both what can and can't be said concerning the modification of the exigency. "They are made up of persons, events, objects, and relations which are parts of the situation because they have the power to constrain decision and action needed to modify the exigence. Standard sources of constraint include beliefs, attitudes, documents, facts, traditions, images, interests, motives and the like; and when the orator enters the situation, his discourse not only harnesses constraints given by the situation but provides additional important constraints—for example his personal character, his logical proofs, and his style."[1]

**content:** textually produced meaning reduced to its propositional level. Content cannot be divorced from form.

**context:** the various circumstances that surround a particular situation, event, and so on, to which rhetors attend in shaping potentially persuasive messages. Variables may include, but are not limited to, the historical moment in which rhetor and audience find themselves, the dynamics of the sociocultural milieu in place, and the nature of the immediate setting (for instance, assumptions and preparation that precede a political speech at a campaign rally surely differ from those that guide planning for funeral remarks to note the passing of someone revered universally). It is the field of operation within which a text is placed, and with which it interacts to produce meaning, action, and effect. Context cannot be divorced from text.

**continual critique:** this phrase assumes that any particular change in human relations (or power differences between people) is not a sign that perfection has been reached; thus, they are open to reexamination. You may not make a change as a result of the critique, but any change in power relations is always open to future reconsideration.

**critic as inventor:** in this role the critic does not conceive of invention as making things up out of nothing, but rather as discerning, within the vast and complex world of signs and symbols, what influences might be present in determining how one's own orientation is formed or altered.

**critical act:** the actual act of performing and sharing criticism. Consists of three parts: the conceptual stage, the communication stage, and the countercommunication stage.

**critical rhetoric:** references a way of approaching criticism that enables the critic to examine relations of power that either inhibit or foster new human relations.

**criticism:** "the systematic process of illuminating and evaluating products of human activity. [C]riticism presents and supports one possible interpretation and judgment. This interpretation, in turn, may become the basis for other interpretations and judgments."[2]

**critique of domination:** This critique has an emancipatory aim, a "freedom from" that which controls the beliefs or actions of others.

**critique of freedom:** focuses attention on "freedom to" be other than what one is at the present moment.

**cultural studies:** an interdisciplinary field concerned with the relationship between culture and power. It focuses on the ways that symbolic action reproduces, resists, and transforms existing power relations and conditions of inequality. This approach to criticism explains how mass media construct, affirm, and sometimes challenge social hierarchies based on categories of identity such as race, gender, class, sexual orientation, and nationality.

**decentering:** references a removal of the role of the speaker as the origin of thought, words, and action in order to focus attention on the context that brings discourse into existence.

**deliberative discourse:** is concerned with the future, and its auditors are asked to make judgments about future courses of action.

**diachronic:** in the context of ideographic criticism, the diachronic dimension explores a society's changing ideological commitments through time by tracing the changes in ideographic usage. In the United States, for example, over the past century <equality> has become an ever more important ideological commitment, and its prominence has come at the expense of other ideographs.

**discourse:** refers to language in use, or more broadly, the interactive production of meaning.[3]

**disposition:** also known as organization; the arranging of the speech's (text's) materials in various structures to achieve a particular effect.

**doxastic:** refers to the role of opinion in forming what we know about the world.

**dramatism:** Kenneth Burke's theory of language and human action. Dramatism contains a number of Burke's central ideas, including the role of language to provide terministic screens, the role of identification in persuasion, the power of form to shape human perceptions and expectations, and the dramatistic pentad.

**dual audience:** criticism often teaches that a key variable for assessing a rhetorical experience is the extent to which a message is adapted to a "target audience." Complicating the task, though, are situations in which the speaker or writer must address a message to auditors with conflicting priorities. Political convention speakers, for example, are often challenged to excite or invigorate the immediate audience of delegates and political professionals, while simultaneously reaching, through the mass media, viewers whose politics differ from those at the convention.

**enthymeme:** generally understood as a syllogism that is missing a premise which is supplied by the audience. The missing premise is understood as an unstated assumption.

**epideictic discourse:** is set in the present and concerns speeches of praise or blame, with the values that hold the audience or society together. Its auditors are being asked to make judgments concerning how well the speaker accomplishes his or her goals.

**epistemic:** refers to that knowledge which is certain. Epistemology refers to the nature of knowledge.

**epistrophe:** a rhetorical figure of speech that has the repetition of the same phrase at the end of each clause.

**ethos:** an interpretation by the audience of qualities possessed by a speaker as the speaker delivers his or her message. Thus, by the way a speaker constructs and makes an argument, an audience will make judgments about his or her intelligence, character, and goodwill.

**exigence:** "an imperfection marked by urgency; it is a defect, an obstacle, something waiting to be done, a thing which is other than it should be."[4] To be rhetorical in nature an exigency must need discourse as part of its successful modification. In any rhetorical situation there will be at least one controlling exigency, and this will convey an organizing principle to the situation and also determine what audience should be addressed.

**exordium:** the introductory part of a speech. It reviews the purpose of the speech, and the type of cause being presented.

**feminism:** a pluralistic movement interested in altering the political and social landscape so that all people, regardless of their identity categories, can experience freedom and safety, complexity and subjectivity, and economic and political parity—experiences associated with being fully human.

**forensic discourse:** is concerned with past acts, and its auditors are asked to make judgments concerning what actually happened in the past.

**form:** linguistic resources that give conspicuous structure to otherwise abstract formulations, typically elements of style, voice, and genre. Form cannot be divorced from content. It can be a pattern that invites our participation; it arouses our desires and promises to fulfill them. We see the power of form when we know a pattern and expect it to be repeated.

**generic antecedents:** modes of expression established by traditional usage and that in turn may shape and give effect to any given instance of textual action.

**generic application:** a deductive approach to generic criticism that begins with a genre that has already been described; it applies the characteristics of that genre deductively to another instance of that genre in order to explain or evaluate it.

**generic description:** an inductive approach to generic criticism that begins by identifying the defining characteristics of the suspected genre, then looks for and carefully examines examples of discourse from that suspected genre for similarities, and then explains discovered similarities in order to identify the characteristics of the new genre.

**generic hybrid:** see *rhetorical hybrid*.

**generic rhetorical criticism:** involves looking for the observable, explicable, and predictable rhetorical commonalities that occur in groups of related discourses as well as in groups of people.

**hegemony:** the process by which the system of social hierarchies, structures, institutions, relations, customs, and values remain stable by generating the voluntary consent of its members.

**homology:** disparate sets of discourse that have a similar underlying structure that orders human experience. Looks more at the formal patterns across discursive elements rather than in content of ideas.

**identification:** an extension of the traditional notion of persuasion, associated with Kenneth Burke, that takes into account unconscious persuasive effects. It is thus the often-unconscious processes by which we align ourselves with others and act based on similarities or shared interests. Identification occurs when you choose a path of action not simply based on weighing the pros and cons of that action, but because you perceive that action as aligning you with other people like you.

**ideograph:** term coined by Michael McGee to designate an ordinary-language term found in political discourse. It is a high-order abstraction representing commitment to a particular but equivocal and ill-defined normative goal. Examples of ideographs, which are usually placed inside angle brackets when discussed by critics, would include <property>, <liberty>, <democracy>, <freedom>, and <rule of law>.

**ideological turn:** Philip Wander has characterized the ideological turn in modern criticism as reflecting "the existence of crisis," acknowledging "the influence of established interests and the reality of alternative worldviews," and commending "rhetorical analyses, not only of the actions implied but also of the interests represented."[5]

**ideology:** any system of ideas that directs our collective social and political action. Can also be "a set of opinions or beliefs of a group or an individual. Very often ideology refers to a set of

**political** beliefs or a set of ideas that characterize a particular culture. Capitalism, communism, socialism, and Marxism are ideologies."[6]

**inartistic proofs:** evidence not created by the speaker but existing in its own right: contracts, wills, and constitutions, for example.

**interpellation:** in cultural theory refers to the process by which ideological discourse constructs subject positions for individuals and groups from which they can make sense of their experience. That is, our own identities are the products of ideology. We internalize ideological discourses that offer us a certain image of our place in the world and then use that image to guide our beliefs and behaviors.

**interpretation:** determining what a rhetorical artifact means. It is the act of the critics trying "to account for and assign meaning to the rhetorical dimensions of a given phenomenon."[7] Such interpretations can focus on the external or internal dynamics of a rhetorical artifact. External interpretations focus on how the rhetorical artifact interacts with the situation that surrounds it, and internal interpretations focus on how different parts of the rhetorical artifact act together in forming a whole.

**intertextuality:** the generation of meaning by the patterns and confluences across texts, where all meanings draw on other meanings.

**invention:** one of the five classical cannons. It involves the discovery and invention of the appropriate materials and arguments for the discourse.

**kinesics:** broadly speaking this is the study of various body movements. Specific to rhetorical studies, it is concerned with using the body to convey meanings and emotions.

**logos:** one of the three artistic proofs, a logic based on reason. This is not a scientific logic, but rather a rhetorical logic, one based upon probability. Involves both inductive and deductive argument structures.

**metaphor:** a figure of speech often used to make new ideas "come alive," often by comparing unlike things to a known thing. For example, "teenage drinking is dynamite in the hands of babies." Such an expression conveys the potential harm of underage drinking more powerfully than the literal, "teenage drinking is dangerous." Although marked historically as a topos of rhetorical style, metaphor's utility as an inventional resource, particularly in constructing arguments, is increasingly apparent.

**motive:** in Burkean theory, the underlying worldview and philosophy of the speaker and the worldview the speaker wants us to adopt. By using the pentad to explore how a speaker explains an action (Should the act be understood as a result of the scene? Was it for a higher purpose?), we can better understand the worldview/philosophy of the speaker. Burke argues that when explaining an action, the choice to emphasize a particular element of the pentad corresponds with a particular philosophical orientation: scene corresponds with determinism, agent with idealism, agency with pragmatism, purpose with mysticism, and act with realism.

**narrative:** a form of rhetoric drawing on the power of stories to help people understand the world and persuade others.

**narrative fidelity:** the degree to which the story rings true in relation to the experience of the audience.

**narrative form:** the combination of characters, plot, setting, and theme.

**narrative function:** the work done by stories in rhetoric. That work includes providing the audience with a worldview and persuading them to accept a new viewpoint.

**narrative paradigm:** the theory developed by Walter Fisher that all forms of communication can be understand as forms of narrative.

**narrative probability:** the dimensions of a narrative that make it coherent.

**nominalism:** suggests that when you hear a general term such as *dog*, you automatically relate it to a specific dog you are familiar with—the general term has no explicit existence.

**orientation:** the way in which you approach the world—your attitude toward what things are good (being vegan) or not (meat) may be one example.

**panmediation:** the interaction of the plurality of media that shape social life.

**paralepsis:** a rhetorical stylistic device used to bring up a subject while the speaker or writer denies actually bringing it up. Particularly used to make a subtle ad hominem attack on one's opponent.

**paralinguistic features:** aspects of vocal communication that move beyond the basic verbal message consisting of proper grammar or argument structure. For instance, varying volume, rate of speaking, or tone.

**paratexts:** the variety of materials including advertisements, movie trailers, and interviews with actors that comment on or refer to a primary text such as a movie, television program, or recording.

**pathos:** one of the three artistic proofs, it is an appeal to the emotions of audience members through the construction of arguments that are designed to induce specific emotional states. Once audiences are in the emotional state, they become more easily moved to a particular action.

**pentad:** the goal of pentadic analysis is not to simply name each of the five parts, but rather to identify the relationships between them and determine which term dominates the others. Consists of five terms. Act: the pentadic term for the action. It answers the question, what happened? Texts that emphasize act demonstrate a philosophy of realism. Scene: the pentadic term for the context in which an action occurred. It answers the question, what was the situation/context? Texts that emphasize scene demonstrate a philosophy of determinism. Agent: the pentadic term for the person who acts. It answers the question, what kind of person performed the act? Texts that emphasize agent demonstrate a philosophy of idealism. Agency: the pentadic term for the means by which the act was accomplished. It answers the question, what technology, method, or technique was used? Texts that emphasize agency demonstrate a philosophy of pragmatism. Purpose: the pentadic term for why an act is performed. It answers the question, to what end or with what purpose did someone act? Texts that emphasize purpose demonstrate a philosophy of mysticism.

**peroration:** the final part of the speech (the conclusion). This section would be used to remind the audience of the main ideas contained in the speech and in persuasive efforts to rouse the emotions of the audience to help induce them to action.

**plot:** the action in the story.

**power:** actual advocates try to influence the course of events in a manner that promotes their interests. Some advocates have more resources (money, access, technology, networks of influential friends) than others. Some advocates press a case on behalf of established institutions and traditional ways of doing things, while others work for groups with little social or economic standing and who find their interests at odds with the status quo. These disparities in power make a huge difference in the ability to influence audiences.

**power/knowledge:** the position that all knowledge is implicated in questions of social power, which is productive and circulates through all levels of society.

**principles of praxis:** serve not as guidelines for criticism, but as ways of conceiving of the rhetorical act and as potential indices to consider when beginning to critique.

**public knowledge:** the knowledge held in general by a community of persons who "share conceptions, principles, interests, and values and who are significantly interdependent. This community may be characterized further by institutions such as offices, schools, laws, tribunals; by a duration sufficient to the development of these institutions; by a commitment to the well-being of members; and by a power of authorization through which some truths and values are accredited."[8]

**rhetor:** another term for communicator.

**rhetoric:** The strategic use of communication, oral or written, to achieve specifiable goals.

**rhetorical artifacts:** Specific acts of rhetoric that critics single out to analyze.

**rhetorical criticism:** the analysis and evaluation of rhetorical acts.

**rhetorical hybrid:** sometimes termed a generic hybrid, discourse that entails traits of multiple classes or categories of speech. Political convention keynote addresses, for instance, may be termed epideictic because the dominant issues are praise and blame. Since speakers employ praise or blame to promote their own party, however, their messages are often equally deliberative or political, as well as ceremonial.

**rhetorical perspective:** a theoretical orientation a critic uses to help guide criticism of a rhetorical artifact.

**rhetorical situation:** a theoretical construct advanced by Lloyd Bitzer. It is "a complex of persons, events, objects, and relations presenting an actual or potential exigence which can be completely or partially removed if discourse introduced into the situation can so constrain human decision or action as to bring about the significant modification of the exigence."[9]

**rhetorician:** in the time of Cicero, an orator-statesman who would use rhetoric as a means of serving the people. Today we use the term to denote one who studies or who uses rhetoric.

**setting:** literally the place where the story occurs, but more broadly the place where similar stories often occur.

**signification:** the process by which meaning is constructed through the relationship among signs that prompt the reader, viewer, or listener to think of something other than itself.

**simile:** often referred to as a metaphor that uses "like" or "as," a simile serves much the same function as its sister trope. Thus, extending the example of a metaphor, a simile might be cast as "lowering the drinking age to eighteen is *like* giving a stick of dynamite to a baby."

**social order:** refers to a system of social hierarchies, structures, institutions, relations, customs, values, and practices that correspond to specific ideological assumptions.

**style:** the use of the right language to make the materials of exposition and argument clear and convincing.

**syllogism:** a major form of logical argument that uses deductive reasoning to arrive at a conclusion. It is based on using two or more propositions that are asserted to be true. The classic form of this argument is composed of a major premise (a general statement), a minor premise (a specific statement), and conclusion. A classic example of this type of argument is all men are mortal (major premise), Socrates is a man (minor premise), and thus we may validly conclude that Socrates is mortal (conclusion).

**symbolic action:** a phrase describing how language operates rhetorically, with particular stress on textual performance, function, and effect.

**synchronic:** in the context of ideographic criticism, the synchronic dimension explores the tension among ideographs at a particular time. During the struggle for civil rights, for example, the two sides clashed over the tension between the rights of <private property> and the commitment to <equality>.

**telos:** in terms of rhetoric, the idea that all rhetorical communication is directed toward some end state or goal.

**terministic screens:** the capacity of language (terminology) to encourage us to understand the world in some ways while filtering (screening) other interpretations out. The specific language we use to describe an object or event draws our attention toward some aspects of the event and thus away from other aspects.

**text:** A provisionally bounded field of discursive action. Text cannot be divorced from context. Generally speaking, a text is a discrete rhetorical artifact that can be analyzed: the text of a speech, the text of a radio broadcast, the text of a debate, the text of a war memorial, and so on.

**theme:** the message of the story.

**topics (topoi or topos):** categories used in a type of systematic brainstorming using predefined categories.

**traditional perspective on criticism:** criticism guided by the theory of rhetoric handed down from antiquity, usually including theories of Aristotle, Plato, Isocrates, Cicero, and Quintilian.

# NOTES

1. Lloyd F. Bitzer, "The Rhetorical Situation," *Philosophy and Rhetoric* 1 (1968): 8.

2. James Andrews, Michael C. Leff, and Robert Terrill, "The Nature of Criticism: An Overview," in *Reading Rhetorical Texts: An Introduction to Criticism* (Boston: Houghton Mifflin, 1998), 6.

3. Robert T. Craig, "Communication," in *Encyclopedia of Rhetoric* (New York: Oxford University Press, 2001), 135.

4. Bitzer, "Rhetorical Situation," 7.

5. See Philip P. Wander, "The Ideological Turn in Modern Criticism," *Central States Speech Journal* 34 (1983): 1–18.

6. Vocabulary.com, s.v. "Ideology," http://www.vocabulary.com/dictionary/ideology. The *Oxford English Dictionary* defines *ideology* as "a systematic scheme of ideas, usually relating to politics, economics, or society and forming the basis of action or policy; a set of beliefs governing conduct."

7. Michael Leff, "Interpretation and the Art of the Rhetorical Critic," *Western Journal of Speech Communication* 44 (1980): 342.

8. Lloyd F. Bitzer, "Rhetoric and Public Knowledge," in *Rhetoric, Philosophy, and Literature: An Exploration*, ed. Don M. Burks (West Lafayette: Purdue University Press, 1978).

9. Lloyd F. Bitzer, "The Rhetorical Situation," *Philosophy and Rhetoric* 1 (1968): 6. According to Webster's dictionary online, http://www.merriam-webster.com, *exigence* [exigency] is "that which is required in a particular situation."

# Index

abortion, 51, 70, 148, 222, 233, 285
accomplishments, 114, 172, 198–99
act/action, 7, 20n34, 52, 150, 153, 158, 175, 259–60. *See also* agent-act ratio; collective action; critical act; scene-act ratio; symbolic action
act-act ratio, 155, 157–58
administrative text, 89n11
advertising, 69–70, 148–49, 151, 204, 211n8, 218–19, 226, 228, 288n35
advocates, 34, 184, 215–17, 223–24
Afghanistan, 42–43
African Americans, 31, 96–97, 101, 116, 209, 228, 230, 262; "Black Lives Matter," 149; Black Power, 170; men, 225; police brutality and, 278; women, 272. *See also* race; *individual names*; *specific topics*, e.g., civil rights
agency, 52, 150–51, 153–59, 161, 163, 255, 259; coercive, 220; free, 226, 230, 235n48; of government, 159; of ideographs, 223; in Obama's second inaugural address, 158–59; pragmatism and, 154, 157; speech as, 221
agency-act ratio, 52, 155–57
agent, 52, 150, 153–54; as effect, 259–60; idealism and, 151, 154, 156, 173; stressing, 159
agent-act ratio, 52, 155–56
agrarian concerns, 159–60
*Alien* (two films), 142
allegory, 99, 101, 128, 132, 142–43, 228, 276–80

al-Qaeda, 53, 71
Althouse, Matthew T., 167–90
American Anti-Slavery Society, 81
American Dream, 16, 160, 178–79, 186, 218, 285
American exceptionalism, 97, 241–43, 276
*American Idol,* 269
analogy, 30–31, 105–6, 170, 220
analysis, 30–32, 290–91; framing, 296; generic, 48, 57; judgmental, 241, 296; narrative, 133–40; two fundamental goals of, 137. *See also specific topics,* e.g., close textual analysis; ideographic analysis
anaphora, 86
anarchy, 65
Andersen, Arthur, 217
anger, 31, 77, 84–85, 137, 140
*Animal Farm* (Orwell), 128, 142, 277
Anthony, Susan B., 79
anti-intellectualism, 231
antiwar movements, 220, 276
apologia, 37n19, 58, 295
architecture, 11–12, 241, 244–45
argumentation, 24, 82, 86, 141–42, 215, 223, 298
"Argument in Drama and Literature: An Exploration" (Fisher and Filloy), 130
arguments, 15, 142, 291; analogies as form of, 31; central, 270; commonplace, 76; metaphor as, 107, 121n3; novels as making, 130; rhetorical criticism as form of, 26; rhetoric of, 298; strong, constructing, 26

Aristotle, 8–9, 49, 70, 72–73, 75, 79, 152
Arnold, Carroll, 75
*Ars Poetica* (Horace), 150
art: importance of form in, 150; rhetorical criticism as, 21–39; texts, artistic density as exhibited by, 94–96, 101
artifact, rhetorical, 21, 30–32, 53–54, 198–99, 201, 289–91. *See also* analysis
artistic proofs, 75–76, 79
Arts and Crafts movement, 241, 243
athletes, 211, 226–27, 230
atonement, 97–99
Attic orations, 75
attitudes, 16, 41, 72, 107, 128, 130, 142, 148, 160, 169, 171–72, 177, 182, 230, 263, 283, 298; naming/nominalist rhetoric, 258; pentadic criticism and, 155, 161; persuasion and, 221; symbolic act and, 256–57. *See also* worldview
audience, 14–15, 41, 45, 70; constructing, for rhetorical events, 71–73; dual, 114; fantasy-theme analysis and, 171; and narrative, effectiveness of, 134–35
Augustine, St., 8, 219
Ausmus, William A., 120
authenticity, 280–81
authoritarianism, 245

Bacon, Francis, 219
Bales, Robert, 175
Ball, Moya A., 171–72, 187
Barthes, Roland, 239, 276
baseball, 227, 232, 235n48, 236n64; "Baseballville," 167–76
Baskerville, Barnett, 30
*Battlestar Galactica* (TV program), 132, 143, 277
Bazerman, Charles, 15
beauty, 70, 89n8; feminine, 200–210, 212n47, 270, 281
behavior, 221
beliefs, 13, 15–17, 26, 41, 72, 107, 130, 167, 175, 186, 243, 256, 277, 298; "behavior and/or belief," 221; similarities in/shared, 55, 170. *See also* ideology; worldview; *specific topics*, e.g., persuasion; stereotypes
belief system tradition, 17
Bello, Richard, 163
Benham, Jessica, 260–61
Benjamin, Walter, 277
Benoit, William, 47–61, 169, 186, 258, 277, 295

Benson, Thomas W., 103
Bergdahl, Bowe, 74
Berlin Wall (Reagan's Brandenburg Gate Address), 43
Berry, Wendell, 160, 165n26
Beveridge, Albert, 7–8
Beyoncé, 274
Bible, 85, 94, 100–101, 292
bigotry, 64. *See also* racism
Bingham, George Caleb, 7
Bitzer, Lloyd F., 41–46, 51, 76, 215–16, 223. *See also* rhetorical situations
Black, Edwin, 22–24, 28, 33, 39n66, 49–50, 103, 110–11, 120, 240; on objectivity and politics in criticism, 63–66
Black, Jack, 202, 204–5
Black, Jason Edward, 39n65, 297
"Black Lives Matter," 149
Black Power, 170
black (race). *See* African Americans
Blair, Hugh, 9
Bliss, Diane, 207–8
Blood, Adam, 215–36, 271
Bloom, Allan, 182
*Blue Bloods* (TV crime drama), 278
Bodolay, Maryanne, 207
Bok, Derek, 181, 184
Bolshevik revolution, 277
Booth, Wayne, 130
Bormann, Ernest G., 167–77, 185–87
*Bowling Alone* (Putnam), 184
Brandenburg Gate Address (Reagan), 43
Brock, Bernard L., 26, 240, 250
Brockriede, Wayne, 21, 26, 28, 224
Brookey, Robert Alan, 204–5
Brouwer, Daniel C., 285
Browne, Stephen Howard, 91–104
Brummett, Barry, 163, 274, 277
Bruner, M. Lane, 241, 245–48
Bryant, Donald C., 14, 19n24, 21, 36n4
Brydon, Suzan, 199
Buescher, Derek T., 285
Burgchardt, Carl, 262
Burke, Kenneth, 32–33, 107, 130, 241, 244–45, 249, 254, 256–58, 263, 265; dramatism and pentadic criticism of, 147–65. *See also* cluster analysis; identification; "master tropes"; ratios
Burkholder, Thomas R., 105–24
Burton, Dan, 136–42
Bush, George H. W., 115, 118

Bush, George W., 42, 48, 53, 73, 109, 119, 124n61, 178, 250, 277, 296

campaign rhetoric, 48. *See also* keynote addresses
Campbell, George, 9, 219
Campbell, Karlyn Kohrs, 50–51, 54, 58, 103, 122n30, 210
Cannon, Lou, 113
capitalism, 16, 157, 173, 192, 200, 218, 246–47, 271–72, 279–80, 288n35
Capote, Truman, 65
carnivalesque tactics, 245–48
Carpenter, Ronald H., 132
Carrington, Edward, 251n25
Carter, Jimmy, 159, 169, 187, 229
Castro, Fidel, 163
Castro, Julian, 55
categorization, 172
causality, 221, 259
Cecil the lion, 254
censorship, 158, 222
chaining, 168–69, 171, 177–79, 183
*Challenger* disaster speech (Reagan), 161
change: fear of, 15. *See also* agency; social change
character, personal, 154–56, 159, 190n72
characteristic, defining, 53–54
characters, 126
Chesebro, James W., 240, 250
children abducted to Saudi Arabia, 126, 135–40
China, 134, 241, 245–48
Chosen Nation narrative, 228
Christian Children's Fund, 77, 90n16
Christianity/Christians, 8–9, 71, 73, 84–85, 99–100, 107, 218, 228, 231
Christie, Chris, 55
Christina of Sweden, Queen, 132
Christine de Pizan, 197
chupacabra, 241–42
Churchill, Winston, 43, 131
Cicero, Marcus Tullius, 8–9, 155, 219, 240, 245–46, 305
circumstances, 153–54, 224
cisgender, 197
Cisneros, J. David, 120
civic life, 65, 270, 284
civil disobedience, 98
civil rights/civil rights movement, 129, 133, 157, 220, 253, 276, 296; synchronic dimension, 223
Civil War, US, 43, 98, 128, 230, 261
clarity, 78
Clark, Thomas D., 58

class, social, 16, 178, 194, 247, 278–80
class inequality. *See* inequality
climate change, 7, 127–28, 284, 298
Clinton, Bill, 77, 169, 178–80, 229
Clinton, Hillary, 87, 96–97
close textual analysis (CTA), 3, 91–104, 119, 250, 270
Cloud, Dana, 221, 225, 233, 262, 265–266, 272, 285
cluster analysis/criticism, 160, 244, 295
coercion, 153, 220, 280
Colbert, Stephen, 261
Cold War, 110, 120, 158, 170, 172
collectivity, 221–23; collective action/behavior, 12, 16, 159, 261; collective agreement, 275; collective bargaining, 227, 230, 235n48; collective decisions, 174, 269, 273–74; collective identity, 65, 97–98; collective interest, 192; ideographs and, 229. *See also* movements
colleges and universities. *See* higher education
Collins, Mary Evelyn, 241, 243–45
Collins, Suzanne, 278–79
colonialism, 285, 297
colonization, 297
*The Columbian Orator*, 81
comedic discourse, 261–62. *See also* humor
common good, 158, 217, 230
common ground, 77, 153
commonplace arguments, 76
common sense, 14, 93, 117, 172, 207, 246, 271–72, 276
communal idealist vision, 176–77, 180–84, 190n73
communal identity, 15
communication, 4, 10–11, 244; critical act, communication stage of, 24–28; critical act, countercommunication stage of, 28; departments of, 9–10; epistemic approach to, 175; narrative as, 131; rhetoric as goal-oriented, 12–14; and SCT, value of, 174
communicator. *See* rhetor
communism, 16, 18, 43, 128, 142, 151, 232, 241; "cancer of communism" metaphor, 110, 120; carnivalesque tactics and, 245–48; McCarthyism/the Red Scare, 230
community, 15, 174, 190n72, 226
Compromise of 1850, 80
Conant, James, 183
concepts, 270; conceptually oriented criticism, 30, 296; conceptual stage of critical act, 23–24

Condit, Celeste, 58, 120–21, 210, 223, 225, 233
confidence, 77, 159
Congress, US. *See* United States Congress
connotation, 275–76
conscience, 83, 230
conservative political perspective, 47–49, 52, 55, 97, 109–10, 119–20, 194, 254
constellation, 50, 54, 215, 224, 262
Constitution, US. *See* United States Constitution
constraints, 16, 41–42, 153, 216, 224, 250, 259, 286
consubstantiality, 16, 127, 244. *See also* identification
consumerism, 218, 232
content, 92–93, 101
context, 70, 162; for critique, 260; cultural, 111; of rhetorical events, recreating, 71; text and, 93–94, 101
continual critique, 256, 260, 264, 266–67
conventional opinions, 65
convention speeches. *See* keynote addresses
"convergent critical rhetoric," 263
cookie-cutter criticism, 87
Cooper, Lane, 88
Cooper, Martha, 106–7
Cooper Union Address (Lincoln), 78
Cornell University, 180
countercommunication stage of the critical act, 28
covenant, 97–100, 228, 231
cowboys, 241–43
*Crafting Equality* (Condit and Lucaites), 225, 233
Cragan, John F., 186
credibility, 74, 76–77, 85, 121, 129–30, 134–35, 138, 140
crime drama genre, 277–78, 287n27
crisis, 45, 53, 133, 136, 159, 217
critic: and courtroom judge, 64; as inventor, 257–58; personality of, 22–23, 32; perspective of, 27, 32; procedures of, 64.
critical act, 23–28, 35, 64, 198, 261, 263
critical essays. *See* essays, critical
critical race theory (CRT), 261
critical rhetoric, 253–68. *See also* rhetoric; rhetorical criticism
critical thinking, 2
criticism, 1, 3, 21, 64, 67–288; conceptually oriented, 30, 296; cookie-cutter, 87; expanding horizons of, 237–88; formulaic, 87; goals of, twin, 291; good/the best, 28, 32, 35, 65–66, 240, 253, 293–94; mythic, 241, 297; objectivity and politics in, 63–66; as performance, 259; perspectives on, 67–236; possibility of, 265; postcolonial, 297; as reason-giving activity, 26; reflexive, 88; traditional, 69–80; writing, 289–94. *See also* eclectic approach to criticism; fantasy-theme criticism; ideographic criticism; metaphor, criticism of; narrative perspective on criticism; objectivity and politics in criticism; popular culture and social media, criticism of; rhetorical criticism; traditional perspective on criticism
criticism, pentadic, of Kenneth Burke. *See* dramatism and Kenneth Burke's pentadic criticism
criticism, pragmatic model of. *See under* pragmatism: pragmatic model of criticism
critique, context for, 260
critiques of domination and freedom, 255–57, 260, 262, 264
Crocker, Ryan C., 139
Crow, Allen, 178
CRT. *See* critical race theory
CTA. *See* close textual analysis
cultural feminists, 193–94
cultural imperialism, 297
cultural studies, 269–71, 270, 276, 297–98
culture: contemporary, 184; narrative's role in, 142; power and, 270–73. *See also* popular culture
Cuomo, Mario/keynote address to 1984 Democratic National Convention, 106, 113–19, 121, 123n55
Custer's Last Stand, 259

"Daniel Webster" (Howell and Hudson), 88
Darrow, Clarence, 156
data, 17, 26–27, 73, 129, 135, 172, 178–79, 182–83, 190n71; ideographs as kind of, 224–25; public opinion, 134; qualitative methods of collecting, 263
*The Day After* (film), 172
debate, 8–9, 17, 49, 53, 75, 95, 109, 182, 289
decentering, 264
decisions, 157, 162, 165n33
Declaration of Independence, 80, 83, 94, 102, 104, 112, 158
deductive approach to generic application, 55–57
defining characteristic, 53–54
deliberation, 15

deliberative discourse, 72, 79
DeLuca, Kevin, 274
demagogues, 64, 151, 162, 223, 230–31
democracy, 8–9, 15, 17–18, 151, 241, 265, 282–83; American, 42, 84–85, 97–98, 117, 151, 218, 269; democracy promotion industry, 108; education and, 176, 178–79, 181–83, 218; liberal-democratic thought, 230
Democratic Party, US, 30, 47, 51, 73, 106, 113–19, 230
denotation, 275–76
Depression, Great, 151
Descartes, René, 9
description, 29–30
determinism, 153, 156, 160
Dewar, Helen, 113
Dewey, John, 179
diachronic dimension, 223, 233
dialogic criticism, 262
dialogues, 199
Dicochea, Perlita R., 262
dilettantes, 246
Dillard, Courtney, 17–18
Dillard, James Price, 121
Dimondstein, Alan A., 113
Diogenes of Appolonia, 240
Discenna, Thomas, 261
discourse, 70, 79–80, 217; deliberative, 72, 79; epideictic, 72, 79; evaluating, 79–80; forensic, 72, 79; ideological, 271; narrative as mode of, 131; political, metaphor in, 108–11; power and, 217–18; LeBron James, surrounding, 225–32; themes in, 172
discrimination, 31, 112, 125, 192, 195, 202
disposition/organization, 75, 77–80, 82–83, 99, 227, 230
Dobson, James, 87, 241, 248–49, 252n29
*Doctor Who* (TV show), 260–61
doctrine, 65, 78, 240. *See also specific doctrines,* e.g., determinism; pragmatism
documents, 41, 74, 76
Dodds, Harold, 181, 183
dogs, 275
Dolan, Jill, 193
dominant ideology, 272–73
dominant term, 154, 158, 160–62
domination, 193, 218, 255–57, 260, 264
Donner Party, 242–43
*Do the Right Thing* (film), 132, 143
Douglass, Frederick, 9, 80–87
Dow, Bonnie, 273, 285

doxastic knowledge, 258
dramatism and Kenneth Burke's pentadic criticism, 147–65
dramatized messages, 171, 187
*Dreamworlds* (I, II, III) video (Jhally), 201
*Dred Scott* case, 261
drugs, war on, 106, 109–10
dual audiences, 114
Dubrofsky, Rachel, 278, 280–82
Duncan, David, 217
Duncan, Mary B., 187

Eastern European protests, 232, 241
East Germany, 245–46
eclectic approach to criticism/eclecticism, 30, 239–52
ecology, 165n19, 165n26, 193
economic inequality. *See* inequality
economics, 20n34, 126, 224
education, 178, 180, 218. *See also* higher education
Edwards, Jason A., 53
effect, 70, 259–60
eighteenth century, late, 9
Eisley, Loren, 120
*eklektikos,* 240
Ekman, Rickard, 178
Eliot, T. S., 21, 65
elites, 17, 108–9, 151, 278
Emancipation Proclamation, 105
embellished speech, 7
Emerson, Ralph Waldo, 94
emic orientation, 33, 38n55
emotions, 14–15, 69, 72, 77, 85–86, 113–14, 129–30, 134, 140, 148, 150, 156, 162, 169–72, 298; chaining and, 169; ideographs and, 222, 230–32; language of feeling, 86
Endres, Danielle E., 263
Endres, Thomas G., 170
end state. *See* goals; purpose; telos
enfoldment, 199
Engels, Friedrich, 157
Engstrom, Erika, 241
Enron, 217
enthymemes, 76, 107, 298
environment, 126, 177, 182, 221, 247, 255, 271
epideictic discourse, 72, 79
epistemic/epistemology, 102, 128, 135, 175–76, 258
epistrophe, 78, 86

equality, 43, 86, 117, 179, 191, 193–94, 210, 218; as ideograph, 222–25, 230, 233.
equal-opportunity fantasy type, 178–79
Esbjornson, David, 240
essays, critical: agrarian concerns, 159–60; close textual analysis of Obama's March 18, 2008, speech in Philadelphia, 96–101; conundrum of loyalty and the market: discourses surrounding LeBron James's leaving and returning home, 225–32; eclectic approach to criticism, 240–41; fantasy themes for college, 177–84; feminist rhetorical analysis of *Shallow Hal,* 200–208; *The Hunger Games* as allegory for class struggle, 278–80; *The Hunger Games* as production of authentic whiteness and natural femininity, 280–81; *Hunger Games* franchise as promotional cynicism, 281–82; Mario Cuomo's keynote address to the 1984 Democratic National Convention, 113–18; "Mr. Douglass's Fifth of July," 80–87; narrative analysis of stories about children abducted to Saudi Arabia, 135–40; purpose and agency in Obama's second inaugural address, 158–59; stressing the agent, 159; using and/or extending a critical orientation, 260–63
ethics, 9, 15, 32, 96, 181, 207, 209, 216–17, 220, 247, 265, 267; situational, 153
ethnicity, 16–17, 31, 55, 93, 116, 194, 207, 218, 262, 286
ethnography, 263, 284
*ethos,* 76–77, 79, 83–85, 100, 130, 176, 232
etic orientation, 33, 38n55
eulogies, 47–49, 51–53, 55, 173
evaluation, 32
Everdeen, Katniss, 278–84
evidence, 171
evil, good versus. *See* good versus evil theme
Ewalt, Joshua, 233
exigence/exigency, 41–46, 94, 96, 216
exordium, 82

facts, 14, 41, 51, 77, 117, 136, 168, 179, 219, 296
Faludi, Susan, 191
family metaphor/family-values discourse, 115–17, 225
fantasy-theme criticism, 167–90
fantasy types, 169–72, 177–79, 185
Farrell, Kathleen, 41–46

Farrelly brothers (Bobby and Peter), 200, 202–6, 208
fascism, 16, 147, 151, 182
feedback, 28, 294
feeling, language of, 86
femininity, 110, 142, 192–97, 209, 280–81
feminism/feminist analysis, 191–213, 274
Feminist Frequency, 198
Ferraro, Geraldine, 31, 113–15, 118
fidelity, 159, 231, 275. *See also under* narrative: fidelity
figures of speech, 78, 86, 88, 105, 111, 118–119, 171
Filloy, Richard A., 130
film: feminism/feminist critics and, 200–201. *See also specific genres and titles*
*Finding Nemo* (film), 199
Fisher, Walter, 49, 126, 130–32, 134, 137, 141–45
Fiske, John, 284
flag, US, 276
flattery, 77
Fletcher, George, 226
Flood, Curt, 227, 232, 235n48, 236n64
Foley, Megan, 120
foreign policy, 108, 125, 140, 276
forensic discourse, 72, 79
form, 150–51, 164n17; content and, 92–93, 101. *See also under* narrative: form
*Form, Genre, and the Study of Political Discourse* (Osborn), 121, 244–45
formulaic criticism, 87
Foss, Karen, 172, 198–99
Foss, Sonja, 11, 29, 37n35, 165n24, 168–69, 198–99
Foucault, Michel, 272
Fox News, 74
frames/framing, 116, 118, 254; competing, motives and, 160–61; framing analysis, 296
Francis, Pope, 217
Franco, Francisco, 151
Frank, Glenn, 181–82
free agency. *See under* agency: free
free choice, 156
freedom, 110, 173, 222–23, 230, 232, 250; critique of, 255–57, 260, 262, 264
freedom of religion, 223
freedom of speech, 222, 230
free market, 231
Friedman, Milton, 217

frontier myth, 241–43
Frye, Northrop, 143n5
Fugitive Slave Law, 80, 83–85
Fulkerson, Richard P., 103
function, narrative. *See under* narrative: function
funerals, 3, 285. *See also* eulogies
future for rhetoric, 17–18

Gaines, Jane, 200
games/game play, 18. *See also* sports; video games
Gardner, Tony, 205–7
Garrison, William Lloyd, 81
Garrisonians, 81, 87
gays and lesbians, 44, 273, 285. *See also* queer rhetoric; queer studies
Gearhart, Sally Miller, 199
gender, 16; hierarchies, 195. *See also specific topics,* e.g., feminist analysis
general theory, 174
"A Generation in Search of a Future" (Wald), 75
generic antecedents, 96
generic application, 53
generic descriptions, 48
generic elements in rhetoric/generic rhetorical criticism, 47–61
generic hybrid. *See* rhetorical hybrid
genre, 3, 47–52, 277
German, Kathleen M., 58n2
Germany, 111, 224, 231; East Germany, 245–46
Germond, Jack W., 114
gestures, 11, 16, 91
Gettysburg Address, 43, 71–72, 89n8, 103
GI Bill, 178, 180
Gilbert, Dan, 227–33
global power structures, 297
global warming, 7, 127–28, 284, 298
goals, 172; of criticism, twin, 291; ideographs as, 222; rhetoric as goal-oriented communication, 10, 12–14. *See also* purpose; telos
good/goodness: good versus evil theme, 119, 124n61, 150, 246; a virtuous rhetor, 245–46. *See also* common good
good criticism: *See under* criticism: good
Goodrich, Chauncey A., 9
Gorbachev, Mikhail, 43
Gore, Al, 128
*Go Set a Watchman* (Lee), 129
government, 120, 149; agency of, 159; complexity of, 108; power, justifications for, 232; separation of church and state, 222. *See also* politics; *specific forms of government*
*Grammar of Motives* (Burke), 148–49, 152–55
Gramsci, Antonio, 271
Grano, Dan, 187
Grant-Davie, Keith, 45
*Gravity* (film), 273
Gray, Herman, 274
Great Depression, 151
Greece, 8, 17
Greek language, 64, 66, 167, 231, 240
Greek mythology, 198
Greek tragedy, 132
Gregg, Richard, 29
Grenada invasion speech (Reagan), 163
Griffin, Cindy, 199
Gronbeck, Bruce E., 37n19, 106
grounded theory, 175
guilt, 60n33, 77, 85–86, 140
gun control, 51–52
Gunn, Joshua, 250

Habermas, Jürgen, 17
Hadot, Pierre, 165n33
Hall, Stuart, 271
Hamlet, Janice D., 210
Hanke, Robert, 210
Hariman, Robert, 266
Harrell, Jackson, 49–50, 54
Hart, Roderick P., 17–18, 186
Hauser, Gerard, 14
health care, 96, 125, 272
hegemony, 187, 218, 271–72, 285; counterhegemonic messages, 272, 279–80, 282, 288n35; popular culture as resource for challenging, 280
"Hegemony or Concordance? The Rhetoric of Tokenism in 'Oprah' Winfrey's Rags-to-Riches Biography" (Cloud), 285
Henry, David, 105–24
Herbig, Art, 263
Hernandez, Miriam, 137–39
Hess, Aaron, 263, 285
hierarchy/hierarchies, 164, 297; gender, 195; social, 270–71, 278. *See also* cultural studies; hegemony; social order
higher education, 18, 24, 163, 168, 176–92, 279
Hill, Forbes I., 69–90
history, 91; historical moment, 103, 265; rhetorical tradition in, 8–10

Hitchcock, Orville A., 88, 201
Hitler, Adolf, 111, 147–48, 151, 224, 231, 258
Hoerl, Kristen, 262, 269–88
Hollihan, Thomas A., 132
Holocaust, 111, 127, 129
homology, 277, 284
hooks, bell, 192, 200, 206
hope, 77–78
Horace, 150
horror films, 277
housing crisis (Foley), 120
Howard, John, 181
Howard, Pokey, 165, 167, 170
Howell, Wilbur Samuel, 88
Hudson, Hoyt Hopewell, 11–12, 69, 88, 89n3
humanities, 22, 91, 102, 270
humor, 161, 199, 203, 207, 261–62. *See also* carnivalesque tactics; jokes
*Hunger Games* (film franchise), 278–84
Hutchins, Robert M., 182
Hutson, Saul, 207
hybrid. *See* rhetorical hybrid
hyperbole, 86, 228

idealism, 151, 154, 156, 173. *See also* communal idealist vision
ideas, 42, 70, 151, 298; controversial, 182; the critic/researcher's, 24, 26, 28, 32–33, 48, 56, 289–90, 292–93; dissemination of, 199; frames as, 296; judgmental analysis of, 296; the media and, 243; metaphors and, 108–9; popular culture and, 270, 280. *See also* ideology; *specific topics,* e.g., close textual analysis; eclecticism; identification; pragmatism
identification, 15–16, 60n33, 127, 148–49, 244, 290
identity: communal, 15; individual, 218, 272
ideographic analysis, 223–25, 232–33
ideographic criticism, 215–36
ideographs, 221–23, 228–29, 232–35, 271
ideological turn, 215–19, 232, 253, 259
ideology, 20n34, 216–19, 221, 254, 271–73; American, 16; changes in, 224; dominant, 272–73; as false consciousness, 225; importance of, 271
"image restoration," 295
images, 41, 91–92, 96, 148, 151, 162, 169, 216, 231–32, 269, 275–76; metaphor and, 105, 110, 112, 118–21; visual, from *Shallow Hal* DVD, 204–5, 208

immigration/immigrants, 13, 17, 97, 113–14, 120, 296
imperialism, 297
implementation, 244–45
impressions of the receiver, 11
inartistic proofs, 75–76, 79
*An Inconvenient Truth* (Gore), 128
Indian Rivers Stadium, 171–74, 176
individual identity, 218, 272
individualism, 151, 178–80, 183–84, 192, 194
individual rights, 231, 237
indoctrination, 218, 248
inductive approach, 47, 52–55
Industrial Revolution, 9
inequality, 176, 270–71, 279–80, 282–83
"infestation metaphors," 111
influence, 244–45, 259
injustice, 83–84, 86, 105, 112, 169, 247, 279, 284
inquiry, rhetoric of, 299
intentions of the rhetor, 11
"internal dynamic," 56
Internet, 245–47; Chinese, 247. *See also* social media
interpellation, 271–72
interpretation, 30–32
intertextuality, 276
*Invasion of the Body Snatchers* (film), 277
invention, 75; critic as inventor, 257–58
Iraq/Iraq War, 18, 48, 71, 73, 119, 134–35, 286
irony, 118–19, 225
ISIS/ISIL, 53, 71, 231
Islam, 71, 131, 140, 231
Isocrates, 219
Israel, 97, 135, 142, 228
Ivie, Robert L., 34, 110–11, 120

Jackson, Jesse, 31, 131, 230
Jackson, Robert, 180
Jackson, Wes, 160
James, LeBron, 154, 215, 225–36
Jamieson, Kathleen Hall, 50–51, 54, 58
Japan, 41–44, 72, 77–78, 132, 134
Jasinski, James, 16–17, 29
Jay Z, 274
Jefferson, Thomas, 102, 151, 153, 160, 181, 183, 245, 251n25
Jenkins, Steven, 253
Jenner, Bruce/Caitlyn, 125
jeremiad, 97–99, 101
Jesus Christ, 31, 131, 228

Jhally, Sut, 201
Johnson, Allan G., 191–92
Johnson, Deirdre, 199
Johnson, Lyndon B., 122n24, 187
Johnson, Mark, 115
jokes, 150, 162, 185, 203, 205–7. *See also* humor
"Jonathan Edwards" (Hitchcock), 88
Jordan, Barbara, 57
Jordan, Michael, 154
journalists/journalism, 45, 73, 150, 181, 225, 233, 258
Judeo-Christian religious belief, 73, 97, 99–100, 218
judgment, 64
judgmental analysis, 241, 296
justice: racial, 276, 284. *See also* social justice

Kafka, Stephanie, 190n71
Kahn, Rick, 51
Kelley-Romano, Stephanie, 132
Kellner, Douglas, 198
Kelly, Casey R., 285
Kelly, Megyn, 74
Kennedy, Edward/Ted, 161, 163
Kennedy, George A., 88
Kennedy, John F., 113, 187
Ketcham, Ralph, 181
keynote addresses, 3, 47–49, 53–58; Cuomo's, to the 1984 Democratic National Convention, 106, 113–19, 121
Kilbourne, Jean, 195
*Killing Us Softly* (Kilbourne), 195
kinesics, 69
King, Andrew, 7–20, 32, 147–65, 258
King, Charles, 152
King, Claire, 285
King, Martin Luther, 97, 105, 112, 132, 157, 224, 276
*King Kong* (film), 198
Kneupper, Charles, 156, 160
knowledge, 1, 14, 176; doxastic, 258; evolving, 175–76; "pre-knowledge," 46n9; public, 42–46; of rhetorical theory and methodology, 141. *See also* epistemic/epistemology; power/knowledge
Knowles-Carter, Beyoncé, 274
Knutson, Roxann L., 169, 172, 187
Kohrs Campbell, Karlyn. *See* Campbell, Karlyn Kohrs
Kopechne, Mary Jo, 161
Kramarae, Cheris, 191

*krisis*, 64
Kuypers, Jim A.: on eclectic approach to criticism, 239–52; "From Science," 248–49; "Hoyt Hopewell Hudson's Nuclear Rhetoric," 89n3; on rhetoric, 7–20; on rhetorical criticism, elements of, 1–4; on rhetorical criticism as art, 21–39

Lakoff, George, 115
language: of feeling, 86; paralinguistic features, 69; and social cohesion, 16; as symbolic action, 152–53; terministic screens, 147–48, 164. *See also* discourse
Launer, Michael K., 45, 46n9
law, 126; ancient Greeks and, 8; conventional procedures of, 64; divine/higher, 157; judge, courtroom, 64; local, 157; and order, 222; rule of, 222; television crime drama genre, 277–78, 287n27; truth/facts and, 219
Lawson, Sean, 274
leadership, 154, 159, 183, 188n29; ideographs and, 223; movement leaders, 297; servant-leader fantasy type, 181
*Lean In* (Sandberg), 193, 211n5
Lear, Gabriel, 164n13
Lee, Harper, 129
Lee, Ronald, 215–36, 271
Lee, Spike, 132
Leff, Michael, 30–32, 104, 107, 120
Left, the, 151
legitimation, 218
Lenin, Vladimir, 157
Lewis, William F., 123n55, 132–33, 143
liberal feminists, 193
liberal political perspective, 49, 52, 55, 109–10, 119, 230
libertarian political perspective, 194
liberty, 8, 44, 82–86, 110, 112, 158, 182, 218, 247; as ideograph, 222, 233
Lincoln, Abraham, 102, 186; the Cooper Union Address, 78; the Gettysburg Address, 43, 71–72, 89n8, 103; Lincoln-Douglas debates, 75; second inaugural of, 44
Ling, David, 161, 163
Linkugel, Wil A., 49–50, 54
literature, 9, 29, 91, 95, 128, 137, 153
Littlejohn, Stephen, 172
Logan, Harold, 183
logic, 14, 76, 82, 86, 89n8, 131, 179, 185, 230–31, 250, 256; logical proofs, 41
*logos*, 76, 79, 130

*Loving with a Vengeance: Mass-Produced Fantasies for Women* (Modleski), 200
loyalty, 225–33, 275
Lucaites, John, 223, 225, 233
Lucas, Stephen E., 27, 104–5
Lutz, Robert, 180
Lybarger, Scott, 46

Mabus, Ray, 136, 138–39
MacIntyre, Alasdair, 226
MAD (mutually assured destruction), 158
Mahan, Alfred Thayer, 132
male centeredness, 192, 196
male domination, 191–92, 196
male identification, 191–92, 196
*Man Cannot Speak for Her* (Campbell), 197, 210
Mandela, Nelson, 18
Manifest Destiny, 242
Mann, Thomas, 151
Mao Zedong, 151
Marcus Aurelius, 132, 165n33
market, 225–32
marketing, 202, 204, 208, 211n8, 226, 231, 281–82
Marx, Karl/ Marxist tradition, 16–17, 65, 147, 155, 194
Massachusetts Anti-Slavery Society, 81
"master tropes," 106, 118
materialism: feminism, materialist, 194; rhetorical/rhetoric and, 215, 219–21, 224–25
Maurer, Lucille, 113
maximalists, 193
Mayer, Marissa, 192
McCarthy, Joseph/McCarthyism, 230, 232
McGee, Michael Calvin, 35, 215, 219–23, 233, 266, 287n13
McGeough, Ryan Erik, 147–65, 258
McKerrow, Raymie E., 32, 253–68
McMullen, Wayne J., 132
meaning, 10–11, 275. *See also specific topics,* e.g., close textual analysis
*The Meaning of Meaning: A Study of the Influence of Language upon Thought and the Science of Symbolism* (Richards and Ogden), 150, 164n16
media, 149, 243; commercial, 269, 273–74, 288n35; global, 297; mass, 10, 17, 72, 148, 151, 169, 270, 275, 284. *See also* social media; *specific topics,* e.g., framing
meditations, 94
medium/agency, 53

megastate, 17
*Mein Kampf* (Hitler), 147–48
Meltzer, Marisa, 207
memes, 275–76
memory, public. *See* public memory
men: hegemonic masculinity, 187, 191–92. *See also specific topics,* e.g., patriarchy
Mencken, H. L., 89n8
messages, 70, 73–79, 171–72; dramatized, 171, 187
metaphor, 105–24; ideology as, 16
*Metaphor in Context* (Stern), 120
metaphysics, 220
method: consequences and, 157; criticism as, 1, 22–23.
Middle Ages, 8–9
middle class, 9, 73, 113, 116–17
Middle East, 126, 135, 142, 169
Middleton, Michael, 263
Middleton, Richard, 104
Miles, Edwin A., 114
Milford, Michael, 132, 143, 277
minimalists, 193
Mink, Lewis O., 127–28
Mio, Jeffrey Scott, 108
mise-en-scène, 71
misogyny, 274
Modleski, Tania, 200
Mohrmann, G. P., 185–86
Mondale, Walter, 113–15, 118
monosemic interpretation, 259
moral dimensions of rhetoric, 14–15. *See also* ethics
Moss, Jean Dietz, 8
motive, 60n33, 152; competing frames and, 160–61
movements, 296–97; movement metaphors, 108; workers', 247
movies. *See* film; *specific genres and titles*
Moynihan, Sean, 200
"Mr. Douglass's Fifth of July," 80–87
Mulsof, Karen, 187
multiculturalism, 17
Mulvey, Laura, 201, 203–4
Murphy, John M., 255, 267
*Murphy Brown* (TV show), 273–74
music, 10–11, 66, 104, 269, 273, 276–77, 286, 298; videos, 201, 274
Muslims. *See* Islam
Mussolini, Benito, 151
mutually assured destruction (MAD), 158

*My Big Fat Greek Wedding* (film), 210
mysticism, 155, 157, 173, 228
myth, 132, 167, 169, 176, 207, 228, 241–43, 262, 276, 285; mythic criticism, 241, 297

naming, 258
"Narration as a Human Communication Paradigm: The Case of Public Moral Argument" (Fisher), 143
narrative/narrative perspective on criticism, 125–45; analysis, 133–40; approaches to, 130–31; audience and, 134–35; fidelity, 131–32, 134; form, 54, 123n55, 126–30, 132–33, 137–40, 150, 229; function, 126–31, 133, 135; importance of, 130–31, 141–42; in literature vs. in rhetoric., 128; paradigm, 126, 130–34, 141, 143; potentials and pitfalls, 141–42; power of, 141; probability, 131–32, 134; rationality, standards of, 134; systematic perspective, 133–35
National Association to Advance Fat Acceptance (NAAFA), 207
nationalism, 16
national security, 74, 222, 231
National Socialism, 111
Native Americans, 97, 116, 194, 259, 285
negotiation, 15, 44, 154, 272
New Academic doctrines, 240
New England Anti-Slavery Society, 81
Nichols, Marie Hochmuth, 11, 22–23, 88, 149, 164n10
Nilsen, Thomas R., 30
nineteenth century, 9
Nisbet, Robert A., 184
Nixon, Richard, 7, 76
nominalism, 258
nonviolence, 159, 245
norms, 15, 23, 94, 246, 283, 298
Nosthstine, William L., 29
novels, 11, 69, 95, 129–30, 142, 154, 278
nuclear power accident (Three Mile Island), 129
nuclear weapons, 110, 120, 134, 158, 172, 220, 247
Nudd, Donna Marie, 191–213, 270

Obama, Barack, 7, 43, 74, 87, 97, 108, 217, 262, 276, 279; executive order on immigration, 13; March 18, 2008, speech in Philadelphia, 92, 96–101; second inaugural address of, 158–59; speech, "A More Perfect Union," 30–31, 93–94, 96, 98–99, 101; "Statement by the President on ISIL," 48, 71; 2015 State of the Union, 179
objectivity: in criticism, 34–35, 63–66; as ideograph, 225, 233
Occupy Wall Street, 255, 274–76, 279–80, 284
Ogden, C. K., 150, 164n16
the "one percent," 279, 284
Ono, Kent, 255, 265, 267, 285
opinions: common, 169; conventional, 65; informed, 14; opinion polls, 115; public opinion data, 134
opportunity, 160, 228, 230–31; equal-opportunity fantasy type, 178–79
*Orange Is the New Black* (TV show), 201, 292
order, 223
organization. *See* disposition
orientation, 150, 160, 254, 263; etic/emic, 33, 38n55; theoretical, 2, 26, 33
Orwell, George, 80, 128, 142, 158, 277
Osborn, Michael, 121, 244–45
Other, 273, 281, 298
Ott, Brian, 262

"Paddling the Rhetorical River, Revisiting the Social Actor: Rhetorical Criticism as Both Appreciation and Intervention" (Black), 39
pageantry, 101
Paine, Thomas, 78
Palmer, Janay, 24–25
Paltrow, Gwyneth, 202–7, 209–10, 212n47
panmediation, 274, 281
paradigm, narrative. *See under* narrative: paradigm
paralepsis, 82–83, 86
paralinguistic features, 69
parallel structure, 78, 85, 93, 298
paratexts, 274, 276, 278, 281–84
*Participatory Critical Rhetoric: Theoretical and Methodological Foundations for Studying Rhetoric in Situ* (Middleton et al.), 263
partisan critique, 34–35
paternalism, 236n64
*pathos*, 76–77, 79, 83–85, 130
patriarchy/patriarchal systems, 142, 191–93, 195–96, 198–200, 209, 211
Patriot Act, 155
patriotism, 7, 116, 218, 276
patterns, 161. *See also* form
Patton, John H., 45
Pavlov's dogs, 152
Pearl Harbor, 41–44, 132

penny dreadful, 242, 251n7
pentad, 52, 60n33, 147–65
pentadic criticism of Kenneth Burke, dramatism and, 147–65
perceptions, 50–51, 175
Peripatetic doctrines, 240
Perkins, Sally J., 132
peroration, 83, 85, 117
Perry, Steven, 111
*Personality and Interpersonal Behavior* (Bales), 175
personality of the critic/researcher, 22–23, 32
perspective: importance of, 162; theoretical, choice of, 32–33. *See also* rhetorical perspectives
persuasion/persuasive communication, 12, 148, 215; credibility and, 129; rhetorical figures of speech and, 78; rhetorical situation concept and, 2; text or speech as representing a persuasive act, 155; truth and, 129; violence and, 197, 199. *See also specific topics,* e.g., close textual analysis; pentad; propaganda
Philadelphia, Obama's March 18, 2008, speech in, 92, 96–101
philosophy, 8–9, 91; "working philosophy," 179
pity, 77, 83–85
*Places in the Heart* (film), 132
Plato, 8, 15
plot, 127, 153, 172
Plus-Size Task Force (PSTF), 207
Poehler, Amy, 198
poetry, 9, 11–12, 43, 87, 89n8, 91, 95, 147, 149–50, 152, 241, 249
Poland, 94, 246–47
police brutality, 278
"Police Lives Matter," 149
policy making, 20n34, 109, 171
polis, 17, 164n13
political correctness, 163, 254
political speeches, 222, 274. *See also under specific speakers*
politics, 9; complexity of, 108; in criticism, 63–66; metaphor in political discourse, 108–11; partisan, 34–35, 96, 113–14, 116, 161; popular culture and, 241–43, 283, 292; religion and, 241–43, 292. *See also* Democratic Party; Republican Party; *specific topics,* e.g., ideology; keynote addresses; propaganda
polls, opinion. *See* opinion polls
polysemy, 143, 284; polysemic interpretation, 259

Pope Francis, 217
popular culture: and dominant hegemony, 280; politics and, 241–43, 283, 292; religion and, 241–43, 292; and social change, 269, 271–72, 279–83
popular culture and social media, criticism of, 3, 269–88
populist movements, 282
Porter, Laurinda W., 187
*The Poseidon Adventure* (film), 285
postcolonial criticism, 297
postmodernity, 226, 231–33
poverty, 9, 17, 112, 225, 272, 279
power, 217–18; contemporary global structures of, 297; culture and, 270–73; discourse and, 217–18; dominant power elite, 16; of generic criticism, 48; government, justifications for, 232; of narrative, 141; the "one percent," 279, 284; relations, 103, 255–57, 262, 265, 269–70, 278; unequal, 15, 261. *See also* advocates
power/knowledge, 255, 271–72
*Practical Criticism* (Richards), 164n16
practical mind fantasy type, 179
pragmatism, 172; agency and, 154, 157; Burke as pragmatist, 147; communication, pragmatics of, 95, 215; criticism, pragmatic model of, 215–16, 223–24; doctrine/philosophy of, 154, 157; keynote addresses, pragmatic aim of, 114; Lincoln's "romantic pragmatism," 186; progressive, 118; rhetoric, pragmatic conception/vision of, 11, 15, 69, 172, 179, 187, 215–16, 221, 223–24
praxis, principles of, 258–59
preconceptions, 290
"pre-knowledge," 46n9
"prescientific," criticism characterized as, 63
presidency, US, 47–49; campaigns, 41, 48–49, 71; candidates, 163; debates, 49. *See also specific presidents*
*Principles of Literary Criticism* (Richards), 164n16
principles of praxis, 258–59
printing press, 9
privacy, 222, 230, 233
probability, 12–14, 23, 73, 76. narrative, 131–32, 134
pro-choice/pro-life, 51, 148
production, systems of, 198
Prohibition, 51
proof, 74, 76, 79, 82, 130, 185. *See also* artistic proofs; inartistic proofs

propaganda, 10, 69, 151, 182, 218, 232, 265, 279–81
property, 222–24, 230, 233, 261–62
protagonist, 126–27, 133–34, 138, 142, 143n5, 153, 157, 227, 277, 292
protest discourse, 253
prudence/practical wisdom, 265, 267
Psaki, Jen, 74
public knowledge, 42–46
public memory, 101, 246–48, 262, 297
public relations, 70, 74, 149, 151, 216, 223, 282
public schools, 180, 218
public speaking, 8, 10, 88, 105, 215
purpose, 49–52, 60n29, 150, 153–55, 157; fulfilling, 159; mysticism and, 155, 157, 173, 228; in Obama's second inaugural address, 158–59. *See also* goals; telos
purpose-act ratio, 52, 155, 157, 160
Putnam, Robert, 184

qualitative research, 175, 255, 263
quantitative research, 175, 255, 283–84
Quayle, Dan, 273–74
queer identity, 285
queer rhetoric, 298
queer studies, 201, 209
*The Quest for Community* (Nisbet), 184
questions, research, 23–24, 291
Quigley, Brooke, 16
Quintilian, 8, 219, 245–46, 251n26

race, 16–17, 73, 93–94, 96–101, 152, 194, 207–9, 224–25, 230–32, 236n64, 248, 261–62, 270, 284–86; critical race theory, 261; *The Hunger Games* and, 280–84; racial justice/injustice, 112, 284; white privilege, 192, 261; *See also specific topics,* e.g., civil rights; postcolonial criticism; stereotypes
"Racechange Is the New Black" (Vats), 286
racism, 31, 99, 119, 207, 225, 262, 281, 297; postracism, ideology of, 286; white supremacy, 192, 200, 231.
Raines, Howell, 113
Rainey, Homer, 180
Rarick, David L., 187
Ratcliffe, Krista, 211n21
rationality, 134
ratios, 52, 155–58
Ray, Julie, 190n71
reaffirmative depiction, 245

Reagan, Ronald, 43, 113–18, 132–33, 154, 161, 163, 169
realism, 153, 158
reality, 185; discourse and, 175; texts and, 161–62
reason, 76, 250
religion, 55, 154, 163–64, 218, 226, 230; American ideology and, 16; freedom of, 83–84, 223; hypocrisy and, 86; loyalty and, 226, 231; "metaphoric clusters," 121; politics, popular culture and, 241–43, 292; religious services, 150; of the researcher, 22; separation of church and state, 222
religious right, 49, 55
Renaissance, 9
reproductive agency, 285
Republican Party, US, 42, 47, 51, 73, 78, 82, 86, 116–17, 158, 254. *See also* Tea Party
researcher (critic). *See* critic
research questions, 23–24, 291
responsibility, 223
revolutionary discourses, 245–46
rhetor (communicator), 11, 45, 46n13, 49–50, 52–53, 55–57, 60n29, 107–8, 111–12, 128, 198, 216, 224, 260, 263–64, 266; judgmental analysis and, 296; perception of, 50; virtuous, 245–46; worldview of, 295
rhetoric, 1–3, 7–20, 89n3, 220–21, 299; critical, 253–68; as epistemic, 176; generic elements in, 47–61; pragmatic conception of, 172; righteous conception of, 172, 187; as situated, 43–44; social conception of, 172–73, 187. *See also* rhetorical criticism
rhetorical artifact. *See* artifact, rhetorical
rhetorical criticism, 1–66, 253–68; as argument, 26; as art, 21–39; close textual analysis, 91–104; the critical act, 23–28; dramatism and Kenneth Burke's pentadic criticism, 147–65; eclectic approach to, 239–52; expanding horizons of, 237–88; fantasy-theme, 167–90; feminist analysis, 191–213; generic, 47–50, 52–54, 57–58; history of, 253; ideographic, 215–36; key issues in, 28–35; of metaphor, 105–24; as method, 22–23; narrative perspective, 125–45; objectivity and politics in, 63–66; overview of, 5–66; perspectives on, 67–236; of popular culture and social media, 269–88; reasons for engaging in, two, 21; traditional perspective, 69–90; writing, 289–94. *See also* critical rhetoric; criticism; rhetoric

rhetorical criticism, key issues in, 28–35; initial approach, 33–34; objectivity or subjectivity, 34–35; theoretical perspective, choice of, 32–33; what to include, 28–32
rhetorical events, 29, 44, 70–73
rhetorical hybrid, 56, 58, 114
rhetorical materialism, 219–21
rhetorical perspectives, 2–3, 26–27, 35, 53–54, 127, 174, 245, 254, 270, 289–90, 295–99;
rhetorical situations, 2, 41–46, 49–52, 60n26, 71, 115, 121, 194, 199, 215–16, 223
rhetorical texts. *See* texts, rhetorical
rhetorical theory/theorists, 3, 9–11, 27, 29–30, 33, 54, 57, 80, 118, 141, 220, 242; contributing to, 291, 293; eclectic criticism and, 239; feminist, 196–97, 199; generic descriptions and, 48; McGee and, 215, 219–20; rhetorical artifact or, 289–90
rhetorical vision, 53, 168, 170–73, 176–77, 179–80, 182, 184–87
*Rhetoric* (Aristotle), 49
rhetoricians, 8–9, 14–15, 35, 45, 69–70, 72–73, 85, 89n3, 263. *See also individual names,* e.g., Burke, Kenneth; Cicero; Quintilian
Rice, Ray, 24–25, 37n19, 72
Richards, Ivor Armstrong, 150, 164n16
Ricoeur, Paul, 115
righteousness, 77, 97, 172–73, 179
Rightists, 110
rights, 230–31, 231, 237
Riley, Patricia, 132, 143
Riley, Richard, 178
*The Ring* (film), 277
ritual forms, 150
Rochester Ladies Anti-Slavery Society, 80
Rodden, John, 182
Romans/Greco-Roman world, 8
romantic comedy ("romcom"), 199
Romney, Mitt, 77
Roosevelt, Franklin Delano/Roosevelt's War Message, 41–44, 72, 74, 77, 102, 116, 121
Rosenfield, Lawrence W., 27, 34–35, 250
Rosser, James, 180
Rossing, Jonathan, 261–62
Rosteck, Thomas, 132, 143
Rountree, Clarke, 152, 162–64
Roush, Pat, 136–39, 141
Rowland, Robert C., 56, 125–45, 277
rule of law, 222
Rushing, Janice Hocker, 142
Rusk, Dean, 75

Russia, 18, 246
rust belt, 226
Ryalls, Emily, 278, 280–82

Sandberg, Sheryl, 193, 211n5
Sapir, J. David, 107
Sarkeesian, Anita, 198
Saudi Arabia, children abducted to, 126, 135–40
scene, 52, 153–54, 156, 265
scene-act ratio, 52, 155–56
scene-agency, 158
Schiappa, Edward, 283–84
*Schindler's List* (film), 262
Schwarzenegger, Arnold, 154, 156
science fiction, 127, 131–32, 142, 242, 277
science/sciences, 22–23, 126, 172, 192, 241, 248–49, 273, 291; "prescientific" criticism, 63; rhetoric of, 299
scientism, 249
Scott, Robert L., 240
Scott, W. Richard, 177
scriptural imagery/allusions, 85, 94, 100–101
SCT. *See* symbolic convergence theory
segregationism, 129, 223
*Select British Eloquence* (Goodrich), 9
self-help, 25, 151, 154
self-interest, 15
self-reliant fantasy type, 178
Selzer, Ann, 225, 233
semantics, 92, 164n16, 225, 241, 249
Senda-Cook, Samantha, 263
Seneca, 165n33
September 11, 2001, 42, 44, 73, 129, 135, 142, 155, 182, 250, 277, 285
sermons, 9, 86, 95–97, 99, 101
servant-leader fantasy type, 181
Sessions, Jeff, 13
setting, 10, 13, 28–29, 118, 153, 155, 168, 172, 185, 259; context and, 71; narrative perspective, 126–28, 133–35, 137, 139–40
sexism, 24, 192–93, 201, 203, 208
sexual orientation, 194, 270
*Shallow Hal* (film), 200–210, 212n47, 270
shame, 84–85
Shields, Donald C., 186
"Shining City on a Hill" metaphor, 113, 116, 118
Shugart, Helene, 210–11
signification, 222, 275–76
Sillars, Malcolm O., 106
similarities, rhetorical, 54–55

simile, 105
Simons, Herb, 253
simplicity, 72, 78
situational determinism, 156
situations, rhetorical. *See* rhetorical situations
skepticism, need for, 141
Skilling, Jeffrey, 217
slavery, 9, 78, 80–87, 97–99, 105, 110, 128, 181, 222, 230, 232, 236n64, 261
Sloop, John, 265, 267
Slotkin, Richard, 297
Slut Walks/"slut shaming," 197
small groups, 169, 175, 185–87
Smart Girls web series, 198
Smith, Craig R., 24, 46
Smith, Gerrit, 82, 90n23
Smith, Hedrick, 113
Snowden, Edward, 226
social change, 10, 35, 147, 221, 255, 262, 264; popular culture, social media, and, 269, 271–72, 279–83
social class. *See* class, social
social conception of rhetoric, 172–73, 179
social inequality. *See* inequality
socialism, 16, 222
socialization, 150, 218, 231
social justice, 247, 262, 273, 278, 283
social media, 10, 18, 36n10, 41, 43, 92, 149, 196, 198, 263, 269–90; Twitter trolling, 274. *See also* Internet; popular culture and social media, criticism of
social mobility, 178
social order, 271–72, 296
social science, 175, 221
Solomon, Jon, 178
Solomon, Martha, 132
Solomon, Robert, 178
sophists, 8
Sopory, Pradeep, 121
Sotomayor, Sonia, 261
source, 70
South America, 94, 290
Soviet Union, 43, 110, 128, 157–58, 163, 232, 245–48, 277. *See also* Cold War
Spaeth, Robert, 184
speakers, 70; exemplar, 10. *See also individual names*
special-interest groups, 17
speech: as agency, 221; persuasive act represented by, 155
speech, figures of. *See* figures of speech

speeches: "great," 9, 43. *See also specific types of speeches,* e.g., keynote addresses
sports, 154, 187, 192, 211n8, 226, 286. *See also* baseball; James, LeBron
St. Antoine, Thomas J., 167–90
Stalin, Joseph, 151, 157
Stanton, Elizabeth Cady, 94, 102
"starting point" for critical rhetoric project, 255
status quo, 217, 282
Stelzner, Hermann G., 77
stereotypes, 31, 47, 86, 93, 128, 209, 283
Sterling, Donald, 236n64
Stern, David, 230
Stern, Josef, 120
Stevenson, Karla, 53
Stoic doctrines, 240
stories/storytelling, 127, 141–42, 174, 243. *See also* narrative
Stowe, Harriet Beecher, 128
Stowers, Monica, 136–40
Strain, Robert, 132
Strauss, Robert, 115
Stuckey, Mary, 242–43
*Stump Speaking* (Bingham's painting), 7
style, 75, 78, 85–86, 96
subjectivity, 34–35, 64, 191, 194, 210, 273, 283
Sun, Ye, 274
Super Bowl, 192, 211n8
*Supernatural* (TV show), 242–43, 292
Supreme Court, US. *See* United States Supreme Court
surveillance, 155, 280
syllogism, 76
symbolic convergence theory (SCT), 168, 173–76, 186–87
symbols/symbolism, 10–11, 19n15, 275, 298; symbolic action/activity, 10, 15–16, 92, 96, 100–101, 152–53, 256, 259, 269–71
synchronic dimension, 223
systems of production, 198

"Tale of Two Cities" metaphor, 116, 118
talk radio, 169, 172–73, 222
Taylor, Susan L., 210
Tea Party, Boston, 157
Tea Party (twenty-first century political movement), 42, 254, 279–80, 284
TED Talks, 195
television, 243; feminism/feminist critics and, 200–201. *See also specific genres and shows*

"Telling America's Story: Narrative Form and the Reagan Presidency" (Lewis), 132, 143
telos, 70, 265–68
term, dominant. *See* dominant term
terministic screens, 147–48, 164
terrorism, 53, 126, 129, 217; War on Terror, 217, 277. *See also* September 11, 2001
Texas rock houses, 243–45
text, 93–94, 270, 274; act emphasized in, 158; analyzing/evaluating, 275–78; artistic density exhibited by, 94–96, 101; context and, 93–94, 101; dominant term, finding, 161–62; as "multiple versions of reality," 161; reality and, 161–62; persuasive act represented by, 155; selecting/constructing, 273–75; as site of symbolic action, 92, 100–101. *See also* close textual analysis
theme, 127–28, 172
theory: epistemic, 175–76; general, 174; grounded, 175; theoretical perspective, 32–33; theory building, 30, 48, 291. *See also* rhetorical perspectives; rhetorical theory
Therborn, Göran, 258
Thevenez, Pierre, 175
third world countries, 297
Thomas, Clarence, 119
Three Mile Island, 129
Tiananmen Square protests, 247
timing, 78
*To Kill a Mockingbird* (Lee), 129
tolerance, 218, 222
Tompkins, Joe, 278, 282
topics/topical thinking, 75
totalitarianism, 80
"toughlove" narrative, 132
traditional perspective on criticism, 69–90
transgender individuals, 125, 194, 197, 298
treason, language of, 223, 226–27, 231
Treichler, Paula, 191
tropes, 92, 106, 118–20, 248
Truman, Harry, 131
truth, 14–15, 32, 129, 218–19
twentieth century, 9–10
Twitter. *See* social media
Tyler, Chaplin, 179
tyranny, 85, 159, 222, 279–80
Tyson, Neil deGrasse, 273

Udall, Morris, 161
*Uncle Tom's Cabin* (Stowe), 128
United States, 16, 218, 272; flag, 276; Founding Fathers, 78, 85, 127, 218; Patriot Act/surveillance of citizens, 155. *See also* American Dream; American exceptionalism; Democratic Party; Republican Party; *specific topics and events*, e.g., Cold War; September 11, 2001
United States Civil War. *See* Civil War, US
United States Congress, 41–42, 44, 72–74, 78, 141, 157–58, 161
United States Constitution, 41–42, 44, 51, 81, 85, 87, 94, 97–98, 230
United States presidency. *See* presidency, US
United States Supreme Court, 44, 94, 119, 235n48, 261
universities: university as microcosm fantasy type, 182. *See also* higher education
*The Unsettling of America* (Berry), 165n26
utilitarianism, 172, 176–80, 183–84, 228

Valenzano, Joseph M., III, 53, 241–43
values, 129, 148, 243
Vats, Anjali, 286
Vatz, Richard, 46n13
Vico, Giambattista, 9
video games, 18, 198, 286
Vietnam/the Vietnam War, 75, 94, 109, 187, 253
violation, 97–99
violence, 161, 193, 197, 199, 220, 245, 274, 286. *See also* nonviolence

Wald, George, 75
Wander, Philip, 215–19, 232, 233n3, 253–55, 259
war, 53; "war" on drugs, 106, 109–10; War on Terror, 217, 277. *See also* Roosevelt's War Message; *specific wars*
Ware, B. L., 58, 295
Warnick, Barbara, 131
Washington, Booker T., 101
Washington, Denzel, 290–91
Washington, George, 85
watchdog fantasy type, 181–82
Watergate, 169
Weaver, Richard, 15
weightism, 200–208
Weiser, M. Elizabeth, 164n2
Wellstone, Paul, 51
Westboro Baptist Church, 285
Westerfelhaus, Robert, 204–5
*The West Wing* (TV show), 242

Whalen, Kristina Schriver, 191–213, 270
Whately, Richard, 9, 219
*White Like Me: Reflections on Race from a Privileged Son* (Wise), 192
whiteness, *The Hunger Games* and, 280–81
white privilege, 192, 261
white supremacy, 192, 200, 231
Wichelns, Herbert, 70, 89n3
Wiesel, Elie, 127
Williams, Raymond, 269
Wills, Garry, 72, 81
Wilson, John, 75
Wilson, Robert, 179
Wilson, Woodrow, 182
Windt, Theodore Otto, Jr., 19n9, 104n3
Winfrey, Oprah, 272, 285
Winthrop, John, 97
wisdom: communal, 15; practical, 17, 265, 267
Wise, Tim, 192
Witcover, Jules, 114

women. *See specific topics,* e.g., feminist analysis
Women Film Pioneers Project (WFPP), 200
Women's History Museum, 198
*Women Speak* (Foss and Foss), 198–99
words, 10–14
workers' movements, 247
working class, 16, 247
worldview, 152, 168, 202, 254, 258, 269, 271; of the rhetor, 295
World War I, 147, 231
World War II, 41–44, 127, 132, 149, 157, 243. *See also* Roosevelt, Franklin Delano
Wright, Jeremiah, 30–31, 93–94, 96, 98–99, 101
writing criticism, 289–94

Yale University, 229, 261
Young, Marilyn J., 41–46

Zagacki, Kenneth S., 187
Zarefsky, David, 105, 122n24

# About the Contributors

**Matthew T. Althouse** is associate professor of communication at the College at Brockport, State University of New York, where he teaches courses in rhetoric and public address. His research interests include dramatistic rhetorical theory and criticism, and rhetoric and religion. He has published in journals such as *Rhetoric Society Quarterly*, *KB Journal*, *Rhetoric Review*, and *Communication Quarterly*.

**William Benoit** is professor of communication studies at Ohio University. He has published over 250 journal articles and book chapters and is the author or editor of fifteen books. The American Communication Association has presented him with both the Outstanding Teacher at a Doctoral Institution Award and the Gerald M. Phillips Mentoring Award. He has served as the editor for the *Journal of Communication* and *Communication Studies*. His primary interests are rhetorical theory and criticism and political communication.

**Edwin Black** (d. 2007) was professor of communication arts at the University of Wisconsin, Madison. He was the author of the seminal book *Rhetorical Criticism: A Study in Method* and a host of landmark essays of criticism. He twice received the Speech Communication Association Golden Anniversary Award.

**Adam Blood** is a PhD student in rhetoric and public culture and a graduate assistant at the University of Nebraska at Lincoln. He teaches classes in rhetoric, professional communication, communication theory, and public speaking. He received his master's degree at the University of Central Missouri and is the debate coach for the University of Nebraska.

**Stephen Howard Browne** is professor of rhetorical studies at The Pennsylvania State University. He teaches courses in rhetorical theory, rhetorical criticism, and social protest rhetoric. He is the author of *Jefferson's Call for Nationhood*, *Angelina Grimke: Rhetoric, Identity, and the Radical Imagination*, and *Edmund Burke and the Discourse of Virtue*. His book on Angelina Grimke received the National Communication Association's Diamond Anniversary Book Award, and he has received the Karl R. Wallace Award from the Speech Communication Association.

**M. Lane Bruner** is professor of rhetoric and politics in the Department of Communication at Georgia State University. He is the author of several books, including *Strategies of Remembrance* and *Repressive Regimes, Aesthetic States, and Arts of Resistance*, as well as dozens of scholarly essays and book chapters on various aspects of language and power. His current research focuses on artificial personhood, the rhetorical unconscious, and the role of poetry in Ancient Athenian politics.

**Thomas R. Burkholder** retired as associate professor and chair at the Hank Greenspun School of Communication, University of Nevada–Las Vegas, where he taught courses in rhetorical criticism, rhetorical theory, and the history of US public address. His scholarly work has appeared in *Communication Studies*, the *Southern Communication Journal*, the *Western Journal of Communication*, and various book chapters. He is coauthor, with Karlyn Kohrs Campbell, of the second edition of *Critiques of Contemporary Rhetoric*.

**Mary Evelyn Collins** is professor of speech communication at Lamar University. Her research interests include folk speech and cowboy humor, child and family advocacy, rhetorical depiction and culturetype as a critical tool in rhetorical analysis, and the intersection of cultural tradition and popular culture forms. She is a past president of the Southern States Communication Association.

**Kathleen Farrell** is professor in the Department of Communication, St. Louis University. She teaches and researches instances of contemporary and historical public argument, argument theory, and argument pedagogy. She has published in numerous scholarly journals, edited volumes, and proceedings. She is the author of *Literary Integrity and Political Action*.

**David Henry** is professor of communication at the University of Nevada. He teaches courses in rhetorical theory and criticism, political communication, persuasion, and argumentation. He has published articles in numerous journals such as the *Quarterly Journal of Speech*, *Communication Monographs*, the *Rhetoric Society Quarterly*, and the *Southern Communication Journal*. He received the 1998 University Distinguished Teaching Award at Cal Poly State University, San Luis Obispo, and shared with all contributors to *Eisenhower's War of Words: Rhetoric and Leadership* the 1995 Marie Hockmuth Nichols Award for Outstanding Scholarship in Public Address. He has been the editor of the *Western Journal of Communication* and the *Quarterly Journal of Speech*.

**Forbes I. Hill** (d. 2008) was emeritus professor, Queens College of the City University of New York. He published in the field of history of rhetoric and public address. He is the author of "Aristotle's Rhetorical Theory" in James J. Murphy and Richard Katula's volume, *A Synoptic History of Classical Rhetoric*.

**Kristen Hoerl** is associate professor of critical communication and media studies and the speakers lab director at Butler University in Indianapolis, Indiana. She teaches courses in media literacy, film criticism, the rhetoric of social movements, and argumentation. Her research explores the role of popular culture in the process of social change. Her articles have appeared in numerous journals, including the *Quarterly Journal of Speech*; *Critical Studies in Media Communication*; *Communication and Critical/Cultural Studies*; *Communication, Culture, and Critique*; the *Western Journal of Communication*; and the *Southern Communication Journal*.

**Andrew King**, professor emeritus at Louisiana State University, divides his time between Baton Rouge and the Catskills where he is engaged in launching The Renaissance Farm, a modern Chautauqua for artists and writers. He is the author of *Postmodern Political Communication* and *Power and Communication* and coeditor of *Twentieth-Century Roots of Rhetorical Studies*. He is a former editor of the *Quarterly Journal of Speech and the Southern Communication Journal*. He was selected as the American Communication Association's Outstanding Teacher at a Doctoral Institution in 1998. His academic interests lie in the areas of communication and power, and medieval and Renaissance rhetorical theory. He is a past president of the Kenneth Burke Society.

**Jim A. Kuypers** is associate professor of communication at Virginia Tech. He is the author or editor of twelve books, including *Purpose, Practice, and Pedagogy in Rhetorical Criticism* (winner of the Everett Lee Hunt Award for Outstanding Scholarship) and *Partisan Journalism: A History of Media Bias in the United States* (a 2014 *Choice* Outstanding Academic Title). He is the recipient of the American Communication Association's Outstanding Contribution to Communication Scholarship Award, the Southern States Communication Association's Early Career Research Award, and Dartmouth College's Distinguished Lecturer Award. His research interests include political communication, metacriticism, and the moral/poetic use of language.

**Ronald Lee** is professor of communication studies at the University of Nebraska–Lincoln. He teaches and writes about contemporary rhetoric and political culture. His work has appeared in the *Quarterly Journal of Speech*, *Political Communication*, the *Western Journal of Communication*, *Communication Studies*, the *Southern Communication Journal*, *Argumentation and Advocacy*, and *Technical Communication Quarterly*. He is the coauthor (with Rachel Friedman) of the recently published book *The Style and Rhetoric of Elizabeth Dole: Public Persona and Political Discourse*.

**Ryan Erik McGeough** is assistant professor of communication at the University of Northern Iowa. He has published in the areas of pedagogy, visual argument, new media technology, and public deliberation.

**Raymie E. McKerrow** is emeritus professor in the School of Communication Studies at Ohio University. He has published in the areas of modern rhetoric, argumentation theory, and critical/cultural approaches to contemporary rhetoric. He is past president of the Eastern Communication Association and the National Communication Association, and he received the Douglas W. Ehninger Distinguished Rhetorical Scholar Award and the Charles H. Woolbert Research Award from the National Communication Association.

**Donna Marie Nudd** is professor of communication at Florida State University and executive director of the Mickee Faust Academy for the Really Dramatic Arts. Her major areas of interest include feminist criticism, pedagogy, radical performance, and adaptation for film and theater. Nudd's essays have appeared in *Text and Performance Quarterly*, *Bronte Society Transactions*, *Communication Education*, and *Liminalities*. Nudd and her lifelong collaborator, Terry Galloway, are co-recipients of the National Communication Association's Irene Coger Award for Lifetime Achievement in Performance.

**Robert C. Rowland** is professor and director of graduate studies in the Department of Communication Studies at the University of Kansas. His many publications include *Shared Land/Conflicting Identity: Trajectories of Israeli & Palestinian Symbol Use* (with David Frank), which won the inaugural Kohrs-Campbell Book Award; *Analyzing Rhetoric*; and more than eighty essays on rhetorical criticism, argumentation, and narrative. He received the Douglas W. Ehninger Distinguished Rhetorical Scholar Award from the National Communication Association in 2011. Rowland's research interests include critical methodologies, public argument, argumentation theory, and political communication.

**Thomas J. St. Antoine** is professor of communication and director of the Frederick M. Supper Honors Program at Palm Beach Atlantic University. His work has been published in the *Southern Communication Journal*, the *Journal of Education and Christian Belief*, and *Research on Christian Higher Education*. He is a former editorial assistant for the *Quarterly Journal of Speech*. His teaching and research interests include the rhetoric of higher education and the rhetoric of place.

**Joseph M. Valenzano III** is associate professor of communication and basic course director at the University of Dayton. He teaches courses in rhetorical theory and criticism, religious communication, persuasion, and instructional communication. His scholarship focuses on the intersection of religion, politics, and the mass media in American culture. He is coauthor of *Television, Religion, and Supernatural* and has also published articles in *Communication Monographs*, *Communication Education*, the *Journal of Media and Religion*, and the *Southern Communication Journal*. Valenzano is the editor of the *Basic Communication Course Annual*.

**Kristina Schriver Whalen** is dean for the School of Fine, Applied, and Communication Arts at City College of San Francisco. Her work has been published in *Text and Performance Quarterly* and *Women's Studies and Communication*, among others. Her research explores the intersection of feminist argument and performative protest and equity issues in higher education.

**Marilyn J. Young** is the Wayne C. Minnick Professor of Communication, Emerita, at Florida State University. She has published numerous articles and book chapters and authored two books, *Flights of Fancy, Flight of Doom: KAL 007 & Soviet-American Rhetoric* and *Coaching Debate*. With David Marples she edited *Nuclear Energy and Security in the Former Soviet Union*. Her research interests are in argumentation, rhetorical theory and criticism, and political (particularly international) rhetoric, especially the development of political language and argument in newly emerging democracies.